Contents

Dedication

This book is dedicated to my parents, who gave me life, support and inspiration to help me navigate the storms of life to the shores of success.

And to my wife Batia. My fifty-five years in America could not have been achieved without her. I hope that this book pays the great tribute she deserves for sticking with me. The following verse from Jeremiah 2:2 expresses my love for her:

I remember concerning you the devotion
of your youth, the love of betrothals, your
following after me in the wilderness, through a
land not sown."

Sam and Batia Regev, celebrating Hanukkah,
the Festival of Lights, 2019.

Gratitude

I did not anticipate, even in my wildest dreams that I would ever write a book, but I did and you, the reader, are holding it. This book began on December 4, 2019 when my friend, C. Mark Smith, an accomplished author, and a wine aficionado, came to my house to taste a new wine I made from one of the Italian red grape varietals I planted in my small vineyard. He liked it so I gave him a bottle to take home and share with his wife. While we drank the wine and munched on with crackers and cheese, I told him that I wrote a short documentation on how and why I got myself into planting a vineyard and making wines from the grapevines I planted. (See Chapter 19.) Mark replied, "Sam, let's make a deal. You give me a copy of that story and I'll give you a free copy of the book I wrote about our former US Congressman, Doc Hastings." When I agreed, he went to his car for a copy of his book and adorned it with his autograph.

My phone rang the next day and the caller introduced herself. "Hi, my name is Marcia Breece, Mark Smith emailed me a copy of your vineyard story and I found it very compelling, especially what happened to your family during the Holocaust."

I thanked her for the complement and said I had more stories about my family who perished in the holocaust.

"Your stories should be published," Marcia replied. After a brief discussion, Marcia agreed to help me publish my book.

Thank you Mark for your friendship and forwarding the chapter to Marcia. You deserve the sole credit of being the person who set publishing this book in motion.

I am fortunate to have Marcia Breece, already an accomplished novelist, to help me publish my book. Thank you, Marcia for your excellent work and encouragement. Seeing to it that my stories are published is your "walk of life" but by your own admission, you learned many things about Israel's history and Judaism you did not know until working with me on my book. Thanks again for walking the extra mile for me.

Saying "Thank you" is not enough to convey my love and admiration to Dr. Francis Marion Summers, my teacher, mentor and guardian angel. You were the only one who supported me and pushed my plea to be admitted during my hastily arranged visit to meet you and other members of your department at UC Davis. They refused to admit me, but you fought for me and convinced them to give me at least the chance of proving myself. Our association turned out to be a very fruitful, with four years of collaboration and friendship as well. You left us and moved to reside in heaven on July 15, 1994 with all the other angels and the cherubim. I agree, wholeheartedly with the In Memoriam note UC Davis released after you passed away stating that you were very much a people person who cared deeply about others with whom you were associated, especially the students and the growers you served. I had never told you, until now, that you gave me one of the greatest compliments I ever got. Before the beginning of one of your classes you approached my desk and whispered in my ear, "Sam, why is it that almost everything that preoccupies you other than your schoolwork is centered around Israel?" Then you gave me your famous fatherly wink and went back to the podium to start the lecture. A big chunk of the stories in my book should give you the answer to that question you asked me fifty-three years ago.

If Dr. Summers was the one instrumental for me getting the Ph.D., Dr. Wyatt Cone is solely responsible for my success after my graduation from UC Davis. Thank you, Wyatt for granting me the Post Doctorate research position at The Irrigated Agriculture Research and Extension Center in Prosser, Washington. It launched my academic career. Batia and I are also indebted to you for setting the motion that gained us the Green Card and the USA citizenship that followed.

Thanks to all my friends and co-workers at the Hanford reservation; we shared many wonderful hours and events together some of which are mentioned in this book.

Last but far from least, my son Raz and daughter Shir. Hopefully, this book will shed some light about your family and how you ended up living here. Thank you Raz for your acumen in Political Sciences and helping your community. Shir, thank you for serving humanity on two fronts, first as a Peace Corps volunteer in Namibia, Africa right after graduating from the university (WSU). Then for serving for almost nine years in the US Navy.

Preface

Writing this book turned out to be a difficult task but choosing a proper title for it was even more difficult. I was not looking for a cute or catchy name, just a title that truly described the nature of the book; a documentation of the milestones in my life as well as a tribute to my family members who were executed by the Nazis during the Holocaust. They did not have the chance to tell their stories and their achievements, so I tried to do it for them.

Fairly early in my adult life I made the decision to come to the USA in pursuit of a higher education. That decision required sacrifices. I realized I was not the first to experience a similar fate. The first verse of The Call of Abraham in Genesis 12:1-3 perfectly describes what I've been feelings since I started my fifty-two-year journey in the United States:

> *"The Lord had said to Abraham, "Go from your country,*
> *your people and your father's house to the land I will*
> *show you."*

I decided to name the book *My Call of Abraham*

Like Abraham, I left my country, my people, my friends and my father's house, and arrived in a foreign land. I was convinced it would be temporary and we would return when I earned my Ph.D. It proved to be a classic tale of easier said than done. My wife and I remained in the USA and became naturalized citizens.

Enjoy reading.

Chapter 1

132 Ben Yehuda Street

My parents illegally immigrated to Eretz Israel/Palestine when the land was controlled under the British Mandate commissioned by the United Nation.

In March 1939, the British government under Neville Chamberlain drafted a policy called The White Paper, in response to the 1936-1939 Arab Revolt in Palestine. The document called for the establishment of an independent Jewish state in Palestine and a similar independent state for the Palestinians within ten years. However, the plan limited the number of Jewish immigrants *(Immigration Certificates)* to 75,000 for five years. It ruled that further immigration certificates would be determined by the Arab majority living in Palestine. Many Jews, my parents included, defied this limitation, and attempted to immigrate illegally. A few ships with Jewish immigrants were intercepted by the British navy and the immigrants on board, many of them survivors of the Nazis concentration camps, were imprisoned in camps the British built in Cyprus. A detailed account of my parent's illegal immigration ordeal is documented in Chapter 3.

This chapter describes the first six years of my life under the British Mandate, living on 132 Ben Yehuda Street in Tel Aviv. Ben Yehuda Street was also known by its nickname *Ben Yehuda Strasse* because so many Jewish immigrants from Germany lived there.

Until 1920, the leaning of German Jews to assimilate into the German and Austrian societies was a well known phenomenon. Jews even served in the army of the Austrian Emperor Franz Joseph. A monumental change took place in Germany and Austria when the National Socialist German Workers' Party or the Nazi Party, was founded and operated in Germany between 1920 and 1945. It was far-right politically, and under the helm of Adolf Hitler. The Nazi Party sought to support what they considered a *pure* Aryan race and planned a campaign to exterminate Jews, Romani, Poles, gays and people they considered mentally ill. The Nazi's zeal to exterminate the Jews was called the *Final Solution* which turned out to be an industrial system of genocide, known as the Holocaust. It culminated in the murder of six million Jews and a million people of other ethnic groups.

It was clear to the Jewish community leaders in Eretz Israel/ Palestine that the Jews in Germany were under dire threat. There was an urgent need to bring them to Eretz Israel/Palestine. There was a sort of a preferential bias toward them. It was expressed by granting them the lion share of the Immigration Certificates allotted by the British authorities. Allegations started to circulate, claiming that David Ben-Gurion, the head of the Provisional Jewish government, wanted as many German Jews as possible to immigrate to Eretz Israel/Palestine. The rationale behind it was the prevailing perception that most of them were considered to be financially well-to-do, highly educated and skilled in highly sought fields such as engineers, architects, medical doctors, etc. Many of them escaped Germany and came to Israel before WWII started. I believe that this immigration wave from Germany peaked in 1935. My in-laws, emigrated from Germany in 1935 and founded *Kibbutz Matzuba* on the Israeli/Lebanese border. My wife Batia was born and raised there.

The Jewish immigrants from Germany were different in culture and mannerism from the Jews who emigrated from Eastern Europe. The two groups mirrored different levels of sophistication and technical advancement. The German immigrants were prompt, dressed neatly and looked more *European* than their peers from Eastern Europe.

Many of the immigrants from Eastern Europe and some of the *Sabra* (Jews born in Eretz Israel/Palestine) resented them and gave them the nickname *yekkes*. Quite a large number of the German Jews resided on Ben Yehuda Street, one of the main and longest streets in Tel Aviv. The *yekkes* brought German habits and a different way of life to my beloved Ben Yehuda Street causing its nick name, *Ben Yehuda Strasse.*

The *yekkes* had a huge impact on the Jewish community in Eretz Israel/Palestine, especially on my hometown, Tel Aviv. The city was founded in 1909 with the idea of becoming a garden city on the sand dunes outside the mostly Arab city of Jaffa. Meir Dizzingoff, Tel Aviv's first mayor, hired a Scottish urban planner, Patrick Geddes, to design the master plan for Tel Aviv. The plan was approved and accepted in 1929 but architectural style of Tel Aviv was determined by the many German Jewish architects, trained at the Bauhaus School in Berlin.

The Nazis considered the Bauhaus School a communist intellectual center but the Bauhaus style became the most influential art and design of the 20th century. The German Jewish architects who immigrated to Eretz Israel/Palestine wanted to recreate the European culture they left behind and adopted their Bauhaus designs to the hot climate of their new land.

It was a difficult architectural and engineering challenge to modify this style of German architecture and to make it functional in the prevailing harsh climate conditions of Tel Aviv. Unlike the solid surface on which the houses in Germany were built, Tel Aviv was situated on a large mass of sand. It was impractical and even dangerous to set the foundations of the new houses on these shifting sand dunes. The Bauhaus architects solved the problem by raising the new buildings on thick pillars, known as *piloti*. The pillars allowed the wind to blow underneath, slightly cooling the apartments above, no one during that era had air-conditioners. The area underneath the pillars provided space for stores, and a variety of businesses and services. Many houses used the area as a playground for the children living in that building. Some creative residents planted vegetable gardens there. We had several of these buildings on Ben Yehuda Strasse. When I asked my father why some buildings were built on stilts, he said, probably pulling my leg, that it was done that way to protect us from the crawling snakes.

The Bauhaus houses were painted white to reflect the sun's heat. There were more than 4,000 houses built in Tel Aviv at that time, giving the city its nickname *The White City*. There were more Bauhaus buildings in Tel Aviv than any other place in the world prompting UNESCO in 2000 to name Tel Aviv a *World Heritage Site* for its Bauhaus modern architecture. The Tel Aviv municipality passed a resolution to preserve and maintain the original Bauhaus buildings but unfortunately some had been torn down and replaced with more modern and taller buildings before the resolution was made. In 2005 the German government and the city of Tel Aviv signed an agreement whereby Germans contributed $3.2 million and created a special fund to preserve these houses for ten years.

Another major adaptation the Jewish architects from Germany made was to change the type of roofs from pitched to flat. Pitched roofs were more suitable for Germany's snowy winters but unnecessary in snow-less Tel Aviv. Ironically, in the winter of 1950, my parents took my sister and me to the roof to see snow for the first time.

The flat roofs of the Bauhaus-style buildings built in Tel Aviv adhered to the Bauhaus architectural philosophy that everything associated with buildings should be functional, and indeed, they were. The flat roofs provided an area to dry laundry, a big plus because only commercial laundromats owned electric dryers. The ones for domestic use were not affordable to most people. The flat roofs also provided some relief from the summer heat where the residents could socialize over cold watermelon and seasonal fruit.

Tel Aviv's searing hot summers forced the Bauhaus architects to design houses with enough light without the need to have the large glass windows used in Germany and other European countries. The Bauhaus architects of Tel Aviv designed smaller, recessed windows to cut the heat and the glare. The stairwell of a Tel Aviv Bauhaus building had long narrow skinny windows, known by their nickname *thermometers*, installed to provide daylight.

Despite the many years that have passed since my childhood at Ben Yehuda Strasse, I remember some of the Jewish immigrants from Germany that lived in our neighborhood. Allow me to introduce to you Berta and Hans who lived on the fourth floor in one of the buildings down the street from us. They did not have children and barley spoke Hebrew. I knew their names just from observing their daily garbage dumping ritual, augmented with a few ounces of German sophistication. Evidently, living on the fourth floor and taking the garbage bucket all the way to the dumpster in the back yard was too much of an effort for Hans. It looked more *sophisticated* for him to stand in the street in front of their building, cap the palms of his hands around his mouth and yell toward their balcony, "Berta... Yooo-Hooo... Berta Yooo-Hooo...." So I learned that his wife's name was Berta. He waited until Berta appeared on the balcony shouting back in German "*Nur eine minute, Hans*" (One minute, Hans) so I learned his name was Hans. A few minutes would pass before Berta reappeared on the balcony with a white porcelain container, filled with their garbage and attached to a rope long enough to reach Hans on the street. She gingerly lowered the can, trying not to spill the garbage. There were times when the wind or her shaky hands caused the bucket to pepper the pavement with their kitchen garbage. After emptying the bucket into the dumpster, Hans would retie the rope and shout, "*Nacho ben ziehen, Berta*" (Pull it up, Berta). Most of the time, pulling the empty garbage can up was smooth and uneventful but occasionally, the wind bounced it back and forth, hitting the walls, and sounding like a jingling church bell.

Then, there was the door-to-door salesman. We did not know his real name but called him *Charlie Chaplin* because of his brisk gait. He was a slim person and immaculately dressed, wearing black, tailor-made trousers and white shirt with a fancy black butterfly bow tie. He looked very European and aristocratic but totally lost. His attire was perfect and proper for the business streets of Berlin or Munich but not the hot sun of Tel Aviv. He perspired profusely. Our *Charlie Chaplin* wore an expensive casquette hat and carried a brown, thin-walled rectangular suitcase that housed the goods he was trying to sell door-to-door. My parents, who emigrated from Poland called his suitcase a *walizka* (Polish for suitcase). The image of the *walizka* he carried is engraved in my mind and resurfaces each time I see pictures of similar *walizkas* carried by Jewish Holocaust victims murdered by the Nazis in the concentration camps.

Charlie Chaplin's business territory was the stretch of Ben Yehuda Street where we lived, Keren Kayemet Blvd. (currently, Ben Gurion Blvd.) and Arlosoroff Street, which is a major street intersecting Ben Yehuda Strasse. There were quite a few three- to four-floor buildings on both sides of the street, making it very hard on him physically. Even now, as I recount my memories of him, I feel his pain and remember how tired he was each time he exited a building after trying to sell his wares. He leaned on the nearest tree to catch his breath and escape the hot, unrelenting sun. I felt uncomfortable each time the doorbell rang and there he was when my mother opened the door. He never spoke a word in Hebrew or Yiddish, the language most Eastern European Jews spoke. He would open his *walizka* and present its collection of spools of sewing thread, needles, hairpins, rubber bands, crochet threads, and the like. Next, he would say in German "*bitte*," as he moved his right hand across the goods. My mother, who spoke fluent German, pretended to inspect the goods and bought a spool or two of the sewing thread she didn't really need. She didn't have the heart to send him away empty handed. We lived on the third (top) floor of the building and heard his "*Danke, Danke.*" (thank you, thank you) reverberating down the stairway as he headed to his next customer.

I have no doubt that our *Charlie Chaplin* was far too educated to be a notions salesman. I strongly believe that he, like many other immigrants to Eretz Israel/Palestine, was a professor, pushed out of his high position at one of the universities when the Nazis took over Germany. Historically, the percentage of Jews in academia was proportionally high in the communities where they lived.

The Nazis deposed a great many Jewish professors from their academic positions and replaced them with less qualified non-Jewish counterparts. Many of the deposed academicians escaped Germany and immigrated to other countries, including Eretz Israel/Palestine and resumed their academic careers. Others were not that fortunate and assumed vocations not even closely related. I am sure that some of them, like *Charlie Chaplin* lived on my beloved Ben Yehuda Strasse.

✡

It was common during that time for more than one family to share an apartment. Our family shared a two-room flat with the Neumann family; Elka, Godek and their two children, Israel and Nili who were the exact age of my sister, Chaya, and I. A wide door separated our room and theirs, so my parents placed the big cabinet that held our clothes and meager belongings next to that separating door. It made a physical barrier between the two rooms but there was no privacy as everyone could listen to what was said in the opposite room.

There are many funny and not so funny stories describing the awkward situations associated with these living arrangements, for example, when a visitor rang the doorbell for the apartment shared by more than one tenant, it created confusion as to who was to answer the bell. It was a bone of contention when the two tenants were not on friendly terms. A practical and popular solution was to affix a small sticker to the doorbell, with the following message: *Please press once for the Cohen family; twice for the Levi family.*

We took turns sharing the small kitchen, the toilet room and bathroom that had one bathtub. Our bath water was heated by a very primitive boiler that burned only small pieces of wood. Each family had to fetch its own wood supply to heat the water they needed.

Theoretically, sharing the flat facilities equally and fairly between the two should have been a simple arrangement mutually agreed upon, but it was not. The flat was owned by Elka's uncle who showed an obvious bias in favor of the Neumann family. They used the facilities whenever they felt like it. We felt somewhat compensated because the flat's only balcony was attached to our room and was used solely by us. It was the *Center of the Universe* for me, where I spent many hours. I still have sweet memories of my hours on the balcony.

We did not have a refrigerator, so my parents managed to buy a second-hand ice box and placed a block of solid ice in its top compartment. The water from the melting ice drained into a container at the bottom. They placed the ice box by my bed.

A truck loaded with long ice blocks stopped by our building every day and honked its horn to alert the neighborhood that ice was available. You told the iceman how much ice you needed, and he cut the proper size off the long ice block using a special cutter. My mother put me in charge of letting her know when the ice truck arrived. She gave me the money and told me to buy a third of a block. She also gave me a special gizmo made especially for carrying ice blocks without touching it with your bare fingers.

It was next to impossible for us to use the single stove in the kitchen because the Neumann family used it around the clock so my mother cooked our meals on a small kerosene burner, inside our tiny room. I let her know when the kerosene man arrived. He announced his arrival by jingling a hand bell. I saw and heard him from the kitchen window and alerted my mother. She gave me the kerosene container and the money to buy what she needed for cooking, and to heat our room in winter.

His special fuel cart was painted red and pulled by a small donkey. Unlike the USA where the fuel is now hauled by eighteen-wheeler trucks, our kerosene was transported by a four-legged donkey. The poor donkey never failed to urinate and defecate on the asphalt next to the fancy De Soto limousines parked at the entrance of Hotel Yarden next to our building.

We took our bath on Friday evening just before *Sabbath* set in. During the entire week, I scavenged through the dumpsters behind the neighborhood grocery stores for wood we stored, covered from the winter rain, on our balcony.

Mr. and Mrs. Gabel, the owners of the grocery store by our building helped with the wood supply. They emigrated from Germany before WWII. My mother used to send me there with a grocery list written in German, and they filled the grocery bag. My mother stopped at their store later and paid the bill. I was a cute little blond boy during that time, and it helped me as the elderly Mr. and Mrs. Gabel, who did not have children of their own, had a soft spot for me. They gave me enough damaged crates to take home for our *Sabbath* bath. I am sure that they, like our *Charlie Chaplin* described earlier, were professionals back in Germany before immigrating to Eretz Israel/Palestine.

The bathtub of our shared apartment also served as an aquarium for the carp my mother and Elka Neumann bought a few days before the Sabbath. These carp were destined to metamorphose from fish living in rivers and sweet water lakes into the famous Jewish *Sabbath* dish known in Yiddish as *gefilte* fish (stuffed fish). They kept the carp alive by filling the bathtub with water and letting the fish swim until the *Gefilte Fish Chef* decided it was time for the carp to meet their maker and become the main entry of the *Sabbath* dinner. My sister and I never touched *gefilte* fish but my father was crazy about the way my mother prepared it. She, too, loved that dish. They both came from Poland where carp were native to the rivers, considered a staple and inexpensive. You can buy *gefilte* fish nowadays at the supermarket here in the USA, but it is not really prepared like a *gefilte* fish. The product sold in a jars is a chunk of ground pike mixed with matzo meal, made mostly by The Manischevitz Kosher Company. Most people slide the Manischevitz-style *gefilte* fish down their throats along with a spoon or two of horseradish.

Using the bathtub was a challenge, especially during the time it was used as the *aquarium*. This situation provided only a very narrow window of opportunity to take a bath before *Sabbath* but I managed to cope with that problem.

The more challenging problem was the possessive zeal shown by Elka Neumann toward the carp she purchased. Although our carp and hers came from the same store, Mrs. Neumann was adamantly sure that her fish was much better than the one my mother bought. My mother bought only one carp whereas Mrs. Neumann bought two or three and always insisted on exactly the ones she purchased. She started tagging her coveted carp by attaching small metallic shower curtain rings to the tips of their tail fins. My mother surmised, "A carp is a carp is a carp," and let Mrs. Neumann worry about it. Mrs. Neumann's method created a problem for me because the rings made an annoying noise each time the carp's tail hit the bathtub's cast iron wall. The noise was amplified by the number of carp Mrs. Neumann bought that week. I could take the noise during the day, but I could not sleep. It sounded like Flamenco dancers and their castanets. Evidently it began to bother the Neumann family as well and Elka stopped tagging the carp with rings and started cutting a notch in the carp's tail.

During the curfews imposed by the British authorities, the shared bathtub also served as a water reservoir. We lived a block from David Ben-Gurion's home on Keren Kayemet Blvd. He was the political leader of the provisional government. Whenever the British Mandate authorities had serious military issues with the Jewish community, they would impose a curfew that sometimes lasted for many hours. Our street and the residential area next to Ben-Gurion's house was a popular target. The British authorities would send a car with a loudspeaker on its roof and announce that a total curfew was to start within the next hour. Anyone caught outside during the curfew would be arrested. The announcement created apprehension as people were not sure how long the curfew would last and if the services such as the municipal water department would operate. Some people, including us and the Neumanns, filled their bathtubs with water in addition to what they managed to store in pots and other containers.

The curfews usually ended whenever the British felt that they had met their objectives. They would send another car with a loudspeaker to inform the community that curfew was over. Their announcement, in Hebrew, still reverberates in my head even after the many years, "Hello, Hello, Ha' otzer butal, Hello, Hello, ha' otzer butal," (Hello, Hello, the curfew is over). The curfews had a bad impact on our family as my father's barber shop was located within the curfew territory and he could not go to work.

Ushering in the Jewish *Sabbath* at Ben Yehuda Strasse was a unique Friday ritual. Three hours before, a car from the municipal religion department drove the entire length of Ben Yehuda Strasse honking its horn to let residents know that *Sabbath* would start in three hours. Soon after that, the orthodox residents would start walking with towels rolled under their arms and head to the *mikve*, (the Jewish ritual bath) in their neighborhood, to cleanse themselves for *Sabbath*. *Sabbath* was a special day throughout the entire country, a *Day of Rest* the bible commanded us to observe. People did not go to work and there was no public transportation from Friday evening until *Sabbath* was over the evening of the next day.

✡

WWII was raging in Europe and foreign soldiers from the British Commonwealth and a few American soldiers spent their off-duty leave in Tel Aviv. The ones I liked the most where the Australians, the Sikhs from India and the Americans.

Two of the American soldiers, probably Jewish as they spoke broken Yiddish, visited my father's barber shop. Their rudimentary Yiddish was sufficient enough to communicate with my father who did not speak or understood English very well. They begged him relentlessly, requesting an invitation to our house for a *Sabbath* dinner. My father found many excuses why he could not invite them. It was not because we were stingy people but because our entire family and belongings were crammed into a single rented room in an apartment shared with another family. Besides, feeding non-family guests a fancy dinner was beyond my parent's financial means.

My father didn't share their request for a dinner invitation with my mom, as he knew it would be an extra burden on her. But the two American soldiers kept coming to get their haircut and requesting an invitation to *Sabbath* dinner. My father finally told my mom about their request. "I don't know what to do about it and how to get them off my back," he said. "I don't like to lose them as clients but most importantly, I hate to hurt their feelings."

My mother, an expert at facing any difficult situation replied, "We have no other choice but to invite them to dinner but tell them about our living conditions and not to expect much. I will cook something for them on the kerosene burner. I bet that these American soldiers are Jewish and miss their home and families. They need this invitation just to satisfy their craving for Jewish warmth while they are in a war and far away from home. It is not the food they are craving, it is a few hours spent with a Jewish family on the *Sabbath*. Next time they come to get their haircut pick a date for them to come and I will prepare something," she said to my father and I could see he was relieved.

That *Sabbath* eve came, and the two American soldiers brought fancy candies for my sister and me and a large cardboard box filled with an assortment of canned beef they managed to scoop from wherever

Figure 1.1 Our family with two America soldiers during WWII, after they had *Sabbath* dinner with us.

they were stationed. They knew that these items were in short supply and knew that my parents would gladly take them even though the meat was not kosher. They also brought us a sophisticated can opener I have no idea why my father referred to the beef as *the bull beef* and can opener as the *Churchill.* That night, my mother prepared her special chicken soup, served with mashed potatoes. For desert she prepared a spongy cake similar to the angel food cake sold here in the USA.

Our American guests enjoyed their visit, their faces glowed like the *Sabbath* candles. I trust that they liked the dinner my mother managed to prepare despite our poor financial situation and no proper place to host them. They took the time to pay attention to me and my sister. Before leaving, they apologized for not bringing a camera with them and asked if it would be OK for them to come again the next morning and take pictures. The photographs were taken in front of David Ben-Gurion's house on Keren Kayemet boulevard. My mother told me this story during one of her visits with us in the USA when I showed her the pictures of the soldiers with our family and asked for an explanation. (Figure 1.1)

✡

My playmates on 132 Ben Yehuda, the *132 Ben Yehuda gang,* included my sister Chaya, Avrama'le, (Rivkah Yakobovitz's son), Srulik (nickname for Israel) and his sister Nili, who were the children of the Neumann family that shared the apartment with us, and Rocha'le (nickname for Rachel). She was the daughter of Mrs. Bendikovski who ran a women's underwear and brassiere business from their apartment on the ground floor. Mrs. Bendikovski had a large display at the street entrance leading to our building. It was empty, no longer in use and it's glass walls had been removed so we used it as our assembly place. Evidently, we all looked cute inside that chamber and it caught the eye of a Mr. Berenstein, the professional photographer who captured us on film. (Figure 1.2) Photographer Berenstein was so proud of this picture he placed an enlargement in the display window of his photography studio.

✡

Mr. Zand, another Jewish immigrant from pre-WWII Germany, owned a stationary store at the corner of Ben Yehuda and Ferdinand La Salle Street.

He sold a plethora of school-related items such as pens, pencils, notebooks, books, and various arts & crafts supplies. I liked his store immensely. It smelled of welcoming sophistication, very much like a well established public library. I loved the smell of a just-sharpened pencil and the ambient smell of a bookstore. To my nose, they were coveted perfumes. It was almost like an addiction. I bought a new

Figure 1.2 The 132 Ben Yehuda Gang
Standing: my sister Chaya (l) and Avrame'le (r), Sitting: Rocha'le Bendikovski (r) and me (l), what a great and happy childhood we had, even without cell phones, iPads and texting.

pencil from Mr. Zand and asked him to sharpen it for me so I could smell the soft wood flakes. Even now, I cling to my old habit of opening every brand new, off-the press book, smack in the middle and savor the irresistible smell of ink, paper and binding materials.

Mr. Zand also sold colorful sheets of paper that I used to build my own fancy kites, otherwise known by the Arabic name *tayara*. None of us used the Hebrew name *afifon*. I don't like to brag about my skill as a kite builder, but I was not just a run-of-the-mill kite builder, I was a Kite Engineer. My friends and I would walk the two-mile path down Ben Yehuda Street that ended at the banks of the Yarkon River. It had plenty of reeds growing along its banks. We split their woody stems into thin strips to build the kite frame. I used three of these slim reed strips as the backbone supporting the head of the kite. We called the wooden reed stems by their Arabic name *booseem*. (We also used the long stem of the reed for our fishing rods and arrows for our bows.) I used a string to loosely bind the three thin strips together at the center and then spread them like a fan. Another string ran uncut around each tip of the strips to produce the hexagonal head of the kite. Another string ran within the area of the kite center where I attached papers of different colors to create patterns which made the head of the kite look like a stained glass window. My favorite design was the Star of David.

La Salle Street was the shortest route from our building to the beach. There was no better place to fly kites than the beach with its pure white/gold sand and the blue water of the Mediterranean, and the beach had no electric poles and wires for the kite's tail to get tangled on and cause brownouts throughout the entire neighborhood.

Mr. Zand also sold special paper designed for covering our notebooks and the books the school loaned us. We had to return the books at the end of the school year, in good condition so covering them was a must. The special paper also helped me with the huge challenge known as arithmetic. The book covers Mr. Zand sold us had the multiplication table printed on them in large bold fonts, we could see them from Mars.

✡

I would like to describe a few visitors to Ben Yehuda Strasse who did not emigrate from Germany and did not reside in our neighborhood. Nonetheless they were frequent visitors to our close-knit community. I remember two in particular. The first character, an unshaven sort of aloof person, wearing dilapidated clothes, talked, non-stop, to himself. I called him *the smoker*. You could not miss him when he was strolling down the street gazing at the pavement in search of cigarette butts. If he came across one, he would put it inside an old candy tin. Occasionally, he'd find a shady spot under a fichus tree in front of our building and take a smoke break. He would shred a few cigarette butts and spread the tobacco onto a cigarette paper and seal it with saliva. He never stopped mumbling to himself except during the time that he was either inhaling or exhaling that poisonous smoke. The guy was an expert at blowing smoke rings. His image always pops up in my mind whenever I see the logo of the Olympic Summer Games with its five interlocking rings representing the five continents.

The pavement in front of our building seemed to be his favorite cigarette butt collecting spot, for two main reasons. The first one was Mrs. Rivkah Yakobovitz who lived on the first floor. Rivkah was a very attractive lady but unfortunately, a very heavy smoker. The balcony was her favorite smoking spot. Sometimes she would start coughing heavily after the very first puff and immediately toss the cigarette to the dirt. It was *the smoker's* favorite spot because he found those almost full-length cigarettes.

The smoker's second favorite place for collecting cigarette butts was the walkway by the entrance of the Hotel Yarden that shared a fence with our building. He was attracted to the sidewalk by the hotel entrance where guests smoked expensive British and American cigarette brands. These cigarettes were made from the American Virginia type tobacco as opposed to the Middle Eastern kind. Most of the local cigarettes were produced by the Dubek cigarette factory which used local tobacco grown by the Arabs. The Virginia tobacco was much stronger and *the smoker* liked the butts of these cigarettes better. He inspected every empty cigarette package oftentimes finding one or two accidentally left inside.

Hotel Yarden was a sophisticated hotel and a popular place among the Britons who served in Eretz Israel/Palestine. It's expensive and stylish restaurant, had tables covered with white linen and an lantern with a small lampshade at the center of each table. On Friday and Saturday nights guests danced to popular tunes of that era played by a ballroom dance-band, similar to Lawrence Welk or Benny Goodman. My friends and I peeked through the restaurant windows. It was a great show for us to watch the band play and the guests having a good time. No wonder I am hooked on this kind music and culture.

Hotel Yarden also housed one of the foreign embassies. The official's fancy cars parked by the entrance outside on Ben Yehuda Street. Major airlines kept their offices there, so my friends and I had the habit of sneaking into the large lobby to collect fliers and glossy booklets from the airline counters. The best treat, without any doubt, were the days when we sneaked into the lobby and managed to charm one of the foreign guests to take us with him or her up and down the elevator. The hotel staff knew that we were from the building next door, so they never raised a fuss as long as we did not enter with dirty clothes and sandals.

My friends and I had our own kind of cigarette addiction, not smoking, God forbid, but collecting empty foreign cigarette packages we found on the sidewalk by Hotel Yarden. We used them to make what I call *cigarette coins*. I am not sure if making *cigarette coins* was a leisure activity unique to us at 132 Ben Yehuda Street or if it was practiced by other cohorts during that era. Collecting *cigarette coins* was akin to collecting stamps of foreign countries but much more glamorous. Each package had the brand's logo or a unique picture at its center. We considered packages of the foreign cigarettes to be more valuable than the ones of the local brands.

To produce our *cigarette coins*, we set our empty packages on the sidewalk in front of our building. It was of paramount importance to select a pavement tile with the perfect rough surface for the job. Then we placed onto it the empty package, logo side up. Next step was to center a metal cap from a Coca Cola bottle with its serrated edges on top of the logo making sure it was centered. We used a bottle cap because of the sharp serrated edge. I'm sure that we were more precise with our production quality assurance than the one used at any of the USA mint producing the American coins. Once satisfied that the Coca Cola cap was placed correctly, we pressed it hard against the pavement tile and rubbed it vigorously until the logo was cut from the cigarette package.

We determined their *exchange value* by how difficult it was to find the empty package of a specific brand. If we wanted to have a coin with a logo we did not have, it required negotiating with the friend that had it. We never used real money to buy the coins. We used our *cigarette coins* instead. The best outcome of our childhood preoccupation and production of *cigarette coins* came decades later when we, as grownups, knew how to manage our IRA, 401K, or any other investment transaction. As a side note, I wish to state that none of us ever became cigarette smokers.

Another visitor to our neighborhood was an elderly Arab fruit merchant with a donkey as old as he was. During the summer season he stopped frequently by our building selling fruit grown in the Arab villages around Tel Aviv. I felt sorry for his old donkey as the old fruit merchant loaded it with two large gunny sacks filled with fruit, one on each side.

I liked apricots the best and I liked the way he announced them, shouting in a very raspy voice *Mish-Mish, Mushamash, Mushamash.* Then he shouted the price per kilo (a kilogram is about 2.2 lbs). We combined our small change enough to buy one kilo. He pulled a slim twig out of the gunny sacks. It had two flat metal pans attached to the tips of the twig to make it into a scale. Then he placed the proper weights on one pan and loaded the *mish-mish* into the opposite pan to match the weight. There was a rope at the center of his scale so after putting what he estimated to be one kilo worth of *mish-mish* he would lift the scale making sure it would be biased in our favor, thus giving us extras.

We liked the apricots for their splendid flavor and aroma, but also for their pits. The nickname in our neighborhood for the apricot pit was *go-ga-lach*. I have no idea where this Yiddish-sounding name came from. I'm not sure if it is a Yiddish term. We collected them to play the *go-ga-lach* game. There were many variations but we followed the rules that we invented. Our version required the players to find a flat area next to a brick or cement wall and dig a small hole touching that wall. The diameter of the depression was similar to that of a drinking cup. Each player put an agreed-upon number of pits (*go-ga-lach*) in the *bank*. Next, we drew to determine the turns, the player who played first, took all the apricots pits from the bank, held them in his palm while standing about two meters from the small depression. Next, he/she threw the pits toward the depression, trying to get as many into the depression as possible. The player earned all the *go-ga-lach* that landed inside the depression. The ones landing outside went back to the *bank*. Each player added an additional *go-ga-lach*, and the game continued with the next player. The game kept going until we decided it was time to do something else.

The elderly fruit merchant lived in Jaffa, the major Arab city bordering Tel Aviv. Many Arab merchants come to our street riding on the back of their donkeys as it was a simpler and shorter commute. The path used the stretch of the sandy beach between Jaffa and our neighborhood, which was located three blocks from the beach. The sandy beach was the popular highway for the Arabs using donkeys and camels (Figure 1.3). After the War for Independence, the two cities merged into one municipality named *Tel Aviv-Yafo*. (Yafo is the Hebrew/biblical name for Jaffa).

Ben Yehuda Street sloped toward the Yarkon River for at least five miles. The yard where we played was about ten meters lower than the hotel entrance. The Hotel Yarden bar was a popular with off-duty British soldiers, no matter what time of the day it was or how hot it was outside. There was one soldier in particular who never failed to get really drunk and loud with his filthy mouth. The people at the bar would kick him outside when he got rowdy and that made him extremely mad and out of control. We knew it was time for us to leave the spot where we played *go-ga-lach* and run for a safe shelter since that drunk soldier had the habit of grabbing one of the bicycles the hotel kept for their guests and throwing it at us, thirty-three feet below. He almost hit us during one of his mad attacks. The fear of drunk people got instilled in my head ever since that incident.

One more reason why we loved the apricot pit, it could be made into a great whistle. It was a labor-intensive job requiring the use of a tile on the sidewalk, the spot where we minted our *cigarette coins*. We rubbed the wider tip against the tile's file-like surface until a wide enough slit exposed the seed. Next, we removed the soft seed and let the empty pit dry in the hot sun. The test came when we blew air across the opening and a whistling tune was music to our ears.

Another of our favorite places was the Abd al Nabi Muslim cemetery at the western end of La Salle Street. It was on a kurkar ridge overlooking the Mediterranean. Kurkar is a type of rock unique to the Levantine coast of the Mediterranean countries such as Israel, Turkey, Syria and Lebanon. It is formed by solidifying the windblown quarzitic sand dune, with the natural carbonate cement. It stretched approximately from the La Salle Street in our neighborhood north to the southern edge of Mount Carmel. All the hills in Tel Aviv were kurkar mounds. The Muslim cemetery was about a five-minute walk from our building so we went there quite often sneaking behind the older boys that lived in the neighborhood.

After we moved away from Ben Yehuda Street, I continued to ride my bicycle to visit the Abd al Nabi Muslim cemetery by myself. I liked the nights in particular, as the pitch-dark Mediterranean was peppered with small fishing boats and the Lux lanterns the fishermen used to attract the fish to the surface. They looked like a swarm of bright fireflies. I brought my crystal radio with me to listen to nice

Figure 1.3 The use of the sandy beach between Yafo and Tel Aviv as a transportation highway by Arab merchants.

music. The place had excellent reception for crystal radios since there were no buildings around. I borrowed one of the three retracting stands (legs) from my father's camera tripod and used it as an antenna attached to the back of my bike.

✡

A few words about the Abd al Nabi Muslim cemetery and its history are in order as it has a significant part in the development of Tel Aviv. The city was founded in 1902 on the sand dunes north of Yafo, a predominantly Muslim city with a few Jews living there. During the Ottoman Empire era, Yafo was under the jurisdiction of the Turkish governor residing in Jerusalem. A cholera outbreak ravaged Yafo in 1902, the year Tel Aviv was founded. In his attempt to stop the cholera from spreading even further, Yafo's district ruler did not allow new burials in Yafo and ordered the opening of two new burial sites outside the city, one for Jews and one for Muslims. The one assigned for Jewish burial, was located where Trumpeldor Street is today. The burial site for Muslims was located on a *kurkar* ridge overlooking the future beach of Tel Aviv. It stood where the Hilton International hotel is located today. The body of Abd al Nabi was already buried at that site along with graves from the nearby Arab village of Sumail (also known as al Masudia) to the east. The Abd al Nabi Muslim cemetery was not a popular burial site among the Yafo Arabs because of its location at the edge of the fast-growing Jewish city of Tel Aviv. Once the cholera crisis ended, they preferred to bury their dead in Yafo's new cemetery at Jebelia. The Abd al Nabi became the main Muslim cemetery for the Arab village of Sumail, located east of Abd al Nabi. The village was founded in the mid-19th century by Egyptian immigrants, most of them farm workers who worked in the fields and citrus orchards north of Yafo. In 1930 the village was incorporated into Tel Aviv.

In addition to the Egyptian farm workers who founded the village, Sumail also attracted Bedouins from the Sinai Peninsula who came during the growing and harvesting seasons. These nomads pitched their tents where they worked. Sumail's population grew even further due to Muslims from the villages in the northern part of the British-Mandate

Palestine searching for jobs. Abd ai Nabi's location on top of a *kurkar* cliff made it a perfect vantage point for our 132 Ben Yehuda gang. We enjoyed gazing at the Mediterranean and the Arab caravans of donkeys and camels loaded with *zif-zif* used by the Tel Aviv brick manufacturers and the house builders building the city. *Zif-zif* was the type of sand excavated at the beach next to the water line and consisted of quarzitic sand, pebbles, conch and mussel shells. Many of Tel Aviv's houses built during that time used a mixture of *zif-zif* and Portland cement. The Arabs hauled it by donkey, camel and wagon.

The extensive excavation of the sandy beaches became an environmental concern. In 1963, the ministry of Housing and Development commissioned a study regarding the effects of *zif-zif* excavation on the shoreline. The scientists determined that the excavation caused the recession of the coast line and should be outlawed and it was, eventually. The environmentalists were pleased with that decision. The construction people did not shed tears over it either because *zif-zif* contained organic elements which made it an inferior building material compared to more modern alternatives.

Toward the end of the British Mandate era in Eretz Israel/Palestine, the tension between the Arab and the Jewish communities worsened so we stopped going to the Abd-al Nabi Muslim cemetery. Ironically, the cemetery became very popular in the minds of the youngsters our age due to a series of children's adventure novels named *Chasamba* written by the author Yigal Mossinson. The series described the assistance a group of Tel Aviv children gave the *Haganah*, which was the Jewish underground military force dedicated to end the British Mandate and establish the Jewish State of Israel. The *Haganah* along with the three other underground groups, *Palmach, Etzel (Irgun)* and *Lechi* protected the Jewish community from the hostile Arab community as well. They all integrated together to from the IDF (Israel Defense Force) upon Israel's Declaration of Independence on May 14, 1948.

Although the book series was fiction, the stories and the actions described there sounded real to us and captured our imagination. Our 132 Ben Yehuda gang gravitated toward the Abd al Nabi Muslim cemetery that our *Chasamba* heroes used as the top-secret place for their night time meetings.

Chasamba is the Hebrew acronym for *Chavurat Sod Muchlat Behechlet* (The Absolutely Absolute Secret Group). We were sure that the spot was located inside the building that housed the grave of Abd al Nabi. Although I had not started elementary school yet, and could not read, I knew every small detail associated with the book just from hearing the older children talk about our *Chasamba* heroes.

✡

There were several mulberry trees growing on La Salle Street close to Abd-al Nabi Muslim cemetery, a habitat for silkworms who fed only on white mulberry leaves. I kept silkworms in a shoe box with holes in the cover. I had to bring fresh leaves every day until they spun a silk cocoon and pupated inside. The Chinese harvested the silk by placing the cocoon in boiling water to kill the pupa, and then they unraveled the single silk thread that made the cocoon. A single silk thread can reach a length of 984 yards. Since I was not interested in the silk business, I let the larvae pupate and emerge as whitish moths from a round hole they cut through the cocoon.

During the summer season, the mulberry trees were loaded with berries, so I came every day to harvest them. One day I got carried away and managed to fill three beach pales I borrowed from my sister. The pales were overflowing with mulberries. I don't know what struck me on that day to become a businessman all of a sudden. I strolled down La Salle Street and shouted from the top of my lungs "Tooteem, Tooteem Le' Mchira" (Mulberry, Mulberry for sale).

As I approached the corner of La Salle and Ben Yehuda Street in front of Mr. Zand's stationary store, a man yelled from the third balcony "*Hey yeled, kama kesef ata ro' tze?*" (Hey boy, how much money you want?).

Delighted by my instant business success, I shouted back "*Shlosha g'roosheem*" (Three *grush*).

"OK son, please come up, bring the mulberries and get paid."

I zoomed up to his flat and emptied the tree pails into the container he placed on the kitchen counter. He paid me the three *grush* and I went home feeling extremely rich and proud of myself.

At the dinner table that evening, my parents asked why my fingers were stained purplish. I told them about harvesting and selling the mulberries to a family living in the building where Mr. Zand's store stood. I showed them the three *grush* I had made. I don't know why, but it did not sit well with my mother who was adamant against me starting to *wheel and deal* with strangers. "As soon as we finish dinner, I want you to go back to these people and return their money, and please don't do it again," she told me.

I went back to my *client's* apartment on La Salle Street and very softly knocked on their door, embarrassed about the whole situation. I was surprised that someone inside even heard me knocking. The man who bought my mulberries answered.

The family was having dinner. "Yes, son, what are you doing here? Do you have more mulberries to sell us? The ones you brought this morning were very good," he said.

"No, but my mother sent me and told me to give you back the three *grush* you paid me. I will take the mulberries with me if you still have them."

"Too late, son" he replied with a big fatherly smile, "We already made a great pudding out of them, see the big bowl on the table, here is a small cup and a spoon, please take some and enjoy it."

It looked too inviting to resist, so I accepted his invitation. It tasted really good. I thanked him again and was about to head home when he said, "Please tell your Mom that I refused to take back the three *grush*."

My mother was pleased that everything turned out well. Many years have passed since the mulberry incident but I still don't understand why my dear mother put an end to my business aspirations but the three *grush* I earned from selling the mulberries had a lasting emotional impact on me.

A few words on what the *grush* was. It is an obsolete item now, relegated to the history of Israel. It was fondly referred to, descriptively as the *coin with the hole in its center*. Eretz Israel/Palestine was part of the Ottoman Empire for 400 years, starting in the year 1517 and ended in 1917 when it lost to Britain in WWI. The *grush* was a currency used throughout the Ottoman Empire and its monitory value varied according to the individual countries under the Turkish rule. After the British conquered that part of the Ottoman Empire, they made the Egyptian lira the official currency from 1918 through 1927. The *grush* represented one hundredth of the Egyptian lira. It was also known as ten mils (one mil being one thousandth of the lira) as minted on the coin. It was an official currency under the British Mandate in Eretz Israel/Palestine from 1927 to 1948 when the British left. The *grush* was a very recognizable coin due to the round hole in its center. The coin became embedded into local folklore.

For example, if you wanted to describe someone who was oblivious to anything other than making quick money, you would say that the person was looking at things "through the holes of the *grush*." To denigrate someone's expertise as worthless, you

Figure 1.4 Grush

would say that "He is an expert worth a *grush*," and God forbid, if you had the misfortune of being poor, you would earn the accolade, "Not having a single *grush* to your soul." To convey the impression that something was worthless you would say something like "Don't buy that, it's not worth a *grush*." And finally, when you wanted to refer to something that happened in the far past you would say, "When the *grush* had a hole."

✡

It should be obvious to the reader by now that I liked La Salle Street very much. I lived on Ben Yehuda Strasse next to it for the first six years of my life. I was too young then to pay attention to its strange name that did not sound Hebrew or Jewish. But as I grew older and started to reminisce on my childhood era I began to wonder why we had and still have, a street with a French sounding name such as Ferdinand La Salle in the midst of Ben Yehuda Street, the bastion where so many German Jewish immigrants lived.

I found out that Ferdinand La Salle was a mid-19th century German Jewish activist and philosopher who lived in Berlin. He founded the Social Democratic Movement in Germany. He estranged himself completely from his Jewish roots. Moreover, at a young age, he wrote how badly he hated the Jews, changed his name and disassociated himself from Judaism. Ironically, his separation from Judaism was not complete. When he was killed in a shooting duel over a woman in

Carouge, a suburb of Geneva, Switzerland, Ferdinand La Salle was buried in Poland at the Breslau's old Jewish Cemetery.

Ferdinand La Salle's checkered Jewish history puzzled me as to why such a negative personality, from a Jewish perspective at least, received the honor of having such a lovely street named after him. The answer is, most likely, that La Salle established the first socialistic movement in Europe. The provisional government of the Jewish community in Eretz Israel/Palestine was definitely socialistic. The largest socialist party within the provisional government already had two establishments on La Salle Street affiliated with the socialists. One was a Kindergarten (pre-school), the other was an elementary school. My sister and I went to the socialist-run kindergarten off La Salle Street.

The A.D. Gordon elementary school founded in 1932 was also known as *Beith Hinuch ba' tazfon* (Hebrew for The Education House for the North). It was built for the children of the blue color socialist workers. My mother worked there in the kitchen and the dining hall for more than ten years. Unlike the regular elementary school in Eretz Israel/Palestine, the school kitchen and dining hall provided a large free lunch for its students. The school was part of the education system during the British Mandate and then an integral part of the State of Israel education system. My father who did not subscribed to the socialistic philosophy sent me to the normal, mainstream Nes Ziona public school on Gretz Street near our building. Looking back, I regret that my parents didn't send me to the A.D. Gordon elementary school as it was a very good one-of-a-kind school.

✡

Socialist *(Mapi)* was the dominant political force ruling Israel for thirty-eight years, during the British mandate and the years after Israel became a sovereign state. David Ben-Gurion, Israel's first prime minister (1930-1954, 1955-1963), lived on Keren Kayemet Blvd which was the first adjacent street south of La Salle Street. The entire La Salle Street area had a very heavy socialistic tint to it so, in retrospect, naming the street after Ferdinand La Salle, the Socialist, was not a strange act after all.

The Jewish socialists in Eretz Israel/Palestine followed the ideology of Aaron David Gordon (A.D. Gordon) who was considered the father of the Zionist labor movement. The socialistic elementary school on La Salle Street was named after him. According to A.D. Gordon's doctrine, the suffering of the Jewish people in the diaspora was the result of their inability to participate in creative and physical labor. Immigrating to Eretz Israel/Palestine, the land of the Jews forefathers, presented an opportunity for them to work the land, reclaim it and bond with it. It was imperative that they should work the land themselves rather than depending on others.

The students at A.D. Gordon School on La Salle Street practiced this doctrine by doing real work in addition to being full time students. They spent two days a week working in the field, owned by the school, where they grew and harvested the food cooked and served in the school's dining hall. During the agriculture off-season, the boys were taught carpentry once a week and the girls were taught embroidery in addition to the normal school curriculum. During the summer recess, the working parents had the option to send their children to the school's full-day summer recreation/daycare center. That included a one-hour mandatory nap so the students brought from home their sleeping bags and pillows. I attended two of their summer sessions and enjoyed them immensely.

✡

From my perspective, one way for the British Mandate authorities to control Eretz Israel/Palestine was to agitate the Arab communities against the much smaller Jewish community, also referred to as *The Yeshuv*. The Arab city of Jaffa shared a border with Tel Aviv. The demarcation line between the two cities ran through the southern edge of the Carmel *Souk*, an open market serving the two communities. The tension between the Arabs and the Jews intensified toward the end of the British Mandate. Both communities wanted the Britons to leave. The hostility coming from the Yafo Arabs intensified as well. Shopping at the Carmel *Souk* stopped being the pleasant event it once was. We continued to go there because it was the cheapest place to buy food. To save the cost of a babysitter, my mother took my sister and me along when she did her weekly shopping

I loved the Carmel *Souk* and its plethora of merchandise, food, clothing and the smell of ethnic foods cooked on the open fires and charcoal. Jews and Arabs intermingled at the market. My biggest fascination by far, was watching the Arab housewives shopping for fresh eggs. They picked an egg from the large tray, formed a circle with their thumb and index finger and positioned the wider end of the egg into that circle. They tilted their heads in the direction of the sun and looked through the egg while rotating it along its vertical axis, as if peeking through a fancy kaleidoscope.

During one visit to the *souk*, I was mesmerized by an Arab housewife, dressed in a black burka, holding a large straw basket. The gold crown in one of her front teeth shone like the sun in its mid-day zenith. She was inspecting the eggs so intensively, I started following her as she moved from one egg stand to the next. Pretty soon I did not see my mother and everyone around me was speaking Arabic. I found myself out of the Jewish sector and well into Yafo at a time of rising hostility between the two communities.

My mother was frantic, to say the least. It was *Te' sha Be' AV*, (the 9th day of the month *AV* in the Hebrew calendar). That date in the Hebrew calendar has been a very bad date for the Jewish people. It was the date when the first and the second holy Temples in Jerusalem were destroyed. It was also the date Jews were expelled from Spain in 1492. Hundreds of pogroms befalling the diaspora Jews for centuries, also happened on the 9th day of AV. My mother was sure I won't survive if I got lost in Yafo. A British policeman had found me and sheltered me at the Yafo police station. Her intuition led her there and we were reunited.

The afternoon of that very same day was as eventful as its morning. While we waited at the bus station, I started tinkering with the hub cap bolts on a different bus that stopped to take passengers. My mother rushed to alert the driver not to move and managed to grab me before the bus took off. My mother fasted on the 9th day of AV every year until she passed away at the age of eighty-nine. She was convinced that God saved me twice on that day.

✡

Although Hotel Yarden next to our building had a fancy restaurant with a dance hall and orchestra, my parents, who were ballroom dancing enthusiasts were looking for a less expensive place to take the entire family for a treat. They chose *Gan Hawaii* (Hebrew for The Hawaiian Garden). Gan Hawaii was a small café and night club on the northern bank of the Yarkon River. Popular during the 1940s, the café was situated in front of the Arab village of Sheikh Muanis, where Tel Aviv University and the Ramat-Aviv suburb are today. The place was built by Ibrahim el Baydas, a resident of Sheikh Muanis on a lot inside the citrus orchard owned by his family.

After WWII ended, the place was expanded when Jewish partners invested and became part owners. Gan Hawaii offered evening entertainment for both Jews and Arabs of Sheikh Muanis, who called it *El Alamein* instead of Gan Hawaii. One Saturday evening at the end of *Sabbath*, we visited Gan Hawaii. It was a big deal for the entire family, especially for me and my sister as the trip included cruising on a motorboat along the Yarkon River.

We rode the bus all the way to the boat docking area, the last bus stop. All the passengers on our boat were headed to Gan Hawaii. The boat's single headlight beam pierced the darkness. It required considerable skill on the part of the boat captain to navigate among the many small rowboats floating with young lovers who found the river romantically enticing that evening.

The commercial motorboats that ferried passengers on the Yarkon River were unique, each one built in a different style and design. They were hand-built at a small assembly yard next to the passenger boarding dock. The engine was small, not powerful or environmental friendly. The smell of exhaust fumes mixed with ladies' perfume was strange and unpleasant.

We got off at the dock next to the club. Although we had reserved a table, my sister and I preferred to sit at the edge of the dancing area, slurping our melting ice cream and watching our parents enjoy their tango. It took great skill not to let the melting ice cream soil our white clothes. We all had a great time at Gan Hawaii and on the boat ride home my parents decided that we would visit the club again.

A few weeks later my parents marked the evening of August 10, 1947 as the day to visit. It fell on Sunday and during breakfast that morning, my mother said to my father with a fierce and determined tone in her voice "Yaakov, we are not going to Gan Hawaii tonight!" Then she told him, in Yiddish, about the nightmare she had that shook her to the core. In that dream, our entire family was enjoying the visit at Gan Hawaii when a fierce gun battle erupted with a few guests killed and many injured. The injured guests were covered with blood, shouting, and screaming.

Many years later, I asked her for the reason she told my father about that bad dream using Yiddish instead of Hebrew. "I did not want to scare you and Chaya with the details of that nightmare," she answered. My mom's scary dream and her intuitive refusal to visit Gan Hawaii on that night saved our family as a big gun fight did take place on the evening of August 10, 1947.

The Gan Hawaii massacre occurred during the time period when the collision between the Arabs and the Jews in communities in Eretz Israel/Palestine reached a new level. Armed Arab gangs were robbing Jewish communities. These violent activities were mostly criminal in nature, but some were also driven by nationalistic zeal. On that night, around 10 p.m., a previous argument between Fausi Abu Kishek, a Bedouin from a village nearby the Jewish community of Herzelia, and Ibrahim el Baydas, the owner of Gan Hawaii, escalated into a violent fight. An armed Arab gang, dressed as British soldiers, stormed into the club while the ballroom dance band played a tango. When the shooting started, Ibrahim el Baydas, the club's Arab owner, pleaded with the gang to stop shooting, but they killed him along with four Jewish guests and entertainers. Some of the guests ran for their lives and hid in the bushes on the river bank. Two other club owners, one Arab and one Jew were among the wounded. The gang robbed the cashier and stole expensive watches and jewelry from the shocked guest. Clearly, it was a robbery but the four Jews who were murdered, gave it a nationalistic angle.

The aftermath of the Gan Hawaii massacre brought more violent collisions between Jews and Arabs at the Tel Aviv-Yafo demarcation area. They lasted four days costing lives and burnt properties on both sides. The *Haganah*, the military force of the Jewish community in Eretz Israel/Palestine, retaliated by killing the Arab man who guided the Gan Hawaii killers to the café. They also killed the Arab who owned the tent from which the killers embarked. The *Haganah* command also located the citrus orchard used as the training camp for that gang and attacked it while they were training for their next terror activity. Most of the gang members were eliminated in that attack but some escaped. The last retaliatory act of the *Haganah* was blowing up the house located in that orchard. However, the *Haganah* soldiers were not aware that seven members of the family owning the orchard were hiding inside the water well below it. The house was demolished and the seven people hiding there perished in the blast. The *Haganah* command paid reparation to the relatives of that family.

As the relationship between the Jewish and the Arab communities under the British Mandate became more violent, with casualties mounting on both sides, the UN General Assembly formed the UN Special Committee on Palestine (UNSCOP) in May 1947. The committee was chartered with the task of finding a solution for the problem. It took the commission three months to formulate a report and suggested partitioning the land into a Jewish state and Arab state. It became known as the *Partition Plan* (Resolution # 181). The plan was announced on November 29, 1947 at Lake Success, NY by the United Nation General Assembly. The plan also stipulated the termination of the British Mandate in Palestine by no later than August 1, 1948. The resolution granted a Special International Regime for the city of Jerusalem. Britain, which ruled Eretz Israel/Palestine since 1917 announced on the evening of February 1947 its intention to terminate its Mandate and leave. Israel, accepted the *Partition Plan* and declared its independence on May 14, 1948, as Britain terminated its Mandate at midnight of that day.

David Ben-Gurion, who was the World Zionist Organization, Chairman of the Jewish Agency for Palestine and the de facto leader of the provisional government of the Jewish community in Eretz Israel/Palestine, declared the establishment of the *Jewish State of Israel* replacing the old name *Eretz Israel*. He would soon become its first Prime Minister. The declaration took place at the Tel Aviv

Museum, known today as the Independence Hall. On the wall behind him during the ceremony, was a large portrait of Theodor Herzl, the founder of modern Zionism. Flags of the new nation hung on each side of the portrait. The ceremony was not publicized, fearing that the British authorities would try to prevent it from happening as well as the fear that the Arab armies would launch a surprise attack on the new state. To maintain secrecy, the participants and the signatories were summoned by messenger early that morning. They were asked to arrive at 15:30 and to keep the ceremony a secret.

At 16:00 it stopped being a secret when the ceremony was broadcast live on the radio. It was the first official live broadcast of Israel radio services named later on as *Kol Israel* (Hebrew for The Voice of Israel). The ceremony and the radio broadcast started at 16:00 as not to breach the *Sabbath*. David Ben-Gurion read the *Declaration of Independence* which he called *The Foundation Scroll of the Jewish State* and asked Rabbi Fishman to recite the Jewish blessing *Shehecheyanu* (Hebrew for *who has given us life*), thanking God for this historic moment of the Jewish people. After Moshe Sharett, the last signatory, signed the declaration, the Israel Philharmonic Orchestra played the *Hatikvah* (Hebrew for *the Hope*) which become the official anthem of Israel. The ceremony concluded with Ben-Gurion declaring, "The State of Israel is established."

Ben-Gurion's declaration mesmerized Jewish communities, and people flooded the streets to celebrate despite the fact that it was *Sabbath* already. I remember that our family and others in the building went to Dizzingoff Street two blocks east. That street was, and still is, a major traffic artery of Tel Aviv and runs parallel to my beloved Ben Yehuda Strasse. The spontaneous celebration lasted into the night. The next morning rumors flew in our neighborhood that David Ben-Gurion, who lived two blocks from us, was about to ride in an open Jeep on his way to a meeting.

It was Saturday, and out of character for public figures to breach the *Sabbath*. Evidently, he got wind that the Arab armies were staging their forces at the borders, ready to invade any second, so he breached the *Sabbath* to be in the command room and meet with other members of *Moetzet Ha'am* (The Provisional State Council). *Moetzet Ha'am* was the legislative body running the affairs of the new state. It was later replaced and became the Israel Parliament, the *Knesset,* after the first election in January 1949. The Judaic laws forbid us to breach and desecrate the *Sabbath* except when observing *Sabbath* would endanger life which was the case that morning when Ben-Gurion drove by our building on his way to *Moetzet Ha'am*.

The Arab's hostility toward the Jews living in Eretz Israel/

Palestine was at its peak following the signing of Israel's Declaration of Independence. A few hours later, on May 15, 1948, the new Jewish State had to defend itself against troops from Egypt, Trans-Jordan, Syria, Lebanon, and Iraq. The danger was exacerbated by having a hostile Arab population living in territories assigned to Israel under the UN Partition plan.

My friends and I were happy for the birth of our country, but as a six-year-old, I didn't fully grasp the significance of the event and the looming danger it brought. To us, the *Ben Yehuda Gang*, it was business as usual so we grabbed the candies our parents gave us to celebrate, headed to Abd-al Nabi Muslim cemetery and the beach below it.

At the intersection of La Salle and Ranak Streets we heard a loud roaring noise coming from the sky above us and saw airplanes heading toward Arlozorov Street, just few houses north of where we stood. Next, we heard the explosion from the bombs dropped on a building on Arlozorov Street demolishing its 4th floor. We run to Mr. Zand's stationary store for shelter.

In addition to dropping bombs, these planes sprayed nearby residential buildings with machine guns. The building at the corner of Arlozorov and Zlatopolski Streets was machine-gunned badly.

The attack my friends and I witnessed on that morning was the first Egyptian air raid on Tel Aviv, and the opening salvo of the 1948 Israel-Arab war for Israeli independence.

✡

The reality of a raging war meant that there was the likelihood of me being killed by the marching Egyptians once they were at the entrance of my hometown. If not by the Egyptian soldiers, my demise would come from one of the Egyptian pilots bombing my city. Many buildings, including our building, did not have underground bomb shelters. When the air raid sirens yelped to warn us of an approaching Egyptian bomber, all the families living in our building rushed to the ground floor and squeezed under the lowest flight of stairs. For our family, it meant having no shelter at all since we lived on the third floor and by the time we reached the ground floor, all the space under the lowest flight of stairs was occupied.

There was an upholstery repair shop on the ground floor next to the entrance of our building. The furniture man was a shy, soft-spoken, likable person. He was not married and lived by himself. The furniture man kept the door open so we saw him building the furniture and then used volatile polishing and varnishing materials. He kept the door wide open to allow circulation of fresh air. At times, the door to his place was closed because he did not feel well. My mother who had a soft spot in her heart for him, brought him hot chicken soup when he was under the weather. He reciprocated by putting mattresses in the stairwell to keep us safe during the air raids. The raids were tough on us especially since my father had been recruited by the *Haganah (IDF)*.

✡

On June 3, 1948, after sixteen raids over Tel Aviv, the Egyptian Air Force stopped bombing when the Israeli Air Force intercepted them. Modi Alon, the legendary young native Israeli, engaged two C-47 Dakota bombers and the two Spitfires that escorted them. He shot down the two bombers while the Egyptian Spitfires fled. The incident was observed by many Tel Aviv residents who didn't know that The State of Israel had started building an Air Force. The Egyptian bombers never showed up again over Tel Aviv.

There were two announced cease fires during the war. The first one began on June 11, 1948 but the fighting resumed on July 8, 1948. A second truce started ten days later, on July 18, 1948 and was broken again in mid-October 1948.

We saw my father only once during the war when he came home for a very short one-day leave during the first official truce. I remember how glad we were to see him alive, and how excited we were about the presents he carried. He brought me a large bag full of empty rifle cartridges and large empty Cannon shells that we later used as flowers vases.

The most interesting present he brought was a large, elongated straw basket. Its opening was covered with a *kufiya,* the traditional Arab headdress. I watched the frantic activities inside the basket as the black and white scarf moved back and forth. He pulled live chicks out of the basket very much like a magician pulling a rabbit out his cylindrical hat. My sister and I were really impressed.

I'm sure that my mother, who was a very practical person, already marked the dates on her calendar as to when to transform those chickens from pets into something more tangible like chicken soup and chicken meal. My father suggested that we should keep them alive on the balcony and harvest the eggs. My mother went along with the idea and it was up to me to work the logistics after my father returned to his unit.

With my father away from home fighting in the war, my mother had to go to work and earn some money. She found a job at the largest towel factory in Eretz Israel/Palestine so she left us at home and made me the *official babysitter* of my four-year-old sister.

Since we all lived in one single room it was obvious that the two chickens would stay on the balcony. We also used the balcony to store large-size items and save the precious space in our room. My sister's old baby crib was stored on the balcony. It was an old-style metal crib, the kind you see on TV documentaries from Eastern European communist countries during that era. It was, basically, a white cage made of metallic frame with vertical rods spaced at narrow intervals.

I created a chicken coop out of the crib, and padded the floor with as many old rugs as I could find to make my chickens comfortable. Then I had to wait for my mother to come back from work and help me take the chickens out of the long straw basket and place them in their new home.

My chickens grew and I felt so proud of myself when I found the first egg. She was the only one who kept doing her job. The other chicken had changed into a very fancy creature with colorful feathers and never laid a single egg. I learned that roosters never lay eggs. This rooster paid with his life and was the first one my mother took to the butcher. The egg-laying chicken had to meet the butcher too when our balcony became messy and smelled like a chicken coop. That was the end of my career as a chicken farmer for a while.

The war that started on May 15, 1948 ended on July 24, 1949 with a Israeli victory. No peace treaty was signed. The war ended with armistice agreements between the belligerents. My father came back, and our family reunited.

✡

During the 1948 War for Independence, we also had our own Jewish War with a violent outcome. It took place between the two main political wings of Zionism. The left-wing Socialists and the right-wing Revisionists differed widely on how to deal with the British.

David Ben-Gurion and his Socialist Party subscribed to the philosophy that the best approach to establish a Jewish state could be achieved only by a massive Jewish immigration to Palestine, cultivating the land and building the cities. They were convinced that the only way to achieve that goal was by cooperating with the British authorities.

The Revisionists, on the other hand, subscribed to the philosophy that the only way to establish a Jewish state in Eretz Israel/Palestine was to retake the land by force.

David Ben-Gurion and his Socialist party were willing to negotiate with the Nazis government to expedite a massive immigration of German Jews to Eretz Israel/Palestine.

Whereas David Ben-Gurion and the leadership felt that they were looking after the interest of the German Jews, the Revisionists believed that under no circumstances should Jews negotiate with Nazis officials.

The Revisionist had purchased a cargo ship, Altalena. The ship was loaded with weapons donated by the French government along with 940 Irgun (Revisionists) volunteer fighters. It left France and intended to arrive in Israel on May 15, 1948, when Israel declared Independence.

The task of incorporating Jewish fighting groups into the IDF, (Israeli Defense Force) including Irgun and Haganah turned out to be very complicated as each group continued to fight the Arabs on its own and planned to keep their own weapons. Nonetheless, on June 1, 1948 the Irgun signed an agreement with the provisional government agreeing to be absorbed into the IDF and to cease its independent weapon purchasing activities.

As the ship was about to depart from France and sail to Eretz Israel/Palestine the Irgun informed the provisional government about Altalena, its weapon cargo and the 940 volunteers on board. Fearing that the ship would be attacked at sea, the Irgun French headquarters tried to keep the departure date secret.

The ship commander decided to leave France on June 11, 1948 and informed the Irgun headquarters in Eretz Israel/Palestine in a cable. The existence of Altalena and its whereabouts was revealed when the Radio London Broadcast service learned about it and put it on the air. Moreover, the ship's departure date, planned to take place on June 11, 1948 was very problematic as it was the first day of the first cease fire. It was feared that the truce would be canceled because one of the stipulations in the cease fire banned bringing new military equipment and fighters into the country.

Menachem Begin, the *Irgun* leader, decided to postpone the arrival of *Altadena* and cabled the ship commander to stay in France and wait for further orders, but it was too late, the *Altalena* had already left.

On June 15, 1948, Menachem Begin met with representatives of the provisional government informing them that *Altalena* had left France, without his knowledge, and that he was on his way to consult with the *Irgun's* upper echelon on how to proceed.

The next day, David Ben-Gurion, the head of the provisional government, realizing that the ship was due to arrive shortly, instructed Begin to anchor at an unknown location far away from densely populated Tel Aviv. Ben-Gurion gave Begin his consent to unload *Altalena's* cargo as quickly as possible at the selected destination.

Menachem Begin, upon securing Ben-Gurion's consent, radioed *Altalena*, sailing somewhere in the Mediterranean, with orders to sail toward Ertez Israel/Palestine at full speed. The *Irgun* high command insisted that the shores of Tel Aviv were their preferred unloading site but representative of the provisional government defense group convinced them to direct the ship to the Kfar Vitkin shore located halfway between Tel Aviv and the city of Haifa further north.

While *Altalena* was sailing toward Eretz Israel/Palestine, Ben-Gurion disagreed with Begin's plan to distribute the weapons because it would create an *army within and army.*

Meanwhile, *Altalena* anchored off the shore of Kfar Vitkin in the late afternoon on June 20, 1948. It took the entire night to unload cargo at Kfar Vitkin but Begin still retained control over the weapons. Ben-Gurion issued Begin an ultimatum to hand over the weapons to the IDF. The ultimatum made it clear that the army would open fire on the ship and the *Irgun* people at the Kfar Vitkin shore should Begin fail to meet the demands.

One of the reasons for having *Altalena* anchor by Kfar Vitkin was to evade being discovered by the UN observers monitoring the ceasefire. This objective failed as a United Nation surveillance plane flew over Kfar Vitkin and recorded the unfolding incident. The stalemate lingered on into the evening and heavy fire exchanges between the *Irgun* and IDF erupted.

Altalena, with Begin in command on board, sailed to Tel Aviv, a city that had many *Irgun* supporters. Moreover, many of the *Irgun* fighters who had previously incorporated into the IDF, left their IDF units and arrived at the Tel Aviv beach after hearing about the crisis and the arrival of *Altalena* with Begin on board.

Rumors were flying claiming that the *Irgun* was planning to forcibly take control away from the provisional government. Ben-Gurion, who was determined to block the arrival of *Altalena* at Tel Aviv at all cost, ordered the IDF air force to attack and sink *Altalena* before it reached Tel Aviv.

The IDF air force commanders tried to recruit the foreign volunteers to attack *Altalena* but all refused, "We volunteered to help Israel against the invading Arab countries, but not to kill Jewish fighters," they claimed. So the order to attack the ship from the air was strapped.

The corvettes of the IDF navy fired at *Altalena* as it was getting closer to the Tel Aviv shore. The corvettes stopped firing at the ship after their *Irgun* fighters, still on the ship, fired back at the navy corvettes with their heavy Bren guns. The fighting between the *Irgun* and the IDF was not limited to the beach but spilled over to the center and southern neighborhoods of Tel Aviv.

Altalena reached Tel Aviv around midnight and purposely ran onto the sand bar next to the corner of Hayarkon and Frishman Streets.

When *Altalena* ran aground, the beach was crowded with journalists and local residents. United Nations observers were watching the unfolding events from a beach front hotel. Ben-Gurion ordered the

IDF to bring more troops and to take control of *Altalena* by force. The heavy shelling of *Altalena* was done from a vacated British army camp located at the northern edge of the Abd all Nabi Muslim cemetery described earlier. One shell hit *Altalena* and started a fire (Figure 1.5 a & b).

IDF troops on the beach joined the fight and fired at the ship with heavy machine guns loaded with armor-piercing bullets. Monroe Fein, the ship's Captain, raised a white flag and ordered the evacuation of *Altalena*. People who could swim did so despite the fact that the IDF soldiers kept shooting. Some *Irgun* fighters refused to surrender, continued their fire and ignored the white flag of surrender.

A gunner who just emigrated from South Africa refused at first to shell the ship but yielded after being threatened with a court martial. A total of eight IDF soldiers refused to obey the shoot-to-kill order against fellow Jews and were court-martialed for insubordination after the incident.

Menachem Begin agreed to leave *Altalena* only after the last wounded person on the ship was evacuated.

The incident ended with a cease-fire agreement on the evening of June 22. The *Irgun* cells within the IDF were disbanded and the former *Irgun* fighters that deserted IDF during the *Altalena* incident went back to their units. A total of 200 *Irgun* members were arrested but released a few weeks later except for five senior *Irgun* officers who were kept for two months until released on August 27, 1948.

Menachem Begin ordered his *Irgun* fighters to cease fighting the IDF and to help in the battle for Jerusalem.

The *Altalena* affair took the lives of sixteen *Irgun* fighters, six of them at Kfar Vitkin Beach. The IDF lost three fighters, two at Kfar Vitkin and one on the beach at Tel Aviv.

✡

I find this act by the *Altalena*'s crew to run aground intentionally, very personal, and interesting because a similar act happened on August 22, 1939, when my parents, along with other 860 Revisionist, arrived at the same stretch of Tel Aviv shore on board the ship *Parita*. (See Chapter 3.)

Figure 1.5 a: Tel Aviv residents watching the burning *Altalena*

Figure 1.5 b: Abd al Nabi Muslim Cemetery, Tel Aviv residents watching the *Altalena* burning after being shelled by the Haganah during the *Altalena* Affair, June 1948

✡

We heard the gunfire exchanges on the beach 700 yards from our apartment, but had no idea what was going on. Our apprehension intensified when we heard the bombardment and shelling. I looked up at the sky each time I heard the boom to see if it came from another Egyptian bomber. Then the plume of heavy smoke from the burning ship reached us. As the event continued to unfold and the initial details became available, all the residents in our neighborhood were urged to evacuate immediately. My mother hastily packed a small suitcase with basic clothes for all of us. The bus services on Ben Yehuda Street stopped operation so we walked the 1.2 miles to my uncle's house. My mother, who was twenty-seven years old at that time, carried the suitcase and delegated me, almost six, to hold my four-year-old sister's hand. We had to pick a safe route to my uncle's house because escaping via the Ben Yehuda Street route was too dangerous. We stayed at my uncle's house one day and returned to our building after the provisional government announced that the *Altalena* incident was over and it was safe to return.

Altalena, ravaged by fire, stayed aground on the sand bar for almost a year after the incident. Adventurers swarmed the ghost ship in search of souvenirs such as burnt rifles and other weapons left by *Irgun* fighters. The children in our neighborhood had an ample supply of guns for our *Police and Robbers* game. A year later, the ship was re-floated off the sand bar, towed fifteen miles away from the Tel Aviv and sunk to the seabed at a depth of 984 feet.

✡

As the years passed, Israel started building and transforming itself into a modern country with a strong IDF (Israeli Defense Force), but the trauma of the *Altalena* Affair lingered on for a very long time. The ship, a ghost resting on the seabed of the Mediterranean, haunted Davis Ben-Gurion and Menachem Begin, the two main players in its drama. David Ben-Gurion became the Prime minister of Israel and the leader of Israel's largest political party (*Mapai*), but he was still fighting Menachem Begin, the leader of the Freedom political party (*Herut*). Begin became the opposition leader of the Israeli parliament, (*Kneset*). The fight between the two was not just an argument between two leaders with big egos, but rather a moral disagreement centered around the question of whether or not it was justifiable for an Israeli government lead by David Ben-Gurion to use government forces (IDF) to kill fellow Jewish citizens who subscribed to a different philosophy on how to establish the State of Israel. Ben-Gurion elected to use force and, in the process, brought bloodshed, costing the lives of both *Irgun* and IDF soldiers. The timing of that decision was wrong as the fledgling country was in the midst of its war for its survival and being attacked by the five Arab armies. Ben-Gurion and his supporters claimed that their decision was absolutely necessary and justifiable in order to impose the authority of the Israeli government against a small section of the Jewish community that he believed was aiming to form a separate army rival to the IDF.

Not everyone bought Ben-Gurion's justification for the bloodshed that happened during the *Altalena* Affair. My parents never talked to me about it, so I never asked questions during the years that followed. I was puzzled by their silence about the *Altalena* incident because my mother and her Jewish friends from Poland, were politically active, and members of the Revisionist movement *Betar*, ones who brought my parents to Eretz Israel/Palestine. (See Chapter 3)

✡

Many years later, during her last visit to the USA, I recorded her stories about her family in Poland as well as her ordeal on *Parita*. Surprisingly enough, she never mentioned the *Altalena* incident and our frantic run from 132 Ben Yehuda Street to the safety of my uncle's home.

The socialistic *Mapai*, the largest political party in the Israeli parliament, along with the other smaller socialistic political parties, had the majority of the seats in the *Knesset* (Israeli parliament). They served as the parliament coalition, and ruled Israel. Menachem Begin and his *Herut* party led the opposition wing of the parliament. The socialists had the tendency to bash Begin and his *Herut* party depicting him as a demagogue, warmonger, fascist, and many other derogatory expletives. These accusations were far from the truth as he was a very educated person and an outstanding orator with a razor-sharp tongue. He definitely was not a demagogue. Begin was a very well-mannered person and a perfect gentleman. Oddly enough, this was how Ben-Gurion's wife, Paula described Menachem Begin. His political opponents claimed that whenever he gave political speeches during his election campaigns, the official car that brought him to the campaign site was led by a column of motorcycles riders, like the ones seen in documentary films showing Hitler's public speeches. I personally, never saw these motorcycle riders his opponents accused him of.

Menachem Begin did not forget or forgive David Ben-Gurion for the *Altalena* incident and let Ben-Gurion and everyone else know his feelings on the matter. He never referred or mentioned Ben-Gurion by name but during the political discussions from the *Knesset* plenum, Begin referred to him as "the other man."

The post *Altalena* Affair collision between the two leaders reached it crescendo in 1951 when the Israeli government made a claim for compensation from Germany. The Israeli government justified the move, claiming that it had to absorb and resettle more than half a million Holocaust survivors because of the atrocities committed by Nazi Germany. It was a huge financial burden on the newly established nation recovering from its War for Independence. When the *Reparation Agreement* was signed on September 10, 1952, between Konrad Adenauer, the German Chancellor, and Moshe Sharett, the Israeli Foreign Minister, a fierce public debate erupted. It was dubbed the *Luxembourg Agreement* as it was signed at Luxembourg's City Hall. Ben-Gurion and his *Mapai* party, supported the agreement, whilst Menachem Begin, his *Herut* party, and the leftist *Mapam* party, all opposed it. The opponents claimed that accepting reparation from Germany was tantamount to forgiving Nazi Germany and absolving it from its genocide against the Jewish people.

There was an additional angle to the leftist *Mapam* party objection to the agreement. Germany's miraculous financial and industrial recovery, made Germany a member of the western world political block, an adversary of the socialistic/communist Iron Curtain block. The socialistic, leftist-including the *Mapam* party, preferred that the State of Israel align itself politically with the Communist block and not with the Capitalists. In *Mapam's* opinion, getting money from capitalistic Germany was an abomination. Moreover, several *Knesset* members from *Mapam* led the Warsaw Ghetto Uprising against Nazi Germany. They considered signing the Reparation Agreement an insult to the memory of Nazi victims.

The proponents for the agreement, led by David Ben-Gurion and his *Mapai* party were more pragmatic on the issue, and claimed that Israel must decide *logically* and not *emotionally*. The reparation was badly needed to build the infrastructure of the new nation and to help with the acute shortage of foreign currency reserves it faced. Besides, that money came from the currency and properties stolen from the Jews. Not claiming it was similar to what the Old Testament quoted Elijah the prophet saying: *"Say to him, 'This is what the Lord says: Have you not murdered a man and seized his property?"* (1 Kings 21:19). The proponents strongly believed that the reparation was essential for the survival of Israel.

> It should be noted that Israel, on its part, paid the German government fifty-four million Deutsche Marks for the properties of the German Templers who settled in Eretz Israel during the Ottoman Empire at the end of the 19th century.

The opponents, led by Begin, considered the agreement from the moral aspect as it implied that Israel forgave the Nazis and absolved them of the genocide they committed against the Jewish people. A debate and a *Knesset* vote on the issue was scheduled for January 7, 1952. The police blocked all roads to the *Knesset* in anticipation of a rally against the agreement, organized by Begin and his *Herut* party. A barb-wire fence was erected around the *Knesset* building and IDF's riot dispersing forces were on standby. It was, and still is, the most severe challenge to Israel democracy as more than 15,000 Israelis showed up for the rally and heard Menachem Begin's fiery speech against the agreement while inside the *Knesset* plenum the agreement was up for a vote. In his speech Begin evoked memories of the Holocaust victims, and reopened the trauma of the *Altalena* Affair and stated that, unlike the *Altalena* incident, when he pleaded to his people not to return fire, this time he instructed them to do so if fired upon.

At the end of his speech Begin led the huge crowd to the *Knesset* building. Riots ensued and the protesters threw stones that broke the *Knesset* windows and interrupted the voting session. It took the police more than five hours to control the riot. Hundreds were arrested. Luckily, there were no fatalities, but 200 protesters and 140 policemen were injured. The session ended with the approval of the Reparation Agreement with Germany by a 61-50 margin.

Looking back at history, I found it interesting and almost an axiom that whenever the *Mapai*/socialists and the *Herut*/revisionists get tangled in issues pertaining to negotiation with Germany, David Ben-Gurion and Begin are the main players and emotions flared causing casualties.

✡

I was ten years old when the deep rift within the Israeli society erupted due to the Reparation Agreement with Germany. At that young age I could not grasp the magnitude or the meaning of what the opponents and the proponents were fighting about. Hence, I did not take sides on that issue. My parents did not talk to us about it and I am not sure if my parents were ironing out the issue between themselves. If they did, they probably were conversing in Polish so we won't understand.

Holocaust survivors who immigrated to Israel filed their own personal reparation claims directly to the German government. They were granted a monthly *renta* to cover their living and medical expenses. They also received monitory compensation for physical and mental suffering caused by the Nazis. Some were also compensated for their properties stolen by the German.

My mother was too proud to file such claims as she felt it was below her dignity to do so. No one could compensate her for the loss of her beloved family. Even in 1952, my mom still denied that her entire family perished in the Holocaust. She refused to accept their demise and to ask for reparation. I elaborated more about my maternal family in Chapter 3.

Now, as a grownup man living in America, the most capitalistic country under the sun, I feel informed enough to pass my own humble opinion as to what side in the Reparation Agreement issue was more pragmatic and beneficial for Israel. Israel has become a technology world power and a top start-up nation. The benefits of the Reparation Agreement was the engine that enabled Israel to achieve that status. Thirty percent of the money was used to purchase the fuel needed for Israel energy and transportation. Israel, unlike its Arab neighbors, did not have any domestic oil or natural gas reserves. Seventeen percent of the money was used to purchase brand new ships for Israel merchant marine. Two of them were passenger's liners which I had the pleasure to use twice. The first time was to sail from Naples to Israel upon returning from my 1964 visit to the USA. The second time was in the summer of 1968 when my wife Batia and I sailed to Venice on our way to catch a flight to the USA for graduate school at UC Davis.

The money was also invested to equip the port of Haifa with modern cranes to load and unload the cargo vessels. The government-owned electric company expanded its infrastructure and upgraded its electric power plants across the country. Israel's railway company, also owned by the government, purchased new diesel locomotives and railway cars, replacing the old steam locomotives. Reparation money also financed the purchase of mining equipment for the Timna, Israel sole copper mine, near the port city of Eilat on the Red Sea. The decision to make this agreement with the German government proved to be the best decision. It also helped heal the wounds of the past and in 1965 the two countries established diplomatic relationship. The list of where the reparation money was invested is a long one and beyond the scope of this story.

For many years I was convinced that I would never see the *Mapai* party and its socialist allies lose the elections and control of the *Knesset*. I was pleasantly wrong as, in 1977 they did lose the election to Menachem Begin, for the first time in Israeli history. He became Israel's new Prime Minister. Begin, who in 1952 led the fierce opposition against the Reparation Agreement with Germany and who vowed to never forgive them, did not cancel the Reparation Agreement but kept it intact. Nor did he cancel or break the diplomatic relationship between the two countries. Menachem Begin, the statesman accused by the socialists and the Israeli left of being a fascist and warmonger was the one who made peace with Egypt and signed a peace treaty with Anwar Sadat.

David Ben-Gurion passed away on December 1, 1973 and did not live to see his archrival assume the position of Israel Prime Minister. Their relationship through the years was stormy. Each one had a different philosophy as to what was best for Israel. Many mutual friends on both sides of the political spectrum, tried to make the two great leaders bury the hatchets but failed. Paula Ben-Gurion kept nudging her husband to leave the animosity from the past and open a new page in their relationship but to no avail. Menachem Begin, in my opinion, was the more accommodating person between the two, willing to let bygones be bygones. When asked one time what he considered to be his greatest life achievement he claimed that not retaliating against Ben-Gurion for ordering the IDF to bomb *Altalena* and killing *Irgun* fighters was his greatest moment as a statesman.

✡

Begin's last act that demonstrated his nobility came in June 1967, on the eve of the Six-Day War when Egypt, Syria and Jordan acted against Israel. I, along with my paratrooper unit, was recruited to fight. The IDF had to wait for the diplomats and the UN to resolve the crisis. Egypt gave an ultimatum to the UN forces stationed at the buffer zone between Israel and Egypt, to leave as it was ready to attack. My comrades and I dug foxholes inside a citrus orchard to protect us from a possible Egyptian air raid. This time though, I was not the child from 132 Ben Yehuda Street being attacked by an Egyptian bomber. This time I was a soldier ready to defend my country. There was an undeniable sense in the air that Mr. Levi Eshkol, the Israeli Prime minister at that time, was hesitant and could not make up his mind to make the right move. David Ben-Gurion, at eighty-one, had retired from political life and lived with his wife Paula in *Kibbutz* Sde Boker in the middle of the Negev Desert. A delegation headed by Menachem Begin, traveled all the way to Sde Boker and asked Ben-Gurion to retake the premiership again at that crucial moment and lead the nation through the war that was about to start. Ben-Gurion declined the request. Right after the meeting ended and Begin left, Ben-Gurion confessed to his confidants that had he known during the *Altalena* Affair Begin's attributes as shown during their meeting at Sde Boker, the Altalena incident would have ended differently. What great leaders both of them were. See Chapter 6 for a detailed account of the war and my participation in it .

Chapter 2

34 Yehuda Hamaccabi Street

Housing shortage was an acute problem throughout Israel after the War for Independence, largely due to the huge influx of Holocaust survivors brought to Israel by the *Israel Jewish Agency* in charge of helping diaspora Jews. The new immigrants were housed either in tents or temporary shacks built from galvanized metal sheets which made the living conditions unbearable during the cold rainy winters as well as the notoriously hot and muggy in summers.

The housing shortage was acute even before the wave of immigrants came to Israel, prompting the major political parties in the *Knesset* (Israeli Parliament) to build apartment complexes for their party members. Each apartment was purchased and the building was managed and cared for by the families living there. During the British Mandate the Socialist Labor Party in Tel Aviv built at least two apartment complexes with several buildings each.

New residential areas were established in remote areas of Tel Aviv where there were no proper roads or infrastructure. The area where we moved was about three square miles of large citrus orchards abandoned by their owners at the outset of the War for Independence.

Menachem Begin's Revisionist political party *Herut,* built at least six apartment complexes for its members. Each building was three-stories high with three entrances and called a *Train Building.*

The General Zionist Party my father belonged to built three such train buildings. There were native black and white mulberry trees and fig trees at the back of our train building. My sister and I and many of the children living there, attended the new public elementary school named Yehuda Hamaccabi (Judah the Maccabi), built by the Tel Aviv municipality. It served the apartment complexes built in that new region of Tel Aviv.

Next to the Revisionist *Herut* apartment complex stood the large complex built by the ultra-socialist *Mapam* party to house its party members. It was odd to have the ultra-right *Herut* and the ultra-left *Mapam* living side by side without bloody fights between them.

Then, there was the ten-building complex, each with three stories, built by the Port Authority for its employees who operated the seaport of Tel Aviv. Their children also attended Yehuda Hamaccabi elementary school.

The South African immigrants association built five three-story apartment buildings in our neighborhood. Mrs. Deborah Livni, my sixth-grade English teacher, was one of the immigrants living in that complex.

There were three separate entrances, dividing our building into three wings, each one with its own street number (32, 34, 36). You could enter the first entrance at 32 Yehuda Hamaccabi Street, climb the stairs to the roof and walk to the stairway doors of the other wings of the building. Each wing also had a laundry room with a large bathtub and clotheslines stretched along the flat roof. It was a great help as none of us had a washer or drier.

Next to our complex to the south was a large apartment complex built by the Orthodox Hapoel HaMizrachi political party. It had twelve three-story buildings housing its members. The orthodox children did not attend our school because under the coalition agreement with the orthodox parties in the Knesset, the religious parties established their own public schools, teaching the regular curriculum in addition to religious studies.

Construction delays caused our family a great deal of inconvenience because we had to vacate our room at 132 Ben Yehuda Street. Ezekiel Goldberg, my father's close friend from their early childhood in Góra Kalwaria, Poland, let us stay in his fancy apartment during the week he and his wife were out of town. It was an act of great generosity and affection on his part, to let my parents and their six-year-old son and four-year-old daughter stay in their immaculate apartment with its expensive furniture, fancy gramophone, hot water available all the time and central heating and air conditioning. These were luxuries our family had never experienced. Ezekiel, or better known by his Yiddish nickname *Chaskel*, was financially secure, as he was an accomplished baker and a member of the largest bread baking cooperative in Israel.

Chaskel was always willing to loan my parents money when they urgently needed to pay bills. He never charged them interest. "Pay me when you can," he told them. My parents always paid him back the minute they had the money. When he learned that my parents were toying with the idea of getting me an accordion but could not afford it, a huge accordion showed up one day at our home with Chaskel's famous motto, "Just enjoy it and don't worry. Pay me when you can." And there I was with an accordion much bigger and heavier than me, forcing me to learn how to play it.

Our apartment complex was not ready for occupancy by the time Chaskel Goldberg returned from his week-long vacation so we found another temporary place to live, offered by my father's distant relatives from Góra Kalwaria. Their flat had a small storage room on the roof that sheltered us from the elements. We slept on folding cots our host managed to scrounge and we used their bathroom. These unsuitable conditions made my parents edgy. They started pestering the construction manager as to why the apartments were not ready. The only answers they got were silly excuses, at best.

During one of those visits, my parents took my sister and me with them to meet the construction manager. We saw a father and his son leaving the Train Building. We followed them to the abandoned citrus orchard by the building where the father dumped a five-gallon bucket filled with human waste. He was a bit embarrassed when my parents stopped and introduced themselves. He introduced himself as Arie Cohen, the owner of an apartment on the floor below us. We also found out that his son Yotam and I were almost the same age, me being three days older. He told my parents that a few owners got tired of waiting so they invaded the apartments they owned even though the toilets, showers, and kitchens were not functional. Quarrels and heated arguments with the construction manager were a daily occurrence. They called him *The Sadist.*

My parents decided to join the group of flat owners and move in despite the lack of facilities. We invaded our flat late at night after *The Sadist* had left.

The question of what to do next was still lingering in the minds of all of the *invaders*. By sheer luck, one of the invaders was a big wig for the Tel Aviv municipality. He managed to force the builder and his construction manager to make the facilities in our apartments operational.

Moving there was a big deal for me and required great adjustment to my new environment. After spending six years in our one room apartment at the urban Ben Yehuda Street, with its wide streets, many stores and bus services, I felt like we landed on Mars. To begin with, we were isolated in what looked like a nature reserve, served by a bumpy dirt road. There was only one public bus which made a few daily trips. Its final station was by our building because it could not go any further due to the huge abandoned citrus orchard.

Less than a quarter mile north of our building was the Yarkon River with a rather dense strip of pine trees along its south bank. At night the few streetlights didn't offer near enough light in the pitch darkness. The entire region transformed into a coyote's kingdom, their yelps never ending. They aggregated along the riverbank but quite a few of them were brave or hungry enough to come all the way to our apartment complex where they toppled garbage cans searching for food. We learned very quickly not to dump our garbage after dark.

Although the pine tree strip along the Yarkon River was an irresistible attraction for us, no one dared go there after dark because of the coyotes. During day light hours, however, it was a nice place to watch fishermen operating a wide fishing net stretched across the river, attached at its four corners to four tall wooden poles, two on each side of the riverbank. The wide net was kept under water for a while before a motor lifted it out. The fisherman operating the motor left enough space between the surface of the water and the bottom of the net, enabling a fisherman in a rowboat to harvest the fish that were about the size of large sardines.

During winter, the ground inside the pine tree forest was covered with yellow oxalis flowers. It was an interesting experience to feel the tangy taste when I chewed the leaves but I was advised by new neighborhood friends, who professed to be experts, not to eat the stuff. "Why not," I quizzed them.

"The hamtzis (oxalis in Hebrew) grows only on the spots were dogs or coyotes have urinated," and according to my newly found scientist friends, that was why the oxalis tasted sour. As the new guy on the block, I took their advice and stopped chewing that plant.

Years later, I revisited the topic and learned that people from other places and cultures chew oxalis to treat mouth sores, sour throat, alleviate thirst and muscle cramps. Some even cook it with sugar to make a dessert. Nowadays, I don't have to go looking for oxalis plant to satisfy a craving for its oxalic acid as I can get plenty of it from eating spinach, broccoli, Brussels sprouts, grapefruit, and rhubarb.

✡

My parents solved their transportation problem by buying two used bicycles and rode to work. Luckily for my parents, there was the municipality day care center (8:00 a.m. to 4:00 p.m.) next to our apartment complex, so they left my sister there. My mother had enough time to come directly from work to bring my sister home from the daycare center.

Since I had already started my first year at the Nes-Ziona public school on Gretz Street, I had to continue going there for almost a year after moving because the municipal elementary school in our new neighborhood was still under construction. It forced me to hop on the first bus that parked next to our building and ride 1.5 mile to the corner of King Solomon and Keren Kayemet Boulevard, then walk an additional mile to my school. I had to catch the bus early enough to be at school by

8:00 a.m. and took the same route back home. My parents made sure to stash extra money in my leather book carrier for the ride home in case I lost the coins I kept in my pocket.

When Yehuda Hamaccabi Elementary School opened, my friend Yotam and I attended the same classes with the same teachers for the next eight years until moving on to high school. We became close friends, almost like brothers, and attended not only the same elementary school but were also active in the same youth movement, followed by the army's basic training camp. His brother Dani and my sister Chaya, also went to school together. (See Chapter 6.)

✡

Our apartment was on the third floor of 34 Yehuda Hamaccabi section of the building and shared a common wall of our living and bedrooms with the Reich family. We also shared the balcony with a cement partition in between. The shared balcony was a very handy feature on occasions when either Mrs. Reich or my mother were in the midst of baking and discovered that she had run out of one or two ingredients. She simply went to the balcony, asked for the missing ingredient. Similar exchanges took place between residents living in the other wings. The architectural design had a great impact, making the residents of the Train Building into a very close community.

We were secular Jews who adhered to the Jewish tradition but did not observe the *Sabbath* or most of laws as dictated in the Torah. Members of the Reich family on the other hand, were orthodox Jews who observed the *Sabbath* and the *Mosaic/halacha* Biblical laws. The Israeli orthodox political party built its own residential complex next to ours, but the Reich family chose to live among the secular Jews. They seemed to like living among us and got along very well with other residents. Sharing common walls and the partitioned front balcony did not seem to bother them. I emphasize this point because *Sabbath* and Jewish holidays could have been problematic.

The Reich family spent weekdays at the kosher dairy restaurant they owned, and came home late in the evening. They were glued to their home from Friday evening when the *Sabbath* started until Saturday evening when it ended.

The shared walls were thin enough to transfer the noise coming from either side. In addition, the majority of the residents did not have air-conditioning, so they kept their balcony doors open to let in fresh air. Most residents living in our building were very considerate, trying not to be noisy. I listened to music on the radio at a very low volume out of respect for *Sabbath* and the Reich family. That was difficult on Friday evenings when my favorite pop music came from *The Voice of Ramallah,* the Palestinian City of Ramallah. They had their weekly USA pop music broadcast at the exact time the Reich family started their *Sabbath* dinner. Later in the evening, the Israeli Military radio station *Galey Tzhal* started a few hours of dance music called *Hamahane Roked* (Hebrew for the camp dances). I used my crystal radio to listen to the domestic broadcast.

My family and the four other families living in our wing became close friends right from the beginning and took turns hosting weekly card games, which usually started at 9 p.m. and went on well into the night. During the summertime they played on the balcony. Playing cards on the front balcony on Friday nights was a popular pass time for the entire neighborhood throughout the entire country. This entertaining activity was jokingly called *Sabbath* Praying. I felt bad for the Reich family on those Friday nights when it was my parents turn to invite their friends for the *Sabbath* Praying. Although the card players were not unreasonably noisy, I am sure that the *Sabbath* observing Reich family was aware of my parents and their non-observing secular guests.

My parents and their friends were also ballroom dancing aficionados. When it was my parents turn to invite their friends, they opened the door separating our living room and the bedroom to create enough space for dancing. When they needed a break from their card game they danced to the waltzes and tangos I squeezed out of my accordion. They considered me a good accordion player. I felt bad about it because the two combined rooms turned ballroom dancing hall were the walls we shared with the Reich family. They never complained about violating the *Sabbath*. They knew that our family would reciprocate and tolerate their *Sabbath*. There were times when their religious activities created noise through the thin wall. For example; when they invited a large group of orthodox friends to what is known as The *Seudah Shlishit* (Hebrew for third meal).

Mr. Reich and his guests were engaged in lively discussions while reciting and studying chapters from *Pirkey Avot* (Hebrew for *Chapters of the Fathers.*) Through the thin walls I heard every word but I was too young to dwell on the topics they discussed. Later, I enjoyed reading through it myself and the wisdom it provided.

I was also exposed to the *Seudah Shlishit,* from the *Sabbath* observers that lived in the large apartment complex the Hapoel Hamizrachi, the orthodox political party built for its members. We all moved to this new area of Tel Aviv at about the same time. Our Orthodox Jewish neighbors did not have a synagogue, so they converted the large pump house and storage building that once served the orchard. Their make-shift synagogue was located in the backyard of our building, and was made from kurkar.

✡

The *Seudah Shlishit* is a special meal eaten by orthodox Jews on the *Sabbath* afternoon. It commemorates the *Manna* God provided for the Israelites as they wondered through the Sinai desert for forty years after leaving Egypt. They were on their way to the Promised Land. The biblical reference for the *Manna* is Exodus 16:25-36. According to the Hebrew Bible, on Fridays, God provided the Israelites double portion of the *Manna*, one for Friday and for Saturday so they would rest and wouldn't desecrate the *Sabbath*, searching for food. That biblical passage specifies Saturday by name three times so it became customary for the *Sabbath* observing Jews to add this extra meal on Saturday afternoon and call it *Seudah Shlishit* (third meal). According to the *Halacha* (Jewish Law) the third meal should be eaten in the afternoon and it is usually the smallest meal.

The *Seudah Shlishit* has a special significance because it is considered to be a *mitzvah* (a Jewish commandment) to eat three meals on the *Sabbath*. There are special *Sabbath* songs sung during the *Seudah Shlishit*. I definitely heard them through our thin walls whenever it was Mr. Reich's turn to host his *Sabbath*-observers inner-circle. Their favorite songs were *Mizmore L' David* (Hebrew: Song of David), Psalm 23, and the 16th century song *Yedid Nefesh* which was composed by the Kabbalist Rabbi Azikri. It evokes pleasant childhood memories whenever I hear these songs sung at my own synagogue. It is also customary to recite a few chapters from *Pirkei Avot* (Hebrew for Chapters of the Fathers), the rabbinical ethical teachings from the *Mishnah* time (starting in the 1st century CE). It deals primarily with ethical and moral Jewish principles.

Here are some examples of the rabbinical teaching compiled in *Pirkei Avot:*

- *Be cautious regarding the ruling power. Because they only befriend a person when it serves all. They appear as friends when it suits them, but they do not stand by a man in his time of need.*
- *In a place where there are no worthy men, strive to be worthy.*

> - *Meet every person with graciousness.*
> - *Your house should be widely open, and you should let the poor be members of your household.*

It took our Jewish orthodox neighbors a few years to build a great, fancy synagogue but in the meantime, they used the pump building. They served the *Seudah Shlishit* meal outside on a long table with a white cloth cover. I watched them from our kitchen balcony and listened to the *Kiddush* (the Jewish blessing over the wine). The main dish was *gefilte* fish (stuffed carp) with salad and red kosher wine or grape juice. Two loaves of traditional braided Challah bread were the most symbolic food on the table. The two loaves signified the double portion of the *Manna* that fell on Friday.

Occasionally, they extended the *Seudah Shlishit* into Saturday evening and performed the *Havdalah*, Jewish service that marks the end of the *Sabbath* and beginning of the new week. It was interesting to watch them light the special *Havdalah* candle with its three wicks all burning simultaneously, and reciting the blessing (*Kiddush*) over the cup of kosher wine or grape juice. Then they passed a special, artistically decorated, container with sweet spices for everyone to smell and remind how sweet the *Sabbath* was. At the end of the *Havdalah* service, they extinguished the candle by dipping it into the cup of the *Kiddush* wine while reciting a specific blessing to show that the wine was dedicated solely for the *Havdalah* service and not just for the pleasure of drinking wine. Some people dipped their finger into the leftover wine and touched their eyes with their wet finger absolutely convinced that this act was a good omen because that wine was used to fulfill a *mitzvah* (a Jewish command). They ended their service by singing *Eliyyahu Hanavi* (Elija the prophet) which is the customary song for most Jews to end the *Havdalah* service.

After a year, they had to rent a place because that section of the orchard was cleared to make room for a another three-story apartment building. I was saddened to lose their *Sabbath* services but even more so losing my favorite fig, mulberry and carob trees. That was one of my favorite places. It had two mulberry trees, one carob tree, and three fig trees loaded with sweet fruit. What else could a boy with a sweet tooth ask for?

The Reich family was not the only orthodox Jewish family living in our wing of the Train Building. The Rudy family also chose to live among us. We had good relationships and mutual respect to each other. Mr. Zerach Rudy and his family lived on the ground level apartment. He was the housekeeper and manager of a large synagogue on Ben Yehuda Street not far from where we lived before moving to our new place. My father visited there on a few occasions so he knew him personally. My father was pleasantly surprised when the Rudy family moved to our building a few months after we did. Evidently, they preferred living on the ground floor to avoid climbing stairs several times a day.

Nonetheless, there was a huge disadvantage living on the ground floor. Laundry was done by soaking the dirty clothes overnight in the bathtub filled with water and detergent. Next, the laundry was hung on the clothesline off the kitchen balcony. Poor Mrs. Rudy got furious when her laundry, completely dried by then, got wet when residents on the upper floors started hanging their dripping laundry above hers.

✡

Living on the ground level apartment provided the Rudy family with a great advantage during the Jewish holiday of *Sukkot* commonly known as The Feast of the Tabernacles. A better English translation is The Festival of Booth. Every year they built a *sukkah* (Hebrew for booth) on the ground adjacent to their front balcony. They ate their meals in the *sukkah* and spent time inside, fulfilling the biblical commanded associated with the holiday: "*You shall live in booths for seven days, all that are citizens in Israel shall live in booths, so that your generations may know that I made the people of Israel live in booths when I brought them out of Egypt. I am the Lord your God.*" (Leviticus 23: 42-43). The Rudy family was kind and always invited the children to sit inside their *sukkah* and enjoy the cookies Mrs. Rudy baked for the holiday.

The name *Sukkah* is the singular of the Hebrew word *Sukkot*. Almost everyone in Israel refers to the holiday as *Chag Sukkot* or simply *Sukkot*. The holiday is celebrated on the fifteenth day of Hebrew month *Tishrei* and lasts seven days in Israel and eight days in the diaspora. The first day of *Sukkot* is observed like a *Sabbath* so no work is allowed as well as other restrictions associated with observing the *Sabbath*. The seven days that follow are called *Chol Hamoed* (Hebrew for Festival Weekdays). These intermediate days are observed like regular weekdays with the exception that only certain work is permitted. The eighth day that follows is called *Shemini Atzeret* (Eighth Day of Assembly) which is a *Sabbath*-like holiday. It ends the Festival of *Sukkot*. It should be noted that when the holy temple in Jerusalem existed, *Sukkot* was one of the three pilgrimages, i.e. *Shalosh Regalim* (Hebrew for Three Pilgrimage Festivals) that commanded the Israelites to take a pilgrimage to the holy temple in Jerusalem. They brought with them offerings to the priests, mostly portions of the season's harvest. The other two Pilgrimage Festivals and their harvest offerings were *Passover* and *Shavuot* (Pentecost).

The *Sukkah* (booth) is a temporary walled structure with a roof made primarily of palm branches or leafy branches trimmed from other tree species. It was used as a temporary dwelling for the farmers during harvest time hence, the *Festival of Sukkot* is strongly associated with agriculture and also known by its second name: *Chag Ha' Asif* (Hebrew for Feast of In-gathering, Exodus 34:22). The *sukkah* served as the temporary dwelling of the Israelis during their forty years of wondering through the Sinai desert after escaping slavery in Egypt. (Leviticus 23:42-43). Throughout the seven days of *Sukkot*, meals are eaten inside the *sukkah*. Some people sleep in the *sukkah* as well.

Mr. Rudy invited us to his *sukkah* to observe and participate in the ritual known as Waving the Four Species. This ritual is a biblical command stating that, "Ye shall take you on the first day the fruit of goodly trees, branches of palm trees, boughs of thick trees and willows of the brook and ye shall rejoice before the Lord your God for seven days." (Leviticus 23:40). The waving ceremony of the four species involves the *etrog* (citron fruit), *lulav* (frond of date palm), *hadass* (myrtle bough) and *aravah* (willow branch). By Jewish law, I was still too young and not obligated to follow the command of waving the four species so I enjoyed just watching Mr. Rudy do it but he was kind and let us try to get the hang of it. Later in life I fulfilled the command and performed the waving ceremony at our synagogue in the USA.

The interior of the Rudy's family *sukkah* was decorated. It is customary for the *Sukkah* owner to hang decoration of the four species and other artwork.

Visiting Mr. Rudy's *sukkah* captivated me so much that *Sukkot* became my favorite Jewish holiday. I managed to convince my close friend Yotam to go along with my plan to build a *sukkah*. He lived on the floor below us and was my classmate at the Yehuda Hamaccabi Elementary school. It was our second year living in the Train Building. My family owned the apartment on the third floor just below the clotheslines running across the long flat roof. The long clotheslines anchored to the walls of the laundry room next to each of the three entrances of the building were in great demand for hanging our oversized laundry such as bedsheets, blankets. These items were too big to hang on the kitchen balcony clotheslines. I *borrowed* that section of the clotheslines above our flat and built a *sukkah* with my buddy Yotam.

✡

It is worth mentioning that the Jewish months are determined by the lunar cycle as opposed to the solar-based cycle of the Gregorian calendar. Because of difference, the Hebrew month *Tishrei* varies from late September to late October on the

Gregorian calendar. Moreover, because both, the Gregorian and Jewish year have twelve months, the Jewish calendar must add an additional month every four years to compensate for the lunar year being shorter than the solar year. The Jewish leap year that has thirteen months is called *Shana Meuberet* (A pregnant year). The extra month is added around April to synchronize the spring season on the Hebrew calendar with the actual time it occurs in nature.

The walls of our *sukkah* were comprised of four blankets which we hung on the metal clothesline with laundry clips. The corner of each blanket was tied to a twine and secured to the floor with a cement block we found at a nearby construction site. We trimmed a few branches of pine trees in the forest by the Yarkon River near our house and decorated the interior with colorful paper chains and pomegranates hanging from the clotheslines. I toyed with the idea of having electricity coming from our apartment.

I was confident that getting electricity from our flat to the *sukkah* would be easy. My uncle Marek, who was an electrician, had his small side business at home, making thermostats to supplement his salary. He was married to my father's sister, Aunt Mala so we visited them often. Those visits provided me with the opportunity to watch him working with the electrical stuff.

My friend Yotam and I sat at the entrance of our building next to the mailboxes and bicycles racks, splicing and assembling pieces of electric wire we scavenged at the construction site nearby. It looked funny due to the different colors of the insulation sheath on the wires. We finished assembling the line just as Mr. Mitelsbach, our neighbor came to check his mailbox. He and his wife lived in the apartment below ours with their only son, Avigdor whom I believe was around eighteen years old at that time. They emigrated from Belgium and I am not sure if they were born and raised there or escaped to Belgium from another part of Europe during the Holocaust. Once in Israel, Mr. Mitelsbach established a factory and manufactured all kind of electrical wires and cables for the construction industries. Their son Avigdor was somewhat mentally impaired for his age and had no friends so Mr. and Mrs. Mitelsbach got him a small dog, he named Fifi.

Avigdor and Fifi were inseparable. My family treated him very nicely so Mr. Mitelsbach had a soft spot for me. Mrs. Mitelsbach however, was less friendly to me and my sister. She had the habit of knocking on our door asking my mother to control me and my sister, making us walk on the tile floors barefoot. "The foot taping on the floor drives me crazy," she complained. My parents could not afford buying rugs to cover the floor, made of ceramic tiles called *balata* (singular) or *balatot* (plural).

Mr. Mitelsbach opened his mailbox, collected the mail and noticed the long electric wire Yotam and I spliced together. "Shmuel, what are you trying to make here?" he asked me, using my Hebrew name.

"We built a *sukkah* on the roof and I want to have a light bulb connected to the electrical outlet in our apartment." I told him the names of the seven children living in our wing that were invited including his son Avigdor.

He was pleased to accept the invitation and promised to send Avigdor when we gathered inside the *sukkah*. Then, he looked at me while holding the electric wire and said, "Kids, this contraption of yours would have electrocuted you and anyone else upon touching it. Shmuel, let's go to your apartment and show me the location of the electric outlet you want to use, and I will measure the length of the wire you need. I'll bring you one from my factory with the light bulb socket already installed. You'll have light in your *sukkah* on *Sukkot* Eve."

Mr. Mitelsbach brought the wire and the bulb socket the next day making sure that it was safely secured to the center of the sukkah. The electric cord extended all the way from my apartment to the sukkah. I thanked Mr. Mitelsbach for his help and reminded him of the invitation to his son Avigdor and Fifi.

Being eight-year-old sukkah builders was a big deal for me and Yotam so I wanted to make it a big show-off event. The best way to do so was to invite our neighbors to celebrate in our *sukkah* by designating it as a "Special Event by Invitation only, Tickets Required." Of course, we did not intend to charge money for the tickets but I felt it would be more impressive if our guest received official tickets with an admission stub.

In my eight-year-old mind, admission tickets meant a piece of paper with a perforated line to mark the separation of the admission stub. I wrecked my brain for a solution. Mr. Mardix came to the rescue, albeit unknowingly. He was my father's childhood friend from Góra Kalwaria, Poland. He immigrated to Israel right after the War for Independence and built a factory that manufactured sewing machines. They looked similar to the Singer brand. They were sold under the brand name Mardix. He sold a brand new one to my parents at cost. I removed the spool and sewed the paper along the admission tab to create the perfect perforation line. Since we all attended the same elementary school we surprised our friends by giving them admission tickets during recess.

The evening at *Sukkah* was a great celebration as everyone came, including the parents. Mr. Mitelsbach and his son Avigdor with Fifi were there too. We thanked him in front of everyone for making sure we had light in the *Sukkah* and he nodded back with a fatherly smile.

There was no school during the *Festival of Sukkot* and *Shmini Atzeret* so we attempted to spend as much time as possible at our *Sukkah* during the days and the evenings. However we could enjoy it for only two days because of fall winds. It was heart breaking to see our beloved *Sukkah* flapping in the autumn wind. The blankets that served as the *sukkah* walls were still anchored to the floor with the cement blocks but all the decorations inside were torn up and gone with the wind. I hated this time of the year and the realization that the great and lovely summertime was gone and the gloomy winter was at our doorstep. No more Jewish holiday until *Hanukkah* which also meant no more school breaks until then. Building the *Sukkah* on the flat roof using the clotheslines became a nice tradition for me and my buddy Yotam for the next nine years until Yotam and I finished high school and started our mandatory military duty.

✡

I spent a total of thirteen years of my life living at 34 Yehuda Hamaccabi Street, ten years prior to serving in the Israeli army and three years attending Tel Aviv University after being discharged from the army. Very nice, warm people lived there. I already mentioned Mr. Mitelsbach and his son Avigdor. I also described the Reich family, our Jewish orthodox neighbor, and let's not forget Mr. Zerach Rudy and his family, the other Jewish orthodox family who invited me and my friends to spend time in his *Sukkah*.

Mr. Rudy continued to affect my life when my parents and Yotam's parents hired him to tutor us for our *bar mitzvah* ceremony at the synagogue where he worked.

Bar mitzvah is a Jewish coming-of-age ritual marking the day when a boy is thirteen and becomes accountable for his own actions. A *Bat Mitzvah* is a similar celebration for girls when they reach the age of twelve. The service takes place at the synagogue during the *Sabbath* morning services. The *bar mitzvah* boy participates in the service by chanting the portion of the Torah associated with that date on the Jewish calendar. It requires a lot of preparation and that's why our parents hired Mr. Rudy. Yotam and I had our *bar mitzvah* at Mr. Rudy's synagogue which was located a few buildings away from 132 Ben Yehuda. Since I was three days older than Yotam, my *bar mitzvah* service took place first and his was celebrated on the next *Sabbath*.

A year after we moved to 34 Hamaccabi Street, the municipality uprooted a long strip of the orchard and built a paved street stretching southward all the way from the pine forest on the bank of the Yarkon

River and to a public square later to become *Kikar Ha'Medina* (Hebrew for the State Square). They named that street *Rechov Kibbuts Galuyot* (Hebrew for gathering of the diasporas). A few years later they renamed it Chaim Weitzman Street, when the first president of Israel died. That area of Tel Aviv was sparsely populated and there were still patches of the abandoned citrus orchard along the way.

The plot that became *Kikar Ha'Medina* Square had a large abandoned citrus orchard where coyotes visited and pierced the silence of the night with their howls. They gave me, a nine-year-old child, a real scary moment. When I lost my bus fare to return home from the Maccabi sport club, I had to walk the 2.5 miles. It was already dark when I reached the desolated *Kikar Ha'Medina* Square. I bumped into the coyotes as I was crossing it. I am not sure who was more scared, me or the coyotes but I took an evasive u-turn. I arrived home very late and my parents were worried as I was not on the last bus that day. When I explained what happened my mother scolded me for not asking someone to loan me the money. "Just to repair the holes in the sole of your shoes would cost more than the bus ticket," she admonished me.

✡

There were very colorful people living in the building behind us. Mr. Konshtat and his wife lived on the ground floor. They both were in their sixties and emigrated from France. They spoke Yiddish but felt more comfortable speaking French. Mr. Konshtat repaired watches. Being French, they liked eating lots of fresh vegetables, especially lettuce. I enjoyed watching his vegetable washing ritual. He placed the raw vegetables in a screen metal basket, dipped the basket into tap water and then went to the kitchen balcony and swung it forcibly left and right, to get rid the water.

The Konshtat's had plenty of opportunity to use their French because Mr. and Mrs. H'aelyon lived in the 32 Yehuda Hamaccabi wing of our building. They were Jewish immigrants from Greece and spoke fluent French. Mr. H'aelyon was a journalist for the Israeli French daily newspaper. The conversations between Mr. Konshtat and Mr. and Mrs. H'aelyon were very loud and animated.

To get telephone service in Israel was extremely difficult during that time, so the Konshtats and the H'aelyons shouted their conversations from balcony-to-balcony. It started with Mr. Konshtat standing at his kitchen balcony, capping the palms of his hands around his mouth and shouting loudly, "Monsieur H'aelyon, Monsieur H'aelyon," and then pausing for a reply. If he was lucky, Mr. H'aelyon came to his kitchen balcony and the two conversed a long time. I was not privy to their conversion as it was in French. If Mr. H'aelyon did not respond, Mr. Konshtat shouted, "Madame H'aelyon, Madame H'aelyon." If she came out, the conversation started flowing. If no one answered the call, he would try again and again throughout the day. I often wondered what these two families were talking about.

Mrs. Binski was another colorful character that enriched my childhood universe. She lived on the second floor of the building behind ours. Her kitchen balcony was close to ours. She kept their kitchen door open and I could see what she was serving for dinner. Unlike her husband and teenaged son, both very shy and quite, Mrs. Binski made sure that everyone within a mile radius knew she was alive and kicking. From the balcony, at top of her lungs she called, "Pani Alroy, Pani Alroy", the lady living in the apartment next to her. Their apartment shared a common wall. When Mrs. Alroy stepped onto the balcony, they talked in Polish for a long time.

Mrs. or Mr. Binski education level is still a mystery to me, but their son David seemed to be very smart, always building large airplane models from balsa wood and special paper. He rode to the Airplane Model Builders Club on his bike carrying the latest model he'd built. The Binski family eventually immigrated to Canada where David became an Aeronautical Engineer. During the time they lived in our neighborhood, Mrs. Binski tried to portray herself as a highly educated member of the elite group of Israeli society. People who lived within a quarter of a mile from her apartment did not have to consult with their calendar to find out that it was 9:00 a.m. Saturday when classical music blasted from her apartment. It drove the entire neighborhood crazy because the only record she played was *Beethoven's 6th Symphony*. She purchased a new one when the old record got scratchy. I have no idea why Mrs. Binski chose Saturday mornings to play her *Beethoven's 6th Symphony*. Perhaps she was trying to impress as many residents as possible. After all, *Sabbath* morning was the time when most people did not have to go to work and children had no school.

Mrs. Binski had the 9 a.m. to 1 p.m. time slot for *Beethoven's 6th Symphony*. Then, at 1 p.m. Mr. Cohen took the airtime to play his favorite Jewish cantorial music. *Kol Israel* (Hebrew for The Voice of Israel), the government-owned radio station, had a weekly program of Jewish Cantorial Music aired at 1 p.m. every Saturday. Mr. Cohen loved it so much and was kind enough to share it with the entire neighborhood at high decibels. It was his clue to Mrs. Binski to let *Beethoven's 6th Symphony* retire until next Saturday.

My father liked Jewish Cantorial Music. It reminded him of his childhood religious school *(Cheder)*. He tried to impress me with his knowledge of who sang what. "This is Yossele Rosenblatt singing, and this chazzan (Hebrew for cantor) is Moshe Koussevitzky," he would say with absolute certainty.

And of course there was the cantor Samuel Malavsky's family, his four daughters and two sons. I did not care too much for that kind of music although some of the Jewish cantors were very accomplished opera singers, like Richard Tucker (born as Reuben Ticker) of the Metropolitan Opera. I knew for sure that a few residents in our neighborhood did not care for that kind of music. You could hear doors slamming shut the minute Mr. Cohen started blasting his program.

Another colorful character, Mrs. Schwartz lived on the third floor next to us. I nick named her *G'everet Avatiach* (Hebrew for Mrs. Watermelon). During summertime Yehuda Hamaccabi Street and the entire neighborhood, became a popular place for watermelon. Several salesman came to our street almost every day with their long wooden carts loaded with watermelon and pulled by a mule. We knew that they had arrived when we heard them shouting *"Avatiach, Avatiach, Al Hasakin, Avatiach"* (Hebrew for "Watermelon, Watermelon, On-the-Knife Watermelon").The term *Al Hasakin* (on-the-knife) referred to the ritual where the buyer expected the merchant to prove that the watermelon he selected was red, sweet, and tasty. The watermelon merchants let the buyer point to the watermelon he wanted to buy. The watermelon merchant picked it up, patted it several times, and squeezed it with his hands while touching the fruit with his ear. I named this phase of the ritual as the *acoustic test* where the merchant pretended to listen to "what was going on inside" before telling the customer, his professional opinion, "This is an excellent choice." It boosted the customer's ego but the customer still wanted to make sure it was the perfect watermelon. That was saved for the last act of the *Al Hasakin* ritual. The watermelon merchant carved a small triangle plug pulled it out, and gave it to the customer to decide how intense the red color was and how sweet the watermelon tasted. If it failed to meet the customer's satisfaction, the merchant opened another melon until the customer was pleased.

Mrs. Schwartz, *G'everet Avatiach,* watched the watermelon merchant from her balcony. The minute the merchant started moving on to a new location and shouting *"Avatiach, Avatiach, Al Hasakin Avatiach"*, she would shout from her balcony, *"Hey Adon Avatiach, cha'ke re'ga, Ani K'var Yoredet"* (Hebrew for Hey Mr. Watermelon, wait a minute, I am going down now.) The watermelon merchant would pull the harness and yell *"HOY'SSA"* ("STOP" in mule language, I guess). I could hear Mrs. Schwartz's wooden slippers taping on the cement stairs like a Flamenco dancer. That was my clue to go to the front balcony and watch her style of selecting a watermelon from the merchant.

Mrs. Schwartz and the watermelon merchant were loud enough for me to hear. When she finally selected a watermelon that looked sexy enough for her she would point to it and let the merchant perform the acoustic test followed by cutting and pulling the triangular sample. Next, she would inspect it visually and taste its sweetness before saying, "I don't think it tastes sweet enough for me. Could we try another one, please," and the poor watermelon merchant would pick another one just to be rejected like the one before. She would finally accept the third watermelon he picketed for her. I am sure that the first two watermelons she rejected were perfect and sweet but Mrs. Schwartz craved attention and needed to feel important so she made him go through the motions.

One day a young guy who never dealt with Mrs. Schwartz before was not willing to play her game. When he cut the tasting triangle from the second watermelon, she rejected it and asked to taste another one, the third watermelon in a row. The watermelon merchant tasted the watermelon himself and said, "I don't see or taste anything wrong with this watermelon. It is sweeter than sugar so what is your problem?"

She looked at him and said, rather bluntly, "Well, it may taste sweet but it does not look nice."

That got the watermelon man really mad as if some stranger made derogatory remarks about his beloved child. The guy lost his temper. Everyone in the neighborhood heard him yelling, "And you, old lady, better go home and look at the mirror. Do you think that you look nice? This watermelon is too good to be wasted on you."

Next thing I saw was Mrs. Schwartz running for her life fearing the merchant would throw the watermelon in her direction. You could hear her murmuring to herself while climbing the stairs, "What *chutzpahn* (Hebrew for fresh), who does he think he is. His poor mother failed to teach him manners."

Although I felt that he was too rough, I sided with him. I never saw her buying watermelon again from any watermelon merchant who came to our street with their mule and cart. Poor Mrs. Schwartz carried her watermelon all the way home from the grocery store, and watermelon grown in Israel are as big and heavy as a full moon.

✡

There was an acute shortage of apartments in Tel-Aviv. Several construction and home building contractors swarmed into our neighborhood and started changing our pastoral environment into an urban landscape of bricks, cement, and asphalt. Excavation machines were staged at the edge of the abandoned citrus orchard next to the 36 Yehuda Hamaccabi. The realization that the days of the abandoned citrus orchard were numbered was very distressing to the children living in the neighborhood. That orchard enriched our childhood. Where else could we find turtles to adopt as pets, not to mention picking the *Shamouti/Yafo* oranges that were growing there.

The bird population of the orchard enticed Mr. Bornstein to play a prank on the children, including his own sons Mordecai and Shmulik who were also members of my *Sukkah gang*. I am not sure what Mr. Bornstein did for a living as I always saw him sitting on the front balcony either reading the daily newspaper, or watching passersby. Occasionally he was there when the mail carrier arrived to distribute the mail into the mailbox. Mr. Bornstein would leave the porch, go to the mailbox, and talk to the carrier. His sons Mordecai and Shmulik attended the same school as the other children in our building.

Mrs. Bornstein, a very attractive woman, was just the opposite of her husband, always dressed well and wore expensive jewelry. It was a bit odd because Mr. Bornstein and his sons wore khaki cloths most of the time whereas she was always dressed as if she was about to walk down the *Les Champs Elysees* in Paris. Oftentimes we saw a neatly dressed, nice looking gentleman about her age taking her out in the evening and bringing her home few hours later. They conversed in Polish. Mr. Bornstein stayed home with the kids when she and her companion were out. Maybe that gentleman was the one showering Mrs. Bornstein with the expensive jewelry she wore?

I am not sure what made Mr. Bornstein play a prank. We were playing at the entrance to the stairway when he came out to check his mailbox. He happened to overhear us expressing our dismay at the fact that our beloved abandoned citrus orchard was about to be uprooted with all the living creatures that made it their home. He collected the mail, inspected it and then asked, "Children, do you want to catch a few birds before they all fly to different orchards?"

Everyone, including his two sons gave him an enthusiastic, "Yes!"

"Very good," he replied "Be here tomorrow morning at 10 a.m. and bring cardboard boxes to keep the birds we catch. Make sure to drill a few holes for the birds to breath." He counted how many of us were there before going back to his flat. We could hardly wait for the next morning.

Everyone arrived on time. Mr. Bornstein came with a straw basket containing brown sandwich bags folded at the top. Next, he gave each one of us a bag and asked us to shake it gently next to our ears and we complied. "Please unfold the top of the bag and check what it has inside," he said, "and be careful not to spill it because it cost lots of money." We opened the bags and checked the contents. It looked to me like coarse sea salt and I wondered how it would help us catch birds. But Mr. Bornstein went on with his instructions before I had the chance to quiz him. "Now, listen carefully on how you are going to catch the bird without injuring it. I would like your bird to be alive and not a dead," he told us in a very serious and convincing voice. "Now, we are going to the orchard. Keep a fairly good distance from each other while searching for a bird to catch. Once you see one that you like, open the brown bag, take a pinch of that special salt, and through it on the bird's tail. You have to aim at the tail as this is the only part of its body that will prevent the bird from escaping." That was Mr. Bornstein last instructions for us, the brave bird hunters.

What happened next was a scene from a comedy where a naïve bunch of children chased birds in an abandoned citrus orchard, throwing coarse sea salt in their direction. As for Mr. Bornstein, he was laughing so hard it was a miracle he didn't wet his pants. Needless to say, none of us realized that it was a prank. We even thanked him for his willingness to take us for another bird hunting expedition the next day. "Hopefully, tomorrow will be your lucky day," he said but it never happened because the next day, the earth mover tractors uprooted the trees.

The earth movers gnawed at the abandoned citrus orchard, clearing the ground for the new municipal high school named *Tichon Ironi Daled*. The bulldozers also cleared the orchard in the eastward direction and extended our *Yehuda Hamaccabi* Street all the way to the Tel Aviv/Haifa highway which was a two-way artery, a far cry from today's multi-lane highway connecting Tel Aviv to the Northern part of Israel. During that time, the number of Israelis owning a private car was minuscule, the traffic on the Tel Aviv-Haifa highway was limited to the public transportation and commercial vehicles, so much so, that on *Yom Kippur* eve, when traffic was expected to be very low, my friends and I would sneak out, go to the highway, and lay on the asphalt for hours not fearing that a vehicle would show up and run over us. Not a very smart *sport*. Luckily, nothing bad happened to us.

Extending our street all the way to the Tel Aviv/Haifa highway provided me with easy access to a hill located at the intersection of the highway and the extended Yehuda Hamaccabi Street. We named that hill *Givat Ha' Kalaniont* (Hebrew for The Anemone Hill) for the beautiful wild anemone flowers that grew there. The northern slope of the hill had a denser population of anemone flowers than the rest but as years went by and the region became more populated, the anemones dwindled as more people picked the flowers. As always the case with a mushrooming urban development, Anemone Hill gave way to a new development with a busy gas station next to it.

They also cleared the citrus orchard on the north side of our street. The bulldozer dug two large rectangular excavations at the approximate dimensions of the future buildings. They were very deep because new building codes stipulated that all new buildings had to have underground bomb shelters.

Providing residential buildings with underground air raid shelters was mandatory as the Israelis knew that despite defeating the Arab armies in 1948, it was just a matter of time before another flare-up.

The bulldozers left the site but the contractor delayed the construction for almost two years. Rainy winters filled the two deep excavations. They stayed full because, unlike the sand dunes on which Tel Aviv was built, this particular site had a heavy clay-type soil that retained water. The neighborhood kids collected chunks of it, and molded it into a fairly sized cube. Next, we poked a hole at the center of each face making sure that the holes were interconnected. The next step was to insert pieces of broken mirror at a forty-five degree angle transforming the clay cube into a homemade telescope. Mothers were scratching their heads trying to figure out where their lipstick mirror had disappeared to. It was a miracle that no one cut his fingers trying to get the pieces of the broken mirror into the telescope.

During the early fifties, the city ordinances pertaining to public safety around construction sites were very lax so the construction company did not fence the two deep excavated trenches. There was a real danger of drowning or getting stuck in the mud. In fact, we built rafts with flat wood boards we "borrowed" from nearby construction sites and floated on them across the deep trenches pretending to be the Israeli version of the Huckleberry Finn floating down the Mississippi River.

The banks of the two excavated trenches were a fertile ground for wild vegetation, predominantly the thorny *barkan* weed (Syrian thistle) that was extremely attractive to honeybees so we had to be careful not to get stung. Moreover, and I hate to reveal, that we used the stems of the *barkan* as our home-made cigarettes by harvesting the dried stems. The stems were hollow so some of us used it as a straw but the more courageous kids lit the stem, inhaled a few puffs, and found themselves coughing and spitting for hours afterward. Perhaps that was the price to pay for having an explorative mind. Good things never last forever and we lost our *Mississippi River* trenches when the construction company finally started building.

✡

When Mr. Mitelsbach, who helped us get lighting to our *Sukkah*, bought a newer apartment in a more upscale building, Doctor Levi, a dentist, moved in. He was a peculiar person. No one knew much about him other than he never got married. During the years that I lived there, I never saw any female companion visiting him. He was hardly at home and spent most of the week out of town working as a dentist in one of the IDF airbases in the south.

My parents bumped into him a few times in the stairway and exchanged pleasantries but he was not a conversational kind of guy. The exchange of pleasantries, however short, gave my Polish-speaking parents the hint that he was not an eastern-European Jew so they quizzed him about where he lived before immigrating to Israel. As it turned out, Dr. Levi was a Bulgarian Jew who studied dentistry in Sofia, the Bulgarian capital. Bulgarian Jews immigrated to Israel after the 1948 War for Independence. There were about 75,000 of them making it the fourth largest immigration group after the ones emigrating from Russia, Romania, and Poland.

The Bulgarian people, under the Nazi occupation, defied Nazi orders to turn in the Jews, and heroically saved 50,000, almost the entire Jewish community in Bulgaria. Bulgarians living in the countryside provided Jews with hiding places and shared their food. The leaders of the Bulgarian Orthodox Church preached to their followers to protest the deportation of the Jews to the death camps in Poland. That plea was effective. In fact, on March 10, 1943 thousands the Bulgarian Jews who had been arrested and kept at detention centers ready to be deported to the Polish camps, were freed as a result of widespread demonstrations of the Bulgarian people. It is sad that Bulgaria, Denmark and Albania were the only European countries whose non-Jewish population mobilized to save its Jewish neighbors during the Holocaust.

The citizens of Albania, a Balkan country, like Bulgaria, were also shining examples of extraordinary compassion shown toward the Jewish refugees during the Holocaust. First occupied by Italy, an ally of Nazi Germany, Albanians refused to comply with the order to provide the Italian occupier with a list of all the Jews residing in Albania. The government agencies went the extra mile and provided these Jewish refugees with fake documents helping them to blend with the native population. When Nazi Germany took control of Albania, the Albanians provided sanctuary to the Jewish refugees arriving from other countries. Albania is the only European country ruled by a Muslim majority, making this extraordinary act even more remarkable. All the Jews were saved except for one family. The Albanians' kindness and assistance toward the Jews was most likely rooted in their highest ethical code of honor known as *Besa* (Keep Your Promise).

The Jewish immigrants from Bulgaria founded their own sport club which they named the *Zionist Association of Maccabi Yafo*. It was founded in 1950 by the chairman of *Maccabi Bulgaria*, Mr. Albert Kiyosso. Their soccer team played for thirty-two seasons in Israel's top division. It was a very popular with the Bulgarian population.

My father, who was an accomplished soccer player for *Maccabi*

Warsaw in Poland, took me with him to the soccer games played at the Maccabi stadium in Tel Aviv and at the Bloomfield stadium in Yafo. I liked attending the games where *Maccabi Yafo* played and I experienced the enthusiastic support of their fans with their nonstop cheer, *"Hi-dhe Maccabi Yafo, Hi-dhe Maccabi Yafo" (Go Maccabi Yafo, Go Maccabi Yafo)*. I found their use of the word *hi-dhe* a bit funny as it is usually used to command a horse to move. The games were held on Saturdays. The kids attending *Yehuda Hamaccabi* elementary school had plenty of discussions first thing on Sunday morning. No one ever failed to brag about how great his team did, and never failed to keep silent if his team lost. One of our classmates, David Nachmias came from a family who emigrated from Bulgaria and was a fanatic fan of *Maccabi Yafo*. We added salt to his injury by shouting at him *"Hi-dhe Maccabi Yafo, Hi-dhe Maccabi Yafo, Hi-dhe Maccabi Yafo"* whenever his team lost. Children could be cruel at times.

I don't believe that Dr. Levi, the Bulgarian dentist living below our flat was a *Maccabi Yafo* fan or a fan of soccer in general. We had a few hilarious situations with him as the clothesline off his kitchen balcony was just below our clothes line. Every once in a while, the wind would blow bras and other women's lingerie belonging to my mother or my sister from our clothesline and land on his, transforming it into a colorful display of ladies' lingerie. That was a major crisis for Dr. Levi. He felt his reputation as the ultimate bachelor was in jeopardy so he had to act promptly. His routine to mitigate the situation was to dislodge the offending garments with a long broom handle as he did not dare touch the items with his hands, God forbid. The situation was exacerbated when the colorful ladies' lingerie he untangled landed on Mr. Rudy, the pious orthodox Jew who probably struggled to explain to his wife and the entire secular neighborhood how the garments came to be there.

We could live with this particular idiosyncrasy of Dr. Levi's because he was a good neighbor. I was 100% sure that he would never get married but I was wrong. Many years after I left the house and moved to the USA I asked my mother who was visiting us, about the whereabouts of Dr. Levi. As it turned out, Dr. Levi had a brother who married a non-Jewish Bulgarian lady and never immigrated to Israel. When Dr. Levi's brother died, Dr. Levi married his sister-in-law and the two shared their time between the two countries. Eventually he sold his apartment and they went back to live in Sophia.

Each of the three wings of the Train Building at 34 Yehuda Hamaccabi Street had an underground bomb shelter for the eleven families. One flight of stairs took you to the backyard exit. The next led to the underground shelter. We tried to keep the place clean and easily accessible not only for the people living in the building but also for strangers who looked for shelter when the air raid siren sounded. There was a rectangular opening in the backyard, covered with cement that provided an escape route in case the exit through the stairway was blocked. We had to use our underground shelter during the Suez Campaign.

✡

On October 30, 1956 a day after the Suez campaign started, the Egyptian destroyer *Ibrahim el Awal* was dispatched to the Israeli port city of Haifa to shell the oil refineries. The ship reached Haifa at 3:00 a.m. on October 31 and began shelling from six miles off-shore. Although discovered at 2:45 a.m. it was not fired upon by the Israeli navy, because there was a US naval operation to evacuate American citizens happening at the time. The fire from *Ibrahim el Awal* did not cause any significant damage or casualties. A French destroyer, *Kersaint*, already at the Haifa port as part of the joint campaign, opened fire on the Egyptian destroyer but missed.

The captain of *Ibrahim el Awal* decided, upon finishing its shelling of Haifa, to retreat, at full speed, to Beirut, Lebanon instead of sailing all the way back to Egypt. He rationalized that the longer escape route to Egypt would make it easier for the Israeli Navy and Air Force to intercept and attack. The Israeli Navy chased the Egyptian destroyer and together with four Air Force jet fighters managed to damage the ship's rudder and turbo generator. The ship was left without power. It surrendered to the Israeli Navy and the Egyptian sailors were taken prisoner. The Israeli Navy recommissioned the ship into the Israeli Navy and changed its name to *Haifa* after the port it shelled. During the *Ibrahim el Awal* we and many other Israelis living along the coastline stretching from Tel Aviv to Haifa, spent all that time inside our underground shelter until the ship surrendered. We did not know what was going on other than hearing the jets flying. It brought me eight years back to my childhood era, living at 132 Ben Yehuda Street trying frantically to find a shelter during the Egyptian air raid on Tel Aviv. During the ship incident we had a full-fledged underground shelter and not one flight of stairs to squeeze inside, like we did at 132 Ben Yehuda Street.

Surprisingly enough, the US objections to the Suez campaign came under the presidency of the republican Dwight Eisenhower and his republican Secretary of State John Foster Dulles, who was a fierce opponent of Russia during the cold war and also against Gamal Abdel Nasser, the leader of the Egyptian regime. The only answer I can think of, while trying to reconcile this paradox, is to speculate on the fact that the Suez campaign took place when John Foster Dulles underwent an extensive colon cancer surgery followed by a long post-surgery hospitalization.

✡

The shared backyard between our train building and the other train buildings behind us was a favorite spot for all kinds of vendors who solicited odd services, reminiscent of the kind they offered in their own tiny *shtetl* before immigrating to Israel. A *shtetl* was a small town or village primarily in Russia and Poland with a large, close-knit Jewish community. Yiddish was the predominant language. The *shtetls* can be traced back to 13th century Eastern Europe when the diaspora Jews experienced relative prosperity and tolerance by the non-Jewish population. Their fortune worsened during the 19th century under the Russian Empire with its poverty and frequent pogroms. The *shtetls* communities were wiped out in the Holocaust

There was a long walkway that provided access from the *Kibbutz* Galuyot Street (now Weizmann Street) to the second entrance of that building. It had a wider paved area to serve the mailboxes of the residents. That area was the vendor's favorite place to loudly offer their services to nearly sixty surrounding households. One vendor offered to repair damaged goose-feather blankets. I'd never heard of that vocation. He carried a tool on his shoulder that looked like an oversized rifle. I don't remember seeing anyone using his services so I have no idea how goose-feathers blankets were repaired. I felt really sad for him and hoped he did not go to sleep on an empty stomach.

The Junk Man visited our neighborhood with his dilapidated buggy pulled by an old mule. He tied the harness to the electric pole on *Kibbutz* Galuyot Street. Next, he walked to the vendors spot, shouting in Yiddish: "*Alte Zachen, Alte ShIech Alte Zachen Alte Shichalech*" (Yiddish for Old Stuff, Old Shoes). He carried a empty gummy sac on his back, shouted until someone wanted to get rid of items, and shouted back, "*Hey, Alte zachen, vart a minut*" (Yiddish for Hey old stuff man, wait a minute). The neighbor would throw down the items for the *Alte Zachen* man to collect. At times, the shower of stuff tossed to the *Junk Man* was quite heavy. Occasionally, clothes and other items thrown down for the *Alte Zachen* man got tangled on the electric line that ran between the two buildings. Clearing them was too dangerous for the residents so the electric company came and in turn lectured us not to do it again. After *harvesting* all the items thrown to him, the *Alte Zachen* man moved on to his next stop. He sold the used items at flea markets in Tel Aviv and Yafo. The Americans have Garage Sales to get rid of old junk, but the Israelis during that era had their *Alte Zachen* to serve the same purpose. The *Alte Zachen* are relics of the past. You don't see them nowadays.

Another colorful character visiting the vendor's spot was the *The Sharpener*. We knew that he had arrived when he shouted at the top of his lungs a long list of his services, *"Shli-fen, Shli-fen Meser Sharpener, Sharpener Sher, Shlayf di gantse kich"* (a somewhat lose translation would be: *Sharpener,…. Knife sharpener, scissor sharpener, sharpener of the whole kitchen*). I am not sure how precise my Yiddish is but that is what I remember hearing as a child many years ago. *The Sharpener* carried on his shoulder a large wooden wheel connected to a foot pedal. His sharpening contraption also had a stand to place the large wheel on the ground. Sharpening was done by spinning the big wheel with his foot on the pedal turning the sharpening stone. It was spewing zillions of tiny sparks like fireworks seen on the Fourth of July in the US. It was fun to watch him work.

The last character frequenting the Vendors Spot, whose visits were deeply engraved into my mind and impacted my mom and I the most, was not a vendor at all. He did not offer any service or try to sell anything. I called him the *Troubadour*. Unlike medieval lyric poets and musicians who sang mainly about courtly love during the eleventh through thirteenth centuries, our *Troubadour* sang about the harsh misfortunes of life. He was an old man, very skinny, with a slightly bent stature. Gray whiskers covered his wrinkled face and his bare gums caught my attention whenever he smiled.

My *Troubadour* hero played a dilapidated button accordion, missing a few notes. We knew that he had arrived when we heard his signature song, *TZena TZena*. That song was written in 1941 by a Polish immigrant who came to Eretz Isracl/Palestine before WWII. He served in the Jewish Brigade of the British army. The lyrics encouraged the Israeli girls to come out and greet the Jewish soldiers. The song became popular in Israel and was played often on the Israeli radio. In 1946 it became popular in the USA when the Weavers sang it in Hebrew. Other American singers performed it as well, with various English translations. The following is an accurate English translation of the Hebrew lyrics.

> *"Go out, go out, go out girls and see soldiers in the* moshava *(Israeli small farming community). Do not, do not, do not hide yourself away from a virtuous man, an army man."*

Personally, I never liked it and considered the song mediocre, but our *Troubadour* captured the attention of the neighborhood. He did not know Hebrew and definitely did not understand what he was singing. He sang only the first verse like a broken LP record, *"TZena, Tzena Margarina Tzena Margarina,"* and did not stop until he saw an audience gathering on balconies to watch his concert. He added the word *margarina* which was the name the Israelis used for *margarine* and not part of the original lyrics. No one had the slightest clue what margarine had to do with the song.

One nice summer morning the *Troubadour* came to our neighborhood. I was enjoying my summer recess, siting in the kitchen with my mother when we heard him singing "*Tzena Tzena Margarina.*" The kitchen door to the balcony was open and I went outside to see who was singing the strange rendition of that song. My mother was not impressed and did not even bother to come out on the balcony. But when he started singing the next song the situation changed completely. I vaguely knew what he was singing because it was in Yiddish. My mother stopped what she was doing, came out to the balcony and saw the frail, bony old man, singing his heart out. When he looked up to see if he had an audience, he saw my mother.

I didn't understand the eye contact between the two but he stopped singing in the middle of the song and restarted from the first verse. My mother went into the kitchen, reached for her purse. When she felt she had enough, she wrapped coins in a paper napkin and returned to the balcony. The *Troubadour* was still singing so Mom shouted to him in Yiddish "*Her Zinger*" (Yiddish for Mr. Singer). He stopped singing and looked at her. She waived to him with her hand holding the napkin stuffed with coins and shouted, "*Piasters, Piasters, cenen ir chapen es?*" (Yiddish for "Piasters, *Piasters,* can you catch it?"). He put his accordion on the pavement, looked at her and smiled, showing his toothless gums and shouted "*Yo!*" (Yiddish for yes). My mother tossed the bundle of coins but he failed to catch it. The napkin burst, spreading the coins all over the place. The *Troubadour* collected the coins he could see. My mother felt bad about what happened, and hoped he would find every single coin she gave him.

I was still puzzled as to why my mother was moved to give him money when he sang the second song, so I asked her, "What is the name of that song?" "*A Bissele Mazel*" (Yiddish for A Little Bit of Luck) she replied. I did not pursue the conversation any further as I was still too young to delve into what that Yiddish song was all about. Many years later I came across it and realized that it was really a description of the misfortune of the *shtetl* people. All of them, the *Alte Zachen*, the knives sharpeners, the feather blanket repairman, the *Troubadour* and many others visited our backyard. They paraded before my eyes, a youngster born and raised in a free and independent Jewish state. The old *shtetl* Jews struggled just to survive financially and were dreaming of a break from their poverty. The lyrics of the second song the *Troubadour* sang that day expressed that so succinctly. It was written by Benzion Viter. Here is the gist of it:

> If I could find a good fortune, a small, tiny piece of good luck, spin the wheel, get me a fortune and happiness, hidden

or stuck. We all laugh and cry, we all suffer, just after we came into being. Oh, where to get a piece, just a tiny piece of happiness, we all miss.

We have hardships, worries and troubles. They never bypass us. We still walk and walk the roads, seeing our days and life passing by while we still wishing to find a good fortune, a small tiny piece of good luck

The poverty and the hardship of the *shtetl* Jews was the norm, unfortunately. Basically, the main three classes of the American society could be classified as The Rich, The Poor, and The Middle Class. The great majority of the Jews living in the *shtetls*, were all poor. Someone, I don't recall his name, claimed that fights between social classes in the Jewish *shtetl* was the fight between the *Kabtzensons* and the *Dalphonsons* (The Poor against the Paupers). They all lamented about being poor and out of luck and, dreamed of better times. A nice example of that theme is the song "If I Were a Rich Man," from the Broadway hit show *Fiddler on the Roof.*

My mother had a hunch that our *Troubadour* would show up again so she prepared the money to give him. I called it the *piasters*, the name she shouted to him when she tossed the coins from our kitchen balcony. This time, however, she put the coins in a small plastic bag. I didn't know what the word *piasters* had to do with the money she tossed to him. I found out years later, that it referred to monetary unit used in the former Turkish Empire in the Levant. It was the equivalent of 100th of the Turkish Lira, or the Egyptian Pound, when Eretz Israel was part of the Turkish Empire.

Mom was right, we didn't wait too many days before *Troubadour* singing, "*Tzena Tzena Margarina*" echoed from the vendors spot. I went out to the balcony and there he was, unshaven, dressed in the same clothes he wore during his last concert. Even my untrained musical ears noticed that more notes were missing from his accordion. Other neighbors came out as well. My mother grabbed the small plastic bag with the money and intended to toss it to him upon finishing the song, "A Bissele Mazel" like she did before. He surprised us by replacing it with the Yiddish song, "My Yiddish Momme." That song was a 1920 classic musical treasure that took on a life of its own to become an ode to Jewish mothers and their unwavering dedication to their children. My mother froze the minute she heard the first verses and became overwhelmed with emotion as he continued.

The *Troubadour's* raspy, crackling voice, the music from his dilapidated accordion and my tearing mother holding the *piasters* bag she was about to toss to him, was a once-in-a lifetime moment. I realized that my *Troubadour* was singing about his own mother as well as my mother's mom, my own grandma who perished in the Holocaust.

My mother did not toss the *piasters* bag but went back to the kitchen, tears in her eyes, chocked with emotions and opened the refrigerator looking for food to give him. She was very selective remembering that he did not have teeth. She packed the food in a brown bag and gave it to me along with the *piasters* bag and told me in a faint voice, "*Ten lo et ze*" (Hebrew for "Give him this"). I took the brown bag and the money downstairs while he was still singing. He stopped as I approached and I gave him the *piasters* bag and the food my mother prepared for him. I could see a bright smile on his face when he counted the money and started munching on the food. "Danken, Danken" ("Thanks, Thanks") he murmured to me and waved to my mother who was watching from the balcony. When I returned to the balcony, he was gone. My mother had regained her composure by then but we did not talk about that particular concert or what the lyrics of the song meant.

I knew that the song was about Jewish mothers, a very sensitive and emotional issue for my mother who was close to her own mom. My mother who left home, rather abruptly to immigrate to Eretz Israel/Palestine, never saw her parents and her entire family again. They were all murdered by the Nazis, execution style, during the Holocaust. My mother always became overwhelmed whenever she heard songs or stories about mothers.

My mother was in total denial for many years, refusing to accept the harsh reality that her family perished in the Holocaust. She also admonished me one time for telling her the truth. Chapter 3 documents her immigration to Eretz Israel/Palestine.

As I grew up I wanted to understand why hearing "My Yiddish Momme," always put my mother into emotional storms. I looked for the lyrics. Since I was not (and still not) versed in Yiddish, I settled for its English translation used when the song was first performed in the USA. The lyrics, written by Jack Yellen, are very powerful and merit being listed here.

> "*Of things I should be thankful for I've had a goodly share*
> *And as I sit here in the comfort of my cozy chair*
> *My fancy takes me to a humble eastside tenement*
> *Three flights up in the rear to where my childhood days were spent*
> *It wasn't much like Paradise but 'mid the dirt and all*
> *There sat the sweetest angel, one that I fondly call*

My yiddishe momme I need her more than ever now
My yiddishe momme I'd like to kiss that wrinkled brow
I long to hold her hands once more as in days gone by
And ask her to forgive me for things I did, that made her cry
How few were her pleasures, she never cared for fashion's styles
Her jewels and treasures she found them in her baby's smiles
Oh I know that I owe what I am today
To that dear little lady so old and gray
To that wonderful yiddishe momme of mine"

The *Alte Zachen* and the knife sharpener eventually stopped frequenting our neighborhood, but the *Troubadour* never came back after performing "My Yiddish Momme." My mother continued to prepare *piaster*s bags and kept some food for him in the refrigerator in case he came again but she gave up after realizing that he was gone. His singing overwhelmed my mother, but it also had a profound impact on me. His singing style, his repertoire, sang in his raspy voice accompanied by a dilapidate accordion, exposed me to the compassion and humanistic virtues of my mother, virtues that she kept until she passed away many years later.

I don't know if *Troubadour* got sick and could not continue coming back or even worse, died. I missed him very much and still remembered him vividly. I am convinced that our *Troubadour* was one of the *Lamed Vav Tzadikim* (Hebrew for 36 Righteous People) the Jewish people believe to exist in the world. This mystical concept in Judaism asserts that there are 36 *Tzadikim* (righteous people) in the world. Their sole purpose in life is to justify before God the existence of mankind. According to Judaism's mystical belief, in each generation, God does not destroy the world, even when humanity reaches its lowest point, because of these *Thirty-six Righteous People* serving as the advocates for mankind. It brings back the biblical story in Genesis when Abraham, the first Jewish Lawyer arguing with God to spare the wicked City of Sodom and Gomorrah if he could show God even one righteous man.

The *Lamed Vav Tzadikim* are also called the *Nistarim* (Hebrew for Concealed Ones) because their identity is unknown. Jewish mysticism says that they emerge out of their concealment and spare us from disasters and persecutions of our enemies. Once the pending disaster is averted the *Lamed Vav Tzadikim* disappear and become anonymous again. Moreover, the tradition claims that identities of the *Lamed Vav Tzadikim* are not known to each other so each one operates alone. The name *Lamed Vav* is the Hebrew acronym comprised of the Hebrew letter *Lamed* with its numerical value of thirty and the letter *Vav* which has the numerical value of six. Summing these numbers together we get the *Thirty-six Righteous Ones.*

Allowing myself to be captured by this innocent and beautiful Jewish mysticism I believe that the frail *Troubadour* who captured my mother's heart and mine, was one of the *Lamed Vav Tzadikim.* He did an excellent job disguising himself as an old, unassuming man with no teeth and playing the life story of our diaspora brethren on a dilapidated button accordion with missing notes. He appeared twice and then disappeared. He did not die. He just showed up at the vendors spot to protect us from something bad happening and then returned to his anonymity.

It is noteworthy that when Senator Henry "Scoop" Jackson, a great supporter of Israel and the Jewish people, died, New York Senator Daniel Patrick Moynihan stated: *Henry Jackson is proof of the old belief in the Judaic tradition that at any moment in history goodness in the world is preserved by the deeds of thirty-six just men who do not know that this is the role the Lord has given them. Henry Jackson was one of those men.*

✡

Our neighborhood and its surrounding region continued to grow with more businesses and buildings. The highway connecting Tel Aviv, Haifa and northern Israel was widened and a larger bridge was built to accommodate the heavy traffic. We graduated from Yehuda Hamaccabi Elementary School and moved on to different high schools. It was a bitter-sweet feeling, growing into a more mature phase of life, the worry-free childhood happiness was gone. No more building my beloved *sukkah* on the roof or the sound of children having the time of our lives.

The long electric wire Mr. Mitelsbach made for me to bring electricity and light into the *sukkah* was no longer needed. And then I revived it once more to bring more pleasant moments to my life. I stripped its plastic sheath to expose the copper wire and used it as my crystal radio antenna. I climbed up on the antenna towers and extended it through the entire length of the building. It gave me great radio reception.

Although my close friend Yotam and I attended different high schools we stayed inseparable as we still lived in the same wing of our Train Building. To see him, I went down one flight of stairs and rang the doorbell. Our parents and the entire card-playing gang living in the wing stayed very close. They continued taking turns hosting their traditional Friday evening card games.

Yotam and I also belonged to the same youth movement, affiliated with the *kibbutz* movement. We spent almost six months at *Kibbutz* Rosh HaNikra on the Israel-Lebanon border prior to being conscripted to the army. The high school he attended was just a few yards from our building and was built on the lot where the old abandoned citrus orchard stood. My high school, however, was more than a mile from our building so I got my daily exercise by riding there on my Raleigh sport bikes, rain or shine.

On my first day as a high school student, at fourteen, for the first time in my life, I wore a pair of slacks. Before that, it didn't matter what season of the year it was, rain or shine, my mother had insisted that I wear only short pants. She was adamant about it, fully convinced that it would build my health and immune system, not to mention my character. She had a great admiration for the people of ancient Sparta and wanted me to be just like them. She boasted that the minute I was born, she dipped me in cold water after bathing me in warm water. It became a habit for me as I got the hang of it and always ended my hot showers with cold water. I am glad my mother gave me this "Spartan" cold water shower and made me wear short pants during the winter.

I continued to go to the beach for my daily swim even during winter, except for stormy and windy days when the surf was too high and dangerous. High school started at 8:00 a.m. and unlike the USA, the Israeli students attended school six days a week (Sunday through Friday). I left my house on my bike at 5:30 a.m. for the two-mile ride to the beach by the Abd-al-Nabi Muslim cemetery that I knew very well from my childhood days living at 132 Ben Yehuda Street.

Next to the beach stood a small cluster of wooden, not very well built houses, *Sh'chunat Machlool*, (the Machlool neighborhood) hastily built at the southern edge of the Muslim cemetery. Calling that location a "neighborhood" is a bit of a stretch as it had no street, walkways, street lights, etc. Just a few improvised structures a few feet apart.

The name *Machlool* was a real estate term in the law that prevailed in Eretz Israel when it was part of the Ottoman Empire. The term applied to an undeveloped stretch of land. In 1920, the British Mandate authorities gave that area between Tel Aviv and Yafo, to the governing authorities of Tel Aviv, who left it undeveloped. Its easy access to the open sandy beach turned it into the Eretz Israel/Palestine version of the American wild, wild west. People just claimed ownership of a piece of land. The third wave of Jewish immigration to Eretz Israel/Palestine from 1919 to 1923 brought many immigrants who fled the pograms and financial hardship in Eastern Europe. A large number of them built their own temporary shack from pieces of wood the waves washed ashore. They also gathered sheets of galvanized metal from construction sites. To make the temporary dwellings rain-proof, the settlers covered the structures with tar paper.

Riots against the Yafo Jews erupted on May 1, 1921 killing thirteen and injuring many more. The riots made more people come to that patch of Tel Aviv beach to build their temporary dwellings. As far as I know, no one paid the Tel Aviv authorities any property tax. A few more years passed and the Machlool neighborhood became a huge urban eyesore and a problematic spot for the city. Strong winter storms, flooding and fires were the main culprits. These shacks were not built to comply with any building and engineering codes.

Oddly enough the Machlool neighborhood with its strange, off-code flimsy houses, did establish two industrial factories. One factory weaved and dyed silk fabrics. The other one processed raw leather. The stink coming from the leather factory was so offensive that the *Haganah* used the location on the factory premises to manufacture guns and ammunition, hiding these activities from the British authorities. I suspect that the people who built their illegal flimsy shacks at the Machlool neighborhood also illegally dumped and disposed building materials and other solid garbage into the sea.

I experienced the result of that illegal dumping as I was injured while swimming there. The sea was at least thirteen feet deep. The area looked innocent and safe until I hit a long rusty pipe, submersed vertically below the surface and anchored to the seabed. It hurt my left thigh causing me to limp for two weeks. Luckily, I was current with my tetanus shot.

Leaving my house at 5:30 in the morning made my ride to the beach easy because traffic was light. I arrived at the Machlool neighborhood, carried my bike on my shoulders and walked on the sandy beach toward the large wooden structure that housed the changing room and showers. It was wintertime so there was no lifeguard on duty. During the summer season, the tower was humming with activities orchestrated by *Aharontzic*, the legendary lifeguard, blowing his lifeguard's whistle sounding like one of Vivaldi's Piccolo Concerto. Legend has it that he saved the lives of 5,000 people during his thirty-five years as the lifeguard on that beach.

I chained my bike to the lifeguard tower and got ready to plunge into the cold, calm blue water of my beloved Mediterranean sea. I waived good morning to the group of ten to fifteen senior citizens who braved the cold winter morning, dressed only in swimming suites and leftover summer tan. There were a few ladies in that group. These *Polar Bears* were busy throwing a large heavy leather ball to each other. They waved back at me. They knew my routine of taking a short swim and then jogging next to the waterline toward the Port of Yafo. The wet compact sand made it easier to run albeit very cold and painful on the soles of my feet. Being the only teenager brave or crazy enough to plunge into the cold water and then jog on the cold beach, gained me the respect of the *Polar Bear* senior citizens. They were extremely kind people and we bonded easily. I knew that I had gained their respect when they made me an *Honorary Member* of their group with the benefit of using the facility and showers free of charge. In their eyes, I was the carrier of their torch to the younger generation.

There were days when I forgot to wear my wristwatch. Still, I was able to tell when to go back home and not be late to school. All I needed to do was watch the main manhole cover at the Machlool neighborhood. It was time to leave the beach when the manhole cover of the haphazardly built sewage system raised, and raw sewage spilled onto the sandy beach nearby. It always happened around seven o'clock when most of the residents were getting ready to go to work and flushed their toilets. It was time for me to leave the beach and get ready for school.

One extremely cold morning, I was taking off my wet swimming suit and putting on my street clothes, I sat on the sand unable to move due to the near freezing temperature. I noticed to my dismay that the Machlool neighborhood manhole cover, my "clock" was raised and the sewage was spilling onto the sandy beach. By the time I was able to move I realized that it would be a miracle if I made it to school on time. I pedaled home as fast as I could, skipped my shower and rushed to school on my bike, arriving just as the bell rang. I took my sit, huffing and puffing when Eva, our English teacher, entered and inspected the class making sure everyone was present. Then she saw my curly hair loaded with sand spilling on my shirt and the table. "*Shmuel*," she interrogated me with her heavy German accented Hebrew, "where have you been and how did you get so much sand in your hair?"

"I went swimming at the beach this morning and failed to leave on time so I skipped taking a shower before coming to school."

Eva gazed out the window and saw the heavy dark clouds and the pouring rain. "Sure!" she said skeptically, she did not buy my story. My friend Uri, who shared the class desk with me, told her that I was telling the truth. All my classmates knew that I was crazy enough to go swimming during the winter. She accepted that and started class.

✡

Tichon Hadash High School was unique and special. It merits a brief description as it had a huge impact in molding my personality during my teen era. Its name, *Tichon Hadash*, Hebrew for *new high school* refereed to a new approach of teaching and philosophy. The school was established in 1937 by a cooperative of German Jewish immigrants who came to Eretz Israel/Palestine before WWII. The school was run by Dr. Toni Halle and Dr. Aaron Berman as its co-principals. Other founders were Dr. Meir Bloch, who taught Bible classes, Dr. Yehoyakim Papporish who taught Geography. He was the author of the geography textbooks used at Israeli high schools. The main objective was to teach students to love the country and be *humanists* at the same time. We were asked to address our teachers by their first names including Dr. Toni Halle. I am not sure why everyone addressed the other co-principal not by his first name Aaron but as Dr. Berman. A most likely answer was that Dr. Berman was a real medical doctor by education. We also addressed our geography teacher as Dr. Papporish and not by his first name Yehoyakim, because that was the name printed on the cover of his geography books.

Unlike the Gymnasia Herzelia High School, with its leaning toward conservatism and bourgeoisie philosophy, my school leaned toward a national socialistic philosophy and opened its doors to the youth movement of the socialist political parties. Most of the students, like me, belonged to *Ha' Tnuha Hameuchedet, Machanot Ha' Olim* and *Ha' Shomer Hatzair*. A few lonely wolves belonged to the Boy Scouts youth movements. High schools operated by the Tel Aviv municipality, required students to wear a uniform. At Tichon Hadash we had no official school uniform. However, most students came to school on Fridays wearing the special *blue shirt* which was the uniform of the socialist movement. Wearing the blue shirt to school on Fridays was not mandatory but the majority of students came from socialist homes.

For many students, attending Tichon Hadash was a natural continuation from the time they spent attending the Beith Hinuch ba' tazfon elementary school (later known as A.D. Gordon Elementary School). That school was founded for the children of the blue-collar workers of the socialist movements. My cohorts who came from Beith Hinuch ba' tazfon were accustomed to wearing the blue shirt on Fridays. (See Chapter 1 for more details about that school.)One day some of the students, whom I considered to be "too socialistic and Zealots" went to Toni Halle, to complain about the students who did not wear the blue shirt on Fridays. Toni, who did not have children of her own but knew each of her students by name and treated them as if she was their biological mother, admonished the complainers with her soft voice and heavily German accented Hebrew, "It does not matter what is the color of the shirt you are wearing. What counts is what is underneath that shirt." It became sort of her motto which let us to realize that the heart beating underneath the shirt must show empathy and understanding toward fellow man.

✡

One of the students who came to Tichon Hadash High School along with his classmates from the Beith Hinuch ba' tazfon elementary school was Daniel Barenboim, a child prodigy. He was born in Buenos Aries, Argentina and immigrated to Israel in 1952 when he was ten years old. Both his parents were professional pianists who started teaching him how to play when he was five years old. His father did most of the teaching and managed Daniel's early musical career. Daniel gave his first public concert when he was seven years old. Israel was extremely excited about having a prodigy immigrating to Israel. His parents sent him to Beith Hinuch ba' tazfon to study and intermingle with the normal Israeli kids his age. Evidently their choice of that school indicated their socialist leaning. My mother, who worked at the dining hall, remembered him as a happy and mischievous child. She claimed to be his favorite member of the dining hall crew because she always gave him an extra helping when he begged for more food, saying that he was still hungry.

Having Daniel Barenboim as a student in our high school posed a problem, albeit a nice one, for Toni Halle. While other students attended English classes, it was unfair to force him to take the class when he was already fluent in Spanish, English, Hebrew, French, Italian and German. Moreover, our school, unlike the other Israeli high schools at that time, fostered classes in Art History, Music and Music History. These classes were mandatory in the school's curriculum even though they were not part of the Israeli Matriculation Tests that all Israeli students must pass in order to be admitted to any Israeli college or university. Toni did not force Daniel Barenboim to take the music classes either. He was by then, a world-renowned pianist playing with major world-famous symphony orchestras. He also decided to persue conducting.

Being a prodigy and an accomplished musician also made him very proficient in mathematics and calculus, so Toni exempted him from these classes as well. She was a great educator and as such she made him take General History, Hebrew Grammar, Hebrew Literature, Bible, Talmud and Sports like the rest of us. Toni believed in equality for all and made him take the Matriculation Tests upon finishing Tichon Hadash, like everyone else.

During the recesses Daniel liked to get together with his old classmates from Beith Hinuch ba' tazfon elementary school and the new friends at our school. He wore the blue socialist shirt every Friday, an old ritual from his former school.

Toni, who knew each of her students, realized that Daniel, being exempt from so many classes, would get bored, so she assigned him the task of being her currier. He delivered written messages from her office to the teachers while they were in the classroom teaching. Our school did not use a PA system and relied on the currier delivering messages when classes were in progress. One day, during my history class, there was a faint knocking on the door. Yosef Izraeli, our teacher, opened the door and Daniel Barenboim gave him a note. Teacher Izraeli read the note, came to my desk and whispered to my ear, "Shmuel, Toni wants to see you in her office right now." I was shocked and tried to figure out what I could have done wrong that warranted interrupting the class and sending me to the principal's office.

I left the classroom and went downstairs to Toni's office with my heart palpitation exceeding the speed limit. The door to Toni's office was closed so I knocked and heard Toni's German-accented voice, "Ya-Vo," (Hebrew for come in). I was shocked to see my parents sitting there looking serious. I wondered what made my parents take time off work to see Toni, I had never had any disciplinary issues in my entire life as a pupil. Toni said, "Shmuel, I am here to arbitrate between you and your parents. They called me and requested an appointment to discuss your after-class activities at the Tnuha Hameuchedet youth movement. They are deeply concerned that your activities as the leader of the younger members at your group takes too much of your time and might compromise your chance of being ready for the Matriculation Tests. So, for the sake of fairness, I would like to hear your side of the story."

My high school was very supportive of the socialist youth movement and encouraged their activities. I expected Toni to support me and she did. But she also paid attention to my parent's concerns. I told Toni that this was the first time I heard their concern. I assured her and my parents that my activities at the youth movement did not negatively impact my grades, and Toni vouched for that. I assured Toni and gave my parents my word that I would quit my youth movement activities at the first sign that my grades were impaired. Toni looked at my parents and said, "Mr. and Mrs. Polonecki (my old surname, see more about my name change on page 83), as Shmuel's educator and with the feedback I am getting from his teachers, I am not concerned at all. I trust that he will keep his word and continue to take his studies seriously. I would like to suggest that we leave things the way they are. Feel free to call me if he does not keep his word. Then he will have an issue with me." Everyone was relieved and felt better when Toni said to me, "Shmuel, go back to your class before the bell rings for lunch recess."

As mentioned earlier, my high school emphasized the appreciation for the Arts and Music and made Arts and Music classes mandatory in its curriculum. Toni encouraged students to visit museums and concert halls. Since my cohorts and I had the fortune and privilege to have the world-renowned pianist Daniel Barenboim, as our class-mate, Toni saw to it that he played classical music for us from time to time. On the morning of Israeli Independence Day, for example, which is solemnly observed as a memorial to the fallen soldiers, we had a memorial service at the school gymnasium and Daniel played Maurice Ravel's "A Pavane to a Dead Princess."

Another exposure to the music world was presented to us when our music teacher, Mrs. Miriam Grossman struck a deal with the Israel Opera to have her students and everyone at Tichon Hadash who was interested, attend the opera's dress rehearsal held at the Israel National Opera House located at Herbert Samuel Plaza by the Tel Aviv beach. The world renowned opera singer Plácido Domingo had signed a two-year contract with the opera. We had the pleasure of hearing him staring in a few famous operas.

Despite the school's socialistic philosophy and political leaning, its outside the box approach to education, along with its emphasis on teaching humanism, the school attracted the elite of the Israeli society during that era. Its reputation drew students from cities outside the Tel Aviv metropolitan like Ranana, thirteen miles away or the posh neighborhoods of Herzelia Pituach and K'Far Sh'maryahoo located nine miles away. They all took the public bus during regular school days. For off-hours school activities their parents brought them to school and parked their fancy cars along the curb. Toni, the devoted socialist, did not like these iconic symbols of capitalism parked by the high school she and her socialist colleagues founded as a bastion of socialism and the working class.

Dr. Toni Halle and Dr. Aaron Berman were very special people in their own right. We did not know much about Dr. Aaron Berman. Many years after graduation, I checked into his history and his professional path as an educator. Dr. Berman was born in Poland, and attended *Yeshiva* (Jewish orthodox religious schools sort of the equivalent of the secular high school). After finishing his Yeshiva studies Dr. Berman studied in German and Swiss universities. In 1913 he received his MD degree from a Zurich university. I don't believe he worked as a medical doctor, most of his life centered on being an educator. In 1936 he immigrated to Eretz Israel/Palestine and belonged to the group of educators that included Toni Halle. He believed, like Toni, that teaching should involve instilling socialistic values along with the humanistic values of Judaism and humanity in general. He also taught our philosophy classes. Dr. Berman wrote several books about the history of education in Israel and several books related to philosophy.

✡

When I was a child and teenager, it was mandatory for Israeli parents to send their children to kindergarten followed by eight years of elementary school. Most of us continued to four years of high school or vocational school but it was not mandatory. Some elected to join the work force, earn money and attended the high schools which taught in the evenings. These schools and their curriculum were under the jurisdiction and inspection of the Ministry of Education.

To be admitted to any Israeli university, a student had to pass six matriculation examinations. Each test covered a specific field, e.g. Physics, Mathematics, History, etc. Each four-hour test was given throughout the country on the same day and at the same time. The entire matriculation exam was stretched into a two-week time-frame. Leaving students about two-weeks to catch their breath before being recruited to the army.

The four-year curriculum at Tichon Hadash High School was structured into two segments. The first two-year segment covered the generic curriculum taught to all the students. During the third and the fourth years, the students elected the fields of their interest or future aspiration so after the first two years these students were separated into four different classes: Literature & Art, Mathematic & Physics, Biology, and Social Humanities. I chose Biology. There was a friendly and healthy rivalry between the four groups adding some pep to being a student there. It was kind of sad when these two years of togetherness ended and the Israeli Army drafted both males and females. I believe that after we left Israel, the administrative structure of the Israeli high school system was changed and modified to look more like that of the prevailing one in the USA.

By the middle of my third year at Tichon Hadash which was my first year on the Biology curriculum path, I realized that I had made the right choice as I excelled in the Biology classes, and worked very well with Frieda, our Biology teacher. Since the Israeli Ministry of Education allowed students attending the Biology curriculum to design and carry out a rather extensive scientific research in lieu of taking the Biology Matriculation test, I decided to take that option. Frieda enthusiastically agreed and gave me her blessing with one caveat, "If you can convince Toni to go along, I will support you," she told me. I had no doubt that Toni would be sympathetic as she always encouraged her students to think out of the box and take on challenges. I was granted an audience with her.

When I met with Toni, I noticed that she was browsing through her small black notebook. "Good morning Shmuel, what prompted you to request this appointment? I hope it is not another argument with your parents about your activities at the youth movement," she said.

"Not at all," I replied. "That issue was resolved at the end of the meeting with my parents a few months ago." Toni looked at me still holding her back notebook and said, "I just consulted with my notebook and I did not see any notes indicating any problems with you being behind with your schoolwork or passing the quarterly tests, so it must be something else that needs my attention and I am ready to hear it," she said with her heavy German accent. I shared with her my desire to skip the Biology Matriculation test, carry out my own research experiments and write a thesis in lieu of the Matriculation test. "I guess you already talked to Frieda, your Biology teacher. What did she say about it?" Toni asked.

"Frieda is 100% behind me, if you agree," I replied.

"Well, Shmuel. You are the first student thus far trying to take this route so I need to check with the Ministry of Education officials regarding their prerequisites and the procedures involved. They also should let us know the scope of the work they want in order to grant you a passing grade in the Biology Matriculation test. Let me also discuss it with Frieda. We will have another appointment once I have the information on how to proceed."

I thanked Toni for her support and was about to leave the office when she asked, "How is Popo doing?" I did not know who she was talking about.

"Who is Popo?" I asked.

"Popo" is your cousin, Shmuel Polonecki who graduated from our school two years ago. He was very popular among his peers so they gave him the nick name "Popo" and that was the name we all used until he graduated from Tichon Hadash.

I informed Toni that Popo had just graduated from the army's Officers Academy as a Second Lieutenant. "He applied to attend the Hebrew University in Jerusalem aiming at Bachelor and Master's degree in Economics," I told Toni, who opened her black notebook and jotted something down.

"I am glad to hear that both of you share not only the same first and last name but also being very industrious," she said as I was about to leave her office. Yet, I could not resist the temptation to share with her the fact that I paid a dearly for having an identical first and last name when we both attended Nes Ziona Elementary School.

"I was a first grader while my cousin was three grades above me. The problem for me was that he was afraid of the immunization shots. Whenever the school nurse called him to get vaccinated, he protested claiming that he already got it and it was his cousin Shmuel Polonecki who needed the injection. The nurse would call me to the nurse's room ready to poke me with the syringe so I protested too, claiming that I already got the injection and she was mistaking me with my cousin. The nurse decided, that since she already drew the vaccine into the syringe and since I was the youngest between the two it stood to reason that I was the one scared of injection. Unfortunately for me, she followed her reasoning and gave me the shot. I had the pleasure of getting some of the vaccines twice. The vaccine against tuberculosis, in particular, was very painful and left a round scar at the injection site so I have two scars." I rolled up my sleeve and showed Toni. I hope she didn't jot this story into her black notebook.

Toni and Frieda got all the information needed to proceed with my project. I started at the beginning of my forth year at Tichon Hadash. I chose to research plant physiology associated with plant hormones/growth regulators and their effects on the plant. For example, how do green plants orient themselves toward the light and what is the physiological process enabling them to do so. A somewhat similar variation of the same question would be the mechanism by which the plant's main root orients itself downward in the direction of gravitational force and its stem grows upward counter to gravity. In fact, if you reorient a growing plant from its normal vertical position and place it horizontally, given enough time, it will make a correction; the bottom part bending itself downward toward gravity for the roots to grow into the ground and the other end of that plant bending itself upward.

My next challenge was to find an expert willing to help me with the project. I called the University of Tel Aviv Biology Department and told the secretary about my intended project and asked her who to talk to about it. "Professor Galinka would be the best person to help you with that," she replied. "He is teaching the Plant Physiology class and its associated lab. I would like to suggest that the principal of your school and your biology teacher contact him to coordinate this project if he is willing to guide you. I know Toni Halle, your principal, very well so I am going to call her personally and get your project up and running, if professor Galinka concurs."

A few days later, Toni summoned me to her office with the good news that the project was approved and Professor Galinka would be happy to be my mentor. "You have to schedule an appointment," she told me and added, "we need to establish some ground rules for you to follow. You will perform the research work and the meetings with Professor Galinka after the regular school hours, and please don't neglect your other classes. I will watch your grades, making sure that you are not slipping because of your project. Last, but not least, performing this project in lieu the Biology Matriculation test, does not exempt you from taking Frieda's Biology classes, labs and the midterms tests.

"Don't worry Toni, you have my word," I reassured her and left.

My first meeting with Professor Galinka went very well. I found him to be a very pleasant and forthcoming person. He set aside a space in his own research lab for me to grow my plants and made sure his assistant took care of them during the time I was in school. He also furnished me with the plant hormones and regulators needed for my project. He had the foresight and understood that the project I took upon myself would benefit me well beyond skipping the upcoming Biology Matriculation test. Professor Galinka wanted me to broaden my horizons so he gave me many reprints of scientific papers relevant to my project. To keep me on my toes he would say, "Shmuel, I left a textbook on my desk. I suggest that you read the section I marked and don't be bashful to ask questions or clarifications." He noticed my apprehension the first time he suggested that I submerse myself into his textbooks so he said to me, "I know it is very challenging for you to tackle as it is written in English but get used to it because if you attend a university, English is the universal scientific language."

Four years later our paths crossed again when I became a student at the Tel Aviv University, took his plant physiology classes and earned my B.Sc. Degree in Biology.

It took me three months of hard work to complete the project and write a thesis along with photographs, charts and tables, and present it to Toni and Frieda upon receiving Professor Galinka's approval. "We need to send your thesis to the Ministry of Education in Jerusalem by special delivery to verify that they received it. Come to my apartment on Dov Hoze street tonight at six p.m. and I will have all the official documents sealed and ready to go." She jotted down her address on a piece of paper. I knew that street and neighborhood very well as it was not far from where I lived on Ben Yehuda Street when I was a child.

I arrived at Toni's apartment on time and rang the doorbell. I was totally surprised that it was not Toni who opened the door but a male who looked like a senior citizen to me. I was puzzled because I never knew Toni was married as I never saw a wedding ring on her finger. I told him who I was and that Mrs. Toni Halle, my principal, was expecting me. He let me into the corridor by the entrance and said, "Wait here please, and I will let Toni know that you arrived."

Toni greeted me and gave me my thesis, sealed in the official school package with the name and address of the Ministry of Education. "Please take it to the dispatcher of the taxi station at corner of Ben Yehuda and Gordon streets and tell him to deliver it, *Go'vayna* (Hebrew equivalent of Collect on Delivery) to the Ministry of Education in

Jerusalem. I already made arrangements with the taxi dispatcher. He will take care of it from there. Please make sure he gives you a receipt and bring it back to me along with verification document that it was sent. I will see you at school tomorrow morning," she said as I left with my precious package.

The shipping arrangement may sound strange in the USA, but Israel at that time did not have the equivalent of the American UPS, or FedEx. Same-day secured deliveries were done by sending the items by a well-established and reputable taxi company.

About a month later Toni summoned me to her office and showed me the official letter from the Ministry of Education exempting me from taking the Biology Matriculation Test. "Congratulation Shmuel for work well done. Dr. Barash who reviewed your thesis gave you the 90% grade so you passed your Biology Matriculation test," Toni exclaimed. "Frieda is not going to be back until Monday but she wants to talk to you before then. Please stop at Frieda's house. I believe she lives not too far from where you live."

Toni did not have to entice me to visit Frieda, my beloved Biology teacher. I always loved visiting her house during the time I was working on that project and needed her consultation. That apartment building was built especially to house the musicians of the Israel Philharmonic Orchestra and the professional musicians were always playing classical music. They practiced at home making my visit to Frieda all the more delightful. A few years later, I got my annual subscription to the concerts of the Israel Philharmonic Orchestra and recognized many of Frieda's neighbors as they entered the stage dressed in their tuxedos. I still don't know how Frieda and her husband lived in that building as neither of them were musicians.

Until I went to Toni's house to pick up my thesis, I thought that she was not married. Hence, I was very surprised when a man wearing slippers and apparently living there, opened the door. I decided to explore her story and solve this intriguing puzzle. After all, Toni knew every tiny detail about us and wrote those details in her black notebook so it was only fair for me to do learn about her.

As it turned out, the man who opened the door for me on that day was a Jewish philosopher, Gustav Steinscheider. Toni and Gustav lived together for many years, albeit, unmarried. They did not have children. Gustav was younger than Toni and not a very industrious person. His extensive education as a philosopher could not land him a job in his field of expertise. He was unable or incapable of making the necessary adjustment living in Israel after emigrating from Germany. Toni had to use her connections to got him a job as a street sweeper for the Tel Aviv municipality.

A somewhat similar situation repeated itself many years later, when the Soviet Union opened its gates and let huge waves of Jewish immigrants out of the country. The majority of them immigrated to Israel. They were highly educated professionals but could not find jobs in their field either because of the small size of Israel job market or their training in a communist socialist economy was not on par with standards prevailing in Israel. Many of the musicians who played in famous Russian orchestras made their living playing classical music on street corners, collecting money passersby put in the tin cans next to them. Their beautiful performances were lost or brutally comprised by the street noise coming from the heavy traffic.

Toni, who suffered from heart problems for many years, finally married Gustav Steinscheider when she was sixty-eight years old so that he would receive her pension when she died. She passed away in 1964, six years after marring him. Her dedication to the Jewish community in Eretz Israel/Palestine prompted her to emigrate from Germany in 1924 when she was thirty-five years old. That was not a simple undertaking for a young woman, coming from a Jewish family trying hard to assimilate into the German Christian society. Her father, who was a judge in the German court system, was told flatly by his superiors that the way to advance himself up the ladder, was to convert to Christianity, but he refused.

When our last year at Tichon Hadash came to a close, we all took the Matriculation Tests, a challenge that stretched into two long weeks. Unlike my friends in the Biology path who had to take the four-hour Matriculation Test in Biology, I was exempt because of the special research project and thesis I wrote.

✡

About three weeks after my last Matriculation Tests I started my mandatory service in the Israeli Armed Forces. I'd just turned eighteen with all the legal rights as an adult. Born and raised in Israel with Hebrew as my native tongue, I felt alienated from anything connected to Poland and the Polish language so I was counting the days until I could replace my last name *Polonecki*, with a Hebrew last name that would better define who I was and my connection to the land.

I chose the name Regev, which is the Hebrew name for the clod of soil created when the farmer ploughs his field. My parents did not like the idea, claiming that the name Polonecki was associated with Polish nobility, but I persevered claiming that I was an Israeli and any relationship to Polish nobility was irrelevant. I applied with the Israel Ministry of Interior for a name change and received my Israeli ID card with the name Shmuel Regev.

The majority of my peers who graduated that year became achievers in the years that followed. They became CEOs of high technology companies, successful lawyers, combat jet fighter pilots in the Air Force, university professors, and successful business owners.

This Chapter dealt with the seventeen years I lived at 34 Yehuda Hamaccabi Street. I have not lived there since my wife and I moved to the USA in 1968. We visited occasionally when my parents still lived there. My mother stayed for a while after my father passed away in 1980. She moved to another location in Tel Aviv and rented an apartment.

The Train Building deteriorated quickly. The new building codes in Israel require each flat in a new building to have a specially constructed room to protect the residents from air bombs. Moreover, the new buildings must withstand the seismic activities typical in the region. Since our Train Building never complied with the new codes, it qualified for Israel's TAMA Plan which called for modification or replacement.

A builder/developer signed a contract with all the owners whereby the building would be demolished and replaced. Each unit owner would get a new, larger unit, with an underground parking space.

My Train Building is currently under the final review by the Tel Aviv municipality. I hope its replacement will be built during my lifetime. It is sad that 34 Yehuda Hamaccabi Street, a significant chunk of my life's sweet memories, is going to be erased. The price of progress.

Chapter 3

Mom and Dad's Illegal Immigration to Eretz Israel/Palestine

My maternal grandparents, Mordecai and Bluma Lipka had four children, two sons and two daughters. The older son, Kuba, was born in 1910 after ten years of efforts to conceive since the day of their wedding. Heniek, born in 1913 was followed by their daughter Rozka, in 1914 and finally, Mom, Yutka, the baby of the Lipka family, born in 1921.

Mom and her brother, Heniek were active in the Betar movement, a Revisionist Zionist youth movement founded by Ze'ev Jabotinsky. By watching the virulent anti-Semitism in Poland and the rise of Nazism in Germany, Jabotinsky predicted the looming Holocaust. The following is a plea he issued to the Polish Jewry on *Tisha B' Av* (the day on the Jewish Calendar commemorating the destruction of the Jewish Holy Temple in Jerusalem by the Romans in the year 70 AD), issued in Warsaw on August 6, 1938:

For the last three years, I have been calling you, the Jews of Poland, the crown of the world Jewry, and warning you, time and time again, that a catastrophe is coming. My hair has turned gray and I got older during these three years because my heart is bleeding, my dear brothers and sisters, because you don't see the volcano that will start spewing the fire of annihilation. I see a terrible outcome. The time to save yourselves is getting short. I know that you don't see it because you are preoccupied with your day-to-day worries but listen to my words on this 12th hour for God sake! Please save yourselves, each and every one of you! While there is still time to do so. The time left is very short.

And one more thing I want to tell you on this Tisha B' Av day:
Those who will be able to flee and spare themselves from the
catastrophe will live to celebrate the great Jewish joyous moment:
the rebirth and the creation of the Jewish State. I am not sure
that I will be alive to see that moment, but my son will, for sure!
I believe in it as I am absolutely certain that tomorrow morning
the sun will rise again. Yes! I believe in it, without a doubt.

Many Jews who heeded Jabotinsky's plea, attempted to immigrate to Eretz Israel/Palestine which was then under the British Mandate. The British government, however imposed limits on how many Jews were allowed into Eretz Israel/Palestine. Then in March 1939, the British government under Neville Chamberlain drafted a policy called, *The White Paper,* in response to the 1936-1939 Arab Revolt in Palestine. The White Paper called for the establishment of an independent Jewish state in Palestine and a similar independent state for the Palestinians within ten years. However, the plan limited the number of Jewish immigrants (*certificates*) to 75,000 for five years. It ruled that further immigration certificates would be determined by the Arab majority living in Palestine.

Jabotinsky's Betar movement devised a plan to bring the European Jews to Eretz Israel/Palestine illegally and save them from the looming Holocaust. Betar agents canvassed the European continent, organizing immigration to Eretz Israel/Palestine. They opened immigration centers in Poland, Romania, Czechoslovakia, Austria, Hungary, Switzerland, France, Greece, Yugoslavia, Bulgaria and England. The planed illegal immigration was called *Aliya Bet* (Hebrew for second immigration) but it was also known by its popular name, *Ali'yat Aph-alpi-chen* which means, in free translation: *The in-your-face immigration,* expressing Betar resentment of the British who limited Jewish immigration to Eretz Israel/Palestine. European Jews flocked to these centers wanting to immigrate to Eretz Israel/Palestine.

Mom was seventeen and a half when she heard about the campaign during one of her weekly Betar youth meetings. When she came home and told her parents about her wish to immigrate to Eretz Israel/Palestine, legally or illegally, her brother Heniek, himself a very active Betar member admonished her for being an adventurist looking for nothing but trouble. My mother and her brother Kuba survived because they were the adventurists.

Her mother suggested that if she really wanted to immigrate to Eretz Israel/Palestine she should do it legally. My grandmother was concerned about Mom's plan because print and radio news reported horror stories about the British stopping the illegal ships and arresting the immigrants. Grandma was also aware of the stories about the British navy firing on the illegal ships and the many immigrants who drowned. Still, Mom was determined to immigrate to Eretz Israel/Palestine. She went to the nearest Betar immigration center and signed up for the next sailing. Four of her friends from the Betar cell joined her.

Mom told her sister, Rozka, about her wishes to immigrate to Eretz Israel/Palestine and admitted that she had no money to pay for it. Rozka was married to Zigi Hirsch, a scion of the very rich Hirsch clan of Golub. Zigi was aware of Jabotinsky's plea to leave Poland. He encouraged my mother to emigrate and promised to give her money for the voyage. Rozka joked that she and Zigi would need someone in Eretz Israel/Palestine to receive them when they too immigrated. When my grandparents realized that Mom was determined and that Rozka and Zigi would sponsor her, they agreed to give her money.

For security reasons and not to alert the British, the Betar regional immigration headquarters kept the information regarding the departure date and the port of departure top secret. Mom's trip to catch the first available ship required traveling by train to a port somewhere in Europe. Betar operatives did not tell her the port location but instructed her to be ready to depart on very short notice. Since it was somewhat odd for a female her age to travel on such a long trip by herself the Polish authorities quizzed her about it. She told them she was on her way to her brother's wedding.

While Mom waited nervously for notice to depart, there was a flurry of activities surrounding this particular voyage. First, a ship had to be found, purchased and modified to accommodate as many immigrants as possible, and a captain and a crew had to be found. A cadre of Betar operatives had to be trained to manage the immigrants on board as well as once they reached Eretz Israel/Palestine. Betar also established absorption centers in Eretz Israel/Palestine to help the new immigrants establish themselves and blend into their new home country. The ship had to be supplied with enough food, water and coal to reach Eretz Israel/Palestine.

Time became critical when the Germans took control of Czechoslovakia in 1938. The Betar immigration center in Prague and its operatives escaped in the nick of time and moved to Paris. Betar operatives narrowed their search to France and contacted a Greek nationalist who owned a few ships. After heavy negotiations they purchased a 1200-ton ship they named the *Parita* which was registered under Panamanian flag. It was anchored in a small port near Marseille. Although it was sea-worthy it was not equipped for hauling people. The *Parita* was built originally to haul coal and had to be fitted with sleeping bunks, kitchens and sanitary facilities to accommodate 800 immigrants. Moreover, the work had to be concealed to avoid drawing the attention of the French authorities.

The immigrants on the *Parita* were comprised of the French Group, the Romanian Group, and the Polish Group. The voyage was arranged primarily for members of the Betar movement. Each participant was asked to pay a certain amount of money based on the number of years he or she had been a member of the movement. Those who could not afford the payment were taken free of charge. The money for their passage came from non-Betar passengers.

Dr. Hecht, a Betar operative born in Belgium, smuggled the French Group, who fled Germany, Poland, and Austria. He led them through the borders of Switzerland, Belgium and Holland until they reached Paris. Once in Paris, he found a small hotel and bribed its owner to let them hide until the *Parita*'s departure day. The group was forewarned not to go outside the hotel lest the police stop them and check for official documents they did not have.

The French authorities were extra vigilant, checking the papers presented by immigrants. It was clear to Betar operatives that France would not allow the immigrants into the country, fearing that they would stay and seek French citizenship. Although they did not declare publicly, other countries in Europe implemented the same policy. Moreover, to avoid upsetting the British government, France did not allow any ship with Jewish immigrants heading to Eretz Israel/Palestine to use its ports. Sadly, the European countries were aware of the virulent anti-Semitism the Jews faced, yet they refused to let them in while condemning anti-Semitism with the same breath. Hypocrisy at its best.

Another problem was sneaking the *Parita* out of port unnoticed. Officials decided that the *Parita* would leave the Marseille harbor after dark, without the immigrants and anchor next to the Château d'If, a tiny island off the coast of Marseille. The immigrants were taken from Marseille by small boat to the *Parita*.

Vladimir Mikhailovich, the ship's captain, was in Marseille coordinating with the boat's owners the exact time and location where the *Parita* would wait for them at Château d'If. The additional challenge was transporting the French group from its hiding place in a Paris hotel to the port in Marseille, and once there, how to take them, by boat, to the *Parita*, anchored off the coast of Château d'If.

Transporting the immigrants from Paris to Marseille via the train went without a glitch. Evidently, whoever forged the official papers did an excellent job as they did not raise suspicions of the French police. Once in Marseille, Betar operatives managed to hide them at Hotel Oasis until the scheduled departure time.

The *Parita* waited at Château d'If. Its forged official papers indicated it was a commercial vessel delivering coal. There was one more complicated hurdle, how to move the immigrants from the hotel to the pier, then load them into boats to the *Parita*. It had to be done quickly and unnoticed. Moreover, the French Group's dilapidated clothing, not typical of real tourists, would raise suspicions.

Luckily, Mr. Waxman, the Betar operative in charge of modifying the *Parita*, developed great rapport with the Greek sailors and merchants working at the port. The sailors agreed to operate the boats and take the immigrants to the *Parita*. One of the Greek merchants who supplied food for the voyage—for a hefty profit—had a soft spot for the refugees embarking on the voyage. He offered to help. Since he was the head of the local Boy Scout band, he staged them far away from the pier. The Greek merchant and his Boy Scout band started marching and playing a very loud concert with their trumpets, drums and cymbals to draw attention away from the refugees boarding the boats. When the concert finished, the immigrants were at Château d'If climbing into the *Parita*.

The ship sailed into the international waters heading toward the Black Sea port of Constanta, Romania to pick up the Polish and Romanian Groups.

About the time the *Parita* left Château d'If, Mom received a telegram from Betar Polish Immigration Center instructing her to be ready to leave for Constanta. Four other members of her group (two boys and two girls) got a telegram stating that, due to lack of space, their trip was postponed by a month and they would leave on the next ship. These friends perished in the Holocaust.

Mom's trip to Eretz Israel/Palestine had three phases: The first phase was a train ride from Warsaw to the town of Shcneytin on the Polish/Romanian border. From there she took a Romanian train to Constanta where she boarded the *Parita*.

✡

My father, Yaakov (Jacob) Polonecki, also joined the Polish group. In addition to word of mouth, advertisements in local Jewish papers reported the *Parita*'s planned voyage to Eretz Israel/Palestine. The advertisement added a measure of urgency to Ze'ev Jabotinsky's plea to the Polish Jews to leave the country while it was still possible. Dad, who was a soccer player for the Jewish sport club Maccabi Warsaw, learned about it from a friend who saw the ad. Dad had wanted, for many years, to immigrate to Eretz Israel/Palestine, so the *Parita* voyage was an opportunity he could not resist.

His affiliation with Zionism stemmed from his mother, Chaya (my grandmother), who was David Ben-Gurion's friend in Plonsk, where they lived next door. Her father was a *melamed* (schoolteacher) who taught

Ben-Gurion in his *cheder* (Jewish classroom). David Ben-Gurion became Israel's first Prime Minister.

✡

Dad was older than my mom who had the bad habit of snubbing men who were not members of her beloved Betar. My poor father, sitting next to my mother, had the disadvantage of not being a Betar member. My future parents did not know each other prior that trip, but rode in the same car locked by the Romanian authorities for fear that the refugees fleeing the Germans would end up staying in Romania. To break the ice, he offered a drink to their friendship but Mom declined.

She asked him where he came from and Dad, who was born in Góra Kalwaria, a rather small provincial Polish town, tried to impress her by claiming that he was from Warsaw. That was not a complete lie, since he had been living in Warsaw for twelve years.

Mom snubbed him again and let him know that she was not going to talk to a man who considered himself a resident of Warsaw. Dad's feelings were really shattered by then so he chose to sit silently and never spoke a word to her through the remainder of the trip.

The enormity of leaving his happy past behind and being locked in a train car with someone who looked down on him, both sailing into an uncertain future, hit him all of a sudden. He reminisced about his beloved friends, still in Góra Kalwaria, especially the mandolin band they founded (Figure 3.1) They had been a very popular ensemble and gave many performances at the I.L. Peretz Library, the center of Jewish culture in town.

✡

The sequence of events that made him leave Góra Kalwaria and move to Warsaw is a story by itself. It shows that my father was as rebellious as my mother. Both planned their future the way they preferred it to be despite the objection of their parents. My mother wanted to immigrate to Eretz Israel/Palestine. My father wanted to escape the yokes of being an orthodox Jew, a future his parents planned for him.

His Jewish orthodox parents worried about him being in his early twenties and still a bachelor when most orthodox men his age where married with several children. Without his knowledge they used the services of a matchmaker. One day the matchmaker found a "good wife" from a "good home" and assured his parents that the bride was as beautiful as a fairytale princess. He fled Góra Kalwaria the minute they told him they'd found him a wife. To escape, he enlisted in the Polish army. (Figure 3.2 a & b)

Figure 3.1 Mandolin Band. Yaakov (Jacob) Polonecki,
second from left, back row

Figure 3.2 a & b
My father, Yaakov (Jacob) Polonecki

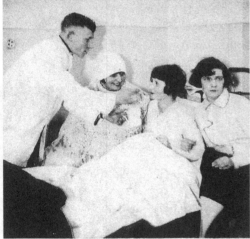

Figure 3.2 c (above) Yaakov (Jacob) Polonecki, (third from right, first row) graduating from the Polish Army Medics Course

Figure 3.3 (left) Yaakov (Jacob) Polonecki with |female patients

While living in Warsaw, Dad had tried to attend medical school but his financial situation wouldn't support the idea so, after basic training he enrolled in the army medics course.

He graduated from the course on March 28, 1929 (Figure 3.2 c) and practiced at a civilian hospital. Evidently he liked the non-Jewish lady patients and they seemed to like him (Figure 3.3.)

When he was discharged from the army, he accepted the invitation to live with his oldest brother, Arie, and his wife, Sara. They wanted his help in the large grocery store they owned.

Things worked very well at first but as the store became very successful, Sara wanted Arie to kick my father out because she did not want him to know how rich they were. Luckily for Dad, his sister Mala also lived in Warsaw with her husband. They owned a successful beauty and cosmetic salon with several employees.

They invited him to live in their spacious house for as long as needed. He accepted the offer and went to vocational school to become a barber.

✡

My father, and his sister Mala, were very good-looking, with deep blue eyes. The blue-eyed bachelor made enough money to buy fashionable suits and hats like the ones they wore in Hollywood movies in the thirties. He dated ladies who were as classy as he was, and he was generous, giving expensive gifts to his friends and the people he loved.

I wrote about how good looking my father was, not to brag, God forbid. His God-given gift saved his niece from the Nazis.

Mala asked the unmarried Catholic manicurist, Baszka, to take her two-year-old daughter to the house of her sister Mariska and her fiancé Sigmund and hid her while Mala fled the Nazis. Baszka, who had a crush on my father, agreed. Chapter 4 tells that remarkable story.

Figure 3.4 Yaakov (Jacob) Polonecki's Warsaw driver's license

✡

In 1933, Uncle Arie, his wife Sara and my father decided to immigrate to Eretz Israel/Palestine. Arie and Sara left Poland first. In Tel Aviv, Arie joined the largest public bus cooperative serving Tel Aviv. He was a bus driver and applied for my father's membership into that cooperative. They accepted my father as a member so Uncle Arie advised him to obtain an official bus driver's license from the Polish government before emigrating.

My father went to driver school in Warsaw and got the license, (Figure 3.4) however, he could not immigrate legally, and work for the bus cooperative. He decided to illegally immigrate as a passenger on *Parita*. That is how he and my mother met on the train going to the Romanian port city of Constanta.

Their paths did not cross during the entire voyage as the ship was very crowded. Although it was upgraded by Betar engineers to transport 800 immigrants, it ended up hauling 860. Plywood boards were installed to partition cargo space into shelf-like compartments that provided the passengers some sleeping/resting space. These compartments were further divided and assigned to individuals or families. My future parents were assigned to different compartments.

✡

Parita's original plan was to sail for six days from Constanta to a rendezvous point in the Mediterranean where small, fast, fishing boats would move them to several beaches along the Eretz Israel/Palestine coast. Betar immigrants would disperse and blend in among the Jewish communities, thus making it difficult for the British authorities to trace the illegal immigrants. Unfortunately, the fishing boats where not at the rendezvous location. The ship waited there for four days until the food and water was consumed. The Betar operatives sent distress messages to headquarters but got no replies. They eventually sailed to the port of Alexandretta (Iskenderun) in southern Turkey hoping to contact headquarters, get new instructions, and buy water and food with money collected from the immigrants.

The port authorities refused and ordered the ship to leave. The *Parita* and its hungry and exhausted immigrants headed to Rhodes. It arrived there on July 31, 1939.

During the war, the island was under the control of fascist Italy. The *Parita* was ordered to leave Rhodes immediately but the immigrants refused to do so unless the ship was resupplied with food and water. The authorities refused. Luckily, tourists on the cruise liner anchored next to the dilapidated *Parita* witnessed the drama. One of the tourists, a Jewish lady, took the initiative and ordered, out of her own pocket, watermelon and beer delivered to the *Parita*. That was not exactly what the immigrants had in mind or hoped for. They needed real food, but it cheered them up a little knowing that someone cared about their plight.

The *Parita* still refused to leave without food and water. The port authorities caved in and supplied only water. The *Parita* still refused to leave. Then on August 2, soldiers from an Italian war ship took control of the *Parita* and forced its captain and crew, at gunpoint, to leave Rhodes and sail to Izmir, Turkey.

The *Parita* arrived in Izmir on August 8, 1939. It was its second entry into Turkey and like its first visit to Alexandretta (Iskenderun), was ordered by the Turkish authorities to leave the port immediately. The hungry and tired immigrants demanded that the port and the Turkish authorities supply the ship with food, water and coal to continue its voyage. The immigrants, already at the point of desperation, felt there was nothing to lose and prepared themselves to resist any attempt to force the *Parita* out of Izmir.

One group of immigrants attached itself to the anchor lifting mechanism to prevent sailing out of Izmir. Another group prepared big signs written in many languages demanding food and water. They waved the signs for all the tourist at the port to see. They also chanted loudly, "ekmek ve su," Turkish for "bread and water." A third group was ready to swim into the port. Finally, the Turkish authorities agreed to supply the *Parita* with food, water and coal after an envoy from Betar upper echelon arrived at Izmir on a private airplane and negotiated with the Turkish authorities. The *Parita* left Izmir after getting resupplied.

They sailed toward Eretz Israel/Palestine hoping to meet the small fishing boats originally assigned to take the immigrants from the *Parita* to the beaches in Eretz Israel/Palestine but again, there were no fishing boats in sight. Most of the immigrants were exhausted, some were sick and in very bad shape. Water and food were completely gone and despair was sinking in. A voyage that was planned for only six days had mushroomed into a forty-two-day ordeal. The Betar operatives on the ship decided to head directly to the beach of Tel Aviv.

As it left the international water and crossed the territorial waters of Eretz Israel/Palestine, the ship's captain, Vladimir Mikhailovich and his chief mechanic refused to continue, fearing the high certainty of clashing with the British Naval ships. The Betar operatives on the *Parita*, with the aid of a few immigrants overpowered them and locked them in their rooms. Other Betar operatives who were veterans of the Betar maritime academy, took control of the ship. They raised the Blue and White Jewish flag, later to become Israel's national flag, and headed at full speed toward the Tel Aviv beach. Avraham Bash was the navigator who steered it directly into the sandbar near the Ritz Hotel (which became the location of the Luxury Dan Hotel). The *Parita* was stuck in the sand and out of commission. (Figure 3.5) It was August 22, 1939, two weeks before Germany invaded Poland and WWII began.

Figure 3.5 *Parita* stuck on the sandbar near Tel Aviv.

Figure 3.6 The *Parita* immigrants being helped off the ship and escorted to the beach.

Once stuck on the sandbar, the Betar men activated the ship sirens at full blast, screeching up and down at sunrise creating pandemonium. Thousands of Tel Aviv residents flocked to the beach bringing food, candies and cigarettes. Those with boats got closer to the disabled ship and whisked away as many immigrants as possible before the British soldiers arrived and surrounded the *Parita*. Some Tel Aviv residents piggy backed as many immigrants as they could and helped them escape the British soldiers. The ship's commander Itzhak Leibovitch and the Betar operatives also escaped. (Figure 3.6)

The *Parita* immigrants who were not able to escape stood on the deck facing the beach shouting and waving to their Israeli brethren who could do nothing for them. British soldiers boarded the ship and started evacuating the immigrants. They were gathered in the Ritz Hotel and the Savoy Cafe. After being checked and provided with medical treatment by the Magen David Adom, (the Jewish equivalent of the Red Cross) the immigrants were jailed in Zarafend, one of the British army camps near Tel Aviv.

Mom managed to escape before the British soldiers surrounded the *Parita*, but Dad was one of those jailed in Zarafend. The immigrants were released ten days later and allowed, officially, to stay in the country. The number of certificates that the captured immigrants received were deducted from the quota stated in the British White Paper.

The British authorities took Vladimir Mikhailovich, the ship's captain and his fifteen crew members to the regional court in Yafo accusing them for participating in the illegal immigration of 860 people. They were also charged for being in Eretz Israel/Palestine without a permit. The defendants were represented by attorney Yakov Shapira, the future Justice Minister of Israel. The captain and the crew pleaded guilty of the second charge and received a one-month jail sentence. They pleaded not guilty for the first charge claiming that they were captured by the Betar operatives and locked in their cells against their will while the ship was still in international waters and not in the territorial water of Eretz Israel/Palestine, and they did not navigate the ship and its immigrants into the sandbar. The court accepted their claim and dismissed the case. The chief prosecutor of the British Mandate disagreed with the verdict and filed an appeal. In January 4, 1940 the Supreme Court chaired by three judges heard Yakov Shapira's defense presentation, dismissed the case and set the defendants free.

The *Parita* was left stuck on the sandbar across from the Ritz Hotel and stayed there for few years, marking an epic event in Israel immigration history. Looters managed to strip items off the ship. Swimmers made her a site to swim to and from, until it was declared a public hazard, destroyed and cleared off the beach.

✡

Six months had passed since Mom and Dad landed on the Tel Aviv beach and went their separate ways. One day while standing on the balcony with his childhood friend Yakov Goldhacht, Dad saw Mom strolling down the street. He chanted, in Turkish, from the top of his lungs, "*ekmek ve su, ekmek ve su*" (bread and water). He caught her attention and unlike their first encounter when she ignored him, this time they engaged in conversation. Dad invited her to come upstairs and join them for coffee or tea but she declined, saying that it was inappropriate for a single lady to visit an apartment with two bachelors. Dad persisted this time and offered to meet again at a different place. She declined again hiding behind the excuse of being "very, very busy." Finally, when she did agree to meet him, she failed to show up due to stormy weather.

✡

Mom had moved in with her aunt Zipora Cohen by the Tel Aviv beach. One Saturday morning, while going swimming with her childhood friend Elsa, she saw Dad sitting on the sandy beach reading a book. After routine pleasantries, he offered to escort her home. Luckily for Dad, she agreed this time. Still, they did not meet again for a very long time.

In the meantime, Dad's brother Arie, and his wife Sara tried to find him a bride. Of course each candidate they introduced came from a very good home and was blessed with very rich parents, the usual qualifications that Jewish matchmakers use to entice a potential bride or groom but Dad was not impressed with their choices. Mom had her share of suitors too. One of them in particular was a very promising candidate. He was also an immigrant on the *Parita*. The guy was very industrious and, during the short time since his arrival, managed to build a very successful soap factory and become rich but she did not marry him.

✡

She finally succumbed to my father's charm and married him on March 25, 1941, so here I am, their son, to write the story of how they met and how they escaped Poland in the nick of time.

Mom's adventurist instinct took her as an illegal immigrant to Eretz Israel/Palestine sparing her the horrible fate of the Holocaust. Other members of her Betar cell were not so fortunate (Figure 3.7)

The rest of the Lipka family escaped Golub-Dobrzyń and fled to Mir, Russia but eventually were murdered, execution style by the Germans. (See In Memory Of.)

Figure 3.7 Mom's friends in Betar Cell in Golub-Dobrzyn, Poland. After the war, Daniel Piniek (center) became a successful surgeon. In order to have a reunion with the surviving Betar Youth Group Members, he bought plane tickets and paid expenses for my mother and the Communist, standing next to my mother (name unknown), to come to his estate in the French Rivera. Officials kept the Communist's wife in Poland so that he would not defect.

✡

On the 14th of September 1939, a month after Mom landed safely on the beach of Tel Aviv, 270 Jews in Golub-Dobrzyń, Poland, were taken out of the synagogues and forcibly transported to the city of Bydgoszcz (Bromberg), tortured and executed in the area of Fordon outside Bydgoszcz. Some were executed in Tryszczyn, also near Bydgoszcz. They were all buried in unmarked mass graves.

The brutalities at Mom's hometown continued on a daily basis but the next major evil occurred in Golub-Dobrzyń on November 9th when money was extracted from thirty-five Jewish families before they were taken away by the Germans, never to be seen again. Many were shot in the forests along the way. A tragic ending to the once-thriving Jewish community of Golub-Dobrzyń.

For years, my mother continued to hope that members of her family had survived while she found comfort with her aunt and distant cousin who had immigrated to Tel Aviv before WWII.

My father's brother and his wife survived the Holocaust by legally immigrating to Eretz Israel/Palestine in 1934. My father assumed that his beloved parents and two sisters, Mala and Sima perished in Poland. It turned out that his sister Mala survived. (See Chapter 4.)

Much of the information about their voyage on the *Parita* was told to me by my mother. Some of my questions were answered in a small book written and published by the survives. (Figure 3.8 a & b.)

אניית ההצלה של מעפילי

"פריטה"

עוגנת בחופה של תל־אביב
ב־22 באוגוסט 1939

Figure 3.8 a Cover of book written and published by survivors of the *Parita*.

Translation:
    Line 1: The Immigrant's Rescuing Ship
    Line 2: "*Parita*"
    Line 3: Beached on the Tel Aviv sandbar
    Line 4: On August 22, 1939
           Note: Hebrew is read from right to left

Figure 3.8 b My parents entry in the book written and published by
survivors of the *Parita*.
Note: Hebrew is read from right to left.

Chapter 4

A Cousin All of a Sudden

When we had an early release from elementary school, and Mom was at work, I walked two blocks to my father's barber shop. I liked those early release days. I usually took my vantage point on top of the wide concrete pillar at the entrance of the building where his shop stood. An ice cream cone at Mr. Berale's kiosk helped cool me on hot days. I liked Berale's kiosk very much. Berale was his nick name, his real name, Berel. He was a wizard in concocting carbonated sodas, with flavors and brilliant colors that put to shame the rainbow that God showed Noah promising no more flood.

Dad's barber shop was located on Dizzingoff Street, one of the major traffic arteries and business sections of Tel Aviv. If you were looking for a fashionable upscale dress or a fancy jewelry store, Dizzingoff Street was the place to go. It was also peppered with sidewalk cafés and restaurants. The traffic was always heavy even then. Public bus line #6 ran along Dizzingoff Street and had a stop close to my vantage point. I developed the habit of watching each bus as they stopped to let passengers on or off. I watched for Uncle Arie, Dad's brother, who was a bus driver on that line. He was a member of the Dan Transit Cooperative which operated the public bus services. Uncle Arie always honked his horn and motioned for me to come on board. He made me his *co-pilot* in charge of turning the traffic signal handle to warn drivers behind us that we were about to turn. In the *good ol'e days*, cars and buses didn't have sophisticated electric signals and used hand signals or a flat metal plate shaped like a wide necktie with its tip painted red. It tilted horizontally to signal that the bus was about to make a turn. I was extremely elated and super pompous for being my Uncle Arie's traffic signaling man.

On days when I was not fortunate enough to ride with my uncle, I sat on the concrete pillar and enjoyed watching the passing cars and the people strolling up and down the street. Mr. Bender's produce store with all its fresh vegetables and the ripe summer fruits was at the corner of Dizzingoff Street and Keren Kayemet Boulevard. A real festival for the eyes. It was a mom and pop business with their two sons helping occasionally. Mr. Bender was a good friend of my father's. He came from Góra Kalwaria, my father's hometown in Poland. Next to Mr. Bender's store stood a flower shop named *Nitzan* (Hebrew for bud) which sold gorgeous cut flowers. Their son Gil was a classmate of mine. He helped at the store, especially on Friday afternoons when Israeli husbands liked to buy a bouquet of flowers for their wives. *Sabbath* was not a real *Sabbath* without fresh cut flowers. Besides, they did not even dare mess with the cardinal rule *happy wife, happy life*.

One of those early release days brought a shocking surprise. As I was scouting the Dizzingoff Street from my vantage point, a couple and a girl a bit older than me, approached the shop, hesitated for a while and then went inside. I'd never seen them before and wondered who they might be. None of them looked in need of a haircut. Besides, they were dressed too European and definitely looked like newcomers to Israel. A few minutes later, they emerged with my father smiling from ear to ear. He introduced them to me in Hebrew, "The Beckman family: Aunt Mala, Uncle Marek and cousin Halina." They had just immigrated to Israel after surviving the Holocaust. They spoke only Polish and Yiddish. I climbed down from my vantage spot and before I knew it, I was flooded with kisses and hugs that only Polish Jewish families are capable of. My ribs were hurting for weeks from the intensity of their hugs. My father closed the shop and we all walked home. It was definitely a big surprise for me to discover that in addition to Uncle Arie and his family, my family included the Beckman's too.

Aunt Mala was my dad's sister. I believe she was a bit older than Dad. She was beautiful with natural blond hair and big round blues eyes. You could not tell her apart from a non-Jewish Polish woman. Her great personality augmented her beauty.

Her appearance saved her during the Holocaust as the Gestapo did not suspect that she was a Jew. Her husband Marek, was strong and very athletic in his appearance. He originally came from a town with a mixed population of Russians and Poles. During the war he joined the partisans and fought against the Germans and was wounded. I always thought that he was Halina's father but I found out years later that Marek was not Aunt Mala's first husband and not Halina's biological father. Aunt Mala's first husband was caught at the early stage of the German invasion to Poland. He was deported to a concentration camp where he died.

Shortly after the war ended, Aunt Mala and Halina stayed with the partisans. The Israeli Jewish Agency, in charge of helping Holocaust survivors, brought them to its special camp. From there the Holocaust survivors were brought to Israel. Marek was brought to the same camp and this is where they met.

Marek lost his entire family in the Holocaust. He was starving and in a bad physical shape when Aunt Mala saw him for the first time. She revived him by feeding him birdseed that she managed to find somewhere. They married at the camp, he adopted Halina and raised her as his own daughter. She was close to him until he died of cancer. For many years, I was not aware of these stories and even after I learned that he was not Halina's biological father, he was still my favorite Uncle Marek. She chose not to reveal the truth to her two sons until the day he passed away. Aunt Mala never provided Halina with details about Halina's biological father. She claimed that a long time had passed since he perished and delving into the past was unnecessary. She was only two years old when he died.

Once the Beckman family started feeling at home in Israel, my cousin, Yitzhak (Isaac) was born to Mala and Marek anchoring the family to Israel. They rented a place in a neighborhood that wasn't far from where we lived enabling me to visit them frequently.

Uncle Marek was an accomplished electrical technologist specializing in assembling electrical thermostats, repairing them as well as fixing almost any kind of electrical gizmos under the sun. Word about his skills spread fast and he eventually landed a full-time job as an electrical technician with the Israel Electric Company, owned by the Israeli government. He also did repair jobs on the side to supplement his income.

I liked to watch him at work. As mentioned before, he was a very strong man, who could not resist the temptation to pick me up and flip me in the air whenever he came for a visit. He had his own technique and expertise, and always made sure I landed on my feet. Unfortunately for my sister, one night when our parents were out to see a movie I tried to perform Uncle Marek's trick on her and she ended up bumping her head on the hard tile floor. It hurt badly and she cried as if there was no tomorrow. I was not sure how to treat her injury and stop her crying so I invented my own medical protocol by rubbing her head with a whole package of margarine I found in the ice box. Eventually the pain subsided and she calmed down. I flunked medical school right then and there. The worse outcome of that fiasco was me trying to explain where a whole package of margarine disappeared to. It was distributed by the government during the food ration era after the War for Independence.

Uncle Marek stopped performing his flipping in the air routine after he learned about my unsuccessful attempt to perform his trick on my sister.

It didn't take long to find something else to amuse me, like watching him testing electrical wall outlets to find out if the electrical line was live. I was mesmerized, watching him stick a tester into the wall outlet and a tiny amber light glowed like a Chanukah candle. I came to the unmistakable conclusion that Uncle Marek was the greatest magician on earth. The Great Houdini paled compared to him.

And then came the day when I decided I had been watching him enough and I should try to imitate his electricity testing routine. My parents were at work so I took my little wooden chair, like the ones you see at the kindergarten, and placed it next to the wall outlet and sat on it. Since I did not have something similar to Uncle Marek's testing gizmo I rationalized that a long nail would do the job just as well. I inserted it into an electrical wall outlet and I can certify beyond any doubt, that the line was *live*. Before I knew it both the chair and I were thrown across the room. I hit my head on the dresser by the other wall. Luckily, sitting on the wooden chair insulated me and spared me from being electrocuted.

Uncle Marek's most profound effect on me was the crystal radio he built for me. It accompanied me throughout my childhood and adolescence, up to my mandatory draft to the Israeli army.

Uncle Marek's Russian roots and his time with his Russian comrades fighting the Nazis influenced his political views. He was a socialist at heart. The minute he got his electrician technician job with the Israel Electric Company he joined its union and always voted for the *Mapai,* party, the largest socialistic political party in the Israeli parliament (*Knesset*). My Aunt Mala also leaned toward socialism so every time they came for a visit I knew for sure that a heated political debate would ensue because my parents subscribed to a more conservative political philosophy. Political views aside, our families where extremely close and affectionate. So much so, that my parents, Aunt Mala and Uncle Marek purchased adjacent grave plots at the cemetery on the outskirts of Tel Aviv and kept joking about it stating that they would continue their political debates at their burial sites.

My cousin Halina had a difficult time from the minute she immigrated to Israel. To begin with, she was not a *sabra* (Israelis born in Israel) and she did not speak or understand Hebrew for a long time. Except for a neighborhood girl about her age named Yardena and her brother, both native Israelis, the other Israeli-born children in the neighborhood were rude and picked on her. They called her the *Yiddishe* (derogatory name for someone who was born in the diaspora, maintains the so-called *diaspora mentality*, does not speak Hebrew and communicates either in Yiddish or the language of the country he or she came from).

My first *project* was to teach her how to ride a bicycle. The street where they lived was a small side street with hardly any traffic so riding bicycles and showing off the many tricks was the favorite pastime for neighborhood youngsters. The kids were expert riders while Halina struggled to balance. The boys watched her fall and never stopped mocking. Two boys in particular, Ehud and Amos, were the worst. I asked them, on numerous occasions, to stop treating her like that but they ignored me. I told my parents and they talked to the boy's parents who promised to talk to their sons. I never noticed any improvement in their behavior toward Halina. My parents also talked to Uncle Arie and requested that he talk to Ehud's father who was Uncle Arie's co-worker. Once again I didn't notice any change in Ehud's attitude toward Halina. Eventually puberty did the trick as the three players succumbed to the power of hormones. Halina transformed from the *Yiddishe* girl into a beautiful chick with a perfect womanly figure. Ehud and Amos also underwent profound transformation, grew taller, needed a daily shave, talked with deeper voices and were in hot pursuit begging for a date. Now it was her turn to ignore them.

✡

As a grown man in his mid-forties, I became aware of Halina's life story before she immigrated to Israel. That phase of her early life is a miracle. She never talked to me or my sister Chaya about her ordeal. Halina's past tormented her for many years, long after she immigrated to Israel, changed her name to Chaya (Hebrew: alive) and finally felt like a full-fledged Israeli. It would take almost forty-five years for her to go back to Poland and retrace the landmarks associated with her ordeal. She hoped to bring closure and put that tormenting history behind her.

As mentioned earlier, Aunt Mala looked like a native Polish beauty queen so it was just natural for her and her first husband to open a cosmetic shop in Warsaw. The shop was located in a Catholic neighborhood so most of their clients were Catholics.

Halina did not remember her father as she was two years old when the German army invaded Poland. The Gestapo caught her father and deported him to one of the concentration camps where he died. Aunt Mala, with her non-Jewish appearance, managed to escape. Halina, on the other hand, looked Jewish and would not stand a chance if the Gestapo came looking for Jews. Aunt Mala brought Halina to an unmarried Catholic manicurist named Baszka who worked at the store and ask her to take two-year-old Halina to the house of her sister Mariska and her fiancé Sigmund.

Mala wanted to make sure that her two-year-old Halina would be taken care of in case she, Mala, didn't survive the Holocaust. She willed the house and all of her possessions to Mariska in the event she did not survive. She extracted a promise from Mariska that she would take care of Halina and raise her as her own child. Mariska took Halina to her house where she lived with Sigmund, her fiancé. Sigmund was not an anti-Semite but he did not like the idea of having a two-year-old toddler, especially a Jewish one, staying with them, but he went along with Mala's plan.

Halina lived with Mariska and Sigmund for almost two years until an upstairs neighbor squeaked to the Gestapo claiming that there was a Jewish-looking toddler living at the floor below him. Sigmund, who saw the Gestapo approaching his flat hid Halina under the sofa. Miraculously she survived and was not killed when the solders stabbed the sofa with bayonets. They stopped searching for Halina only after Mariska and Sigmund bribed them to leave. It was a close call. However, the upstairs neighbor was adamant in his belief that there was, for sure, a Jewish-looking toddler hiding in the flat below his and again called the Gestapo and suggested, loudly that they come right away and do a better job this time. Sigmund, who got the wind of it somehow, woke Halina up, dressed her and loaded her onto a meat delivery truck belonging to one of the residents living there. He sandwiched her between two freshly butchered cow carcasses. Their blood was still oozing, staining Halina's clothes and face. He drove the truck to a nearby Catholic convent and orphanage. Sigmund told the mother superior that he found Halina wondering aimlessly in the street, covered with blood. He begged her to admit Halina to the orphanage. To make his case more convincing he presented Mother Superior with the "official document" he forged but said he found it in Halina's coat. The document stated that she was a Christian orphan. Halina was accepted and stayed there for the next four years until the war ended.

The orphanage provided Halina with shelter and protection as it was safer place for her than staying with Mariska and Sigmund. Yet, there was not enough food at the convent to feed the orphans. Her nourishment comprised of a few potatoes or a slice of bread when it was available and some watery murky soup. The nuns made sure the orphans would become good Polish Catholics. They taught them how to kneel, how to pray and never skipped an opportunity to drill into their heads that *the Jews killed Jesus.*

Clothing was also a major problem for Halina because the orphanage had very few sets of clothing and shoes. If someone else got there first, she had to walk barefoot that day and wrap herself with some curtains she managed to find somewhere in the convent. Not having a pair of shoes was the most difficult agony for Halina and other orphans because they couldn't play outside. The only thing for her to do during those unlucky days was to gaze at the world from the window on the second floor.

After escaping from the Warsaw ghetto, Aunt Mala found a job as a maid for the Ewings, an extremely anti-Semite family who liked to boast of not hesitating to unleash their mean dogs at any Jew they found. Ironically, the Ewings did not realize that their trusted maid was a Jew. Aunt Mala, the proud person that she was, found it extremely difficult to bite her tongue and ignore the numerous ant-Semitic diatribes she heard at the Ewing's household.

The Ewings lived not too far from the orphanage but Aunt Mala didn't know that Halina was there. Mrs. Ewing visited the convent occasionally as a volunteer and also donated money for the orphans.

Mother Superior was obsessed with the *Snow White and the Seven Dwarfs* fairytale. Once a year the orphans enacted the show for the public. She invited Mrs. Ewing to attend. Mrs. Ewing enjoyed the performance and raved about it to Aunt Mala. She also mentioned in passing, that one of the dwarfs looked somewhat different than the other orphans and was extremely adorable. She was talking about Halina.

When the war ended, Halina was eight years old. During the four years at the Catholic orphanage she became a devoted Catholic. She also contracted tuberculosis.

Aunt Mala searched for Mariska and Sigmund's house looking for Halina but the house was ravaged during the war. She found no trace of Mariska and Sigmund. Worst of all, Aunt Mala had no clue if Halina had survived. She started searching all the orphanages in the area looking for Halina. She remembered Mrs. Ewing's story about the orphanage at the convent and the *Snow White and the Seven Dwarfs* show. She also recalled Mrs. Ewing stating that one of the girls playing a dwarf was exceptionally adorable and looked different than the rest of the orphans, so Aunt Mala headed toward the convent. As it turned out, that was one of Halina's *out-of-luck* days when she could not find shoes her size and had to stay inside instead of playing outside. She was spending the morning with another unfortunate orphan who also could not find a pair of shoes. They were gazing at the world through the second-floor window when Aunt Mala, dressed in a leopard-skin fur coat, started walking up the path to the convent. "My mother had a fur coat like that," Halina told her friend. The coat was Aunt Mala's favorite, reserved for the most important and joyous family occasions before the war. Mala put on that fur coat when she visited the orphanage hoping that its uniqueness should register subconsciously in Halina's mind and help Halina recognize her mother. That rational paid off.

Although she looked very fashionable wearing that fancy coat, she had nothing to wear underneath but a few cotton rags she managed to salvage somewhere. Mala told Mother Superior that she would like to volunteer at the orphanage. Mother Superior was thrilled that someone was willing to help, so she wasted no time and introduced Aunt Mala to the orphans before she could change her mind.

Aunt Mala started hugging each orphan very close to her while chatting with them, enabling her to inspect each one from head to toe paying attention to details. She told Mother Superior that she was doing this *get-to-know-you* ritual to gain the orphan's trust. But that was a cover-up to conceal the fact that she was in search of unique body marks. When she got to Halina, her encounter and chatting lasted longer and was more intense. She managed to sneak a brief inspection of Halina's neck and there it was, Halina's birthmark that only a real mother would remember. Aunt Mala's close inspection of Halina did not escape the watchful eyes of Mother Superior so she asked Halina, "Do you know who that lady is?"

"Of course," Halina replied, "she is my mother."

My aunt stayed calm and oblivious to Halina's reply, lest her relationship to Halina be revealed. The birthmark she saw on Halina's neck cleared any doubt in Aunt Mala's mind. Yet, there was always the possibility that Halina's spontaneous response could have been expected from any lonely child orphaned by a long war who was yearning for his or her lost parent.

Aunt Mala started working daily at the orphanage. She knew for sure that Halina was her daughter but she did not show any preference toward Halina so as not to raise suspicions. She developed a plan to snatch Halina from the convent.

Halina did not behave as if she recognized Aunt Mala as her mother. Evidently, her answer was more of an impulse or wishful thinking rather than confirming a true fact. One day, at the end of her shift, Aunt Mala snatched Halina and ran to the partisan's hideout. There is no doubt that Mother Superior knew who took Halina and why, but Mother Superior never called the authorities.

Traveling to the partisan's hideout was emotionally difficult for Aunt Mala as she came from a very traditional Jewish religious home. Her brother Yaakov, (my father), went to a *Cheder* (a religious Jewish school, somewhat similar to the grammar school in the American education system.) It was taught by an orthodox rabbi, yet, her daughter Halina was by now a fully indoctrinated Catholic. Traveling with Halina and being with her around the clock, broke her heart, seeing Halina kneeling and crossing herself every time they passed the numerous statues of Mary along their way. (And there were many of them for sure.) At one point it was too much for Aunt Mala to bear, so she asked Halina if she loved Jesus. Halina did not hesitate before answering with a resounding, "Yes" and blamed the Jews for killing him. Aunt Mala did not say anything. When they finally arrived at the partisan hideout, Halina was very sick, malnourished and suffering from tuberculosis. They had to shave her head completely as she was infested with lice. That was her physical and medical hardship. Her emotional anguish was even worse. The Jewish partisans at the camp took away her crucifixes and told her bluntly that she was not Christian but Jewish like them and her mother. Many years later, as an adult, living in Israel and a mother of two, Halina admitted that the minute of that revelation of her Jewishness at the partisan camp was the lowest point of her life. Moreover, she felt condemned because she belonged to the *people who killed Jesus*. She blamed Aunt Mala for bringing all this misery on her and wondered why she took her away from the convent.

The years went by, the Beckman family felt secure financially and had a very comfortable life, and blended very well into the Israeli society. They took my mother's advice and bought a brand-new condominium in Ramat Aviv, a popular suburb of Tel Aviv, next to the Tel Aviv University campus. Halina finished high school, continued her college education and became a certified elementary schoolteacher. She taught until her retirement.

I was always amazed at her command of the very complex grammar rules of the Hebrew language, and the richness of her Hebrew vocabulary, all from a girl who did not speak a single word of Hebrew when she immigrated to Israel.

Despite the many years that passed since they left Poland, Aunt Mala never forgot Mariska and Sigmund's bravery and human kindness. She kept writing to them through the years and also sent them care packages loaded with food items that were hard to get in communist Poland. She also helped them financially upon learning that it was very difficult for Sigmund to find a job after being stigmatized for sheltering a Jewish girl during the war. It was a noble gesture from Aunt Mala to reciprocate and help Mariska and Sigmund when they were facing dire financial hardship.

Then came the Israel's 1967 Six-Day War when Egypt, Jordan and Syria attacked Israel. Egypt's loss to Israel had an indirect impact on the communication between Aunt Mala and Mariska. The defeat at the hands of Israel was a painful blow to iron-curtain countries like Poland. Anti-Israel sentiments and anti-Semitism in Poland reached its climax. Under these circumstances, it was dangerous for Mariska and Sigmund to continue corresponding with Mala. They asked Mala to stop communicating with them until further notice.

Aunt Mala resumed corresponding with Mariska and Sigmund in 1986 right after the collapse of the Iron Curtain and the Russian's hegemony. Poland, no longer under the Russians, became friendlier toward Israel. Finally, in 1989 Aunt Mala flew to Poland to visit them, almost thirty-nine years after she begged them to hide her two-year-old Halina from the Gestapo. The reunion was very emotional.

More years passed and Aunt Mala's health deteriorated and she was placed in a nursing home. Halina, a married woman now, going by her Hebrew name Chaya (alive) and a mother of two sons kept communicating with Mariska and Sigmund, albeit intermittently. When Aunt Mala died, communicating with them became more sporadic because although fluent in Polish verbally it was difficult for Halina to write in Polish. She finally gave up sending letters all together. In her last letter she gave them her phone number and suggested that they call her collect whenever they felt like talking to her instead of using the mail services.

A few weeks later Halina's phone rang and the person on the other end of the line introduced himself as Michael the son of Mariska and Sigmund. He broke the news that his parents had passed away. He also told Halina that his mother told him everything about Halina and the way his parents saved her from the Germans. He told Halina that he considers her his own sister, the one that he never had. Shortly after that phone call he landed in Israel for a two week visit as Halina's guest. It was a very intense and emotional visit for both of them. They spent long hours exchanging notes and deepening the bond between the two families intertwined by the horrors the Holocaust.

A few more years passed after Michael's visit and then in 1995 Halina mustered the emotional strength to visit Michael in Poland and replayed her childhood history, with all its traumas. Growing up in Israel helped ease the pain of Halina's childhood in Poland but those years failed to provide her complete closure. Once in Poland, he took her to his old house, her first hiding sanctuary when Aunt Mala hastily trusted her to Michael's mom. The house was destroyed during the war. Ironically, the only part that was still standing was the room where Halina hid under the bed when the Gestapo came looking for her. Halina stood there, almost paralyzed and overwhelmed with emotions and then started crying uncontrollably for a very long time.

At Halina's request they traveled to the city of Góra Kalwaria or *Ger* as it was referred to by its Jewish inhabitants. It was the birthplace of her mother, Aunt Mala, and my father. They grew up there and moved to Warsaw later on. Once a thriving Jewish center with its famous Rabbi (*The Ger Rabbe)* the city had only one elderly Jew still living there at the time Halina visited. This elderly Jew was in charge of taking care of the Jewish cemetery which was in terrible condition. She searched for the headstones for Polonecki, our paternal family name and Richeiser, the family of her biological father who perished in the Holocaust but she did not find any of them. Still to this day I am very disturbed because I have numerous pictures of the beautiful marble headstones with their Hebrew and Yiddish inscriptions that stood on those graves. The headstones were there before the war. Evidently, the marble headstones were taken and used as building material.

Michael's last gesture as Halina's host was to take her to the site of the convent where she lived as an orphan during the war. The convent was razed to the ground a few years after the war ended to make room for a new hospital for treating children with cleft palate. The site also housed a few sanatoriums for tuberculosis patients. Michael and Halina managed to find an old nun living in that neighborhood who volunteered to walk with them and show them around. She pointed to where the convent and the orphanage used to be. It brought Halina back in time, recreating the minute when she first saw her mother, the lady with the leopard skin coat walking along the path leading to the convent in search of her lost daughter. That era was long gone, disappeared into the oblivion. The convent and the orphanage were gone too. And there she stood, sad and deeply disappointed that the convent and the orphanage were not there for her to see. Still, there was a silver lining and a pleasant surprise. As they were about to leave the site, they came across a statue of one of Snow White's seven dwarfs standing there, alone, like an orphan. The nun, who showed them around did not know what that statue meant or how it got there but Halina, *the most adorable dwarf* who impressed Mrs. Ewing at the annual show knew who that statue was and how it got there. For the first time in her life, she felt the closure she had been searching for.

It was time for Halina to end her expedition to Poland and go back to Israel. First, she was a *Jewish toddler* destined to die at the hands of the Gestapo just for being a Jew. Secondly, she was a *Polish Catholic orphan* taken care of and brainwashed into Christianity by nuns at a catholic convent and thirdly, she was the *free Israeli Jew* living in a Jewish state with its own Jewish army protecting its citizens, a sanctuary place for Jews around the world. During her early childhood she knew that she was Christian, felt and prayed like one. She wore a crucifix necklace and then someone burst her bubble telling her that she was Jewish. Still it did not change her conviction and mindset that she was a Christian. Even after a few years following her immigration to Israel, living there and absorbing the Israeli and Jewish culture, she still got excited seeing churches and visiting them. The harsh and demeaning treatment she received from the Israeli-born children in her neighborhood did not help to dispel these feelings.

Talking about her past was always painful. The 1995 visit to Poland brought closure and was the determining factor enabling Halina to part from her past as a Christian. Upon reaching this significant milestone in her life she recorded her story and documented it as a testimonial at the Washington D.C. Holocaust Museum archive and at The Holocaust Museum in *Kibbutz Lochamei Hagettaot* (Hebrew for The Ghetto Fighters).

✡

Halina's story would not be complete without a few words about her husband, Pinchas Singer, who also resided in Ramat Aviv, where Halina lived. He was Aunt Mala's most favorite suitor for Halina. Aunt Mala was adamant and made sure that Halina and everyone else under the sun concurred with her choice of Halina's groom. To begin with, he was *polani* (Hebrew slang for someone of Polish Jewish decent, culture, mannerism and mentality). And let's not forget that he spoke Polish, fluently. Moreover, Pinchas was very good with numbers, auditing and balancing business books and as such was a well-respected and sought after CPA. He was the chief CPA for Mekorot, the government-owned water monopoly that developed and managed Israel's water supply. Aunt Mala knew, without a shadow of a doubt, that if Halina married him, she would be financially secure and live comfortably for the rest of her life. Halina succumbed to her mother's prodding and Pinchas charm and married him.

I liked Pinchas Singer very much. He was a very quiet, soft-spoken gentleman always willing and ready to help others. He was well respected at the company so when I found out that Mekorot had temporary summer jobs assigned for high school students on their summer recess or those who just finished high school and about to be drafted to their mandatory service in the army, I applied and listed his name as a reference. I did it without his knowledge as I tried to avoid allegations of nepotism. Needless to say I got the job.

A few years went by, I got married and moved with my wife Batia to the USA in pursue of a Ph.D. degree. My contact with Halina and Pinchas became limited to the elaborate family reunion dinners my mother gave in our honor every time we crossed the ocean and visited Israel. They had two smart sons, born after we left Israel. The older one earned his Ph.D. degree in computer science and then moved to the USA to work on his post-doctorate project.

And then *destiny* tested my cousin Halina through one more traumatic ordeal, as if she had not had enough already. She and Pinchas were in a car accident while visiting his family in Brazil. He was killed instantly and she was seriously injured. Her legs and hips were smashed so badly the Brazilian doctors who treated her in the emergency room told her that she would never walk again.

But *destiny* had a change of heart and helped Halina. Her childhood friend Yardena, who never mistreated Halina like the rest of the neighborhood children, was a medical doctor running the infectious diseases department in Israel. Yardena flew Halina from her hospital bed in Brazil directly to the orthopedic surgery department at the Israeli hospital where she worked. Yardena *babysat* Halina through the many months she was hospitalized until she could walk again. Her deep love and commitment to her longtime friend, nurtured Halina and brought her back to life. She is walking now close to normal despite the many implanted metal bones and screws.

Living in a different continent makes my communication with Halina limited to seeing her during *Sabbath* family reunion dinners when we visit Israel. This family tradition was passed on to my sister after my mother passed away. I treasure these *Sabbath* dinners and the quality time together so we can reminisce on our intertwined past. Time is of the essence as both of us are getting old. To me, Halina symbolizes the person who managed to face so much turmoil and challenge through her life, yet survived against all odds and lived to tell her story.

Chapter 5

Mom's Search for her Brother Kuba Lipka

My son, Raz, and daughter, Shir, were born in the USA and became US citizens at birth. My wife, Batia, and I became naturalized US citizens in 1982. I felt guilty depriving my parents and mother-in-law of the joy of being grandparents. I also deprived my children of the affection only grandparents could give. It was kind of replicating my own childhood too, as I never knew my maternal and paternal grandparents, or uncles and aunts as they were all murdered by the Nazis during the Holocaust. Unlike my US-born friends, my childhood was shadowed by the Holocaust.

Mom and her older brother Kuba were the only Lipka family survivors. Kuba felt that Poland was too backward compared to the westernized countries. Upon getting an engineering degree he left with a friend for Brazil and never returned to Poland.

I still have vivid memories of my mother obsessively listening to the daily broadcast called *Ha'Mador lechpoos Kroveem* (Hebrew: The Program for Searching for Relatives). The sole purpose of this program was to help Holocaust survivors locate relatives or friends that managed to survive the Nazis. Listening to these daily broadcasts was difficult for me, a six-year-old boy, to comprehend mainly due to its impact on my mother. I had to listen, attentively, to this radio program when the broadcaster announced the name of a survivor who was looking for relatives or friends that might have ended up in Israel. Attention to detail was of paramount importance making sure to announce the *Katzenic* number tattooed on the person's arm in case he survived a concentration camp. Sometimes the radio announcer described body markings in detail, such as unique scars, moles, etc. Date of birth and the village/city they came from were also given. I don't know for sure how successful the program was, but it provided a glimpse of hope, "Maybe today will be my lucky day."

In the years that followed, I started to grasp the magnitude of my mother's agony and trauma. I am sure that every day she hoped for a miracle, that a relative would be found, but deep inside she knew that was not likely. Nonetheless she listened to those daily broadcasts until the program was terminated.

✡

I remember the very first annual *Yom HaShoah,* the Holocaust Memorial Day, observed in Israel. It started with a siren during which everything stopped for two minute of silence. Buses and cars halted when the siren started. Drivers got out of private cars and stood by the vehicle. Pedestrians stood silently until the siren stopped. This is how the Israelis honor the memory of the six million Jews who perished in the Holocaust.

One day I was by the kitchen window looking at the main street below when the Memorial Day siren sounded. My mother who was cooking dinner, gazed out of the window but did not stop. When I asked her why she didn't stop and pay homage to our family and all the people who died in the Holocaust she got extremely angry and admonished me with a very strong and forceful conviction, that her parents and the entire family did not die. She was adamant that they survived the war and we would soon be reunited. I had never heard such a stern voice coming from her. It was triggered by my innocent belief that her family perished in the Holocaust. I learned after that incident not to raise the issue or talk to her about the family.

Deep inside me, a young boy who was born in Israel and not in Eastern Europe, I felt that my family would not rise from the ashes and come back. My mom, however, was in a complete denial for a long time, refusing to accept the harsh and painful reality. She finally accepted that her family, the entire Lipka clan, was murdered by the Germans. Many other Jewish families, children and babies included, where shot at the same trench by the Germans and their local anti-Semitic collaborators. The Germans, promised to spare the Jews if they would bring them money and their valuables. They took the money and valuables and then killed them anyway.

Upon accepting the demise of her family, my mother found the strength to visit the Yad Vashem Holocaust Museum in Jerusalem, fifty-eight years later (June 22, 1999). She gave a deposition for each member of her family. The depositions included an original photograph of each family member, date of birth, and the date and place where they were murdered. I was not aware that she made the depositions at Yad Vashem, since I was already living in the USA at that time. I learned about it from a friend in Israel who was in the midst of exploring his ancestry and the fate of his family during the Holocaust and came across her depositions. (See In Memory Of.)

✡

The only survivor of the Lipka clan besides my mother was Kuba Lipka, her older brother. He was Mordecai and Bluma Lipka's first-born child, born in 1910. Kuba was a handsome youngster, an accomplished athlete and a soccer player. (Figure 5.1.) My grandparents sent him to technical school and then to college where he earned his civil engineering degree. The objective was for him to run and manage the family power plant and the family's timber and lumber processing plants. Kuba was Mom's idol and by her own account, he loved her the most because she was the baby of the family. He was always clean, neat and dressed fancily. After getting his engineering degree at the age of twenty he felt that a small town like Golub-Dobrzyń was too small and suffocating for him. Before long, even Poland was considered too small for him. He managed to receive a temporary deferment from the Polish Army and traveled with his friend to Brazil and settled in Rio de Janerio. Kuba's friend returned to Poland but Kuba Lipka never returned despite a letter he sent to his parents promising to at least come for a visit.

Once in Brazil, Kuba established a chain of franchised gas stations. Unfortunately, the business never succeeded financially as he kept losing fortunes because of the very frequent military coups typical to Latin America. Each new military dictatorship declared that all old debts owed by the citizens to their debtors were null and void yet he, as a businessman, was forced to pay his debts. His good reputation remained untarnished but financially, he was broke and could not keep his promise to visit his family in Poland. There was also the possibility that the Polish government would not extend his deferment and would force him to serve in the army.

Kuba loved racing cars. He bought them

Figure 5.1 Kuba Lipka

and raced in numerous races. My grandmother did not like to hear about her son's *un-Jewish* hobby and lifestyle in Brazil. She wrote to him about her concern but he always wrote back trying to calm her by saying that in Brazil the only things that die because of his driving style are the wild pheasants that have the misfortune of crossing the road during a race.

My uncle Kuba Lipka was very uneasy about his Polish origin so he claimed to be of German decent. In 1939, at the age of twenty-nine, he married a nineteen-year-old gymnastics teacher. In a letter to his parents in Poland he joked that he married at the very old age because in Brazil, unlike Poland, it was customary for the man to get married at the age of twenty. Kuba's friend who first went with him to Brazil told Bluma (My grandmother) that, to his knowledge, there were no gymnastics teachers among the Jewish community of Rio de Janeiro. So she suspected that my uncle married a *Shik'se* (gentile lady). She never grilled Kuba's friend on whether or not his wife was Jewish. Mom's sister, Rozka, did ask the friend about the origin of Kuba's wife. The friend, trying to be helpful and to sweeten the pill of Kuba marrying a non-Jewish wife, said that she was a decedent of a *Sephardic* Jewish family, or *Marrano* Jews that practiced their Judaic lives and origin secretly for fear of being executed.

After arriving in Eretz Israel/Palestine, my mother wrote to her mother requesting Kuba's address in Brazil. My grandmother wrote back that she did not have his address because his car racing career took him all over the country. He assigned a family to collect his mail and used their address as his own, but she lost that address during the Lipka's hasty escape to Russia when the Nazis invaded Golub-Dobrzyń. She promised to try to locate that Brazilian family but the Germans murdered her before she had the chance.

Throughout her entire life, my mother tried ceaselessly to find my uncle, Kuba Lipka. She even placed ads in the major newspapers in Brazil. She was deeply disappointed and mad at him for being unwilling to reestablish the family ties. I can serve as a witness to her ceaseless attempts to find him and to reestablish and preserve whatever was left of the Lipka clan. Her first attempt to reach him was through Dr. Lerner, a Brazilian Jew who immigrated to Israel. Unfortunately, Dr. Lerner could not shed any light on the whereabouts of Kuba Lipka. Mom contacted the Rio de Janeiro police but they had no record of a resident named Kuba Lipka.

Mom's third attempt to locate my uncle was through an affluent Jewish family living in Rio de Janeiro who claimed to have known him. It is still unclear to me how she managed to get their names and address. In the meantime, Dr. Lerner, who had been associated with the Israel *Aliyah* (immigration) office was sent to Brazil on a four-year assignment as the head of the *Israel Aliyah Center*. Mom gave him the name and address of the Jewish family who claimed to know Kuba. According to new information gleaned by Dr. Lerner, Kuba left Rio and moved inland to a very remote province. According to Dr. Lerner's source, Kuba knew that his sister Yutka (my mother) survived the Holocaust and was living in Israel. He promised the people who informed him about the whereabouts of Mom, that he would contact her but he never did. Mom made, through that family, several more pleas to him but he ignored them. Finally, she gave up.

According to Dr. Lerner's assessment of the case, Kuba Lipka was determined to severe all connection to his Jewish past and family. Dr. Lerner decided to try one more time to reach Kuba. This time it was through a third party who happened to be a friend of a friend of Kuba Lipka. Sadly enough this last attempt was terminated after that third party advised Dr. Lerner that a friend of the friend's wife was a *lady of ill repute*. Dr. Lerner, being the official representative of an Israeli government agency, was not comfortable proceeding with his efforts on my mother's behalf and jeopardizing his reputation in the process.

It has been hard for me to comprehend my uncle's despicable behavior and the emotional torture he caused my mother. Through the years, I tried not to talk with her about Kuba until her last visit to us in the US. During that visit I recorded her stories on a tape recorder. The account presented here is from one of the recordings.

After her funeral on October 8, 2010 I found old correspondence while cleaning her apartment including a letter from Dr. Lerner. Here is a translation of the letter:

January 19, 1960

Dear Mrs. Yutka Lipka,

I am very sorry to inform you that according to the letter I received from Brazil in reply to the details about your brother, please be advised that Mr. David Eisenberg met your brother about a year ago and asked him for his home address but he refused while commenting that he resides at the outskirts of Rio. He did acknowledge that he was aware that his sister in Israel wanted to contact him but he was adamantly not interested.

Respectfully,

Dr. Tzvi Lerner

Chapter 6

Education Story

For as long as I can remember, a self-taught education and gaining knowledge was an important part of my life. I have a soft spot in my heart for all my teachers, especially the ones that taught me during my eight years in the elementary school. The relationship with my main teacher, Moshe Ben Mordecai who taught us during the last two years at the elementary school was the warmest and the closest by far. Our personal relationship lasted way after I moved on with my life. Perhaps this kind of revelation is somewhat strange and perhaps irrelevant to someone born and raised in the USA and attending school here, but not to someone who is the product of the Israeli society and its school system. The striking difference between the Israelis and the Americans was that we were grouped into learning class from the very first day in elementary school and continued as a group throughout the entire eight years before high school or vocational school. The only way to break this connection was when a family moved to a different city or school district. This kind of system and the fact that we all lived in the same neighborhood fostered and built a deep family-like friendship between us, and in many cases continued all the way through our high school and even through our mandatory military service.

My close friend, Yotam, who was three days younger, and I lived in the same wing of the train building since the day it was built. We spent our eight years of elementary school in the same class with the same teachers. We spent four years of high school attending different schools and then reunited and served the six months of military basic training together in the same squad. The same situation repeated itself with his younger brother Ron and my sister Chaya. They both spent their eight years of elementary school in the same class and taught by the same teachers who taught me and Yotam two years earlier. My parents and theirs were close friends. As a matter of fact, the nine families residing in the same wing of the train building were close friends and all the children of that wing went to the same elementary school. (See Chapter 2.)

The nine families had an unbroken habit of meeting every Friday night, at the place of a different family's flat to play cards as well as ballroom dancing to the music aired by the radio station especially for Friday. Although I was happy to see these grownups having a good time I had to pay the price for that every once in a while when it was my parents turn to have the ballroom dancing party in our apartment with me navigating my huge accordion that was ten times bigger than me. I entertained them, playing tango and other ballroom dancing music they had watched in Fred Astaire movies. Their favorite tango by far was my version of *La Comparsita*. I must confess that to this day, I get hives every time I hear *La Comparsita*. My father was a great dancer and a great gentleman matching the description *debonair* to the letter. The weekly get-togethers became an integral part of the lives of the nine families and they kept a very precise schedule of whose turn it was to invite the others. The flight schedules of the best airlines on earth paled compared to the neighbors' scheduling their Friday night card games and ballroom dancing get-togethers. None of us where rich financially so they played cards using matchsticks. No one had air-conditioning so no ballroom dancing took place in the summertime.

The same scene repeated itself along Yehuda Hamaccabi Street where you were hard pressed to find a balcony that did not host card players. Since Friday was the day when orthodox Jews had their *Sabbath* prayers, people called the non-observer Jews who played cards on Friday nights, *The Sabbath Praying Groups*.

As you see, we, the children and our families were a close-knit society both in school and in our after-school hours. This closeness was kept for many years, but dwindled as we grew up, went our separate ways and the parents passed away.

✡

Yotam's girlfriend, Talia, lived in the house across the street from our house and Mira, my girlfriend, lived few blocks from us, next to a pine forest by the Yarkon River. Mira was a bit afraid of the coyotes who yelped loudly every evening at sunset, so I would escort her home just to ease her mind. It was the year 1950 one year after the War for Independence ended and they just started building our neighborhood. It was not densely populated during that time and was situated next to a huge citrus orchard left by its Arab owner during the war. There was plenty of ground to play. (See Chapter 2.)

Yotam, Talia, Mira and I were very close friends and attended the same classes through the entire eight years at Yehuda Hamaccabi Elementary School. The four of us got our education and personal fatherly attention from Mr. Ben Mordecai, our main teacher, or

Mechanech (educator in Hebrew). We had great admiration for him and he reciprocated by pampering us with uncompromised love. We knew the boundaries between the time he dealt with us as our *teacher* and the time he was our *fatherly mentor* away from school. We always went to class prepared and well versed in what he taught us the day before.

Teacher Ben Mordecai's love for us and the rest of the pupils in his class was very deep-seated as he and his wife Erma were childless. Erma was a gymnastics teacher and taught children in her home pouring her motherly love onto her students like her husband did. In a sense it is safe to assume that we all were the children they never had.

Yotam, Mira, Talia and I, took the public bus to visit teacher Ben Mordecai and Erma on the eve of every major Jewish holiday and during spring vacation. Once we were ushered into their apartment, their warm smiley faces beamed as they showed us Erma's famous cookies and other goodies associated with the Jewish holiday. After the first round of goodies, we had to endure *Erma's inspection*. She made each of us stand erect by the wall and moved our bodies around until she was satisfied that we demonstrated perfect posture. She would not let us go until we promised, honest to God, to maintain it from that moment until *the end of time*. And if we did not work on improving our posture, God forbid, she warned us that we would get *scoliosis*. I am not sure if we were afraid of medical condition or just the terrible sound of that word.

Admittedly, there were times when Yotam was less than enthusiastic about visiting our beloved teacher and his wife. I threatened to tell his mother so he decided to join us.

Our close relationship dwindled away when Yotam, Talia, Mira and I attended a different high schools. Since Yotam and I lived in the same building we kept visiting teacher Ben Mordecai and his wife especially during the high holidays and Passover.

More years passed and our beloved teacher retired. He and Erma sold their apartment and moved to a government-run condominium complex built for senior citizens who did not require the aid of caregivers. That was about the same time that Yotam and I started our military service. Yotam stopped communicating with teacher Ben Mordecai but I exchanged letters. He always answered, addressed them to "My Very Dear Student Shmuel."

More years passed and Erma passed away leaving teacher Ben Mordecai a very lonely widower. My mother, who worked at the supermarket across the street from their building, had the opportunity to chat with him quite often when he came to the store for his weekly shopping. She made sure to update him on how I was doing in the army and passed his messages on to me. I tried to visit him during short leaves during my service. I kept visiting him after my discharge from military service and the three years at the Tel Aviv University.

By the time I moved to the USA, teacher Ben Mordecai's health had started to deteriorate. He was bed-ridden and no longer able to do his own shopping so my dear mother made sure to visit him and kept him company for an hour or so to ease his loneliness. And then the inevitable sad news came in a letter from Mom that my beloved teacher and mentor Moshe Ben Mordecai Jabotinsky had passed away. I hope that he understood what a huge impact he had on me.

✡

Mr. Joshua Holtz, the school principal's approach was the opposite of teacher Ben Mordecai's extreme kindness and support. Mr. Holtz taught arithmetic, which unfortunately was not my forte. He was very poor at explaining the subject and was not patient with the students who were a bit slow understanding the material. His people skills were poor as well. We had to learn everything by heart and repeat it to him like parrots, using the exact same words and sentences he used. He never took the extra time to explain the subject in a way that we would understand. If a student missed the correct answer he made a mockery of him or her in front of the entire class. It took a long time to recover from the humiliation. To this day, I still wonder what made him so nasty and mean. I have no idea why he chose me to pick on. After all, I was very popular with my cohorts and the other teachers. I was elected several times as the best student in gymnastics, and the 400 and 800 meter running champion. Add to that my performances as a stand-up comedian reading my humorous monologue at school and on our after-school gatherings on Fridays nights.

One day he summoned my parents to his office for a meeting without me. Mom and Dad were concerned and thought that perhaps it was a disciplinary issue associated with my behavior at school. Principal Holtz downloaded a long list of his *issues* with my academic performance. Maybe he had some grounds to complain when it came to arithmetic, but he was dead wrong when it came to the rest of the curriculum as I got good grades from the other teachers. Bluntly speaking, he lied to my parents about my performance. He told them in a very authoritative voice, "Your son Shmuel is a *gornisht* (Yiddish for *good for nothing*) so better enroll him in a vocational school so at least he will learn something useful." He informed them that he would not sign the recommendation papers needed for my admission to the municipal high school system.

Preventing me from being admitted to the municipal high school system meant a huge financial burden for my parents who chose to send me to a private high school. The annual tuition charged by the municipal high school was considerably lower than the private sector.

Principal Holtz's refusal to sign me into the municipal high school was a blessing in disguise as I ended up going to a very special high school named *Tichon Hadash* which in a free Hebrew translation meant *New High School*. *New* denoted the school's approach to educating its students. Ms. Tony Helle and Dr. Berman founded the school and served as its co-principals. They strongly believed that students should excel not only in the academic curriculum but even more so in social duties to society and the country. The school was what could be defined nowadays as *progressive* with a strong socialistic leaning. Coming from a family with a more conservative philosophy on the political spectrum, forced me to make some mind setting adjustment. Every Friday we had to wear the blue shirt of the socialist political parties in Israel, *Mapai* and *Mapam*. The socialistic leaning of the school worked in my favor since they kept the tuition low and reasonable making it affordable for families struggling to make ends meet. (See Chapter 2 for more details.)

Principal Holtz's cruel and blunt opinion of my academic ability, sent me on a perpetual, never ending drive to self-educate in fields and topics outside what was needed in school. I worked very hard to compress all the new information I gained through reading, into my little head hoping that I would be able to retain it, retrieve it and use it, in the future. It became difficult to achieve a balance between schoolwork and gaining outside knowledge without scarifying time spent with friends.

It was also hard on my parents who refused to accept Principal Holtz opinion. Right after their meeting with him, my father placed an order for the *Hebrew Encyclopedia.* Although they were struggling financially, they spent a lot of money so I would have that *fountain of knowledge* at my disposal. The publication of the encyclopedia took many years to complete and was still an on-going project when I left Israel for the USA in the summer of 1968. Nonetheless, there was enough material published for me to read and absorb. Before I knew it, I had gained so much knowledge through reading the encyclopedia that I became the undisputed Trivial Pursuit champion among my friends.

I gravitated toward the medical-related articles and data printed in the *Hebrew Encyclopedia* almost to a point of being addicted. I would start browsing the minute each new volume arrived. I leafed through the pages, cover to cover making sure not to skip any medical disorders, treatments and medications as well as the applicable bibliography. I studied the material in depth, especially the ones that piqued my interest. The medical dictionary became my best friend at that time, almost like a new bible.

Before I knew it, my knowledge of medical disorders, diagnostics and the current treatments was quite substantial. Friends at school started calling me *Doctor Polo* (my surname was Polonecki at that time. (See Chapter 2). I must confess that I began to like the sound of doctor attached to my nickname, *Polo*.

During a two-week community service in a *kibbutz* (a special agricultural community) located on the Israel-Lebanon border I was dispatched to work with their hired construction worker, a young Arab from the nearby village of *Arab al-Aramsha* also on the Israel-Lebanese border. We poured concrete while building platforms and stairs for the new residential houses in the *kibbutz*. I got carried away and used a long nail to carve *Dr. Polo* into each new slab. I made sure to engrave the date as well.

"Don't you think you're a bit brazen?" asked Chalifa, the foreman who supervised our work.

"No! Not at all," I replied. "One day I will come and visit you with my doctorate diploma in my hand. I am not sure how long it will take and that is why I engraved the date, but I will come back with it for sure."

My Arab co-worker added, "Chalifa, al hakim, Bolo be-areph il kooll," meaning, "Dr. Bolo knows everything!" He always called me Bolo instead of Polo. (Most Arabs cannot pronounce the letter P so it sounds like B.)

✡

Usually, the terms addiction and obsession have a negative connotation but I don't believe that my addiction and obsession to gain knowledge was negative. It never abated after Principal Holtz's rough talk with my parents and is still strong today. His curse helped me numerous times throughout my life, a blessing in disguise.

In December 1961, during my military service, I was sent along with eighty other soldiers to serve thirty days on Mount Scopus overlooking Jerusalem. The first campus of the Hebrew University was built there. Albert Einstein was among its founders, a member of the Board of Governors and the chairman of its Academic Committee. He also delivered a scientific lecture during his visit to Mount Scopus in 1923. His fund-raising activities as well as his academic advisory capacity had a great impact on the success of the Hebrew University. And then the Israeli War for Independence broke out in May 15, 1948.

On April 13, 1948 a convoy of 105 university staff members comprised of scientists, doctors and medical personnel along with a few patients on their way to Mount Scopus were attacked by an Arab mob, killing seventy-five people. The British soldiers there did not attempt to protect the victims, instead, they prevented the Jewish forces from entering the area to rescue the convoy. The war ended on March 10, 1949 with Israel defeating the armies of the seven

Arab countries that attacked Israel in an attempt to wipe it off the map. However, Jordan ended up controlling East Jerusalem, Mount of Olives, Judea and Samaria on the west bank of the Jordan River. There was no peace treaty signed between Israel and the defeated Arab countries. The only agreement was a cease fire that defined the borders between them. It became known as *The Green Line*. Mount Scopus and the Hebrew University campus were designated as an Israeli enclave with an Israeli jurisdiction and a buffer zone separating it and the Jordanian jurisdiction. A UN observer separated the two jurisdictions and monitored for any violation of the cease fire agreement.

The gist of the agreement was for Israel to control all civilian activities inside the Mount Scopus enclave and take care of the campus but the Jordanians were left in control. No academic teaching or research activities were conducted there. The agreement between the two countries stipulated that there would be no military presences other than eighty policemen protecting the property. The Jordanians allowed only bi-weekly access to Mount Scopus. Every two weeks, a maintenance convoy with its equipment, tankers of potable water and trucks with food supplies, along with the eighty policemen were assembled at the site known the *Russian Complex*. From there the convoy was escorted by the Jordanian Legion vehicles, crossed the *Mandelbaum Gate* which was the crossing point separating West (Israel) and East Jerusalem (Jordan). From there the convoy was escorted to the enclave through the Jordanian neighborhood of *Sheikh Jarrah* following the same route as the convoy ambushed on April 13, 1948.

Since the agreement allowed for only eighty policemen and excluded the presence of any military on Mount Scopus Israeli soldiers were disguised as *policemen*. Our commanders sent us to a training center where we were taught how to talk and behave like policemen. They issued each of us a police uniform with a large ID number pinned to the jacket. We had to memorize the ID number and shout it out upon a command from our commander. We were instructed to finish any verbal interchange with him with a, "Yes sir," instead of *"ken ha mephaked,"* (Hebrew for "Yes my Commandant") used in the army. We were drilled until it became second nature for us. We had a *dress rehearsal* the day before our departure to Mount Scopus.

On the date we left for Mount Scopus we gathered at the Russian Complex assembly yard, under the watchful eyes of the Jordanian representative and the UN observers. Each indoctrinated *policeman*, announced his name and ID number before he was motioned by the *Police Commander* to board one of the two armored personnel carriers waiting for us. It was a silly game since the Jordanians knew that the eighty Israeli *policemen* were actually Israeli *soldiers* dressed in police uniforms. Yet any slip of the tongue such as announcing your military ID number instead your police ID number, or replying with "Yes My Commandant," would be an embarrassment.

We were each given an antiquated Canadian rifle and five bullets if I remember correctly. We had to manually load a single bullet and eject it after each shot before reloading the gun for the next shot. We were each given one hand grenade. After the staged *police* roll call at the assembly area, we boarded two armored personnel vehicles, leftover from WWII and the 1948 War for Independence. Once seated inside the vehicle the doors were locked and two Jordanian legionnaires sat with us and blocked the door at the back of the vehicle. Two more Jordanian legionnaires sat on the front fenders outside all the way from Jerusalem to Mount Scopus. I felt bad for the driver as he had to navigate the vehicle looking through a tiny slit. The Jordanians claimed that it was done to protect them from us spying and collecting sensitive data. We were concerned about our safety because the two Jordanian legionnaires traveling with us and guarding the vehicle door, had automatic rifles. We made sure that two of our strongest crew members, with physiques of body builders, sat next to a Legionnaires and pretended to remove imaginary dirt from underneath their nails using a very hefty Swiss pocketknife. I got the impression that the two Jordanian legionnaires were scared more than we were.

Our convoy included large tankers of potable water because the Mount Scopus enclave was not connected to any municipal water system. The bulk of the water used on the enclave was rainwater collected from the roofs through the gutter system down into the basements, which served as storage pools. The water was mighty cold during December. Shaving in the morning was a huge undertaking, almost a miracle. One very cold morning I wished I had a total anesthesia while shaving.

The convoy reached Mount Scopus and stopped by the British cemetery at the enclave entrance. The cemetery was established by the British government for the British soldiers who died while fighting against the Ottoman Empire during WWI. We got off the armored personnel cars and marched to an assembly hall for an initial briefing while the water tankers and the trucks with the food and maintenance supplies entered the enclave. They navigated a U-turn on the narrow road by the cemetery and faced in the direction of Jerusalem ready to go back to the Russian Complex with the empty water trucks, empty supply truck and the eighty *policemen* who had served their thirty-days.

We assembled in a hall for the initial orientation given by the enclave commander and were divided into four groups. Each group was assigned to a specific location on Mount Scopus, served one week in that location, then we rotated to another location serving another week, and so on.

The first assignment my group received was to serve at the Ratennoff building which was the Hebrew University Medical School building. It was situated next to the western perimeter of the enclave overlooking the old city and the eastern side of the wall surrounding it. The postcard-like scenery excited me as I watched the city King David, my king, built as the capitol of the Jewish kingdom. The Domes of the Rock and the Al-Aqsa mosque nearby were the prominent figures of the east Jerusalem skyline, a pleasing sight for the eyes and for taking pictures. However, I could not escape the sad feelings that these two Muslim shrines stood on the ruins of my holy temple, destroyed by the Romans in the year 70 AD, when they took my people to Rome as servants.

The Dome of the Rock mosque was surrounded by tall construction cranes working to refurbish it with a new layer of gold donated by Saudi Arabia. There was a small forest between the Ratennoff building and the western perimeter of the enclave with a row of cedars trees along its edge. We spent our days inside the Ratennoff building doing surveillance work and recording the movements of the Jordanian Legion's vehicles traveling the highway connecting Jerusalem and the city of Ramallah. We also surveilled the activities at the Jordanian Police Academy. By far, the most popular surveillance job was what we fondly described as *The Blonds Alert* when every morning at 7 a.m. sharp, our powerful binoculars and telescopes followed two blond sisters walking to school along the dirt road meandering out of the Arab village of *Anata*, (the biblical *Anathoth*, the home town of the prophet Jeremiah.) They were so cute and the blond hair was an unusual feature among Arab natives. We jokingly claimed that they were born as the result of love affairs between local females at Anata and one of the British advisors to the Jordanian Legion. A blond Norwegian UN observer was another option to consider.

From sunset to daybreak, we spent our time staged in a little shack in the forest between the Ratennoff building and the western perimeter of the enclave. Each one of us had a shift patrolling the perimeter. We had orders to shoot if necessary. That was a tricky assignment as it occurred just before Christmas and I dreaded the likelihood of shooting and killing Jordanian youngsters sneaking close to cut cedar branches to sell as Christmas trees to their Christian neighbors.

✡

I treasured my off-duty time during my Ratennoff assignment. Visiting deserted labs and doctors' offices was a surreal experience. I gazed through an open door at a scientist's white lab coat, left on the back of a chair ready for the next day. A nagging feeling gnawed inside me.

Perhaps there was no *next day* for that scientist. He was part of the convoy ambushed by the Arabs on its way to Mount Scopus. Maybe he was one of the seventy-five people killed. There I was, thirteen years later, standing in that deserted lab, in a deserted building that once hummed with research work designed to better human life.

In another lab I noticed microscope slides beside a microscope probably staged for the next day. Again I was tormented by whether or not the scientist showed up the next day or perished in the ambush. While standing next to the microscope slides, I started reminiscing about my high school biology lab, cutting living tissues, fixing and staining, and looking at them under the microscope. For a minute I forgot that I was a soldier guarding the Hebrew University campus on Mount Scopus. I felt more like a colleague of the scientists who worked in that lab.

The most memorable leisure time for me at the Ratennoff building by far, was leafing through the medical textbooks I found on the tables and shelves. I attempted, frantically, to fill my secret notebook with the names of as many diseases and disorders as I could. There was so such information to choose from not to mention the photographs posted in those textbooks, it blew my mind. I was squeezed for time as my assignment at the Ratennoff building was only for one week. I had to limit myself to the diseases and disorders with the most interesting photographs and the ones I sensed to be important. I read my notes during my off time while smoking my pipe which helped me to concentrate.

The southern perimeter of the Mount Scopus enclave was adjacent to Mount of Olives, the ancient Jewish burial site, lost to Jordan during the 1948 War for Independence. The Jordanians desecrated the cemetery, removed the headstones and used them as building materials and floor tiles for their latrines.

On the north side of Mount of Olives, bordering Mount Scopus, stood the Church of Augusta Victoria and the hospital bearing the same name. The church and the hospital were built in 1910 and named after the wife of Kaiser Wilhelm II. The church was built on a strategic, elevated position on the mountain which made it a perfect choice for the Ottomans and the British to build a fort later on. The hospital treated the British soldiers during WWI. At the end of the 1948 War for Independence, Mount Scopus and the Hebrew University became a non-military buffer zone managed by Israel, whereas the Church of Augusta Victoria and the hospital became a buffer zone managed, supposedly, by the UN from 1948 to 1967.

Then on June 6, 1967 the Six-Day War broke out when Egypt, Jordan, and Syria combined their forces and attacked Israel. Victorious Israel took over east Jerusalem, the old city as well as Mount of Olives and the Church of Augusta Victoria. Israel also took Judea and Samaria area, known as the West Bank.

✡

My thirty-day service on Mount Scopus had its own intrinsic dangers that manifested in a serious of armed confrontations with the Jordanian Legion. After all, we, the eighty *policemen* with our dinky antiquated rifles were no match for the well-entrenched and well-supplied Jordanian legionnaires who outnumbered us. The civilian population around us was no less hostile. We were surrounded by an ocean of hostility. The muezzins called their Muslim followers to prayer five times a day. Their loud chanting through the megaphones echoed through the Kidron valley between east Jerusalem and our post.

At the end of the 1948 Israel War for Independence, a Cease Fire Committee had been established between Israel and Jordan with the participation of the UN and its observers. The committee determined the borders between the two countries leaving Mount Scopus and the Hebrew University campus there under Israeli jurisdiction, an enclave surrounded by the Jordanians. They controlled access to the enclave allowing a one day access every two weeks under supervision. Protecting the area was not doable due to the ill-equipped *policemen*.

The Jordanians could not resist the temptation to encroach on the area and grab more Israeli land. To stop the land grab by the Jordanians from further escalation, the Israeli army used its *policemen* to patrol the unmanned areas around Mount Scopus. These became known as *Sovereignty Patrols* and were scheduled by the enclave commander. They were carried out at different areas and different times to avoid a predictable schedule. Serious shooting incidents occurred from time to time.

The longest sovereignty patrol was the *Gan Shulamit* (Hebrew for *Shulamit Garden*) covering the eastern unmanned area of the enclave. It usually started at the university physic building which served as the enclave command headquarters. The patrol had several paths to walk through but all of them covered the eastern perimeter of the enclave. It was the most dangerous sovereignty patrol no matter which path was chosen as each path took us out of the vision of the command center. Once there, we were at the mercy of the Jordanian snipers or the hostile residents of Isawiya, the village nearby. To make matters worse, we could not call the command headquarters for help since radios and walkie-talkies were outlawed by the cease fire committee. The only communication methods allowed were runners.

After a week serving at the Ratennoff building we moved to the physics building when the commander decided to schedule another

Gan Shulamit sovereignty patrol. I was one of the *policemen* assigned to it. The knowledge of how dangerous this patrol was, made me apprehensive since a serious attack on that patrol took five lives three years before. Suddenly, I was in the thick of it and walking the same route and being watched through the cross-hairs of Jordanian snipers.

✡

Three years earlier, on May 26, 1958 at 13:20, Jordanian Legion snipers ambushed a sovereignty patrol in the Gan Shulamit area. The Jordanian snipers hid behind a stone wall inside a pine forest next to the patrol path. The ambush occurred at the dead spot out of sight of command center. The patrol returned fire. One of the patrolman was injured forcing its commander, a corporal, to send a runner back to headquarters to report the incident and summon help. The patrol commander stayed with the wounded patrolman and treated his injury while the other two soldiers returned fire.

Intelligence reports obtained after the incident revealed that there were eleven Bedouin snipers. Based on the runner's report, the enclave commander ordered the use of machine guns. That was not effective as the snipers were well protected by the wall and kept shooting at the trapped patrol. The only effective way to silence the Jordanians was to shoot 81mm mortars into their hideout. However, the use of mortars was forbidden by the ceasefire agreement. Hence, the enclave commander did not get permission from his superiors to use mortars.

Thirty-five minutes into the ambush the enclave commander assembled a rescue patrol comprised of six *policemen* and a second lieutenant. They left headquarters at 13:35 on the rescue mission. They encountered a fierce barrage of gun fire the minute they reached the sloping open terrain. The rescue commander attempted to reach the ambushed patrol despite the massive fire and was mortally wounded. The medic who was part of the rescue patrol could not reach him because of the massive gunfire. Although the enclave commander could not see what was going on at the ambush, he could hear the intensity of the gunfire and ordered massive gunfire toward the snipers. That enabled the rescue medic to reach the wounded officer. Noticing the severity of the officer's injury, the medic called the enclave commander, using an *illegal* radio to request a second rescue team equipped with a stretcher to carry the officer. A second rescue team of two *policemen* headed by a sergeant was sent with a stretcher to bring the wounded lieutenant and was fired upon as well, losing its sergeant to a sniper bullet. Two more *policemen* were wounded trying to reach the wounded officer.

At 14:30, one hour and ten minutes into the ambush, the enclave commander contacted the headquarters of the local UN observers in charge of supervising the ceasefire agreement to report the incident in progress. The UN commander contacted the Jordanians who informed him that there was a shooting incident going on in the area around Mount Scopus and that they suffered a few casualties. Two UN observer teams arrived at 14:50. One team entered the enclave. The other team entered Isawiya, the village nearby, under heavy suspicion that its residents were also shooting at the ambushed patrol.

The escalating situation prompt the enclave commander to stage *illegal* heavy machine-gun fire from the top of the headquarters building in preparation for another rescue mission. The fact that an *illegal* heavy machine-gun was staged while the UN observers where in the building revealed the gravity of the situation. At 15:00 the enclave commander received the order from his superior to stop the fire coming from the enclave in order to enable the UN observers to do their inspection.

The fire from Mount Scopus stopped at 15:30 but the Jordanians kept shooting at the trapped soldiers. The UN team reported that they saw the injured and the dead at the ambush site but could not reach them because of the Jordanian fire. At the same time a message arrived from the UN headquarters stating that they ordered the Jordanians to stop the fire starting promptly at 15:30. Still, the Jordanian snipers kept shooting. The UN commander called the enclave commander at 15:45 notifying him that UN forces could do nothing until Jordan officially announce its agreement to a ceasefire. They did so at 15:50 but broke it again five minutes later, shooting at the trapped patrolmen from the Church of Augusta Victoria. Despite the Jordanian's violation of the cease fire, the UN officer assigned to the enclave requested that the Israelis stop firing. The enclave commander agreed to hold the fire for a while as it was in line with a similar recommendation received from his commanders in Jerusalem forty minutes earlier.

When it became obvious to the command in Jerusalem that the Jordanians ignored the UN observers and had no intention of de-escalating the crisis, they instructed the enclave commander to position heavy *illegal* weapons at their preassigned strategic locations on Mount Scopus. A larger rescue force equipped with *illegal* weapons was standing by. The command in Jerusalem also issued an ultimatum to the UN command and let them know that since they failed to force the Jordanians to keep the ceasefire and since the UN had failed to reach the trapped patrolmen, Israeli forces would use the *illegal* weapons within the next thirty minutes. Jordan, who started the incident, would bear the consequence.

This put some pressure on the UN command to be more aggressive in its efforts to reach the trapped patrol despite the fact that the Jordanians kept shooting. The enclave commander informed the UN observers that he was sending stretchers to rescue the injured patrolmen and the dead. This time the observers managed to get closer to the ambushed patrolmen but could not remove them because the Jordanians intensified their fire. Colonel Flint, the commander of the UN observers was able to finally reach the wounded patrolmen and was hit himself by the Jordanian snipers. The other UN observers attempted to rescue him but failed do so.

The Jordanians had the audacity to contact the headquarters of the UN command at 17:20 to tell them that they, the Jordanian Legion, could not control the *wild* and *undisciplined* Bedouin snipers. The death of Colonel Flint was confirmed at 18:30 by another UN observer who was able to sneak inside despite the heavy fire. Another call from the UN command informed the enclave commander that there was nothing the UN could do and suggested waiting for the dark to resume the rescue efforts.

At 19:30, when darkness set in, a large force left the enclave, rescued the trapped patrolmen, and recovered the bodies of two patrolmen and Colonel Flint, the commander of the UN observers. Then at 21:40 the bodies of two more patrolmen were recovered. One of them was the commander of the original sovereignty patrol.

This serious incident finally ended around 22:00, after eight and a half hours of cynical and cruel ceasefire violation by the Jordanians. It took four Israeli lives and the life of one UN Colonel who tried to oversee and implement the cease fire agreement signed by both Jordan and Israel.

Soon after the incident, the biased anti-Israeli UN machine blamed Israel for the death of Colonel Flint and started an investigation. As it turned out, upon removal of Colonel Flint's body from Mount Scopus to the Shaare Zedek hospital in west Jerusalem, the UN doctor accompanying the body was able to remove the bullets. They were sent to Sweden for forensic testing and were identified as bullets used by the Jordanian snipers during the incident. The Jordanians purposely killed Colonel Flint to shift the blame of the entire incident to Israel.

✡

Now it was my turn, three years later, to do the Gan Shulamit sovereignty patrol along with six comrades, walking the same path through the dead spot where enclave command could not see us. Would we be unfortunate like the comrades three years before and get ambushed or would our patrol be able to complete its mission without incident?

We were uncomfortable, each patrolling with an antiquated gun and a single hand-grenade facing well-equipped Jordanian legion with its heavy weapons pointing at us. This time, with the grace of God, we completed our patrol without incident. I let out a sigh of relief and enjoyed the aroma of *Sabbath Challah* (sweet bread) coming from the enclave bakery. *Sabbath the Queen* as she is called in our prayer book was approaching Mount Scopus.

I counted going on the Gan Shulamit sovereignty patrol and not being hurt as a blessing. However, I had my own share of violent engagements with the Jordanian legion later on in my military service.

✡

Having been a paratrooper in the Israeli army, I was regularly summoned, as a civilian, to refresh my parachuting skills. During my three years at the Tel Aviv University for example, I had to take time off from my classes, go to the airbase, jump from the airplane and then return to campus with my hair and body dusted with sand from the dunes.

In addition to the annual parachuting practice I also had a mandatory thirty to forty-five days of active reserve duty. Besides war-game drills, including jumping from airplanes, sometimes we were called for active duty serving on the borders between Israel and its Arab neighbors. Our paratrooper reserve duties also meant combat activities if necessary.

Such was the case during the Six-Day War. Our brigade was ordered to parachute into the Egyptian Sinai Desert and prevent their advance toward Israel. However, since the Israeli tank battalion successfully defeated Egyptian forces in the area, the high command re-assigned us with the task of fighting the Jordanians and taking the Latrun region, a territory taken by Jordan during the 1948 War for Independence. After we took over the Latrun region we advanced eastward through territory controlled by Jordan from 1948 till the 1967. Our brigade reunited Jerusalem by taking the Old City (East Jerusalem). Unlike my time as a *policeman* on Mount Scopus in 1961, this time I had the honor of really fighting the Jordanian legion.

✡

I got married in October 1967, four months after that war and was soon called back for thirty-day reserve duty. This assignment was different from the ones we had done before, and took place on the western bank on the Jordan River not far from the Palestinian city of Jericho. We were tasked with intercepting the PLO terrorists who crossed the Jordan River on their way to infiltrate deeper into Israel, carry out terrorist activities and suicide bombings in public places. These terrorists received the full support of the Jordanian Legion.

We did not have a permanent camp, or structures for sleeping and shelter from the elements during the cold month of December. Instead, the army supplied us with a special coat with its lower part designed to turn into a sleeping bag to cover our legs while we slept. In the evenings, after dark, we traveled along the bank of the Jordan River, chose a spot and waited a few hours then moved to a different location and laid our ambush at a spot overlooking the river itself. The main objective was to intercept the infiltrators at the waterfront. Infrared vision devices were our major surveillance instruments.

All the fire exchanges occurred during pitch-dark. We aimed toward a location on the river where we thought the infiltrators would cross or we aimed toward the area where night vision instruments showed activity. At sunrise, another group patrolled the area looking for evidence such as wound dressings stained with blood or other indications that potential infiltrators suffered causalities. The wound dressing and other first aid items they found were the type used by the Jordanian Legion.

My next engagement with the Jordanian Legion happened during the same thirty-day reserve duty on the bank of the Jordan River near Jericho. Our platoon was assigned the task of inspecting the Israeli section of the Allenby Bridge that runs across the Jordan River and connects Jordan and the territories to the west. Stopping there and surveying the Israeli section of the bridge meant a symbolic act of Israeli sovereignty over that section. There was no official international border between the two countries except a new cease fire line running through the middle of the bridge.

This seemingly easy task, turned out to be another lethal incident with the Jordanians. Just as we stepped onto the Israeli side of the bridge, a group of Jordanian legionnaires marched in our direction, and stopped at the line marking the border between the two countries. All of a sudden, one of the legionnaires fired at us and killed one of my comrades, a successful dairy farmer. They all ran away and took cover inside their foxholes on bank of the Jordan River. There was no way for us to shoot since civilian cars and trucks were parked there. The situation escalated and became an international incident within a very short time. Our brigade dispatched a large force, with heavy weapons, ready to cross into Jordan in retaliation, a policy that was practiced during that time. The retaliation force was combat-ready and waited for the *go* order while the upper echelon of the Israel Defense Ministry, The Foreign Ministry and the UN, where trying to contain the crisis.

Evidently these efforts succeeded in preventing a major conflict between Israel and Jordan. No retaliatory action was carried out and the large force summoned, returned to base. It left me with very bad feelings and the conclusion that perhaps somewhere in the decision-making circles, *our lives,* as soldiers, had a low *numerical value* on what I call a *reaction/retaliation magnitude scale.* Retaliation is warranted if the number of casualties suffered exceeds a predetermined value on the *reaction/retaliation magnitude scale.* Evidently, one dead comrade did not justify a full scale fight with the Jordanians who provoked the incident like they had with the Gan Shulamit ambush on Mount Scopus a few years earlier. It left a bitter taste in our mouths, and a heavy feeling in our hearts knowing that the incident also produced a widow and two orphans.

A week later and during the same thirty-day reserve duty we were patrolling the area near Jericho when we heard an explosion about a mile away. Then the radio called us with an urgent request to move to that area and help the brigade just shelled by Jordan. The explosion we heard came from a single mortar shell fired by the Jordanian Legion. It was another cynical provocation and injured one soldier.

When we arrived at the scene we saw the soldier with a shattered tibia. He was in great pain and bleeding badly. Next to him stood the doctor assigned to the unit. It was clear to everyone at the scene, that the physician was completely shocked and confused, stricken with paralysis, and unable to treat the wounded soldier. There was no time to waste. My thirty day service at Mount Scopus, the knowledge I gained at the Ratennoff Medical School library became useful.

An inner voice pushed me to treat the wounded soldier as best I could. I asked two of my comrades to help stop the bleeding with a tourniquet while I searched for the morphine syringe. I found it and squeezed the drug into the thigh of the uninjured leg.

His injury was impossible to treat in the field. I asked his commander to radio for an evacuation helicopter. While we waited, I removed dried chunks of soil and dirt clinging to the torn muscles and the shuttered tibia. The sight of the shuttered bone was ingrained in my head and will probably haunt me for the rest of my life. I never realized how white human bones are, (or at least the tibia bone). It was whiter than fresh snow. The never-ending swarms of house flies kept landing on the wound. I felt utter contempt toward the flies, God's creatures, and wondered why He created this despicable species.

The evacuation helicopter arrived and rushed the wounded soldier to the Hadassah Hospital in Jerusalem. With all the commotion associated with treating him on top of his incoherence from the morphine and blood loss, I didn't get his name. I only knew that his first name was Abraham.

When we returned to our camp-site, I was summoned to the commander's tent and given commendation. I told him that after all the years that my friends teased me by calling me *Dr. Polo,* I finally had the chance to present my *credentials*. I also expressed my wish to know how the wounded soldier was doing. A few hours later I was told the sad news that Abraham underwent a lengthy operation and lost the lower portion of his right leg.

Chapter 7

Meeting Batia and My First Trip Abroad

Sooner or later, everyone develops a profile that best defines the character, attributes and idiosyncrasies of people they know. With some people, reactions and actions are predictable which helps us navigate out of sticky situations.

One of the forensic tools used by investigators and psychologists, is *graphology*, the study of handwriting, employed as a tool to analyze a person's character. I decided to develop my own version, hoping it would be as good as the prevailing standard graphology. Striving to always learn new and different things was in my blood, and besides, it sounded exotic to me and merited my attention.

First, I divide all of the people I thought I knew well, character-wise, into behavioral groups where a specific, easy to define, character was shared by all individuals in that group. For example grouping people into introverts, extroverts, aggressive people, industrious people, etc. I also designated special groups to those individuals with one character that was very unique and not encountered every day. For example, individuals with an outstanding artistic talent.

Next, I rationalized that each person in my *character bank* had matured through the years and developed his or her own unique handwriting that could be used as a *proxy* for their character types.

I found volunteers from the *character bank* willing to sit in front of me and write on paper with no lines, a text that I dictated to them. Then I studied those papers in depth looking for any unique features in the handwriting. I rationalized that the same handwriting features would repeat themselves every time that person wrote on a piece of paper. The same features would show up again and again because they typified, in my mind at least, the person's characteristics.

When I met people for the first time, I glanced at their handwriting to see if they happened to write something or they carried with them documents they wrote. If they did not have any, I found some plausible reason for them to write something for me. As our encounter was about to end I would light my pipe with its Erinmore Irish tobacco or the Dutch Amphora and ask their permission to express my personal impression of their characters and merits. The pipe was extremely essential to gain their respect and confidence in me as the *subject matter expert* substituting for the fancy diploma that I did not have.

Most of the people I tested told me outright that I was correct with my analysis. A few disagreed with some of the points I listed but overall, they agreed, I wasn't far off.

✡

The person that disagreed with my analysis the most, was Batia Guggenheim. Luckily for me, it did not prevent her from becoming my girlfriend and later on to be courageous enough to be my wife. I took it as a sign that perhaps I was not too far off with my graphology analysis of her. Before I met her, the reputation of *Polo the Graphologist* was already circulating among her peers in the *kibbutz*. One of her classmates knew me from my stint as a medic at the summer camp on Mount Carmel. I tried to help that girl find a publisher for a poetry book she wanted to publish. She told Batia about me and my graphology prowess and Batia's letters started arriving in my mailbox soon after that. Being a good-mannered person, I answered back with letters of my own. Evidently it made her a celebrity among her peers who asked her to forward their handwriting for analysis.

The argument with Batia about the accuracy of my graphology analysis continued through the postal service. I did not know what she looked like and she did not know how I looked.

Things started to change when Batia and her classmates from her *kibbutz* moved to Beit Berel, a location in the Sharon Valley near Tel Aviv, for their last year of high school. Beit Berel served for many years as the high school of the *kibbutzim*. The students lived in Beit Berel during the school year and went home to their own *kibbutz* during the holidays and the summer recess.

✡

The *kibbutz* (Hebrew for gathering) is a unique system invented in modern Israel and exists only there. It is a socialistic farming community, with some industrial factories acquired or established later on for the purpose of economic diversification. The first *kibbutz*, Degania, was founded in 1910 near the shores of the Sea of Galilee near the location where the Jordan river starts its long descend toward the Dead Sea. The *kibbutz* movement was conceived, originally, as a utopian Zionist movement driven by a socialistic philosophy and ambition to erase the negative and oftentimes derogatory stereotype of the diaspora Jews. Most of the diaspora Jews, especially the ones living in Eastern European countries like Russia and Poland, did not own any land and suffered from violent antisemitism. The first newcomers of these idealistic people were called the *halootzim* (Hebrew for pioneers). They took the risks and moved back to the Jewish ancestral homeland as free people cultivating the land from which they got expelled by the Romans 2000 years ago.

Batia's *kibbutz*, Matzuba, was founded on February 14, 1940, 2.8 miles east of the Mediterranean and 1.4 miles south of the Israel-Lebanon border. It was founded by members of the *Young Maccabi Movement* immigrating to the land of Israel from Germany, Austria, and Czechoslovakia. Both Batia's parents came from Germany so hearing German spoken there was not something out of the ordinary.

At first, the *kibbutz* members lived in small tents that were cold and wet in the winter and hot and muggy in the summers. Windy days were no picnic either.

During the Israeli War for Independence in 1948, Matzuba and the nearby *kibbutz*, were under an Arab siege that was lifted only after the Israeli military campaign Ben-Ami drove the hostile Arab forces out of the West Galilee region. However, since the war was still raging, the *kibbutz* decided to evacuate the children to a youth village by Kriyat Bialik, a small city next to the port city of Haifa. The children's parents stayed in the *kibbutz* to defend it. Batia was a toddler during that time. The children returned at the end of 1948 after *Campaign Hiram* cleared the entire North Galilee region and drove off the Arab forces.

Figure 7.1 Tent occupied by *Kibbutz* Matzuba member

✡

In one of her letters, Batia told me about a scheduled visit to a drama theater in Tel Aviv. I replied suggesting that if she was willing to meet with me instead, I would wait for her at the entrance of the iconic Tel Aviv Habima Theater. I also promised to bring her back in time to take the bus with her class mates. I proposed the Habima location as the place to meet because it was easy to find. She agreed to skip the show.

I arrived at Habima twenty minutes early and took my vantage point leaning on the handrail surrounding the theater entrance. It was a perfect spot to survey the square below. Since I had never seen her or a photograph of her, I felt that it would be next to impossible to recognize her among the passersby on a busy Saturday night, when Jewish Sabbath ended and people were went out for recreation.

Not being a person who gives up easily I watched the people strolling at the square. I narrowed the scope of my search and filtered it to only the females that looked her age. I am not ashamed to admit that I was bias and paid extra attention to all the beautiful girls parading down at the square. I was sure that Batia was beautiful. After a while I noticed one young teenager walking back and forth across the square looking in all directions probably for me, *Polo the Graphologist.* So I called her attention to where I was standing followed with the statement, "If you think that I am going to chase you, you are sadly mistaken." She momentarily froze, looked up and saw me. I went down to the square and asked if she was Batia Guggenheim from *Kibbutz* Matzuba and she rewarded me with a nice, "Yes."

I introduced myself and asked at what time she must meet her classmates and go back to Beit Berel. We had about three hours to get acquainted so I suggested that we take the bus to my parents' house. I promised to bring her back in time to meet her classmates.

Riding the bus to my house, having coffee and cookies and taking her back to meet her classmates did not leave too much time, but I managed to learn that her parents were founders of the *kibbutz* and she was working at its kindergarten taking care of the toddlers during her after school hours.

When it was time to catch the bus back to Beit Berel, we arrived on time but there was no bus in sight. We kept waiting and waiting until the nagging feeling that we missed the bus started sinking in. I called a taxi and asked the driver to take us to Beit Berel located about eighteen miles east.

It was pitch dark all the way to Beit Berel and the place looked completely deserted when we arrived. We found out later that the charter bus was late and left Tel Aviv long after we took the taxi. Realizing that

Batia and I were the only people there I asked the driver to wait for me while I escorted Batia to her room. I made sure that she was safe and the doors were locked. I asked her not to open the door until her classmates arrived back from Tel Aviv. She promised and I took the taxi back to Habima square.

It was after midnight so I missed the last public bus and had to walk eight miles home. Luckily for Batia, her classmates arrived from Tel Aviv soon after I left and started interrogating her with questions like, "How did the date with Polo go?"

I'm not sure what Batia told them about me but judging from my subsequent encounters with them, I felt that I gained their stamp of approval, albeit at a price, as I was flooded by a tide of new requests for my graphologist analysis from her classmates with Batia as the go-between. For the first time in my life I had a *secretary*.

Batia and I kept communicating via mail and in one of my letters I told her about my decision to quit my *graphologist job* as it was taking too much of my time when I just starting my first year at Tel Aviv University. At that stage I had to invest all of my attention in studying and could not waste my time doing graphology.

Another reason to shy away from my graphology activities came when a nice lady started crying when I finished describing her character. I was appalled by that reaction and I asked if I had done something wrong or crossed some unchartered boundaries. "Not at all," she replied and then confessed that all her life she had tried hard to conceal many of the characters and the idiosyncrasies I was able to detect just by glancing at her handwriting. She felt as if her privacy was compromised and anyone with some graphology talent could uncover her secretes. I started to feel that my graphology hobby was infringing on someone else's privacy and I should stop.

✡

The academic stage of my life began in the fall of 1964, two years after finishing my mandatory military service. I was admitted to the Tel Aviv University for a bachelor degree in Biology (BSc). Tel Aviv University had just received its teaching credentials from The Ministry of Education and opened its gates to new students.

Students who had their mind set on a specific field for their graduate work, invested all their efforts into getting the highest finale grades in the courses considered essential to their field, with little effort toward the course considered insignificant to obtain the master or doctorate degree. The overriding concern was to pass with at least eighty percent average grade in those courses significant to your advanced degree. This practice enabled students to be admitted to the

Tel Aviv University Graduate but proved detrimental when I applied to UC Davis. (See Chapter 8.)

I chose human endocrinology, the study of human hormones as my elective course. It was taught by a guest professor from the Weizmann Institute of Science. For my research work and thesis I elected to study plant hormones, plant regulators and their commercial use in fruit production. I was so captivated, I ended up, at UC Davis, where the world's expert of that field was teaching.

✡

A description of the huge difference between the strict prevailing European teaching methodology in Israel when I studied, compared to the one practiced in the USA, is warranted to underline the difficulties I faced as an Israeli graduate student attending an American college like at UC Davis. To begin with, all the candidates who were admitted to the bachelor's program, were lumped into one class that followed a three-year curriculum of mandatory courses. They would be granted the degree upon passing the final exams of that curriculum. So the student would stay with his/her peers as a class for the entire three years unless someone dropped out the university or did not pass the required tests.

The American system allows the student flexibility in choosing courses, the time they are taken and the number of credits taken per trimester or semester as long as the curriculum required to obtain the degree is completed eventually. The Israeli/European system does not provide that flexibility. The curriculum for any specific degree is set by the university and has a precise schedule. You must pass in order to move to the next trimester.

For example, calculus, physics, and inorganic chemistry were required courses during the first year of my bachelor's degree in biology. These classes were given twice a week during the entire first year in school. There were no midterm exams, only one final exam at the end of the school year covering everything taught in the course.

We were graded by the actual percentage of correct answers and not by the *curve* used when I studied at UC Davis. Under the Tel Aviv University system, if you failed a final exam, you got another chance to take it a month later and if you failed again and the course was required you were not allowed to advance to the second year of the three-year bachelor program. This left you with two choices, either quit your academic aspiration or bite the bullet, register again and join the new class that was assembled a year after you started. You had to retake the required courses that you didn't pass the year before.

The second year in the Biology Bachelor degree program had

the same format as the first one, namely, you *must pass* mandatory curriculum with no flexibility of choosing courses. Failing in any of the mandatory courses prevented you from advancing to the third, final year of the program. The third year in the program was somewhat different than the first two as it allowed you to select two major courses, usually in the field that you planned on pursuing during your quest for a master's degree or a doctorate later on in your academic career. These optional courses were given during the second and third trimester of the final year. The first trimester was still comprised of the mandatory courses required to get the degree. You also had the option to perform your own original research in one field, in lieu of taking the course in that field and its final exam. Choosing that option required you write a thesis and with final approval from the professor.

✧

A few months after I started my studies at Tel Aviv University, a friend and former member of a *kibbutz* located five miles from Batia's *kibbutz*, offered to take me with him for our annual reunion with our friends, now members of that *kibbutz*. We were all ex-paratrooper comrades, they elected to stay in the *kibbutz* after finishing the military service.

My friend and I had elected to leave the *kibbutz* in search of an academic degree. I spent some time at the reunion and since Batia's *kibbutz* was nearby I decided to surprise her with an unannounced short visit. My friend was very kind and agreed to take me there and to pick me up. I figured out that three hours should be enough for a first visit, to meet her mother and to explore if this friendship would flourish into something more serious.

My friend dropped me at the *kibbutz* dining hall promising to come back in three hours to pick me up. I went inside and asked where I could locate Batia Guggenheim. The person who offered to help me gave me a surprised look, not expecting that she had a date with a stranger that was not a member of Matzuba. He probably considered me a real weirdo when I asked directions to Batia Guggenheim's place and not referring to her by her name Bati used by the locals. He also informed me, "Since *Sabbath* has set in, she will be at her mother's place." I was struck by the beauty of the path to her mother's house.

When he knocked on the door, the lady inside replied in heavily German accent Hebrew, "Come in, the door is unlocked."

"There is someone who came to visit Bati," he said, and left as I entered the room. Batia and her Mom were surprised by my visit. I'm almost sure that Batia's mom was even more surprised to see that her daughter had a young lad coming all the way from Tel Aviv to see her.

The record player was playing a symphony and the shelf was

full of classical music albums. I felt utterly insecure for a moment, I was extremely deficient in the classical music area to say it mildly. I realized that I would need to catch-up if I wished to develop my friendship with Batia.

✡

Back in Tel Aviv, I started listening to live concerts of the Israel Philharmonic Orchestra on the Israeli radio and committing the symphonies and famous concertos to memory before my next visit to Matzuba. It started to grow on me, but I did not mention anything to Bati in any of my letters to her.

Before heading to the train station, I had to take care of one more thing before my next visit to Matzuba and that was to be more familiar with classical music especially the masterpieces played on Batia's mom's record player. Upon finishing the last class at the university, I stopped at the music store on Brenner Street specializing in all kinds of classical music. They supplied the musical scores to the Israel Philharmonic Orchestra. I asked the owner, an accomplished musician in his own right, for his professional suggestion on what record to buy as my first *musical gift* for Batia. I begged him not to embarrass me with a bad selection, or he wouldn't see me again. He pulled Vivaldi's *The Four Seasons* off the shelf, inserted it into a nice plastic bag, handed it to me and said, "Take this one, you can never go wrong with that record," and he was 1000% right. I am currently looking at it as I am typing this story and my other nick name *Shmulik* is written in Batia's handwriting at the top of the record jacket.

It was the first record of a collection that grew as the number of my visits to Matzuba grew as well. After I subscribed to the Israel Philharmonic Orchestra, suggestions from the owner of the music store became unnecessary. I purchased the records of the music they played at the concerts.

I guess that the stars were perfectly aligned for me to schedule a Friday-through Saturday *pilgrimage* to Matzuba and spend time with Batia. Although Israel is a small country travailing from Tel Aviv to her *kibbutz* was a logistical challenge. I was at the mercy of the public transportation system. Moreover, since I traveled on Friday, I had to reach Matzuba before *Sabbath* started and the public transpiration stopped until the *Sabbath* was over on Saturday evening. It meant taking the Tel Aviv/Nahariya train for eighty miles and from Nahariya I still had to catch the last bus to her *kibbutz*, which was another twelve miles.

I managed to arrive at Matzuba on time. It was the bus's last stop before returning back to Nahariya with Matzuba passengers before Sabbath set in. Upon arrival, the bus stopped at the round square by the *kibbutz* tall water tower. Batia was waiting for me. Other *kibbutz* members were waiting there as well to meet their guests or family members. It was kind of embarrassing for me to notice the zillions of pairs of eyes staring in disbelief at Batia and her nice looking stud, (as some of my female classmates at the university used to call me) unfortunately nothing of that is left after the many years that have passed.

✡

Classical music was playing in the background while Esther, her mother, was busy loading the living room table with cookies and cakes to go with what was supposed to be coffee. It occurred to me that if I was to continue visiting, I would need to be in charge of making the coffee.

I handed Batia the Vivaldi's *Four Seasons* record and she played it as we drank the watery coffee and enjoyed the cookies and cakes. The entire room transformed into a bastion of sophistication. The owner of the music store was right. His *You cannot go wrong with that record,* reverberated in my head while Vivaldi took us from one season to the next.

Esther's room held a huge treasure of books, almost all of them in German, which indicated she was an avid reader. Hebrew was her second language which she spoke very well, albeit with a thick German accent. Her room was always the focus of attraction of Batia's age group, classmates and friends. Other people came to her seeking advice and wisdom to help with whatever bothered them. She had the gift of listening to other people and their concerns, always keeping the door to her house unlocked. People felt free to help themselves to a cup of coffee or tea as if it were their own home.

✡

A few words about communication in those days are warranted as they were before the Internet and email. Another problem was the scarcity of private telephones as only a small portion of the population in Israel had phones and many of the lucky ones had to share with other users making it a party line. Moreover, Bati's *kibbutz* had two phone lines; one at the entrance to the dining hall and the other at the *kibbutz* office. If I decided to call the number at the entrance to the dining hall and ask the responder to summon Batia Guggenheim, I had no guarantee he or she would find Batia. Also consider that these were cost-prohibitive long distance phone calls. Communicating through the postal services was the only practical option.

During subsequent visits, when I was looking for something like sugar, or cream for my coffee, I asked one of the *regular guests* at her home to show me where she kept them.

My most favorite spot at Esther's home was the balcony overlooking the west horizon with the blue Mediterranean Sea shining three miles away. A big spiny ziziphus spina-christi tree, a native to the area, grew by the balcony, providing cooling shade from the late afternoon sun. We enjoyed its small pinkish-orange sweet fruits and the many birds that made it their home. No wonder the ancient Egyptians loved this species and used its leaves and fruits for their cosmetics and medicine. Moreover, current day research revealed that extract from its leaves are effective as anti-inflammatory agents and anti-bacterial as well. And for my Christians readers I might add that the ziziphus spina christi tree is believed to be the very tree from which Jesus crown of thorns was made.

When it was time for *Sabbath* dinner, we all put on our *Sabbath* clothes and strolled to the dining hall. We shared a table with old-timers of the *kibbutz*. Batia's mom introduced me as, "Bati's friend from Tel Aviv and a former member of *Kibbutz* Rosh HaNikra." The dining hall was fully occupied with the other members enjoying the excellent *Sabbath* dinner on tables covered with white tablecloths, unlike weekdays. It brought back memories of *Sabbath* dinners I had in my own *kibbutz*. With the *kibbutz* being a small community, the presence of any stranger let alone one sitting by Batia was an anomaly and I sensed the many eyes in the dining room watching me attentively. After a few more visits to Matzuba and the *Sabbath*, my novelty status evaporated and I became a fixture. This time I felt, for the first time, like a part of the family.

After the *Sabbath* dinner we returned to Esther's house, had dessert and chatted about my studies at the university and Batia's upcoming mandatory military service. I tried my best to leave a good impression on Esther and to get her unspoken approval for future visits.

When the time came for Esther to retire, Batia took me to the building where she and her classmates lived. I spent some time chatting with them as well. A few of them already knew me from being the medic at their summer camp on Mount Carmel. Others were curious to see *Polo the graphologist* for the first time. We spent some time at her room before she took me to the room she had reserved for me. It belonged to a classmate who went to Haifa for the weekend.

The Matzuba dining hall (*chadar ha' ochel* in Hebrew) was the center of the community in the *kibbutz*. It was the place where you eat three meals a day with other members of the *kibbutz* sharing a table with them while other members pushed a cart full of the menu. Each member had his or her own turn to serve the food. Other members had their turn to clean and make sure the dishes were washed and cleaned ready for the next meal.

On special holidays, such as Passover Seder with its special ritual meal commemorating Moses leading the Israelites out of Egypt, the tables were linked together so *kibbutz* members and their guests sat as one big family. It is noteworthy that Jesus Last Supper with his disciples was a Passover Seder.

The dining hall was also the place where all the important decision-making sessions were held through an *asepha klalit* (Hebrew for general meeting) with all *kibbutz* members present. Issues were decided by majority rule. For example, if you wished to pursue an academic degree you presented your request to a special committee that handled issues raised by members of the *kibbutz*. The next step was for the special committee to present your request at the next general meeting for the *kibbutz* members to vote on. If the members voted in your favor, you attended the university and all the expenses were paid by the *kibbutz*. But if your request is turned down, you were left with two choices; accept their verdict and move on with your life or quit the *kibbutz* and study on your own.

Being a first-time guest and the gentleman who still was not sure whether or not to commit to a more serious relationship with Bati, the lovely and innocent person, made it necessary for me to behave correctly. I allowed myself just to give her a nice warm hug that got me close enough to notice how blue her eyes were. I thanked her for the lovey time. I didn't know her emotional state at that moment as she stayed cool. She told me to be ready around 9:00 o'clock the next morning so we could have breakfast on her mother's balcony.

The roosters' cock-a-doodle-doo-ing woke me up and I got ready for breakfast. Batia came to pick me up and we strolled down to her mother's house for breakfast on the balcony with its picturesque view of the Mediterranean. I noticed that Esther loved hard cheeses, especially smelly Roquefort. She didn't mind making the twelve-mile trip to Nahariya to buy it. I must admit that I loved it after my first bite, so she started buying extra just in case *Shmulik* come for a visit.

I was, and still am, very particular about the quality of the coffee I drank, but during that breakfast, I had to settle for the Landwer cheap coffee sold at the *kibbutz* general store. It was a fine powder with no aroma to speak of. The customary way to drink it was to put a spoon-full of powder into your cup, add sugar and hot water, making yourself what it is known as *Café Botz* (mud coffee). You drank it black or added cream.

I returned as Batia had captured me with her charming personality. On my next visit, I brought portable Italian espresso device and treated Batia and her mother to the heavenly flavor and aroma of real coffee.

My expeditions to her *kibbutz* became few and far between as I struggled with physics, calculus, and chemistry knowing full well that flunking the finals of these required class would kill my academic aspirations. However, we kept communicating through the mail.

✡

Toward the end of my first year at the Tel Aviv University, students were flooded with enticing *See-The-World* deals from ISTA, the Israeli student organization's travel agency. My childhood friend Yotam and I decided to use their services and planned a trip to the USA, with a short stop in Paris where Yotam's cousin, a nice young beauty queen lived. Yotam was also a student at Tel Aviv University studying for his CPA degree. He was always great with numbers.

We elected to spend up to a week in New York City where he had two uncles and I planned on staying with my mom's childhood friend from Poland who immigrated to Israel and then to the USA few years later and became a naturalized citizen. From there we planned to cross the country riding a Greyhound Bus. It offered unlimited trips anywhere in the USA and Canada for 99 days at a cost of only $99.

I wrote to Batia about my USA trip a week before we left, promised to contact her upon my return, and schedule another visit to Matzuba.

From the first day of the trip, it became clear that the *good deal* was far from being a bargain. The first shock was to discover that our original TWA nonstop flight from Tel Aviv to Paris was really a flight to Rome on a small non-jet Icelandic Airlines plane with propeller engines. In Rome we had to change airlines and boarded an Air France Carvel plane headed to Paris-Le Bourget airport instead of the main Charles De Gaulle listed on the itinerary.

I felt apprehensive during both flights as they were my first flights EVER on a commercial air plane. I felt naked sitting without my parachute on my first flight as a tourist. The altitude of the commercial flights were also a first for me since the highest jumping altitude was around 600 feet but sitting in a commercial flight I felt height fear as the airplane was flying close to God's gated community. Another first for me, unlike in the past where I landed on the ground via parachute, this time I landed still sitting in an airplane seat.

What was supposed to be a four-hour non-stop flight mushroomed into a ten-hour ordeal as we arrived in Paris very late at night. Compounding our misery, we'd left sunny Israel with only our short sleeved shirts to arrive during a Parisian rain shower. I am sure that it took a few hours for the taxi driver to ready the vehicle for the next passengers. After hanging our wet clothes in the bathroom and sliding into to dry clothes we rushed to see the cancan show at the famous Moulin Rouge Theater. A flock of beautiful and slim ladies with gorgeous legs performing the cancan dance entertained us. For sure, these dancers were not the caliber of the Bolshoi Theater prima ballerinas, nevertheless we enjoyed every minute of it. It also became very apparent that these dancers were not graduates of the Girl Scouts, but the show was very entertaining.

The next morning, we met Yotam's beautiful cousin who took us to a tiny restaurant for lunch. It gave her the opportunity to tell us, with her French-accented English, how great her recent visit to Israel had been. It was her first visit to Israel. She spent a few days in *Kibbutz Evron*, near Nahariya and not too far from Batia's *kibbutz*. She was there visiting Yotam's uncle and aunt who were founding members.

We had more than six hours before our non-stop flight from Charles De Gaulle to JFK was supposed to take off so we asked her to call the airline to confirm our flight. Sure enough, our streak of surprises continued as TWA switched us to the Icelandic Airlines departing from the Paris-Le Bourget airport instead of Charles De Gaulle. To add salt to injuries, they put us on a propeller-engine airplane and not a jet. To ensure that the plane had enough fuel to cross the Atlantic we had to land at the Shannon Airport in Ireland for refueling. I was furious and used all the exploitive names in the dictionary to vent my frustration with the Israeli Students Travel Agency. My only comfort was the fancy Briar pipe I bought at the duty-free shop and the Erinmore tobacco I coveted so much.

The trans-Atlantic flight was noisy, bumpy and long as hell. I thought it would never end or it would end with us ditching into the ocean. I wish I had one dollar for every air pocket we hit. The sinking sensation was new despite my previous parachuting activities.

We finally landed at JFK and my jaw dropped when I saw the city skyscrapers piercing the skies. Passing Immigration and Border Control was uneventful but clearing through the custom station was a different story all together. Being a pipe aficionado put me in big trouble with the agent manning the inspection station. He found the little pipe tobacco can I had in my backpack. He opened it and discovered it contained a very fine white powder instead of pipe tobacco flakes. I could see the glee in his eyes, fueled by his 1000% conviction that he just caught a notorious drug dealer coming to make a fortune on the streets of New York.

"What is the white powder you have in here," he asked in a stern voice with the authority to put me in jail. I told him that my friend and I were about to embark on a cross country tour using the Greyhound buses and the white powder was laundry detergent. Coming from Israel I was not aware of facilities called laundromats. The inspector did not buy my story and summoned his supervisor. The supervisor asked me the same question and I gave him the same answer except this time I challenged them to dip their finger in the white powder and taste it to confirm that it was detergent. They both declined and tossed the can into the big garbage bin where they threw fruit and other food items that were not allowed into the USA. The supervisor asked to see my passport and I noticed from his facial expression an interest in it. He also knew the correct side to open and browse through it as Hebrew is written from right to left. He became friendlier and more accommodating. In retrospect, I believe that the gentleman was Jewish with a warm heart and soft feelings toward native Israeli Jews.

A taxi dropped me at the house of my mother's childhood friends and then took Yotam to his uncle's house. Since the next day was Friday, we decided to stay for *Sabbath* with our hosts and inaugurating our Greyhound bus adventure on Monday morning.

✡

The first spot on our *must see* list was Niagara Falls. In Israel we had domestic home improvement devices called Niagaras used to flush the toilet by pulling a long chain to release the water. It was about time to see the real Niagara Falls.

We arrived at the Greyhound bus terminal and showed the clerk our *$99 for 99 days* special tickets and got aboard the bus to Niagara Falls. We traveled light with only our small backpacks. Fortunately, mine contained another pipe tobacco can filled with laundry detergent. I needed that powder to do my laundry throughout our trip.

Coming to the giant USA from a tiny and young country like Israel, was an eye-opening experience for us. I was amazed by how nice the Greyhound bus looked, its cushioned seats, and the air conditioning feature which made the ride anywhere smooth and comfortable. And there was the great amenity of having a toilet inside the bus, a concept that never existed in Israel bus services during that era.

Going from New York City to Niagara Falls was a short trip relative to the vastness of the USA. We decided to milk the Greyhound $99 ticket deal to the max by using the bus as our *home away from home* for at least three weeks. We had to develop a plan on how to implement it. Other than the short run from New York City to Niagara all the other places we planned to visit entailed long hours riding on the same bus and in some cases having our bus exchanged to a *fresher* one at some point along the route. Although the bus provided the solution of where to sleep, we still had to tackle the question of where to eat. Luckily, we discovered the American diners tailored for people who accept munching on a hamburger patty between two buns peppered with toasted Sesame seeds as a bona fide dinner. To make sure the hamburger patty did not feel lonely or boring to the hungry mouth, the diner blanketed it with lettuce, a big chunk of raw onion, mayonnaise and melting cheese. To close the deal, they also gave us a cardboard basket full of french fries, or *chips* as we called them.

The diner served a cup of coffee charging only ten cents. I ordered one cup and it was fresh and very good. I finished it at a speed of light and before I knew it, here came the waitress with a coffee carafe with fresh, just brewed coffee. She smiled at me and filled my empty cup. I was stunned by her gesture and finished that cup to the last drip. Then the same waitress came again and poured another cup of fresh brewed coffee. At that point I began to think that the waitress had a crush on me. I had not experienced that kind of excellent service or coffee cup refilling ritual in Israel. It simply overwhelmed me. I realized that I was working the poor waitress to death so I started drink my coffee at a slower pace. I was wrong as she stopped again at our table, gazed at my coffee cup, still at the half-full mark and asked in a very sweet voice, "Would you like me to warm your coffee?" This really threw me off and I said, "Yes. Please." What superb service this lady provided, she went the extra mile to warm it for me. I reciprocated and left a fat tip and commended her before we left the diner. From the expression on her face I was sure she tried to figure out what type of accent came out of my mouth. She told me that it was the policy of all the diners and restaurants in the USA to charge only ten cents for a cup. All the refills were free of charge.

Going to the bathroom was most challenging and complicated during the entire Greyhound trip. True, we had a toilet on the bus and it served its purpose at first but it was too small for comfort and after a while I started feeling as if I got a life sentenced with a solitary confinement for a crime I did not even commit. We needed to find a better solution. We used the large restrooms at the Greyhound bus stations where our bus driver stopped for refreshing and relaxation. The very first time Yotam and I went into the restroom we were shocked to find that the Americans charged ten cents to enter and use it. The user had to feed a dime. Ten cents for a visit was an expensive proposition, especially for me, the coffee addict who needed ten cents for the cup of coffee and all the free refills that came with it. A quick calculation revealed that with the huge amount of coffee I drank and paying ten cents in the restroom, we would go bankrupt before we finished the trip.

What we did to alleviate this problem was to choose a good vantage point right at the entrance to the restroom and the minute we sensed movement coming from one of the stalls we were on the alert. We sprinted to the door before its spring mechanism locked it shut. You should see the expression on the faces of the people at the facility. I felt somewhat vindicated when I saw some of our fellow passengers from the same bus using our method during the next stops along the route. There were always emergencies when you did not have the option of waiting. In situations like that we made sure that no one was at the entrance and when the coast was clear we slide ourselves through the wide space between the locked door and the floor.

After touring Niagara Falls and absorbing its beauty, vastness, tremendous energy and the fine water mist that engulfed us, we hopped on a Greyhound bus to Chicago.

The scenery was not something to call home about but we looked forward to visiting Chicago since both of us had friends to stay with for the night, willing to show us some of the highlights of Chicago.

I stayed with another of Mom's childhood friends from Poland who immigrated to the USA before Hitler invaded. Once in the USA she married a man from their town who also immigrated to the USA before WWII. He was an artesian baker, so they opened a bakery with a store attached to sell their baked goods. The business was very successful, making them financially comfortable. They flooded us with baked goods, making sure they would last until we reached Salt Lake City, our next destination.

They had only one child, a nice-looking daughter, about to finish high school and go on to college. They were extremely nice to me and went out of their way to make sure that I paid attention to their daughter. My mother forewarned me before leaving on the trip that the mother hosting me would play matchmaker. I continued to be cordial but thanked God I was leaving Chicago the next day.

My friend Yotam spent the night with family relatives, Jack Schlopak and his wife. Jack had a very nice jewelry store downtown where he sold and repaired high-end watches. His store also sold 35mm cameras. We visited his store and I bought a Yashica camera for me and Bulova gold watches for my parents. Although my relationship with Batia at that point was still in the exploration stage, a gut feeling told me that is was just a matter of time before I would succumb to her charm and be her official boyfriend. I went with my heart and bought her a nice necklace watch.

We headed west to San Francisco with a one day stop in Salt Lake City, Utah, and brief stops in Reno, Nevada and Sacramento, California. That was a very long ride and took a heavy toll on us so we decided to spend the night in Salt Lake City hotel not too far from the Mormon Tabernacle. We also discovered the Safeway supermarket chain. It soon became our main source of food and saved us lots of money.

We visited the Mormon Tabernacle, and learned about the Mormons, their history and how they traveled across the vast territories heading west until they stopped at their current location. Their practice of giving places and landmarks Hebrew names taken from the Old Testament, like Zion, Jordan, Moab and their social system of taking care of their members intrigued me.

When it was time, we hopped on the bus to Sacramento, California. The stop in Reno, Nevada was long enough to enjoy the scenery but more importantly, to operate the fancy gambling machines. We, the uninformed, provincial Israelis coming from a country where gambling was outlawed, did not know how to operate any of those machines with their bells and whistles. Finally, a bystander who watched us with disbelief on how ignorant we were, showed us what handle to pull and how many coins to insert. I don't remember if I won anything, but I felt that I'd need to take a *Gambling 101* class next time I set my foot in the USA. Later on, I learned that gambling is outlawed in the USA except the state of Nevada where it is a major contributor to the economy.

The ride on Interstate 80 highway took us from Reno to Sacramento. The scenery became astonishingly beautiful as the bus climbed up the Sierra Nevada Mountain ridge and then rolled toward the Sacramento valley. I was admiring the beautiful postcard scenery while frantically photographing color slides with my new Yashica 35mm camera. Once in Sacramento we went to a diner next to the Greyhound depot and ordered our *traditional* hamburger/french fries combo and of course, the ten cent cup of coffee with its unlimited refills. We got on board the Sacramento-San Francisco bus and continued to *the city by the bay*. The long ride from Salt Lake City was tiring and I struggled to stay awake and not to miss UC Davis and the famous city of Berkley when the bus passed by them.

Although Yotam and I obtained international driver licenses before embarking on our trip, we decided against renting a car and driving in San Francisco. The heavy traffic there was too much for us so we did our sightseeing by walking, except for the ride on the iconic cable car. Walking was great cardio exercise, especially after the long sedentary life as Greyhound passengers. But walking in San Francisco put us in big trouble too as we walked on the margins of their busy highways when there were no sidewalks.

We also failed to pay attention to the warning signs posted along our path. We walked our merry way when we heard a loud siren behind us and two armed policemen ordered us to stop where we were. They got out and asked for an ID or a driver license which I learned later on is the common document to serve as your ID. The USA does not use or issue ID cards for its citizen like we have in Israel. We showed them our international driver licenses. This put us in even deeper trouble as they realized that we are foreigners and perhaps undocumented, God forbid. Now they wanted to see our passports. Once again we experienced the extra interest shown by US Government official unfamiliar with how to open an Israeli passport as it must be opened and read from right to left. I had to explain that to the officers and they were convinced at last that we were in the USA legally.

After verifying our identity and checking all our official documentations, the policemen informed us that we committed two violations that prompted them to activate the siren. The first violation walking in areas closed to pedestrians. The second violation, the worst one, was trespassing and entering into a military zone. Realizing that we were there by innocent mistake the policemen helped us into their patrol car and whisked us away to safety. We thanked them profusely and promised to spare ourselves from similar situations in the future. To this day, from my experience thus far, I considered USA policemen and law enforcement agent to be very courteous, polite, and kind.

From San Francisco we traveled to southern California and visited Los Angeles, Hollywood and Disneyland adding these attractions as feathers to our traveler hats. The weather was nice and warm unlike foggy and misty San Francisco during the time we were there. The southern California weather reminded us of Israel. The ride along the interstate highway revealed the huge agricultural nature of that state making it the state where most of the domestic fruits and vegetables are grown.

When it was time to start heading back toward New York, we chose short visits to Flagstaff Arizona, the Grand Canyon, and Washington DC. We needed to reserve some money and stamina for the trip back to Israel via Switzerland. Beside, riding for so long on the Greyhound bus and living on hamburgers, french fries and coffee compounded by lack of decent sleep and hot showers started to take a toll on us. We were more than happy to go back to New York City.

Stopping and touring the Grand Canyon and its beauty was the highlight and the justification of going through Arizona. It also presented us with the opportunity to visit a Native American reservation and see *the real thing* rather than reading Karl May's fictional novels about *Old Fire Hand* and his trilogy about *Winnetou*, a fictional Native American hero; books that I read during my adolescence. I found it funny that these novels about American Indians were written in German by a German novelist who never set foot near an Indian reservation. I marveled at the beads, craftsmanship and artifacts I saw at their souvenir store and visualized how beautiful Batia would look wearing a nice beaded necklace. I bought one for her, of course.

Our next stop was Washington DC where we visited all the *must-see* attractions. After seeing the beautiful and impressive mountainous landscapes in the western states, riding through the flat landscape and the never-ending stretch of corn fields was somewhat boring. The most exciting event during that stretch of our bus ride was a major car accident between our bus and a Trailways company bus, Greyhound's main competitor at that time. I am not sure which driver was at fault, but not too long after the Highway Patrol officers did their inspection and gave the drivers the applicable reports, an empty Trailways bus picked all of the passengers from our bus and drove us all the way to Washington DC. I expected to hear some juicy swears and bad language exchanged between the two drivers like they do in Israel, but these two American drivers were very well behaved. It made me feel good to witness such refreshing civility while trying to resolve an unpleasant situation.

We finally arrived at the New York Greyhound bus depot where we started our trip almost three weeks before. We were tired and started to believe that if we sat on another Greyhound bus, our bodies would assume the shape of the passenger seats. I swore to never again ride on a Greyhound bus, EVER, but I was patently wrong as I repeated the same long ride four years later when I came back to the USA, a married man, to attend the University of California Davis campus. (Chapter 8.)

Yotam and I allowed ourselves two more days in New York to recover, then flew to Zurich, Switzerland to start the final leg of our overseas trip.

After landing, we headed to Lucerne and found a small hotel to spend the night and have a nice breakfast. I don't remember what they served for breakfast, but I remember quite vividly the pure silver artisan-made coffee carafe. The coffee was in a much higher league than the coffee we had in the USA. I dubbed it *European style coffee*. I am still wondering if its unique taste came from the way it was brewed, or the type of the coffee beans used. Most likely it was the combination of the Artisan carafe, and the old-style European breakfast table covered with a white tablecloth. I have sweet memories every time I see a coffee ad in the glossy pages of European magazines.

After the great breakfast and coffee at our hotel we took the lake cruise from Lucerne to nearby Mount Pilatus. To reach the mountain we went on the Mount Pilatus Cogwheel Railway considered to be the steepest railway in the world. It was built in 1889 and takes you to the top on a 2.6-mile track with a forty-eight percent gradient. It has a unique tracking mechanism called cogwheel rail designed to prevent the car from jumping off the tract due to its steep gradient. In 2001 the unique engineering of the Mount Pilatus cogwheel railway granted it the recognition of Historic Mechanical Engineering Landmark by the American Society of Mechanical Engineering. For a native Israeli like me who never left Israel, going up the mountain on such a steep angle was quite an experience. For the first time in my life I was on a real mountain and not just a tiny mound we Israelis have the *chutzpa* to call a mountain.

Getting off the Mount Pilatus cogwheel was a striking experience with the breathtaking view of steep huge mountains, evergreen forests and green meadows below. There was also the lake with boats sailing across it. I could attest to the fact that all postcards coming from Switzerland are genuinely describing its beauty. Here again I started to complain about Moses and where he led my ancestors.

We wished to stay longer at Mount Pilatus and absorb the beauty but our schedule was really tight as we planned to visit the Swiss town of Geneva which was famous for, among other things, its numerous international agreements known as The Geneva Conventions. Of interest were conventions related to wars between countries. Perhaps the following information is not true or simply a figment of my imagination, but I recalled that during my military service in the Israeli army, we were told that the shape and the design of the bayonet attached to our rifle conformed to the Geneva Conventions. While being trained at the parachuting school they told us that shooting at a paratrooper descending to the ground was against the Geneva Conventions. It was OK to kill him once he was on the ground. The practicality of these conventions seemed questionable or a joke to say the least. Personally, I am convinced that whoever coded these statements into a convention was *under the influence* of something. Still, I had to see Geneva.

We took the Mount Pilatus-Lucerne lake cruise back to Lucerne in order to catch the train to Geneva. We got on board the cruise ship and sat inside the passenger's hall instead of standing on the cold deck. We sat just above the ship's engine room with its large glass window which provided the passengers a nice view of all the activities inside the engine room.

The sight of the old grandpa-type person attending and operating the engine caught my attention. He was dressed, head to toe in a blue coverall and kept oiling the engine parts with an old fashioned oiler you see nowadays among collectible items on antiques websites. He was squirting the oil into spouts and then wiped them with a red rag until the chrome was shiny bright. The entire engine room floor looked so clean you could eat your dinner off it. I am sure that elderly mechanic spent his entire professional life working on that engine, keeping it and the engine room in good shape, running without a glitch.

I started to have some ambivalent feelings toward this Swiss obsession with cleanliness, promptness, and their perfect attention to details. Yes, I wished I would see these values implemented in Israel too, but then again, I kept asking myself where were the Swiss people when six million of my people were murdered by the Nazis during the WWII. The Swiss nation chose to stay neutral and prospered while other nations fought Nazi Germany and suffered major destruction. Why didn't the Swiss people open their doors for my people trying to escape the Holocaust? Why did the Swiss people let the Nazis keep their money in Swiss bank volts? Or why paintings and art collections stolen by the Nazis from their Jewish owners were hidden in Switzerland while their legal owners were sent to the gas chambers at Auschwitz? Europe was in flames and my Jewish brethren were murdered by the Germans while the only thing the Swiss people did was *yodel* and pretend that the world went on, *business as usual*. So in the end I became less impressed with Switzerland.

Back in Lucerne, we went to the station to catch a train to Geneva. When the clerk at the ticket window started talking to me in Swiss German I said, "English please," so he replied with German-accented English, "Where to you like to go?"

"Geneva" I replied and opened my wallet to pay for the tickets.

"Genève?" he asked me.

"NO sir," I replied back, "we would like go to Geneva."

The clerk did not relent and kept saying, "Genève?"

I was as stubborn as he was and kept asking to go to "Geneva."

Then it occurred to the clerk that perhaps there was a language barrier going on between us so he asked me with a very reassuring tone that now he figured out where we wanted to go and asked, "Genova?"

I exclaimed with a loud voice of relief, "Ya Ya," like I noticed the Swiss saying during conversations, something equivalent to the American's "Yeh." Well, I made a humongous mistake that cost us dearly later on. There is an old saying of our sages that, "Life or death depends on the tip of the tongue," and it sure did when I bought the tickets to *Genova* arguing with the ticket agent in Lucerne.

The train coming from Zurich entered the station shortly after we purchased the tickets. We got on board and sank into the nice cushiony seats by the window ready to enjoy the beautiful lush green landscape along the route. It was the first time for us to ride on a train powered by electricity, unlike the diesel locomotives used in Israel. The Swiss train traveled smoother and quieter. With an estimated 164 mile distance between Lucerne and Geneva, I expected to be in Geneva within three hours at the most. I started to get bad vibes when I did not see any signs along the tract referencing major cities ahead of us, or distance in kilometers, etc. I expected from this important route running between major cities such as Bern, the Swiss capital and Lausanne not to mention Geneva. Moreover, the train was traveling in a southeastern direction instead of the southwestern direction I expected it to go. The landscape also started changing from what I considered to be the typical Swiss postcard type to more of the humid subtropical weather like the northern parts of the Adriatic/Mediterranean Sea. My next shock came when our train stopped at a town called Lugano and people who got on board spoke Italian and not the Swiss German. Deep in my heart I began to realize that the train we were riding on would not take us to Geneva. I drew on the last ounce of my optimism, succumbed to denial and believing that somewhere along the railway they would switch to the Geneva-bound train. After the fact, I learned that Lugano is a town in southern Switzerland in the Italian speaking canton of Ticino and has the largest Italian speaking majority outside Italy.

The train left Lugano and traveled about thirty more miles before stopping at a very large station that looked to me like a junction point where trains change destinations and let passengers switch trains to their final destination. For a moment I was relieved believing that they would switch us to the train heading to Geneva but my wishful thinking bubble burst when cars from our train were separated and towed to other cars and locomotive while we stayed connected to the same locomotive that took us from Lucerne. My next shock came when two policemen wearing uniforms I had not seen in Switzerland entered our car and asked passengers for passports and visas. As it turned out, we were at the Swiss-Italian border crossing and these two policemen were the Italian border control agents conducting their inspection similar to these done at any international airport.

While inspecting our passports and realizing that we were foreigners one of the border control agent asked us, in a very broken and rudimentary English, where we were heading. I told him that we were on our way to Geneva. He paused for a minute, nodded his head from side to side murmuring "No, no," trying to explain that we were on the wrong train which was about to cross the border into Italy. To make maters worse, the agent said that we could not continue riding into Italy since our Italian visa, issued in Israel did not allow for multiple entry. We already used one entry when we entered Rome on our flight to Paris.

Our original plan to fly back to Israel via Zurich after visiting Geneva was no longer practical. The two agents showed signs of impatience as the train was about to continue its route into Italy. We pleaded with them but the agent in charge said that there was nothing they could do and we better leave the train right there. Miraculously, my attention for details saved us out of crisis at the twelfth hour, as I noticed tobacco stained on their fingers, they were heavy smokers. We presented them with an offer they could not resist. We *bribed our way* into Italy by giving each one of them a full carton of American Parliament cigarettes my friend Yotam, a smoker, purchased at the JFK duty-free shop.

The train crossed the border into Italy shortly after the policemen left and our unplanned journey into Italy started. For a long time after we crossed the border I wondered how we ended up in Italy and not in Geneva. I racked my brain searching for an answer which took me back to my conversation with the tickets clerk at the Lucerne train station. It never occurred to me that a name for a city could be pronounced differently or with different nuances depending on geographical regions, or different languages. It could also be spelled differently. To me, Geneva was called Geneva and that was it. The clerk at the station however knew it by its French Genève or ville de Genève as the French-speaking Swiss people call it. So when he asked if we wanted to go the Genève and I kept insisting on Geneva he consulted with his destinations chart showing the location in Europe the train served. Finally, the name Genova popped up. When he asked me, "Genova?" it sounded close enough to *Geneva* I exclaimed with my stupid, "Ya Ya." What a grave mistake it was, because Genova is the Latin name for *Genua*, which we use for it but, on the clerk's chart it was called *Genova*. Interestingly enough, Genua/Genova is the sixth largest city in Italy and the birthplace of Christopher Columbus.

The Geneva-Genova fiasco put us in quagmire as we were supposed to fly back to Israel on Swissair and since we already left Switzerland I was afraid that our Swiss visa was issued for a one time entry. I didn't want to get stuck at the border on our way to fly out of Zurich.

We explored alternative ways to go back to Israel. I knew that the Israeli-owned shipping company Zim had a regular round trip voyage between Haifa Israel and Napoli (Naples) so we called their Napoli Office from the Youth Hostel where we spent the night. We were told the ship *Moledet* would depart to Haifa in five days and the only available tickets left were for a shared dormitory in the lower level without windows. We jumped on the opportunity to go home and reserved two tickets.

We were still at the very northern part of Italy, close to the Swiss border so we were under immense pressure to travel the long distance to Napoli and be there before the ship sailed to Israel. The fastest and safest way to do so was the train that took us into Italy. We didn't dare leave the train except when it stopped for five to ten minutes, allowing us to sprint to the platform and grab an Italian pork sandwich and a 1.5 liter, straw-wrapped bottle of Chianti the sandwich vendor sold us. I found this menu as good as or even better than the menu at the diners along our Greyhound bus tour.

We got more relaxed and at ease after realizing that we were ahead of schedule and would reach Napoli perhaps two days earlier than the ship departure day so we stopped in Milan and visited the iconic La Scala opera building. We spent the night at a local Youth Hostel that also served a huge spaghetti dinner. It was housed in an old church with crosses and religious icons adorning every empty space. Although I considered myself a secular Israeli Jew, I still felt uneasy surrounded by the religious ambiance. For the most part, through history, Jews living under the Catholic rules endured persecution. The expulsion from Catholic Spain in 1492, and from Catholic Portugal in 1496, not to mention the forced conversion into Catholicism are few examples. After the spaghetti dinner with its huge volume of sauce we slept on a two-level bunk bed with other strangers in the same huge hall. I tied my Yashica camera and backpack to the frame of the bed by my side so no one would steal my *fortune*. The next morning, we took the train to Napoli.

After a few more stops, meat sandwiches and bottles of Chianti, we finally arrived in Napoli and went to the Zim shipping office to get our tickets to Haifa, Israel. The ship was leaving the following afternoon so we found a cheap hotel for the night.

The ladies at the reception desk, who looked like a mother and daughter, did not appear to be too sophisticated dealing with world travelers. At least that was my impression while watching the older lady perhaps in her fifties, inspect our passports. The older lady took us upstairs and showed us to our room.

From my very first glance at our room, I realized that our hotel was not in the *four star* league. When I opened the chest drawer on which a small lamp was standing to see if they had the a copy of the Gideon Bible, like our Salt Lake City hotel had, then I found original pornographic photographs of naked ladies as well as boxes of unused disposable flash cubes. The bathroom was different than the ones typical to Israel and the motel chains in the USA. To begin with, it did not have a shower but a large four-legged white bathtub, the kind probably used by Queen Victoria or Marie-Antoinette. And then there were all kinds of enamel pans, pitchers and funny looking rubber flat bags staged by a strange looking small stool. We realized that this was not what we considered a *bona fide hotel*. It was too late to find a better place so we tried to get some sleep. I left a few small lights on to avoid stumbling into the furniture.

I was awakened in the middle of the night to the noise of someone carrying a bunch of keys and trying to unlock our door. At that moment I started worrying about all the legends I had heard about Napoli being a bastion of the Italian Mafia. The next thing we knew, the mother and daughter entered our room, almost naked offering us their services. Shocked and half asleep we managed to yell at them from the top of our lungs, "No! No!" and pushed them forcibly out of the room. Next, we barricaded ourselves by placing the beds vertically against the door and reinforced it with all the furniture that we could put our hands on. We did not stop building our fortress until I felt absolutely confident that even the armies of the mighty Hannibal Barca, Attila the Hun and Genghis Khan combined won't be able to invade the room. Needless to say, we were no longer in the mood to sleep so we sat quietly until sunrise hoping that no more surprises were in store for us.

At daybreak we tried to sneak out unnoticed but we were greeted by the mother/daughter team, now properly dressed, with warm wide smiles and the sweetest, "*buongiorno*," (good morning in Italian) greeting as if nothing happened during that night. I replied with a sweet, "*buongiorno signore*" (good morning ladies) and motioned with my hand toward the door to indicate that we were leaving. One last, "*Ciao*," (bye) and we were heading to the port. Unlike the night before, they looked so pleasant and innocent I thought we met Mother Theresa and a young Madonna right out of Italian paintings and sculptures.

We walked the short distance from the hotel to the port, went to the border control inspector who stamped the *Exit* stamp notification in our passport without raising any fuss about our adventure at the Swiss-Italian border. We were rushing toward the Zim's passengers departing hall, but this time not for fear of missing the ship but from the euphoric sensation of GOING HOME that swept over us. Once on board, the crew ushered us to our dormitory that became our home for the three-day voyage. Then it occurred to me that the ship's Hebrew name *Moledet*, (homeland) was a perfect fit for the occasion. Three days later when we saw the golden dome of the Bahai Shrine on Haifa's Mount Carmel and *Moledet* entered the port we knew that we were finally home.

Chapter 8

UC Davis: Part 1

The warm spot in my heart toward the United States started after the 1948 War for Independence. The United States' foreign aid, including shipments of basic food items, helped Israel during that difficult time. (See Chapter 18.) The packages were stenciled with the USA foreign aid emblem. To this day, I am thankful for the generosity of the American people. I also remember the care packages with clothes my mom's uncle from Brooklyn sent us along with toys for me and my sister even though he struggled financially.

Another factor that kept my interest with the United State was the fact that my sister and my brother-in-Law moved to Forest Hills, New York and went to college. Both received their bachelor's degree there. My brother-in-law continued his graduate studies and earned a master's degree in Economics from Rutgers University in New Jersey. Their three children were born there as well. Unfortunately for my parents, a wide ocean separated the nuclear family they had built.

My affinity toward the USA intensified during my studies for my Bachelor's degree in Biology at Tel Aviv University. I was exposed to research work done at UC Davis when I wrote a paper on Plant Physiology. A gut feeling told me I would eventually go there. My first step in that direction was to take the so-called Test of English as Foreign Language (TOEFL) required by some English-speaking universities. The TOEFL measured the ability of individuals for whom English was a second language. When I found out that the Zionist Organization of America (ZOA) center in Tel Aviv offered the test, I registered and took it. I didn't realize how difficult the test would be for someone who read and communicated in Hebrew.

Fifty-six years have passed since I took the TOEFL but I still remember some essential details. It lasted 2.5 hours with only a ten minute mandatory break. The test was comprised of four parts: reading, listening, speaking and writing. I don't recall if the company administrating the test sent me my overall score or sent it only to the American universities I listed when I ordered the test. Two colleges,

The University of Arizona and Fresno State College in California, notified me by mail that I passed the test to their satisfaction.

My academic quest for master and doctorate degrees in the USA had to be put on the slow burner for a while due to three factors. The first one was the Six-Day War that erupted in June of 1967. I was attending the second trimester of my last academic year of the bachelor program. Being a paratrooper, I was called for active military duty, liberating Jerusalem, the West Bank (Judea and Samaria) and the southern tip of the Syrian Golan Heights. A few of my classmates and some of the instructors were also called to their military units. For the classmates who were not called, the lectures, and homework assignments continued as scheduled. It was difficult for soldiers to switch back to being students. We took our final exams a month after the war and completed the three-year bachelor degree program.

I married Batia, my girlfriend, four months after the Six-Day War ended. Our wedding was held in Matzuba, her *kibbutz*. It was officiated by Rabbi Keller, the orthodox rabbi from Nahariya, the northern-most coastal city in Israel. Rabbi Keller provided for the religious needs of the nearby *kibbutzim*. Rabbi Keller made me sign the Jewish *ketubah* (Jewish marriage contract) witnessed by Batia's two class mates from her *kibbutz*. (Figure 8.1 a and b.) A huge crowd attended our wedding including all the members of her *kibbutz*, my family from Tel-Aviv, my friends from the army and my *kibbutz* were there to celebrate with us.

Figure 8.1 a and b.   Left: the *ketubah* I gave Batia. Right: Rabbi Keller, who officiated our wedding, watching me sign the *ketubah*.

Figure 8.2 The *kibbutz* planned music and dancing

The *kibbutz* put together music and dancing that put any Hollywood production to shame. We still have many photographs and super 8 movie film that recorded the event. (Figure 8.2.) The *kibbutz* wanted us to live there as full-fledged members but we had a different plan and elected to move to Tel Aviv where we rented an apartment. Batia, being my girlfriend for almost four years, knew about my wishes to pursue the academic dream of getting master and doctorate degrees from a US university and agreed to go along. To this day I consider myself a very fortunate man and thank her for her support. With her consent and blessing, I started sending my applications to the universities I considered best suited for achieving my goal.

Right after the wedding, I was called for forty-five days of active military annual duty, serving with comrades from the Six-Day War. We knew each other very well making our reservist duty feel like a family reunion. As mentioned in Chapter 6, we were dispatched to the western bank of the Jordan River close to Jericho area, with the task of intercepting the PLO terrorists trying to cross the river, infiltrate Israel proper and commit terrorist attacks. It was a tough assignment that postponed my admission application to the University of California at Davis, my top preference. We also postponed our honeymoon.

Waiting to get any response from the universities was very difficult and discouraging. Friends who were familiar with the universities in the USA and reviewed my grades reassured me that I was more than qualified to be admitted to any graduate school. Still, waiting for replies made me edgy and I felt that a change of plan was warranted. My brainstorming mechanism clicked in high gear. *If not now, then when?!* I asked myself.

First we needed new Israeli passports and a B-2 visa to the USA.

Still, I had not received a reply from any of the universities. By the time we obtained the passports, I was willing to take even higher risks. I had the approximate dates when the next academic quarter started in the USA, so I purchased round–trip airline tickets for me and Batia along with the iconic Greyhound $99/99 days tickets. I told myself, *If the mountain will not come to Muhammad, then Muhammad must go to the mountain.* I decided to go to UC Davis and knock on their doors until they admitted me. I wouldn't be ignored any longer. We packed our clothes and other personal items and sent them to my sister's address in Forest Hills, NY.

One day, upon entering the foyer of my apartment building I noticed a white enveloped, typical to the ones used in the USA, sticking out of my mailbox. My hands were shaking and my heart palpitating as I opened the mailbox. The letter came from UC Davis, the top university on my "short list." I had been waiting for that moment for a very long time and finally someone at UC Davis replied to my admission application to its graduate school. A moment later my heart sunk when I read their July 17, 1968 reply. (Figure 8.3.)

UNIVERSITY OF CALIFORNIA, DAVIS

BERKELEY · DAVIS · IRVINE · LOS ANGELES · RIVERSIDE · SAN DIEGO · SAN FRANCISCO   SANTA BARBARA · SANTA CRUZ

OFFICE OF THE DEAN   DAVIS, CALIFORNIA 95616
   OF THE GRADUATE DIVISION

July 17, 1968

AIR MAIL

Mr. Shmuel Regev
Jeuda-Hamakabi 34
Tel-Aviv, ISRAEL

Dear Mr. Regev:

The Dean of the Graduate Division has reviewed your scholastic records but regrets he is unable to accord you admission. Competition for gaining entrance to the University of California, Davis, is keen; and the quality of scholarship indicated by your transcripts does not meet the standard we have found necessary to establish for acceptance. We hope you will find it possible to continue your education in another college of your choice.

Sincerely yours,

(Miss) Sue Armstrong
For the Dean of the Graduate Division

SA:lj
cc: Entomology

Figure 8.3 Rejection letter from
Dean of the Graduate Division at UC Davis

All my dreams were shuttered. I was frozen for a second standing by the mailbox. I regained my composure rather quickly and climbed to our apartment on the third floor. The last thing I needed was another resident entering the foyer and seeing my long face. "What are we going to do?" Batia asked when I showed her the rejection letter.

"What do you mean by asking me, what are we are going to do?" I retorted back. "I am going to fold this letter very neatly, put it in my pocket and take it with me to the United State because we are going!"

At that point we had the airline and Greyhound Bus tickets in our hands and the packages with our clothes were already in transit to my sister house in Forest Hills so I was not going to back out of our plan. "And remember," I told Batia, "We have not taken our honeymoon yet, so let's consider going to the USA as our belated honeymoon. We owe it to ourselves." She deserves huge credit for following me into the uncharted path at the early stage of our life together. I have always told her that in life, if you aim at something which is on the opposite bank of the river, you must jump in and swim to the other side and get wet in the process. And get wet we did!

Since our flight to the USA was to depart from Zurich, Switzerland we purchased a one-way voyage to Venice, Italy on the Israeli ship *Moledet*, departing the Israeli port of Haifa. It was the same ship *Moledet* that my friend Yotam and I took in 1964 from Napoli to Israel at the end of our trip.

We spent one night in Venice and next day took the train to Lucerne, Switzerland enjoying the scenery along way. We were fortunate to find a room at the same small, family-oriented hotel that my friend Yotam and I stayed in 1964. Batia was happy to experience the nice European ambiance at the breakfast table with its white tablecloth and perfect coffee, poured out of the antique carafe like I did when I was there before. From Lucerne we took the train to Zurich, flew to New York, landed on August 21, 1968 and stayed at my sister's house.

My sister's house was sort of crowded when we arrived. She had just given birth to her first child, Eilat. My mother had arrived two weeks earlier for the birth of her first grandchild. It was clear to me that the sooner Batia and I moved out, the better.

I mailed UC Davis an express letter, addressed to the School of Agriculture Entomology Department informing them that I was an Israeli visitor looking for a graduate school. I would be in the UC Davis area around a specific date and wondered if they would be kind enough to grant me a short meeting to explore what their department had to offer. I picked the Department of Entomology as I rationalized that not too many candidates were interested studying that field, hence I would stand a better chance of being accepted. In my letter I mentioned the fact that I already sent my application to the Graduate School a few weeks earlier and still waited for a reply. Obviously, I did not mention the rejection letter from the Dean of the Graduate School. It was well secured in my pocket.

The reply arrived a few days later, signed by Professor Stafford, informing me of their willingness to meet if I was in the area. I hopped on the next Greyhound bus.

Once again I was thankful for the Greyhound Bus Company's $99/99 deal. This particular ride was extremely important. Time was of the essence as I had to be in Davis on time for the meeting, forcing me to ride, non-stop, all the way to Davis. I arrived there at night and found a small hotel next to the bus station. I booked for the night and enjoyed a hot shower and a comfortable bed after the long ride across the continent.

The next morning I took another shower and made myself presentable for my 11:00 a.m. meeting. I ate the (included) continental breakfast and walked the few blocks to campus. I located the Department of Entomology building and still had more than an hour until the appointment so I set on the bench next to the building. My brain generated numerous scenarios on how the meeting would go. I tried to formulate answers to the questions I thought they would most likely ask. At a few minutes before 11 a.m. I headed toward the Entomology building searching for Dr. Stafford's office. A student showed me where Dr. Stafford office was located.

My heart was racing when I knocked on his door. No one answered so I knocked again, a bit harder the second time and heard a "Come in," so I entered the office with my backpack still on my back and introduced myself as "the guy who sent the request for a meeting." I showed him the letter he sent me.

"Oh! Yes! Of Course!" he replied, "why don't you sit down while I ask two of my colleagues to join us." I felt apprehension as it was going to be "three against one," situation. A few minutes later he came back with his colleagues and introduced us. We all shook hands while Dr. Stafford gave me a brief description of who they were, their field of expertise and the courses they taught. He introduced himself as the *Taxonomist* whose specialty involved identifying insects considered major pests of commercial fruit trees. He looked to me like he was in his mid-fifties. The next professor was Dr. Judson, the *Insect Physiologist,* who seemed to me to be in his late forties. The last one, with a crew-cut was Professor Francis Summers who looked older than the rest. He was an *Acarologist* teaching and researching mites and ticks.

It should be noted that the professional expertise represented by the three professors were essential for agriculture and pest control management to ensure ample food production. California was and still is, the major food and fruit producer of the USA. In fact, before UC Davis was transformed into a university with several different colleges, it was California's most important agriculture college and research center known as *Cal Aggie* (California Agriculture).

Now it was my turn to introduce myself, my academic background and my aspiration to advance my academic career. I told them about my acquaintance with UC Davis through a project I had done during my bachelor's degree in biology. It dealt with the physiology of fruit production and based on the research of UC Davis's Professor Julian Crane who was the world expert in the field. They all knew him, he was a staff member of the Plant Physiology Department next door.

At first they raised eyebrows when I mentioned that specific research since my letter to Dr. Stafford I mention my request to be admitted to their Entomology department and not to the Plant Physiology Department so I reminded them that my degree was in Biology, Plant Physiology included.

I kept thinking, *So far so good,* while trying to boost my self-confidence and keep my composure as I faced this *tribunal trio*. It was not easy. To begin with, my poor brain had to absorbed what I heard in English, translate it to Hebrew and then formulate a reasonable and convincing answer in Hebrew and then answer in English. It was quite a challenge. In addition, I tried to predict their decision regarding my application for admission by gauging their tone of voice and facial expression. After each question they posed to me, I kept thinking, *Are they friends of foes.* I noticed that both Dr. Summers and Dr. Judson seemed relaxed and smiled a lot while talking to me in a soft *fatherly* voice. Dr. Stafford, on the other hand, was stern and business-like so I was not at ease with him. Among the three of them, he talked the least during the interview.

At one point Dr. Summers interjected and informed me that UC Davis had maintained an extensive research and professional collaboration with The Hebrew University of Jerusalem faculty of Agriculture. He mentioned a few names and asked if I knew them. I admitted I did not as I was a student at Tel Aviv University. Then, out of the blue, Dr. Stafford looked at me and asked in his stern voice, "Mr. Regev, I don't understand why you are still trying to be admitted to the Graduate School at UC Davis and scheduled this appointment with us when you already received an official rejection letter from the Dean of the Graduate Division declining your request on the ground that your transcripts did not meet the standard deemed necessary for acceptance." The silence that followed his statement was deafening. I am sure that everyone in the room heard my heart beating louder than the huge drums of the UC Davis marching band.

I paused deliberately for few seconds to give the impression of not knowing what he was talking about and I replied as calmly as I could, "I did not receive the letter you are referring to." He pulled a copy of the same rejection letter I had in my pocket. I went along and pretended to read the copy he gave me. He offered to make me a copy.

"So where do we go from here?" I asked Dr. Stafford while the other professors sat silently.

"There is nothing we can do other than to suggest that you try to apply to colleges in the Bay Area or southern California."

I was not sure how genuine Dr. Stafford's remarks were so I decided that I had nothing to lose at that point and the only sliver of hope for me was resorting to chutzpa (audacity, in Hebrew/Yiddish). I mustered every ounce I had in me and retorted back, "So why did you schedule an appointment to see me, making me travel all the way from New York City to Davis just to tell me that I would not be admitted?"

The three professors looked surprised. "No, that is not completely correct. You wrote that you would be traveling in the UC Davis area and asked if we were willing to talk to you, so I agreed, out of courtesy, but still there is nothing that we can do about the graduate school rejection."

Dr. Stafford was adamant and very clear on that, making me ready to admit a painful defeat. I picked up my backpack and was about to thank them for their time when I noticed Dr. Summers looking at his watch, "Gentleman, it is lunch time. I don't know about you but I am hungry. Why don't we take a lunch break, discuss his case and ask Mr. Regev to come back at 1:30."

Dr. Judson concurred, leaving Dr. Stafford in the minority so I was asked to return back at 1:30 p.m. Dr. Summers showed me where the cafeteria was located. I was about to go when he took my hand and said, "Sam, don't carry your backpack around, let's put it in my office. You're coming back at 1:30 aren't you?" He winked at me with smiling eyes. I was speechless and felt I had met my guardian angel. I left my backpack in his office and went to the cafeteria.

When I came back at 1:30, the three professors were waiting for me. Dr. Judson and Dr. Summers were smiling at me. Dr. Stafford was the spokesman for the three of them and explained to me the decision they'd made. Dr. Stafford looked at me and said, "Mr. Regev, as the letter from the Dean of the Graduate Division stated, your transcripts from Tel Aviv University did not meet the standard acceptable for admission to the Graduate Division at UC Davis, there is nothing that we can do at this stage to change it. This decision is out of our jurisdiction. Nonetheless, we took into consideration the fact that you flew all the way from Israel to the USA and then crossed the country to meet with us. We would like to offer a suggestion for you to consider. It is a complicated proposal so feel free to stop me at any time if you have questions." He paused and waited for my reply.

"Please go ahead and let me know the details and what I can do to help my case."

"To tell you the truth," Dr. Stafford continued, "the decision to reject your acceptance to the graduate division was not made by UC Davis. It was made on the advice of the Dean of Graduate School at UC Berkeley."

I was shocked by this revelation because UC Berkeley was a different university, I didn't see how they got involved in the application process. "How come?" I asked.

"Mr. Regev," he replied, "you graduated from a very new university and no one at UC Davis was familiar with it or its credentials. Moreover, no one here knew how to convert your transcripts from the percent format into the GPA format used here so the Dean of the Graduate Division forwarded your application and transcripts to his counterpart at UC Berkeley, who was better qualified to address this issue due to a long time collaboration with the Hebrew University of Jerusalem."

That rationale riled me up, big time, so I asked what method they used to convert my transcripts into the GPA format. According to Dr. Stafford, the UC Berkley people wanted to *play it safe* and subtracted 10% from each grade, lowering my academic scores markedly. As a result, my 90% grades were changed to 80%, the 80% scores became 70%, 70% reduced to 60%.

It should be noted that during my tenure as a student at Tel Aviv University, the requirement for admission to the master's degree program was predicated on having a combined average of 80% or higher in the courses considered prerequisites in those fields *only*, so I channeled all my efforts into those fields. Unfortunately for me, the Dean of the Graduate Division at UC Davis denied my application for admission based on the transcripts *conversions*. I managed to control my anger. If I had some misgiving about telling Dr. Stafford that I never received the Dean's rejection letter, it stopped bothering me after they told me about the convoluted way they had calculated my academic scores.

"Anyhow," Dr. Stafford continued, "Here is what we could do so you could start studying at UC Davis, but you must decide very soon because fall quarter starts a month from now." Then he described his *admission plan* by which I would be admitted to their Entomology department as a *Limited Status* student.

"What is *Limited Status*?" I asked.

"It means that, for the time being, the school would not consider you a graduate student despite the fact that you did receive a bona fide bachelor degree from Tel Aviv University. You would be allowed to attend our graduate courses and take the exams but you would need to pass these courses with at least a B or better. If you do, we will reevaluate our decision and remove the *Limited Status* restrictions."

I agreed to take their offer and promised to do my best. I thanked them profusely for their time and efforts on my behalf. I assured them that I would be back on time to take care of the registration before the fall quarter started.

Dr. Summers ushered me to the entrance of the building and showed me a shortcut to the campus exit gate and the street to the bus station. He winked at me again as he shook my hand. "Don't worry, Sam, I am 100% sure everything will be all right. I am looking forward to working with you."

As he entered the building, I felt immense gratitude toward this warm hearted human being. I noticed that he called me *Sam* rather than, *Mr. Regev*. I took it as a good omen and rushed to the Greyhound bus station to travel back to New York City to pick up Batia and bid farewell to my mother who was about to return to Israel.

The clerk at the bus station told me that my bus would arrive within an hour. It would follow the same route that I took coming from New York. For a change, I felt in full control of the situation and decided to call Batia with an update. The Greyhound clerk was supper nice to me and helped me make a collect call to my sister's house. It was a brief call. I promised to give all the details once I was back in New York.

Traveling back to New York gave me time to reflect on what I had gotten myself into and the difficulties in store for us. I considered the nagging question of *can we make it?* The monumental hurdle was being able to pay the $1200/year out of state tuition fee because I was not a Californian resident. I tried to figure out where to borrow the money. Another tuition-related problem was the *Limited Status* designation. It was the policy of the UC Davis graduate school to grant a tuition waver to any graduate finishing the quarter with a 3.5 GPA or higher. If too many students qualified, the dean of the graduate school would raise the qualifying GPA to 3.6 or higher, as needed. The *Limited Status* designation excluded me from that money saving option.

✡

Deciding to come to the USA to live and study put me at odds in the eyes of some Israelis who had known me personally for many years. There was a stigma attached to my name, almost like the sign affixed to Cain's forehead as told in the Old Testament.

Allow me to elaborate a bit more on that point so that the reader can better understand the emotional and mental conundrum I was getting myself into. To start with, there are, roughly speaking, three types of Israelis, in the eyes of the Israelis, at least. The first one is the *sabra* (native) who was born, raised and still lives in Israel. The second type who was born and raised in the diaspora and then immigrated to Israel making it his/her home. This type is the *Ole* (ascender or going up in Hebrew). The *Ole* is looked upon very favorably by the native Israelis and gets lots of help from the government. The third type of Israeli is known as the *Yored* (descender or going down). This person left Israel for whatever reason to live abroad.

Often, financial or personal advancement are the core reason for leaving Israel. The *yored* is not looked upon favorably. The United States has been the most popular country for the Israelis to immigrate to. As of today, there are close to million Israelis living in the USA, still, there are some Israelis that stigmatize them as *yordim* (plural) with its negative and almost demeaning connotation.

The negative sentiments toward a yored really bothered me as some people characterized me as such, albeit not to my face. It manifested itself in several ways such as *"What's wrong with the Israeli universities, are they not good enough for him?"* or *"He likes to make money in the USA,"* etc. The thoughts of the likelihood of my reputation being tarnished as a *yored*, kept tormenting me through the entire ride back to New York but I did not abandon my plan to return to Israel upon receiving my Ph.D. Those who considered me *yored* would have great satisfaction, if I failed. Failing to fulfill my goal was not an option.

I finally arrived in New York City and took the subway to my sister's house where Batia and my mom were anxiously waiting to hear how my visit turned out. I told them about my interview with the three professors at the Entomology department who agreed to admit me to their department. I did not bother with the *Limited Status* details as I already knew that my mother was not too happy with my decision to study in the USA. In fact, she had confronted Batia when I purchased the airline tickets. "How is he going to find the money to pay for the tuition, let alone living expenses?" she asked Batia.

I am sure my parents had valid concerns, or maybe they hated to see me leaving them alone in Israel since my sister and her husband were already in for the USA. The sadness of realizing that their little birds matured, spread their wings and left their nest started to sink in.

During supper I pressed the fact that we needed to go back as soon as possible to find a place to live and register for fall quarter. We left the next day. I was glad to start the journey into my academic future at UC Davis but deep sadness set in when I realized that I might not see my family for quite a long time.

We arrived in Davis after three days on the Greyhound bus. The bus stopped in Salt Lake City but we did not spend the night. During the short stop the bus made in Reno, Nevada I showed Batia the machines in one of the gambling places next to the bus depot. As usual, people were glued to the machines searching for the elusive *Pot of Gold* that would make them filthy rich. I am sure that no one found it by the time our bus left for California.

The bus was huffing and puffing in high gear as we climbed through the Sierra Nevada mountains and crossed into California. To this day, I am not sure if it was a *good omen* for the new phase in our life, but the Mamas and Pappas' popular song, "California Dreaming" was playing on the bus radio as we descended into the Sacramento Valley. My heart still palpitates whenever I hear that song.

We reached Davis in the early afternoon and checked in at the same hotel I spent the night during my interview about a week earlier. I suggested that we walk to campus to get familiar with it. Once there, I came across a directory sign listing various points of interest. The *Foreign Students Office* caught my eye. We climbed the stairs leading to the second floor, knocked on the door and I introduced myself and Batia as Israelis and *newcomers* to UC Davis. "Oh, you are from Israel?" the lady exclaimed, "we have several Israeli students on campus. There is also a *Hillel House* on B Street next to our office. One of the Israeli students gave us the address to Hillel House where he lives. I suggest you contact him." She gave me a map of campus and the adjacent streets making sure to draw a big circle around the Hillel House location. "And one more thing that might be of interest to you," she continued, "There is the Israeli Student Organization of UC Davis run by Ephi and his wife Nili. I don't recall their last name, though." We thanked her for the tremendous help and valuable information and headed to Hillel House.

We saw two young people sitting on lawn chairs in front of the house. They were drinking beer and conversing in Hebrew. I approached them and asked in Hebrew if this was Hillel House. The one who looked the younger of the two answered in the affirmative so we introduced ourselves. "Are there any Israeli students at UC Davis?" I asked in Hebrew.

"Yes, of course," the younger guy replied, in Hebrew, "Shalom, my name is Ronny and I am one of them, and this is Avi. I am attending the Veterinary school here, trying to follow my father's footsteps. He is a veterinarian in Ramat Hasharon, Israel. Avi also studies Veterinary Medicine. I live in this house and take care of it but the director of the UC Davis Hillel organization is Professor Larry Rapport. He is teaching at the Plant Physiology Department. He is a great guy," Ronny told me.

I asked Ronny and Avi to recommend good but inexpensive

apartments not too far from campus. Ronny suggested that we could stay at the Hillel House until we found a place to rent. We accepted his offer but would come the next day as we already booked a room at the hotel. "See you tomorrow morning," I said.

"Yes, the morning hours would be perfect for me to show you the large apartment complex on Avenue H," he said as we shook hands.

We arrived the next morning with our small suite cases. Ronny pointed to one of the rooms and said, "This is your room until you move to your own apartment. Why don't you put your suitcases there and, lock the door? I'll take you to the apartment complex I mention yesterday," he said

"Sounds good to us," I replied and we all rode in his car. I don't recall what car he drove but it looked fancy to me. Evidently, it was beneficial for Ronny to be the son of a veterinarian in Israel. Ronny took us to the large apartment complex that he believed would be suitable for us and he was right. I named it *The Green Apartments*. If someone asked me where I lived, I could say, "I live in the green apartments on Avenue H."

The apartment complex was comprised of four rectangular two-stories buildings, two along Avenue F and two on Avenue H near the railroad track with a chain of railcars a mile long. The apartment manger, sensing my concern about the proximity to the railroad track, reassured us that the railcars just park there and were hardly used. There was a large swimming pool between the front and the back rows of the buildings. The manager's office and the maintenance buildings stood next to the pool. When the manager asked for my name I told him, "My Hebrew name is *Shmuel*, but you can call me *Sam* if you wish"

"You bet," he replied with a warm smile, "My name is Sam *too*," he beamed at me. "It's your lucky day. I just finished preparing a two-bedroom apartment on the second floor of Building D by the railroad track. Would you like to see it?" We agreed and he took us there.

"How much is the monthly rent," I asked as we climbed the stairs leading to the apartment. I knew full well that whatever he said would be expensive for us, as I had only $500 in my wallet after paying the $1200 for the out of state tuition.

"The monthly rent of that apartment would be $100 which is a good bargain. Don't you agree? You get a fully furnished apartment with appliances, beds and window air conditioner. Moreover, the electricity and water bills are included."

I promised the manager I'd let him know our decision within a day or two. "Call me soon. I can't leave the apartment vacate for more than two days," he said. He gave me his business card as we left.

Ronny took us back to Hillel House where we spent the night in the room he set up for us. We slept on the floor since the house was used as a meeting place for Jewish students and not for Jewish visitors looking for a bedroom. Although staying there was very inconvenient, I did not like to sign the rental contract at the Green Apartments as we had very little money at our disposal. We planned on staying at the Hillel House for as long as we could while figuring out a solution for our money crunch. This hope was dashed the next day when a red-haired gentleman came to the house and knocked on the door of our room. "Where's Ronny," the gentleman asked me. I told him I had no idea where he was. "And who are you and what are the two of you are doing here?" I sensed the irritation in his voice. I explained to him who we were and the fact that Ronny invited us to stay in that room for the time being. "It was wrong of him to do that without my authorization. I will talk to him about my disapproval the minute he shows up. I am sorry but you cannot stay here. Please pack your stuff and leave."

Unfortunately, our first encounter with Dr. Larry Rapport, the director of UC Davis Hillel House was sort of brutal and forced us to head directly to the Green Apartment complex and look for Sam the manager. I knocked on the door to his office and was relieved to hear his, "Come in, please."

"Mr. Sam," I said as we shook hands. "We would like to move to the apartment you showed us yesterday if it is still available."

"Very well," he said and offered us chairs. "It will take a while before we are done with the paperwork so better take a load off your feet," he said and pulled out the contract documents for us to read and sign. I confessed my ignorance regarding rental contracts used in the USA and asked him to explain each line we were signing. Despite Sam's explanations, it still sounded very intricate to me so I asked him to give it to us in a plain English what the contract said. We signed the contract and I hoped that "Sam the Manager" was a man of integrity and would not screw "Sam the Foreigner."

"I need an ID from both of you," he said to Batia and I. I pulled out my Israeli ID card which had several pages to it. He checked it from all sides and upside down and exclaimed, "What the hack is that?

"That is my official Israeli ID card," I answered.

"It won't work here in America, do you have a social security card?"

"What's a social security card?" I asked. He pulled a card from his wallet and showed it to me. He finally agreed to use my international driver license in lieu of an ID document. "Last thing I need from you before giving you the keys is the $100 rental for the first month," he said and I gave him the money leaving us with only $400 cash. The urgency of finding additional funds started to sink in. We put our suitcases in our new apartment and walked back to Hillel House.

When we arrived, Ronny was very apologetic about the incident with Dr. Rapport. I told him not to bother about it, we already moved to the Green Apartment. Our main concern at that point was to obtain some basic items such as bed sheets, blankets, cooking utensils, etc. I thought it would be good idea to visit Linda, the lady at the International Students office for suggestions so we left Ronny and headed there. "How do you like Davis thus far?" she greeted us as we entered her office. I told her about the apartment we found and then she asked me for Batia's name. "You introduced yourself and your wife the other day but I am not good at remembering names, although I am very good remembering faces," she said.

So it was Batia's turn to take the initiative and introduced herself. "Hi, I am Batia which means *God's Daughter* in Hebrew, but feel free to call me Bati."

"What a nice name," Linda said, there are not too many Batia's around here so I will definitely remember it." She pointed to the coffee maker at the corner. "It is fresh, I just made it so, please help yourselves. There is cream and sugar there if you like." She did not have to ask me twice as being a *coffeeholic* I poured a cup for me and Batia and complimented her about how great the coffee tasted. I felt at ease and relaxed at that office so I asked her, jokingly, "Linda, where do you like me to leave the tip?" I am not sure if she realized that I was joking when she said, "Oh, you don't need to do that."

"Is there anything else that we can do for you today?" Linda asked me, so I asked where to get second-hand items like bed sheets, blankets, household goods, etc. and most importantly, a job for Batia. "I cannot help you with your first question other than suggest that you go to what we call Garage Sales this weekend and I am sure that you'll find the items you need. Better yet, talk to the manager of your apartment. His storage room is probably full to the brim with items left by previous renters. He would be more than happy to give you whatever you need," she said. "As for a job for Batia, it just happens that a young lady came just recently requesting names of female students willing to babysit for her three-year-old during the day when she teaches at the nearby elementary school. Sheila Weiner is her name. Why don't we call her right now?" She called Sheila to inform her that she found a young lady who was interested in babysitting. "Her name is Batia and based on my personal impression, she seems to be the perfect match for the job," she assured Ms. Weiner.

"Why don't you send her to my place now if possible because I will be out of town during the weekend." She gave Linda the address and directions to her house.

"Oh, by the way, Ms. Weiner," Linda added, "they are newcomers to Davis so don't be upset if they get lost and show up a little bit late. Hey, and one more thing, sort of heads up, you will have to train your ears for their accented English which is good but tainted with Hebrew."

I was not amused by this disclosure from Linda but I was absolutely certain that Batia would get the job when we heard Mrs. Weiner saying that was no problem. She was also Jewish and exposed to Hebrew in the synagogue when she was growing up. We wasted no time and left to meet Sheila.

We were pleasantly surprised when we arrived at Sheila's house as it was located about a block from our apartment. Moreover, we found her to be a jovial and attractive lady. Judging from the amount of cookies and refreshments she offered us I sensed that she got a good impression of us. Then she introduced her blond toddler, Steven and told him that Batia was going to be his babysitter even though we had not discussed what the job entailed or the hourly pay rate. I believe she introduced Batia as *your babysitter* just to gauge his reaction, hoping for his approval. He played with his toys while she described Batia's job responsibilities. She should be at Sheila's house at 7:30 am and work until 3:30 p.m. Monday through Friday. She also confided that she was a divorcee but had a fiancé, a veterinarian teaching at the Vet school on campus. They liked to go out on Friday nights so there would be more babysitting hours for Batia beyond the regular weekly schedule. Facing the deep crisis of not having money to sustain ourselves, we felt mighty rich when Sheila offered to pay Batia 60 cents per hour. We accepted her offer.

An important factor helping Sheila to select Batia for the job was her experience taking care of the toddlers at *kibbutz* Matzuba. However, the most important factor was that our apartment was next to her house making me available when I was not on campus taking classes. Let me elaborate more on that. Although Sheila's three-year-old son was a healthy growing toddler, he was prone to have epileptic seizures whenever he got high fever brought about by a simple cold or childhood ailment. His body had to be cooled down fast and given the proper tranquilizes to prevent irreversible brain damage. The pediatrician told Sheila that it was a temporary problem bound to resolve itself as he grew older. She would train Batia on how to help him though these episodes. I assured Sheila that I would come if Batia needed my help. Luckily, it never happened under our watch as Batia was on top of the situation giving Steven the proper medications to prevent the convulsions.

The two-day weekend was about to set in so we left Sheila and Steven. "See you on Monday at 7:30 Batia," Sheila said. "Please be on time so I won't be late for school."

"Don't worry, I'll be on time," Batia assured her. We left and walked to our apartment. We stopped at the office and asked the apartment manager if they had some bed sheets, blankets and basic utensils in the storage room that he could spare until we could buy our own. "Here, take whatever you need to get you started. It'll reduce the clutter," he said and complained about all the junk previous renters left behind. We grubbed as many items as our arms could carry and retreated to our apartment. It was a bit embarrassing, I could not escape the piercing glances of the sunbathers at the swimming pool.

Now that we'd secured a steady income, albeit puny, I urgently needed more cash for registration. The $300 tuition for the upcoming quarter. Our $99/99days Greyhound tickets had not expired yet, so I decide to take the bus to San Francisco and visit Dr. Arthur Ganz, a friend of Batia's mom from the time they lived in Germany before WWII. Esther, Batia's Mom, gave us his phone number and address as a point of contact in case of emergencies. Our financial situation fit that definition. She told him about us living in Davis and asked him to help us if needed. I called him and introduced myself, explained the situation and asked for a $500 short term loan to pay for the initial registration. I gave a sigh of relieve when he agreed and asked us to come to his house and sign the proper papers. I gladly agreed and gave him the estimated arrival time of our Greyhound bus and he promised that someone would meet us at the station. "And please don't eat anything," he warned me. "You are invited for dinner at 6 p.m. with my wife, son and daughter-in-law. She was born in the USA but her family roots could be traced to several generations residing in Jerusalem," he bragged. We took the Greyhound bus to San Francisco that coming Saturday.

When we arrived at the San Francisco bus depot the driver sent by Arthur Ganz was there to take us to Arthur's home. For the first time in my life, I experienced the luxury of being driven in the latest model black Lincoln Continental. Born, and raised in Israel, I was not accustomed to such royal treatment, let alone having our own chauffeur. The next shock hit us upon arriving at Dr. Ganz mansion, or should I say *castle*. A maid dressed in a black uniform and white apron ushered us to the living room. Everything there, including the maid, was so *European,* especially when she kept saying, "Bitte" (German for please) in a thick German accent.

Arthur Ganz entered the room soon after we sat on the sofa and shook our hands warmly. He looked like a man in his mid-seventies, full of stamina. He introduced himself as a close friend of Alfred Brumlik, Batia's maternal grandfather. "We will talk about your venture into UC Davis during dinner but better get the loan business now before the other guests arrive," he said and took us into his study. He wrote a check for $500 and handed it to me. "Here it is," he said. "I trust you and Batia so there is no need for special memorandums to make it official. I know that you will pay it back when you can." I put the check in my wallet. We thanked him for helping us and we joined the guests at the dining table.

Dinner was sumptuous and served by the German-speaking maid we had met earlier. Expensive silverware and china plates adorned the table. Different bottles of expensive French red wines were on the table waiting for Arthur Ganz to decide which one to uncork first. Everything there radiated the aura of the good life. Arthur read the labels on the wine bottles and then handed one to the maid to pour. When we started the first entrée Arthur Ganz pulled out an expensive gold pill box peppered with tiny diamonds glistering like stars and took the medication he needed with the meal. Some guests engaged us with questions about our lives in Israel and why we had come to the USA.

Overall, the visit was great but I did not want to miss the last Greyhound bus to Davis so after finishing the desert I asked Arthur if it would be OK for his driver to take us back to the bus depot. We said farewell to the other guests and promised to keep Arthur abreast on our progress at UC Davis. I reassured him that we would pay back the $500 loan and left. When we arrived back home I started filling out the application and registration papers. I was eager for registration week that started the next day.

I had until 3:00 p.m. to register and I decided to stop at Professor Summers's office to get his blessing and suggestions as to how many unit credits to take and the courses to choose for the coming quarter. I still had the great impression of him from my interview only two and half weeks earlier. I was at ease and relaxed when I found the door to his office open and him sitting by his desk browsing through the *Cal Aggies*, the UC Davis campus newspaper. "Come in Mr. Regev," he greeted me warmly. "How was the trip back to New York to pick up your wife and return Davis?" He pointed to the empty chair.

I told him about finding an apartment and that Batia started her first day of babysitting for a Jewish teacher living next to our apartment. "That is a great start," he said, "it looks like you're settling in and beat the system. Please, I need time to find the paperwork, can you come back in fifteen minutes? I should be ready by then." I went outside and caught up on my sun tan before I was about to become a bookworm borrowing inside textbooks.

When I returned to Dr. Summer's office I noticed a folder bearing my name sitting on his desk. "The department assigned me to be your academic advisor and guide you through your studies in our department," he said. "It will be a bit complicated because of your Limited Status admission restrictions but I'm sure it will be a temporary inconvenience," he promised me. "In order for us to remove your *Limited Status* restrictions, you must finish the quarter with a minimum average of 75%. Since this will be your first quarter studying and communicating in English, I suggest that you take only two courses, my Insect Morphology course and Dr. Norman Gary's Apiculture course dealing with the physiology of honeybees and their hive."

I left Dr. Summers and went to the registration office and handed them the completed forms. I listed the courses I was going to take during the fall quarter and the number of credits as per Dr. Summers' suggestions. The clerk glanced briefly through the documents and said that everything looked fine and asked for the $300 quarterly out of state tuition. I gave her the money and thought that I was finally finished with the registration phase, but I was wrong. The clerk consulted the folder they had on me and said, "although we have the results of the TOFEL English test you took in Israel, the University of California system has its own English proficiency criteria so you are required to take our test and pass it before the quarter starts." She scheduled the test the next day at 1:00 p.m. at the Foreign Languages Department. I took the test and passed it to their satisfaction and counted the days before school started.

I called to give my sister our address and informed her about starting my career as a UC Davis student. It had been almost two months since I sent packages from Israel to her address in Forest Hills. She still had not received them, but promised to forward the packages the moment they arrived.

My next concern was how to move around without a car, a necessity I could not afford. I had to a find a solution for commuting from my apartment to the campus and back. Getting groceries at the store was not an issue as I managed to walk the half mile from the apartment to Safeway. Once again, Ronny the veterinary student came to my rescue offering a pair of used lady's bicycles that someone dumped on the lawn of the Hillel House. "You can have them if you want," he told me, "but they were designed for tiny ladies and not for large males like you.

I told him I did not care as long as they would carry me from point A to point B. I would probably be the joke of the town when people saw a grownup person riding a tiny lady's bike. I accepted his offer and rode back to the apartment.

Batia started her job as Steven's babysitter and bonding with him. Sheila was extremely happy about choosing Batia. One day I stopped at Sheila's house to see Batia. Sheila happened to be there and notice me glued to the black and white TV when Walter Cronkite aired news from Israel. I told her that we had been missing news from our home. My jaw dropped when she gave us that TV set to take home. "It is for the two of you. Please take it as I have extra sets."

✡

The first day of the quarter finally arrived. I felt elated and remembered a similar moment in my life when, as a first grader, I walked to my first day of elementary school. However, starting my first day at UC Davis was different. All of a sudden, the cruel and insensitive statement Mr. Joshua Holtz, the principal of my elementary school, made to my parents kept echoing in my brain. "Your son Shmuel is a *gornisht* (good for nothing) so better enroll him in a vocational school so at least he will learn something useful." *Sorry Mr. Holtz,* I told myself while I rode my lady's bike, *See, we didn't listen to your advice and I will prove you wrong.* I tasted the sweetness of revenge.

Dr. Summers was in the classroom when I entered. He shook my hand and asked how I managed to find my way through the labyrinth of the registration process. I told him it was not too difficult but I didn't expect the extra English proficiency test. Then he pointed to an empty seat in the front row next to his podium and said, "This will be your permanent seat while you attend my class this quarter and please save the one next to you for Guillermo."

"Who is Guillermo?" I asked Dr. Summers.

"He is a foreign student from Venezuela and since my class is the first class both of you are taking in English, I insist that you sit close to the podium. It will help me keep an eye on you so I don't lose you during my lecture because of the language barrier."

I thanked him for his concern for us. I took my seat and looked around to familiarize myself with the new surroundings. I counted twenty students, none of them looked foreign. And then Guillermo entered the classroom, and stopped to greet Dr. Summer. It was obvious the two had met before.

"Guillermo, I would like you to meet Mr. Sam Regev a native of Israel and a new student at UC Davis, just like you. I want the two of you to sit next to me for the entire course so I can monitor your comprehension during my lecture. And please don't stress yourselves over the language barrier. I will make sure it won't stand in your way." I shook Guillermo's hand.

Dr. Summers started the class describing his expectations: coming to class prepared and doing the homework assignments. He sounded very flexible and accommodating, unlike some of my teachers at Tel Aviv University. Dr. Summers was assigned to be the advisor for both Guillermo and me. Although both of us were foreigners and far away from home, Guillermo was much better off than me. To begin with, he was an official employee of the Venezuelan government sent by their Department of Agriculture to get a master's degree from UC Davis. His tuition, apartment and living expenses were paid by his government on top of his monthly salary that was wired to his bank account in Davis. *What a lucky guy*, I thought. *Your only work is to study."* Although he was from Venezuela and spoke Spanish, he looked perhaps Inca with darker skin, and facial features like I saw on documentaries coming from that part of the world. He had a friendly personality and we became good friends.

Dr. Summers tested our knowledge through biweekly tests that covered the material he taught during that period, instead of taking one long final exam at the end of the quarter. The final grade was comprised of the average grades of these biweekly tests. It was difficult to memorize the insect morphology, especially for foreign students like Guillermo and me. Moreover, the financial burden of *Limited Status* forced me to study and pass all exams with flying colors so that I could be removed from the restrictions.

My efforts paid off as I finished my first biweekly test with a straight A. Guillermo flunked the test and got panicky. Dr. Summers was aware that Guillermo knew the material well but failed because of the language barrier and the stress was too much for him to overcome. To help him, Dr. Summers suggested that Guillermo answer in Spanish and his answers would translated by colleagues fluent in both English and Spanish. Guillermo agreed to retake the test during lunch time on Friday. Sadly enough, it did not work. He got so stressed before the test, he was taken to the campus hospital, suffering from a nervous breakdown. I never saw him again as he returned to Venezuela, leaving his empty seat next to me. It made Dr. Summers very sad as well and demonstrated once again how he cared for his students

I did well in Dr. Gary's Apiculture course by simply burying myself in the textbook and working hard to get an A on his biweekly exams. Dr. Gary's classes were very interesting, especially the social structure of the beehive, the division of labor and tasks among the individual bees in the hive. The presence of a queen in the hive determines the wellbeing of the hive. Dr. Gary had a great personality as well, which made taking his class a pleasant experience.

Dr. Summers's request that I sit by his podium turned out to be a non-issue as everything went smoothly. However, sitting in that spot and getting A's on tests allowed superstition to take hold on me. I might flunk if I moved from that spot. Sitting there also exposed me to Dr. Summers's sharp eyes and inquisitive mind. One day after dismissing the class, he stopped by my seat and gave me his famous eye wink and said to me, "Sam I noticed that you were taking notes during my class. What were those strange characters you were using?"

I told him that I was taking notes in Hebrew. "These characters have been used for at least 2000 years."

"But you were writing from *right to left*."

Now it was my turn to teach Dr. Summers. I explained that Hebrew is written and read from *right to left*. In biblical times, Hebrew was engraved into stone using chisel and hammer. I showed him the fonts on a page from the Israeli newspaper I picked up at the Hillel House. "Hebrew characters were designed as simple straight lines to make it easier to chisel into the flat hard stone. The right to left direction is because most people are right-handed making it easier to hold the hammer in their right hand and the chisel in the left hand while carving the letters."

"Gee, I did not know that. There is always something new for me to learn," he said in a jovial tone so I felt at ease to describe to him how difficult it was to be a foreign student.

"Dr. Summers, when you teach the class I hear what you say in English, and my brain translates into Hebrew as close as possible to what you meant and then I have to comprehend your message. If I need to respond, my brain starts to formulate an answer and translates it into English as close as possible to what I mean to say. This convoluted process must be done as fast as possible to prevent you from waiting too long for my reply. That's why I'm almost always among the last students to finish exams."

It felt like a long sermon on my part and as if a big boulder rolled off my chest when he said, "Don't worry Sam, you are doing great. Thanks for sharing this information with me."

A few more weeks passed by and our packages from Israel had not arrived. When fall season began I had only three presentable shirts and pants to wear. And then the season's first rain poured while I rode my tiny lady's bike. My white dress shirt and jeans stuck to my body as if I just finished swimming ten laps in an Olympic swimming pool with my clothes on. Before going to Dr. Gary's Apiculture class, I went to the men's room removed my clothes and wrung them the best I could. I tried to enter the classroom unnoticed and took a seat at the very back of the classroom. A student who knew me from Dr. Summers class approached and asked me if I would be able to last through the entire one hour lecture soaked like that. I gave him the same reply popular in Israel for people in a similar situation and said "Don't you worry, I'm not made of sugar and won't dissolve."

When the class was over I stopped at the International Students Office to use their phone to call my sister about the packages. Linda, the secretary, said "Poor Sam, I saw you riding on your bike in the middle of the heavy rain and felt sorry for you. How can I help you?" I explained to her the situation with the packages with our clothes which I mailed from Israel two months prior. Linda placed a call to my sister in Forest Hill to check on the status of the shipment. I offered to pay for the call but she refused claiming that they were there to assist me and my fellow foreign students. My sister came through the phone speakers telling me that the shipment arrived and she forwarded the packages to my Davis address. I told her that we never got them. A few months later I got a letter from my parents telling me that the US Postal Services shipped them back to Israel instead to my address in Davis. Nonetheless, there was still a happy ending. Dr. Schechter, the fiancé of Batia's boss had shirts and pants to spare and they fit me perfectly. He gave me enough cloths to last until the end of time.

Batia and I did not have much of a social life. I spent every minute studying and preparing for the biweekly tests as well as helping her, occasionally at Sheila's house. Sheila had spread the word on what a great a babysitter Batia was and that I accompanied her whenever she had babysitting jobs in the evenings and late at night. Other families started calling her asking for her service. Most of the callers were professors on campus.

Occasionally, I took a short break from studying and we accepted Ronny's offer to join him on his weekly grocery shopping at the members-only Gemco shopping club in Sacramento. It was much cheaper than the stores in Davis. You had to be a member so Batia and I joined. I remember buying a loaf of sliced bread for 19 cents and Ronny filling his car with gasoline to the tune of 19 cent a gallon. Wow! Those were the days. Unfortunately gone forever.

It was nice of Ronny to take us on his pilgrimage to the Gemco. Still, not having a car of our own made us very uncomfortable and dependent on someone else's good will. At times it felt as if we were imposing on him but we were too poor to even think about buying a car. I was pinching pennies and kept track of how much Batia earned each day. I ran a small notebook which we nicknamed, *The Bible* where I recorded every penny earned and every penny spent. Our total expenses, including the $100 apartment rental, was $180.41. The many hours of babysitting brought in $224.25, a whopping earning of $43.83 in the black.

Being a graduate of the *t'zena* (Hebrew for austerity) era in Israel following the War for Independence, helped me to live as frugally as possible. Now, living in Davis I relived food shortages. There were days when I visited Batia at work, she opened the refrigerator and said, "Look what I found in the garbage can outside. It was not there yesterday."

She pulled out raw ground meet still wrapped in its original saran plastic cover. On some occasions the package was opened and partially used. I took the meat to our apartment and mixed it with enough oat meal to extend it for the entire week in the form of hamburger patties or meat loaves made mostly of oat meal with a token amount of meat. This creativity became more complicated on those Monday mornings when Batia found the hamburger in the garbage can outside. Was the meat tossed there on Friday after she left for the weekend or was it dumbed there on Saturday or Sunday? There was the risk of poisoning ourselves.

I devised a bioassay to check the safety of the meat. I immersed the meat in a pot of water and placed it in our refrigerator for few hours. I watched closely for gas bubbles coming out of the raw meat. I decided to take the risk and cook it very well if I saw no bubbles. If I did see gas bubbles released or if the meat smelled funky, I tossed it into the garbage bin outside. We watched for any stomach discomfort and hoped we would not end up at the campus hospital with food poisoning. Luckily, both Batia and I are still around, fifty-two years later. Evidently my *scientific method* worked. Nonetheless, I discourage adopting the method.

✡

Although burying myself in textbooks, lecture notes keeping my mind occupied with academic chores, I could not escape the homesick moments that led me to question whether or not I made the right choice, moving so far away from my beloved home, family and country. The geographical distance from my parents, Batia's mom, and my close friends brought deep homesick feelings. I started to miss the closeness of the Israelis, and culture of the Israeli society. If I were to describe, in one sentence, the essence of Israeli society, I would say that, on regular days they could be mean and chew each other apart, but when their tiny country faced external threats and tough times, this inner bickering evaporated and the country transformed into one big family.

Unlike the gigantic mass of land of the United State physically separating families, Israeli families stay in close proximity due to the tiny size of Israel. So every Jewish holiday, or simple family events such as birthdays, become an excuse to get together and have a happy family reunion. I was deprived of these precious moments by my own decision to land myself in UC Davis.

Another striking difference between the two countries is that whereas there are plenty of Jewish holidays that are cause for family reunions throughout the year, American family holidays are mainly *Thanksgiving* and *Christmas*.

One day, while shopping at the Safeway, I noticed an employee stocking huge bags of frozen turkey in the open freezer so I asked him what was going on. He looked at me as if I just landed from mars, "It's Thanksgiving time, man." I didn't want to show my ignorance by asking what Thanksgiving was and its association with turkey, so I just said, "Of course, I almost forgot," and left.

Our apartment was a block away from the city public park and the city library next to it so I stopped at the library to familiarize myself with the Thanksgiving holiday. A lady at the reference books section asked me what I was looking for. I told her that I was a new comer to UC Davis who knew nothing about Thanksgiving. She introduced herself as Mrs. Assardo a volunteer at the city library while her husband taught Spanish at the Foreign Languages Department. Most of her volunteering time was spent helping Spanish-speaking foreign students become more proficient in English. She described Thanksgiving to me.

"We live a few blocks from the library and would like to invite you and your wife to a Thanksgiving dinner at our house. Please talk to your wife about it and bring a good appetite with you. We'll have a huge turkey and I hate to eat leftovers weeks after the holiday is over." I gladly accepted her invitation.

The Thanksgiving feast with the Assardo family was very pleasant. By then I knew quite a bit about the holiday and the stories associated with it. I empathized with the *Mayflower* pilgrims landing in America and the harsh conditions they faced in their new surroundings. They would have perished if not for the help of the indigenous people.

I was puzzled as to why the turkey plays center stage on that holiday. One of my comrades in the paratroopers was a farmer who raised turkeys commercially and supplied the major supermarkets in Israel. He loathed that bird with a passion, telling me how stupid they were. Mr. Assardo started slicing the turkey's breast into thin slices with a long electric knife and I kept saying to myself, *Boy! These American are equipped with everything.* It was obvious he was skilled at slicing and had quite a few Thanksgiving dinners under his belt. The conversation at the table went very well although I did most of the talking since the Assardo's where Church-going Catholics and showed great interest in life in the *holy land* and how modern Israel was compared to its biblical past. That particular Thanksgiving dinner at the Assardo family presented Batia and I with the opportunity to be Israeli Ambassadors at large. I have no question in my mind that they enjoyed our company and we were glad they invited us to share Thanksgiving with them.

✡

Time flew by and it was our turn now to celebrate two major holidays, The Jewish New Year which fell on September 23, 1968 and *Yom Kippur* (the day of Atonement) that came ten days later. This time, the celebration was completely different from previous years. Now we were living in a different country, away from family and friends and surrounded by a Christian society that continued its daily life oblivious to the Jewish high holiday. It hit me hard to realize that the only place to really feel the essence of the Jewish culture, holidays and way of life was in Israel and to some extent, some dominantly Jewish neighborhoods in the diaspora.

On *Yom Kippur,* Jews are commanded to fast for twenty-four hours, depriving themselves of any food and water. They spend most of the time in the synagogue praying for forgiveness, atoning for the wrongdoings and disobeying God's commandments.

I remember going with my father to the neighborhood synagogue on *Yom Kippur* eve for the *Kol Nidrei* opening prayer. I also joined him the next morning and spent the time outside the synagogue with my friends while our fathers were inside participating in the *Yom Kippur* services and the *Yizkor* service honoring family members who passed away. It also observed the Jewish martyrs and victims murdered by the Nazis. Although my friends and I were still younger than *Bar Mitzvah* age (thirteen years old) thus not obligated to practice the Jewish laws, fasting on *Yom Kippur* included, we fasted and bragged about it. To earn the accolade of being a minor and fasting like the adults, we had to prove that we fasted. The acceptable proof of that was for us to stick out our tongue in front of the other kids, i.e. *the referees.* If the back of your tongue was white, you passed the test. If it was not white, you were considered a liar.

My first *Yom Kippur* outside Israel was shocking. For the UC Davis Jewish community, comprised mostly of progressive professors and professionals, it was acceptable to have the *Yom Kippur* service performed at one of the local churches whereas an orthodox Jew would rather die than pray a Jewish religious service inside a Christian church. And there I was inside a Christian church observing and hearing the progressive diaspora Jews of Davis chanting the *Kol Nidrei,* the solemnest prayer in Judaism, inside a local church with a huge cross hanging from the roof above our heads. I never attended any of their religious services again.

Christmas time and the end of academic quarter were fast approaching, forcing me to double my study sessions at the apartment. I had to finish final exams with the highest grade I could in order to convince professors Stafford, Judson and Summers that I was worthy of being a graduate student and get the *Limited Status* restrictions removed. I stayed at the apartment most of the time and studied unless it was absolutely necessary to be on campus. I thought that staying at home would provide me with the quite environment I needed for maximum concentration but this was not meant to be. Just the opposite. After Batia left for work I started studying for Dr. Summers final exam of the quarter. I cleared the dining table and spread my books and notebooks.

The dining area had a very wide window just above the lawn and the swimming pool. The pool was covered with heavy tarp for the fall and winter seasons. When I gazed through my window I saw Sam, the apartment manager, assembling a large plastic doll which I was not familiar with. I learned later on that the kitschy doll made of sturdy cheap plastic was Santa Clause. Sam checked that all the light bulbs inside Santa worked before asking his wife to help him hoist it to the roof of the swimming pool storage shack. Next, he anchored Santa with metal wires to the roof to prevent the wind from blowing Santa to the North Pole.

Sam made sure that a tape recorder played Christmas songs around the clock. Being a manger with a reputation for paying attention to the tiniest details and executing any job to perfection, he saw to it that the speakers would play at the right volume, meaning a loud distraction that ruined my concentration and prevented me from studying. I was not alone with that problem. Other foreign students living in the apartment complex faced the same problem as we all tried to prepare for final exams.

As the day of the final exams drew closer, my stress level skyrocketed. One morning, after Batia left for work and the Christmas music blasted from the swimming pool area, I reached my breaking point. I went to Sam's office, "What can I do for you, Mr. Regev?" he asked in his polite and soft voice.

I explained to him my situation and the absolute necessity for me to pass the final exams at the top of my class, otherwise I wouldn't be admitted to graduate school. "Playing the Christmas music around the clock and so loud, is a distraction for me. Is there any way to minimize it a bit?" I asked him politely. I expected him to be considerate and accommodating.

Suddenly his face turned red and the tone of his voice became hostile, "Listen to me Sir!" he shouted at me. "You don't like our Christmas songs, ah? What are you? A communist?" He continued to shout at me from the top of his lungs. "This music will be played until Christmas is over so get used to it, Sir. You are in America now and not Israel, so stop complaining," he said while turning the volume up even louder, showing me who was boss. I realized that it was a lost battle so I left without saying another word but promised myself to leave the apartment complex at the first opportunity.

I tried to study using ear plugs but that was not the best alternative. Unfortunately, for many years following this incident, I could not stand Christmas songs and the Christmas season. *Father Time* did his magic, the Christmas season doesn't bother me anymore. In fact, I'm glad to see how much happiness that music brings to little children and my Christian friends. Moreover, Batia loves the Christmas songs and I take my sweet revenge by telling my Christian friends that most of the great iconic Christmas songs in American were written by Jews. For example, the song "White Christmas" was written by the American Jewish song writer Irving Berlin.

The days of the final exams came at last. I took the tests and I read my answers several times before submitting them. The tests were in the essay format and not multiple choice. Although I had to write my answers in English I preferred the essay format as it was the type of tests they used in Tel Aviv University where I studied. There was no question in my mind that I would make numerous spelling and grammar mistakes so I jokingly forewarned, both Dr. Summers and Dr. Gary that I would answer their test questions using *Shakespearean English* and *ancient spelling*. Since the school break between fall and winter quarters started right after the final exams I gave them a stamped postcard with my address to send my final grade. Naturally, I was apprehensive for a few days until I saw the letter A on both cards. Dr. Summers took the extra effort and jotted a very large, "Great Job, Sam," to boost my morale. It made my day.

Now, that the pressure to pass my first academic quarter at UC Davis with a straight A GPA was gone, I allowed myself to relax a little and contemplate how to remove the Limited Status. Although I was indebted to the three professors who assigned the *Limited Status* as their only way to circumvent the rejection letter, I felt it would be beneficial to fight their decision. Since Dr. Summers was assigned as my advisor, I asked him to reconvene his three colleague and have a meeting with me to discuss my request to remove the *Limited Status* and he agreed.

I worked hard on what to say to the three professors who held my academic future in their hands. How could I convince them to lift the restrictions. I practiced my sermon and got a huge boost in that direction a few days before the scheduled meeting, when an official letter arrived congratulating me on making the Dean's list, Figure 8.4. I was mighty proud as I thought it would help convince the three professors to grant my request to be a bona fide graduate student.

UNIVERSITY OF CALIFORNIA, DAVIS

KELEY · DAVIS · IRVINE · LOS ANGELES · RIVERSIDE · SAN DIEGO · SAN FRANCISCO   SANTA BARBARA · SANTA CRUZ

COLLEGE OF AGRICULTURAL AND
   ENVIRONMENTAL SCIENCES
AGRICULTURAL EXPERIMENT STATION
OFFICE OF THE DEAN AND ASSOCIATE DIRECTOR·

DAVIS, CALIFORNIA 95616

January 9, 1969

Mr. Shmuel Regev
1224 F Street, Apt. #9
Davis, California

Dear Shmuel:

    Dean Meyer and I congratulate you on your excellent
scholastic achievement for the past quarter. Your name
has been placed on the Dean's Honor List of the College
of Agricultural and Environmental Sciences.

    We hope you will continue to excel in your studies,
and will prepare yourself for future leadership.

                Sincerely yours,

                T. A. Nickerson
                Associate Dean
                College of Agricultural an
                Environmental Sciences

TAN:ns:ym

Figure 8.4 Dean's List letter from T.A. Nickerson

✡

My scheduled meeting with the three professors was held at Dr. Stafford's office, same as before. Dr. Stafford was his usual business-like self. Dr. Judson was smiling at me while Dr. Summers honored me with his, now famous, smile and eye wink. I was 100% sure that it would be my lucky day but it wasn't. I recited my sermon about being a serious student deserving to be admitted to the graduate college and asked them to remove *Limited Status* restrictions. "My grades prove my point," I told them while presenting the letter from the Dean.

Dr. Stafford, who was the spokesperson for the three said, "Sam, we would like to congratulate you on your achievement thus far but you must realize that one quarter is not enough for us to change your status."

It hit me like a thunderbolt and I was silent for a while before asking them what their expectations were.

"Well," Dr. Stafford replied, "We would like you to enroll for another quarter, still as a *Limited Status* student and see if your final grades next quarter warrant changing your academic status. You will need to stay on your toes next quarter as it will be more difficult for you to repeat your success from last quarter."

I did not know how to read his statement. Was it advice or a warning?

To be honest, I deeply resented their decision to keep me on the *Limited Status* for another quarter. I found it demeaning especially since I already earned a Bachelor's degree in Biology from Tel Aviv University.

The three professors who decided to keep me on *Limited Status* caused a harsh financial situation. My perfect 4.0 GPA entitled me to a tuition waiver had I been considered a graduate student. It forced me to scramble for an additional $300 for the upcoming winter quarter tuition.

Frustration set in but then I remembered Dr. Summers' warm attitude and compassion towards me since the first day we met, so I mellowed and moved on. I chose my courses for the winter quarter, registered and paid the tuition. I prayed that I could find second-hand textbooks at the student bookstore. I also prayed that Batia would be swamped with extra babysitting hours to help us keep our heads above water.

Chapter 9

UC Davis: Part 2

Finishing my first quarter (fall 1968) at UC Davis with a straight A average and having my name placed on the Dean's List boosted my morale. Yet it was a bittersweet feeling for me because the three professors did not take me off the *Limited Status* restrictions. I had no other option but to go along with it, albeit grudgingly. I turned in my registration papers and paid the $300 out of-state tuition, which was difficult emotionally as well as financially.

The Christmas season and the Christmas break at UC Davis were around the corner. The speakers on the roof of the storage shack by the swimming pool were playing Christmas songs at full blast. I did not wish to provide Sam, the apartment manager, with another opportunity to call me a communist, so I let it go. Besides, I had a more serious issues to deal with.

Our USA B-2 tourist visa, issued at the American Embassy in Tel Aviv on July 23, 1968, would expire on July 23, 1969. We entered the USA on August 21, 1968 and I became student shortly after that. I needed to change my status to *student*. It started a nightmare that Batia and I hadn't bargained for.

Upon starting the winter quarter, I wrote a letter to the immigration and naturalization office in Sacramento requesting a change from tourists to student and spouse of a student. It was well into the winter quarter and I still had not heard from the immigration office. Then, two separate letters finally came while I was in the midst of preparing for my first quarter final exam. Each of us received an official summons to appear, in person, for a separate interrogation by Inspector Jones (not his real name). The interrogation dates and time were not negotiable so I had to drop my preparations for the final exam and show up at inspector Jones' office on that day. Ronny, the Israeli Veterinary student drove us there as we did not own a car.

The meeting with Inspector Jones was our first encounter, ever, with the US Federal authorities. I showed him our passports and my UC Davis Student ID card. Inspector Jones gave us a brief description of the process. Each of us would be interrogated, under oath. He started with me first and browsed through the application forms I sent prior to our appointment. Most of the answers to his questions were already included in my application. As the interrogation continued, his attention shifted to my financial situation and my ability to support myself as a full time *out-of-state* student. He was very thorough in his questions about the financial situation, yet very polite and courteous. Then he summoned Batia for her interrogation so I left the room. She too was interrogated about our financial situation. When he finished the interviews, he gave us back our passports and told us to return to Davis and wait for an official letter. We shook hands and left feeling that we made a good impression.

I resumed my studies for the final exams but I found it very difficult to concentrate after Inspector Jones's interrogation. His focus on our financial situation made me apprehensive. And sure enough, a few days later we received a letter from him requesting names of US citizens willing to attest to the fact that we could support ourselves financially while studying at UC Davis. I called Linda at the office of the International Student Services seeking her advice on the matter. She called back with the advice of their legal expert urging us to provide inspector Jones with the names. It was time consuming and took me away from my studies.

I racked my brain thinking of who to contact and chose Batia's boss, Sheila and Mr. Herman Auerbach, a high school friend of my mother from the time they both grew up in Poland. He became a successful HVAC engineer. I provided Inspector Jones with their names, addresses and phone numbers. I also gave him Dr. Arthur Ganz's name, after getting his consent to do so,

I felt that everything was under control. A few days later I received a letter from Dr. Ganz saying among other things that:

>.....*Don't think I forgot your nice letter of October 14, but it took me some time to find out what you need and how to proceed. Now, I have to discuss your case with the competent Department of the Immigration Services, but in order to do that I need either the original letter they sent you or a copy of the letter. Then, I have to go there once more and I'll keep you posted about the outcome."*

From our first experience with Dr. Arthur Ganz and the dinner at his house a few weeks earlier, I knew that he was a man of his word and would contact the immigration office on our behalf to resolve the visa problem. After all, he was the man who lent us $500, interest free, an open loan without a payoff date.

On November 11, 1968 a letter arrived, telling us he contacted the immigration office and got the information they needed with regard to our case. The letter stated, among other things:

> *"Dear Samuel and Batia:*
> *Referring to our yesterday's phone conversation, I send you the enclosed:*
> *Letter of the US Department of Justice*
> *Letter of Guaranty of ourselves for Sacramento.*
> *Hoping that this will meet the evidence of your qualification they asked for.*
> *Please let us know about the outcome."*

The letter to the immigration office letter was signed by Arthur and his wife. (Figure 9.1)

I was extremely happy to receive his letter which arrived at the time when I was fully immersed in my books and lecture notes studying for the quarter final exams. I mailed a short letter to the immigration and naturalization office in San Francisco informing them that Dr. Arthur Ganz was involved. I included a copy of his guarantee letter on our behalf which stated very clearly, that Batia and I would not become a *public charge.*

Arthur's guarantee letter reduced the stress somewhat. Unfortunately, his letter turned out to be a false peace of mind as I received another letter from the immigration office dated January 8, 1969, indicating that it was not going to be smooth sailing for us as it was more of an ultimatum than a letter from Assistant District Director for Deportation. (Figure 9.2)

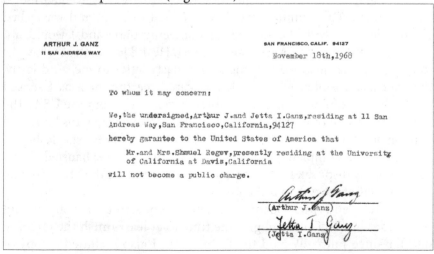

Figure 9.1 Letter from Arthur Ganz

```
                                                          PLEASE REFER TO THIS FILE NUMBER

        UNITED STATES DEPARTMENT OF JUSTICE          A18 501 494; 495
       IMMIGRATION AND NATURALIZATION SERVICE
                  630 Sansome Street
               San Francisco, California
                   January 8, 1969


       Mr. & Mrs. Shmuel REGEV
       1125 "H" Street, Apt. 29
       Davis, California 95616

       Dear Mr. & Mrs. REGEV:

            With reference to your letter of December 30,
       1968, you are granted until February 1, 1969 in
       which to voluntarily depart from the United States.

                          Sincerely,



                          G.C. Cochran
                          Assistant District Director
                          for Deportation
```

Figure 9. 2 Letter from G.C. Cochran

Mr. Cochran's letter was very disturbing, came at the wrong time and posed an extremely difficult situation. To begin with, it came when I was just starting my second quarter at the university. The letter forced me to drop my studies and devote all my time and energy to dealing with the Immigration and Naturalization bureaucrats in San Francisco. Secondly, up to that point in the application process, the immigration office never specified what exactly they wanted me to provide them. Dr. Arthur Ganz already talked to them and was asked to provide them with the affidavit guaranteeing Batia and I would not become a burden on the American taxpayer. He did just that, so what was the problem that justified sending such a nasty letter to me. And lastly, the conclusion sentence of that letter scared me the most as I sensed the likelihood of Batia and I being forcibly removed from the USA. The unpleasant vision of immigration marshals with their big guns knocking hard on our door with the handcuffs ready to put on our wrists, flashed in my mind. I felt completely helpless knowing that I had exhausted all the options at my disposal. I was too poor to even entertain the idea of hiring an immigration lawyer to plead my case.

I did send Mr. Cochran a letter requesting that he would reconsider his decision and give me time to at least finish the ongoing quarter since I already paid the full tuition. I also included a copy of the affidavit guarantee that Arthur Ganz and his wife gave them. I attached the letter stating that my name was listed on the Dean's List. I hoped it would convince Mr. Cochran that I was a serious student who came to the USA to advance my education and not for any other reason.

I continued to study for the final exams despite the difficulty to concentrate. I managed to finish the winter with one A and two Bs instead of the straight A I hoped for. My total GPA for the two quarters was 3.6, out of the 4.0 possible. My mind was wandering wildly as I expected a reply letter from Mr. Cochran to arrive any day, but it did not show up in my mailbox. And then the February 1, 1969 deadline for me to leave the USA voluntarily came, and still I had not heard from the immigration office. Their marshals did not come knocking on our door either. I began to suspect that perhaps the *big wigs* at the immigration office were still debating among themselves on how to handle my case. I decided to register for the spring quarter despite the fact that I still did not have a student visa.

After registering for the spring quarter I met with Dr. Summers to discuss my future curriculum. I reminded him of their decision to keep me on a *Limited Status* restrictions for winter quarter. Their reasoning for doing that was to evaluate my academic capability because I was a foreign student. At least this was what they told me. I opened my discussion with Dr. Summers and said, "I just finished the quarter as *Limited Status* student as per your decision. I feel that my grades and being placed on the Dean's List warrants taking me off the *Limited Status* restrictions." I was surprised to be so assertive and I hoped he did not take me as being *fresh*. "Congratulation, Sam," he replied, "we already received official copies of your grades and removed the *Limited Status* restrictions. Welcome to the UC Davis Graduate School." Dr. Summers' words were music to my ears. From that moment on, I would be allowed to apply for the college tuition waiver if my quarterly GPA exceed 3.5. I informed Dr. Summers that I was still in limbo as to when the immigration office would grant me the visa change.

I continued chugging along as a graduate student. It was my third quarter at UC Davis but still no word from the Immigration and Naturalization office. I convinced myself that those people were not in a big rush to review my case and probably had larger potatoes to fry. And then, two certified, requested signature, letters dated May 26, 1969 arrived. One addressed to me, the other to Batia. Both letters were Notice Of Denial explaining why the immigration office turned down our application for a visa change. (Figure 9.3)

UNITED STATES DEPARTMENT OF JUSTICE
Immigration and Naturalization Service
San Francisco, California

REFER TO THIS FILE NO.

A18 501 494

Date: MAY 26 1969

Shmuel Regev
1125 "H" Street, Apt. 26
Davis, California 95616

NOTICE OF DENIAL

Your Application for change of nonimmigrant status to student

_____ has been denied for the following reasons:

Although you have presented affidavits of support from a Sheila B. Weiner
and a Herman L. Auerbach, you have testified under oath that you receive
no support from either person. You testified that your entire source of
income in the United States is through your wife's employment as a baby
sitter. The Immigration and Nationality laws do not permit a visitor or
the spouse of a student to undertake employment in the United States.
Consequently, you have not shown that you possess the financial means to
support yourself and your wife while you are pursuing a course of study
in the United States.

If you desire to appeal this decision, you may do so. Your notice of appeal must be
filed within 15 days from the date of this notice. If no appeal is filed within the time allowed, this decision is final. Appeal in your case may be made to:

☐ Board of Immigration Appeals in Washington, D. C., on the enclosed Form I-290 A.

☒ Regional Commissioner on the enclosed Form I-290 B.

If an appeal is desired, the Notice of Appeal shall be executed and filed with this office,
together with a fee of $10. A brief or other written statement in support of your appeal may
be submitted with the Notice of Appeal.

Any question which you may have will be answered by the local immigration office
nearest your residence, or at the address shown in the heading to this letter.

Sincerely yours,

CERTIFIED MAIL
RETURN RECEIPT REQUESTED
Enclosure(s)   Acting District Director

Form I - 292
(Rev. 1-10-66)

Figure 9.3 Notice of denial

Batia's letter was identical except for the following paragraph:

> *You were admitted to the United States as a visitor
> for pleasure on August 11, 1968. A change from one
> nonimmigrant classification to another nonimmigrant
> classification may be granted in certain instances to an
> alien who has been lawfully admitted to the United States
> as a nonimmigrant and has continued to maintain that*

*status. Your husband has testified under oath that his only
means of support as a student in the United State is through
your employment as a babysitter. A nonimmigrant visitor
to the United State is not permitted to accept employment.
Consequently, you have failed to maintain the status to
which you were admitted and are statutorily ineligible for
change of nonimmigrant classification.*

Receiving these letters was by far the lowest point of our lives
in Davis and the seriousness of our situation began donning on me.
I realized I was running out of options. It negatively affected my
concentration. The nightmarish visions of US immigration marshals
coming to our apartment to forcibly deport us, started to resurface and
distracted me from my studies even more. I knew that this time I must
recruit the big wigs at the UC Davis Office of the International Student
Services to help me.

I wasted no time and rushed there with copies of the two letters
and showed them to Linda. She glanced through the letters and said,
"Sam this is a very serious matter so I need to delegate it to my boss."
She scheduled an urgent appointment with her boss for the following
day. "Let me make a copy of the letters. Please make sure to bring with
you all your past correspondences with the immigration officials in
San Francisco," she said before I left their office.

The next day I met Linda's boss, Mr. John A. Seeley, The Associate
Dean of the UC Davis International Student Services to discuss my
situation and the options, if any, to resolve it. Mr. Seeley was very
sympathetic to our plight and eager to help. He came to our meeting
well prepared. When I saw copies of my official transcript laying on his
desk, I got the hunch that he would use my scholastic achievement as a
bargaining chip dealing with immigration on my behalf. I apologized
for the fact that Batia did not join us as we could not afford her taking
time off from work. I sensed the urgency of the matter when he said
to me, "Sam, the officer who issued the Notice of Denial to you and
Batia pushed it aggressively to make it difficult for you to comply as he
granted you only fifteen days to appeal his decision, let alone providing
supporting evidence to back your appeal. I believe it was intentional,
to make it difficult for you to comply and easier for him to deport both
of you. His timing is also problematic for me because he deliberately
chose sending these denial letters knowing full well that you are in
the midst of the quarter final exams. It is urgent that you request an
extension for more time to produce the documents supporting your
appeal because the fifteen days he gave you won't be enough. You must
send your letter as a certified, return signature requested."

John Seeley read the letters again and said, "It is very clear that the San Francisco immigration people are fixated on your lack of financial resources so we need to work on changing their mindset. Pardon my asking this, but do you have an active bank account in Davis?"

"No, we don't," I replied. "Let's face it, the sixty cents per hour Batia earns for babysitting does not leave much to open one."

"I fully understand your dire financial situation but there is no other way around it," he said. "You must open a checking account in Davis, otherwise the immigration office in San Francisco won't budge. I am 100% convinced. You need to open that account *now!*" I heard the urgency in his voice. "Based on my past experience with the immigration people, an account with a balance close to $5,000 *at all times* may move them in your favor."

His candid assessment of my situation shocked me to the core. "How do you expect me to come up with that much money, other than taking it at gunpoint from someone?" I exclaimed, utterly frustrated.

"I don't expect you to do that yet, both Linda and your professors attested that you are a smart guy so I trust that you will be creative and find a way to get $5,000 into a new bank account in Davis," he said and switched his attention to Batia's Notice of Denial letter. "She should send a separate certified, return signature requested letter requesting an extension as well. I intend to argue and try to convince the immigration officials that her acceptance of the babysitting job offer was done innocently and not an intentional violation of the immigration law," he concluded. "You have lots of work cut out for you so better start tackling it now because time is really of the essence. Good luck and keep me posted," he said. I left his office and went home to write the letters he suggested.

I mailed our letters on June 18, 1969 and received the immigration office reply on June 25, 1969. (Figure 9.4.)

That task was the easy part. How in the world was I going to get $5,000 to deposit in a new bank account in Davis? That hurdle looked insurmountable. I was tempted, at first, to call Dr. Arthur Ganz for a $5,000 loan in addition to the $500 he already loaned us two months earlier but I loathed to impose on him again so I called my sister instead. "Be creative," that's what John Seeley urged me to be so I let the creative side of my brain churn a plan that should work, provided that my sister would go along and the immigration offices would buy it.

I called my sister, described the problem and asked for her collaboration. "I need $5,000 in my local bank account," I told her, "otherwise I stand no chance of the immigration people changing my tourist visa and let me continue to stay under a student status," I tried to impress on her.

PLEASE REFER TO THIS FILE NUMBER

UNITED STATES DEPARTMENT OF JUSTICE

IMMIGRATION AND NATURALIZATION SERVICE

A18 501 494
A18 501 495

Sacramento, California
June 25, 1969

Mr. Shmuel Regev
1125 "H" Street, Apt. 26
Davis, California 95616

Dear Mr. Regev:

Reference is made to your letter of June 18, 1969 in which
you request an extension of time to secure documents to
support your brief in appeal of the denial of your application for change of nonimmigrant status.

You are hereby accorded until July 5, 1969 to submit such
a brief. If you fail to submit the brief by that date your
appeal will be forwarded to the Regional Commissioner for
his decision based upon the existing evidence.

Sincerely,

George T. Patterson
Officer in Charge

CERTIFIED MAIL
RETURN RECEIPT REQUESTED

Figure 9.4 Letter from George Patterson

"Are you out of your mind?" she raised her voice at me, "$5,000 is a huge sum of money for us to give."

I was afraid she would hang up on me right there. "Listen, Chaya," I said, "I am not asking for a loan, what I need is just to show the immigration office that my bank account at Davis has a balance of around $5,000 at all times. If you send me a $5,000 check, I will park it my bank account. I promise not to touch that money. It would make no difference for you where you keep that money, either in your Forest Hills bank account or mine. I promise not touch it." I gave her my word to send the $5,000 back, with interest the minute I got my student visa. I gave a sigh of relief when she finally agreed to send a $3,500 check claiming that $5,000 would create a liquidity problem for them. I thanked her and promised to put the money in a separate saving account to maximize the interest she would get. I made sure to send her copies of the monthly bank statements to verify that her money was safe.

I wasted no time when the check arrived and rushed to the Bank of America branch near campus and opened a joint checking account where we deposited the cash Batia was getting from her babysitting job. I opened a separated saving account and deposited my sister's check. I waited few days for the check to clear and stopped at the bank to request a written statement on their letterhead to the effect that we had accounts with them. (Figure 9.5)

I rushed to see Mr. John Seeley upon receiving the letter from the bank. It was a close call because I received it on July 2, 1969, three days before my deadline to submit my brief and the documents supporting my case. When I arrived at his office, he was already dictating to Linda a letter on my behalf to the immigration regional commissioner in San Francisco. John stopped dictating and took a look at the letter from the bank. He glanced at it briefly, nodded with his head in approval and added it to the documents I provided earlier. "Have a seat and let me explain what I have been doing while you were working on opening a bank account." I will be brief as this letter must be typed and mailed today in order to meet the deadline. I was confident you would find a way to get the money, so I took the initiative and talked to Dr. Summers about the problem you are facing. He was shocked to hear about the denial letters and professed not wanting to lose you as his student. As you know by now that Dr. Summers is approaching retirement and considers you his last graduate student before ending his long and lustrous academic career. He gave me all the information

Figure 9.5 Letter from Bank of America

I needed along with his opinion of you and your academic capability. In fact, I am incorporating that information into the letter I am writing to the regional commissioner. It will be sent today as a certified, return signature requested mail. I hoped that this time they will grant you and Batia student and student spouse status." I thanked John for his excellent job advocating my case and left.

As promised, John Seeley's letter was finished and sent that day. It was written on official UC Davis, Office of International Student Services letterhead and included all the documents supporting my appeal. John gave me a copy of the letter, it sounded convincing. I also hoped that my official transcript would convince the commissioner that I was a serious student and not merely someone who entered the USA for the sole purpose of making money. (Figure 9.6)

A week later I stopped at Linda's office to check if they had heard anything new about my appeal. "We have not heard from them yet but I know that they received our letter. Here is the signed signature requested card that went with John's letter. At least we know for sure that the immigration people received your appeal before the deadline," she said and forewarned me that it might take a few more days before I would hear from them. "So what should I do in the meantime?" I asked. "

"Just continue your business as usual, being a student and going about your life as if your appeal for a change of status was granted," she replied and that's exactly what I did.

The good news from John Seeley's office came a few weeks later, informing me that our appeal for change of status was approved and the case and the files were transferred to Inspector Jones of the Sacramento branch. As a reminder, it was Inspector Jones who initially interviewed us and started the commotion that almost ended up getting us deported. John Seeley contacted Dr. Summers with the great news and thanked him for his testimonial about me and my academic achievement. John let him know that he included it in his letter and it helped my case tremendously. I trust that Dr. Summers was relieved, realizing that he was not going to lose me, Sam from Israel, his last Ph.D. graduate student before retiring. I promised him that I would carry out exemplary research and Ph.D. dissertation and present it to him as a retirement gift. I could tell from the glee in his eyes that he believed whole heartedly that I meant each word of my promise.

The change of status from tourist to student did not take us out of the woods, by any means, as it did not resolve our dire financial situation. I was not allowed to work and neither was Batia. Nonetheless, we needed to continue her babysitting job knowing full well that she was breaking the immigration laws.

UNIVERSITY OF CALIFORNIA, DAVIS

BERKELEY · DAVIS · IRVINE · LOS ANGELES · RIVERSIDE · SAN DIEGO · SAN FRANCISCO   SANTA BARBARA · SANTA CRUZ

OFFICE OF
INTERNATIONAL STUDENT SERVICES   DAVIS, CALIFORNIA   95616

July 2, 1969

Regional Commissioner
United States Department of Justice
Immigration & Naturalization Service
San Francisco, California

                                        Re: Shmuel Regev   A18 501 494
                                              Batia Regev   A18 501 495

Dear Sir:

This letter strongly supports the appeal of Mr. and Mrs. Shmuel Regev for
changes of non-immigrant status to that of student and student spouse.

Dr. Francis M. Summer, Mr. Regev's academic adviser, informs me that he
is beginning to demonstrate splendid capability in scholarship. Further,
his adviser indicates that Israel and other countries in the Middle East
are in short supply in individuals trained in Acarology. A few such
specialists are needed when countries are concerned with development agriculture of public health alterations. Mr. Regev is currently enrolled in
a Master's degree program and hopes to pursue a Ph.D. degree. His speciali-
zation within the general field of Entomology is Acarology.

I have reviewed the briefs both Mr. and Mrs. Regev are submitting for your
consideration. The statements are true to the best of my knowledge.
Mrs. Regev's unawareness of immigration law related to employment and the
apparent misinformation she received regarding this provided the background
for her acceptance of babysitting employment. She did not intentionally
violate the law.

The resources available to the Regevs are clearly identified and substantiated in their briefs and file. In my judgment based upon our estimates
of the costs related to an education at the University of California at
Davis, the resources available to the Regevs are sufficient to meet their
expenses.

I seek your discretion in acting favorably upon these appeals. It seems
the broader moral aspects of the case which relate to the ability of this
fine student to continue his education in a needed field of training while
his wife remains with him and his desire to return to Israel outweigh the

---

Regional Commissioner   Page 2   July 2, 1969

statutory justification for the denial of his original application. This
suggestion is made recognizing Mr. Regev's commitment to his educational
objective and his ability to support himself and his wife without her
employment income.

Sincerely,

JOHN A. SEELEY
Associate Dean of Students
International Student Adviser

JAS:bh

cc: Shmuel Regev
     Dr. Francis M. Summers

Figure 9.6: Letter from John A. Seeley

We still owed the $500 Dr. Arthur Ganz loaned us and I was eager to pay it back as soon as possible. There was no viable alternative other than asking Sheila and everyone else needing Batia's babysitting services, to pay her in cash rather than check and they all agreed. Even to this day I feel uncomfortable knowingly breaking the law, but we did not have any other choice.

Taking me off the *Limited Status* restrictions and considering me a bona fide graduate student helped to reduce our financial burden a bit as the university awarded me the tuition waver benefit. I did not have to worry about grades because my total GPA was close to 4.0. I was awarded the tuition waiver for the remaining eight quarters I studied and earned my Ph.D. I finished each quarter with a 4.0 GPA.

An additional, albeit unexpected, source of income came from the Dean of the Foreign Languages Department requesting me to teach Hebrew during the 1969 spring quarter. I was asked to substitute for the professor who regularly taught the course while he was on a sabbatical, and teaching Hebrew at the Department of Foreign Languages was legally allowable by the immigration laws. Luckily, he gave me the textbooks and the exercises material already prepared by the regular professor. I was able to squeeze this job into my crowded schedule taking the courses I needed for my own degree. The Hebrew course I taught was held once a week for one hour. It was popular among the students because of its Satisfactory/Unsatisfactory grading. Needless to say, all my student finished with the *satisfactory* grade.

Time flew by and I got more comfortable being a student and chugged along with my studies. Batia continued babysitting for Sheila and other UC Davis professors, making sure that they paid in cash. The last thing we needed was for the *immigration hawks* to find out and kick us out of the country for good. Earning sixty cents an hour forced us to take the risk and Batia worked as many hours as she could. We hoped that it would be enough to take us to my graduation date and return to Israel with my Ph.D. Dr. Summers also helped our financial situation by offering me a summer job assignment to help with his research on pests damaging California's burgeoning almond industry. The Almond Growers Association gave him a grant to hire me for a research project. I enjoyed the trips we made across the state, visiting almond orchards. The cents and dimes that kept trickling our way were deposited into our Bank of America checking account. We were very vigilant to keep the balance around $5,000 at all times, in case the immigration people were snooping on us.

The euphoric feelings of being a bit richer for a change, prompted me to revisit my Wish Bucket. It had several wishes on the short list but all dwarfed compared to the urgent need to have our own car. Commuting around town riding on the funky dilapidated lady's bike Ronny gave me was impractical and a pain in the neck as well as the butt. Riding the bike during the winter rain was not pleasant. Besides, someone stole the bike one day when I was in the classroom and left it unchained. Last but not least, asking other people to give us a ride for shopping became uncomfortable and an embarrassment. We needed a car, badly, the sooner the better.

I started looking around hoping to come across a good deal that would fit our budget. An opportunity presented itself, unexpectedly, when Pablo Garcia, a medical student from Mexico, overheard me talking to another classmate about my interest in buying a car. We all took Dr. McClelland's Medical Entomology class. Pablo was already a practicing medical doctor from Mexico who came to UC Davis Medical School for special training not available in Mexico at that time. The spring quarter was his last and he and this family were leaving a few days after the quarter ended. Pablo owned a blue Volkswagen Square Back model and was willing to sell it to me for $300. I never owned a car before, yet the $300 price he asked sounded like a reasonable offer compared to the price-range I saw in town. "It would not make us broke," I convinced myself. "I don't want to buy a *cat in the sac* I told him, so I need to see the car and drive it before making any commitment. Why don't you bring it to my place on Saturday," I suggested.

Pablo agreed and brought the car on Saturday. It looked nice and drove well so Batia and I agreed to buy it. I liked Pablo's personality and the fact that he was a medical physician exuded an aura of confidence and integrity making him an unlikely person to cheat me out of my money or sell me a lemon. I trusted him and paid him the $300.

Having a car gave us the freedom of not depending on others to take us to do the weekend shopping at Gemco. More importantly, it allowed us to entertain visiting Batia's newly discovered relative, Carl Baer, who lived in Santa Clara near San Francisco. Batia's paternal grandmother's maiden name was Betty Baer. Batia was named after her. To this day I don't know the exact details of how he was related to Batia's grandma but Carl bore the same last name. Batia's mother gave us his address and phone number before we left Israel. Having a car presented us with the opportunity to travel the 104 miles separating Davis and Santa Clara and visit him and his family. I picked up the phone, introduced myself and scheduled a visit. Since he worked as a cashier at a Safeway supermarket in Santa Clara, we scheduled a visit during a weekend when he was off. Batia and I planned on having a short visit but Carl insisted that we come on Friday night and spend the *Sabbath* with them. I agreed but stressed the fact that we should leave on Saturday afternoon as I had some class assignments to finish.

The trip to Santa Clara was surprisingly easy. At first, I was a bit apprehensive since it was my first long distance drive in the USA. Adding to my apprehension was the heavy traffic in the Bay Area. Moreover, we did not have the luxury of GPS in those days, I had to rely on a California road map, making sure not to miss the exit. We left Davis a bit earlier to give us some extra time in case we got lost. We arrived early and Carl's wife, Berta, ushered us into the living room, offered some cold drinks and said that Carl was on his way home from work. When he arrived and we talked for a while, I noticed that he was in pain. A minute later he pulled a chair, sat down and murmured "Excuse me, but my feet are killing me. I will be right back as I need to soak them in warm water."

Carl looked to be in his early sixties and ready to retire. While he was busy taking care of his swollen feet, Berta revealed that the supermarket chain where he was working did not allow its cashiers to work at the cash register while sitting on a stool like they do in Israel. "There are days when his feet hurt so much he has to put on a bandage to sooth his sore ankles. It is that bad," she added.

I took his predicament very personally as my mother also worked as a cashier at Israel's largest supermarket chain until her retirement. Every time she came for a visit she got shocked anew to see her American counterparts working at the cash register while standing on their feet. Batia and I became advocates for the American cashier workers and whenever we befriended a favorite cashier, we would send the corporation's CEO a letter suggesting a change of policy to allow them to do their job sitting instead of standing on their feet for the entire shift. Unfortunately, we were not too successful.

When Carl returned we set at the table for the *Sabbath* dinner, lit the *Sabbath* candles and recited the Kiddush blessing over the wine. A Challah (sweet Jewish bread baked for *Sabbath* and holidays) that Carl brought from the kosher section of his supermarket was at the center of the table. We recited the *hamotzi,* the special Jewish blessing over the bread, and started the *Sabbath* dinner. It was a nice gesture from the Baer family to invite us for *Sabbath* dinner, the first one we had since we left Israel. It rekindled the warmth of a *Sabbath* dinner with a Jewish family. During the conversation we learned that Carl and Berta had one daughter who was attending graduate school at UCLA. We were invited to come again on *Rosh Hashanah* (Jewish New Year) and to meet their daughter who planned to come home for the holiday. We gladly accepted their invitation.

It had been almost thirteen months since we came to UC Davis and the Jewish high holiday season starting with *Rosh Hashanah* was just around the corner. It reminded me of Carl and Berta Baer's invitation to visit and meet their daughter. I called Carl to confirm our plan to come for a short get-together but we won't stay overnight. They were happy to hear that we would visit. "Other than you, Batia and our daughter, we don't have close relatives in the USA to celebrate the Jewish holidays with," Carl confessed to me.

When *Rosh Hashanah* arrived, we loaded our thermos with coffee and packed more than plenty six-packs of the Safeway brand bubbly soft drinks and headed to Santa Clara. As a side note I would like to add that thus far, I liked the VW square back we bought from Dr. Pablo Garcia. It was spacious enough and rewarded us with excellent miles-per-gallon performance. The flip side of this success story was the realization that VWs and gusty windy days are mutually exclusive. Driving my VW on windy gusty days was a bit tricky, and required constant praying to the Almighty, interspersed occasionally, with the use of the f-word while holding tight to the steering wheel and staying on the road. I was very happy that the day we left for Santa Clara was a calm day with barely any wind.

The ride was smooth and uneventful. Being a *coffeeholic* I enjoyed the coffee Batia poured into my cup. We were approaching the first hilly stretch of the highway not too far from Vacaville when the engine made strange rumbling noises and began losing power. I pressed the accelerator pedal all the way to the floor to give my poor VW more stamina but to no avail. Then we heard a boom sound from the back of the car housing the engine. A rod from one piston got loose and went through the engine block, setting the engine compartment on fire. Luckily, I was driving on the right lane and the car had enough inertia for me to navigate it to the side of the road. I rushed to the back, opened the hatchback and removed the cover of the engine compartment. A fire was still burning like a candle at the spot where the piston rod pierced the block. We did not have a fire extinguisher so I reached for the six-pack of Safeway soda pop, shook them vigorously to maximize the pressure inside the can. I opened a few cans and unloaded the soda onto the raging flame.

The soda squirted out of the can foaming as if there was no tomorrow. The popping noise upon opening the cans was music to my ears and reassuring as I noticed that the flame dyeing right at the spot it originated. Luckily, most of the back of the car survived in relatively good shape.

To this day I am not sure how the soda pop extinguished the flame. Was it the carbon dioxide bubbles? Most commercial fire extinguishers generate carbon dioxide gas which is heavier than air and suffocates the fire as a result. Or maybe it was the artificial sweetener. Perhaps it is not a far-fetched thought, though, since all the nutritionists under the sun have been preaching that artificial sweeteners are very bad and would kill us one day. I will let you be the judge, but the soda pop killed the raging fire in my engine.

"So now what?!" I asked myself, trying to evaluate the situation. Batia was worried too. This fiasco happened before the cell phone was even invented so how in the world I was going to summon help? I believe that my guardian angel was watching over us as very soon after I controlled the fire, a California Highway Patrol trooper stopped by our disabled VW and offered to help. Evidently, someone passing by saw what happened and alerted the Highway Patrol on his two-way radio.

The trooper took a look at the engine, still flooded and dripping with soda pop. He nodded his head and said, "Sir, I hate to be the bearer of bad news, but this engine is beyond repair. Do you live nearby?" I told him we were from Davis and on our way to Santa Clara. "Well, you cannot leave your car by the side of the highway so you either tow it to Vacaville, which is not far from here or take it all the way to Davis, which would cost you more because of the greater distance. Anyway, I am going to call the towing company. Someone will be here shortly. I'll revisit this spot to make sure your car was towed." He called the towing company, described our car and the exact location. I thanked him for his help, we shook hands and he was gone.

It took less than half an hour for the towing truck to arrive. A burly driver stepped out, shook my hand and debated with himself as to the best way to tow our car. "Where would you like me to tow you?" he asked. "UC Davis," I answered and could see from the expression of his face that he noticed my foreign accent. I expected him to ask for my nationality but he did not. Instead, he said to me, "Sir, towing your car to Davis will cost you close to $150, how are you going to pay for my towing service?"

I pulled out my Bank of America checkbook and said, "I'll write you a check."

"Sorry Sir" he said "I trust you but my boss won't allow me to accept personal checks. It is either a bank cashier's check, cash or credit card. Being a poor foreign student excluded me from getting a credit card so I told him we did not have one. I expected him to leave us there but evidently he had a good heart and was willing to help. "Didn't you say you have a checking account with Bank of America?" he asked.

"Yes that is correct," I answered.

"Here is an idea, why don't I take both of you to the Bank of America branch here in Vacaville and they will cut the cashier's check we need. It sounded an acceptable solution to me, so we hopped on his truck and we all went to the bank. The teller at the bank verified my ID and called the Davis branch to make sure I had the account there before issuing the cashier's check. Before leaving the bank I asked to make a short phone call to Carl Baer to tell them about our misfortune and to apologize for not being able to come.

The tow truck driver took us back to our disabled VW and we headed back to Davis after he mounted our car onto his truck. It had been a long day for us and I was tired and not in the mood to engage in a long conversation with the truck driver. I tried to limit the scope of the conversation just to the issue at hand, namely his suggestions as to what were the best options to fix the car. I explained that being a student with the burden of paying out of state tuition, buying a different car was not an option. He understood my situation and suggested that I should call the junkyards around Davis and look for a used VW engine of the same model. It sounded like a reasonable solution for me, financially. We finally arrived home and the tow truck driver unloaded our car at the apartment parking space. A new era of financial uncertainty and tribulation was in store for me and Batia. I could see, in my wild imagination, the immigration vultures hovering around us waiting for our demise.

We talked to Sheila and her fiancé, Ron about our new situation and asked for suggestions on how to resurrect our car. They both suggested we talk to their neighbors, Bob and Judy Chen. "Bob is a Mechanical Engineering professor on campus and should come up with a plausible solution," Sheila suggested and added, "I know that you babysit their son Jason, occasionally."

That was a splendid idea and I contacted him right away. They lived in our neighborhood. Bob came and inspected the engine. He was the kind of guy with the reputation of paying attention to details. He recorded the *incriminating evidence* with his fancy Polaroid camera, taking pictures of the damage and then gave me his assessment of what he saw. "Sam, the engine is beyond repair so you need to order a factory-made engine or rebuilt engine from the VW dealer. The other option is to get a used engine salvaged from one of the junk yards around here," he advised me. It was not a shocking revelation as it was more or less, what the towing truck driver told me. "Just give me few days to explore if Sears or Montgomery Ward stores have it by any chance," Bob suggested and left. As expected these companies did not carry the VW engine I needed, so I had to fold back to the junkyard option.

There was a small car repairs garage close to the hotel where I spent the night during my first visit to UC Davis. That small garage had a catchy sign with huge letters shouting WE FIX FOREIGN CARS. Being a foreigner who also owned a foreign car, I felt that I found my *match made in heaven* and decided to stop there during my lunch break the next day. I brought with me the Polaroid pictures of the damaged engine Bob Chen took, entered the garage office and talked to the guy sitting behind the counter who was munching on his Big Mac and french fries. "What can I do for you," he asked me after conquering a big chunk of the Big Mac and wiping the mustard and ketchup smeared around his mouth and nose. "Yes, I hope you could help me with my VW Square Back engine. Your sign boasts that you fix foreign cars, so can you fix this car?" I said and I put the photographs on the counter for him to see. "Holy crap," he exclaimed, "you did a good job busting your engine. How did you do that?" he asked and I did my best to tell him what happened.

To prevent his imagination from going wild and seeing the dollar signs popping up in his mind, I stressed upon him the fact that as a self-supported foreign student with limited resources, the only option I could afford, money-wise, was to salvage a similar engine from a junkyard to replace the busted one. I also asked for the free estimate advertised on his sign. He looked at me and said "I'm the owner here but Johnny is the mechanic who knowns how to repair foreign cars. He's on lunch break now so why don't you leave these pictures here and come back in twenty minutes, he should be back by then."

I came back after twenty minutes. "Hey Johnny," the garage owner shouted. "The guy owning the VW car is here, would you please come up front to meet him and explain the options we discussed while he was gone. Don't forget to bring the estimates with you." Johnny stopped the repair work he was doing and came to meet me. He wiped his greasy hands with a red rag before shaking my hand. He had strong arms covered to the last inch of skin with elaborate tattoos. I was convinced that Johnny was a mechanic blessed with the gift of paying attention to the tiniest detail, as could be judged by the intricate details of the tattoos showing naked nymphs adorning his arms. We agreed that Johnny would try to get a used engine, operational and in decent conditions. We also agreed to a price ceiling of the entire repair job not to exceed $400. Honestly, I had no idea what was a reasonable price for such a repair job.

Our daily lives in Davis became hectic and warranted having our own telephone. I finally called the phone company and subscribed for their party-line option. It meant sharing the same phone line with another subscriber, yet having a different phone number. It was not the ideal service for me but it fit my financial situation. I was astonished by the speed it took the phone company to install my phone. We had it hooked and operational the next day. The first call I made was to the garage and gave them my phone number and checked the status of the repair job. "We found a few engines but we're still haggling with them about a price that would meet the repair cost we agreed upon," the owner told me on the phone. He promised to call back when a deal was finalized and the engine was in their garage. The garage called a few days later and asked me to bring the car. Once again, Ronny came to the rescue and helped me get the car to the garage where Johnny, the mechanic with the colorful tattoos, started resurrecting it.

It took Johnny more than a week to replace the busted engine with the one salvaged from the junkyard in Sacramento. Evidently, the engine did not quite match the type and the design of the original engine installed at the VW factory in Germany, so Johnny the mechanic, had to improvise and performed numerous *alterations* on the junkyard engine. He cut the lines and plugged the ends whenever he couldn't find the spot where they should be connected. Many lines ended up being orphans with one end loose. Nonetheless, when I saw him turning the key and starting the engine, I firmly believed that I was watching a miracle performed by no other than Harry Houdini, the greatest magician. And when I saw Johnny backing my VW out of the garage it felt like a child watching a magician pulling a rabbit out of his black cylinder hat. That was definitely a "WOW!" moment for me.

I drove with him on the highway and around town to check the car. It ran well, albeit with less pep than it had with its original engine. Johnny assured me that the engine would improve in time. We returned to the garage for the final negotiation on the price and settled for $350. It was a hefty expense for Batia and I to bear but what other options did we have? "Don't worry," I told her, "I will find a way to recover the money," which was more wishful thinking than conviction. We drove the car back to the apartment, enjoying our newly restored freedom of mobility to the tune of $350.

Driving our revived VW home from the garage gave us a few elated minutes but soon the reality of The Day After started to sink in, threatening to crush me and my aspiration to finish UC Davis with the coveted Ph.D. The odds of surviving the looming crises were next to none. I felt that my doomsday was approaching at the speed of light. Whatever we managed to save up to that moment, evaporated when our car engine was destroyed. Just before the engine problem, I had entertained the idea of sending my sister the $3,500 she let me park in my Bank of America account but the cost of replacing the engine and the need to have some money for rainy days scrapped that idea.

There was no way that our salvation would come from Batia's babysitting job which was a clear violation of the immigration regulations to begin with. I could not even dare going to the Office of Foreign Students Services and share with Mr. John Seeley our new problem after he had worked so hard preventing our deportation earlier. He and Linda did not know that Batia continued her babysitting job. Just think about it, our only crime was the sheer sad truth that we were financially poor. I told Batia we did not have any other option but for me to find an off-campus job on top of being a full-time student. And that's exactly what I did knowing full well that the Regev's household had two, not one, immigration law violators. I felt utterly ashamed of myself for compromising the trust between us and the staff at the UC Davis Foreign Students Services so I kept them out of the loop and did not share with them my intention to get an off-campus job. I kept Dr. Summers out of the loop as well. After all, he wrote an enthusiastic testimony in my behalf that was included in Mr. John Seeley's letter to the immigration regional commissioner.

The time I allotted to studying got stiff competition for my attention as I became an avid browser of the help wanted ad in the *Davis Enterprise*, the daily local newspaper. And one day, a glimmer of hope finally arrived. Evidently, when the stars and the constellations got perfectly aligned with the sun. I noticed an ad stating that, "Help is needed in our circulation department. Please contact Mr. Harry Whitehouse at the *Davis Enterprise* to schedule an interview." I hadn't the faintest idea what a circulation depart was or what the job entailed, nonetheless, I picked up the phone and talked to Mr. Harry Whitehouse who scheduled an interview for the next day at lunch time. I was excited to have the appointment, yet apprehensive at the same time fearing that my deep Hebrew-accented English would torpedo this sliver of hope.

The *Davis Enterprise* newspaper was located not far from the Davis Lumber Home Improvement and Construction store. The two businesses shared the same alley where I usually parked my car while shopping there, so I parked my VW at my regular parking spot. I entered the lobby and told the receptionist I had an appointment with Mr. Harry Whitehouse. "Where can I find him?" I asked the nice lady.

"Harry's office is at the back of the building right where our offset printing press is. Just look for a white-haired, slim sixty-year-old chain smoking grandpa," she said half-jokingly and I knew that with her detailed description there was no way I would miss him. "Just go to the other side of the building and knock on the door and they will let you in," she said.

I thanked her and found the back door that she told me about. I knocked on it several times but no one answered so I returned and told her that no one opened the door.

"They might be printing today's paper and didn't hear you or they got too busy to leave the running press. Let me take you there through the back of our lobby," she replied and led me there. The noise from the running press was deafening, I barely heard her saying, "Harry's office is up there," as she pointed to a wide elevated wooden platform built above the floor. The space between the floor and the elevated platform served as the storage area for the huge roles of paper used to print the *Davis Enterprise.*

The receptionist left and I climbed the stairs leading to the deck housing the circulation department. I looked for Mr. Harry Whitehouse and bumped into a man in his mid-sixties busy stocking a candy vending machine with a wide selection of candy bars, the ones coveted by the youngsters celebrating their trick-or-treat Halloween rituals. "Excuse me sir," I said. "Are you by any chance Mr. Harry Whitehouse? I am looking for him."

"Yes I am, son," he answered and removed the burning cigarette from the corner of his mouth. "What can I do for you?" he asked.

I introduced myself and said, "I am the guy who called you yesterday about your help wanted ad.

"Oh yes," he replied, "I'm getting sick and tired placing that ad every other week. People come and go like this department is a revolving door. They don't last here for more than a week or two. They quit without even calling me to let me know," he lamented. "Are you like them or do I stand a better fortune hiring you?" he finished preaching to me and put the cigarette back to his mouth and inhaled." Smoking in a place like that or inside buildings was not outlawed during that time so it did not bother me. Besides, I was a pipe smoker myself.

"Mr. Whitehouse," I replied, "I cannot answer your question because you haven't described the job. How many hours per week would I work and what is the hourly pay rate?" I asked him.

"Of course, of course," he said to me, "Just let me finish stocking this damn candy machine before the paperboys show up and don't find their favorite candy." He loaded few more candy bars, locked the vending machine, inserted a dime to verify it was working OK, pulled out the candy bar, and gave it to me. "Hey, this is for you. I can see that you have sweet teeth," he said and started showing me the ropes.

My job was to help Harry Whitehouse run the delivery aspects of The *Davis Enterprise* newspaper, making sure subscribers' papers were delivered on time by the young paper carriers called paperboys. It was a five-day weekly job Saturday and Sundays were the days off. "See the long counter with its many shelves by the walls over there?" he pointed. "Each opening in that counter is numbered and assigned to a paperboy. You have to be here at noon every day when the press is running and printing the daily paper. The pressmen know how many copies we need and place them on the cart over there. He usually prints extra copies for the newsstands located at different locations around town. You don't have to worry about those, Fred takes care of that. He will show up later on." Harry stopped lecturing for a moment to light another cigarette

"Who is Fred?" I asked.

"We are co-father-in-laws. Fred's daughter is married to my son. Anyhow, as you can see, the offset press machine is located on the floor down there and we are up here so you will have to do some muscle work to bring copies up here. Most of the time the press will be done by the time you show up for work so the pressmen crew will bring the copies here. I will give you the list of our paperboys and how many subscribers each one has. Your job would be to put the correct number of copies they need inside their bin. On days where the newspaper has inserts coming from other printing companies, you will have to put them there as well. Make sure the paperboy inserts them into our paper."

Harry paused for a minute and pointed to a table by his vending machine and said, "This is your office. It has a phone to answer subscribers complaining about the paperboy failing to deliver their paper. It is your job to first, calm them down, apologize profusely, and take their name and address. Promise the subscriber that you, personally, will deliver the missing paper today by six p.m. at the latest. You will have to do that on your route to our paperboy in the El Macero neighborhood as it is too far away and dangerous for him to ride his bike all the way here to pick up his papers. You should record the mileage associated with these special deliveries to get reimbursed for using your own car. Make sure to give me the name of the paperboy who failed to deliver the paper and I will check what happened. We also need to hear the paperboy's side of the story associated with the complaint. If this is a recurrent issue, we subtract the cost of any missing delivery from his check at the end of the month. In some cases, we have to let the bad carrier go."

Harry looked at the clock and said, "The paperboys will start showing up in less than an hour and this place will transform into a wild zoo. I hope I didn't scare you with my description of your job. Are you still interested? Think you could handle the stress?"

I sensed from the tone of his voice that he wanted me to take the offer so I gave a rather lengthy reply. "Mr. Whitehouse," I said, "just to let you know, after serving in the Israeli army and fighting in the Six-Day War and surviving, I am confident I would be able to cope with all the mayhem these kids have in store for me, and yes! I will take the job."

Harry looked at me and said, "Sam, from the first minute you opened your mouth and started talking to me I noticed your foreign accent but I did not want to be impolite and nosy by asking what nationality goes with that unique accent. Now I know where it is coming from. Welcome to the USA." His 100% approval of my origin as well as giving me the job was noticeable in his voice and smiling face.

"Harry, you are not the first one and won't be the last to wonder where my accent comes from. In fact, I am always ready to address that question when it pops up by saying that the accent comes from my mother tongue Hebrew which was also spoken and preached by Jesus, hence, I feel that I am in a good company, don't you think so Harry?"

"Of course. Of course," Harry replied so I felt at ease to elaborate more on my Hebrew-accented English and explained that it had a very unique origin. "It is a cocktail of the accents imparted on me during school. The first four years in the elementary school my English teacher, Mrs. Livni, had immigrated to Israel from South Africa. Then it was Shifrah, who immigrated from Brooklyn New York and taught me English for the first two years of high school. And last but not least, for the last two years of high school, I had Eva, a Jewish immigrant from Germany, who taught English grammar and literature. Her German-accented English was so thick you could cut it with a knife and break the blade. So now you know why I sound like the United Nations when I speak English."

Harry seemed to be impressed with what I said. He reached for his wallet, browsed through it and pulled out a photograph of a nice-looking young man dressed in a US Air Force uniform, "I give you a large credit for serving in the Israeli army and fighting in the Six-Day War. I have great respect for people like you and my son who serve their country. My son David is probably in Vietnam as we speak," and handed me the photograph of his son so I could see it closer. "He is the pilot of a huge Air Force cargo airplane. He transports supplies and war materials needed by our troops in Vietnam. The airplane he flies is so huge it needs four crew members to fly it; my son the pilot, he has a co-pilot, a navigator and a communication officer." He went on and showed me a photograph of the huge airplane. I was so impressed and uttered a big "WOW!" Harry described how sophisticated that plane was with all its gadgets, bells and whistles, trying to impress me even more. The one gadget that impressed him the most was the navigation system. "My son and the navigator don't need to work hard to find the exact location over the globe where the plane is at any point in time. They have a super duper gizmo that does it for them in a split second." Many years later when I recalled that conversion, I realized it was the GPS devise he was talking about. It was a big deal then, but abundantly available to the public nowadays.

It was obvious that Harry Whitehouse was very proud of his son but also worried sick about the danger his son was facing in Vietnam. Our conversation that day took place during the height of the Vietnam War with its heavy American casualties. These painful statistics were revealed extensively on the hourly TV news of the major TV network channels and polarized the American society. UC Davis was a calm campus whereas UC Berkeley campus, not far away from us, was the epicenter of the anti-government protesters nicknamed the *peaceniks*. These protesters collided, violently, with the police forces. The ex-movie actor, Ronald Reagan was the Californian Governor at that time and they referred to him as the *Pig*. He later became a very popular president of the United State. During the Vietnam War era, *UC Berkley* and *tear gas* became synonymous to me.

"So Sam, are you taking this job? I hope you will," Harry asked me again, forgetting that I already told him I was interested.

"Yes I will take the job provided you keep in mind that I am also a full-time graduate student at UC Davis." I assured him that I would to do my best to avoid conflicts between my two responsibilities. I urgently needed the job he was offering me. I never told him about the VW car fiasco or my saga with the immigration office.

"That is great, Sam, let's go to the front office and I'll introduce you to Phil, the owner. We need his blessing and signature on the application documents. I'm sure he'll hire you, so I am expecting you to report to work tomorrow at noon," Harry said and took me to see Phil.

Phil was the kind of owner who did not micromanage the place but was very vigilant that no employee would bring the *Davis Enterprise* embarrassing publicity. Phil asked what I was doing at UC Davis as well as the unavoidable question, "I hear an accent, what nationality is that?" Harry Whitehouse did not lose a second and started reciting my resume and harped on my credentials even though he just met me for the first time an hour before. "Better hire him Phil. Now! Or else," he joked.

"Or else what?!!" Phil played along with the small talk.

"Well, I have to warn you that Sam is an ex-paratrooper in the Israeli army and fought in the Six-Day War two years ago so better be nice to him."

Evidently, Phil was impressed by then and shouted "Hey Debra, please come here and see who Harry Whitehouse got to work for us at the circulation department. I need your seal of approval."

Debra came, shook my hand and introduced herself as Phil's wife and the bookkeeper for the newspaper. "Welcome to the *Davis Enterprise* family," she greeted me and gave me a few more papers to fill out and sign. I sensed that she was a religious Christian as she commented about how happy she was to have a new employee who belonged to the *chosen people*.

I started my job the next day. I was relieved that during my interview with Harry and with Phil no one asked me if I, a foreign nationalist, was allowed to work and be gainfully employed. Harry was already there and the press was running at full speed, spewing the paper off the press. I was afraid I would not be able to synchronize my speed of collecting the printed copies off the running belt without losing a finger or two. After a while I was able to catch up and yet, I was extremely happy when the press stopped and we had the copies we needed for the day. I took them and climbed the stairs to the circulation department on the deck. Harry gave me the paperboy roster, their bin numbers and how many copies each one needed. He also gave me the name and address of the paperboy who lived in El Macero. "Sam, you better tie his bundle of newspaper, otherwise the wind will blow them all the way to Sacramento if left untied on his driveway. Remember to record the mileage you drive using your car. You will get a separate reimbursement check in addition to your salary. Phil pays his employees every Friday so don't forget to pick up your checks before going home on Friday."

Working at the *Davis Enterprise* circulation department provided me with a perfect opportunity to be exposed to a wide spectrum of human behavior. I realized that both the paperboys and their adult subscribers were the world's microcosm. Like Shakespeare said, "The world is a stage and we are merely the players." So there I was, watching big drama for free, five days a week.

I wish to describe, for the sake of posterity, a few of the characters of the drama that played before my watchful eyes. I am using the term *sake of posterity* because time has changed and the accounts I am describing happened during the heydays of the printed newspaper era. My stint at the *Davis Enterprise* happened fifty-one years ago when most people got their information, from reading the newspaper and watching the evening news on the TV. With the advent of the Internet, smart phones, iPads and tablets, the era of the printed newspaper has been in a steady decline and is about to have its last breath. Who knows, maybe my description of the hours I spent working with the paperboys and their subscribers is more like a Requiem for a dying era rather than a description of the characters in a vivid *play* I watched.

To start with, let me introduce you to Jimmy, a very pleasant and well-mannered paperboy, always showing up on time. Jimmy never failed to say, "Good afternoon," to me and Harry. He took his paper route very seriously and was adored by his subscribers who showed their affection with the substantial tips he deserved. This guy had a head on his shoulder and knew exactly what to do with the money and tips he earned. He was determined to go to college and made sure his earning ended up in the college fund he kept at the bank. Jimmy had the habit of neatly rolling the papers I left inside his bin. He tied each one with a rubber band so it won't separate when tossed onto the subscriber's front yard. His paper vest was clean and organized with each rolled paper standing as straight as a soldier. You did not need to worry about Johnny's future. I gave his parents a straight A for raising such a jewel.

The next character in the play, Freddy, a nonchalant paperboy who didn't give a damn. He carelessly rolled his papers, tearing half of the front page while wrapping them with a rubber band. He would not unroll the paper upon discovering that he forgot to include the weekly supermarket inserts with the attractive coupons. He was oblivious to the fact that these coupons were the ones most housewives loved to have a special scissors dedicated to clip them. "It's a waste of time and effort to remove the rubber band and put in the inserts. No one bothers reading this junk anyway," he would murmur to me or Harry whenever we called his attention to his carelessness. Freddy was an additional source of income for me because I had to take replacement copies to the home of every subscriber who did not get their inserts. Unfortunately, Freddy failed to shape up. Harry gave up and fired him, reluctantly. "You have to teach them responsibility," he said to me, apologetically. I noticed sadness in his voice when he said that.

And there was Roger, the paperboy without the sense for time or conviction to come to work on time. Showing up late was his trade mark. It made me wonder if he was using a wristwatch or a sun dial to tell time. Another idiosyncrasy of his was the never-ending complaints to Harry Whitehouse about the candy vending machine. "Harry, your damn candy vending machine took my fifteen cents but didn't give me a Milky Way," was his mantra. This ritual had been going on long enough for Harry to finally realize that Roger was making up this accusation as he had a craving for this particular candy and attempted get an extra one for free. Harry kept some extra bars of Milky Way in his cabinet and gave one to Roger just to get him to leave and deliver the papers on time.

The characters and the personalities of the other paperboys were for the most part a variation of the ones I described. And then, there was the soft-spoken, vulnerable Danny who captured my heart and thoughts for a very long time, well after I left my job at the *Davis Enterprise* and graduated from UC Davis. He was a good paperboy, with a perfect work ethic. His big disadvantage was being smaller and more fragile than his peers. Coming to work was a painful experience for Danny, every single day. Youngsters of that age group could be nasty and cruel to their peers who appeared to be physically vulnerable. Danny was easy prey and bullied by some of the physically stronger boys.

They were very creative with their harassment of him whenever Harry or I were busy and not aware of what was going on. Since each paperboy had to buy his own rubber bands for wrapping his papers, some of the bullies were stealing Danny's as he was in the midst of wrapping his papers before starting his paper route. He would come to my desk, shaken and teary eyed to tell me what had happened. I would usually open the supply cabinet and gave him a new bag and told him to sit by my desk, finish wrapping and start delivering the paper. This nasty harassment of Danny stopped only after I caught some of the paperboys who were stealing Danny's rubber bands. I charged their accounts for all the bags of rubber bands I gave Danny.

Evidently, the temptation to harass him was irresistible. The bullies were creative and came up with new tricks to play on him. They would vent the air out his bike tires while he wrapped his papers. Then they came inside to tell him he had a flat tire. We realized it was a prank when the pressman pumped air into Danny's bike using the offset press air compressor and sure enough no puncture was found. The bullies upgraded the harassment level by hiding Danny's bike somewhere around the building when Danny was inside. It was getting too late and he needed to deliver the papers so Danny called his Mom who came to help him. The bike was missing until the janitor found it in the large garbage bin. The non-stop harassment of Danny started to have a negative impact and interfered with our circulation operation not to mention the emotional impact on Danny. The poor soul was ready to quit his paper route but Harry and I convinced him to stay, promised to find the culprit and put an end to it. Harry Whitehouse, who knew all the paperboys, found out who orchestrated the harassments and fired the boy.

Danny stayed with us for almost a year and then quit his job. I admired him for enduring the pain and the abuse caused by his peers. It was physical pain as well when they shot rubber bands at him from a close range when Harry or I were not present.

Danny's harassment saga reminded me of the testimonial accounts I heard from Jewish immigrants, many of them Holocaust survivors, who told me about their own experience growing up among the gentile bullies. It finally occurred to me that there were many Danny's among the Jews living as a minority amidst the gentiles of Eastern Europe. They were harassed, beaten and abused on their way to and from school. They did not escape being harassed even inside the school, with not much protection from the gentile and oftentimes anti-Semitic teachers.

If dealing with the paperboys challenged my sanity to the max, dealing with some subscribers' with their never-ending complaints was not much different. Most of my dealings with the subscribers were very pleasant and complimentary to their paperboys and to me about our good service. A few however, were not very nice and sounded more like a perennial loser venting his/her frustrations with how life was treating them. We always took every complaint seriously, but the lion share were without any merit. Harry and I tried to reason with what I called the *professional complainers* but it was a lost battle. Take Mrs. Rodgers for example who most likely, had a dedicated alarm clock, set to the time I usually showed up at the circulation department. Her timing was perfect as the phone on my desk always rang as I was climbing the wooden stairs. I would pick up the phone, catching my breath and answer the call using the sweetest voice I could muster and said, "Sam Regev from the circulation department speaking. May I help you?" And before I knew it the caller on the other side of the line said, "This is Mrs. Rodgers calling. Your damn paperboy almost broke my front window last night. He threw the paper at our window instead of leaving it nicely at the entrance as we asked him to do a zillion times already." Her squeaky voice pierced my ear drum.

"Sorry to hear that Mrs. Rodgers," I replied and promised to deliver her paper to her door step myself in the evening. "And please, don't hesitate to call me if it happens again," I told her and kept my promise.

A few days later Mrs. Rodger would call again to complain with the same story but being more forceful this time. I would apologize again and promise to talk to her paperboy and promise to deliver her paper myself. A few more days passed and she called with the same ritual, "Your damn paperboy almost broke my front window last night..." But this time she recited her *mantra* in a much higher octave and decibels. She was rowdy and really irritated and took it out on me. Dealing with her and her paperboy was too much for me so I told her that she should better talk to Mr. Harry Whitehouse, my boss or better yet, just try to get out when the paperboy comes and talk to him in person. I also gave her the paperboy's phone number to call whenever she had any issue with him. For the sake of being fare to the paperboy, he never received any complaint from his other subscribers. I have no idea what Harry Whitehouse told her but she never called me again.

And then there were subscribers eager to jump on me, tearing me apart if, God forbid, the paperboy did not deliver the newspaper at the very spot they told him to. For example: "Your paperboy tossed the paper and it got stuck on the tree in the front yard. It is too high for me to reach," Or "Your paperboy threw the paper on the front lawn and it got completely soaked by the sprinklers. I need a replacement please." Most of the calls came on Wednesdays when the supermarkets printed their weekly inserts with special deals and coupons. Oftentimes, the paperboys forgot to insert them. There were days when Harry got impatient with the ladies complaining and their paperboys. He capped the mouthpiece with his hand and whisper to me, "Sam, you have a way to talk to these ladies. She is all yours," and gave me the phone to deal with the hot potato still screaming on the other side of the line. It was annoying and rewarding at the same time because Phil, the newspaper's owner, paid me for the extra miles I drove, delivering the replacement papers and inserts to appease those subscribers.

The fear of being caught by the US immigration office was weighing heavily on my shoulders and preoccupied my thoughts ever since the engine mishap of my VW. It forced me to work, illegally, despite the fact that both Batia and I agreed not to do so. So here I was, trying to mitigate the financial conundrum I got myself into and started violating the terms of my F-1 student visa. I was risking my plans and academic future for a mediocre job paying peanuts. It bothered me a great deal so I decided to contact Inspector Jones at the Sacramento Immigration Branch to discuss the issue. I chose to speak specifically with him because he was as the one who interviewed Batia and I when we first asked to upgrade our tourist visas to student and student spouse visas. The risk of being deported was very real, but it became imperative that I should do something about it despite the inherent risk.

I figured out that my best chance to win Inspector Jones support, if any, was to show him my official UC Davis transcript and any other documents showing that I was a serious student focused on getting my academic degree. There were two upcoming events that could augment my claim. The first one was simply the final exams of the current quarter, which I finished with a straight A. The second event, which carried even more weight was the successful passing of the Qualification Test. Passing it would be a significant part of my tool chest if and when I was going to meet Inspector Jones and plead my case.

✡

Earning a Ph.D. in the USA was my ultimate goal. I did not anticipated complications from the US Immigration and Naturalization office. Our financial situation was precarious, to say it mildly. We lived on a shoestring for a long time not knowing what the next day would bring. I had to move as fast as I could, trying to achieve my goal and return to Israel as Dr. Samuel Regev. I started looking for academically acceptable ways to shorten the path to the Ph.D. I found out that in some cases, the university would allow a student to skip the MSc degree and work directly toward the Ph.D. I found it hard to believe, at first. None of the graduate students in our department and the ones that I knew on campus, took that shortcut so I decided to explore the option with Dr. Summers, my trusted mentor and advisor.

> ✡
>
> The following is a brief explanation of the Qualification Test, an important prerequisite to initiate a Ph.D. program. Usually, the normal path from the BSc. (Latin abbreviation for *Baccalaureus Scientiae*) Degree to the Ph.D. (Latin abbreviation for Philosophiae Doctor) degree in sciences, passes through the MSc (Latin abbreviation for *Magister Scientiae*). Most people refer to it as the *Master's Degree*. Having a *Master's Degree* defines your professional qualifications and experience. It serves as proof of your higher level of skills and knowledge in an area of expertise. Earning the MSc degree requires the graduate to design and perform an original research work, and then write a thesis detailing the work. A similar process repeats itself when a graduate student holding a MSc degree shoots for the Ph.D. It requires a wider spectrum of advanced scientific knowledge and expertise in a specialized field.

My meeting with Dr. Summers was productive. I learned more about the option as well as the pros and cons associated with it. The main benefit for me was shortening the path toward achieving my academic dreams and returning to Israel. Doctor Summers on the other hand, tried to convince me to get the MS degree first, and then the doctorate. I reminded him the never-ending struggles Batia and I were facing just to survive financially, "The faster I can get the Ph.D. the better." I did not say a word about my illegal off-campus job at the newspaper.

"That is exactly the reason why I recommend that you get a master's degree first," he replied. "If you to skip the MSc degree, start on your Ph.D. and then something happens that forces you to quit, you will return back to Israel empty handed. Earning the MSc degree would at least leave you with a valuable academic degree in your hand," he tried to reason with me. Admittedly, Dr. Summers' rationale was compelling, but my gut feelings convinced me that taking the time to earn the MSc degree under our dire financial situation carried more risks than just shooting directly for the Ph.D. I was determined to stick with my original plan and told him so.

"Well, in that case we need to assemble a committee to evaluate your qualifications to skip the MSc," he told me and added, "this option is granted only to graduates with the highest GPA scores. I don't worry about that requirement since you are more than qualified. The committee would be comprised of three professors from our department, one professor from the UC Davis Plant Physiology Department, and one professor from the Entomology Department in UC Berkley with the stipulation that he does not know you. As your mentor and advisor, I would be one of the professors from our department. Then he gave me the punch line and said, "You should know that the committee will grill you for four solid hours, or even longer as we deem necessary, and if you fail you will have to wait two quarters before being allowed to take the Qualification Test again. Do you still want to go ahead?" he asked me, just to make sure I understood what I was getting myself into.

I paused for a few seconds realizing the enormity of my decision and told Dr. Summers that I was willing to take my chances.

"Very well," he replied and asked me to give him two to three weeks to assemble the qualifications committee and schedule a date agreeable to all participants. I was appreciative of the fact that he went along with my plan to skip the MSc degree. Having secured his concurrence, I felt free to ask his explanation as to the nature and definition of the Ph.D. degree concept. "Dr. Summers, here is a riddle for you to resolve that still confuses me. Both the bachelor's and the master's degrees clearly state that they pertain to science so what is the connection between the Ph.D. and philosophy? I am going to be a scientist, not a philosopher, definitely not like the ancient Greek philosophers or their modern counterparts."

"That's exactly the purpose of the Qualifications Committee. It is a tool to gauge your readiness and capability to generate original ideas and methods for solving problems. This capability requires a vast knowledge of what you have gained through the classwork and your thinking process on implementing that knowledge into practicality. Hence this wide spectrum of your knowledge and thoughts is better defined as philosophy rather than science. It would behoove you to be original and creative with your answers to the Qualification Committee's questions."

I thanked him for the heads-up. Since the quarter final exams were going to take place within the next three weeks I asked him to let me finish with the finals before scheduling my session with the committee. He agreed.

I finished the quarter with another 4.0 GPA. I obtained an official up-to-date copy of my UC Davis transcript to show Inspector Jones, who I planned on seeing shortly, to discuss my job at *Davis Enterprise.* I also passed the Qualification Test and was allowed to start my studies and research work associated with my Ph.D. thesis. "If these two pieces of supporting evidence won't convince Inspector Jones that I am a serious student and let me keep my puny job at the newspaper, then nothing will," I told myself. I overcame my fear and hesitation, picked up the phone and called him to schedule an early morning appointment so I would be back in time for my job at the newspaper. The meeting was scheduled for the following week. I was worried sick, fearing that I was bringing my academic dreams and achievements at UC Davis to an abrupt end. "Only a fool would believe that Inspector Jones would let you go, scot-free, after hearing that you and Batia had been working illegally, despite your first brush with the immigration office," I kept telling myself.

It should be noted that I did not disclose to the UC Davis Office of Foreign Students Services and Mr. John Seeley who helped us with the immigration office the fact that both Batia and I were working illegally.

My *D-Day* arrived, finally, and I was on my way to meet Inspector Jones in his Sacramento office. I did not sleep the night before as my apprehension reached a new height. I was a little more relaxed when I entered his office and was pleasantly surprised to see him smiling when we shook hands. He pointed to the seat by his desk and motioned me to sit. "How has school been treating you and what brought you here today?" he asked and scribbled something in his notebook.

"So far so good," I replied and showed him the official copy of my transcript and the excellent grades I had gotten. I also mentioned my passing the Qualification Test, starting my research work and experiments associated with my dissertation. "I can handle and manage the academic aspects of completing the program and getting my Ph.D., but I am not so sure I will be able to reach that goal after all."

"Why is that?" he asked.

Thoughts of, "Now he is going to set the trap for me," were storming in my brain. I decided to tell him the truth, albeit, without mentioning my VW engine disaster.

"Inspector Jones," I said in the calmest and convincing voice I could summon at that crucial moment, "Dr. Summers, my academic advisor and mentor, is going to retire after I am awarded my Ph.D.. As such, he does not have funds to support the costs associated with my research. Other professors, who are not retiring soon, generate funds when they are listed as co-authors on scientific papers associated with the research they funded."

Inspector Jones seemed to be very attentive and kept jotting down notes in his notebook. I continued to plead my case. "The only way for me to carry out the research and write the dissertation, is to pay for materials and some off-campus services out of my own pocket. I have been fortunate to befriend graduate students willing to let me use their labs and instruments, but I need to bring my own materials. I am more than halfway from completing my studies and writing the thesis. I hate to stop in the middle for lack of funds. I need to work a few hours off-campus to get the extra funds while still attending the college as a full-time student. The circulation department at the *Davis Enterprise* newspaper offered me the hours I need, so I came to see you today to ask your permission to accept their offer so I can finish my Ph.D. and return to Israel with my diploma."

There was deafening silence when I finished my plea. Inspector Jones did not even look at me when I finished, as he was still busy jotting down whatever his thoughts were at that moment. When he finally finished writing, he looked at me and then at his watch and said, "I recorded all the information you gave me today. I need to evaluate your situation as you described as well as your past difficulties with the Immigration and Naturalization office in San Francisco. It will take me a few days, or most likely, two weeks, to reach the final decision so why don't you go back to Davis and wait for my official letter. I will also contact the UC Davis Foreign Students Services and let them know about our meeting today since they have helped you before."

I was somewhat alarmed by the fact that I was about to leave his office without a definite yes or no answer. It meant continuing to work illegally at newspaper. Evidently, I was not thinking coherently for few seconds and succumbed to his smiling face. When he got up from his chair and shook my hand and I was about to leave, my tongue slipped very badly and I asked him, innocently, "So is it OK for me to keep the job?"

Inspector Jones set back in his chair, looked directly in my eyes and asked, "Are you working at the newspaper already?"

"Yes," I replied and instantly realized that I made a terrible mistake and tightened a thick noose around my neck with that stupid question.

"As I said before, go back to Davis and wait for my official letter," Inspector Jones replied. I left his office with a sunken heart.

I drove back to Davis as fast as I could and headed directly to the Office of the Foreign Student Services. I felt utterly stupid. My long face and shaky voice revealed my frustration level. Linda, my friend at the front desk, was smiling from ear to ear when she greeted me. It looked as if she knew something I did not know. "Linda, I am coming directly from Inspector Jones's office. I goofed *big time*. I'm sure they will kick me out of the country soon so you better consider this visit to your office, as a farewell visit," I told her.

"Relax Sam, Relax! Inspector Jones called us right after you left his office and said that he had never, in his entire carrier, met such a determined and serious student. He was so impressed with you and would like to help you get the Ph.D. One way he could do that was by giving you his permission to work at the *Davis Enterprise*, or any other job for that matter." That revelation was music to my ears orchestrated by all of my guardian angels up there in the skies.

I never received the official letter Inspector Jones said he would send. According to Linda, he probably felt it would be better for him and all parties involved to close his eyes and ignore my violation. He was 100% confident that I would finish my studies and get my degree so why rock the boat? From that moment on, he became one of my guardian angels disguised as an immigration inspector. I kept writing to him about my progress and achievements and informed him the day I received my Ph.D..

I kept him informed about my academic progress after leaving UC Davis to accept the post doctorate research assignment with Washington State University. Armed with the US immigration laws and regulation at his disposal, he could have easily crushed my dreams and career by deporting me. He let me fulfill my dreams and aspirations and I will remember him fondly for the rest of my life. What a compassionate man he was after all.

Chapter 10

UC Davis: Part 3

Inspector Jones' permission for me to keep my job at the *Davis Enterprise* was a great boost to our financial situation not because the newspaper paid me lots of money but because I tried to do all types of jobs there, squeezing as many working hours as I could because of the puny minimum wage they were paying. I ended up working an average sixty-one hours a week at the newspaper on top of the twenty hours a week I spent on campus being a student.

Although I was hired to help Harry Whitehouse run the *Davis Enterprise* circulation department, at minimum wage with no benefits, I looked for other assignments there to increase my hours. Despite its small subscriber's base, the *Davis Enterprise* also printed the Cal Aggie, the UC Davis daily paper and the weekly papers of nearby cities such as Rancho Cordova. It also printed the Wednesday food advertisements inserts for other newspapers. The pressmen had their hands full so I offered to help. My first job helping them was to clear the printed copies off the moving belt at the end of the press machine. I had to tie them in small, marked bundles and set them aside for the out-of-town customers to pick up. Some nights were busier that others as more than one paper was printed. The pressmen were busy cleaning the different press compartments and checking ink color.

I have no idea how old the offset press machine was but it had its own share of bad days. The machine malfunctioned, putting the pressmen under huge pressure to have it up and running before the paper delivery time. Describing the concept of offset printing is beyond the scope of our story but I will try to touch upon some of the basic steps involved in producing the newspaper that were relevant to my story.

The description that follows pertains to what was the norm when I was working there more than fifty-one years ago.

✡

The daily and weekend news was written by several full-time writers. They came every day and typed their articles on typewriters. That was before personal computers, let alone word processors, and spell check. Once the story was typed, it was given to the typesetters who used a special typewriter that printed the text on light sensitive paper. Then another person processed these strips of photographic papers and pasted them onto a layout frame the way they would appear on the printed page. The layout person also pasted the photographs in the appropriate spot on the layout.

The original photographs had to be converted into a half-tone images, comprised of discrete tiny dots rather than continuous tones. It is sort of similar to pixels in digital images.

Both the halftone dots and the pixels of the digitized images give the illusion of continuous lines and images. Next time you have access to a powerful magnifying glass, focus on a picture from the newspaper or book and you should be able to see them.

The pressmen developed the roll of film the reporter shot and produced the half-tones the writer chose to include in the article. These tasks required having a small darkroom at the *Davis Enterprise.*

When the layout person finished pasting the text and the photographs comprising a whole newspaper page to be printed, the layout pages were given to the pressmen to be photographed on Kodalith film and chemically processed with Kodalith photographic developer in the darkroom. The end result was a very large photographic negative, the standard dimensions of a newspaper page.

The Kodalith negative was placed onto a thin aluminum plate with its smooth surface pre-coated, more or less, analogues to the use of the *enlarger* used by a photographer in the darkroom. After exposing the Kodalith negative onto the aluminum plate using the strong light, it was treated with the plate manufacturer's special processing developer, washed with water and mounted into the press machine compartment assigned to the applicable newspaper page.

> I don't recall how many units like that the offset press at the *Davis Enterprise* had, but they were several of them and each had two aluminum plates mounted, one for each side of the paper running through the press. The next step was for the pressmen to fill the ink containers in each printing compartment and finally start the initial run to make sure that the printed paper looked correct.

I didn't mean to bore the reader with the somewhat lengthy description. My intention was to illustrate the labor-intensive tasks the pressmen at the *Davis Enterprise* faced.

There were only two pressmen. Even on a normal day, getting the paper off the press in time was a challenge for them. On days when the press machine was acting up or any delay at the layout department, these two pressmen were under immense pressure. "Sam to the rescue," was my mantra. I would finish my circulation department job, hop in my car to deliver the paper to our paperboy in El Macero and then rush back to help the pressmen. I learned their tasks by simply watching what they did.

My innate curiosity and drive to learn their job became useful and a game-changer one day when the two pressmen were way behind and I took the initiative and processed the aluminum plates for them. There were days when I took the pictures of the layout pages and processed them with the Kodalith developer and then burned the images onto the aluminum plates and stayed to help the pressmen start printing. Everyone was happy. The pressmen were happy to get an extra hand. Phil was happy since he didn't have to hire a third pressmen when he had me to do the job at minimum wage. I was the happiest as it gave me more hours on my paychecks. When we finished the pressmen took a short break to grab something to eat while I helped load copies on trucks. I did not have too much time to rest, since we had to print the daily Cal Aggies issue before sunrise.

My job activities at the *Davis Enterprise* became the norm for me and my days extremely long, leaving almost no time to rest or sleep properly. I still had to attend twenty hours a week of classes on campus and then make a short stop at home to change my cloths, drink my coffee, eat my sandwich, leave a note for Batia, who was already at her babysitting job, then rush to the newspaper.

The *Davis Enterprise* became my second home. The only opportunity for Batia and I to have dinner together was during weekends as there were no classes and the newspaper was less busy. The weekend also enabled me to spend more time with my books and lecture notes.

My usual weekday started around noon at the circulation department when I met with Harry Whitehouse, my boss, and discussed our plan for the day and gloss over the list of the newly irate subscribers I needed to pamper because their paperboy mistreated them. I collected the copies off the press and filled the paperboy's bins with the copies for their customers. If the press was still printing the newspaper, I would collect the copies off the press and take them up to the deck. If I had some free time before the paperboys arrived I would process the offset aluminum plates or the Kodalith negatives for the pressmen. When all the paperboys were ready to leave and deliver the paper, I left to deliver copies to that day's irate subscribers and bring copies to our paperboy in El Macero. Next, I had to rush back to the *Davis Enterprise* as the pressmen were about to finish their late lunch break and start printing another publication. I helped with the Kodalith processing and preparing the aluminum plates and then collected the copies of whatever we printed off the conveyor belt and set them aside for the driver of that publication to pick up a few hours later.

It was a tail chasing job, keeping me awake and on my feet for sixteen hours but my shift at the *Davis Enterprise* was not over, as we were still waiting for the *Cal Aggie* layout pages to arrive and print on time. While we waited, I borrowed several red rags from the pressmen, and used them as my pillow and crawled under the deck bellow our circulation department and tried to take a nap, squeezed among the huge rolls of the press paper stored there. I had to share the place with the many mice and rats living there. At first, I nicknamed my refuge spot Motel-6 but since there were more than just six rodents there with me I started calling it My Underworld.

When the *Cal Aggie* people showed up on time, around midnight, we prepared the material for the offset press and finished printing the paper around 3:30-4:00 am. That allowed time for me to go home, shower and take a short nap before dashing to my classes. After class I returned to the newspaper. Most of the time we ended up printing the *Cal Aggie* too late for me to go home. I dashed directly to my classes, tired and exhausted. I was able to keep this schedule for a long time but every once in a while it caught up with me.

One night we were way behind schedule as the *Cal Aggie* people were late. I dashed to class directly from the newspaper. It was Dr. Larry Rapport's Plant Physiology class, the head of the Hillel House that kicked Batia and me out of the room. Dr. Rapport and I amended our relationship right after the incident. He was very supportive and tried to help me whenever he could. He was one member of my Ph.D. Qualification Test committee that approved my application to skip the MS degree and shoot directly toward the Ph.D. So there I was, sitting in his classroom with my dirty work clothes. I was tired and not very attentive. He stopped by my chair and whispered in my ear, "Sam, I want to talk to you after class so don't rush out like you have been doing lately."

"Let's go to my office" he said.

"Larry, I am too dirty to enter your office so let's go to your greenhouse instead."

We entered the greenhouse were his graduate students kept their experiments and opened a window as the place was hot and muggy. In the presence of students and in the classroom I always addressed him as Dr. Rapport but outside the academic environment he was always Larry to me. Larry looked at me and said, "Sam, this is the first course you are taking from me and as agreed by your Qualification Test committee, Plant Physiology would be considered your minor field of interest. I am very pleased that you have been getting A's on the weekly quizzes and the midterm exams but I couldn't help noticing your extreme fatigue lately. What's going on?"

"It is a very long story and I don't know when your next class starts," I said, trying to extricate myself.

"Don't worry about it. We have all the time we need. Tell me what's going on."

Larry never knew about our struggle with the immigration authorities, or the *Limited Status* my first two quarters. He looked at me with disbelief as I unraveled the story.

He paused for a while and finally said, "Sam, you cannot continue like this. It will kill you before you even get your degree. I would like to help take the financial burden off your shoulders. Why don't you switch fields and get your Ph.D. from our department? You will be my graduate student and since you already passed your qualification test and granted the OK to skip the MSc degree, you should get the Ph.D. in Plant Physiology under my mentorship. Dr. Summers is retiring and has no grants but I have plenty. I could fund your research work and thesis. I could also grant you a steady income as my Teacher Assistant. Ephi (Larry's Israeli student) just finished his Ph.D. They are moving back to Israel next month. Why don't you take his place?"

I was overwhelmed by Dr. Rapport's sensitivity and generosity. He was what is known in the Jewish culture a *mensch* (a good human being). "Larry, you caught me by surprise with your generous offer. Let me discuss it with Batia and call you back. I am afraid I've gone quite a distance with Dr. Summers and switching fields now could mean a substantial delay," I told him realizing deep inside that Larry's offer came, unfortunately too late to be a game changer for me. It was very seductive but I had started to see the light at the end of the tunnel I had started under Dr. Summers. I did not have the heart to turn down Larry's offer outright. I called him the next day to inform him that my decision was to stay the course and not switch fields. Larry understood my situation and continued our friendly relationship.

My mentor and advisor, Dr. Summers, was the professor who taught the Insect Morphology course and the Acarology (the study of mites, ticks) classes. His research project during my time under his mentorship centered on the predatory mite Cheyletus malaccensis. His work was taxonomic in nature and dealt primarily with detailing the external features of that group of mite for the purpose of identifying them. Naturally, he wanted me to have my Ph.D. research done along the line of his expertise.

Taxonomy (the science that deals with classification of organisms) was not my cup of tea. Instead, I was exploring other angles of research work, to be more in line with physiology, biochemistry, genetics and the like, while using Dr. Summers Cheyletus malaccensis mite as my *guinea pig*. It meant befriending people in different departments along the line of my interests and learning the tools they used in their own research.

I befriended Willy, a South African graduate student at the Enology department who did biochemical analyses on the components of red wines fermented from different grape varietals. He had come to UC Davis, considered the Mecca of Enology, to receive his Ph.D. and return to South Africa where he had a job at a large winery in Cape Town. He taught me how to apply gas chromatography in my research which I continued to use heavily during my Post Doctorate academic career. Willy also taught me the fundamentals of making good wines which I relied upon during my wine making stint later on. (See Chapter 19.)

I also befriended Robert, who I met in cytogenetics class. Robert was working toward his Ph.D. in genetics. He showed me how to prepare slides and apply special staining techniques to enable watching chromosomes under the phase contrast microscope. Robert taught me how to take photographs of these tissues with the microscope camera. Unknowingly, he was instrumental in my delving into photographing chromosomes and then processing the high definition photographing film using the special chemical developers I invented for that purpose.

I had some research ideas that required the help of a real biochemist and the proper instruments to carry them out. For that I recruited my Israeli friend, Uzi Reiss who was working on his Ph.D. thesis in food science. Batia and Uzi were both born and raised in a *kibbutz* and came to the USA directly from their *kibbutz*. Those who are familiar with the *kibbutz* concept and its socialistic culture should appreciate that such a move was a great jump and required a huge adaptation in life style. (See Chapter 7.)

Uzi and his wife Ziva, landed first in San Jose California where he studied at the San Jose State College and earned his BSc degree. Uzi's Ph.D. advisor and mentor at UC Davis was a Jewish professor with enough research funds to support him thus alleviating the financial burden I faced. Uzi taught me the Spectro photofluorometric tracings technique that I applied in my thesis research. I also learned from him the use of Thin Layer Chromatography (TLC) analysis methods. He let me use the instruments and the various chemicals needed for the analyses.

Our friendship grew stronger after we moved to the university-owned Solano Park students apartment complex. Uzi, his wife Ziva and their son Ori lived there too. Upon getting his Ph.D. they returned to Israel where Dr. Reiss got the job of managing and running the cosmetics production department of The Helena Rubinstein plant in Migdal HaEmek, Israel. He is still the expert in cosmetic lotions and creams coveted by ladies all around the world. In fact he never failed to brag to me that he is the smear champion of the world smearing millions of ladies. He later left Helena Rubinstein and opened his own cosmetic factory on the Golan Height producing special cosmetic products made from the Dead Sea Minerals. We are still close friends.

And then, there was my friend and countryman, Dr. Eliezer Benjamini, from the Department of Medical Microbiology, UC Davis School of Medicine who helped me with the cytological radio assay aspect of my research. Oddly enough, we both were, by definition, Entomologists because he got his Ph.D. from the Entomology Department of UC Berkley and I was about to get mine from UC Davis. We were Entomologists by name only since our research interests were more in the realm of physiology, and biochemistry. Dr. Benjamini got a professorship at the Department of Medical Microbiology at the UC Davis Medical School and became the Dean of UC Davis Medical School.

Dr. Summers was a Taxonomist, in the midst of finishing his research and summarizing his findings to be published in a professional in Acarology journal. Dr. Summers considered his last paper along with my Ph.D. thesis to be the finale of his long and impressive academic career. My frequent visits to the departments to meet my friends who helped me, caught his attention and he asked me one day, "Sam, are all of these people your Israeli friends?"

It caught me by surprise and I said, "Some are indeed Israelis but others are people I met while taking classes and got interested in their scientific work. We became friends and they offered to help me with my research."

Dr. Summers paused for few seconds and I sensed from the look on his face that he was not too happy about it. "Sam," he said, "Officially, I am your academic advisor and Ph.D. mentor who would approve and sign your diploma so I don't understand what these people have to do with your Ph.D. research."

I was not sure from the tone of his voice whether he was angry or his feelings were hurt. "Dr. Summers, of course you are my advisor and the sole person to approve or disapprove my research and Ph.D. dissertation but I have some ideas that I wish to explore and include in my thesis if they substantiate some of my hypotheses. For that I need to utilize the instruments that these friends have and their help. It would be best for us to set aside enough time for me to outline my Ph.D. research scope and what I wish to explore in addition to the taxonomy aspect of the research. I hope that you will give me your blessing after hearing my proposal."

Dr. Summers agreed and scheduled a meeting.

I was somewhat apprehensive, afraid it would turn out to be more of a confrontation than a discussion about my research approach and its scope. Dr. Summers asked me to be at his office during lunch break. When I arrived he was having his favorite lunch, sipping black coffee and munching on a large chunk of Swiss cheese. I was surprised to see Robert Witt, his technician, who shared the office with Dr. Summers. Since Dr. Summers was about to retire the department gave him a rather small office that also served as his lab. Robert Witt was allotted some space in that small room. To make the room even more crowded, it also served as my lab whenever I needed the stereoscopic microscope.

I had a good rapport with Robert. He was a devoted Christian, always asking me questions about the Old Testament after I showed him my bible written in Hebrew. "See Bob, I was teasing him, I read and speak the same language the Bible was written in while you have to read the King James version." He kept telling me how fortunate he was to work with me, one of the *Chosen People*. Robert was helping me with some of the experiments that needed attention while I was in classes or at the *Davis Enterprise*.

"Well Sam, let's hear your Ph.D. research proposal and how you plan to expedite it." Dr. Summers started the conversation. "I hope that it is not radically different from what we and the Qualification Test committee discussed and approved a few weeks ago," he added, putting me on the spot.

I chose my words very carefully, "Dr. Summers, as a Taxonomist, you have been drawing Cheyletus malaccensis for a number of years now. You are familiar with the tiniest detail, every *seta* (Latin for bristle) and every demarcation sign on its body. You know about its life cycle and its biology. We know that it reproduces through parthenogenesis where an unfertilized female produces only males. If the female is fertilized the progenies produced are females. That is what you taught us in your Acarology class. Bringing genetics into the picture, it stands to reason that a Cheyletus malaccensis male should have only one half of the chromosomes (haploids) that a female has (diploid). I don't know what this number is and I haven't found any information about it in the literature. Do you know the haploid/diploid number unique to our mite?"

"No, I don't know what that number is and I am not aware of anyone else looking into it, so what is your plan to resolve the question?"

"To start, I would try to prepare specimens of males and females and stain them with a specific dye that shows affinity to DNA and watch the tissue under the microscope. Hopefully I would be able to see and photograph the chromosomes and count how many each sex has. That's why I asked for Robert's help in the genetics department. I could use their powerful microscope with its sophisticated camera, learn their methods of preparing specimens and staining techniques. Hopefully, I will be able to capture the chromosome on the photographic film and incorporate the photograph into my thesis."

Dr. Summers thought for a while, "what if you aren't able to see the chromosomes, then what?"

"Still, the objective of proving that the males are produced from unfertilized eggs and the females from fertilized ones, could be proven by using DNA content as proxy. Males should have one half of the DNA compared to the female."

"Sounds too complicated to me," he said, "but go ahead and tell me how you plan to perform this task?"

"That's why I went to my friend Dr. Eliezer Benjamini from the Medical School's Medical Microbiology department. He agreed to order the radioactive C14 thymidine I need to soak into the oatmeal we feed the flour mite, Acarus siro, the prey of the Cheyletus malaccensis. The next step would be to count the radioactivity in CPM (counts per minute) per milligram of dry weight of both sexes using Dr. Benjamini's liquid scintillation counter. He agreed to take care of all the necessary steps and regulations associated with handling radioactive materials."

It was unmistakably obvious that Dr. Summers was upset and irritated but he motioned me to continue with my presentation.

Next, I explained my time spent at the Food Science department and the Enology department.

"Yes I am curious about that too," Dr. Summers said. "How in the world are food science and wine making related to our mite?"

"Dr. Summers, have you noticed that during the molting process, the quiescent nymphs become attractive to the males? Several males may hover around until these quiescent nymphs finish their final molt and always turn out to be females. I believe very strongly that the quiescent nymphs produce a sex-attractant chemical to lure the male.

A similar courtship of molting nymphs by active males is well known for spider mites. So if indeed the molting female nymph produces a chemical that serves as sex attractant, I plan to look for any significant biochemical differences between the males and females of Cheyletus malaccensis and identify the sex attractant if they produce one. Usually some pheromones or sex attractants are volatile chemicals and I believe that by using the gas chromatography method I will be able to isolate and identify that chemical, if our mite produces it. My friend Willy at the Enology department agreed to help me with that as they use it with their wine analyses on a daily basis. As for the other biochemical components that might be involved, I plan on analyzing extract from females and males using Thin Layer Chromatography and Spectro Photo Fluorometric analyses techniques. My friend Uzi Reiss at the Food Science department agreed to help me with that using their instruments and also contribute all the reagents I need. Well, that is, in a nutshell, the explanation for my desire to expand the scope of my research beyond just the taxonomy of our mite," I told Dr. Summers.

There was a long and tense silence. Robert Witt, Dr. Summers's technician, pretended to be looking hard through the microscope but I knew he was trying not to miss anything. I sensed that my revelation was something that Dr. Summers did not anticipate. It took him a while to collect his thoughts and formulate his reply.

Then, it was Dr. Summers's turn to lecture me about the situation I created with my wish to expand my Ph.D. research beyond the scope of his expectations. I didn't notice animosity on his part when he broke his silence and said, "Sam, if you're so interested in the biochemistry, genetics and physiology, you should have gone to one of these departments to get your Ph.D. but you chose our Entomology department and me as your advisor and mentor. The proposal I just heard is not in line with my own field of expertise. So people who know me and read your dissertation and the resulting scientific publications will realize that I was not associated with your research. I will support you and help you switch to other departments if you chose to do so."

I felt that the atmosphere at Dr. Summers's tiny office/lab was getting charged so I had to be extremely careful with my replies. I let him know, in no uncertain terms, that I would like to finish my Ph.D. under his mentorship. "I strongly believe that if I am successful with the research I just presented, it would open new facets to the research in the Acarology field. You will be the co-author of any scientific paper coming out of my Ph.D. thesis. That is the best way I can think of to acknowledge your contribution."

I saw a warm smile adorn his face and I realized he took my words as a big compliment. "Sam, thanks for considering me as your co-author on any future scientific publications stemming from your Ph.D. research, and knowing you and the kind of research you plan to carry out, I am confident that such papers will see the light, yet I cannot lend my name as your co-author."

"Why is that?" I asked.

"As I stated before, everyone in the Acarology field knowns my area of expertise. Reading publications that deal with cytogenetic, DNA and biochemistry with my name as co-author will raise too many eye browses. People realize that I was not the one who guided you. But more importantly, I am confident that your research in these areas will yield impressive results because they already make sense to me, so this is your moment to shine as a young scientist. You should be the one who gets all of the credit and the limelight."

I was very moved. He gave me even more incentive to succeed. The onus was on me now. I was so relieved. The meeting had the potential to become acrimonious but turned out to be very pleasant.

After the meeting with Dr. Summers, I made a brief stop at the medical school for a talk with Dr. Eliezer Benjamini. "Eli, I just came from a lengthy meeting with Dr. Summers where I described using the DNA measurements as a proxy to prove that the Cheyletus malaccensis females are diploid and should have twice as much DNA as the males. He was not too happy at first and protested that this approach was outside the scope of his expertise. Since you also got your Ph.D. from the UC Berkeley Department of Entomology please do me a favor and see him in person. Talk to him about the way we are going to carry out this experiment. It will keep him abreast and give him the sense that he is a participant rather than an outsider."

"I'll do that," Dr. Benjamini promised and let me know that he already ordered the C-14 radioactive-labeled thymidine. I always marveled at his multi-faceted attributes and knowledge including being an accomplished violinist and member of the Davis classical music orchestra.

Dr. Benjamini's somewhat unconventional path to a Ph.D. in Entomology, ending as the Dean of UC Davis Medical school, provided me with the opportunity to dispel some of the false perceptions of the real and tangible field of interest any scientist gets into. For example: Gregor Mendel, a 19th century Moravian Augustinian monk, is not remembered for any pious work he did. He is recognized as the Father of modern genetics for his hybridization experiments with pea flowers and the distribution of genes in the progenies. Another example is the wide use of the common fruit fly Drosophila melanogaster. Due to its rapid life cycle and the ability to produce a large number of offspring per generation it is used in genetics, physiology and other research areas. In fact, there have been several Nobel Prizes awarded for research that used the common fruit fly. So a scientist who does research using Drosophila fly is a Geneticist not an Entomologist.

Or how about all the scientists using mice to test new drugs, or to produce large numbers of identical antibodies through the process known as hybridoma (Monoclonal antibodies). Whatever their field of expertise may be, they are not Zoologists just because they work on and with mice. This discussion could go on for a long time but my point is that although Dr. Benjamini and I got our degrees from the Department of Entomology, it did not make us Entomologists. He used insects to do his physiology-related studies at UC Berkeley and I used the mite Cheyletus malaccensis in my physiological/genetics research. It took Dr. Summers a while to come to terms with that truism.

When Dr. Benjamini talked with Dr. Summers about the issue we got his blessing.

A few weeks later I had the pleasure of showing Dr. Summers that my experiments at Dr. Benjamini's lab went very well and indeed, the Cheyletus malaccensis females had twice as much DNA as the males, validating the observation that the males are produced from unfertilized eggs. I was not the only one elated with the findings. Dr. Summers was smiling from ear to ear when I showed him the results and he even gave me his trade-mark eye wink.

"I am still working to show you the exact number of chromosomes the males and females have."

"Knowing you, I am sure you will."

I left his office to see my friend Robert, the geneticist to work on finding the chromosomes of the mite and photograph them. This research aspect of my thesis turned out to be more difficult than I had bargained for. The first step was to be able to see and identify the chromosomes as such, and not mistake artifacts as chromosomes. I was fixing and staining the mites with a specific biological stain that showed affinity to DNA (in this case, the chromosomes) and then positioned them at the center of the microscope's field of vision.

I was successful doing that but the pictures I took through Robert's microscope did not show the chromosomes on the print. It was worthless because I did not have a photograph to show that the female had twice as many chromosomes (four) than the male (two). It drove me nuts. I located a spot on the slide showing the chromosome at the center of field vision, focused the image and said to Robert, "Here it is, you take the picture, develop the film and then print the photograph like you do in your own research. We should see four chromosomes on the print exactly as we see them at X1000 magnification."

"Will do," he said and asked me to stop by at his lab the next day on my way to the *Davis Enterprise.*

I stopped at Robert's lab the next day. "Sam, I'm as frustrated as you are." I developed and printed the negative we took yesterday but the four chromosomes we saw through the microscope lenses do not show up on the print. The only thing I can see is a dark stained area where we saw the chromosomes under the microscope. The photograph is useless as it does not show the details we need."

This problem hit me at the time when had I just started delving into the hobby of photographic film developing and printing. I had read enough about the subject and was familiar with the jargon used by the self-ordained experts.

"Robert, what kind of developer do you routinely use to process the film loaded in the microscope camera?"

"I found the Kodak EMS D-19 Replacement Developer to be the best for taking pictures of chromosomes, for my research at least. But the specimen of my genetics research are plant tissues whereas yours are mites. Maybe my methodology is not suitable for your material. I'm sure that this problem is solvable with not-too-difficult modifications. See if you can come up with some ideas and we'll do some trial and error attempts to solve the mystery."

I was more determined than ever to find a solution.

People who knew me, never failed to accuse me of being an ultra-stubborn person so the hurdle of not being able to produce photographs showing the Cheyletus malaccensis chromosomes challenged my reputation. Personally, I did not consider it to be stubbornness. I called it, "Sam's perseverance" the same trait that has been pushing me throughout my entire life, including my constant struggles at UC Davis and the US immigration people.

I suspected that the developer used by Robert was too active or harsh on the latent image recorded on the film silver halide emulsion and compromised the resolution of the recorded image. Resolution, by definition, indicates how close adjacent lines can be to each other and still be seen, visibly, as two lines. If I was right, the aggressive character of that photographic developer caused the latent images of the four chromosomes on the film emulsion to merge and therefore did not show as four separate lines on the printed photograph. I had some ideas on how to explore and validate my hypothesis. I discussed my hypothesis with Robert.

"So what do you suggest?" he asked.

"Let's use the same spectroscopic film that we have been using but let's process it with the Kodak D-76 Developer instead. It is less aggressive than your high contrast Kodak EMS D-19 Replacement Developer. The Kodak D-76 Developer should give us a fine grain and normal contrast, at least this is what Kodak literature claims." I said.

"Let's do just that. I have enough of this developer in powder form to make one gallon aqueous solution. I kept a few of the microscope slides showing the chromosomes we photographed a few days ago. You find the spot on the slide that you wish to photograph and I'll process the film and produce the prints. I'll have the results by tomorrow. It should be your moment of truth, Sam."

"I'll be at your lab tomorrow morning and don't even dare give me bad news. I'll accept only good news," I joked. We took a few photographs of both the male and female chromosomes and I rushed to my job at the newspaper.

I could hardly concentrate during my morning class on campus as I was eager to dash to Robert's lab and face the *moment of truth*. When I arrived he was waiting for me sipping his black coffee and offered me a cup. "Sam, when you count your blessings, you should add a new one to your list. Here are your *freaking* chromosomes," he said and handed me a few photographs showing the illusive chromosomes we had been trying to capture on film.

The chromosomes were beaming at me from the glossy prints. Now I could substantiate my claim that the Cheyletus malaccensis female has double the number of chromosomes as the male. I already showed Dr. Summers the result from my C14-labled DNA experiments. "Wait until I show these to Dr. Summers, I'm sure he'll be happy that the field of Acarology has new bells and whistles coming out of his lab."

As expected, Dr. Summers was excited to see the photographs showing the chromosomes of the male and female mite he had been studying as a Taxonomist for years. "Can you imagine?" I asked him. "This rather complicated creature that you watch under your stereoscopic microscope and determine to be a male is developed and governed by only two tiny chromosomes and the female by four chromosomes," I said, trying to exude some measure of authority. After all, I discovered it in spite of his initial discouragement. I explained the reason for the long time it took to capture the image of the chromosomes on the photographs. "I switched to a less aggressive film developer and bingo, they appeared."

Dr. Summers inspected the photographs very closely and said, "Yes, the quality of the photographs is adequate enough if your objective is just to document the number of chromosomes of our mite. If you want to publish this research in the proper scientific journal, you must improve the contrast to make your pictures more printable."

I totally agreed with his suggestion and started working on the contrast issue. I knew the exact chemical ingredients and the concentration per liter of the developer Robert used, that gave us too much contrast as opposed to the Kodak D-76 Developer which enabled showing the chromosomes on the photos but at the expense of the contrast. My gut feeling led me to believe that perhaps inventing my own custom-made film developer could be the way to go. Before I knew it, I found myself spending a substantial amount of my time browsing through photographic chemistry textbooks. Luckily, Robert had his own mysterious way to find some of the exotic ingredients I needed to produce my concoctions. The best way to evaluate which of my own developers would give the best results was to order a 100 ft. roll of the film Robert used in the microscope camera, splice smaller footage from that roll, long enough to record five to six frames. We spooled the small unexposed film into the 35mm film cartridges and loaded the camera. Once the pictures were taken, I used film developers I formulated to develop the images.

I finally got the optimal results as far as details and contrast were concerned and Dr. Summer's approved. I kept the formula of that developer as my *trade secret* thinking that I might use it in the future. And sure enough I did. A company I worked for a few years later tested my high definition film developer, and found it superior to the Kodak developer they had been using to process the aerial photographs taken by the U-2 reconnaissance airplane. Their photographic lab started using mine.

If you grew up knowing only digital cameras, and printers, the chemistry of photographic processing sounds medieval. "Splicing and spooling photographic films? D-76 film developer? High contrast fine grain film developer? What are you talking about Man?" But the chemistry of processing both black and white and color film and prints became a significant part of my adult life. (See Chapters 14 and 16.)

Time flew by and the normalcy of a crisis-free period started to settle in. My research work was going very well, yielding the significant results I needed to validate most of the hypotheses in my thesis. I continued to work more than sixty hours a week at the *Davis Enterprise* and twenty hours on courses and research. Then, I received a letter that validated my hard work and scholastic achievement as a UC Davis student. It came from Phi Kappa Phi, the National Scholastic Honor Society, UC Davis Chapter. It was dated February 18, 1971. (Figure 10. 8)

I took the liberty to brag and to prove that I came to the USA to study. I made a copy of that letter and sent it to Inspector Jones at the immigration office in Sacramento. After the initiation banquet on May 26, I also sent him a copy of the certificate. (Figure 10.9.)

PHI KAPPA PHI

National Scholastic Honor Society
University of California, Davis Chapter
Davis, California

February 18, 1971

Mr. Samuel Regev
Department of Entomology
U.C.Davis
Davis, California 95616

Dear Nominee:

The University of California, Davis Chapter of the Honor Society of Phi
Kappa Phi has elected you a member.

Phi Kappa Phi is a national honor society founded in 1897 which now has
121 chapters in colleges and universities. The Davis Chapter was established
in 1954. Phi Kappa Phi is the only national honor society which chooses its
members from all branches of learning. The highest standards of scholarship
are used in the selection. Members are chosen from the upper five percent of
the junior class of each college of the University, from the upper ten percent
of each senior class, and from the upper ten percent of candidates for advanced
degrees in the Graduate Division and in the professional schools. Your election
to membership is a recognition of your high scholarship in the University of
California.

Acceptance of this bid to membership involves a total cost to you of $18.50.
You will be initiated at a banquet arranged in your honor by the local chapter.
You will receive from the National Society a key or pin, a certificate of member-
ship, and two year's subscription to the Phi Kappa Phi Journal.

In order to be a member of the society, it is necessary that you complete
the enclosed form and return it with your check in the enclosed envelope as
soon as possible. Your check must be received by April 5.

The initiation banquet will be Wednesday, May 26 at 5:30 p.m. in Freeborn
Hall. You may make reservations for guests, if you wish, at $3.50 each. Your
check for these additional reservations must reach me by May 21.

Sincerely yours,

Elizabeth Baker

Mrs. Elizabeth Baker
Chapter Secretary
Office of Admissions

EB:kb
enclosures

Figure 10.8 Phi Kappa Phi Letter

Figure 10.9 Phi Kappa Phi certificate

✡

Using my resurrected Volkswagen to deliver the newspaper to our El Macero paperboy and to the irate subscribes, indicated that installing a used engine was the cheapest solution but the car had no pep. In fact, my electric shaving razor had more power than the engine the mechanic installed. The thoughts of, "Sooner or later you'll have to get rid of it," started to permeate my head but I managed to resist the temptation to get another car as we had other priorities.

Batia's boss Sheila and her fiancé, Dr. Ron Schechter, the veterinary professor, were about to get married and move to San Diego. We needed to find another babysitting job with people who would agree to pay in cash.

Sheila's next-door neighbors were US Naturalized Swedes. Oscar, the husband, was a professor in the Economic Department. We knew them very well from Batia's occasional babysitting of their two sons. They knew about our ordeal with the immigration authorities. Realizing that Batia was going to lose her babysitting job, they looked for a new babysitting job for Batia. It just happened that Oscar's colleague,

Laurence, a professor at the Economics department, just lost his wife to cancer and was looking for a dependable babysitter to stay with his two boys when he was teaching. Oscar told him about Batia. Laurence invited us to his house to discuss the job and let his two sons inspect the babysitter candidate.

There was one issue that had the potential to torpedo her getting the job. Although Batia looked as slim as a twig, we were expecting our first baby sometime in early April so we let him know about it in case he preferred to hire someone else. It didn't take long for him to make up his mind and Batia was hired on the spot. "She could work until it's close to the due date and my mother will come from New York to help until Batia is back at work."

Laurence's mother arrived from New York two weeks before Batia's due date and was very pleased, "Everything here is *spick and span*," she told Batia, referring to a popular commercial household cleaner sold by Proctor and Gamble. The product's name was a metaphor for something neat and clean.

The next issue on the agenda, albeit, a happy one was where to live once our first baby was born. As always, money was tight for us and we elected to stay in our one bedroom university apartment, on the 3rd floor. Now I had to master another skill, *being a young father*.

✡

Paying for medical services as compared to today's charges is even more striking than bread prices at the time. While I was a student at UC Davis, my monthly premium through Kaiser was $13 a month for Batia and me. The co-pay for any office visit was $1 per visit no matter how long it was. When Batia got pregnant, the prenatal care and the delivery was a flat package that cost us $99.

Paying for having our first baby was the easy part. Ushering the baby into this world was something different as it required preparation on my part. So Dr. Summers and the other doctors that were involved with my studies at UC Davis, were delegated to the back seat, releasing the front to Dr. Ferdinand Lamaze and Dr. Benjamin Spock, my two new gurus who taught Batia and I *Parenthood*, the right way (in their opinions, of course).

I was adamant, as an expecting father, to be part of Batia's preparations for the delivery as well as being in the delivery room. I became familiar with the childbirth classes developed by Dr. Lamaze. The classes taught the expectant mother ways to reduce the pain associated with the delivery process. I concentrated mainly on learning his breathing techniques and would coach Batia while pushing the baby through the birth canal.

In retrospect, I can attest to the fact that it sounds great on paper but mostly wishful thinking in real life and the reality in the delivery room. It just happened that the wife of a student living in the house next to us was a certified Lamaze childbirth instructor and held a weekly class at her apartment so we took the class.

There were several couples expecting their first and the fear of the unknown was the glue that bonded us together. I am sure that to the people strolling by the instructor's apartment with its windows open during class, it sounded like a bunch of male chauvinists shouting at their poor wives, "Push."

The instructor forewarned the husbands, that is was quite possible that instead of getting the wife to act on our, "Push" command we would most likely get a good measure of profanity leveled at us. It was hard for me to imagine my dear wife Batia doing that. The Lamaze instructor also advised the expectant mothers how to prepare and what to include in the famous suitcase that you grab on the way to the hospital when labor starts. So there we were, a bunch of Americans learning the Lamaze Childbirth technique as if it were gospel. But let's face it, there are billions of mothers around the world who give birth without a Lamaze diploma.

Everyone was eagerly waiting for Batia's due date, including Esther, Batia's mom who flew all the way from Israel to be with us for the birth of her first grandchild. Being a practical lady, she filled her suitcases with cloth diapers that the textile factory in her *kibbutz* manufactured and was known for throughout Israel. I'm talking about cloth diapers you secure with safety pins. Yes! You heard correctly. We were still too poor to afford disposables.

My main concern was our VW as the engine from the junkyard was getting worse and I was afraid I would end up delivering my own child on the side of the highway.

On the night of April 10, 1971, 11 p.m. Batia's water broke so we rushed to the Kaiser hospital in Sacramento. I don't remember ever being as pious as I was during fifteen miles to Sacramento, praying that the VW engine wouldn't stall before reaching our destination. It sounded funny but my prayers did the job.

Upon arrival one nurse ushered Batia into the hospital delivery wing while another nurse gave me the proper attire before allowing me to be the best Lamaze coach ever. "You sit here, dear," the nurse told me. "I'll call you when they're ready. Her contractions are still far apart and she is only few centimeters dilated," she said with an authoritative conviction in her voice.

"Oh boy!" I was mumbling to myself feeling extremely important. Our medical team dumped their beloved imperial measurement system and switched to the metric system just for me and Batia to determine her dilation in centimeters.

After midnight I got really worried as no one came to take me into the delivery room and the thoughts of medical crises or complications started running in my head. Two more hours passed, and I, the greatest Lamaze coach, was still unemployed. Finally, the nurse came and said "Your wife is still in labor. You have a son but he is a breech baby so we are waiting for another doctor to come and help with the delivery. Unfortunately, you won't be allowed into the delivery room during the delivery so you can take off the gown."

Although I took the Lamaze class, the term a *breech baby* was a new term for me. I asked her what that term meant. "Your son changed his position in the uterus. He would pass through the birth canal with his legs first and not with his head first, the position in the majority of deliveries. That's why your wife's labor is longer than usual and also the reason why we called another doctor to help in case they decide to deliver your son through C-section. That is also why they won't let you be in the delivery room. But don't worry, your wife is in good hands," she reassured me.

That was a long night and I was the only expecting father there. Finally, after eleven hours of hard labor my son Raz entered the world with his legs first and his head last. No C-Section was needed and I became a father of an eight pound, eleven ounce son. I felt relieved that everyone was healthy and no complications surfaced. Still I felt somewhat deprived when he was delivered without me showing of my Lamaze expertise. I felt like shouting, "I want my money back," then the inner voice in me said in a soothing voice, "Relax Sam, there will always be the next time for you to shout at Batia: "PUSH, PUSH PUSHHHHH."

The nurse took me to the room where Batia and Raz were. Batia was exhausted from the long labor. I thanked God and the doctors that everything turned out OK in spite of the complicated delivery.

I left for Davis and promised Batia I'd be back early in the evening with her Mom. I drove back with the car windows wide open to prevent me from falling asleep at the wheel after the long sleepless night. When I got home I told Batia's mom the news and explained why the delivery had taken so long. I grabbed something light to eat and told her to be ready by 5:00 p.m. to visit Batia and Raz. She was excited and started loading her 35 mm Konica camera ready to take pictures to show off when she returned to her *kibbutz*.

The mother-daughter reunion was understandably touching. After losing her husband when Batia was three years old, Esther never remarried. Now her married daughter was a mom herself, Esther's first beautiful grandson. They brought him to Batia's bed for breastfeeding. We had such a good time together. I told Batia to enjoy every minute in the hospital where everything was taken care of because in a day or two, we would return to the real world of navigating parenthood on our own.

The next day, Batia looked much stronger and eager to go home. The nurse said that barring unforeseen problems, she would be released the next day at 10:00 a.m. "Please come thirty minutes early for the crash course for first-time mothers on how to care for the newborn. It will behoove you, as a first time father, to learn as well," the nurse told me.

"Don't worry I'll be on time," I assured her.

It was nice to have Esther with us during that time as she kept Batia company while I was attending classes, doing my research and carrying the *Davis Enterprise* on my shoulders.

✡

I worked frantically to prepare our apartment to accommodate our new family member. I found a crib at The Used Furniture Library, a large storage building where students left behind household items. Raz would sleep in a crib in our tiny bedroom and Esther would sleep on the couch in the living room that I also found at the furniture library. This couch was ugly and very heavy. I had to carry it up to the third floor all by myself. That was a huge undertaking and I felt almost like the Greek Mythology Sisyphus pushing the huge boulder up the mountain. Luckily, unlike Sisyphus, I did not drop the couch and was able to carry it up to our apartment. Then, I had to struggle for another thirty minutes to navigate this freaking couch through the narrow door to our apartment. I learned two important lessons from my saga with the couch on that day. First, whenever you buy any furniture and/ or appliances *always* think about how you're going to shove it into or out of the door without taking the door jamb along with it. The second lesson I learned was to *always* have a great respect to the people who work for moving companies. These people are wizards and magicians handling these items.

I was cussing and swearing at that couch but, nonetheless, it had the last laugh because as the song says, *What's Goes Up Must Come Down*. The day we left Davis, I had to take it through the same stupid apartment door, down the stairs and back to the furniture library, all by myself. As I am writing about the coach, many years after the fact I feel somewhat guilty and unfair toward that couch as it served us loyally during the many times Raz got sick with a bad ear infection. Generally he was a very healthy baby but was prone to ears infections. This problem resolved itself as he grew older, but at Davis, when he was sick, I took him to the living room, let him sleep on that coach while I slept on the floor next to him and watched that he was OK.

There was one more issue for me to resolve before bringing Batia and Raz home and that was a place for Batia to change Raz's diapers. Poor Raz had to settle for an ironing board that Batia pushed against the wall to ensure it wouldn't tip over.

Everything was ready so I made the trip to the hospital one more time while Batia's mom stayed in the apartment. This time, our lousy VW decided to give us a hard time and stalled on the way home. It was a typical Sacramento Valley hot day and being stuck without air conditioning with a three-day-old infant was not exactly fun. I opened the engine compartment at the back of the car and tinkered with few parts and luckily the engine started again. I spent the rest of the trip praying that the VW won't stall again and also reciting my new mantra "Get rid of this stupid car the first chance you have."

The next concern on the agenda was what to feed our ever-hungry Raz. He was getting doctor's prescribed multivitamins drops containing fluoride but feeding him with the popular Similac or Enfamil baby formulas was cost-prohibitive so I needed to address this issue as the supply given to us upon discharging Batia from the hospital was gone. Breast feeding was not always enough. From my apiculture class I learned that honey contains about 38% fructose and 31% glucose, both are easy to digest so each table spoon of honey would provide Raz with at least 46 kilocalories of food energy. Protein and fats could come from milk so I chose the 12 ounce cans of evaporated milk that cost fifteen cents apiece at the Safeway store or sometimes cheaper when it was on sale. It had a very long shelf life based on the expiration date listed on the label so I didn't worry about it going bad after few days.

Evaporated milk is produced from regular milk by removing 60% of its water content. My first trial of *baby formula* was diluting one portion of evaporated milk with one portion of boiled water and then adding 1 tablespoon of US Grade-A clover honey. Raz seemed to like it, and wasn't crying as often. To make it a bit tastier I reduced the dilution rate of the evaporated milk a bit. But the *seal of approval* came during our first postnatal visit with the pediatrician. Dr. Smith was very pleased with Raz's weight gain and overall progress. He taught Batia a specific massage practice to perform on Raz's legs, to help straighten them since he was a breech baby and it had affected his legs slightly.

When he asked what we were feeding him, I mentioned my formula and its composition. Dr. Smith paused for a minute and then told me that some pediatricians are against feeding honey to infants but he, personally, did not notice any ill effect. He left it up to us to decide whether or not to continue its use.

A year later, I guess that the baby formula I invented did a great job as the pediatrician was happy with Raz's developmental progress. There was one thing the doctor disliked about our parenting practice. "You have to stop confusing him with your switching back and forth between English and Hebrew. Please choose one language and stick with it," he admonished us and we chose English.

Batia's Mom, Esther, stayed with us until the end of May 1971 and helped Batia while I was splitting my time between classes, doing my research and working sixty-one hours a week at the newspaper.

Then on May 26 at 5:30 p.m. Esther had Raz all to herself as Batia and I attended the Phi Kappa Phi initiation banquet. We ate our meal at the speed of light and left for home as we were on edge leaving Raz for the first time with someone else, albeit, his grandma. Esther savored the minutes with him and her entire visit with us. She went back for Israel with many photographs to fill her apartment and show members of her *kibbutz*.

✡

The thirty-day maternity leave ended and I modified my weekday routine so I could bring Batia, Raz and his plan pen to Laurence's no later than 7:00 am so that Laurence could leave for work and Batia could make sure that his sons were ready for school. Laurence's work schedule was not fixed so I couldn't predict when I would need to take them home. When she let me know when to pick her up, I would leave *Davis Enterprise*, pick them up, throw the playpen in the car, take them home and return to my job. There were days when she and Raz had to stay at Laurence's house from 7:00 a.m. until after midnight as Laurence, a widower, started dating. Here again, I had to stop what I was doing at the offset press, drive my family home and return to work until around 6:00 a.m. Most of the time, my classes on campus started at 8 o'clock and I was really tired by then.

Needless to say, the crazy schedule and waking Raz on these crazy hours was not easy on him or Batia, making me feel guilty to the core. It was also difficult for Batia. In addition to the physical strain of keeping the house clean and seeing to it that the Laurence children were ready to go to school, she had to deal with Laurence's mother who was still there.

The old lady did not stop complaining about Batia's work and about Raz being there. It made me mad because it was her son who made the choice to hire Batia not hers. And if before Raz's birth she was commending Batia on how the house was *spick and span,* now she was looking with a magnifying glass to find a speck of dust or something to complain about. She could not comprehend that babies cry sometimes and she would blow her top whenever Raz cried in his playpen. Batia checked on Raz while the old lady scolded, "Don't go in there. Let him cry, it is good for his lungs," proclaimed Oma the *Pulmonologist*.

Laurence's romance flourished as judged by the number of times he asked Batia to stay until almost midnight as he and his fiancé went out. I guessed that marriage was on his mind when he decided to move from the nice house he purchased with his late wife, to a larger, fancier house with a swimming pool owned by his fiancé.

Raz was fourteen months old when Batia started working at Laurence's new place. He was walking and played with Laurence's sons during the day, so I stopped taking his playpen to Batia's workplace.

Batia had to be extra vigilant, making sure no one drowned in the pool, including Raz. We simply locked the gate to the pool and hid the key in a safe place out of the children's reach. The house was located in a neighborhood of mostly UC Davis professors. One of them was my Human Physiology professor.

Laurence and his fiancé finally got married. She worked on campus and both left just before 8:00 am. It was more difficult for Batia when summer recess started and Laurence's sons stayed home most of the time.

✡

Since I no longer needed the VW to haul Raz's playpen, I felt it was an opportune time for us to get rid of the trouble-making, pain-in-the-neck VW square back. I drove to the Toyota dealer that kept a few VW beetles on his lot and traded it with a nice looking top performing white beetle. It drove like a charm and was very dependable.

When summer break at the university started, Laurence and his wife Jennifer, asked us to move to their house and take care of the boys and the house, while they went on a one-month honeymoon in Europe. Evidently they felt comfortable enough to let us take care of the children and the house.

Laurence prepared a very lengthy *To Whom it May Concern* legal document and even longer *To Do* and *Not to Do* instructions that looked more like someone's Ph.D. thesis. We were told what doctors to take his sons to, his preferred hospital in case hospitalization was absolutely necessary. We were not allowed to use the pool but he wanted me to clean it every two days to prevent the growth of algae. And, "The water level in the pool must be in the middle of the blue tiles at the bar on which the thermometer hangs." He also made me the gardener of the property which meant mowing the grass every ten days and watering the flowerbeds twice a week. There were many instructions regarding the son's activities such as: "The boys come in and out of the house only through the garage." There is NO ball playing in the backyard, ONLY in the front. After dinner, the boys do not play out front; only in the backyard." I was also told how to clean the kitchen and its fancy appliances. And the Formica! God forbid if I dared cleaning it with scouring powder. All of these extra chores were in addition to Batia's job as the boys' babysitter.

I don't recall how much he paid for our services but is was extremely low and bordered on taking advantage of us. Laurence told us to buy our own food and share it with his sons. It did not occur to him that he should be the one paying for his son's food. Luckily for us, the boys were crazy about the puddings I made from scratch and chose to eat the pudding more than real food.

Then came the phone call the evening before he and his wife were to return from Europe. I picked up the phone and it was Laurence telling me to drive 166 miles round trip from Davis to the San Francisco International airport to pick them up at about 10 a.m. "Use your own car and don't bring anyone with you because we have large suitcases."

I was in complete shock as it was not planned. Being their chauffeur was not part of the deal. And why should I cram their suitcases into my tiny VW beetle when their two spacious cars were sitting in the garage? I was fuming mad but at that point there was nothing I could do but tell him that I would be there and hung up the phone.

The next morning I filled up my VW beetle with gasoline and drove to San Francisco International airport, a place I had not been before. It took me a while to find a paid parking spot next to the terminal. I missed a few classes as well as a few hours of work. I was still mad at both of them and hardly said anything during the drive home.

I am still fuming mad at him forty-eight years later. He never offered to pay even for the gasoline and the parking fee at the airport. There was no thank you or any token of appreciation from him or his wife. Just a cold calculated taking advantage of our volatile financial situation. It sounded strange to admit that a few weeks later when he told Batia that they no longer needed her babysitting service it was music to my ears.

Now Batia had plenty of time to be with Raz. Since we lived on the third floor, it was necessary to cordon off access to the stairs leading all the day down to the large grassy knoll between the houses. I built a fence and gate to keep Raz from falling or leaving our apartment on his own. Although we lost the babysitting income, my job at the *Davis Enterprise*, the tuition waiver I received due to my high GPA, and Batia's occasional evening and weekend babysitting kept us financially afloat so we paid Arthur Ganz the $500 he loaned us when we first came to Davis. I was nearly finished with all the required courses and seminars pertaining to my Ph.D. degree. My research work, and the experiments to produce the data supporting my hypotheses were almost complete, including the photographs, charts and diagrams which I did myself instead of hiring someone else. It was time to start writing my thesis, realizing that, at last, I was at a touching distance from fulfilling my lifetime dream. The staff at the International Student Office told me I would be able to stay up to eighteen months with the student visa and then stay out of the country for two years before coming back. I was looking for the most productive way to spend these post-graduation months.

The most attractive option was to search for a postdoctoral research position somewhere in the USA. I was looking in the professional journals for scientists who worked in my area of expertise and published their research work but there were very few of them. I found only three universities. One was Dr. Wyatt Cone, a professor at the Irrigated Agricultural Research and Extension Center, a branch of Washington State University (WSU). The other one was a professor at the University of Florida and the last one was a researcher at a university in Manitoba, Canada. The one from Florida and the one from Manitoba replied to my inquiry saying basically the same thing, "Sorry, your research and credentials are impressive but we have no funding for a postdoctoral position." The inquiry letter I sent to Dr. Wyatt Cone remained unanswered for a long time. I wrote to him after finding publications in professional journals describing work done at his lab by a postdoctoral student from New Zealand. The work was similar to my own studies on pheromone and sex-attractants.

Not hearing a reply to my letter was torturous. Waiting for Dr. Cone's letter became a daily obsession. Our phone was on the wall by the small kitchen sink so I kept a dry towel close to me when I washed the dishes in case Dr. Cone called.

My afternoon routine involved driving Raz to the park by the green apartment's complex where Batia and I first lived. Once there, I secured him into his favorite swing and I pushed, facing the north, in the direction of my new Promised Land, the State of Washington hoping to hear good news from Dr. Cone.

This daily ritual lasted a long time and always ended with disappointment. It brought back to my mind the prophecy of Jeremiah 1:14. I was expecting a pleasant event coming from the north in the form of Dr. Cone's acceptance letter, but according to Jeremiah the only thing coming from the north was nothing but evil as it said, "Then the Lord said unto me, out of the north an evil shall break forth upon all the inhabitants of the land." Every day that passed without hearing from Dr. Cone just reinforced that prophecy in my mind. "Jeremiah was absolutely right so I better forget about the postdoctoral option," I told myself.

The days became shorter and summer was already gone but I kept taking Raz every evening to his favorite swing. I was behind him and pushing the swing in the north direction. Superstition started to take hold of me. I kept the going to the swing park ritual fearing that stopping would cause bad luck. My days as a student were over and all my efforts were funneled toward writing the rough draft of my thesis. I went to the department to use the photography dark room for processing photographs and charts needed in the rough draft of my thesis. I used the typewriters and the department's letterhead and sent letters to more universities as I searched for a postdoctoral position. The rest of my time was split between working at the *Davis Enterprise* and staying home with Batia and Raz.

The holiday season was fast approaching and brought memories of my first Christmas at Davis four years earlier and my collision with Sam, the apartment manager where we first lived. He accused me of being a communist for not liking loudly played Christmas songs.

"You will have to spend another Christmas in Davis," my inner voice told me as no postdoctoral offers came in the mail. Nothing! A complete drought. And then the miracle happened and the phone rang. I almost fainted when I heard, "Hi, this is Dr. Wyatt Cone form the WSU Irrigated Agriculture Research Center in Prosser, Washington calling. You sent me an inquiry about a postdoctoral position."

"Of course I remember sending that request almost four months ago but I gave up on that since no one replied," I retorted.

"Well, I have to apologize for that." Dr. Cone said. "In case you don't know, our research center is a branch of the Washington State University system but the main campus, the administration and our Entomology department are located in Pullman, Washington, 167 miles east. This slowed down the communication, plus the fact that your letter arrived when I was out of town on my one-month summer vacation. Anyhow, the reason I'm calling now is to let you know that a postdoctoral offer from me is on its way to your address and I hope that you will accept it. Time is of the essence so the offer was sent to you from Pullman via express mail. If you accept it, you must complete all the paperwork, sign it and mail it back to us express mail. It is just a formality. As far as I'm concerned, I already approved your request and secured the funding. You will have to be in Prosser before Christmas. The sooner, the better."

"Thanks for your offer," I replied enthusiastically. "Of course, I am accepting your offer and we will be in Prosser before Christmas," I assured him.

"That's great, but since Christmas and the holiday season is just around the corner we need to find you a place to live. I have a real estate friend downtown and I asked him to reserve a place for you to stay temporarily until you find an apartment to suit you and your family."

I thanked him again for being proactive.

"See you soon, Sam," he said when he hung up the phone.

I felt so euphoric, convinced that God was shining upon us for a change and the angles clapped their hands in approval.

My life was pushed into high gear the minute I hung up the phone. It was a special moment for us and our dinner tasted sweeter than ever before. Right after dinner I went to my desk at the university and collected the rough drafts of my thesis, the charts and photographs and put them together into a big binder. It was a strange but awesome realization that my entire original research ideas and scientific work at UC Davis could be put into one binder to be handed to Dr. Summers the next day. I was sure that he would be very happy to hear that I was granted a postdoctoral job at Washington State University.

I also left a note on Carl's desk to call me as soon as possible regarding the car he wanted to sell. Carl, was a Post Doctorate student from Germany who came to UC Davis with his wife, was about to go back to Germany. Carl brought his car with him when he came from Germany. It was a brand new VW Square-back, similar to the one that plagued me for a long time but a newer model and in immaculate condition. Upon his arrival to Davis he had to take his VW to the authorized dealer to modify the engine to comply with California's new antipollution code. He and his wife liked to travel north to the Pacific Northwest region, Oregon, Washington and British Columbia, Canada. Visiting Seattle was his favorite expedition. The many trips he made indicated to me that his VW car was very dependable and in good shape. Carl was proud to show that he brought his car all the way from Germany and affixed noticeable oval D decal to indicate it came and belonged to a German visitor currently living in the USA.

Carl called me that evening. I broke the news to him about my new job and offered to buy his car. He was interested and confessed that I spared him the trouble of looking for a buyer while he prepared to return to Germany. We agreed on the price and the date I could possess it. Once I secured a larger VW to take us and our meager belongings to Washington State, I place an ad in the classified section on the *Davis Enterprise* trying to sell my VW beetle. I was astonished by how fast it sold. In only two days an air force officer from Sacramento came with his wife, looked at it, took a test drive on the highway and bought it. It was nice of him to send us a thank you note a few days later, telling us how great the car was and the excellent job I did taking care of it.

Dr. Cone also called to let me know that the administration office in Pullman received all the papers I sent. "Everything is ready for you, including the place for you to stay." He gave me the name and address of where to go upon our arrival in Prosser.

Dr. Cone also sent brochures and pamphlets published by the City of Prosser Chamber of Commerce describing his hometown. Carl, my German Post Doctorate colleague, always spoke highly of the beautiful Pacific Northwest and State of Washington where he and his wife felt at home. "It is the evergreen state and reminds us our own country with its evergreen trees, snow-covered mountain peaks, almost like European Alps," he said while showing me some of the impressive photographs he kept on his desk. Yet, the glossy brochures Dr. Cone sent me, no matter how glossy and colorful they were, showed barren rolling hills and yellow wheat fields ready to be harvested. Not even a trace of evergreen trees and the alpine mountain peaks Carl told me about. The pictures showing Prosser made me wonder if they had electricity there. Nonetheless, I was more than eager to start a new chapter in my life.

It seemed that my clock was ticking way faster than normal as the departure day came extremely fast and it was time to leave Davis, a place that had became our home for four and a half years. It was time to say farewell to many people that had become part of our lives. I hate farewells as they are emotionally taxing for me. The day before our departure I went to say the last goodbye to Harry at *Davis Enterprise* who gave me what I considered to be my life-line job right after my first car broke and other problems threatened to ruin my academic dreams.

I also stopped to chat with the Offset Press crew who taught me about lithography and the photographic darkroom jobs that became an integral part of my life. I talked to Phil the owner of the *Davis Enterprise* and his wife thanking them for the warm and sympathetic attitude toward me not to mention the flexibility they showed by accommodating my work schedule to fit my class schedule.

I made sure to stop at Dr. Benjamini's office for a last chat and thank him for his tremendous help and support in my effort to add more pizazz to my thesis. He did a great job convincing Dr. Summers to let me spread my wings further.

The most difficult farewell was with Dr. Summers, my mentor and advisor, who never lost faith in my ability to achieve and fulfill my academic dream. I know for sure that he was the only one who supported me on that important day when I came to the meeting requesting admission to their department. He convinced his colleagues to let me in. Dr. Summers shook my hand, held it for a long time and said, "I went over the rough draft of your thesis and marked a few notes and ideas for you to consider. I'm almost done and will leave the package inside the drawer by your desk so you can pick it up tonight. It is a great thesis. I am so glad you expanded into other scientific disciplines. I expect a few interesting scientific papers coming out of it," he said as we embraced for the last time. I promised to visit him in the future but history proved me wrong as it was the last time I saw Dr. Summers, my wonderful saint.

We left for Prosser, Washington the next morning. We had to leave the apartment empty and clean so I took everything we did not need down to the furniture library next to our building. I loaded our belongings into the car the evening before. The only items of value were the black and white TV Sheila gave us and the Fisher stereo system we purchased through the Israeli Students Organization. It was made for 110/220 dual voltage and 50/60 cycle that could be used both in the USA and in Israel.

It is not hard to imagine that we were squeezed to the max as our car was not large to begin with. The speakers were the heaviest items and took most of the space but they became instrumental to our safety on the slippery highway the next day.

And there was one more final job that I had to do before leaving the keys to the apartment. I had to take the famous freaking heavy couch all the way down to the furniture library, all by myself, mind you. I had to struggle from the third floor. It was very early in the morning and people were still asleep. I'm still perplexed where I got the muscle strength to do that job. Maybe God loaned me, temporarily, some of the strength the biblical Samson had. I was huffing and puffing upon pushing the coach through the furniture library storage place.

With Batia and Raz in the car, I made a final stop at the university to pick up the rough draft of my thesis Dr. Summers left with his corrections and suggestions. I took a last farewell look at the place, my sanctuary and a second home for over four years. It was a bit sad but a new future was waiting for us. I dashed back to the car, and placed the thesis under the driver seat and said to Batia and Raz, "Let's go, people, we have a very long travel ahead of us," and started the engine.

✡

We never saw a single flake of snow falling throughout the entire time we lived in Davis. Our winters had a few rainy days but no snow. Evidently, the mighty King of the Universe considered the Regev's move from Davis and to Prosser, Washington as a very significant historical event and signified it by creating blizzards and icy temperatures the minute we left town. It lasted for the next five days. The only time I had experienced a few minutes of snow was in 1950 when snow was falling in Tel Aviv and my parents took my sister and me to the roof to see. So dressing properly for snowy days, preparing the car and driving in these conditions was foreign to me.

According to the road map, taking Interstate 5 all the way to Portland, Oregon was the best route. From there, we would go east along the Oregon side of the Columbia River on Interstate 84 then the exit onto Highway 97 near the John Day Dam. From there we would cross the Columbia River bridge and continue east on Washington State Route 12 until reaching the exit to State Road 241 at Patterson. Route 241 would take us directly to Prosser, provided we didn't get lost. I described that route in detail for the reader to appreciate the difficulties associated in finding the correct roads while driving that route for the first time in my life with next to zero visibility.

"This is California, so this snow covering the windshield is a fluke and will go away quickly," I assured myself as we left Davis and drove north on Interstate 5. But that was wishful thinking. The snow kept pilling on the windshield. The windshield wipers got frozen when I squirted the windshield with the plain tap water I'd filled the container with. What did I know about snow and driving in that kind of climate? NOTHING! The muddy slush thrown on the car from the big eighteen-wheelers coming from the opposite lanes compounded the problem so I had to stop the car and tried to clear the windshield manually. I was wearing my tennis shoes, stepped into a paddle and broke the thin icy crust. My toes got numb making me walk like a ballet dancer performing Tchaikovsky's Swan Lake ballet.

We crossed the California-Oregon State line and continued north to Portland. The blizzard got worse. I was afraid to stop driving other than short restroom stops at the gas stations making sure the car had enough gasoline. We ate the food we brought with us from Davis. Raz hardly slept and started to get tired and edgy. Still I kept going in search of a decent motel with a hot dinner but did not find any. It started to get dark and Raz was crying hard, both hungry and tired so we absolutely had to stop somewhere.

I spotted a large area crowded with many eighteen-wheelers, with their engines running, non-stop. There was a very small dilapidated, one level building that had seen better days. It had a neon motel sign so we stopped there for the night. We were the only guests. They had a tiny restaurant adjacent to the lobby so we ordered the basic hamburgers and french fries and milk for Raz. We ate very fast and went to the room, gave Raz a quick bath and took showers ourselves. It was nice to be in a warm place for the first time that day. We had a long drive ahead of us the next day so we went to sleep right away. Despite the long drive through a constant blizzard the entire day, I could not sleep because of the roaring diesel engines. Moreover, the diesel fumes permeated our room. To this day, every time I smell even one molecule of diesel fume, my memory takes me back to that sleepless night at a place in Oregon called Wolf Creek.

We left very early the next morning, skipping breakfast as I wanted to escape that place. I promised Batia and Raz that we would treat ourselves to a real breakfast at the first Denny's that came our way. The blizzard had stopped somewhat during the night but the highway was still covered with large patches of solid, compacted snow. Raz was back to being himself and had the tendency to sneak into the space between my seat and Batia's. We had to put him back into the back seat since driving a stick shift was neither safe nor easy with a toddler standing there. I spotted a Denny's just as we entered the outskirts of Portland and stopped to indulge in well-deserved treat. I was under immense pressure to be in Prosser before evening so I ordered extra hamburgers and french fries and asked the waitress to put them in doggy bags. Pressed for time, we left Denny's, continued driving, took the exit to Interstate 84 and headed east along the Oregon side of the mighty Columbia River. This geographical region is also known as the Columbia River Gorge, with its undisputed beauty. It is also notorious for being a very windy region, coveted by wind surfers flocking there in the summertime. And sure enough the Columbia River Gorge lived up to its reputation. There was compact snow on the highway and snow floating like tiny dust particles generated by the cars in front of us.

Raz kept standing at the space between my seat and Batia's, refusing to sit in the back. He was more interested in watching the road and the scenes outside through the windshield. Not knowing any better and the fact that I had zero experience driving in that kind of blizzard, I kept driving at almost seventy miles per hour as that was the posted speed limit. It didn't occur to me that I should drive slowly in this kind of a weather.

I continued driving eastwards on Interstate 84 looking for the exit sign to Road 14 that would take us to Road 221 leading to Prosser. I noticed that the scenery along the highway, both on the Oregon and the Washington sides had changed dramatically from the evergreen forests with its big pines trees into nothing but basalt rocks and sage brush.

I was driving pretty fast, too fast for the prevailing weather and road conditions. I was looking frantically to any road sign listing some of the landmarks indicating that I was on the right tract. The most significant one should have been the ones such as, "Highway 97, Route14, John Day

Dam, Patterson, Prosser, Pasco, Richland" but I did not see any.

I am almost sure that I was driving seventy miles per hour when all of a sudden I saw a road sign with the name Pasco so I slammed on the breaks. The car slid badly and lost traction. By the grace of God nothing bad happened to us. I am sure that we were extremely lucky that all our belongings and the heavy stereo speakers crammed into our VW saved us from sliding off the road. The car finally stopped and I managed to reverse to the intersection of Interstate 84 and Highway 97.

We crossed the bridge to Washington state over the Columbia River, exited to Route 14 and then to Route 241 to Prosser. These were very narrow two-way roads. I drove very slowly after my rude awakening. I also wondered where all the big mighty trees were, that the State of Washington bragged about. Years later, a friend explained the puzzle. "Sam, Washington is indeed the evergreen state. West of the Cascade Mountains has abundant rain and is green from the forests and the meadows. However, east of the Cascade Mountains, the state is green from all the dollars coming from its agriculture commodities like wheat, apple and cherry orchards, asparagus, hops and its burgeoning wine industry.

We finally arrived in Prosser and met Dr. Cone's real estate friend. He took us to the place where we would stay until we found a permanent place we liked. The minute we entered, I realized we should find a better one as soon as possible, which meant, "First thing tomorrow morning." To begin with, the place was a one room apartment in the basement below the realtor's office. It was located just below the street walkway so we could hear people walking in the street above us. Dr. Cone left a message that he would be at our place by 10:00 a.m. the next morning and also invited us for dinner at his house in the evening. We were so tired, we took showers and went to sleep. I decided, before retiring for the night, to go outside, find the garbage dumpster and dispose all the garbage that got piled in our car since we left Davis. I left our apartment with a grocery store bag full with garbage and walked on the walkway in search of the dumpster. It was the first time in my life that I experienced *black ice*, the kind of ice that is as a clear as a glass but extremely slippery. So I landed on my behind while the garbage dispersed all over the place. It hurt quite a bit but at least I learned, firsthand about the existence of black ice.

The next morning, Dr. Cone met with us at the underground world his real estate friend prepared for us. We found him to be a very pleasant, soft spoken and a smiling person. He looked very strong, physically, more like a farmer than a scientist. I found out later that he was also cattle rancher as well as a beekeeper. He was producing raw honey with a unique taste I had never tasted before. His manners and overall appearance fit his origin, the State of Montana where he visited often to see his parents and brother who was a physician. "Please, stop calling me Dr. Cone," he begged us, "Everyone here knows me as Wyatt."

There was no question that Wyatt developed great rapport with Raz when he came to meet us that morning. Wyatt picked him up and talked to him like a grandfather. It rekindled anew when we went to dinner at Wyatt's home that evening.

I asked Wyatt if he could take us to see other potential places to rent because the underground apartment was not suitable for us.

"I have an idea, why don't we drive to Grandview, which is seven miles west of here. I'll check with the manager of the apartment complex were my former postdoctoral student lived. He is a native of New Zealand and just left for home. Maybe it is still available or they have other apartments vacated." It sounded like a good idea to us and we all hopped into his car.

Wyatt took us to Grandview, a small town of 3,500 residents, west of Prosser and on the highway to Yakima, the next big city in the area. I was glad to see that they had a Safeway and a Sears store. We stopped at an apartment complex comprised of two ramblers parallel to each other, separated by a common lawn, car parking space and storage sheds. Each building had three separate apartments. Wyatt knew the manager, the Gunter family, who lived in the first apartment facing the street. He knocked and an attractive blond lady with a cute little blond girl standing by her. She greeted us and said to her daughter, "Christine, say hi to these nice people."

Christine was shy, held her doll, and said, "Hi."

The manager seemed to be our age and Christine looked like Raz's age. I liked that place, even before Wyatt asked Judy, the manager, if they had any apartments available. He introduced Batia, Raz and me saying that we were Israelis and I would be working for him at the Irrigated Agriculture Research Center in Prosser.

I believe that he was harping on how great we were, trying to dispel any notion that Judy might have considering us as risky tenants, always late paying the rent or ruining the property. But the more he trumpeted on how good we were, Judy's face beamed with excitement. "Yes, by the grace of God, we just happen to have the two-bedroom unit at the end of this building." She pointed to the third apartment. "It is ready and I will see to it that their son has a mattress to sleep on and double bed for them. I will bring some utensils for the kitchen, but unfortunately, I don't have a dining table," she apologized.

"Don't worry about the dining table, I have one to loan them," Wyatt told Judy.

I told Judy that we'd like to move in the next day.

"You could move even today if you wish. It will be ready for you in the late afternoon," she promised.

"I want you to live by us so we will be blessed through you," she said with a genuine excitement.

"How come?" Wyatt asked, puzzled by her statement.

"Wayne and I are very religious Christians. My parents, who live in Burien on the other side of the Cascade Mountains, are very religious too so having this nice family, members of the chosen people will be a miracle and blessing for us. It is a good omen that you brought them here on Friday just before the Jewish Sabbath in few hours. Please, bring your belongings and move in. You can sign the contract some other time, as I'm not worried about you," she said and went inside her unit, got the key and showed us our apartment, a place that would become our home sweet home for the next four years. Since we were invited for dinner at Wyatt's house that night, I told her that we would spend another night in Prosser and move in the next morning. "I cannot wait until Wayne comes home from work and hears about you. See you tomorrow," she said and walked with us to Wyatt's car.

What a great day it was for everyone involved. I never felt so welcomed, almost like a celebrity. Wyatt too, was happy for us and said to us half-jokingly and half seriously, "I didn't realize there were benefits associated with being The Chosen People."

I told him that throughout Jewish history, Holocaust included, there were more liabilities than benefits. Often times, Jewish people agonize and ask God, "Why don't you choose someone else for a change?"

We spent the second night at the underground apartment. Wyatt let the Realtor know that we found an apartment in Grandview and would leave the next morning. Wyatt showed me the simplest route to drive to his home that evening to join the Cone family for dinner.

It was snowing during the evening just before we left but the driving was not bad at all compared to our drive to Prosser. We had a good time with Wyatt's family. Wyatt's wife, Vera was very warm and kind and so was his daughter who was studying at the WSU main campus in Pullman, and home for Christmas break. His son was still attending Prosser High School. Later on, after graduation, he stayed in Prosser to manage the family cattle business on the acreage Wyatt owned. To my knowledge he still very successfully manages the family business.

It was late in the evening, way past Raz's bedtime when we left. A new day was in store for us in the morning. I cleaned the underground apartment where we spent our first two nights in Prosser and drove to Grandview. When we arrived, Judy, the apartment manager and her husband Wayne were waiting for us. Wyatt had been there earlier to deliver the kitchen dining table he loaned us. He told Judy and Wayne that we were on our way.

Wayne placed a mattress in the room we selected to be Raz's. They left a nice welcome cake and card on the dining table, and loaded the refrigerator with basic food items and milk. Wayne showed me our parking space and storage facility.

We were all set to start the Grandview Phase of the Regev family.

Chapter 11

Grandview: Part 1

I thought it would be a good idea to get familiar with the route to my new job at the Irrigated Agriculture Research and Extension Center, so we decided to take a drive there. The last thing I needed was to get lost and show up late for work on Monday morning. It was a fourteen mile round trip from our apartment. On the way back we stopped at the Grandview Shopping Center comprised of a Safeway, a pharmacy and a post office. It was a shock for us to discover that Grandview and Sunnyside, the next city west of us were both heavily populated with Mexican immigrants.

Monday morning the receptionist told Dr. Cone that had I arrived. A minute later he came to the lobby, all beaming and jovial, shook my hand and introduced me to Evelyn, the receptionist, and the rest of the administrative staff. The research center was a joint collaboration between Washington State University (WSU) and the United State Department of Agriculture (USDA). Dr. Allison managed the center so Dr. Cone took me to his office to introduced me. I found him to be a very polite and cheerful person who looked to me like English gentlemen I'd seen in the movies.

Dr. Allison asked me about the years I'd spent as a student at UC Davis and when I had last visited Israel. I told him that we had not been there since we left in June 1968 so the homesick feelings haunted us. Next, he pulled a folder and said, "Sam, Dr. Cone is your professional boss, but, actually, I'm your real boss because I'm the one who signs off on all the hiring, raises and promotions, so you will have to be nice to me," he winked with a smile when I promised I would. "And by the way, since you are a native of Israel, I would like you to know that a few years ago I had a beautiful time while representing the USDA at an international conference in Jerusalem."

Dr. Allison got up, shook my hand and said, "It's nice meeting you. Good luck with your new job. We're mailing the admission papers to Pullman, the main campus of WSU. I don't know if Dr. Cone told you, but your post doctorate research assignment grants you faculty member status. You should receive your official faculty member card within a week."

As we left, Dr. Cone looked at his watch and said, "It's almost ten o'clock. Most staff members stop at the lunchroom downstairs for a fifteen-minute coffee break, so let's stop by and I'll introduce you to whoever is there. I have a few people I want you to meet. If they aren't there we'll go to their offices or labs after lunch."

The ritual of shaking hands and introducing myself began the minute we entered the lunchroom. I was surprised that although the place was an agriculture research center and an integral part of academia, the people I met were unassuming, and easy-going. Everyone there was on a first name basis so I started calling Dr. Cone, Wyatt.

Wyatt enjoyed introducing me and harped on the fact that I was Jewish and a native of Israel. It broke the ice like magic and worked in my favor because that part of Washington State was a bastion of devoted Christians. Grandview, with a population of 3,500 people, championed seventeen different churches. I became a celebrity when Wyatt mentioned my religious affiliation and nationality, pushing me up the pedestal for being a native of The Holly Land and member of The Chosen People who speaks Hebrew, the language of the Old Testament.

Meeting staff members enjoying their coffee break was a pleasant experience except for the somewhat painful handshakes. The worst came from the staff members who were also farmers and wanted to impress me by squeezing my hand as if they were trying to get the last drop of milk out of a cow's tit.

I also learned that the research center and the region surrounding it showed a politically conservative bias. The USA was still recovering from the trauma of the Vietnam War. One of the coffee drinkers who seemed to be in his fifties, probably a field laborer as judged by his soiled clothing, approached me and shook my hand. "Hi, my name is Bob. I heard that you just graduated from UC Davis," he said. "I hope they didn't corrupt your mind with their crazy leftist ideas. I don't know about you, but I'm sick and tired of watching the lousy UC Berkley students protesting the Vietnam War. They even had the gull to call Governor Ronald Reagan and the police *pigs*. What's wrong with those stupid Californians?" Bob continued ranting, "They're even trying to steal water from our Columbia River and divert it to their stupid state."

I didn't know how to extricate myself from the situation so I tried to be diplomatic and told Bob, gingerly, that I was not a US citizen and as a guest in the United State, I felt it was not right to make negative comments about what I saw around me. Up to that point, he still liked me. Then I blew it completely when I admitted that I liked George McGovern, the Democratic presidential nominee who lost to Richard Nixon. Bob terminated his chat with me rather abruptly. I could see the expression of contempt on his face.

I told Wyatt about the confrontation, "Who were you talking to?" I discreetly pointed toward Bob.

"Damn it," he whispered. "That's Bob Smith. He takes care of our hop fields. You and Bob will be working together, and you're both paid by a grant from the Hop Commission. Don't worry, I'll take care of it."

I was relieved to hear Wyatt's reassurance.

"Let's go upstairs to my office, we need to finish the paperwork and send it to the WSU main campus in Pullman. We need their approval before your name is added to the payroll data base."

As we headed to the stairway, a nice, neatly dressed man yelled, "Wyatt, wait a minute."

Wyatt introduced us. "Sam, I would like you to meet Dr. Jim Elgin, our forages and pastures expert. He works for the USDA."

"Are you living at 409 Avenue J, in Grandview," Dr. Elgin asked.

"You're 100% correct, you must be working part time for the FBI or other federal agencies spying on me."

"Not at all," he assured me. "My family and I are members of the First Methodist Church on the corner across from your apartment. I saw you when we left the church on Sunday. There are four of us living in Grandview. I'd like to invite you to join our carpool. We take turns and save money."

I thought it was kind of him to make the offer. I enthusiastically accepted. That way, Batia would have our car at her disposal, and no longer be imprisoned at home with a three-year-old toddler.

"Very good," Dr. Elgin exclaimed. "I'll pick you up tomorrow morning at 7:30."

Dr. Elgin didn't need to honk or knock on my door. The gravel area by our kitchen door made enough noise to alert me. A tall guy was sitting in the passenger seat. "Good morning Sam," Jim greeted me. "I would like to introduce you to Mel Hagood. He's my neighbor and also works for the USDA. And by the way, we go by first name only. I would like to be addressed as Jim and not as Dr. Elgin."

I entered Jim's car and shook Mel Hagood's hand before sitting in the back seat. Mel informed me that he was the USDA group expert on irrigation scheduling and water use management. "What a coincidence, Sam, I'm also a graduate of UC Davis. How do you like Grandview and this part of Washington?" asked Mel. "I like it here very much and I bet you will like it too. My wife, Pat, is the writer for the *Grandview Herald*. She was excited when I told her about you being an Israeli.

Don't be surprised if she contacts you for an interview," he said just as we pulled into Dr. John Kraft's. Dr. Kraft was the research center Plant Pathologist working on plant diseases caused by the Fusarium fungus.

The geographical region where we lived, known as the Yakima Valley was a thriving agricultural region with cherries and apple orchards. It also had a large number of Concord grapes and Niagara grape vineyards. The Seneca Fruit Company in Prosser produced frozen grape juice concentrate and supplied the entire USA.

At that time, vineyards were in their infancy. Doing research to find the best wine varieties for the climate and soil, Dr. Walter Clore was the viticulturist at the research center. The State of Washington later became the second largest wine producing state after California.

The Yakima Valley was also known for growing hops, mint, asparagus and potatoes, keeping several scientists at the research center busy. The Irrigated Agriculture Research and Extension Center gave advise on pest control, lawn care and vegetable gardens. Residents frequently stopped at the front desk and ask the receptionist to summon the right scientist for help. Being a small community, people went directly to the office of the expert, and brought samples of the infected plants.

Food grown in the region (Prosser, Grandview and Sunnyside) was processed and shipped to the entire USA and the world. Prosser for example had a plant that produced french fries and other potato-based products. Wayne Gunther, my apartment manager, worked as an engineer at that plant.

The processing plant hired one or two inspectors to certify that their products were kosher. This opened a larger customer base for their products

Yakima Valley grew most of the hops for world's beer industry. Several processing plants pressed the hop flowers into long bales and shipped them to brewing companies across the USA and Europe.

Harvesting activities were labor-intensive. Mexican residents furnished the manpower in the Yakima Valley's asparagus and hops fields, and cherry and apple orchards. That explained why the first thing I noticed upon arriving to Grandview, was the prevalence of Spanish speaking people.

"Here we are," Jim Elgin said as we pulled into the parking lot in front of the research center. "Sam did you memorize the route and feel comfortable to drive to work yourself?"

"Don't worry Jim, " I retorted back, "if I managed to navigate all the way from Tel Aviv to Prosser, I'm sure I'll be able to do it."

"Good," Jim smiled, "next week you'll have the great honor of driving us to work." We all exchanged pleasantries with Evelyn, the receptionist. I discovered rather quickly that she was respected by everyone working there. I stopped at the supply room next to her reception counter to get pads and pens and went upstairs to Wyatt's office.

"How do you like the carpool?" he asked.

I told him I was pleased with carpooling as it made the car available to Batia so she wouldn't be anchored to our apartment with Raz. "We found a public park close to our apartment with swings and carousels and she plans on taking him there today."

"That's great, looks like you're getting settled pretty fast. Let me show you your office and you can get settled here as well."

My office was across the hallway, just opposite his. It was a small room with a working counter, two microscopes and a small cabinet. "Sorry to squeeze you like this," Wyatt apologized and pointed to a large environment-controlled chamber that occupied most of the room. "I purchased it for Jim Jackson, my last post doctorate research associate. He needed a small temperature and humidity–controlled growth chamber for his research on the Red Spider Mite, a major pest in the hop fields. We still haven't discussed what your research project will be. Give me a few days to prepare a list of areas I wish to explore. In the meantime, feel free to arrange your office the way you like and walk to our hop yards. Nothing is growing yet but it would be beneficial for you to get familiar with the yards and their location," Wyatt told me. "I bet you've never seen this type of crop before. By the way, since you don't have a phone in your office, please feel free to use mine."

Our carpool headed to Grandview at 5:00, dropping John Kraft at his house first. I was next. "Mel Hagood will pick you up tomorrow morning," Jim said when he let me out. I thanked them and knocked on the kitchen door for Batia to let me in.

Dinner was on the table. Raz hugged me, letting me know that he had missed me. He also let me know that Batia had taken him to the park. Batia said that the phone company scheduled an appointment to install our phone the next morning. They apologized for not having enough private lines. We had to settle for a party line. Judy Gunther, the apartment manager had invited Batia and Raz to her apartment so Raz and her daughter Christine could play together. Christine's toy chest was much larger than what Raz had. I was glad to hear that it was a smooth and easy day for Batia.

After clearing the dinner dishes, we moved to the living room and watched the evening news on the black and white TV, then returned to the kitchen for our ritual coffee and cookies. The doorbell rang. The man at the door, who looked to be in his early fifties, was accompanied by a well-dressed lady holding a large straw basket. "Are you Doctor Sam Regev?" he asked, I nodded. "Hi, I am Dale Burgeson and this is Shirley, our Grandview Welcome Wagon lady. May we pay you a short visit or do you prefer we come some other time?"

"Of course, come in," I replied, a bit surprised. "We don't have furniture yet, so I have to apologize for the inconvenience. May I offer you a cup of coffee or tea?"

"Oh no thank you," the man replied. "We're not going to stay too long. We just came to introduce our lovely city to you. I am the chairman of the city's Welcoming Committee." The committee was created to help newcomers to Grandview. Trust me, Shirley will see to it that your arrival to Grandview and living amongst us will be as sweet as the goodies she brought in this basket."

Dale and Shirley were very nice and answered some of the questions we had about our new hometown. Dale revealed that he was the local State Farm Insurance agent. "What a coincidence," I exclaimed. "We were covered by State Farm when we lived in Davis and I'm looking for a local agent." I sensed his pleasure in finding a new client.

Then I disclosed, "State Farm probably has my name on its list of Trouble Makers."

"Why is that?" he asked. "You look like an innocent and easy going person."

I told him about the fight I had with State Farm which ended with the California State Attorney General office in Sacramento. "Wow, what did State Farm do?"

"Well, I sent a letter to the State Attorney General complaining that State Farm charged me and my foreign student peers exorbitant fees compared to what they charged USA citizens for the same coverage."

"That's the first time I heard about it," Dale said.

"They justified their unfair practice by telling the Attorney General that foreigners pose a higher risk to State Farm because if a case reaches the court and jury notices our foreign accents, they automatically side against us. Anyhow, I won the case and the Attorney General's office forced State Farm to refund the extra money they charged all their foreign clients at UC Davis. I'm sure your colleague at the Davis branch didn't like me after that."

"Don't worry Doctor, it won't happen here I promise," Dale replied. He referred to me as Doctor rather than using my first name, a habit that he never let go. Our families became close friends through the years and his habit of addressing me as Doctor or Doc stayed despite my endless request for him to stop. Shirley noticed that Raz was already busy tasting the candies he dug out of the basket she brought for us. She told Batia about a preschool in town and suggested that we should enroll Raz. Batia promised to look into it. It was close to Raz's bedtime so Dale gave me his business card and asked me to call him when I was ready to switch my policy. We thanked them for the wonderful welcoming gesture and promised to stay in contact.

The next morning Mel Hagood stopped to pick me up. Jim Elgin was sitting in the front. We rode all the way to the research center. "Why did we skip John today?" I asked Jim.

"John is not a regular member of our carpool. His job takes him on the road a lot so we reached an agreement. We pick him up occasionally and he chips in with his share of the gas expenses," Jim explained. "Also, Mel is not going to be here tomorrow morning so it will be only you and me, you're the driver. I live in the brown house next to the church parking lot across the street from you. I'll be waiting at seven o'clock."

"You bet," I replied as we reached the research center. I threw a cheery, "Good Morning," at Evelyn, who was making a pot of fresh coffee.

"I left a few documents for you and Wyatt to sign," she advised me. "They arrived from Pullman yesterday and should go back to the administration office with today's mail." I left them on Wyatt's desk."

Back in my office, I started browsing through the research notes Dr. Cone's post doc had left.

Wyatt showed up for work a little bit late and asked me to join him in his office. "All the documents pertaining to your research associate position arrived from Pullman," he said and gave me my Faculty Membership card. "Please keep it in your wallet. It gives you some benefits beside the honor of being a Faculty Member of the Washington State University," he said. "This is the contract between you and the university. It is renewable every year as long as I'm getting the grant funds to pay your salary and research expenses. Dr. Allison already approved and signed it so now we need your signature. Please keep the yellow copy for your own records."

I took the signed documents downstairs to Evelyn who added them to the outgoing mail.

I returned to my lab/office a little bit disappointed that Wyatt did not discuss what he wanted my research project to be. From all the notes, it was evident that the proposal he had submitted to the Hop Commission to support his last post doctorate associate did not involve any biochemical or physiological methodology. I decided to introduce these disciplines into our research. The grants Wyatt received were to find the best, economical way to control the infestation of the mite. The female spins a web, which protects the colony that infests the leaves. The mites caused heavy damage to the foliage by sucking the plant's nutrients. The end result was a significant reduction in yield.

The behavioral pattern of the spider mite was similar to the predatory mite Cheyletus malaccensis that I used in my Ph.D. research. (See Chapter 10.)

I jotted down an outline of my research proposal and decided to wait for Wyatt's direction. Two weeks went by and Wyatt still hadn't presented me with any research plan. I suspected that he wanted me to bring some ideas to the table. I asked him to set aside some time for me to present my suggestions and we scheduled a meeting for the next morning.

I came to our meeting well prepared and with a copy of the scientific paper he and his former post doctorate researcher published in one of the professional journals. It described the behavioral pattern of the two-spotted spider mite male guarding female deutonymph and mating following her last molting. I pointed to the photographs, "From these photographs and the description in the article, I suspect that we have an identical situation to what I observed in my Ph.D. research."

"What could you add to that study?"

"I would attempt to find and count how many chromosomes the females and the males have and demonstrate, if my hypothesis is correct, that the female has twice as many chromosomes as the male. I would also try to look into evidence indicating the presence of pheromones the quiescent deutonymph produces to attract the male. If the findings suggest that pheromones play a role, I will try to isolate them and identify them chemically."

"So what do we need to pursue the research?" he asked, becoming more excited as I talked.

"For the study of isolating and identifying the pheromones we need a gas chromatograph, I have not seen one here. I'm not privy to the funding, but it would be a shame if we don't try to look for the pheromone role in our mite."

"Why is that?"

"The pheromones in acarology have never before been isolated and chemically identified. It could open a new approach to mite pest control by using natural agents instead of insecticides."

At that point Wyatt was sold on the idea. "Just give me a week to explore the financing angle and how to get a gas chromatograph."

"That would fit my schedule as well," I told him and informed him that my mother, who was visiting my sister in New York, called the night before to let me know she would arrive on the weekend.

"I would be thrilled to meet her."

"Of course," I assured him. "You and Vera are invited for the special Jewish cuisine my mother is an expert at preparing."

"We have a deal," he said as I left his office.

I had never been to the Tri-Cities airport (serving Richland, Kennewick and Pasco) so I asked Wyatt for directions. My mother's flight was scheduled to land late Thursday evening so I left Batia and Raz at home and drove the thirty-five miles from Grandview to the airport in Pasco. She was very tired from the long flight. She had to change planes in Chicago which meant changing gates, not an easy task for my mother who did not speak English.

On the drive home I told her that Wyatt, my boss, and his wife would come for dinner on Sunday to meet her. I also gave her an early warning that we just moved into our apartment and hardly had the basics. "Don't worry *Mulee Le*," she answered, using one of the names she invented to express her affection. "You know we are a tough and strong family and I am sure we will survive this *balagan*, (a slang word used in Israel to denote chaos)."

It was a few minutes after 11:00 p.m. when we arrived home. Raz was already asleep. I was glad the door to his room was closed, I wasn't sure what Mom's reaction would be when she saw him sleeping on a mattress on the floor. She insisted on sleeping on the couch after taking a hot shower.

Twenty-one month old Raz had never met my mother, he had seen her only in photographs, so it took him a while to decipher who he found sleeping on the couch that morning. It finally occurred to him that the *stranger* was *Sabta Yudit* (Hebrew for Grandma Yudit). The photographs of her that we had been showing him helped him recognize her. The commotion he created woke her up and the first meeting between the two was a very happy one, indeed.

We prepared breakfast while she got up and made herself presentable. It was funny to watch Mom and Raz trying to bond, he was not too fluent in Hebrew while my mother's English was very rudimentary. After breakfast we took a walk around the neighborhood. Judy, our apartment manager, was waiting for us as we came back. I introduced my mother to Judy and her daughter Christine. Mom liked both of them right away and promised to get together more during the week she was to stay with us.

When we returned to our apartment I reminded Mom that Dr. Wyatt Cone, and his wife would visit us on Sunday, and that I had told him she was a great cook. "They are eager to munch on something they have never tasted before. Do you have any suggestions?"

"Of course, they should try my *tshulent*. I am sure they will talk about it well after I am back in Israel."

"What a great idea," I agreed and made sure it was not going to be a huge undertaking for her. After all, she came for a visit and to enjoy herself. My mom was adamant about showing off her *tshulent* so I let her run the show.

✡

Tshulent, also known as *cholent*, is a traditional Jewish stew that is simmered for twelve hours or more, usually overnight, and eaten on Sabbath at lunch. This ancient cooking practice originated in Judah, most likely during the time of the second temple in Jerusalem. It served to conform with the Jewish law stated in Exodus 35:3, "You shall not kindle fire in any of your dwelling places on the Sabbath." Jews were prohibited from *kindling* a fire on the Sabbath but there was no prohibition on *maintaining* a fire that started before the Sabbath began. Some families prepared their *tshulent* at home and brought it to the bakery where it simmered in the oven for twelve hours. By the time the *tshulent* was served, its ingredients acquired a very brownish tint. The stew was served boiling hot so it got the Hebrew name *hamin* which derived from the Hebrew word *ham* (hot). Its basic ingredients are meat, beans, potatoes and barley, but there are many variations to the basic recipe, some add wheat kernels, and even whole eggs in the shells.

On Saturday morning, we shopped at Safeway and my mother selected all the ingredients she needed. Timing was of the essence as Mom had to prepare the raw ingredients for the stew and bring it to a boil by 2:00 p.m. so it could simmer for twelve hours before our guests arrived.

My mother went the extra mile and added a chicken neck skin stuffed with a mixture of flour, margarine and chopped onion. First, she sewed one end of the chicken neck skin with a needle and thread, then stuffed the mixture inside and sewed the other end before adding it to the mixture.

I offered to help her but she declined, it was her show. However, she did let me peel the onions and get my eyes teary. As the hours passed by I realized that Mom's *tshulent* was going to be great. The fragrance wafting from the pot was out of this world but I didn't dare lift the lid. The aroma evoked sweet memories from my childhood at 34 Yehuda Hamaccabi Street, where my best friend Yotam, a great *tshulent* addict, always got scolded by his mother for lifting the lid and *stealing* a big chunk of it.

When Wyatt and Vera arrived, Raz was happy to see Wyatt. I introduced them to my mother who was all smiles but could not say much in English. She was fluent in *Polish, German, Hebrew* and *Yiddish,* languages my guest did not speak so I became the official translator.

Wyatt, a native of a small farm in Montana was surprised to learn that my mother and her family where from a small rural community in Poland and owned a timber forest and mill that produced lumber for the entire region. They also owned and operated the sole electric utility plant supplying electricity to the nearby towns. Moreover, her brother-in-law and his family where the authorized agent and distributors of American-made agriculture equipment and machines. He was impressed with my agricultural linage not to mention the fact Batia was born and raised in a *kibbutz,* which is a farming community unique to Israel.

I apologized for the inconvenience of squeezing around the dining table, but Wyatt and Vera felt at home in our tiny kitchen and enjoyed Mom's *tshulent.*

"See you tomorrow at work, Sam," he said as he and Vera were about to leave. They thanked my mother profusely for the lovely dinner and the companionship we had together. "I know that you are going home to Israel. I promise I will take good care of Sam for you," Wyatt said to my mother and won her heart.

"You picked the perfect boss," she told me after they left.

I had to go to work the next morning as Wyatt expected a sales representative from Hewlett Packard to stop by to discuss the gas chromatograph. It was Mel Hagood's turn to be the carpool driver so I left our VW with Batia and my mother. Mel and Jim stopped to pick me up, and after the Monday morning ritual of "How was your weekend.... etc. etc." Mel said to me "Sam, you know my wife is a senior writer for the *Grandview Herald* newspaper. Dale Burgeson and Shirley, the Welcome Wagon lady, told her about meeting you. She's eager to interview you and your family for an article. Would you be willing?"

"Of course," I told him, "but forewarn her that she chose the most boring person to interview, and it's a big risk to her journalist reputation."

"Oh, please don't give me that," he replied. "Dale already gave her his impression of you. He told Pat she must interview the Regev family."

I told Mel it should be an interesting meeting because my mother was visiting from Israel. "Oh, my wife will be thrilled to hear that," Mel exclaimed. "I'll tell her not to forget to bring the camera."

✡

Pat Hagood arrived equipped with a tiny tape recorder and a sophisticated professional camera making me feel for a brief second that we were real celebrities. In retrospect, that was probably not too far from the truth in Grandview, a town of 3,500 residents.

Grandview Herold, January 11, 1973

CENTRAL WASHINGTON resembles their homeland in some respects, members of the Shmvel (Sam) Regev family have discovered. Dr. Regev is employed at the Irrigated Agriculture Research and Extension Center, and the family is living in Grandview. From left, they are Mrs. Regev (Batia), Regev holding son Raz, and Regev's mother, Mrs. Judith Polanecki.

Israeli Family at Home Here

"We had studied English in school since we were very small, but when we came to this country and learned that the English we had learned was English English, rather than American English, so that we had some difficulty in understanding, and being understood, our confidence was shaken." With these words Dr. Shmel (Sam) Regev described his early impressions of the United States.

Dr. Regev and his wife, Batia, are recent newcomers to the area. Originally from Tel Aviv, Israel, they came to Grandview after four years at Davis, Calif., during which "Sam" earned his doctorate at the University of California, Davis. Dr. Regev explains that he is known as "Sam" in this country, as people find his given name too difficult to pronounce. He is employed at the Irrigated Agriculture Research and Extension Center, working with Dr. Wyatt Cone in insect physiology.

The Regevs find the climate and terrain of the area simi-

lar to those in Israel. Asked about differences between this country and their homeland, they remarked on the scarcity of day care centers, and on the fact that persons in Israel are generally much better informed about events in this country than are Americans about Israel.

Their concern about day care centers revolves around Son Raz. Raz was born in nearby Sacramento while the Regevs were at Davis. He's now 21 months old — and a most happy outgoing little fellow, who has the advantage of learning to speak two languages, Hebrew and English, at an early age. His parents had hoped that a day care center could help with the English. "I want him to learn English correctly, not with my accent," his father explained.

Now a guest in the Regev home is Sam's mother, Mrs. Judith Polanecki. She recently arrived after a visit with a daughter, a new mother, in New York.

Asked about hobbies and

other interests, Sam grinned and remarked that, while at Davis, he had worked 60 hours per week for a newspaper, the Davis Enterprise, as well as working toward his doctor's degree, so he had little time for outside activities. Mrs. Regev mentioned reading and music as among her special interests.

The Regevs maintain a link with their native land, to which they plan eventually to return, through a newspaper. Printed on very light weight stock, it comes to the Regevs by air mail. In showing copies to the reporter, they pointed out that reading is from right to left, rather than from left to right as in American publications.

The Regevs have been in the area about three weeks. They are living at 409 Avenue J, Grandview, Apt. 3.

When the reporter-photographer snapped a picture of the family, bright-eyed Raz said something which sounded unfamiliar. "He's saying 'Thank you' in Hebrew," explained his mother.

I introduced my family and talked briefly about UC Davis. Pat reminded me that she and Mel lived there when he studied for his master's degree. After a while, I wasn't sure who enjoyed the session more. As the interview progressed, I sensed that her questions were asked to satisfy her personal curiosity more than for writing the article. My mother enjoyed the interview but could not follow what was said. Occasionally I had to pause and translate so she won't feel left out. There were times during the interview that my mother wanted to express her opinions or feelings so she asked me in Hebrew to translate and convey her thoughts to Pat.

The interview was a smashing success for all participants. I was pleased with the article because it introduced me and my family to the community with the value-added benefit of helping Mrs. Hagood's journalism career. My mother was thrilled to see herself in the photograph Mrs. Hagood published. I had to go to the *Grandview Herald* office to buy a few extra copies for her to take to my sister in New York and to brag about to her friends and relatives in Israel.

Soon after the article was published I received a letter from the Israeli Consulate in San Francisco that provided services to northern California, Oregon, Washington and British Columbia. The consulate informed me they had received a copy of Mrs. Hagood's article. "You did a marvelous job. Please let us know if you need any help, now that you are the 'Israeli Ambassador to Grandview, Washington.'"

I wrote back right away thanking them for their kind words and requested all the literature, books, and pamphlets they could send me to help with my PR task. And more importantly, I asked if they knew of any Jews living within a fifty-mile radius of Grandview. I concluded my letter, "It's lonely being the only Jews in this wilderness."

A week passed and UPS delivered a heavy box filled with the material I requested. There was also a note suggesting that I should contact Dr. Milton Lewis of Richland, Washington. "I believe he is Jewish, but don't quote me, better check yourself. There is nothing to lose," the consul wrote, and furnished Dr. Lewis's phone number. I'd never heard about Richland but sure enough it was on the map.

Back at work, I told Wyatt about the letter from the Israeli consulate with the name and phone number of a person whom they suspected to be a *member of my tribe*. "I'm going to call him tonight, what would be the best time to catch him?"

"Well," he replied, "avoid calling at dinner time or during the evening news on TV. Anytime between 8 p.m. and 9 p.m. would be proper."

"Thanks for the advice," I said and promised to give him a report the next morning. "Wish me luck please, it's getting sort of lonely being the only Jewish family around here."

After eating dinner with Batia and Raz, and watching the *Walter Cronkite Evening News*, I was eager to talk to Dr. Lewis but the other party line subscriber was on the line. I tried several times. It was almost 8:30 p.m. when the phone line was free, and at last, I heard the dial tone. A few rings and a voice on the other end of the line said, "Doctor Milt Lewis's residence, this is Milt, who is calling please?"

I realized I reached the right place but the doctor title through me off. I didn't know what kind of doctor he was. It could be a medical doctor or a Ph.D. *What the heck,* I thought to myself, *I'm a doctor too so I should mention my own degree like he did.* I said, "Good evening Dr. Lewis, this is Dr. Sam Regev calling from Grandview, Washington. Israeli consulate in San Francisco gave me your name and phone number."

"What can I do for you?"

I told him that I had just moved from UC Davis upon receiving a post doctorate research assignment with WSU research center.

"Why did the Israeli consulate in San Francisco give you my name and phone number?"

I told him about the article the *Grandview Herald* and that the people at the consulate got a copy and contacted me. "I asked them if they knew of any Jewish people living close to Grandview and they sent me your name and phone number."

"This is your lucky day, Sam," Dr. Lewis replied. "Just to let you know, I am also a graduate from the University of California. I got a Ph.D. from the UCLA physics department. I accepted a job offer as a physicist at the Hanford reservation and moved from Los Angeles to Richland, Washington. We have several Jewish families residing here so we founded our own synagogue. It's not affiliated with the Orthodox, Conservatives or the Reform movements of Judaism. Hold on for a minute, I need to consult with my wife for a second, I'll be right back." A few minutes later he returned and said, "Sam, are still you there?"

"Yes I am."

"Well, here's the deal. Next week, after the Friday Sabbath service, we're having an out-of-town guest, speaking about the activities of his organization helping to get Soviet Jews out of the iron curtain and settle them in Israel or the USA. Our family is hosting him in our house for the weekend. We would like to invite you and your family for Sabbath dinner with us after which we will all go to the synagogue for the services and lecture."

I thanked him for the invitation and told him we would be honored, except that we had a twenty-one-month-old son and as newcomers, we didn't know anyone well enough to babysit.

"Not a problem, Sam," said Dr. Lewis. "My two daughters and my son will take care of him at my home while we go to *shul*. You can pick him up afterward."

It sounded like an offer you cannot refuse so I accepted it after getting the *Yes* node from Batia. "I'll mail you my address and simple directions to my house," Dr. Lewis promised at the end of the conversation.

Dr. Lewis had revealed that he worked at the Hanford Site, a place I had never heard of. It also clarified a remark I heard later referring to the city of Richland as a city with more Ph.D.s per square mile than any other city in the USA. The Hanford site and the non-profit Battelle Northwest Research Company, located in Richland, were probably the reason for that claim.

✡

I learned that the Hanford Site was founded in 1943 as a component of the Manhattan Project. The site was located in this arid region of south-central Washington. Its sole purpose was a full-scale production of plutonium needed to make the nuclear bombs dropped over Hiroshima and Nagasaki, Japan during WWII. The B-Reactor was the first full-scale plutonium producer in the world. The reactor was designed by the nuclear physicist Enrico Fermi, an Italian physicist, considered to be the architect of the atomic bomb and the creator of the world's first nuclear reactor. Enrico Fermi was awarded the 1938 Nobel Prize for physics.

I found a great interest in Enrico Fermi, who was not Jewish but his wife, Laura Capon was. A few months before receiving the Nobel Prize and noticing the threatening situation of anti-Semitism in Mussolini's Italy, Fermi became concerned about the danger to his wife and his two children. (Jews by the *Halacha* Law). He was alarmed when Mussolini issued the *Manifesto of Race* that considered the Italians to be pure members of the Aryan race but not the Italian Jews. The manifesto was published on July 14, 1938 and a few weeks later, fascist Italy enacted it into law. Initially the law applied only to foreign Jews, but changed to include Italian Jews on September 2, 1938.

Enrico Fermi was determined to escape Italy with his wife and two children before it was too late. In a letter to a fellow scientist in Ann Arbor, Michigan, he described his dire situation and implored his colleague to consider offering him a research position in his lab or with any other suitable opportunity in the USA. He posted the letter from Lugano, Switzerland, an Italian-speaking region close to the Swiss-Italian border, hoping that the letter would avoid interception.

Fermi and his family slipped out of Italy in 1938 and immigrated to the USA where he was eventually recruited to be part of the Manhattan Project.

His father-in-law perished in Auschwitz gas chambers on October 23, 1943. Enrico's sister-in-law pleaded with her father to take shelter at her house near Rome with a few other Jews but he was convinced his career as an admiral in the Italian navy would protect him.

I have heard similar stories about Jewish veterans being deported to the Nazis concentration camps and gassed to death despite showing their Nazis captors all the medals they had been awarded for their bravery serving in Emperor of Austria, Kaiser Franz Joseph's army during WWI.

During the Cold War between Russia and the USA the Hanford Site added nine more nuclear reactors and five plutonium processing facilities, to produce the USA atomic warheads. An excellent account describing the history of the Hanford Site, the Manhattan Project and the B-Reactor was written by Robert L. Ferguson and my friend C. Mark Smith in a book titled *Something Extraordinary* published in 2019. The site along with the Battelle Pacific Northwest Laboratory became a research facility associated with nuclear technology and the handling of radioactive wastes released into the ground at the Hanford Site and the Columbia River.

✡

On the day we planned to have dinner with Dr. Lewis, I left work early to provide leeway in case we got lost. It was be a simple ride to Harris Street in Richland, a rather long street that runs south/north, along the bank of the mighty Columbia River. The area on Harris street where he lived looked plush and affluent. I discovered later my impression was correct as most of the influential members of the synagogue lived in that sliver of Harris Street and its vicinity. Dr. Lewis's house was next to the riverbank. I realized he loved the river, judging from the large motorboat parked next to his garage.

I rang the doorbell. Dr. Lewis opened the door and greeted us cheerfully with a *Shabbat Shalom* (Hebrew for a Peaceful Sabbath) and ushered us to the living room to meet the out-of-town guest. We shook hands and introduced ourselves while Rhoda, Dr. Lewis' wife, made the final touches in the dining room.

No one there could escape my heavy accent so I knew that the, *Where are you from?* question would follow. This time it was Mrs. Lewis who did the interrogation.

"Milt told me that you are Sam and Batia Regev," she said to me.

"Yes, that is correct and I would like to commend you for pronouncing our name correctly. Not too many people do."

"So where are you from?"

"I am from Tel Aviv and Batia is from *Kibbutz* Matzuba in Israel's West Galilee next to the Israel-Lebanese border."

"No, absolutely not, Mr. Sam Regev, you are not from Tel Aviv," she corrected me, and I could see the mischievous glee in her eyes. "You are Sam Regev from the *Negev*," making Regev rhyme with *Negev* which is the largest desert of the southern part of Israel. Landscape and climate-wise it resembles the desert area of Washington State east of the Cascade Mountains. The huge difference between the two deserts is the fact the *Negev* does not have a mighty river like the Columbia River.

She noticed I was surprised that she mentioned the name *Negev* so she told me that she and Milton had visited Israel several times and traveled through the *Negev* desert on their way to Eilat on the southern tip of Israel by the Red Sea. "So remember, from now on you are Sam Regev from the *Negev*," she declared. From that moment on whenever we met, Rhoda Lewis never missed the ritual of asking me "How is Sam Regev from the *Negev* doing?" or "What does Sam Regev from the *Negev* think about this?" She continued to do this for forty-three years following our Sabbath dinner at her house. She passed away and I miss it.

Raz was well behaved at the table and Rhoda made sure that he ate some of the food served the guests. Then her two daughters took him to their room to play. "I don't like to rush anyone but we should leave soon so I'm serving coffee and desert and after that we should leave for the synagogue." Then she looked at me and said, "Sam Regev from the *Negev*, I hope you are a good singer because we are a singing congregation and like to sing part of the liturgy."

I confessed that my singing was more like a frog's croaking.

"Oh don't worry, you should hear Meir's singing."

We left Raz with Milt's daughters and followed his car to the synagogue. "Welcome to Congregation Beth Shalom," Milt told us and pointed to the two-story residential building the congregants purchased a few years before and turned into their place for worship and socializing. "We have a great turnout tonight because of our guest speaker. Usually, there are fewer cars in the parking lot. Let's go inside and I'll introduce you to other members," he said and held the door opened for us.

The first couple we met in the foyer next to the sanctuary was Dr. Bob Franco and his wife Eileen. Bob was one of the synagogue founders and worked as the chief surgeon at the Kadlec hospital in Richland. "Are you from Israel?" Dr. Franco asked me as we shook hands. "Where did you serve in the army?"

"I was just a paratrooper,"

"Wow! What a coincidence, I'm a former paratrooper myself. As a military doctor I parachuted several times into Italy during WWII. Welcome to Beth Shalom." He added, "Oh by the way, have you met Meir Elkin, the gentleman standing over there? He is also a WWII veteran. He helped the British army build roads in Burma. He is also a founder of Congregation Beth Shalom."

The service was about to start so we took our seats in the sanctuary. It was quite an experience for me to participate in a Jewish Sabbath service in a place referred to as a *Synagogue* but didn't looked like one, at least not like the one I attended with my father while we lived at 34 Yehuda Hamaccabi Street. The Arc, which housed the *Torah Scrolls*, was a simple cabinet with a wooden replica of the *Two Tablets* depicting the *10 commandments* on its top. An Eternal Light hung from the ceiling above it. A simple white curtain covered the Arc.

Congregation Beth Shalom and its synagogue served the Jewish community of the Tri-Cities, which was not big enough to have a full-fledged rabbi, so it relied on its own members to serve as the lay religious leaders conducting the services throughout the year except for the Jewish high holidays *Rosh Hashanah* (the new year), and *Yom Kippur* (the day of atonement) when they hired an ordained rabbi.

On the evening we came to the synagogue with Milt and Rhoda, Meir Elkin was the leader. The service sounded a little strange and foreign to my ears as it was conducted mostly in English. Some of the prayers were sung to tunes I had never heard before, certainly not in the orthodox synagogues in Israel. I also found it unusual that, unlike the services in Israel where praying is natural and spontaneous, the service at Congregation Beth Shalom appeared to me like a directive leveled at the congregants by the service leader who conducted the service from the *bimah* (Hebrew for podium). The entire service was interspersed quite often with a directives like: "Please turn to page 123 in the *siddur*," (Hebrew for prayer book), "Please rise," or "You may be seated."

The rising and sitting repeated itself throughout the service. I whispered to Batia, "Is this a place of worship or a kosher gym?" Then the congregation's president made announcements from the podium. His session was relatively long until Dr. Lewis cut it short by reminding everyone that we had an out-of-town guest speaker waiting and it was getting late.

The guest speaker was a member of an organization dedicated to working to persuade communist Russia to let its Jewish people immigrate to Israel. It was the modern-day Moses pleading with the Egyptian pharaohs to *"Let My People Go."* A request of any Russian Jew to leave for Israel meant a jail sentence and many of them ended up somewhere in Siberia. These became known in Israel as *Asiray Zion* (Hebrew for prisoner of Zion). Their case was championed by dignitaries like the Russian physicist Andrei Sakharov, the Washington Senator Henry "Scoop" Jackson. Both were pushing the Kremlin to release the *Prisoners of Zion* jailed in the Russian gulags and to let the Russian Jews immigrate to Israel. His activities on behalf of the Soviet Union Jewry made him the co-sponsor of the Jackson-Vanik Amendment, which provided clout over Russia by denying normal USA trade relations with any country that practiced restrictive emigration policies.

The guest speaker started answering questions from the congregants but it was getting late for us so I told Dr. Lewis that we must leave. We thanked him and Rhoda for their invitation and the great dinner. "Hope to see you again, Sam Regev from the *Negev*," Rhoda recited as we left. Raz was asleep on the couch in their living room. We thanked the Lewis's daughters for babysitting.

"Oh the pleasure was ours. He is very cute. Please bring him again, soon," the oldest daughter said.

"You bet."

"Mission accomplished," I told Batia when we got home. "At least we know that there is a synagogue and a Jewish Community not too far from us. I hope we left a positive impression with the Lewis family and the congregants we met."

✡

Pat Hagood's article was instrumental in helping us find the Jewish community in the Tri-Cities. It must have reached other communities as well. Two weeks after the article was published, I received a nice, handwritten letter from Kevin Moor, a student at the Toppenish High school, requesting that I come to their school and talk about Israel. I was surprised and even flattered that students in a city located within the Yakima Indian Reservation, showed an interested in Israel. I wasted no time, accepted the invitation and scheduled a date for my talk.

This event took place during the era when personal computers and laptops were not widely available to the public. Lectures and presentations were accompanied with color slides projected onto a large reflective white screen. I contacted the Israeli consulate in San Francisco and requested brochures and pamphlets about Israel to give to my young audience in lieu of a color slide show.

On the day of my scheduled talk, I stopped at the school office, introduced myself and gave the secretary the name of the student who arranged my presentation. "Oh Yes, it was Kevin Moor but Mr. Smith is the teacher of that class so why don't you wait here while I summon him for you," she said and left the office.

"Good Morning Dr. Regev," he greeted me and shook my hand. "I hope I pronounced your last name correctly."

"You did a great job," I assured him. "Please tell me the main highlights describing your profile, so I can properly introduce you to the class."

I was surprised to see so many young faces staring at me after Mr. Smith's introduction. A few days before the presentation, I was debating with myself as to what format or approach I should use as I wanted it to be informative and interesting while trying to avoid sounding like a travel agent. I decided to play it by ear and select my approach on the spot after I had the opportunity to gauge my audience.

"Good morning students," I started my presentation, "My name is Dr. Sam Regev but I prefer people address me simply as Sam I rarely mention the doctor title because I sense a mental barrier. Some perceive me as a showoff, harping on my degree and, they suppress any free exchange of ideas, fearing they would be perceived as *uneducated*. Yet, my personal advice for anyone who elects to pursue a higher education is to aim for the highest degree in the field of their interest. In academia, the Ph.D. Degree is the highest degree to earn, so shoot for it. That was what I did when I enrolled at the University of California at Davis, I told myself, *Sam, you left your country and family in Israel and traveled all the way to the USA, so better push yourself and strive for the highest academic degree.*

My dear wife, Batia, disagrees with my opinion, "For God sake," she always admonishes me. "You worked so hard and scarified so much of yourself, me and Raz so use this well-deserved Ph.D. title."

I still try to argue with her, and retort, "Yes, you are right, but *Dr. Sam Regev* sounds more like I'm a gynecologist rather than a *scientist*." We reached a compromise whereby I use the doctor title in cases that require it.

I felt at ease and relaxed as my presentation progressed so I decided to add personal details I thought would be interesting to my young audience. "Have you noticed my foreign-accented English?' I asked them, "Well, my native language is Hebrew, the same language my ancestors used to scribe the Hebrew Bible or the Old Testament as you call it. It is the language my ancestors spoke in the The Holy Land a few thousand years ago. Allow me to reveal to all the devoted Christians in this room that Jesus spoke with the same accent I have so I feel I am in a good company. Some of the Jews that lived during that era, Jesus included, also spoke Aramaic, still it had the same Semitic accent and used Hebrew fonts." Sensing that I had their full attention, I picked one of the Hebrew books and place it in front of a student sitting in the front row, "Hi, I am Sam Regev, what is your name please?"

"I'm Curtis," the nice-looking lad replied.

"OK Curtis, would you please open the book for me."

Curtis picked up the book, looked at it from side to side, top to bottom, then opened it and looked perplexed. "What is that?" he asked loudly enough for the entire class to hear.

"The text on the book cover was not written in English yet you assumed that the book starts from its left side so you opened it there. That book was written in Hebrew so its left cover is where it ends not where it starts.

"Hebrew is written from right to left, not from left to right like English, so the beginning of a Hebrew book is on the right side of its cover. Also please notice that the Hebrew characters are squares comprised of straight lines. In ancient times, text was carved into a flat stone using chisels and hammers. Most people are right-handed and it was easier to carve the text into the stone as straight lines and from right to left." To make my point, I went to the blackboard, and jotted an entire sentence in Hebrew. I started on the right edge of the blackboard. Mr. Smith, the teacher was sitting in the front row, so I looked at him and said, "Teacher Smith, your Israeli counterparts love Hebrew very much, especially when they need to write on the blackboard."

"Why is that?"

"Well, just watch this and judge for yourself. If am a teacher in an Israeli school and write something on the blackboard and oops I notice I made a mistake, I continue writing but erase the mistake with my elbow before the students notice." I demonstrated my point while writing on the board.

"Wow! That is neat," teacher Smith exclaimed.

"Yes Indeed" I retorted, "Too bad you can't do this trick with English."

So far so good, you're doing fine, my inner voice told me, half way into my talk. "When you graduate from Toppenish High School, there will be many options available to you," I told them. "You can join any branch of the military and make it your career, or go to college. Another option is to join the workforce in the profession that suits your interest or financial goals. Your Israeli counterparts however, have a predetermined path, namely, mandatory service in the military. It is a great honor and some even hide medical issues that might exempt them from mandatory service. Israel students about to finish high school must study and pass six matriculation tests. If they don't pass, they will not be admitted to any Israeli university. The six tests stretched over two weeks when I took them.

"Shortly after taking the matriculation tests, both genders are conscripted to the Israel Defense Force (IDF). When I was your age and finished high school, I served my mandatory thirty-two months of active duty. My female counterparts, served their twenty-four months unless they got married or were exempted on religious grounds. After serving the compulsory military service, we are assigned as reservists and continue to serve in the military, undergo additional training to stay current or we're given active duty assignments. In my case for example, as a civilian, I had to show up at my reserve unit and parachute from the airplane several times a year in addition to at least two to three weeks of military training and service. There were several occasions where I left my morning classes, went to the air force base for a short practice with the parachute, jumped from the airplane into the large sand dunes next to my university. I brushed off the sand, changed back into my civilian clothes and rushed back to my classes.

"The military service turns you into a mature and responsible person, better fit to handle the challenges of life as an adult. You also serve the country you love." I told them I did not plan on turning my presentation about Israel into a *sermon* but there I was already in the thick of it and decided to finish. "Let's do the simple arithmetic," I told them. "I am thirty years old. Thirteen years ago, I was at the same phase in my life that you are now. During those years I fulfilled my active military duty, earned my BSc degree at the University of Tel Aviv, fought in the Six-Day War, got married, came with my wife to the USA, went to college and earned my Ph.D. degree. I also have a son born here. I mention this information to illustrate to you the importance of setting a plan for your future and then stay focused until you fulfill it."

I got the impression that the information I presented was a new revelation for them. It forced them to accept the fact that there are other countries and other cultures, where the mindset and norms practiced by their peers are very different from theirs.

It was time for me to show the young audience a little bit of my beloved and colorful country so I distributed the glossy brochures that came from the Israeli consulate. They were really shocked to see the big cities, the sandy beaches of the Mediterranean and the exotic fish and coral riffs of the Red Sea. I enjoyed hearing, "Wow!!" when they saw the pictures of people floating on the Dead Sea next to a floating cup of coffee while reading the morning newspapers as if they were sitting in lounge chairs.

"How can they do that?" someone asked and I explained that the concentration of the salt and other minerals in the Dead Sea exceeds 25%, thus giving buoyancy so you can't sink. Some were laughing when they saw pictures of people smearing black mud they collected from the seabed all over on the bodies. "This mud is loaded with minerals that help fight psoriasis and other skin ailments," I told them. I mentioned that the surface of the Dead Sea is the lowest point on earth, 1380 feet (420 meters) below sea level.

I finished my talk and thanked them for inviting me and bearing with my heavy accent. I left my business phone number and address in case they wished to contact me in the future. Mr. Smith thanked me in front of the class and walked with me to my car. He paused for a second and said as we shook hands, "There are many anti-Israel, anti-Semite people who wish for Israel's demise. I believe you gained new friends for Israel with your talk today." These warm words from a stranger living in a small community by an Indian reservation in the state of Washington and far away from any sizable Jewish population kept reverberating in my head and warmed my heart all the way to Grandview.

Two weeks later, in a letter, Mrs. Johnson, a Prosser High School teacher asked if I would be willing to talk to her students about Judaism, its religious laws and traditions.

I called her from work, "I would be happy to talk to your class. I just gave a talk to the Toppenish high school students and it went very well."

"Yes, Dr. Regev, I know. That's how I got your name and phone number."

"What kind of talk do you have in mind?" I asked. "As you know it's not easy to keep these young students attentive during lectures like mine, especially when the material isn't part of the curriculum or on a test."

"Here is the story, I was browsing at the Walden Books Store when *The Chosen* by Chaim Potok caught my eye. I decided to buy it. From its first paragraph until I finished, I was captivated. The main heroes are two Jewish boys, most likely the same age as my students, so I made it a reading assignment. The school library purchased extra copies making sure there would be enough for everyone in my class to read it and write a report. When we had a discussion about the story, it became apparent that although my students liked the novel they didn't grasp the meaning and significance of the Jewish concepts and terms described in the novel. I couldn't help them as I am not Jewish. Then I heard about your talk at Toppenish and thought you would be able to explain these issues to my students and me."

Mrs. Johnson sounded so kind and polite there was no way I could turn her down, "Mrs. Johnson , I accept your invitation but I must confess, I've never heard about *The Chosen* and Chaim Potok. Please give me two weeks to find a copy, read it and then meet you and your students.

"I will send my copy with Dr. Cone tomorrow. He lives not too far from me."

I thanked her for sparing me the time to look for a copy, "Any day in the morning will be fine with me."

"How about Monday February twelfth at 10:00 a.m.?"

I marked it on my calendar.

✡

The Chosen, published in 1967, describes the lives of two teenage boys growing up in Williamsburg neighborhood in Brooklyn, New York in the 1940s. One is a modern orthodox Jew, with a great potential to become the mathematician his father wants him to be, but the boy wants to become a rabbi. His father is a Talmudic scholar and writer who teaches at his son's school. The father is also an activist pushing for the creation of the modern state of Israel. The other teenager is an ultra-orthodox, very brilliant Hasidic Jew. He is next in line to replace his father, the ultra-orthodox rabbi of his Hasidic community, who followed him en masse when they escaped Bolshevik Russia and came to America. The ultra-orthodox teenager does not want to take his father's place. He wants to study psychology.

I'd like to add that in 1990, seventeen years later, I had the pleasure of hearing Chaim Potok. He came to lecture at Whitman College in Walla Walla, Washington and we convinced him to come to our Congregation Beth Shalom after his talk. He conducted a short evening service followed by a lecture and an informal Q&A session. Most of the questions centered on *The Chosen* and the other books he had written. Sadly, he died in 2002 of brain cancer.

Chaim Potok was a multi-faceted person. He earned a BA degree in English literature from Yeshiva University and became an ordained Conservative rabbi after four years studying at the Jewish Theological Seminary in New York. Being an ordained rabbi, he joined the US Army and served in South Korea as a Chaplin. After his military service, Rabbi Potok joined the faculty at the University of Judaism in Los Angeles, moved to Jerusalem in 1963 to work on his Ph.D. dissertation. In 1970 he received his Ph.D. in Literature from the University of Pennsylvania. His first novel, *The Chosen*, was on the New York Times best seller list for thirty-nine weeks. A movie based on the book was released in 1981 and won the Prize of the Ecumenical Jury at the 1981 World Film Festival in Montreal.

✡

After reading the book, I was not surprised that Mrs. Johnson's students were perplexed and curious about the lifestyle and the path of growing from teenager to adulthood, the two heroes of the novel had to endure. For Mrs. Johnson 's students, growing up in remote, Prosser, Washington, the only time they came close to a Hasidic Jew was, probably, watching the movie, *Fiddler of the Roof*.

My presentation went well and provided my young listeners with plenty to consider. From the questions they asked, it was evident that they were astonished that Orthodox Jewish youngsters must navigate their lives torn between religion and the secular world, a world completely different from their lives in Prosser. The book encouraged them to evaluate orthodoxy of any faith.

✡

While I was preoccupied with planning my research, as well as giving my high school talks, Wyatt received a quote from the Hewlett Packard sales representative, offering a top-of-the-line gas chromatograph they used as a demo. Wyatt scheduled the date for representative to demonstrate its features. "Sam, you are the expert and have worked with gas chromatograph in the past. I'm not familiar with that field so I will count on your judgment. If the price is right and the machine is what we need, we will purchase it."

I was pleased to hear that, "Here's the list of the thin layer chromatography supplies I'll need to start the research while we wait for the gas chromatograph."

We both went to greet Mr. Howard when he arrived. He was slim, and well dressed for our side of the Cascade Mountains.

"We'll need to move the gas chromatograph from my car to your office," Mr. Howard said. The instrument looked impressive but rather heavy.

"My office is on the second floor so let me bring a dolly. Sorry, we have no elevators in this building," Wyatt said apologetically.

My muscular boss grabbed the heavy instrument, pulled it out from the back seat of Mr. Howard's car and onto the dolly. We struggled up the stairs with the dolly and navigated to the lab next to Wyatt's office.

Mr. Howard explained how the instrument would perform the tasks I needed in my research. "Granted, this instrument was a demo but it is in great condition, guaranteed to serve you for many years," he assured us. "And, if you decide to purchase it, I'll enroll Dr. Regev in our three-day training class in Vancouver, British Columbia, three weeks from now. This class covers all the basic tasks and procedures you need to know in order to operate the gas chromatograph. I will be at your disposal in case you need help with the instrument."

"Sounds fair to me and the price is right," Wyatt told him, "send me the paperwork and the official offer to submit to the head of my department in Pullman."

"I'll do that as soon as I'm back in my office in Bellevue."

The application and reservations for my enrollment in the next training class arrived few days later. I mailed the completed forms back to Mr. Howard. The purchase agreement was approved by our department in Pullman. Two weeks before the class in Vancouver, Mr. Howard scheduled a one-day appointment to install and set up the gas chromatograph. He showed me the basic features and how they were different from the brand I'd used at UC Davis. Mr. Howard knew what he was doing and everything was working well after he installed it and verified it was working properly.

Batia and I had to use our Israeli passports with a valid student and student wife visa since taking the class meant exiting the USA into Canada and reentering. Our USA-born son, Raz, was a citizen and did not need a visa, nonetheless, the Israeli consulate added him to Batia's Israeli passport. We were invited to stay with Batia's friend, Ilana, and her lawyer husband, Jerry.

Batia and Ilana had the opportunity to re-live the time they had together at *Kibbutz* Matzuba. While I was in class, Ilana took Batia and Raz to see the sites of beautiful Vancouver. Ilana who didn't have a child at that time bonded instantly with Raz.

The three–day class was a great experience except that I gained a few pounds after falling in love with the Continental Breakfasts and Danish pastries they served. Through the years we kept visiting Ilana, as Vancouver, BC became one of our most favorite places.

The good time in Vancouver, BC made it difficult for us to readjust ourselves to small-town life in Grandview, but it was time to get my research project up and running.

Detailing the research work I did is beyond the scope of this story but I will highlight a few successes. I was able to isolated the pheromone the female spider mite produced to attract the males. One practical application of this finding was spraying the hops, or any plant infested with spider mites, at the first sign of infestation, to confuse the males so they couldn't locate and fertilize the females. The infestation should be reduced commercially to acceptable levels because the unfertilized female produces only males, thus reducing the mite population.

My thin layer chromatography and gas chromatograph analysis determined that the pheromone was farnesol, a natural component in the green leaves of the host plant. I needed a third analytical method to confirm the identity of farnesol. In my opinion the best method was mass spectrometry. I asked Wyatt if he knew of someone in Pullman with mass spectrometry expertise. Wyatt was eager to publish my findings *as is* even without the mass spectrometry. I convinced him it would be worth our while to have that additional confirmation.

"Here is where our research project stands right now," I told Wyatt. "I isolated farnesol as the pheromone that attracts the two-spotted sider mite male to the female but I need mass spectroscopy analysis to prove the compound is, indeed, farnesol."

"That sounds logical to me, so why don't you do that?"

"I plan to extract the body fluid of the quiescent females being guarded by the males and run that extract through the gas chromatograph to collect the pure farnesol as it leaves the detector. The final step is a Mass Spectrometry analysis provided we can find someone in Pullman to analyze it for us."

Wyatt promised to contact the Chemistry Department in Pullman for help. Later he came to my office beaming from ear to ear, "I talked to Dr. Manning in the Chemistry Department. He agreed to analyze our sample. They have an opening on Tuesday next week. It should give you enough time to collect samples for the chemists to analyze. I would like to join you to see the process and get their input regarding our research."

"That's great," I concurred. "Besides, I have never been to our Pullman campus so I hope you'll show me around."

"Be prepared for a four-hour drive. I would like to hit the road no later than 6 a.m."

The entire region was wheat country with a few houses standing alone in the midst the rolling hills. I wondered what happened if they needed emergency medical attention or a pre-harvest fire caught in the surrounding dry wheat field. It would take a long time for help to arrive.

When we arrived in Pullman and met Dr. Manning at his lab, the mass spectrometer was up and running. I gave him my samples. "I strongly believe they are farnesol. I hope you agree," I told Dr. Manning.

He injected the first sample into the detector port of then gas chromatograph and connected it to the mass spectrometer. The next few minutes felt like an eternity, waiting for the results that would validate all the work I had performed since becoming Dr. Wyatt Cone's research associate.

I guess, God decided to shine on me. Dr. Manning gave us the long chart generated by the mass spectrometer, "Gentlemen, based on your thin layer chromatograms, the gas chromatograph analysis supplemented by today's mass spectrometry result, no one will question your assertion that the chemical in question is indeed farnesol. However, just to be 100% sure I suggest that you collect another sample and we'll run it through again," Dr. Manning told us and we agreed.

"Sam will call you and schedule another visit when he has the sample ready," Wyatt told him. "Now that he knows how to find your lab, there is no need for me to come along. We would like to thank you and your staff for helping us. If you happen to be in our area please visit us at the Research Center. Dr. Clore, our viticulturist, is experimenting with different grapevines as he works hard to turn Washington State into wine country. I'm sure you would like to taste the great wines his viticulture department makes."

Dr. Manning accepted the invitation.

After preparing a large enough sample of farnesol for the next mass spectroscopy analysis, I called Dr. Manning and scheduled the date. I drove the nearly 300 miles round trip between Grandview and Pullman and noticed that for most of the time I was the only car on that road. I took the back road through the city of Kahlotus, a small town of around 190 residents. I was sure there were no police on duty to cite anyone for speeding. I was joking to myself that if I would get stopped by a law enforcement officer, it would be them stopping me for directions after they got lost. To be fair, this road springs to life late on Friday afternoon as students from the Tri-Cities attending WSU campus in Pullman head home for the weekend. I enjoyed driving the rolling hills and listening to Mozart's *Requiem* playing on my stereo. It became the must play musical piece each time I headed to the Pullman campus.

I was pleased to hear Dr. Manning say, "Sam, todays results are identical to the ones we saw last time so I am 100% confident that the compound of interest is farnesol. Just for my own curiosity, what are you going to do next with that information?"

"I need to perform one final test to demonstrate that farnesol from the quiescent female attracts the male. I plan to run a bioassay, placing tiny lumps of PVP powder soaked with synthetic farnesol onto a small piece of hop leaf and then add few males to see if they are attracted to the clumps, and show the same guarding/palpating behavior they show towards quiescent female."

"That's a great idea, please keep me posted."

I thanked him again for his indispensable help as I left for the long trip back to Grandview. I was euphoric with the results and eager to be back home and share it with Batia and Wyatt. I evidently pressed the pedal a little hard and arrived home faster than usual.

I was the carpool driver the next morning so I picked Jim Elgin and Mel Hagood and headed to work. I apologized for not riding the carpool twice lately and explained I had gone to Pullman for mass spectrometry analysis related to my research work. I described the highlights of my research work for Wyatt and my impression that he was happy with it. "It's time for me to become a bit famous," I told them.

"How are you going to become famous?" Jim Elgin teased me. "Please let me know the trick"

"Well, the minute we arrive at work, I will set the bioassay experiments and if they prove my hypothesis about farnesol being the pheromone attracting the male spider mites, I will write a scientific paper about it. Once I have my final draft ready, I'll submit it to one of the reputable professional scientific journals in my field."

"That's the way to go," Jim agreed with me.

"I still have some mixed feelings about publishing my research findings right now" I confessed.

"What's wrong with publishing your papers now?" Mel Hagood interjected.

"Well, Wyatt always introduces me as Dr. Sam Regev but as of now, I have not submitted my Ph.D. dissertation, hence I have no official Ph.D. diploma from UC Davis," I lamented. "It is a shame because other than typing, the work is completed and ready to be submitted."

"So what is the problem, man?" Jim said. "Just type it and send the whole package to the university."

I told him that it wasn't that simple. They required the dissertation to be typed on special archival paper, using specific secretarial formatting that I was not familiar with.

"No big deal, Sam," Jim said to me. "My wife does secretarial work for our church and she typed my Ph.D. dissertation. I'll talk to her tonight and see if she can type yours."

"That would be great. I really want that diploma adorning my wall."

The next morning Jim told me, "Just get her the paper UC Davis requires and she'll type it for you."

I ordered the paper from the UC Davis student bookstore and gave it to Jim a few days later.

He brought me the first few pages his wife typed. "What is the verdict?" he asked and received a loud "Great." Jim's wife was a fast typist and did an excellent job. Lucky for me they'd just purchased the most advanced IBM typewriter, with its unique ball-shaped typing head so the end result looked very professional. It took me about a week to put together my entire dissertation, embedding all the photographs, tables and charts, adhering to the required format. I mailed it to the Graduate School Administration Office along with an identical copy to my mentor, Professor Summers.

Then I bit my nails, waiting for UC Davis to decide to either accept my dissertation and grant me the Ph.D. degree or require additional work. Then, Dr. Summers' letter dated on March 1, 1973 arrived addressed to Dr. Samuel Regev. It contained a request for a few extra copies.

Dr. Summers fully spelled my title and made sure to underline it. The gist of the letter was as follows:

> Dear _Doctor_ Sam:
>
> The enclosed materials show that you have fulfilled all of the requirements (except one) for the Ph.D. degree. The remaining requirement is to supply copies for the Department of Entomology and for Dr. Benjamini.
>
> You should receive a diploma within eight weeks after returning the yellow card and you may participate in the commencement exercises on or about June 15.

So all of the peregrinations of earning an advanced degree are now over for you, and you and Batia can live more leisurely and without the daily worries of graduate school.

Congratulations, and good luck.
Sincerely,
F.M. Summers
Professor of Entomology

The official Ph.D. diploma arrived a few weeks later satisfying the dream I started thirteen years early when I carved Doctor Shmuel Regev on a fresh cement walkway. (See Chapter 6.) Holding the Ph.D. diploma in my hand felt good and humbling knowing that I kept my word.

With the objective of getting the doctorate degree achieved, it was time to let the scientific community be aware of the research work I had done thus far. I showed Wyatt my diploma, "Boss, it's about time for both of us to become famous."

He smiled at me and asked, "I am all for it but what is your plan to achieve that goal?"

"I have all the photographs, charts and data associated with my research of the Two Spotted Spider Mites. I'm ready to write our first scientific paper on the topic. It will be my first scientific publication, provided it passes peer review and an editor is willing to publish it. It would also be a first for you because this one is loaded with biochemical and physiological analyses our Acarologist peers are not accustomed to. It would also present you with an opportunity to show the Hop Commission that the grants were well spent, and our findings are practical, reducing the mite damage in the hop yards throughout the Yakima Valley."

I could see from his facial expression that he agreed with me.

"Give me about two weeks to write the rough draft and I'll give it to you along the way to make your corrections and add your comments. Once you've corrected my English and polished the text, I'll submit it to the *Journal of Environmental Entomology* where you published your previous paper. I expect this paper will pass the peer review but I have no idea when the paper will be published. In the meantime, we should create a color slide show describing our research. The Hop Commission should be the first to see the presentation."

"Very well, you work on the research part and I'll prepare the slide presentation."

✡

Having my Ph.D. meant that my dissertation was accepted and I felt it merited being published as well. I found myself working simultaneously on three different scientific papers, one pertaining to my post doctorate project with Dr. Wyatt Cone. The other two papers were based solely on the main sections of my Ph.D. dissertation. The first one described the biology, and the role of sex attractant pheromones in the predator mite that Dr. Summers was working with. The second was on cytogenetics.

I wrote to Dr. Summers revealing of my intention to put his name as a co-author of these papers since I had worked on my Ph.D. thesis under his mentorship. Dr. Summers replied right away, adamantly refusing my gesture. The gist of his refusal was summarized in one sentence: "Sam, these two research projects were your original ideas and methodologies, especially the cytogenetics and the DNA analyses you did with Dr. Benjamini. I am flattered that you give me credit as the co-author. Just to remind you that at first, I was not too happy your research gravitated towards these fields outside my field of expertise, but in retrospect I am glad you insisted on doing that research. It turned to be an exciting research. I am glad you were my last graduate student and your thesis and the scientific papers will brighten my retirement starting a few months from now."

I wrote him back and assured I would find a proper way to acknowledge his involvement and contribution to my work.

I completed writing the paper and sent it to *Acarologia*, a quarterly, peer-reviewed open-access scientific journal that covered all aspects of research in the field of mites and ticks. Although the journal was located in France, it published its articles in English. I was notified by the editor that my paper was received and was under peer review. It was accepted for publication few months later.

Overall, it took about one year from the time I sent the manuscript to *Acarologia* and the day it was printed and distributed to journal subscribers. It felt great when a package of twenty complimentary reprints arrived in the mail.

The footnote listed in the papers published in *Acarologia*, stated, "*A portion of a dissertation submitted in partial fulfillment of the requirement of the degree of Doctor of Philosophy, University of California, Davis.*"

The Acknowledgment paragraph stated, "*The author would like to express his thanks to Professor F.M. Summers for his ideas and encouragement.*"

✡

Soon after it was published I started receiving post cards and letters from all over the world requesting reprints of the paper. The complimentary reprints the editor sent me were gone fast so I had to order more, and paid for them out of my own pocket. The post cards that kept coming and it felt very flattering, realizing that other people who never knew me before found my work interesting and useful enough for them to ask for a reprint. The excitement of feeling recognized went up a notch when I started seeing my work cited and referred to in the references section of the scientific papers of others.

Wyatt was aware of the post card requests for reprints that came from all over the world. In fact, on days when I had to take the day off or take my son Raz for an appointment with the pediatric, Wyatt collected the post cards from my mailbox and put them on my desk. One day he asked me "Sam, how do you feel about all of the requests for reprints?"

"It's rewarding and let's face it, scientists and the actors performing on the stage have something in common, they crave applause and we crave requests for reprints."

The other scientific paper that came out of my dissertation centered on cytogenetic. It detailed the quantitative analysis of the DNA content and determine the number of chromosomes the predatory mite, Cheyletus, Dr. Summers studied and let me use some of the colonies he raised. That research found that males were produced from unfertilized eggs and females from fertilized eggs. It was the first time that research actually proved this fact.

I published it in *Genetica*, a peer-reviewed scientific journal covering research in the field of cytogenetics, cytotaxonomy and ecological genetic. The journal editing group was part of the Institute of Genetics, State University of Utrecht, in the Netherlands. It brought me great pride when this prestigious journal, that accepted papers from all over the world, accepted and published my paper.

Admittedly, I was partial towards that particular part of my dissertation research because it initiated my interest in the chemistry of photography. I was able to detect and record the number of chromosomes unique to the mite I studied only after I compounded my own original film developer to process the films. (See Chapter 10.)

The footnotes listed in the paper published in *Genetica*, stated, *"A portion of a dissertation submitted in partial fulfillment of the requirement of the degree of Doctor of Philosophy, University of California, Davis."*

At the end of the *Genetica* article, just before the References paragraph, I stated, *"The author would like to express his thanks to*

Professor F. M. Summers and to Dr. Eliezer Benjamini, University of California, Davis for their assistance in this work. The author used the laboratory facilities of Dr. Benjamini in his radio assay work."

I sent reprints to Dr. Summers.

✡

With three of my scientific papers published in international professional journals, more requests for reprints arrived in the mail. I had to order more from the publisher. These requests for reprints made me feel proud but occasionally, they were tricky as well because most of the postcards came from overseas. The colorful, beautiful and unique stamps caught the eyes of my colleagues. I had to politely turn down requests for the stamps. I explained that they were my trophies and a legacy I wished to keep for myself and my children. (Figure 11.1)

My weekdays were filled with interesting moments and excitement, but Batia's were more challenging, especially on the days when I drove the carpool. She was stuck at home with Raz for almost ten hours. Interfacing solely with a 2½-year-old toddler was the most difficult time for her. Even nowadays she reminds me of that hard time even though more than forty-eight years have passed. The days I was picked up by my car pool were easier for her because she had our car. She took Raz to the park and then shopped at Safeway. Raz liked watching *Sesame Street* so we bought him a Cookie Monster puppet, his favorite from that show. On the days when I was the carpool driver she walked with him in the vicinity of our apartment or he played with Christine, the daughter our apartment managers.

Figure 11.1 Request card for a reprint of my scientific paper.

One afternoon, while playing with Christine, Raz rubbed his ears complaining they hurt. Up to that time, none of us had visited any doctor in Grandview. Although I was insured through my job with WSU, they did not furnish me with the list of local doctors. "Don't worry," Judy reassured Batia. "I'll call our good friend, Dr. Don Woods, who is also a member of our church and ask him to see Raz. I will let you know as soon as I hear from him. He is a very good Christian," she added. Judy called back shortly and said that Dr. Woods would stop by our apartment right after dinner. When I arrived home from work we hurried with our dinner and got ready for Dr. Wood's house call.

Dr. Woods turned out to be a very nice and jovial person, who did not look much like a doctor except that he was holding a stethoscope and an otoscope. "What a great pleasure to finally meet you", he exclaimed when he shook our hand. "Judy Gunther told me all about you and the fact that you are native Israelis. We love Israel and as a devoted Christian, I plan on visiting there one day but first let's see what's going inside Raz's ears."

Batia sat on the couch and held Raz while Dr. Woods examined him. "Yes, he has a mild ear infection in both ears. Ken's Pharmacy is closed now so let me take you with me to my clinic and I'll give you free samples of antibiotics. It should clear his infection. It is nothing major to worry about," he assured us. Batia and I thanked him for making a special house call and the free medication he was going to give Raz. I wanted to acknowledge his willingness to help us and I said "Dr. Woods, I insist on paying for your time."

Dr. Woods refused, saying "You can pay for this visit by telling me *everything* about Israel when I come for a follow-up. See you next time," he told to Batia and Raz and took me on a short drive to his clinic.

He opened the door, turned on the lights and I noticed the sign *Donald Woods, D.O., Family Practice* posted on the door. "Welcome to my clinic," he said. "Now that you know where we're located, if you or your family need medical attention, just call to schedule an appointment. If we have no openings, I'll stop at your house like I did tonight," he told me while browsing through a cabinet full of samples from pharmaceutical company reps. "Here it is." He pulled twelve vials. "This is a recently approved antibiotic. You can add it to Raz's orange juice or give it to him with a spoon. I'll stop by your apartment next week to see how he's doing but call me earlier if he's still suffering from the ear infection."

I thanked him for his help and the antibiotics. "Let me take you home. It's probably Raz's bedtime," Dr. Woods said while turning off the light and locking the door.

Raz was asleep when I arrived so Batia and I decided not to wake him. I told Batia where the clinic was located in case she or Raz needed medical attention while I was at work. We drank hot tea and munched on a cookie left on the table from Dr. Wood's visit. "You go to sleep," I told Batia. "I need to read the instructions and information about the medication."

I sat at the kitchen table ready to learn more about it. I was puzzled about the sign, "Donald Woods, DO, Family Practice" and wondered what DO meant. "If he's a real doctor, why isn't MD posted next to his name?" I asked myself. The DO vs. MD titles confused me so I consulted the phone book looking for other clinics in Grandview, and found one that had a pediatrician with the MD title next to his name. I withheld giving Raz the free samples of the medication Dr. Woods gave me.

I became apprehensive the more I read the pamphlet that came with the medication because the word *syphilis* was mentioned too many times. "For God sake" I said to myself, we needed medical help Raz fight an ear infection, not *syphilis.*" I felt a rage start to boil inside me and decided not to give Raz the medication. I consulted the phone book looking for other clinics in Grandview, and choose the pediatrician with the MD title listed next to the name.

I called Jim Elgin first thing in the next morning telling him not to pick me up since I needed to take Raz to the doctor. I also left Wyatt a voice message on to let him know I'd be late for work. Right after breakfast I called the Grandview clinic and secured a 10:00 a.m. appointment. We arrived fifteen minutes early as it was Raz's first appointment which required filling all their paperwork. We were sitting at the waiting area for a while before a nurse showed up at the lobby with a folder and looked inside the folder. I could hear her brain whirling, and clicking hard trying to figure out how to pronounce the first and last name of their new patient, so I decided to spare her the agony, "If you are trying to figure out how to pronounce *Raz Regev* here he is.

"Yes, of course," she retorted. "So tell me again how to pronounce it correctly." I went through the motion again and pronounced it in Hebrew. "What nationality is that?" she quizzed me.

"Hebrew," I told her as she ushered us into the examination room.

While waiting for the pediatrician to come, I noticed a small book similar to the one I'd seen at Raz's pediatrician at Kaiser Permanente in Sacramento carry in the large pocket of his white lab coat. I glanced at the book sitting on the desk of the Grandview pediatrician, and copied the information printed on its cover. It was the *Handbook of Pediatrics, 10th Edition* by Henry K. Silver, C. Henry Kempe, and

Henry B. Bruyn. I determined, in light of what happened the evening before that I should get a copy of that manual of my own to guide me through Raz's next medical issue.

My friend, Dr. Benjamini from the UC Davis medical school who became the Dean of UC Davis medical school ordered it for me. I used it quite a bit after that incident but now I keep it as a souvenir from the *Old Days*. The pediatrician finally entered the room, examined Raz and confirmed the ear infection diagnosis. "Here is the prescription for him. I am going to call Ken's Pharmacy. It should be ready for you when you stop there on your way home. Use all the medication and call me if Raz still has problem," he told us upon leaving the room. I felt relieved because this time I took Raz to a real MD and not a DO. I didn't mention the visit with Dr. Woods and the free medication he gave me.

Judy, our apartment manager was outside watching Christine playing on the lawn when we came back from the clinic. I confessed to her that we took Raz to the Grandview clinic instead of having Dr. Woods as Raz regular physician. "I believe it would be better for a toddler at his age to have a *pediatrician* rather than a *general practitioner*," I said and she agreed. "By the way, Judy, I thought you said Don Woods was a doctor but I'm not sure he is."

"What makes you say that?" she replied with a noticeable tone in her voice.

"Well, the sign on the door to his clinic said DO a title I have not heard before." I said to justify my skepticism.

"DO stands for Doctor of Osteopathic Medicine and is equivalent to Doctor of Medicine. You can check it yourself," she said and entered her apartment.

Since she put me on the spot, I decided to explore the MD vs DO issue and I'm glad I did. I discovered she was absolutely right. DOs are medical doctors like MDs. A DO graduates and is licensed from the *osteopathic medical school*, has the same responsibilities, privileges and rights as the MD graduating and licensed from a *medical school*. The curriculum at the medical school and the osteopathic medical school is identical. Both require the two years of core studies of the biomedical and clinical studies after which the students must complete additional two years of core medical training in their special fields. Unlike the MDs the DOs are also required to study close to 500 hours of the human bones and muscle manipulation and that is where the *osteo* part of their title comes from. I discussed the issue with Batia and admitted I made a mistake thinking Dr. Woods was not a real doctor. I also admitted to Judy that I was wrong and thanked her for making me research the issue. I begged her not to mention it to Dr. Woods, and she agreed.

✡

Mrs. Pat Hagood's article about us, along with my talks to the students at the Toppenish and Prosser high schools raised the awareness of the community to the uniqueness of the newcomers living amongst them. Just being native Israelis from the Holly land made us special to this predominantly Christian community. Moreover, belonging to the *chosen people* made us very important because as I discovered later on that a Christian who succeeds to convincing a Jew to accept Jesus and convert to Christianity will secure his/her place in Heaven. It was just a matter of time before devoted Christians visitors, mostly ladies, came knocking on our door, almost daily, with a sheaf of glossy brochures showing Jesus. They came as a team of two, introducing themselves politely, named the church they were affiliated with and handed me one of the brochures they felt would be attractive and interesting for me to read. That was followed with an invitation to come to their Sunday service. At that point I would start to politely resist their attempts to proselytize us, so I told them that we were born a raised as Jewish and intended to stay Jewish.

The great majority of the proselytizers did not accept the fact that we were not going to convert and the encounters escalated into theological debates when I mentioned we had no intention of converting to any other religion.

"But you must accept Jesus as your savior and become a full-fledged Christian in order to secure a place in Heaven," the interlocutors preached to me.

"Who said that?" I asked them.

"The Holy Bible says so, you better read it," they urged me.

At that point at the conversation, I turned the tables on them and gave my sermon. "My wife and I were born and raised in Israel, the Jewish state. We speak Hebrew, the same language our forefathers, the Israelites, have been using for more than 2000 years. Your King James Version is not the original Bible. The Bible was written in Hebrew, mine is the original. Studying the Bible is mandatory school curriculum from the first grade of elementary school all the way to finishing high school. Moreover, being well versed with the Bible is part of our Matriculation tests required for being admitted into any Israeli university. As you can see, the Bible is an integral part of our lives."

To make my statement even more compelling I went inside and grabbed a book that showed a nice picture of a page from the ancient *Dead Sea Scrolls.* The text, handwritten on the parchment by the ancient Hebrew scriber, was a chapter from the book of Isaiah. I also picked up the Bible I was given at the Army initiation ceremony. I opened that Bible at the chapter shown in the picture of the *Dead Sea Scroll* and said, "See for yourself, the text looks and reads the same now and as it did more than 2000 years ago." I started to read to them aloud from the text shown on the scroll.

"Jesus was Jewish and talked both Aramaic and Hebrew, like you just heard me reading to you, so why should I divorce myself from the *real thing*?" I asked.

At that point they gave up and left us alone.

When Judy Gunther first told us about Dr. Woods she said he was a *good Christian* and a very devoted one. I noticed that, firsthand, when he visited again, presumably to check how Raz was doing but I suspect his real motive was to discuss religion with me. First thing he did upon entering our apartment was to check Raz's ears, taking his otoscope from his bag, "and this is from Gale, my wife," he said and pulled out a tasty looking cake. "I hope you like it."

"Well, we're going to check how good the cake is, right now. How about munching on it with the coffee I'm going to make after you check Raz's ears." I said, holding Raz while Dr. Woods checked Raz.

"The infection is gone and his ears are cleared," Dr. Woods declared. I told him, apologetically, that we found a pediatrician to monitor Raz's well being while he is still a toddler. Dr. Woods had no hard feelings. When the coffee was ready and I served it with Gale's cake. "Please tell your wife the cake is great and we appreciate her nice gesture," I said and really meant it as the cake was really good.

We were chatting and enjoying the coffee and cake but then the conversation turned into a political and religious exchange between me and Dr. Woods. It was triggered when he asked how it was it for me living away from Israel and residing in a small community like Grandview.

"Living far away from my homeland, parents, family and close friends is extremely difficult not to mention being surrounded by a different culture and language," I explained "But the most difficult minutes for us are watching the news reports from Israel, showing the terrorist attacks on the civilian population in addition to the Arab suicide bombers," I added. I expected to hear some consoling words from him but he did not utter even a single consoling word to express empathy or understanding how Batia and I felt about the events at home.

Instead he said, "The tribulation that is going in Israel, sounds very bad but actually these events are necessary and destined to happen. It is God's plan and there is nothing you or anyone else can do to prevent it from happening."

It made my blood boil. I wished he would take whatever was left of the cake and just leave but I found myself asking, "Why is that, please give me one reason to accept your justification for horrors the

Israelis are facing on a daily basis."

"I am aware the Jewish people don't deny that Jesus ever existed, but they refuse to accept him as their messiah. For us devoted Christians, Jesus is the messiah and he will reappear on earth again. We call this event as *The Second Coming*." Dr. Woods paused and pulled a small New Testament out of his bag and leafed through it.

"There are some preconditions that must be fulfilled, albeit dreadful, before His second coming. They include great suffering, wars and earthquakes. I know that you don't believe in the New Testament or consider Jesus your Messiah but I'm going to read Matthew 24: 6-7, 'Jesus told his disciples that just before his second coming, war would fill the earth, nation shall rise against nation and kingdom against kingdom.'" He was riled up and so was I.

He was excited about the glorious future Jesus promised. I was riled up because all the suffering of the Jewish people had endured through the years, including the recent terrorist attacks. I was expected to go along with the grand events the Christians believed in. "It is all in the Bible," he kept telling me and showed me the New Testament time and time again. At that point, I felt the debater sitting as guest in my house sounded more like a preacher at the Sunday services than a doctor. I started calling him Don.

"So Don, please tell me, what is the significance of Jesus's second coming to you and other Christians in the world. What does it have to do with Israel?"

"Because you have not read the New Testament you are not aware that Israel is the focal point all of these dramatic events, and Jerusalem is the epicenter. According to our truth, Jesus ascended to heaven from the Mount of Olive, located on the east side overlooking Jerusalem. He will return to the very same place. This will be his Second Coming as mentioned in Acts 1:9-1 of the New Testament and in Zechariah 14:4-5 in your Old Testament. His second coming will start at the millennium which is the 1000-year reign of Jesus. The righteous dead will be resurrected and ascend to Heaven.

"We believe that the purpose of the millennium is for Jesus to establish himself as the King in Jerusalem and sit on the throne of King David. This is the fulfillment of the promise God made to Israel promising the Messiah will coming again and also keeping the covenant he made to Abraham." Dr. Woods paused for a minute.

At that point I had to let my rage come out, "Don, you are not the first person to tell me that all the turmoil facing Israel and the Jewish people is *good*." I felt very strong resentment and disgusted that our suffering satisfies these Christians because our suffering would bring them their savior and salvation. They didn't say it to me directly I can still sense this glee from the tone of their voice and facial expression when they think they associate whatever happen in Israel as an assurance to His Second Coming.

"Sorry, Don," I said to him, "I don't accept your Christian rationale that these painful events in Israel are *good* because they are prerequisites for Jesus's second coming. Israel was re-founded by the Jewish people to be their home and the Jewish State, a refuge for every Jew so please stop using us to gauge when your Jesus is coming back. We are not waiting for him." I was adamant and I hoped he understood where I stood on that matter but, evidently his didn't. Instead, he kept lecturing.

"The Jewish people are waiting for the messiah, we, the Christians, believe Jesus is the messiah, the very same one you are waiting for. He ascended to heaven from the Mount of Olive. He promised he would come again to the same spot but before this second coming, there would be a short period of great suffering, hardship, persecution, famine and wars. Most of us refer to this period as the Tribulation. What is going on in Israel has paramount significance, that's why we're watching closely, lest we miss the signs of his second coming." Dr. Woods said while leafing through his bible.

"Oh, here it is," he said. "Here is it what your own Jewish prophet, Zechariah, prophesied about the wars around Jerusalem: '*I will gather all the nations to Jerusalem to fight against it, the city will be captured, the houses plundered, the women ravished. Half of the city, exiled but the rest of the people will not be cut off from the city.*

Then the lord will go forth and fight against those nation, as when he fights on a day of battle. On that day, his feet will stand on the Mount of Olive which is in front of Jerusalem on the east. And the Mount of Olive will be split in its middle from east to west by a very large valley, so that half of the mountain will move towards the north and the other half towards the south.

And you will flee by My mountains valley, for it will extend to Azel, and you will flee just as you fled before the earthquake in the days of Uzziah king of Judah. Then the Lord my God will come, and all the holy ones with him.'" (*Zechariah 14:2-5*)

Dr. Woods closed his bible, looked at me and said, "All the turmoil and suffering Israel endures does not surprise me or any *real* devoted Christian, but trust me, my friend, from what we see going on in your beloved Israel indicates the Messiah is coming and will bring redemption and salvation to the believers and the Jewish people, the defenders of Judah. I empathize with the Israelis and the rest of the Jewish people for all the suffering they endured including the Holocaust, but this is God's plan and there is nothing that we can do to stop it." Dr. Woods spoke with conviction and certainty.

"So why is it always happening to the Jewish people?" I asked him "Why is it always Jews who must carry the burden?" I fired back.

Dr. Woods replied, "If you read the bible, cover to cover, you will find that God chose the Jewish nation, its people, and the land of Israel as uniquely His. He made a covenant *only with them* and not with other nations. Admittedly, he placed a big burden on the shoulders of the Jewish people. God chose you to be a light to the world and to usher the arrival of the Messiah. We, the devoted Christians, take God's warning seriously, that *those who bless Israel will be blessed in return and those who curse Israel will be cursed.*

Although these words were somewhat soothing to my ears, Dr. Woods managed to add fuel to the fire, "All the turmoil and suffering brought upon the Jewish people has been punishment for not obeying God. He still loves his chosen people and will redeem them."

"Well, Don, just to let you know that we feel that with all the burden and the honor of being HIS CHOSEN PEOPLE, and being persecuted in every corner of the world He dispersed us, not to mention the six million of my brethren who perished in the Holocaust, why doesn't he *leave us alone and chose other people for a change.*" I was really upset at that point. I felt I had reached a dead end, and banging my head against the wall as Dr. Wood recited quotes from the Bible he carried with him. I saw his lips moving but he was really talking to the walls. I wasn't listening.

A few days later the phone rang and it was Dr. Woods calling. *Oh, please God, please spare me from another theological discussion with Don like we had the other day,* I told myself but his voice sounded very friendly and cheerful.

"Shalom Sam, this is Don calling. Are we still friends after the heated discussion?"

"Of course we will always be as long as you promise not to try to convert Batia and me to Christianity," I replied.

"Oh, not to worry, I am not going to do that. The reason why I'm calling is to make up to you for the hard time I gave you during my last visit. Are you Batia and Raz available this coming Saturday at noon?" I told him we would be available. "Great" he said enthusiastically, "I would like to take the three of you with me to Portland."

"We appreciate your offer but Portland is 195 miles away and it would require more than three hours behind the wheel in each direction. I better decline the offer. Nonetheless, it is very nice of you to offer to take us to Portland."

"Hey Sam, who told you we are going to drive there? I am going to take the three of you in my private airplane. I need to meet someone at the Portland airport and coming back right after the meeting. I figured that after the hard time I gave you the other day, you deserve the thrill of flying with me to Portland. So what do you say is it Yes or No?"

"Don, what a shocking and pleasant surprise," I replied and promised to discuss it with Batia and let him know.

I talked to Batia about Don's offer. It sounded like an opportunity for us to have a bird's eye view of the beautiful Pacific Northwest and the Columbia River Gorge so I called him back to let him know we would be waiting for him on Saturday. It was news to me that he flew airplanes and even owned one. This revelation intrigued me because up to this point the only things I knew about him were that he was a family doctor and a very devoted Christian.

I needed to know more about my *private pilot* before entrusting him with our lives. I talked to Don's very close friend, Judy Gunther. "Judy, Don Woods invited us to fly with him to Portland this coming Saturday. I didn't know he was a pilot, let alone a private plane owner. Have you flown with him yourself?"

"Yes indeed. Don is a licensed and accomplished pilot and owns a plane. You are fortunate to get the invitation to fly with him because he seldom makes such an offer to people other than family and close friends. He has accumulated many flying hours as he combines his medical skills and his piloting skill. He frequently takes time off from his own busy clinic and goes on medical missions to Mexico and various other countries in Central America to treat their poor citizens free of charge. In fact, his Christian medical missions took him across the world. He spent time in Africa, Asia and Europe. Take my advice and accept his offer," she said and I took her word for it.

Don showed up at on Saturday at noon, knocked on the door and said "Are you ready? Let's go the airport in Sunnyside where I keep my airplane." He kneeled down so he could talk to Raz eye-to-eye, "Raz, do you want to fly up in the sky?" and pointed to the blue skies above adorned with white puffy clouds that looked like lambs. Raz nodded up and down. "I guess this is a *yes* so let's go."

It took us less than fifteen minutes to drive to the Sunnyside airport that served small private airplanes and a few agriculture spraying airplanes. Dr. Woods parked the car and we walked to his small Piper airplane. He walked around the airplane making sure everything looked right. "Wait for me in the shade here while I am taxi to the aviation fuel pump and fill it up. I'll come back and pick you up," he said before he started the single engine. When he came back, he stopped the engine, stepped out, and helped us climb into the cabin.

We sat behind his pilot seat. Batia, Raz and I were really squeezed in and I started to doubt that we would be able to enjoy the flight. Don started the engine, consulted with all the gauges, talked to the control tower and gave the information about our destination, etc.

The sensation my body felt during takeoff was much different compared big commercial flights. I held Raz close to me and sensed some apprehension on his part, as he had never flown before.

I had a hard time, mentally, since all of my previous flights were one-way flights. During my military service, I got into a Nord military plane, took off and jumped out with a 40-80 pound tarp sac, loaded with equipment, attached with a rope to my torso. I couldn't jump on my own, so two crew members pushed me off the plane, leaving me at the mercy of God and the force of gravity. Once the canopy opened I had to release the heavy sac off my torso and let it dangle below me on the twelve-foot rope attached to the harness of my parachute. Any slight wind transformed me into a fancy pendulum comprised of the heavy tarp sac, rope, and parachute. Being a living pendulum also meant that if the sac hit the ground and I was at an angle relative to the ground, I landed on my butt and it hurt. There was one jump, when the impact was so hard on my behind, the crystal of my watch popped out, and my pants were totally ripped. I finished the drill wearing only my underwear. I am sure the enemy would die of laughter rather than the bullets I shot at him. I was sent to one week of physical therapy to help my back.

Flying inside Don's plane made me feel completely naked as I did not have the parachute attached to my back or the emergency parachute attached to my chest. I also missed the heavy tarp sac loaded with equipment. I felt like a baby deprived of his *security blanket.* The awkward feeling got worse when every light wind rattled the small Piper airplane. Moreover, whenever we hit air pockets my stomach dropped to my feet as the airplane lost elevation. The situation got worse the closer we got to the Columbia River Gorge, known for its windy conditions. The winds there were so strong, it was heaven for wind surfers on the river but not for people flying above it.

The worse part of the entire flight was for me to see Raz hurting and suffering from a very bad pain in his ears brought about by the fluctuating air pressure during the entire flight. I started praying that we would land in the Portland airport soon. It was hard for me to fathom the idea that Raz would have to endure the same torture on the return flight. "Thank God" I found myself saying when Don said we were about to land in Portland. By then I was oblivious to the flight thus far as I paid more attention to how Raz was doing and worries about would the drop in altitude would do to his ears upon landing. I hardly peeked through the windows to watch the actual landing. Then we heard a loud noise the minute the airplane touched the asphalt landing strip and started shaking as Don tried to stop the airplane.

"Oh Shit!" Dr. Woods exclaimed. "We got a flat tire when we landed, are you OK?" I assured him that we were fine. Don radioed the airfield management to dispatch someone to move the airplane and repair the punctured tire. We waited until the help arrived. The technician drove us to the airfield's small terminal building and returned to the airplane to repair the tire. "It would take them close to hour and a half to fix the flat tire and inspect for any damage to the landing gear so please make yourself comfortable here while I call the guy I have to meet," he said and headed to the public phone at the corner of the waiting area.

Dr. Woods introduced us to the Portland resident he was meeting with and after few pleasantries they moved to a different table to discuss whatever they had on their agenda. I learned later that he was a member of a Christian group doing missionary activities in Africa and wanted to include Don on its upcoming mission. The flat tire and the time needed to fix it put us behind schedule, forcing Don to cut his meeting short. The ordeal of squeezing ourselves into the small plane repeated itself, and we took off. We still experienced the air pockets and the winds shaking the airplane but it was not as bad as it had been flying to Portland. When we landed in Sunnyside, I felt like kissing the ground, a custom of devoted Jews, when landing in Israel for the first time. I did not kiss the ground, but made myself a vow to never again fly in a Piper airplane. I never have. Don took us home and asked how we liked the adventure. I managed to be polite, thanked him for his kind gesture and told him it was a great pleasure, marred a bit by the discomfort Raz experienced during the flight. We were really tired, went to sleep and felt lucky knowing that we still had all day Sunday to recover from that flight.

From an early age I was good at sports as my parents enrolled me with the Maccabi sport club. My father was a soccer player with the Maccabi Warsaw and wanted me to belong to the Maccabi club because it was not affiliated with any of the socialistic political parties in Israel like the H'Apoel sport club was. I didn't like to play soccer but I loved to go with him to the soccer matches every Saturday. Instead of participating in the Maccabi soccer activities my parents enrolled me in the gymnastics program during the winter and its swimming activities during the summers. I was a good swimmer and participated in various competitions throughout Israel. I still keep a few documents citing my earning the first or second places in the swimming competitions. I was good at gymnastics too and earned accolades in that sport as well.

In high school I channeled my energy into long distance running. It gave me quality time to brainstorm all kinds of problems. Jogging became a daily routine which I kept for thirty-seven years starting in 1968 at UC Davis and stopped on the advice of my orthopedic surgeon following my knee replacement in 2015.

I have the sweet memories of the few marathons I ran with my daughter, Shir, who always beat me. I believe she inherited the running gene from me. She was a member of her school's cross-country running team and ran 50 marathons including at least one marathon in each continent under the sun. She even run a marathon in Antarctica, befriending the penguins there and plunged, under the supervision of a medical doctor, into the cold water of the ocean.

In Grandview, I usually ran between 10:00 p.m. and midnight. This crazy schedule enabled me to spread myself between work and being a husband and father. My jogging route was not far from our house. I showed it to Batia in case of an emergency or I failed to return home. The first few nights were uneventful but then, when I was jogging around midnight, I was on the last stretch of my route, huffing and puffing trying to catch my breath while negotiating an uphill slope, I noticed someone was standing in the middle of the walkway. As I got closer I discovered it was a sheriff deputy motioning me to stop. "What is your name sir and what are you doing here this late at night?"

"My name is Sam Regev and I am jogging, as you can see," I replied.

"Well sir, people here don't jog this late at night."

I made the mistake of being a smart aleck and said, "Of course, Grandview is a small sleepy town and we just moved here from UC Davis, California where many people jog 24/7 and the police don't stop them."

His body language and facial expression revealed how mad he was.

"Sir, this is Grandview Washington, not Davis California," he replied and asked again for my name.

"Samuel Regev," I said and requested an explanation.

The young police deputy did not budge and said, "I don't know who you are and what you're doing here this late at night. Do you have any papers to show me that you are indeed Samuel Regev?"

"I never jog with my wallet or any personal papers, You should jot down my name and address which is 409 Avenue J. just around the corner and verify for yourself that I am who I am. And you still didn't answer my question, why did you stop me?"

"Well, the old lady living by the church called us several times during the last few weeks complaining about a stranger running late at night. She even suspected that he was a burglar. We were obligated to look into her complaint but every time I arrived at the scene you were already gone. Today is my lucky day. I caught you."

"Am I free to go now?"

"Yes, you can go for now but I'm going to do more research about you," he said. I was 100% sure he was not joking.

I resumed my jogging and noticed that he followed me to verify that I did enter the apartment at 409 Avenue J.

The next evening I decided to change my jogging route lest the old lady call the police again. I surmised that the safest route would be to run down the street from my apartment all the way to Harriet Thompson Elementary School and then run loops around the perimeter of their grassy sport field. *It's the size of a football field so running around its perimeter should trim off a few pounds,* I said to myself. Besides, who would see me running there that late at night?

I began to enjoy my new route and the pleasant nights. I reached the school and I circumnavigated the grassy stadium field several times until I felt I'd burned enough calories and headed home. I congratulated myself for selecting that new route with its serene quietness where no one bothered me. Moreover, the school stadium was next to Safeway's manufacturing plant that made margarine and peanut butter. The nights when they were making peanut butter were terrific as my nostrils got overwhelmed with the aroma. *You could not ask for a better place to jog,* I told myself. I showed Batia my new route.

A week later, around 10:00 p.m. I'd run several loops when a policeman appeared with a huge flashlight. "Oh, it's you again," he said. The voice sounded familiar but I couldn't see him because I was blinded by the strong beam of his flashlight. I got my vision back when the same policeman who had stopped earlier turned the flashlight onto his little notebook. "Oh here it is," he exclaimed. "You must be Samuel Regev from 409 Ave. J?"

"Yes Sir, I'm the guy."

"So let me ask you the same question I asked you last time, what are you doing here, in the dark, this late at night?"

"As you can see, I was exercising," I replied, realizing that I was a smart aleck again.

"Sir, this place is under the jurisdiction of the school district so until I talk to the school principal and get the school district's input as to whether or not they allow you to run on the premises, you'll need to leave."

I jogged back home although I was not sure about the legality of what the policeman had just told me. Still, it was very obvious I was not included on his list of *Most favorite People.* I didn't hear from him after the incidence so I resumed jogging although earlier in the evenings.

On Saturday morning, following that incident, a person who looked to me like a farmer, knocked on my door and introduced himself as Glenn Rayburn. "Are you Sam Regev?" he asked

"Yes I am, Glenn, what can do for you?" I replied.

"I read the article Pat Hagood wrote about you in the *Grandview Review* and I was intrigued by the fact that you and your wife are native Israelis. I am a history buff and a great admirer of your country. I own a few cherry orchards. One is very close to your apartment. I just came from there and as you probably know, the cherry picking season is about to start and I had to bring ladders and buckets for the cherry picking crew. I decided to take my chances and stop at your place to introduce myself, hoping that you will be kind and tell me about Israel," Glenn explained and apologized for bothering me.

"Oh, God no! You're not bothering me at all but I'm puzzled, how did you know where to find me."

"Officer Thompson was one of my students at the Harriet Thompson Elementary School, I'm the principle there. He told me that he had been following you for quite some time. He saw you running at the stadium and he was worried about the safety and security of our buildings. He remembered taking your name and address when he first caught you on Euclid Road at midnight. He revealed your name and address so here I am. I remembered seeing the article about you and that's how I found you."

It was kind of flattering to see someone going through the effort to find me, seeking my friendship and expressing love for Israel. I invited him in and called Batia and Raz to meet him. "Mr. Rayburn is here," I called and asked them to join us.

He interrupted me abruptly, "No, no, no, please call me Glenn," he insisted, rather forcefully.

"Glenn" I continued, "I must confess that when I saw your clothes I was sure you were a farmer but now you tell me that you are the elementary school principal. Pardon me for asking, but how do you reconcile being a person devoted to two so different occupations."

"Yes, I have my hands full taking care of my cheery orchards but my official job is being principal. Both my wife Margaret and I earned a BA degree in Education from Eastern Washington University and both of us have been teachers ever since. Anyhow, before I forget, please feel free to jog around the stadium to your heart's content. I told Officer Thompson to leave you alone; you have my permission be there. He is a very nice guy. I'm sure you won't have any more trouble." Glenn picked up Raz and asked, "Raz, do you like cherries?" Raz nodded his head in the affirmative. "So here's a deal for you, when the cherries are ripe and ready to eat, you come with your mom and dad and help them pick cherries off my trees. I'll let you eat all the cherries you want. Would you like to do that?"

Raz nodded his head again to indicate the deal was sealed. It was obvious that Glenn, the elementary school principal was an expert on how to talk to children.

I continued jogging the grassy stadium at Glenn's elementary school without being stopped and interrogated by Officer Thompson. The peanut butter fragrance was a pleasant bonus adding to my jogging stamina.

A week passed and Glenn called me on Friday evening and said, "Be ready tomorrow around noon, the cherries are loaded and the fruit is ripe. Make sure Raz is not dressed in his best clothes because it will be messy."

The next day, he parked his pickup truck on the gravel area, "Sam, take your own car and follow me because I have to work at the orchard until dinner time. I need to stage everything for the picking crew. They will be here on Monday morning. The Prosser packaging plant requested my cherries and the harvest from the other cherry growers in our region. The packaging plant received a large order from Japan. I hope it won't rain until the harvest is done because any rain would destroy the cherries."

"How's that?"

"Rain will cause the ripe cherries to split, rendering them unfit for the highest quality grade and the Japanese customers are very finicky about the cherries. I could sell part of rain-damaged harvest to pie and jam manufacturers but their payment wouldn't cover my cost."

Glenn's cherry orchard was less than a quarter of a mile from our apartment. There was a little house at the entrance which Glenn owned and rented. "I don't charge much for the rent because I need a steady renter to live here, take care of the property, and keep an eye on the orchard. I grow two cherry cultivars for you to enjoy. The red ones are the Bing cherries which our Japanese customers prefer. The yellow/pinkish looking cherries are the Rainier cherries. Some customers like them as well."

I was impressed how well Glenn took care of the orchard. I also noticed that there were only a few Rainier cultivar trees. I asked Glenn "If the Japanese prefer the Bing cherries, why do you also grow the Rainier cherries?"

"Well Sam, I have to give Mother Nature a hand," he replied. "The Bing cherries require cross pollination which means they must be pollinated from a different cultivar to produce the fruit. The Rainier cultivar is a good cross pollinator for the Bing cultivar," Glenn explained. "Pick the cherries that are easy for you to reach so you don't need to climb on the ladder. Just pick the easy ones. Oh, and one more thing I forgot to tell you, it's most likely your first time at picking cherries. Feel free to pick as much as you want and eat some as you pick, but I must warn you that many people who eat too many cherries at once, find themselves anchored to the restroom with a nasty diarrhea."

We picked enough cherries to fill our refrigerator, thanked Glenn and invited him to visit us again and answer all his questions about Israel. He was thrilled to accept the invitation and became a frequent visitor to our house and in the process managed to become Raz's proxy grandpa.

Glenn's frequent visits provided him with the opportunity to learn everything he wanted about Israel. He brought with him the books about Israel he had accumulated through the years. It was a bonus for me and for Israel because whatever he learned during each visit he shared with his staff at school, his cherry grower friends and his son, who was a schoolteacher in the Seattle area.

One day he said, "My daughter Mary is home from college this weekend. I want you to meet her and my wife Margaret, please come for a barbecue this Sunday. I still have a few pounds of Bing cherries I harvested from the trees in front of my house and I'd like you to have them. They are huge," he said, trying to entice us to come, but it wasn't necessary because as foreigners living far away from our homeland and family, enjoying a close relationship with people like Glenn and his family was a blessing and eased the pain of homesickness.

Figure 11.2 Raz Regev and Washington State
Representative Margaret Rayburn

Glenn and Margaret's house stood in the midst of a small cherry orchard not far from our neighborhood. We were pleased to meet Margaret who was an attractive, pleasant lady. Both she and Glenn were natives of eastern Oregon. Her early years were spent at her parent's ranch raising livestock, bailing hay, and harvesting wheat. Unlike her students, who rode to and from school on yellow buses, she rode her horse or rode in a sleigh during the snowy days of winter.

Batia and I became absorbed talking to Margaret and didn't noticed that Glenn's daughter Mary confiscated Raz and started pampering him, marveling at his blond hair and blue eyes. She projected a very soft and sophisticated personality.

Margaret and Glenn had two children, their son Jeff who lived in Seattle, could not take the time away from college that weekend. Their daughter Mary was younger than Jeff. Margaret too, fell in love with Raz.

In my wildest dreams I never expected Raz and Margaret to intertwine fourteen years after that barbecue when she was a Washington State Representative of her district. She served in Olympia and chaired the Washington State Agriculture and Rural Development Committee. Being an educator herself, she also served as a member of the House Education Committee. When Raz was in his last year in high school, he spent a week in Olympia being her page. (Figure 11.2)

✡

The article Mrs. Pat Hagood wrote about us, continued to haunt me. This time it was a phone call I received from Mr. Ed Kronski, a resident of the Bay area. "I organize group tours to Israel, tailored to devout Christians. I got your name and phone number from the Israeli consulate in San Francisco. They suggested I contact you. I will be visiting a group of believers in the Wenatchee area and plan on driving down to Grandview to meet you. I have many issues I wish to discuss with you and wonder if you would be kind enough to help me," he said on the phone.

I agreed to help him provided the meeting would take place during the weekend. "How about next Saturday around noon?" he asked and I agreed.

"Grandview is a tiny spec on the map so you won't have any problem finding my apartment, especially coming from the Bay area and its heavy traffic congestion," I told him to park on the gravel by my kitchen door since that was the only space available for parking at our apartment complex.

Saturday came and I heard the sound of car tires on gravel. I peeked through the kitchen window at the large Ford Lincoln that had seen a better life before arriving at my kitchen door. The car door opened and a bald-headed oversized gentlemen extricated himself from the driver's seat. He straitened his jacket and knocked gently.

I introduced myself as Sam Regev but Ed Kronski corrected me and said, "Don't be shy Sam, your landsmen at the Israeli consulate in San Francisco showed me the article the Grandview newspaper published about you so I know that you are Doctor Sam Regev," he said with a great determination in his voice.

"Please let me explain what I am doing for a living," Ed said when we set on the couch in the living room. He opened his attaché case and gave me his business card. "As you can see from my card, my wife Eva and I own and operate Promised Holy land Tours, Inc. Our travel company specializes in taking devout Christians on a two-week tour to Israel. Once there, we visit the most significant locations mentioned both in the Old and New Testaments. Eva and I are their tour guide and we try to re-live some of the historic events that occurred at a specific site as described in the scriptures. We usually have one trip a year. Occasionally we add an additional trip if there is high demand. The most popular time is during Easter. The Israeli consulate in San Francisco, who told me about you, considers the tours I take to Israel as a propaganda bonanza for Israel because these tourists become great advocates and supporters of Israel upon returning. The consulate supplies us with the glossy brochures and pamphlets they obtain from the Israel Ministry of Tourism. To make the visit even more authentic we fly only with the Israeli airline El Al, the airplane crew speaks Hebrew like their forefathers 2000 years ago."

Ed Kronski paused for a minute so I took the opportunity to thank him for helping Israel and introducing the country to his Christians clients and turning them into great allies of Israel. "So, tell me Ed," I asked him, "How is Promised Holy Land Tours related to your current visit to Wenatchee before coming to see me?"

"Believe it or not, these people saw my ad in one of the Christian magazines and contacted me requesting information on our tours so I decided to visit them. To be correct, the church of this group was not in Wenatchee but in the nearby city of Cashmere." Ed elaborated on the issue. "I know that you are Jewish, but I am not sure how familiar you are about what we, the Christians, define and believe as the Trinity. So let me explain briefly. We believe that God interfaces with us, as three distinct co-equal persons:

- God the Father, who is our Creator and the judge. The one described in the Old Testament.
- God the Son, Jesus Christ, who reveals himself as a human being and lives among us, i.e. his people.

- As the Holy Spirit, or the Holy Ghost representing the power of new life. The New Testament identifies it as the Spirit of Christ and the Spirit of Truth.

However, not every Christian denomination accepts the Trinity concept. For example, the Mormon Church, Jehovah Witness, and the Unitarian Church don't accept it. The group I visited in Cashmere belongs to a small denomination that does not believe in the Trinity concept so they named their church The Church of God Faith of Abraham. Their message is very catchy due to referencing Abraham, the first human being accepting the concept of monotheism, the existence of one God only. In the past I did not solicit my Israel tours to Christians who did not believe in the Trinity until I got a request from the Church of God Faith of Abraham for information about my Israel tours. I must admit, they were very interested in joining my next expedition to Israel after I sent them pamphlets about it. I am sure, you would find these people very interesting and great supporters of Israel. Do you mind if I tell them about you?" Ed asked me

"I don't mind at all. Now, I have a friend who I am sure would be thrilled to meet you and hear about your Israel tours. Do you mind if I call him right now and see if he is available to join us?"

"That would be great," Ed replied so I called Dr. Woods.

"Don, I have an out-of-town guest who came for a one-hour visit, I strongly recommended you come to my house and meet him. He is a very devoted Christian like you and I prefer that you hear directly from him what he is doing for a living."

"Of course, give me a few minutes."

When Don arrived, he chatted a little bit with Raz who was playing with Christine. I introduced my guests to each other and said, "Ed, I would like you to meet my good friend Dr. Don Woods who wears so many hats. He is a medical doctor, an accomplished pilot and a very devoted Christian. Dr. Woods, I would like you to meet my new friend, Ed. Kronski, who is an expert on showing Israel to devoted Christians. I'll let him elaborate more on what he does for a living."

Batia joined us and with cold drinks and cookies. I was more than 100% correct with my hunch that Don Woods would be excited about Ed's guided tours to Israel. He inspected with great interest the glossy brochures and the booklet Ed received from the Israel Ministry of Tourism. After Don checked the last pamphlet Ed showed him, Don asked, "Mr. Kronski, could you stay in Grandview as my guest, come to our church tomorrow and give our fellow worshipers a presentation on your next tour to Israel. You have persuaded my wife and I to travel with you. I'm sure more people from my church will go with us. What is the minimum number of people needed to make this tour worth your while?"

"Ten participants would be the minimum. Talking to your church would be great. I stopped here in Grandview for a chat with the Regev's and planned to return home but I could stay with you tonight and go to the Sunday service tomorrow."

"Great," Don said. "I need to make a short stop at my clinic. I'll be back in half an hour to pick you up. Sam, thanks for introducing me to Ed. I expect you to show up at my church tomorrow to hear Ed's presentation. Are you coming?" He seemed confident I would say "Yes." I promised to come and he left. Half an hour later Ed Kronski followed Don home. "See you tomorrow," they both said as they left.

Ed Kronski's presentation was a great success. Four more people joined the tour in addition to Don and his wife, including Don's son and daughter. Ed also established contact between Don and the people at the Cashmere Church of God Faith of Abraham. One of them was an avid pilot like Don so they had a common interest exchanging notes about flying in addition to discussing the holy scriptures. I knew that sooner or later someone from that group would contact me so I gave Ed the OK.

Then the Nelsen family invited us to spend Saturday night and Sunday. I was asked to talk to the congregation about Israel.

The Nelsen family was extremely accommodating, but that visit was one of the poorest judgments I ever made. Raz started showing the early signs of an ear infection. He wasn't in pain, and didn't have a temperature so I decided to go ahead with my speaking engagement. Batia was not too happy with the decision and expressed her reservations. She sensed that his early signs would develop into a more serious infection. Moreover, the weather forecast predicted foggy nights and mornings. She went along, nonetheless because I was eager to keep my promise.

The drive to Cashmere was uneventful and we spent the night at the Nelsen's house. Raz's ears started acting up and the earache interfered with his sleep. We had to comfort him which made it a sleepless night for all of us. We could hardly wait for Sunday morning. When I heard Mrs. Nelsen preparing pancakes for breakfast, I asked her if there was a clinic nearby to take Raz to a doctor because his ears were giving him lots of pain. "Let me call Dr. Miller, the pediatrician here in town." Luckily, he agreed to open his clinic at 9:00 a.m.. Sure enough, it was another of Raz's recurring ear infections. Dr. Miller ordered a prescription for antibiotics at the pharmacy in Grandview and gave us a days' worth of medication samples.

Dr. Miller gave Raz an antibiotic pill to swallow, then Raz picked one of the daily newspapers off the clinic journal rack and started browsing through it while I asked Dr. Miller why Raz was so prone to ear infections.

Dr. Miller explained that at this stage of Raz's development, the eustachian tube that connects his throat and the middle ear is a straight horizontal line and therefore it is easy for fluids from his throat to get inside the ear. The ears get plugged which causes the pain. "But don't worry. The majority of cases are resolved when the child's skull grows, causing the eustachian tube–middle ear connection to slope at an angle steep enough to minimize the chance of liquid from his throat reaching his middle ears.

As we left the clinic Dr. Miller commented, "I was watching your son. I have never seen a three-year-old toddler show so much interest in a daily newspaper. He could have picked one of the many children's toys but was glued to a daily newspaper. I suggest you follow up. Maybe this will develop into something more significant in the future. Dr. Miller's observations were correct. Raz had become addicted to reading newspapers and political magazines and eventually earned a BA degree in Political Science.

We returned to the Nelsen's home. Batia and Raz stayed with Mrs. Nelsen and I went with Mr. Nelsen to give my talk. I tried to be as professional and relaxed as I could but it was very difficult knowing that there was a long, torturous, fog-laden drive ahead of me. Nonetheless, the talk went very well and I was amazed at how well versed these people were with the Old and New Testaments. They kept flooding me with questions which kept me longer than anticipated. When we finally left Cashmere I drove the 128 miles at a snail's pace with my nose glued to the windshield. I could hardly see the road a few feet in front of us. While I was busy driving, Batia was busy praying. When we finally reached home I admitted that she was right. Going under these conditions was poor judgment on my part.

Chapter 12

Grandview: Part 2

Things were going well for us, both at work and at home. My research produced more findings and ended up as scientific papers published in the peer-reviewed professional journals. I was listed as the principle author and Wyatt as the co-author. The stream of postcards requesting copies of my published papers kept coming so I decided that having more than five scientific publications merited efforts on my part to shoot for an Assistant Professor position with one of the major US universities. I started brushing up my resume.

As Raz grew older, we enrolled him with Mrs. Baker's pre-school held at the local Methodist Church. The facility was well equipped as the church used it for its Sunday School. The time he was at the pre-school, left Batia with a few hours of quality time to do whatever she wanted, especially on days when I left our car at home. Raz enjoyed the time at the pre-school but his days as the sole *star* of the Regev family dwindled as we were expecting another baby.

Living in a different country, away from home, family and culture, made it difficult to build genuine, deep friendships. Nonetheless, we were fortunate to build solid relationships with my boss Dr. Wyatt Cone, Glenn Rayburn and his wife Margaret, Dale Burgeson and his family and with Dr. Woods and his wife. They all helped us ease the homesickness we felt at times.

Dr. Woods came by one evening and said, "Shalom Sam, just to remind you that the entire Woods family is leaving for Israel this coming Saturday morning. We are flying to JFK to join Ed Kronski, his wife and the other members of the tour group. We will be boarding the El Al mid-night flight direct to Tel Aviv. I decided to stop by and get some final input from *the expert*."

I was pleased knowing that I had some part in his family's trip to Israel. They would cherish their visit for the rest of their lives. "El Al is a Jewish airline. Going with El Al will provide you with security and protection from terrorists like no other airline. Their pilots are former combat pilots in the Israeli Air Force, so obviously they have plenty of experience. Your flight should have an undercover air marshal protecting you from being hijacked. The flight attendants also served mandatory military service after finishing high school. They are gorgeous and if you come back disagreeing with me, I will rush you to the eye doctor imminently. The food served is *Glut Kosher* (Yiddish for 100% Kosher) so please spare yourself from the embarrassment and don't ask for a cheeseburger. Mixing milk and meat is forbidden according to the *Halacha* (Jewish Law). The law states *"Do not cook a young goat in its mother's milk."* This dietary law is mentioned three times in the Torah: Exodus 23:19, Exodus 34:26 and Deuteronomy 14:21."

"Thanks for the warning," Dr. Woods replied. "My son David and I are crazy about cheeseburgers, but I promise we won't order them."

There's another major benefit to flying a Jewish airline," I told Don and asked him if he knew what section of the plane was reserved to their tour group.

"What difference would that make?"

"It could make a huge difference," I replied. "If you're seated in the back section of the plane, you'll have an experience unique to El Al. It will indirectly *add value* to Ed Kronski's tour. Your flight is leaving at midnight on an eleven-hour non-stop transatlantic flight to Israel. Daybreak will come not long after your departure from JFK. For you, Sunday is a holiday but for Jews it is the first day of a regular week. The majority of your fellow passengers will be observant Jews. The start of a weekday calls for the *Shacharit* (the morning service) and putting on the *tefillin* (phylacteries). Moreover, there are some prayers that require a *minyan* (a quorum of ten adult male Jews). I bet you a million dollars that as the new day dawns you will see these observant Jews start summoning fellow Jews to come to the back section to put on their *tefillins* and pray the *Shacharit*. This section of the plane would be crowded. It also happens to have toilets located there which won't be available to you for quite a long time. Personally, I found it hilarious that only on El Al flights, the toilet area transforms into a *Place of Worship* and Pilgrimage Site.

"What are *tefillins*?" Don asked. "Just give me the gist of it and I'll study it in more detail tonight."

"*Tefillin* are two small black cubical leather boxes with straps to attach them to your body. One *tefillin* is wrapped around the arm, the other one is placed on the middle of the forehead.

"It sounds odd and complicated," Dr. Woods interrupted me.

"Maybe it sounds odd and complicated but each leather box contains a scroll of parchment inscribed in Hebrew with the verses from the *Torah* (*Pentateuch*, the five books of Moses). They are affixed onto the arm and the forehead of observant adult male Jews during the morning prayer on weekdays, but not Sabbath and Jewish holidays. The verses inscribed on each parchment inside are from Exodus 13:9, Deuteronomy 6:8 and Deuteronomy 11:18. This should explain to you why they are placed on the arm and the forehead. These are divine commands and serve to remind the Jewish people of God's intervention, rescuing them out of Egypt. I am not sure how accurate the translation of your King James bible is. Here is the translation I prefer:

> *9 And it shall be for a sign unto thee upon thy hand, and for a memorial between thine eyes, that the law of the LORD may be in thy mouth; for with a strong hand hath the LORD brought thee out of Egypt (Exodus 13:9)*

> *8 And thou shalt bind them for a sign upon thy hand, and they shall be for frontlets between thine eyes (Deuteronomy 6:8)*

> *18 Therefore shall ye lay up these my words in your heart and in your soul; and ye shall bind them for a sign upon your hand, and they shall be for frontlets between your eyes (Deuteronomy 11:18)*

✡

Don phoned me upon returning from what he called, "My lifetime tour to the Holy Land. Sam, the flight was exactly the way you described. The orthodox passengers started assembling at the back of the plane at daybreak. They strapped on their *tefillin* and started their morning prayers. Our group was seated at the midsection and not at the back where they gathered at their "Synagogue." Before they started, I talked to the guy who appeared to be their self-appointed prayer leader and explained who I was, and asked permission to observe their service. He was kind, appreciated my interest and gave me the OK. It was so interesting; I also observed their *Ma'ariv* evening prayer. Now I understand why you told me that flying to Israel on El Al makes the flight more interesting than a non-Jewish airline."

A few weeks later we went to his church, saw his slide show and listened to his account of the places they went and his personal impression of Israel.

✡

As mentioned in Chapter 10, my Ph.D. research work drew me into photography and the chemistry associated with processing film and paper. I became very proficient and did all the photographic tasks associated with my thesis. I had decided to make it a hobby once I had more leisure time.

With my research for Wyatt in full swing and producing published scientific papers, and with Raz growing up nicely, we had a little more discretionary income. It was an opportune time to begin my hobby. Moreover, during that time, commercial color film processing and printing did not exist in Israel, forcing the Israelis sent their color film to labs in Europe for processing and printing. I made a vow not to return to Israel without mastering the ability to process my own color film and prints. I also aimed at developing my own color slides and super-8 movie film.

I was lucky to find a store in Los Angeles tailored to photography aficionados and made them my sole supplier. They were Israelis so I could seek advice in Hebrew for a change. I purchased several film processing tanks to process various color film sizes. One kind was designed specifically for processing the color prints I produced by using the Beseler printing projector I purchased.

I ordered a Ricoh Single Lens Reflex SLR camera, with telephoto and close-up lenses. I also purchased a super-8 movie camera. Camcorders were not commercially available. To save money, I ordered 35mm film in 100-foot rolls, but living in a small apartment posed a problem. Unlike black and white photography where you could use a red light to see what you were doing, processing color film and print papers required complete darkness. I devised my own method for spooling the 100-foot rolls into 36 frames per roll, using my parka as a portable dark room. I staged the items, still packed in their light protective covers, inside my long parka, closed its zipper and did all the necessary manipulation with my hands accessing the items through the coat sleeves.

For all other activities requiring complete darkness, I waited until Batia and Raz were asleep so I could use the laundry area by the kitchen as my photography lab. I stuck a large bathroom towel between the kitchen door and the floor to block the light coming from the street. Upon finishing my processing session, I made sure to fold the towel neatly and put it back in the closet so Batia won't get mad at me the next morning. I used my Beseler enlarger to project the color negative images onto the print paper and then processed it in a special drum. I rinsed it and left it to dry overnight. It was nice to brag about it the next morning when Batia saw the pictures.

It was vital for me to clean up my photography mess before going to sleep because color photography chemicals are very poisonous. I had to make sure my family won't be exposed to them.

Processing the films of the super-8 color movie was a different challenge altogether. I had to find a place to dry many feet of wet film. Batia was not too pleased when she got up in the morning and found the full length of movie film meandering on a twine stretched inside our apartment.

✡

Our second baby was due sometime in late October or early November. Batia's mother, Esther, got excited and started preparing for a visit to be with Batia for the birth as she did when Raz was born. This pregnancy though, caused much anxiety on our part. It stemmed from our impression, right or wrong, that the local prenatal and baby delivering services were not at par with that of the Kadlec hospital in Richland. We were toying with the idea of using Kadlec but rushing Batia to a delivery room thirty-six miles away during late October/ early November with the high probability of stormy weather, seemed too risky. Besides, all the *experts* told us that the second delivery is much faster than the first one, so there was no guarantee that we would reach the hospital in time. We decided to take Dr. Wood's advice and contracted the Osteopathic hospital in Sunnyside, eight miles west of us where he had visiting privileges.

Batia's mother arrived from Israel in mid-October. We had a good time together and received an extensive update on what had happened in the *kibbutz* since she visited us when Raz was born. The morning of November 5, was somewhat gloomy, yet there was no indication that a snowy day was in the making when I left for work. I felt at ease knowing that Esther was at Batia's side. Around noon Esther noticed Batia's discomfort, "You must call *Shmulik* and tell him to come home right now."

"There is no need to call him; he will be home in four hours."

"But you don't look OK to me," her mother replied.

"I'm going to take a shower and I'll be fine," Batia said.

At 5:00 p.m., I headed home uttering the F-word as it started to snow. It was dark and the huge snowflakes slowed me down considerably. The twenty minute-drive took close to an hour. Batia was in labor when I finally arrived. I helped her stretch onto the back seat and headed to the hospital in Sunnyside. The drive was nightmarish, I could barely see the side of the road let alone the road signs and exists. I was sure we wouldn't make it in time. I feared I would have to deliver my own baby somewhere along the road in the midst of a blizzard.

I guess our guardian angels took mercy on us. When we arrived, the nurses rushed Batia to delivery, but they didn't have the time to prepare the room. The bed was cold and the room wasn't heated. The nurses paged Dr. Butler who she saw during the prenatal care and was assigned to deliver our baby. He finally arrived and took control of the situation.

This time I was in the delivery room. I don't recall what exactly triggered Dr. Butler to draw me into a political discussion about Israel and the Middle East. I thought he should pay attention to Batia and my baby rather than discussing politics.

"It is a beautiful baby girl, Mr. Regev," he said to me while slapping my daughter to initiate her initial cry. The nurses cleaned her and Dr. Butler checked both baby and mother. "Your daughter and wife are fine," he said. "Congratulations. Do you have a name for her?"

"Yes we do," Batia said, "her name is *Shir*. The Hebrew word for *song*."

"What a beautiful name," he replied and the nurses agreed. "I will come tomorrow to see how you and Shir are doing. Nurses Dottie and Marsha will take you to your room. See you tomorrow," he said to Batia then stopped by where I was sitting and said, "It was interesting discussing Israel with you. Just so you know, my colleague, Dr. Don Woods told me all about you and Batia. I am also a devout Christian so I couldn't resist the temptation to talk to you tonight. I am sure Dr. Woods will visit tomorrow," he said and I thanked him again for taking care of Batia and Shir.

I was amazed at the time it took Batia to deliver Shir. With Raz she labored for almost eleven hours, whereas it took Shir only thirty minutes to become a citizen of this world. It was still snowing heavily when I drove home and told Esther she had a new granddaughter. She was elated and glad she'd traveled all the way from Israel to be part of the happy event.

The next day, I took Esther and Raz to the hospital to see Batia and Shir. Batia looked stronger and happy to have us there. Esther was excited to see her new granddaughter and I promised to send her photographs of Raz and Shir, frequently enough to fill the walls of her home in the *kibbutz*. I could sense that Esther's extreme happiness holding Shir was somewhat marred by the realization that the sweet moments she had with her only family would come to an end in a few days.

Dr. Woods arrived, as promised, and congratulated us. He looked at the medical chart that was attached to Batia's bed and assured us everything looked good. I introduced him to Esther and said that she came from Israel to participate in the birth of her granddaughter Shir.

"I understand that she came here from Israel, yet I can trace some German accent," Dr. Woods whispered.

"Yes, she was born in Germany but emigrated with her friends from Germany to Eretz Israel/Palestine where they established their own *kibbutz*."

Two days later, we were happy to be back home and put Shir in the crib we'd staged in our bedroom. Thus far she proved to be an easy-going baby who didn't cry too much. Raz had to adjust, realizing that from now on he would have to share the *stardom* with Shir. I let Batia relax and enjoy the time with her mother. I never considered myself a chef, nonetheless; I prepared a nice dinner from scratch.

Esther's departure day came and after a lengthy deliberation we decided that the entire family would take her to the airport in Pasco, a forty-four-mile drive in each direction. Batia felt that she and Shir could handle the drive. Trying hard to ease her departure pain, we promised to visit her soon, and waived goodbye as the plane took off.

Our apartment felt empty when we came home from the airport. The reality that we were a family of four, living far away from our parents, relatives, and close friends started to sink in. *Life goes on and so should you* I said to myself as another issue related to dealing with the US immigration office was coming soon and I needed to tackle it correctly.

✡

I was still traumatized from our ordeal with the immigration offices in Sacramento and San Francisco. (See Chapter 9.)

When I received the post doctorate research associate position with Washington State University, my student visa was still current, however, it was about to expire while I was still in the middle of our research project, and no longer considered a student. I had to come up with a solution, and fast. The H-1 nonimmigrant visa addressed my situation and the H-4 nonimmigrant visa for Batia. The H-1 visa would allow me to stay as long as my post doctorate position lasted, and allowed for multiple requests for renewal. I sent applications to the Immigration and Naturalization Office in Spokane, Washington. I explained my situation and included a letter from Dr. Cone stating that he was financing my research and salary and would continue to do so in the foreseeable future.

The waiting game and anxiety started the day I sent the applications. I hoped the Spokane office would be more accommodating than the Sacramento and San Francisco offices. Working with any government agency requires a lot of patience, a commodity I did not have at that stage in my life.

The new visas finally arrived allowing me to have a deep sigh of relief, but there was one mandatory stipulation. The Spokane office had sent the documents to the Tel Aviv embassy. We should have the new visas stamped into our Israeli passports at the American Embassy in Tel Aviv, in person.

Granted, getting our H-1 and H-4 visas approved was a great deal for us, but it also complicated our lives because it forced us to fly to Israel but we had no other choice.

I was so happy things with the Immigration and Naturalization office went smoothly it was cause for celebration. "Let's have a short visit to Vancouver, British Columbia and enjoy ourselves before embarking on our visit to Israel. We haven't been in Vancouver since I attended the Hewlett Packard class," I suggested to Batia and she agreed.

Shir was almost ten months old by then and seemed to enjoy our frequent rides to Yakima or the Tri-Cities to shop at the Columbia Center Mall, or K-Mart in Yakima. I was confident she would survive the nearly six-hour drive to Vancouver. Since we planned to visit Israel the first week of September, we decided that going to Vancouver two weeks before our flight would be reasonable so I made a three-night reservation at the Vancouver downtown Travelodge. The next thing I had on the agenda was to acquire my first credit card.

Being strapped for money for most of my life in the USA, I never even thought about applying, trying to spare myself the embarrassment of being rejected. However, with the upcoming trip to Israel and Vancouver, I decided it would be great to have one. I was ignorant about the kinds of credit cards available at that time although VISA, Master Charge and American Express rang a bell. Then, on our next visit to JC Penney, I noticed their advertisement for the JC Penney Credit Card and I decided to see if they would offer me one.

I approached the lady at the counter and asked for the application forms. She cheerfully handed them to me and highlighted the lines for me to fill in. I told her that I was new at filling out an application for a credit card. "Oh! Don't' worry, it's simple. Just do it here at the counter and I'll help if you need it."

I filled in the information she marked with her yellow marker but I was still concerned they would deny my application so I used my doctor title.

The lady at the counter glossed over my application and assured me that everything looked good. "The card should arrive in your mail shortly."

The card arrived a week later but it looked different from standard major credit cards, it was narrower and orange but no one could miss the *Dr. Samuel Regev* embossed into the plastic. In retrospect, it was a mistake to include my title, especially when we bought low-priced items trying to save money. I could sense what was going through the cashier's head, "What a stingy, cheap doctor. Doctors make tons of money and this dud only buys clearances items." Maybe it was all in my head, but I stopped using the card in the store. I used it only for orders I placed on the phone. I still have an emotional attachment to that particular credit card because it was *my very first card ever*. I kept it for forty-five years before closing the account.

The ride to Vancouver was uneventful until we reached the US/Canadian border at Blaine, Washington. There is a small park called Peace Arch between the Canadian border and the US border. Visitors can park their cars, use the public restrooms and cross the border within the confines of the park. We used the park facilities and ate the food we brought from home. It was a sunny pleasant day to enjoy. All of a sudden it occurred to me that we'd left the USA and that park was really a *no man's land*. What was our legal status as far as the US Immigration and Naturalization office was concerned?

My gut feeling told me not to cross into Canada. I did not want to alarm Batia so I told her I needed to check something with the officers at the Canadian border station and would be back soon. The officer at the counter looked friendly and asked, "May I help you sir?"

I showed him our passports and the names of Shir and Raz added officially to Batia's Israeli passport by the Israeli consulate in San Francisco. I mentioned that both were born in the USA and were American citizens. "Our F-1 and F-2 visas are going to expire shortly and our H-1 and H-4 visas were approved and are waiting for us at the American Embassy in Tel Aviv. We have purchased the airline tickets to go to Tel Aviv in a few weeks before our student visas expire."

The Canadian officer looked at our Israeli passports and said to me, "Sir as far as I'm concerned, I have no problem letting you and your family into Canada but I would like to suggest that you turn around and head back towards the US border station. Just join the line of cars crossing into the USA. I hope they will let you in. Good luck to you and visit us again," the gentleman said as he gave back our passports. I thanked him and returned to the picnic table where Batia and the children were waiting.

"We cannot continue to Vancouver and must return back home to Grandview, if they let us in," I told Batia as we got back into the car. I made a U-turn and headed towards the border crossing lane into the USA. "What happened? What did they tell you at the Canadian border station?"

"It is complicated and I am not sure what our situation is. We will find out when we try to cross into the US," I told her while driving into the inner-most lane, closest to the border station building. The line of cars was long, especially the one I chose. Shir started crying and from the smell I knew she needed a diaper change. We didn't change it because of the haste of leaving the park.

Finally, it was my turn to approach the booth. I saw the border control inspector entering our license number into the computer. He stepped out of his booth and asked for our documents. He got closer and inspected the car and saw Raz and Shir in the back seat. From the vibes I sensed by just watching his long and frowning face, I realized the interaction with this particular officer was not going to be smooth. My worries deepened when he started interrogating me.

"How many days have you been in Canada and what was the purpose of your visit there?"

At that point it didn't feel like this was routine protocol by a border control officer genuinely doing his job. It felt more like someone with the authority to play a *Cat and Mouse* game with me, trying to hurt me before swallowing me alive. He knew that we had not been to Canada because we didn't have the Canadian entry stamp in our passports, yet he kept asking where in Canada we visited and the purpose of that visit. "Sir, we are coming from the Peace Arch Park and we did not cross into Canada today."

"Why is that?"

"We were on our way to visit a friend in Vancouver, BC. Your Canadian counterpart at the Douglas station, advised us not to cross into Canada before checking with you, and that is exactly what we are doing now. Our new H-1 and H-4 visas are waiting for us at the American embassy in Tel Aviv, Israel.

"Sorry sir," the officer said, "I cannot let you return to the USA."

"Why not?"

"Since your F-1 student visa is going to expire shortly, I have to consider you a foreigner trying to enter the USA without the proper visa."

"The student visa has not expired yet so I am still allowed to be in the USA."

"Yes, it has not expired yet, but if we let you in now, it will expire soon while you are still inside the country, illegally without a current visa. We have many cases like this with illegal aliens, mostly farm workers, living in that part of Washington state." I could sense his distaste for foreigners.

Since the incident took place during the normal working hours of the Immigration and Naturalization office in Spokane, I told the officer, "Why don't you call the immigration office in Spokane and check for yourself the validity of what I am telling you. Ask them to check File Number Spo-N-590."

"Everyone can give me stories like this. The only thing that I go by is whether or not your passport has the new visas. "I am not going to call any office to verify your story and let you back into the USA."

It became clear to me that this officer was type of person who got intoxicated by the power of his uniform and the plethora of badges. Showing everyone *who calls the shots*, gave him the pleasure.

I had nothing to lose at that point and decided to let the officer know I could play his game and be less polite if needed. I got out of the car, opened the back door and pulled out the baby seat with Shir and her soiled diaper. I held the seat with Shir next to him and raised my voice loud enough for other people to hear, "Sir, you are giving me and my wife a hard time because we are foreigners, aren't you? But my son and daughter were born here and they are AMERICAN CITIZENS and you have the audacity of not let us take them home. Here is my AMERICAN CITIZEN DAUGHTER. As you can see and smell, she needs a diaper change badly. So here is the diaper. You do it," I said and gave him a clean diaper. "We are not going to move the car," I said fiercely in my Hebrew-accented English. A few minutes into the commotion, another officer who looked like a supervisor showed up at the booth and asked, "What's going on sir?"

I tried to explain the situation and then I pointed to the line of cars stretching all the way to the Canadian border, "I am not responsible for the long line, your officer is the one responsible." I told him what I told the officer, stating that he even refused to contact the Spokane Immigration and Naturalization office to verify the details I gave him. "I even gave him the file number pertaining to our new visas but he still refused."

"Please, give me the file number and the passports and I'll be back." He returned a few minutes later, "Let them return to Grandview."

From the tone of his voice, I got the impression that the officer who gave us a hard time would have to wait a long time for his next raise. The supervisor advised me not to leave the USA until our upcoming flight to Israel.

"That was a close call," I told Batia. We stopped at the first rest area on Interstate 5 to change Shir's diaper, FINALLY!

✡

I chose El Al for our trip but we had to fly from Seattle to JFK on United Airlines. We were still strapped for money so we drove 184 miles instead of flying to Seattle.

We parked our car in the driveway of Dale Burgeson's mother's driveway, near the Seattle Tacoma airport. We first met Dale Burgeson when he and the Welcome Wagon Lady visited us. (See Chapter 11.) Dale and his family became our close friends. His mother promised to watch our car until we return from Israel. Dale dropped us at the airport and promised to pick us up when we returned. What a great friend he was and still is.

This trip to Israel was special for us not only because of the precious visas but also because it was our first visit to our homeland since we left six years earlier as a *married couple*. Now we were returning as a *family of four*. I told Batia, jokingly, "I hope they won't stop us at the Israel customs booth, and charge us a steep fee for importing foreign goods i.e. Raz and Shir." The flight from Seattle to JFK was fine, both Raz and Shir behaved very well, thank God. Once at JFK, the saga of switching from the domestic to the International terminal was as hard as parting the Red Sea. That airport was not too friendly, especially for families with babies and toddlers. Luckily for us, we had purchased an umbrella stroller to carry Shir. It could fold and unfold as needed.

We arrived at the El Al gate around five p.m. local time and found out that our midnight flight to Israel was rescheduled to three a.m.. It meant a torturous ten hour stay at the El Al boarding area with a 3 ½-year-old toddler and a ten-month-old baby, with no food or diapers. I could not see my family suffering through this so I looked for a solution. Since my sister Chaya and her family had returned to Israel, the only other person I knew living in New York was Daphne Cohen, an Israeli close friend who married a Jewish high school mathematics teacher from New York. I looked for her number in the phone directory, chained to the public phone booth.

I was relieved to hear her voice and she was shocked to hear mine, it had been so many years since our paths went different directions. I explained that we were stuck for the next ten hours at the El Al waiting area.

Daphne cut me short and said, "*Shmulik*, I am leaving home right now and will be at the terminal shortly. You will stay with us, have dinner and rest a little bit before I take you back to the airport. I hope to recognize you after the many years that have passed."

That token of affection relaxed me a bit knowing that Daphne always kept her word. I returned to Batia and the children. "Remember my friend Daphne, I've told you about? She is coming to take us to her apartment and she will bring us back in time to board our flight." Batia was relieved to hear the good news.

An hour passed and Daphne showed up. I briefly introduced her to Batia and the children and she drove us to her apartment, located not too far from the airport. "*Shmulik*, you have not changed much since I saw you last time."

"Yes I have," I replied. "To begin with, my bathroom scales would disagree with you but more importantly, I now have my Ph.D."

"How about that, *Dr. Polo* is a real doctor now. Congratulation, *Shmulik*."

"Daphne, before I forget, we need to buy diapers for Shir. We left her diaper supply in the car in Washington," I said when I noticed a supermarket next to her building.

"Don't worry, I'll send Jacob to buy a small pack of diapers. On the plane, they will give you all the diapers you need, but let's have a light dinner first. You must be starving."

Daphne introduced us to her husband Jacob, a Brooklyn native who spoke Hebrew with a Brooklyn accent. "Here is your room," she said, then sent Jacob to buy the diapers. "Why don't you give Raz and Shir a bath while I prepare the dinner."

That was a thoughtful idea that Batia accepted wholeheartedly.

The children were sleepy at the dinner table so after munching on a little food we let them sleep in the room. Batia joined them after a while. Jacob retired for the night as he had to teach the next day. Daphne and I stayed at the dining room table, catching up and sharing stories of what had happened to us through the years.

✡

I met Daphne in the summer of 1962 after being discharged from the army. Both of us were recruited to serve as medics in the youth summer camp on Mount Carmel for high school students. Oddly enough or perhaps by the stroke of luck, a few years later, I ended up marrying one of those teenagers, started a family and now all of us were reunited because a delayed flight.

Daphne and I remained close friends after the summer camp on Mount Carmel. She came to visit me in my *kibbutz* a few weeks later and I realized she was aiming for a more serious relationship. At that time, I had decided to leave the *kibbutz* to attend the university. I told her I was not the right person for her and she understood my reasoning. We remained close friends.

Daphne was a special lady with her own Holocaust survivor story. She was reluctant to talk about it but she shared bits of information she had heard from her mother. I had a friendly relationship with her mother and visited her in her Jerusalem home through the years. Talking to both Daphne and her mother about their Holocaust ordeal I found out that Daphne and her twin sister along with their mother were all part of what became known as the Teheran Children's saga.

Once they arrived in Eretz Israel/Palestine, Daphne's mother was determined to start a new life and married a Holocaust survivor. They had a daughter together, a native of Israel, the Jewish State that became their sanctuary. Daphne loved her stepsister and her stepfather, the only father she knew.

✡

I never talked with Daphne or her mother about the details of the transfer from Iran to Israel so I researched the Teheran Children's Saga.

On September 1, 1939, the Nazis invaded Poland and started massacring the Jews including Daphne's father. Her mother, a young widow with twin baby girls, managed to escape Nazi-occupied Poland. There were many Polish orphaned children among them, as well as children who were separated from their parents and families, never to see them again.

When Germany invaded Russia on June 22, 1941 more Polish refugees fled deeper into Russia. At the same time, the British army and the Soviet Red Army collaborated and occupied Iran so Poles who escaped from Russia migrated to Iran.

With plenty of Polish expatriates in Russia, a Polish Army was formed on Russian soil by a Polish General, Władysław Anders. That army was also known as Anders Army. Many Polish refugees, Jews included, followed the Anders Army wherever it went.

In 1942, a number of units from the Anders Army were deployed into British occupied Iran. Among the civilians that followed were close to 1000 Jewish orphans and some Jewish children accompanied by only one biological parent, like Daphne, her sister Lea and their mother. It was of paramount importance for the Jewish Agency to bring them to the Eretz Israel/Palestine, still under the British mandate.

The Jewish Agency reserved enough certificates to bring the Jewish orphans and their adult escorts to Eretz Israel/Palestine. The task of deciphering which orphan was Jewish and which one was a Polish Christian was a complicated task since many of the Jewish orphans, traumatized by the war, refused to admit their Jewishness. Nonetheless, they were eventually identified.

On January 3, 1943 the Jewish Agency managed to transport 716 Jewish orphans and their adult escorts by truck to the Iranian seaport at Bandar-e Šāhpūr on the Persian Gulf. From there they sailed to Karachi, Pakistan, and continued via the Arabian Peninsula to the Egyptian city of Suez. The last leg of their journey was a train ride from Suez to a warm welcome in Eretz Israel/Palestine.

✡

I woke up my family and let Raz and Shir eat something light before Daphne rushed us to the El Al terminal. The US airport security was minimal at that time. However, at El Al security all checked luggage was opened and searched before the security expert cleared the bags for loading. Only then were the boarding passes issued. The same protocol repeated itself at the boarding gate where the security crew checked each carry-on item and questioned the passengers about where they had been in the USA, if they packed their own luggage and if anyone they did not know asked them to deliver *a gift* to someone in Israel. This of course took time and explained why we needed to arrive early.

When it was time for us to board, we thanked Daphne for her hospitality and kindness. Batia started moving towards the boarding gate pushing the stroller with Shir and I was holding Raz's hand. I turned to Daphne and said, "We will meet again sometime in the future but now please go home and get some rest. Thanks again."

A nice looking and a very pleasant flight attendant ushered us to our seats. Raz had his own seat between Batia and me, Shir sat/slept in a bassinet attached to the wall in front of our seats. She seemed to like it throughout the flight. "We have more than half an hour before takeoff, it's a good time to change the baby's diaper," said the flight attendant, handing Batia a diaper. Batia thought it was a good idea.

Once the plan reached the cursing altitude, the crew served a light meal. We were really hungry and devoured the meal despite the odd hour.

The El Al Trans-Atlantic flight took about eleven hours squeezing us into a cramped airline seats with not much leg room. But the thought of coming back to my Israel, and seeing our families again was a great reward. Showing Raz and Shir to their Grandma and Grandpa was worth it. We landed in Israel on September 3, 1974. My brother-in-law met us at the airport and drove us to my parents' house on 34 Yehuda Hamaccabi Street, where I grew up.

The trauma of fighting with the US Immigration and Naturalization officer at the Canadian border a few weeks earlier was still fresh in my mind so the minute bus services started running, I rushed to the American Embassy on HaYarkon Street to claim our visas. The clerk stamped the visas into our Israeli passports, but there was one stipulation. The visa was limited specifically to the sponsoring employer, the clerk at the embassy made sure to add a handwritten note specifying that I was working for Dr. Wyatt Cone. He also added a written note to that effect below Batia's visa. (Figure 12.1) This note was significant because the holder of an H-1 visa cannot change jobs or move elsewhere without a visa change.

Figure 12.1 Our H-1 visas

Chapter 13

Returning to Israel

Our first visit to Israel six years after Batia and I left for the USA gave us quality time with my parents, Batia's mother, my sister and her family, not to mention close friends that we dearly missed. The visit presented me with an opportunity to reunite with my Aunt Mala, her husband Marek and my cousin Halina, all major characters in this memoir. Our visit also gave my parents precious time with Raz and Shir. My mother invited everyone who knew me to my parents' home to show off her *Son the Doctor* and her cute little grandchildren. And, of course, it was a homecoming to my beloved 34 Yehuda Hamaccabi Street where I grew up.

Living six years in the USA had an impact on the way Batia and I behaved and felt, we had become *Americanized*. Suddenly, we realized how badly we missed the manners and the etiquette most Americans practice. They were in short supply while we were in Israel. The Israelis seemed to be more aggressive, albeit friendly, but living under constant threat from their enemies made the Israelis less relaxed than their American counterparts. It also manifested itself in the way they drove and their willingness to take risks.

All too soon it was time to say farewell. The El Al security protocol instructed us to bring our suitcases to their main office at the El Al tower building in Tel Aviv a night before the flight for inspection and to stay there under their watchful eyes. The security crew was in charge of taking luggage to the cargo hold. This protocol sounded annoying but in reality it was a great free service; we didn't have to carry the heavy bags to the airport and undergo the security procedures there.

The long flight went smoothly. Then we took the five-hour flight from JFK to Seattle where our friend Dale Burgeson was waiting and took us to his mother's house. We thanked her for letting us park our car there and I gave both of them miniature figurines of the nativity scene carved out of olive tree wood from Jerusalem.

The drive from Seattle back to Grandview was somewhat difficult because we had been traveling for many hours but the local clock showed that we had gained time just by flying from the Middle East to the Pacific Northwest.

✡

Back at work, I continued my research and published a few more papers. However, I started applying to every open Associate Professor position announcement by US universities. Obtaining such a position turned out to be extremely difficult. Universities pre-selected their candidate but created a fake Search Committee to show compliance with the government's Equal Opportunity regulations. I received letters telling me how impressed they were with my resume and research work followed by the notice that a candidate had already been selected and wished me luck in my endeavor.

It was time for me to look for a better path to secure the future wellbeing of my family. Dr. Cone still had funds to continue my job, and with my H-1 visa I did not have to worry about the immigration and naturalization. The visa was valid as long as I was working for Dr. Cone.

Applying for the green card was a better option as its holder is not limited to the amount of time he/she is allowed to remain legally in the USA. The green card allows the holder to work in any job in the USA or its territories and to come and go from the USA at will as long as the card has not expired and a valid passport from their country is maintained. Remembering the saga we had at the US/Canadian border made me more eager to have a green card. (See Chapter 12.) I talked to Wyatt about my intention and he promised to help. His support was paramount since immigration and naturalization required a testimonial document that my services and expertise were essential and beneficial to the USA.

I sent my green card request to the Immigration and Naturalization office in Spokane, Washington and received the paperwork to be filed by me and Wyatt. Wyatt did a great job describing the merits of my expertise and my research work. I was unaware that he also sent a letter to Dr. Summers, my UC Davis Ph.D. mentor, asking for his professional opinion regarding my capability. Dr. Summers, a retiree by then, provided the letter. (Figure 13.1)

Dr. Cone's letter stated that according to his professional judgment, my research work saved the farmers in our region lots of money. A few weeks later, my Green Card request was approved. It was ironic that seven years before, the Immigration and Naturalization ordered Batia and I to leave the USA just because she was babysitting for few cents per hour. This time however, they allowed me to take any job in the USA.

UNIVERSITY OF CALIFORNIA, DAVIS

BERKELEY • DAVIS • IRVINE • LOS ANGELES • RIVERSIDE • SAN DIEGO • SAN FRANCISCO SANTA BARBARA • SANTA CRUZ

COLLEGE OF AGRICULTURAL AND
ENVIRONMENTAL SCIENCES
AGRICULTURAL EXPERIMENT STATION
DEPARTMENT OF ENTOMOLOGY

DAVIS, CALIFORNIA 95616

January 7, 1975

Dr. Wyatt C. Cone
Department of Entomology
Irrigated Agriculture Research and
    Extension Center
Washington State University
Prosser, Washington 99350

Dear Dr. Cone:

Dr. Samuel Regev, Research Associate in Entomology in your Department, has requested that I send a statement to you regarding the professional qualifications demonstrated during his residency in the graduate school, University of California, Davis. The purpose is to support Sam's application to the U. S. Immigration and Naturalization Service for a change from an H-1 visa to a permanent residency type of visa. I have no reservations about supporting this for such an industrious scientist because the nature of his present employment on special grant funds places him in a vulnerable position should the present funds be terminated for reasons of changes in the grantor's budget.

I have great respect for his capabilities as an insect physiologist with special interests in the physiology of mites. As you well know, the mites of agricultural and medical importance are very small animals, and investigators concerned with their form and functions must be well trained in the use of various kinds of microscopy and exquisite micro-analytical techniques in biochemistry. More than most other students within my sphere of acquaintence, Sam was quite aggressive in acquiring techniques and skills of great variety, more than required by his indicated courses of study. He cultivated friendships among faculty and staff in other departments here—for example in cytogenetics, botany, vegetable crops, medical physiology and toxicology—and really worked at the business of extending his range of technological capability.

Dr. Regev's greatest asset is his innate creativity. To a marked degree, he constantly generates ideas about avenues of research. In this respect I suspect that he will ultimately outstrip most of his contemporaries in solid productivity. Given a favorable environment in which to develop, I believe that Sam is destined to become an outstanding research biologist.

Sincerely,

F. M. Summers
Professor Emeritus

FMS:jkc

Figure 13.1 Letter from Dr. Summers

I also started looking for an academic position in Israel and let my friends there know that I was available and would return to Israel if a serious offer was on the table. I sent them my resume and a list of my publications. I had no great expectations that this effort would land me a job in Israel so I was surprised when two offers came.

One offer came from the professor at the Ben-Gurion University in the southern city of Baer Sheva in the Negev region. She was an expert in the field of tropical diseases transmitted to humans and animals by ticks. She was also managing the Institute of Tropical & Infectious Diseases located in Nairobi, Kenya. "Here's my offer," she wrote to me, (in Hebrew of course), "I want you to be my research scientist in Kenya for two years, after which, I will try to create a permanent position for you with the Ben-Gurion University. I need to fill the position in Nairobi fast so you don't have too much time to deliberate."

I asked her to give me few days to discuss the offer with Batia and also to consult with Dr. Cone. She agreed.

On the surface, the offer was very attractive and sounded prestigious, running a research project for the Institute of Tropical and Infectious Diseases. However, my gut feelings warned me away for it. To begin with, the offer was only for two years and the promise to grant a position at the Ben-Gurion University in Israel sounded like *pie in the sky*. Besides, leaving Dr. Cone, with an unfinished project was out of the question. On top of that, I strongly believed that it would have been unfair and unwise on my part to take Batia, and my small children to a not-too-stable African country just as Jomo Kenyatta, their aging ruler, was about to die. I turned down the offer.

Then came a suggestion from Dr. Katz from the Faculty of Agriculture of the Hebrew University in Jerusalem that had the potential of a permanent faculty position later on. Its Faculty of Agriculture was located in Rehovot, twenty-one miles south of Tel Aviv.

I wrote him a letter, inquiring about an open position with the Faculty of Agriculture, stuffed it inside an airmail envelop and mailed it. To my surprise Dr. Katz replied to my letter and presented me with creative suggestion for a possible faculty position. The part of his letter relevant to my case stated:

> The Israeli government started a campaign to attract Jewish scientists from around the world to immigrate to Israel and work in the academia. To entice the Israeli universities and research institutes to participate, they presented a plan whereby the university would establish a research group comprised of several Jewish immigrants with the expertise applicable to the research project the university chose to

pursue. The government required that the leader of the research group be an Israeli. The government guaranteed those universities that accepted the plan enough money to pay for the first year salary of the scientists and to cover the cost of the research for a year, provided the university would take over from the second year on and hire the members of the research group as its regular staff members. My plan is to make you the leader of the group and hire you right away. Once in Israel, we will recruit the other members of the research group, depending on how much funding the government will give us. So I need to know if you wish to go along with the plan. Time is of the essence so I need a YES/ NO answer right away.

I discussed this proposal with Batia and she went along with my inclination to say yes. It was a way to return to Israel and resettle among our families and friends. I also discussed the plan with Wyatt and the likelihood that I would go back to Israel but promised to finish the project for which he hired me three years earlier. I phoned Dr. Katz and accepted his plan.

"I am glad you did. I am sending you the application stating your name as the group leader. Please fax me the personal information pertaining to you and your family so I have a head start. I am already familiar with your publications and the research you do for Dr. Wyatt Cone, so I will write a research plan to submit to the government. The likelihood that the government will approve the application is high so I suggest you start wrapping up your research with Dr. Cone. If everything goes well and the plan is approved, I want you to be in Israel starting in June 1976 so you have about a year to finish everything and return to Israel."

The proposal started to look promising. I first learned about Dr. Katz from Dr. Summers, my mentor at UC Davis. He and Dr. Katz had collaborated in the past and co-wrote a few scientific articles in the field of mite taxonomy, but I had no idea if he had the clout needed to make this plan a reality. In the back of my mind I had nagging doubts that it won't happen, yet I had to act with the premise that it would. It meant wrapping up the ongoing research experiments at that time and starting new projects.

It also meant putting the final touches to my various photographic chemical kits for processing color films and papers and perhaps starting a business on the side, once in Israel, to process films and prints and save the amateurs the need to send their work to Europe.

As an Israeli student returning from studying abroad, I was

exempt from paying custom tariffs on appliances, cloths, electronics and various household goods including furniture.

There were a few special deals offered by the Israeli student organization headquartered in New York City. I purchased our first Fisher stereo system through them just before moving to the State of Washington. It had a dual voltage setting to use in Israel with its 220 Volts or the 110 Volts used in the USA. I had to buy a special adapter for the record player because the alternate cycles of the electricity in Israel is 50 cycles per minute compared to the 60 cycles my stereo system had. Without that speed adapter the nice classical music LP records would sound distorted.

I was on the phone with a store in Brooklyn, told them what items we wanted and the price. We agreed to purchase the items the minute Dr. Katz's plan was approved and it was time for us to move back to Israel.

As it turned out, Dr. Katz was extremely fast regarding his research plan proposal. I got an express letter from him during the first week of March 1976, informing me that the plan was approved and urged me to complete all the hiring documents and mail them back to him ASAP. "Time is of the essence. You need to report to work at the Faculty of Agriculture by July 1, 1976." He tried to impress upon me the urgency. In my reply I expressed my objection to quit my research project so abruptly and leave Dr. Cone in a very delicate and embarrassing situation. The Hop Commission granted us research money to pay my salary and perform the research they needed and here I was, thinking of leaving. It was unethical, so I wrote back to Dr. Katz, explaining the situation and the fact that I would try to be there as soon as it was practical. "Please explain the urgency to justify leaving my project so abruptly," I wrote to him.

His reply came express mail. "You have to move fast and be here no later than July 1, 1976. Time is of the essence because if you don't the government will withdraw its approval and will give the funds to someone else."

At that point I felt that what he and the government were expecting was unacceptable. His justification for rushing me to Israel did not make sense to me and I did not believe it came from the government. It was tantamount to forcing me to make a decision at a gun point. I replied that I would be there as soon as I could but there was no guarantee we would make it by July 1, 1976 and if the government withdrew its approval, so be it. Once in Israel I found out that he pushed me to be there by July 1, 1976 because he was sitting on his suitcases on his way to a one year sabbatical in Fresno, California and wanted me to be at my job so he could leave.

I discussed my new situation with Wyatt and assured him I would not leave without finishing the research and writing the scientific paper. I revealed my suspicion they would not grant me tenure forcing me to return to the USA. "Sam, don't sweat too much about it. I trust whatever decision you make," Wyatt comforted me and it made a great deal to me.

There was another issue with Dr. Katz's plan, immigration and naturalization regulations had the potential to complicate my life again. If I took the job in Israel, we could lose our coveted green cards and once lost, it would be next to impossible to get them again. The holder of a green card is not permitted to be out of the USA for a period longer than eleven months but I was offered a job that would require me to stay out of the USA for at least one year, or longer if the University gave me a permanent job as a faculty member. Bottom line, I was forced to decide whether or not to lose my green card in favor of an offer that had the likelihood of being *pie in the sky*.

I called the Spokane Immigration and Naturalization Office, provided the file number they had on me and requested to talk to the officer who approved my green card.

"Officer Richardson speaking, may I help you sir?"

It was my chance to present him with a *what if* scenario associated with the green card

"Officer Richardson, I seek your input regarding my green card. I was offered a research collaboration position with my Israeli colleague at the Hebrew University Faculty of Agriculture. I am aware of the regulation requiring me not to be absent from the USA for more than eleven months. However, it is unlikely that this research project can be completed within such a short period. I hate not to finish the research project or even worse, lose my green card. Is there any stipulation allowing me to stay in Israel to complete the project without losing the card?"

"When does your project in Israel start?"

I told him I had to be there by July 1, 1976.

"There is a way to address this issue. I will mail you the application form. Put down in writing what you have just told me. Please fill it out right away and mail it back to me. I am familiar with your file here and I don't see any problem with approving the forms I'm sending. Here is the most important part of the procedure. I am going to include in my approval letter, a *White Booklet* serving as extension of your green card. It has a deadline associated with it. If you find out that you cannot finish the assignment within the eleven months, you must send this booklet to the American Embassy in Athens, Greece. They will extend your green card until June 28, 1978. However, it is mandatory that the embassy in Athens get the White Booklet by March 1977. They will mail it back to you with the proper extension for you to return to the USA without border control confiscating your card and deporting you back to Israel at your own expense. Please be informed that this is a onetime extension."

The application forms arrived a few days later. A week after I sent the completed forms back to him, I received his approval for extending my green card along with the White Booklet I should mail to the US Embassy in Athens should I need to stay in Israel for an additional eleven months. It gave me a sense of security and allowed me to gamble with Dr. Katz's plan.

I was confident I would be able to wrap up my research for Dr. Cone in time and arrive in Israel by July 1, 1976, so I called the store in Brooklyn to finalize the purchase of the items Batia and I decided to bring to Israel. The store manager moved them into a special storage facility waiting for our instructions.

Our plan was to use Bekins Transport Company to ship what we had in Grandview and to collect the rest of our shipment at the Brooklyn warehouse. And we ordered more items that kept coming via UPS and pretty soon I began to grasp what it meant *to sit on suitcases*.

✡

The reality that our life in the USA might be coming to an end started sinking in and it saddened me despite the bright side of returning home. I felt the need for a farewell visit to our favorite places such as Mount Rainier, Vancouver, Victoria Island and Butchart Gardens. Accepting that soon we would also leave our friends and colleagues was also hard. I knew that we would dearly miss Dale and Marilyn Burgeson, Dr. Woods, and Glenn and Margaret Rayburn. I shared the Faculty of Agriculture offer with them and the possibility of us staying in Israel. Dr. Woods, who already visited Israel was excited, "Great, now I will have someone I know personally the next time we visit Israel." I assured him he would always be a welcome guest. (See Chapter 11.)

Another issue that complicated our preparations was how to keep our car up to the absolutely last minute. The mother of a child in Raz's school knew a teacher who was looking for a car to buy. I offered her our car at a very low price on the condition that we would use it until the last minute and leave it at the Pasco airport the morning we flew to JFK. She agreed. I even gave her my extra key so I could leave the car locked. During that time, the Pasco airport was a small-town family-oriented airport, with no parking fees. People could leave their car for the duration of their trip, so leaving the car for her to pick up was no problem.

Realizing that we won't be able to wrap up everything and be in

Israel by July 1, as Dr. Katz requested, I told him the earliest El Al flight I was able to get was leaving JFK on the fourth of July and landing in Israel on July fifth.

I called the store in Brooklyn to let them know we would be leaving for Israel on July 4 and told them the Bekins Transport Company would stop by their warehouse and pick up the items we bought. I scheduled an appointment with the Pasco office of the Bekins Transport Company to come on July 1, to pack our belongings and ship them to New York City to be consolidated with the items we purchased from the Brooklyn store into one crate and ship it to Israel.

The last week of June 1976 was really crazy as I had to get rid of things that we were not going to ship. I made numerous trips to the city dump. I asked Wyatt to take back the dining table and the chairs he loaned us. The last week saw us as the greatest customer the McDonald's Corporation ever had in Grandview.

We had to squeeze some time to visit our friends and say farewell; a very difficult and emotionally-taxing chore. By Friday our apartment was almost empty but I still had more trips to the city dump. Luckily, I did not have to take the couch as Judy Gunther, the apartment manager and friend suggested I should live it for the next renter.

At around 11:00 a.m. we drove to the Best Western Motel in Pasco and checked in for Friday and Saturday nights. After having lunch at Denny's, (our favorite diner at that time) I told Batia to relax at the motel with Raz and Shir while I went back to Grandview.

It was almost evening when I finished cleaning our apartment and gave the keys to Judy and Wayne Gunther. Final hugs and *Thank you for your friendship* and *We will meet again in the future,* concluded a three-year friendship between our families, and I headed back to Pasco to Batia and the children. It had been a very hectic day, so after dinner at Denny's, we retired early.

Saturday was a sort of farewell to the Columbia Center Mall in Kennewick, the shopping mecca of the Tri-Cities. The mall was packed to capacity as this was the weekend preceding the Bicentennial 4 of July, 1976. I felt drawn to the JC Penny store so we entered and I noticed the cashier who issued my very first credit card. I waived to her and she waved back. She knew us very well by then. We were convinced that we were going home for good and purchased Raz and Shir all the clothes, parkas, etc. in sizes to fit them until they become adults. All of these items were packed and on their way to Israel.

We had to be at the Pasco airport at 6:00 a.m. so we returned to the motel and went to bed early. I couldn't sleep as this particular trip home to Israel was different than the previous one. It was a voyage into the unknown and a new start for our family.

Sunday morning, I dropped Batia and the children at the entrance to the terminal and parked the car at the small parking lot for the teacher who bought it, locked the car for the last time and rushed to join Batia and the children at Republic Airline.

All the passengers were seated when the pilot announced that there would be a slight delay as air control tower had given landing permission to a Piper plane; that is how small and provincial the Pasco airport was.

To this day I have to convince myself that the following incident really happened, but it really did.

I saw the Piper land and taxi toward the terminal but our door remained open and the boarding stairs remained attached to the plane's entrance. There was no sign we were going to take off. Some passengers, including me, started looking anxiously at our watches fearing we would miss our connections. Then I heard some conversation between the flight attendant and a person at the boarding stairs. She looked at the passenger list and waived to the person to board and follow her. Everyone thought the delay was to allow another passenger to board the flight so my jaw dropped when I saw the flight attendant pointing in my direction and leading the man toward us.

It was our dear friend Dr. Donald Woods who flew his Piper and taxied it next to our plane. All the passengers turned in our direction and watched the drama as Dr. Woods stopped by our seats and said "Sam and Batia, I was out of town when you left Grandview, so I didn't have the chance to say farewell to you, Raz and Shir. I know where you are going to land eventually, which is a land very dear to me, as a Christian. We had our heated religious debates at times and I respect your feelings but I want you to respect my feelings too. I would like to you give this gift so you remember Gayle and me." He shook our hands and gave me a wrapped package. "Please don't open it now, I would like you to open it when you arrive in Israel."

The boarding stairs were removed. The flight attendant locked the door and the pilot taxied to the runway for our takeoff. I was overwhelmed with Dr. Woods's gesture of friendship.

When we finally had the chance, we opened the present. It was Hal Lindsey's best seller *The Late, Great Plant Earth* dealing with Jesus, the second coming and the lengthy discussion Dr. Woods and I had in the past.

Chapter 14

Faculty of Agriculture, Rehovot, Israel 1976-1978

I did not have the chance to take an adequate rest after the long cross Atlantic flight to Israel because Dr. Katz was on edge waiting for me at the Faculty of Agriculture and ready to leave for his sabbatical in California. I had to be there to sign the paperwork and finalize the establishment of the research team I was selected to manage.

Dr. Katz signed the general power of attorney authorizing me to sign for him, if needed, during his one-year absence. He also introduced me to his graduate student, Rami who was working on his Ph.D. under Dr. Katz's guidance. "Please help Rami with his Ph.D. research while I'm gone."

Next he handed me the classified ads with the heading *Apartment for Rent*. "I marked a few apartments near the campus. Now, let me introduce you to the secretaries running our department. I asked them to help you get organized. Here is the key to our office and the lab. I'm leaving tomorrow afternoon so if you still have burning questions for me, please call me at home." He jotted down his number. "Good luck to you, I will be in touch once I'm settled in Fresno."

This initial meeting was very hasty, to say it mildly, and Rami, the graduate student sensed my bewilderment, "Don't worry Shmuel, I'll help you navigate this place. And by the way, I saw the apartment list Dr. Katz gave you and I would like to suggest you take the one on 5 Etzel Street. It is located in a new building and a five minute walk from this office. You should contact them first thing in the morning as I don't believe it will stay on the market for too long."

I thanked him for his advice and his offer to help me. "I have to catch the bus to Tel Aviv, so I will see you tomorrow," I said and headed to the bus station at the entrance to the campus.

The next morning, I followed Rami's advice and called the owner of the apartment at 5 Etzel Street. We scheduled an appointment to meet at the apartment at 1:00.

Then I took the Tel Aviv-Rehovot bus and met Professor Goren, the head of my department. I introduced myself and chatted a bit with the secretaries while asking for basic office supplies. Next I started arranging my office so it would look presentable. I was not too impressed with my office and my lab as it was not much bigger or more elaborate than the one I had during my post doctorate work at the WSU. "What the heck," I said to myself, "as long as I have the right equipment and supplies, I will manage to do my best." It was time to meet the apartment owner.

The five-story apartment building was two blocks from campus and brand new. The owner was waiting for me at the entrance to the lobby. "Hi, I'm Dr. Moshe Raphael, Ph.D. from Tel Aviv University. From our phone conversation yesterday, I learned that you are a Ph.D. yourself, what a nice coincidence," he said.

I gave him a brief description of my academic credentials and the work I was going to do at the Faculty of Agriculture. Dr. Raphael pointed to the balcony on the first floor and said, "This is the apartment balcony, as you can see, you have only one flight of stairs to climb. The apartment faces a quiet ally and not the busy Etzel Road. The apartment is new. It is not furnished but I put a refrigerator and a small gas stove in the kitchen."

"This is a brand-new perfect apartment that you bought so why do you live in Tel Aviv and not in this apartment?" I hoped I didn't raise his ire with my question.

"I was offered a position with the Weizmann Institute here in Rehovot, just across the street from your campus so my wife and I decided to register with the builder and bought the apartment just as they started building. Then a much better offer came from Tel Aviv University as head of their physics department so we moved to Ramat Aviv next to their campus." His answer sounded reasonable, so I asked to see the apartment.

It looked spacious and nice, albeit almost naked because other than the refrigerator and the small gas stove, there was nothing there, not even curtains. "Dr. Raphael, I like the apartment and its convenient location but not having any basic items, such as furniture, makes it difficult for me to decide. The cargo with our personal belongings is somewhere in transit but I have no idea when they will arrive. The apartment does not even have a dining table and chairs where we can eat."

Dr. Raphael thought for a while, "I have an extra kitchen table and four chairs that I could bring if it would help you, but other than the kitchen dining set, I have no other household items to offer."

I was really in a tough situation at that point. We could stay with my parents until I found a fully furnished apartment but that could take a long time. Then there was the issue of where to store the furniture and appliances we bought in the USA. It was better for us to have our own place and wait patiently for our belongings to arrive. Moreover, Dr. Raphael's apartment was close to my office. I would be available in case of emergencies or when Batia needed my help. I felt I really did not have a choice. My gut told me there was a high likelihood that someone else would grab that apartment in a jiffy.

"Here is the phone number to reach me. Please call me when the kitchen dining set table is in the apartment and I'll come with my family, sign the rental contract and get the keys," I said. We shook hands and I went back to my parents' place and told Batia I found an apartment for us not far from my office. I knew for sure she was as eager as I was to move out of my parent's apartment.

Since we did not own a car, I asked my brother-in-law to take us to our apartment. I borrowed a skillet, a few pots, a kettle and towels from my parents and sleeping bags and blankets from my sister. When we met Dr. Raphael at the apartment to sign the rental contract he showed me the kitchen dinning set. He took me to the balcony and showed me where the grocery store was and suggested I should go before they close for the day. My brother-in-law waited for Dr. Raphael to leave and then exclaimed, "For God's sake, Shmuel, this apartment is empty, how are you going to manage living like gypsies. It's insane!"

"Don't worry, Momo (his nickname), we will manage."

He looked skeptical. "Call me if you need my help or a ride," he said and left for home.

Batia gave me a list of what we needed for breakfast and lunch the next day and I rushed to the grocery store before it closed. When I came back, we made the smallest room into Raz and Shir's bedroom. We spread a sleeping bag on the floor for each of them and covered the open window with a bed sheet. I hoped the ceramic tile floor was not too hard on their little backs. Batia and I took the larger room next to the balcony and transformed it into our bedroom by spreading the largest sleeping bag we had on the tile floor. I realized it won't be comfortable living in these conditions. I prayed it won't take too long for our belongings to arrive.

There was a nice public playground close to the apartment, a real blessing as it made Batia's life a bit easier, taking Raz and Shir to play while I was at work.

✡

Because of the haste by which Dr. Katz left for his sabbatical, we didn't have adequate time to discuss the research project he wanted me to carry out. After talking to Rami, Dr. Katz's doctorate student, I felt I had enough information to write and perform my own research plan.

Rami, a year older than me, worked full time for the Israel Ministry of Agriculture serving as an extension expert, with expertise in growing and cultivating cut-flowers in greenhouses. These flowers were exported daily to Europe and distributed to other parts of the world. He worked on his Ph.D. under Dr. Katz guidance and was squeezed for time because his employer granted him only few hours a week with pay to work on his research.

Rami lived in Rehovot so I was eager to ask him about living there, such as a recommendation for a pediatrician and family doctor, good preschools, supermarkets, etc. When he came into my office I bombarded him with questions. I felt bad as it sounded almost like an interrogation, but he was kind and patient and provided the information I needed.

I also learned that in addition to his extension job advising the cut flower farmers, he also worked with the Israeli strawberry growers, mostly Israeli Arab farmers. He told me about the problems associated with growing strawberries under plastic tunnels. I decided to focus my research interest on its mite infestation, a problem similar to the one I did for Dr. Cone during my post doctorate work in Prosser, WA. I asked Rami to take me with him to one of the strawberry farms next time he went. "Why don't we go next week?" he said. I marked it on my calendar.

✡

Living in Israel, after eight years in the USA, was not easy. It required drastic adaptation to the prevailing bureaucracy leftover from the socialistic mindset and philosophy the founders of Israel brought with them from Russia and Eastern Europe. It did not sit well with me, a person spoiled by the capitalistic and efficient way of doing business in America.

The complexity and knowhow associated with sending man to the moon, paled compared with what was required for the Interior Ministry Office in Rehovot to give us new Israeli ID cards, and to assign Israeli ID numbers for Raz and Shir. It was exhausting.

Not having a car made life difficult as the lion's share of my days were spent walking from point A to point B and back. Living at the apartment we just rented, also meant making a one-and-a-half-mile pilgrimage to the nearest Super-Sol supermarket. Going to that store was easy but carrying the heavy grocery begs home was difficult. I told Batia I would rather starve to death than let her walk to the Supper-Sol to buy our groceries.

I knew from past experience that Raz would get an ear infection sooner or later. Unfortunately, my prediction materialized and I had to take him to a doctor. I asked Rami to recommend a trusted family doctor and he suggested Dr. Stein. "He is our family doctor, so tell him I sent you." Rami gave me directions to Dr. Stein's "clinic", located downtown near the open market. I wrote the term "clinic" with quotation marks, because unlike the USA where the vast majority of the physicians checked and treated their patients in a clinic or hospital, the Israeli patients went to the physician's apartment for medical attention. One room in the physician's apartment was designated as the "clinic" and if there were several patients waiting, they all set in the corridor by the entrance to the apartment. The door had opaque frosted glass to provide "privacy," another bad joke, because you could hear everything that was said inside. By sitting in the doctor's "waiting room" you knew that poor Mr. XYZ, suffered from a bad case of hemorrhoids. Mrs. ABC, on the other hand was a bit luckier as she came to see the doctor because of her week-long constipation.

To be fair, I know that the situation has improved markedly over the years, as Israeli doctors became more sophisticated and adopted American standards.

With no bus service available from where we lived to Dr. Stein's clinic I had to walk two miles carrying Raz on my shoulders. It was a hot sunny day and Raz had a high temperature. We finally arrived and took a seat. We were alone in the waiting area, but I could hear the conversation and watch images behind the opaque glass door. When the patient left, Dr. Stein peeked out of the door and motioned for us to enter. I introduced myself as a newcomer to Rehovot, just back from the USA after finishing my studies there.

Dr. Stein was checking Raz's ears when the door opened, without a knock, and a middle-aged woman popped in and started chatting. They conversed in Polish as he stopped examining Raz. Their chat lasted for quite a bit and it made me angry so I took the liberty to interrupt, "Madam, who gave you the right to barge in and infringe on the patient's privacy, let alone interrupt Dr. Stein. His appointment was with me and my son and not with you. I would like you to leave this room right now, because if you don't we will leave and go directly to the HMO office that hired Dr. Stein and file an official complaint not only with the HMO office but also with the Israeli Medical Association."

I could sense Dr. Stein was scared as he frantically gestured with his hand for her to leave the room but she did not. He signaled her again to leave and said, "*Szybko*" (Polish for quickly). She left the room slamming the door so hard I thought the glass would break.

It took Dr. Stein a while to regain his composure. "I totally agree. It was not proper for her to enter the room the way she did, but this is not the way to talk to a lady older than you."

Needless to say, I disagreed with his admonishing me, "Dr. Stein, we just arrived from living in the USA for eight years where you would be sanctioned by the authorities if you allowed such an incident to happen. You allowed a stranger to barge into the examination room and infringe on the patient's privacy. You were a willing participant in what that woman did. Moreover, you ignored my son. Please write down the diagnosis and the prescription my son needs and we will leave."

Dr. Stein prescribed antibiotics and wrote on the prescription pad, "for ear infection," so that was his diagnosis.

"Let's go home," I said to Raz and carried him on my shoulders for the two-mile stroll home with a stop at a pharmacy along the way.

At the playground near our apartment, Batia befriended a young lady about our age who was there with her baby. The lady recommended a private preschool nearby so we jumped on the opportunity and sent Raz and Shir there thus freeing the mornings for Batia. Since we did not have a car the close proximity of that preschool was a blessing.

✡

Back at work, Rami took me to a strawberry field near the Arab city of Taibeh in central Israel, twenty-three miles northeast of Tel Aviv. The region is known as the Triangle and predominantly Arab. Rami had contacted the farmer beforehand and scheduled a convenient day to visit.

When we arrived, the farmer was busy uncovering the long sheet that made the plastic tunnel. It exposed the strawberries to the sun and aerated the crop. "See all of the damage this damn insect is causing," lamented the farmer in Hebrew with a thick Arabic accent. "I have four different varieties of strawberries and each one shows a different degree of damage. Do you have any idea why? This is an edible commodity so the government imposes strict restrictions on what, when, and how much I am allowed to spray. It makes life complicated."

Rami pointed in my direction, "Dr. Regev, my colleague just arrived from the USA and he has extensive experience with this kind of problem. Let us take samples of infested leaves to identify exactly what the pest is. We can tell you with certainty that it is definitely not an *insect*. It is most likely a *spider mite*. We will contact you the minute we identify the pest and give you the current recommendations on how to control it," Rami promised the farmer as we left.

✡

I asked Rami if we could return to Rehovot via the city of Herzliya, on the central coast of Israel north of Tel Aviv. "I knew that the Kodak Corporation opened a photographic processing lab in Israel, licensed to Delta Inc, located in the Herzliya Pituach district, next to the Acadia hotel by the beach. I would like to stop by and talk to the manager about my expertise in color photography and see if they have an open position for me. I don't have a car and wondering if you would take me there."

"Of course, but I didn't know about your knowledge in that field."

"My curiosity led me to many different disciplines, and the chemistry of color and black and white photography is one of them. I developed my own original processing formulas. Maybe I will delve commercially into that field but right now I must concentrate all my efforts to show progress as the leader of the Research Team hoping for a permanent job with the faculty. And by the way, I know that you worked on your Ph.D. thesis under Dr. Katz's guidance, however, I have no idea what kind of research you're doing. Perhaps we should spend some time talking about it, maybe I can help you while he's gone."

When we arrived at the Delta lab, I was pleased to notice that public bus stations to and from Tel Aviv were located nearby, a huge plus for me should I get a job there. Rami and I went upstairs and were greeted by the receptionist. "May I help you," she asked while folding the Israeli ladies magazine she was browsing through.

"Yes," I said and introduced myself as a person with plenty of knowledge in the color photofinishing business and wondered if they had any open positions. "Let me page Mr. Abramson, the lab manager."

Mr. Abramson came and shook our hands. I instantly realized I was talking to an America Jew who spoke Hebrew with a deep Brooklyn accent. "What can I do for you?" he asked Rami.

"It's me sir who wants to talk to you. Rami is my colleague at the Faculty of Agriculture and my chauffeur today." I described the extent of my knowledge in his business and asked if they had an open position that I could fill. I made sure to use all the appropriate jargon, believing it would open the door for me. Evidently it worked as Mr. Abramson said, "In fact, I need very badly, someone to produce good quality color inter-negatives from the color slides our customers bring in. We produce color prints from their color slides. I had to place the orders on hold because the quality of the prints produced from the inter-negatives the last guy did were off-color. If you are up to the challenge you could start right now."

I explained to him that I was a full time researcher at the Faculty of Agriculture in Rehovot. However, I would be available after 4:00 p.m. and work a few hours as I was at the mercy of the public transportation.

"That's fine with me. I'm flexible," Mr. Abramson assured me. "Why don't we start the paperwork now, and you can report to work tomorrow at 4:00 p.m."

"That's a deal," I said and the receptionist gave me a sheaf of forms to complete at home.

"See you tomorrow, Shmuel."

"Boy, I was so impressed with all of the fancy words and terms you heaped on the poor guy," Rami said when he drove me home. When he dropped me off at my apartment, I reminded him again my wish to learn more about his Ph.D. thesis and help him with the research.

The next day, I did not go home directly from work, as I had to rush to catch the public bus to the Tel Aviv central bus station. From there I hopped on the Tel Aviv-Haifa bus to Delta Inc. On good days, when traffic was not too heavy, this ordeal took me close to an hour and a half. I walked to the lab and told the receptionist Mr. Abramson was expecting me to report to work today. She paged him.

I followed Mr. Abramson, "Welcome to your workstation," he said when we entered a small, dimly lit, windowless room. "Here is the 35 mm camera attached to our specially designed binocular where you mount the color slides. You load the camera with a Kodak Color ISO 100 film and illuminate the slide to evaluate the image you see through the binocular and use your best judgment as to the optimal camera shutter speed and lens aperture to produce a sharp print with the best color rendition. When you're done, take the inter-negative to the room with the automatic film processor. We process the film with the Kodak C-41 chemistry." I knew what he was talking about. Kodak C-41 process was the world's standard for developing color negative film regardless of brand. I had already devised my own C-41 original formula. "Shmuel, the stage is yours, so do your stuff. Call me if you need my help or have any question."

The *need-to-do* basket was full of envelopes containing color slides. I used my own judgment as to what was the best setting for the camera and produced the inter-negatives. The next day when I reported to work, Mr. Abramson was beaming. What a great job you did yesterday," he said and showed me the prints produced from the inter-negatives I had created.

I tried to be humble, "Oh, it's not me, it is the photographers who shot the slides. They are the ones deserving accolades."

"Oh, don't be shy. I am sure the clients will be happy," he said with his Brooklyn accent. I reminded him that I would work until 8:00 p.m. and then leave to catch the bus home.

✡

To be clear, the reason why I took this job was not to make extra money. It was to learn about the basic equipment needed to run a color photofinishing lab and the operation and QA routines required to run them. I browsed through the user's manual of these machines and studied Kodak's official daily QA protocols. It was an extra load on my brain but I did not mind because it was my dream to open my own color photography finishing lab sometime in the future.

I had misgivings about the lab's method of producing the color prints from the color slides, the job I was hired to do. I knew that their method was not the way it was done in the USA. Yet, I was afraid to discuss the issue with Mr. Abramson, lest he fire me before I scooped all the information I needed. Moreover, every passing day, hastened my decision to bail out soon because working my job at the faculty and then rushing to the photography lab, meant coming home after 10:00 p.m., when the children were asleep and Batia half asleep after long hard day with the children. Not having a car did not help. I tried to compensate them for the many absent hours, by staying home longer in the morning before leaving for my office but it wasn't nearly enough. Moreover, being a guy who always abhorred wasting time, I found the time I spent on the public bus to Delta Inc., cumbersome and futile. I began looking for a way out.

Then came the week when I felt I had all the information I wanted to glean out of my association with Delta Inc. and decided to quit my job. I explained to Mr. Abramson that my research work at the faculty of agriculture started to take more of my time and the long commute from Rehovot to the lab was squeezing me to the limit. "I am going to quit at the end of the week so you have enough time to find a replacement."

"I hate to lose you but I understand your situation and appreciate you telling me in advance. Remember the huge basket full of color slides the last guy left?"

"Mr. Abramson, thanks for being such a nice boss and I hope I am not going to make you mad by telling you that there is a more efficient way to make color prints from color slides."

"How?"

"Using inter-negatives is a very convoluted production process, but I was afraid to tell you, fearing you would fire me on the spot." I expected to be escorted through the front door.

"Do you mean we don't need to use inter-negatives?" he asked in disbelief. "How can you do that? I am eager to know the secret."

"It is very simple process," I said. "You skip the inter-negative step because both Kodak and Fuji Corporations make special color print paper designed specifically for that purpose. You place the color slide in the enlarger and project the image onto the print paper like you do making prints from color negative film. The chemistry embedded into the surface of this special paper assures the print shows the correct image and not the reverse."

"Are you sure about that?"

"Yes, I am sure, because I did it myself many times when I wanted to make 8 x 10 enlargements of my children that I captured on Kodachrome slides. In fact, here is the proof." I pulled out a copy of the *Modern Photography* magazine I subscribed to and showed him the paper listed in the advertisement section.

"How about that!" He took the magazine to the photocopier to copy of the page.

I sensed some embarrassment on his part so I tried to console him. "Mr. Abramson, this is a new product that just hit the market so I am sure that sooner or later it will reach Israel as well."

"Thanks for calling my attention to it," he said and promised to explore it further. I worked there until the end of the week as promised, but they had not found a replacement by the time I left.

✡

I liked Rehovot very much and had been familiar with it before it became a town. I remembered my childhood when I spent a week each summer with my cousin Zelig who was a native of Rehovot. It was a small rural community then, surrounded by citrus orchards. His father, Yakov Lipka, was my mother's cousin. My mother's maiden name was Lipka. Our families reciprocated each year and Zelig spent a week with us in Tel Aviv.

When we turned eighteen, we both changed our last names to Hebrew names. I changed mine from Polonecki to Regev and he changed his from Lipka to Eshhar. We also served in the same paratrooper battalion as reservist after completing our mandatory military service. We both fought in Israel's 1967 Six-Day War and we each earned a Ph.D. Zelig became a professor of immunology with the prestigious Weizmann Institute just across the street from the Faculty of Agriculture. Whenever I had ideas I wanted to explore, I crossed the street and went directly to his lab to see if he had the equipment I needed at his disposal.

✡

Zelig Eshhar became a world-renowned immunologist after inventing a unique way to produce specific anti-bodies to fight cancers instead of using the poisonous chemotherapy approach. He earned the 2005 Israel Price Award in Medicine, the Israeli-equivalent to the Nobel Prize in Medicine. In 2019, after the process was approved by the FDA, a major American pharmaceutical company purchased the patents that were associated with his invention.

✡

Despite my emotional attachment to Rehovot, as time went by, I realized that renting that particular apartment and living in Rehovot was not practical for us and the mistake needed to be corrected ASAP. Without a car and living in an apartment that did not have basic household items, started gnawing me.

The only association with my family was our Saturday afternoon dinners when my sister and her family came to our apartment and brought my parents with them. My mother loaded my sister's trunk with pots and containers filled with the Sabbath meal she cooked. Not having a decent dining table and chairs for all of us to sit forced us to let the children eat first. Then they went to the playground while we ate our dinner.

My mother was shocked when she saw that we all slept on the floor on sleeping bags, and we felt like we were exiled from the civilized world. For Batia, making a phone call to her mother in *Kibbutz Matzuba*, meant going a quarter of a mile to the nearest public phone booth with a handful of *asimones* (Israeli phone tokens). I started searching for a solution.

✡

I must digress a bit and mention that after the many years being strapped for money my parents finally started to enjoy living comfortably. My mother, ever practical and the champion of taking educated risks, had learned about a new residential development at Tel Aviv's northern district, north of the Yarkon River. This development, still on the drawing board, was to be named Ramat Aviv. It was to be located on the east side of the Tel Aviv-Haifa highway. This area was also zoned to house the main new campus of the Tel Aviv University. The government-controlled residential construction company advertised that there would be a lottery for anyone interested in purchasing an apartment in the new buildings in Ramat Aviv. There were many people interested, so it was almost a miracle if you won.

My father, ever the skeptic when it came to winning lotteries, told her not to waste her time.

"You cannot win anything unless you try," she admonished him. "And just so you know, I convinced Mala (my dad's sister) to come with me and participate in the lottery. It took me a very long time but she submitted her name." And then she asked him ""What is wrong with the Polonecki family when it comes to taking risks?" anyhow, "This one is not going to kill us,"

As it turned out, she was absolutely right and both she and Aunt Mala won the right to purchase an apartment in Ramat Aviv.

Another digression related to the apartment my mother purchased in Ramat Aviv evolved around my sister Chaya and my brother-in-law who had also returned from the USA.

My brother-in-law's family owned a large citrus orchard in Hod Hasharon, a small community fourteen miles northeast of Tel Aviv. The family had a small brick house surrounded by white citrus blossoms, a pastoral location. When my sister and brother-in-law decided to return to Israel, they chose that place in the midst of the orchard as the perfect location, however, the house was too small. They decided to replace it with a larger, custom-designed house that would meet their needs. Since it took time to build their dream house, they had moved into the lottery apartment my parents bought in Ramat Aviv. The timing was perfect for my sister because the apartment was ready when they needed it.

My mother saw our miserable living conditions at the same time that my sister's dream house in Hod Hasharon was almost ready. Mom suggested that my sister move to her new house and vacate the apartment in Ramat Aviv so we could move in. The timing was perfect, also, because Raz would soon start his first year of elementary school.

Thanks to my mother's quick thinking, I broke my rental contract with Dr. Raphael after only six weeks, and moved to Ramat Aviv. The landlord was understanding and did not raise any fuss. I just paid him for an extra month's rent and that was it. Momo, my brother-in-law helped us move our meager belongings from our apartment in Rehovot to Ramat Aviv.

The moving company representative informed us that our belongings were due to arrive in Israel any day, so we didn't buy any household goods. I borrowed a folding table and chairs and the cotes my sister and I slept on for many years when our parents didn't have enough money to buy real beds.

Moving from our Rehovot apartment to Ramat Aviv was like a new lease on life for us. All the tenants in that building were young couples around our age and had children about Raz and Shir's age. The building had a large backyard for them to play and socialize with their peers. Our front balcony faced west with a great view to the Mediterranean's blue water and beach, and we enjoyed the fresh breeze coming from the water. That was a great plus because the buildings during that time did not have air conditioning so people installed window units. We relied on the sea breeze. The building's entrance lobby was the center for the young ladies residing in our building and Batia took advantage of it when she was looking for a good preschool for Shir.

Everyone told her, "Take Shir to Gan Malka," a private preschool run by a lady named Malka (Hebrew for Queen). It was located on our street not far from our building. There was no traffic on our street as it functioned more like a long ally running between the buildings. It was a blessing as we did not need to worry about our children being hit by cars.

We enrolled Raz as a first grader at Alonim Elementary School, a three-minute walk from our building. Batia and I were apprehensive, because up to that moment he communicated in English. We met with Zehava, his first grader teacher, and aired our concerns. "Don't worry too much about the language barrier. From my experience he will start speaking Hebrew in no time at all."

I still doubted it would happen. And then an unexpected miracle; Raz started talking fluently in Hebrew a week before school started. To this day I accuse him of pulling my leg.

We had an even greater concern about Shir because she did not speak at all. When Batia took her to Gan Malka for registration, Malka suggested that we take her to a speech therapist because Shir should have talked by then. Either by luck or a divine intervention, she started talking the day the preschool started and has never stopped bubbling in Hebrew.

Our good fortune got a huge boost when the Bekins Transport representative called to inform us that the crate with our cargo had arrived and I needed to meet him at his office in downtown Haifa. "You must bring the Bill of Lading, your Israeli passport and documents showing that you studied in the USA. We need to present all the paperwork to the customs people in order to get your tariff exemption. Don't forget to bring your checkbook as you will be charged the custom's processing fee, and my service fees as the licensed agent handling cargo on your behalf."

"It sounds like customs people are tough and picky guys."

"Mr. Regev, all the items in your cargo are exempt, however, the customs inspectors must pay a fortune for these items if they wish to buy them because of the tariff. It makes them jealous of people like you and they inspect everything you've brought in your crate with a microscope. It may not be fair to you but unfortunately that is human nature. Anyhow, could you be here tomorrow or the next day because the company will start charging you for storage if you don't release your belongings within a week from this phone call."

"Hey, I'm more eager than you are to get my belongings out of there. I'll take the first train from Tel Aviv to Haifa and meet you in your office at 9:00 a.m."

The next morning, I gave him the Bill of Lading and he compared it to the list the company gave him to present the customs officer. The two lists matched. "Let's go to the port to release your cargo."

We headed to the port entrance, a few blocks away. It was the second time in my life I had been inside that section of the port. The first time was during my mandatory military service. The military exercise involved boarding the navy barges that landed us onto the beach very much like the allies did during the invasion of Normandy in WWII.

After clearing the security booth at the port gate, we headed to customs. The officer was polite and did his job in a very professional manner. I brought with me the invoices of each item listed on the Bill of Lading to show that we purchased just the very basic household appliances and not the expensive ones rich people purchase to impress others. The customs officer wrote down each item we brought in my passport. I paid the processing fee and he gave us the clearance paperwork.

A few days later, a big truck arrived. The movers started prying open the walls of the wooden crate and took out the heavy appliances first. Each one had its own large cardboard box, which they left in the alley next to the entrance of our building. These large cardboard boxes were a bonanza for the children of the entire neighborhood. They converted them into *homes* and soon the entire alley looked like a homeless neighborhood like the ones we saw in big cities in the USA.

The boxes also presented a potential health hazard. I asked the moving crew to take the junk with them when they left. "Part of the bill I paid your company included the disposal of these empty boxes and cleaning any mess at the end of the job."

The moving crew finely left after placing the heavy refrigerator and the washer and dryer into their assigned locations. We tested the basic items needed for cooking and put our table and chairs in the dining area. It started to feel like home, finally. Raz and Shir got their separate rooms and enjoyed sleeping in the beds we had purchased in Grandview.

Our living room also looked great after I assembled our contemporary sofa made of a light pine frame and fluffy cushions. We purchased it from the now defunct Montgomery Ward store in Sunnyside.

Next came the Grundig black & white TV which was manufactured in Germany and compatible with the Israeli electric 220V and 50 cycles.

Unlike TV service in the USA, which is a private industry earning its revenues from airing commercials, radio and TV services in Israel at that time were owned by the government who charged an annual fee to support its Israeli Broadcasting Authorities. Moreover, the TV broadcasts were limited to a very few hours in the afternoon for the children to watch programs on the educational channel. The evening broadcasts were geared toward adults and presented the news and sports events. There was no color TV broadcasting in Israel during that time and no Cable TV. I had to erect an antenna to receive the broadcast. It took me back to my early life at 34 Yehuda Hamaccabi Street when I climbed like a monkey on the antenna tower and stretched a copper wire between our tower to the adjacent one, in order to enjoy the music coming from my crystal radio.

We relied heavily on our stereo system for the nice classical music, always available on the Israeli radio. We also had a substantial collection of classical music LP's we brought with us.

There was a small windowless room in the apartment that I turned into my photography dark room. It was completely dark, yet, having no windows, it was somewhat hazardous to be there for too long because of the fumes. Although using a small fan helped somewhat, not having a central HVAC system in the building made it an issue. I also made sure to lock the door when I was not there to prevent Raz and Shir from inadvertently entering.

Batia and Shir became my models, posing for the camera, holding Kodak color charts so I could take photographs, process the negative and then print the picture using my own film and print paper developing kits. I evaluated the performance of my formula by comparing how close the color rendition of the prints was to the ones shown on the Kodak color chart. I was glad I had the foresight to bring an ample supply of color print papers. They were hard to find in Israel during that time.

✡

I started to spend more time on my research project and also talked to Rami about his Ph.D. thesis. "I have problems with my research, and it drives me crazy," he confided.

"What's the problem?"

"I finished one research area of my thesis showing the mechanism by which the mite I am working with survives the winter. It does so by laying special eggs known as diapause eggs into crevices in its host plant. The eggs stay dormant during the winter and hatch at the start of spring. I even have nice pictures of them taken with an electron microscope," Rami said and pulled the photos from his attaché case. They were very impressive, indeed. "The problem is Dr. Katz. Each time I present him with a new research idea to incorporate into my thesis, he turns it down, claiming it is outside his field of expertise. All he wants me to do is stick to the taxonomy of that mite.

It makes my life complicated and I have limited time I can devote to my thesis. If this problem continues I don't see any chance I will be able to finish my research and earn the Ph.D. in my lifetime."

I empathized with him and offered to help. "Dr. Katz did not leave me any suggestions on topics he wanted me to research as team leader. That leaves me a free hand to pick and choose, so let me help you put some pizazz into your theses."

"What do you mean?"

"Well, I am not too familiar with the biology and life cycle of your mite but I won't be surprised if its unfertilized eggs produce only males and the fertilized ones produce females. Some of the diapause eggs in these pictures are most likely unfertilized and I am willing to bet that only males would hatch from them. I have plenty of experience with this kind of research and already published a few scientific papers on the topic. I would like to offer my help. How about finding the chromosome number of your mite, I predict the female will have twice as many chromosomes as the male. I have photographic darkroom equipment at home so I will process the film we capture with the microscope and make prints for your thesis. Just buy boxes of print papers and I'll do all the photographic work needed for the thesis. I'll show you how to make the charts and graphs required. It will be your choice to either do them yourself or pay someone to do them for you. I will photograph and print them as well.

"Another area of interest should involve some chemical evaluation. You mentioned noticing the difference in the infestation rate of your mite on different species of host plants. I suggest we look into the possibility that these differences are associated with the level of chemicals such as farnesol in the host plant's leaves. We'll need a gas chromatograph so make sure to talk to a researcher here that has one. I will authorize taking funds from my own research and purchase the columns you need."

Rami could not hide his enthusiasm and accepted my offer. It sounded to him as a lifeline for his stuck thesis. "My gut feeling tells me that my hypotheses regarding the cytogenetic and sex-determining mechanism of your mite species is correct and would make your Ph.D. thesis a very significant one. Dr. Katz would not dare reject our data. I'm sure that the Ph.D. committee would overrule him and grant you your diploma," I predicted. "Oh, and one more thing I need to tell you, because this part of your thesis is my idea and my contributing to your research, I would take his rejection personally and join you fighting him. I have nothing to lose because from what I have sensed thus far I doubt the faculty will grant me a position during the second year as stipulated in their agreement with the government," I confessed to Rami. "I don't like to alarm you but we need to move fast because the faculty gave me a letter granting my position for only one year so better use me while I am still here."

Then I was called for military reservist training exercises in the Negev desert and could not help him for two weeks. When I came home I got chickenpox from my children and could not commute to Rehovot.

Rami took a week off from his job, brought a microscope he borrowed from our office and we worked on his research at my apartment. He was not concerned because he had had chickenpox during his childhood. As time went by, he worried that his Ph.D. thesis was too comprehensive and impressive with its scope and findings.

"What's the matter?" I asked him.

"I hope it will go well, because anyone who knows Dr. Katz and his reputation as a mite taxonomist would realize right away that he was not the one who mentored me with this kind of research and analysis techniques."

"Rami, I don't like to sound like a broken record but how many times must I tell you not to worry. He won't dare deny your research under my guidance."

✡

Looking back, the eighteen months we lived in Ramat Aviv was the best time of our lives. The children were happy, had many friends and thrived. (Figure 14.1) I commuted to work by taking the early bus to the Tel Aviv Central bus station and a bus to Rehovot from there.

Batia's day started by dropping Raz at elementary school and then walking Shir to Gan Malka preschool. The path to Gan Malka was quite a long one and required climbing many flights of stairs. There were days when Shir had a hard time climbing the stairs so Batia carried her while singing to her. After dropping Shir at Gan Malka she continued to her own job working with preschoolers at the Na'Amat daycare center established by the socialistic political parties to help working mothers.

Raz liked first grade and his classmates. Zehava, his teacher was an excellent educator and fully connected to her students. Schools in Israel, both elementary and high school were, and still are demanding (Figure 14.2) and students attend six days a week. Israeli pupils also studied English as a mandatory foreign language from fourth grade through high school and took the Matriculation test in English.

Figure 14.1 Raz and Shir in Ramat Aviv

בְּכַמָּה יוֹתֵר?

כְּתֹב בְּכַמָּה יוֹתֵר!

כְּתֹב הַסִּימָן וּבְכַמָּה יוֹתֵר!

$$\frac{1}{4} \times 4 \;\square\; \frac{1}{4} \times 8$$

$$\frac{1}{4} \times 8 \;\square\; \frac{2}{4} \times 8$$

$$\frac{1}{4} \times 12 \;\square\; \frac{2}{4} \times 12$$

$$\frac{3}{4} \times 4 \;\square\; \frac{2}{4} \times 4$$

$$\frac{2}{4} \times 8 \;\square\; \frac{3}{8} \times 8$$

$$\frac{4}{4} \times 12 \;\square\; \frac{3}{4} \times 12$$

Figure 14.2 Assignment from Raz's arithmetic book issued by the Israel
Ministry of Education and used by Israeli first grade pupils six months
into their school year. Translation of instructions above equations:
Left: Write by how much. Right: Write the sign and by how much more

✡

My parents still lived at 34 Yehuda Hamaccabi Street, not too far from
Ramat Aviv. It was only a five-stop ride on the public bus to visit the
children. Everyone gained from that, trying to catch up the time lost
during our life in the USA. My father never missed an opportunity to
babysit Raz and Shir.

Saturday afternoons were the best time of all. My sister and
her family and my family had Sabbath dinner at our parents' house.
There was no public transportation running during the Sabbath so my

Figure 14.3 Cousins, Back: Nofit, Eilat, Raz, Nave. Front: Shir

brother-in-law came to Ramat Aviv and picked us up in his car while my sister drove the children in her car directly from Hod Hasharon to our parents' apartment. It was great to see my children sitting with their three cousins, having a special table all for themselves. (Figure 14.3) The grownups sat at the dining table, and everyone enjoyed the great meal and desert my mother prepared. From the corner of my eye, I could see food containers staged inside the kitchen so I knew there would be plenty of food and my mother would insist that we take leftovers home with us.

I established another custom at our Ramat Aviv apartment. Every Friday I made *falafel*, middle eastern cuisine made of ground garbanzo beans mixed with my secret spices. The unique aroma filled the stairways of our entire building. The residents liked it except for Mr. Shapiro, who swore that his wife's gefilte fish (stuffed ground carp) smelled better.

There were three precious events during the time we lived in Ramat Aviv which I cherish to this day. The first one was watching the Maccabi Tel Aviv basketball team win the European Cap championship on April 7, 1977, for the first time in Israel history, beating Russia's CSKA Moscow. The entire country came to a halt with everyone glued to a TV screen. It was sweet revenge for Israel since Russia supported the Arab countries with weapons and supplies to be used against Israel. Russia was furious at Israel for defeating their clients during the Six-Day War when Israel smashed the Egyptian air force and armies trained and equipped by Russia.

The second event was the change of the Israeli government on May 17, 1977, when Menachem Begin's *Herut* revisionist political party won the election for the first time since Israel gained its independence twenty-eight years earlier. Begin beat the alliance of the socialist political parties that ruled the country until then. My father belonged to the General Zionist party (a centrist political party) and my mother was a devout member of the *Herut* party and a member of its Betar movement. It was the Betar movement that brought her to Eretz Israel/ Palestine on the *Parita*. (See Chapter 3.)

I was elated that Begin won. His sore losers told the public to be prepared for endless wars with the Arab countries because Begin was a warmonger. They were pathetically wrong as Menachem Begin was the first Israeli leader to negotiate a peace treaty with Israel's strongest enemy, Egypt. Anwar Sadat, the Egyptian leader, made the bold and courageous first move in that direction, and landed in Israel on November 19, 1977. He was the first Arab leader to officially visit Israel and speak to the *Knesset* (the Israeli parliament). We, and the entire country, were mesmerized and hugged the TV screen. We watched with utter disbelief when his plane landed, he came out and walked on the red carpet. This historic visit was followed by peace negotiations between him and Menachem Begin, mediated by Jimmy Carter, the US president at that time. The peace treaty between the two former enemies was signed at the White House on March 26, 1979, with Begin and Sadat as the signatories. Anwar Sadat paid with his life for his courageous foresight. He was assassinated on October 6, 1981, while watching the Egyptian army's annual parade.

✡

Because I was granted a USA green card with a one-time allowance to extend it by an additional eleven months living outside the USA, I had to watch my calendar closely. As describe in Chapter 13, I was instructed to send the special White Booklet to the American Embassy in Athens, if I needed to stay in Israel beyond the eleven months, or the green card would be voided. The instructions required sending the White Booklet no later than ninety days before the *eleven-month green card anniversary*. Since I did not see any indication that the Faculty of Agriculture would hire me for the second year, I decided to send the White Booklet to the American Embassy in Athens. "A USA green card is too precious to lose," I kept telling myself. A month later, the White Booklet arrived with the eleven-month extension approved. I felt more at ease.

The work I performed for Rami's thesis went very well and I felt it was more than enough to grant him the Ph.D. diploma. I told him that once his thesis was accepted, approved and his Ph.D. diploma was issued, I would like to publish it in one of the peer-reviewed journals, and create a few scientific papers. The papers would be published with his name and my name would appear as the co-author. Rami agreed. My own research project regarding resistance and susceptibility of different varieties of strawberry plants to spider mites went well and was published in the professional journal *Entomologia Experimentalis et Applicata* in January 1978.

The journal was part of the world-renowned *Springer Netherlands*. The abstract of the paper was posted in the publisher's SpringerLink Journal Article for readers who wanted copies. I am citing this publication in particular to prove that I executed my part of the deal that Dr. Katz negotiated with the Israeli government. As far as I was concerned, the fund used to conduct that research was money well spent as it gave the strawberry growers a tool to gauge which variety to plant in order to minimize the damage to their crop from the carmine spider mite. Unfortunately for me, the Faculty of Agriculture did not keep their part of the deal.

✡

Being in Israel revealed to me an expertise I was not aware my mother had, namely, fighting the orthodox rabbis who served as judges at the Israeli rabbinical courts.

The rabbinical courts ruled over issues such as Jewish marriage, divorce or even deciding who is a Jew, using the Jewish *Halacha* laws, which is still true today. Everything beyond religious legal issues were the jurisdiction of the Israeli civil judiciary. You could get married at a lawyer's office or the civil court and be considered a couple in the eyes of the Israeli government, but that marriage was not considered legal in the eyes of the rabbinical court.

Also, the Israel Law of Return grants Israeli citizenship to any Jew upon entering the country and living there. It was enshrined in the Israeli legal code to ensure that Israel became a sanctuary and a refuge for Jewish people around the world. The trauma of Jews being persecuted by pogroms and the Holocaust was a painful reminder that the Jewish people needed a country where they could escape to safety.

A non-Jew who wishes to become an Israeli citizen must apply for citizenship the same way it is done in the USA for example. Being an Israeli citizen granted all the benefits and privileges the country offers.

There were many unique stories about Holocaust survivors who lost their entire family, husbands, wives, children, yet survived and were brought to Israel by the Jewish Agency. There were complicated painful cases where a Jewish man married a non-Jewish woman and were brought to Israel by the Jewish Agency. For most of these non-Jewish Polish wives, living in Israel offered a much better life because of the higher standard of living in Israel, as Poland became a communist country under the control of the Soviet Union. In addition, with so many Polish Jewish immigrants living in Israel, language was not a significant barrier because there was always someone who spoke Polish.

Although not every one of those non-Jewish wives wanted to go through conversion to Judaism or had the mental strength to do so, they maintained a Jewish family life and raised their children as Jewish. These wives were considered full-fledged Israeli citizens with all the rights granted to the Israelis. However, in the eyes of the rabbinical court they were considered *Shikse* (a non-Jewish female) with some very severe implications associated with that status. For example, the children of that marriage were considered *mamzers* (Hebrew for illegitimate), unless she underwent a full-fledged orthodox conversion to Judaism. Otherwise, the children could not have a Jewish wedding or be buried in a Jewish cemetery, just to mention a few of the severe problems this situation could cause.

My mother knew such a mixed couple. The catholic lady saved the life of her Jewish neighbor by hiding him in their attic during Nazis occupation. They got married in Poland right after the war and immigrated to Israel to start a family. To spare her Israeli-born children the stigma of being *mamzers* she asked for a hearing at the Haifa rabbinical court. My mother promised to be at the hearing to give her morale support and testify on her behalf.

My mother presented the rabbis of the court with a glowing testimony about her friend who saved a man's life and married him after the war. Mom also emphasized that the lady and her husband kept a Jewish home, observed Jewish traditions and raised their children as Jews.

Three rabbis presided over the case, serving as *dayan* (Hebrew for a rabbinical judge). Other people who knew the couple also gave supportive testimony. Afterward, the rabbi who led the hearing told my mother and the other witnesses that they could come back in half an hour for the decision however, my mother and the others preferred to stay in the court room.

The tension was high when the three judges returned. The lead rabbi, looked at the folder in front of him and said to the couple:

> *"The testimonies about you and how you adhere to Jewish way of life and tradition were very impressive but we at the rabbinical court were asked to determine whether or not your marriage is Jewish according to the* Halacha *(Jewish law). We did not see any marriage certificate papers from an ordained orthodox rabbi signed by witnesses. We also did*

not see any ketubah *(a Jewish marriage contract) signed by the rabbi who officiated the wedding and signed by two witnesses verifying that the husband signed the* ketubah. *We are sorry but have no other choice but to deny your request to be considered a Jewish Couple according to the* Halacha."

There was a deafening silence. The other witnesses stayed silent thinking there was nothing they could do to sway the rabbinical judges' verdict but my mother had no intention of taking their denial as gospel.

"I caused a huge *vagirass* in the court hearing hall," she told me latter, using the term *vagirass* she probably invented herself and had used many times in the past to describe raising Hell or mayhem. I attest to the fact that her *vagirass* was ten times higher in intensity on the *Mayhem Richter Scale.*

"So what did you do?"

"I stood up and shouted at the lead judge, *"Tit bishoo La-chem, Bu sha Ve' cher Pa, Ha' Isha Hitzila Nepesh Chaya ve'atem mit'naha geem Ka-cha?"* Hebrew for "You should be ashamed of yourselves. What a shame and disgrace. This woman saved a living soul and you are behaving like that." I was still fuming mad and shouted, "You are rabbis, yet did you forget what the Talmud teaches us? Whoever saves one life saves the entire world." (Sanhadrinn 4:5 in Yerushalmi Talmud).

"So, what happened next?" I asked. "Did they kick you out of the hearing hall for shouting at the rabbis? You know, those rabbis are *Holy cows* and you are not supposed to shout at them."

Figure 14.4 A *ketubah* is a Jewish marriage contract stipulating the rights and responsibility of the groom to his bride. It outlines what the wife gets if the couple divorces or in the case of the untimely death of the husband. The *ketubah* goes back to ancient days, as early as the year 440 BCE.

"Not at all," she answered to my surprise. "They started discussing and deliberating among themselves for a few minutes and then the lead judge said to us, 'On second deliberation, in light of the testimonies we heard, the compelling plea from Mrs. Polonecki, and the other witnesses, we decide to consider their marriage a Jewish Marriage. We took into consideration that this woman saved the life of a Jewish person, married him, adopted Judaism and raises her children as Jews.'"

I still don't believe this miracle happened but it did, and made my mother mighty proud of herself, and rightfully so.

The husband was so overwhelmed with the rabbis' decision, he promised he would give his wife a *ketubah* signed by a rabbi and two witnesses. (Figure 14.4)

✡

We had been in Israel for almost eleven months and could stay an additional eleven months without losing our green cards provided we landed on USA soil before midnight on May 28, 1978. The funds to keep me and my research team employed during the first year would run out within a month and yet not a single word from the faculty, I decided to talk to Professor Goren, the head of our department. I told him I needed to know the status of my employment.

"Oh, don't worry, Dr. Regev, I am working on that just now as we speak," he assured me.

A few days later he stopped by my lab and said, "Good news Dr. Regev, our request was granted and funds to keep you employed will be provided by The Richter Foundation. Congratulations for winning it," he said and shook my hand. "We are going on Thursday to the campus in Jerusalem for a big ceremony honoring all The Richter Foundation winners. Be here at 5:00 p.m. and we will drive there in the department car. At the ceremony, when they call your name, we will go to the podium and I will describe you, the work you did and hand you the plaque. It will be followed by the traditional hand shaking ritual for the photo op."

I tried to keep my cool and did not say anything as the entire deal appeared to be a premeditated stinky fraud.

We drove to the Hebrew University campus in Jerusalem and participated in the ceremony and reception honoring the winners of the Richter Foundation awards for that year. As my name was called we both went to the podium where Professor Goren harped on my achievements and why I was nominated to receive it. Based on his enthusiasm, I thought for a moment that I was standing on the stage receiving the Noble Price. I got my plaque and shook the hand of whoever he was.

We sneaked out and drove back to Rehovot as soon as we could.

"Why don't you stop by my office tomorrow afternoon so we can discuss the Richter Foundation award and your salary for the next year," Professor Goren said as we arrived at the Faculty of Agriculture.

I took the bus home, preoccupied with the thought that Dr. Katz and Professor Goren had used me to siphon funds from the government. I felt that the creation of a research team comprised of Jewish scientists who immigrated to Israel, was not a serious and honest effort on the part of Dr. Katz and the Faculty of Agriculture Department of Entomology. I shared these feelings with Batia when I arrived home.

"Why don't you wait until after the meeting with Professor Goren tomorrow and see what kind of a deal the Richter Foundation award is."

"I doubt it has anything good for us. While continuing to play the dummy who doesn't know what they're doing, I need to start planning our next move."

The meeting with Professor Goren confirmed my suspicion. The Faculty of Agriculture negated its promise to make my position permanent. They did not live up to their agreement and awarded me with the Richter Foundation Award instead. It was nothing more than a stipend that would put my family below the poverty line should I count on it as my main source of income. It had no benefits such as medical coverage, pension, vacation time etc. which I did have during my first year there.

It was very demeaning of the Dr. Katz and Professor Goren to even offer me that award. I was able to conceal my outrage and contempt, and even thanked him for awarding me the Richter Foundation stipend. I left his office and headed home to tell Batia what the faculty had in store for me.

"What are you going to do now?"

"Remember the US Immigration and Naturalization White Booklet I sent to the American Embassy in Athens? Well, it extended our green cards. We can go back to Prosser. We have until May 28 this year. I'm working on that but don't say anything to anyone. Please keep it top secret."

Next I contacted Glenn and Margaret Rayburn, our close friends and our children's *proxy grandparents* when we lived in Grandview. I alerted them that we would return to Grandview no later than May 28 because things did not work out well for me, job-wise. "I am not sure I will find a job with Dr. Cone, my former boss, but we will come back, nonetheless, as not to lose the green card. I would also like to pursue my plan to open a 1-hour photo processing shop at the Columbia Center Mall in Kennewick and use the processing chemicals I developed while living in Grandview." I ended my letter, jokingly saying, "If you promise to *behave*, I will consider making you my business partner."

No sooner than I sent it, a telegram from Glenn arrived. "Don't do anything. I am coming to Israel on Monday next week to discuss your 1-hour photo processing shop idea. Pick me up from the airport." I broke the news to Batia and informed Rami I would be busy with a guest from the USA and wouldn't be at work for a week.

I was not surprised that Glenn showed interest in my tinkering with the chemistry of color photography because many times he saw the pictures and the color slides I processed in our apartment in Grandview, but I was surprised that he took such a great interest in my dream of having the 1-hour color finishing store at the Columbia Center Mall. So much so that it merited coming to Israel on a short notice to discuss the idea.

I picked up Glenn from the airport. He chose to have the Israeli experience and flew with El Al, the Israeli national airline. "They gave me a special deal to stay at the Dan Hotel next to the beach so let's go there first. You know me, a farm boy from eastern Oregon who never flew such a long flight, I need to rest a little bit. The Trans-Atlantic flight wore me out," he said from *both sides of his mouth*, one side complaining while the other side apologizing for being worn out.

"Glenn, I must apologize for not owning a car so we will take the airport taxi directly to Dan Hotel. It's a great hotel, by the beach.

Figure 14.5 Shir Regev, Raz Regev
and Glenn Rayburn

When I was in high school, I ran the beach every morning and went swimming in the winter before going class." We arrived at the hotel relatively fast as the traffic was light. "I'll pick you up in the early evening to have dinner in our apartment and visit with Batia and the children.

"I can hardly wait to see Raz and Shir."

Later, I found him waiting for me in the lobby and marveling at the white sandy beach and the Mediterranean Sea. "Sorry, the sun is shining from the west now but tomorrow morning when the sun is shining from the eastern horizon, you will see how blue and clear the water is," I bragged about my favorite sea on earth. I could not resist the temptation to take him outside the wide lobby door and walk to the area on the sandy beach. Glenn, do you see this area over there? This is the beach area where my parents arrived illegally to Eretz Israel/Palestine on the *Parita*. (See Chapter 3.) The ship ran into the sand bar on purpose so the Briton won't direct it to Cyprus and keep the Jewish refugees in concentration camps. I will tell you about their story sometime during your visit."

There was a big happy celebration when Glenn and I entered our apartment. Both Raz and Shir were happy to see their *Grandpa proxy* from Grandview. (Figure 14.5) Glenn was amazed at how they had grown. Shir did not speak at all when we left but she spoke only Hebrew after going to Gan Malka so she talked to Glenn in Hebrew. Raz had communicated with him in English in Grandview but forgot his English when he started the first grade. He also talked with Glenn in Hebrew. We were our children's translators.

When we had finished dinner and enjoyed ice cream for desert, Glenn said to me, "Sam, I have only one week in Israel and I want to squeeze in as much as possible. I know I cannot crisscross Israel in such a short visit so what do you suggest I should see this time."

"How about we stay in Tel Aviv the entire day tomorrow so you can overcome jet-lag. I'll come to the hotel and we'll walk along the beach all the way to Jaffa and its ancient port. Then we'll visit the colorful *Souk Hacarmel* with its unique ambiance. I don't want to overwhelm you so we'll return to the hotel for you to take your *siesta*. You'll be our guest for supper. The next day we should take the daily guided tour to Jerusalem that leaves your hotel at 7:00 a.m. I'm sure you'll like it.

I suggested that for the last trip I should rent a car and Glenn agreed with my plan. "We will visit my former *Kibbutz*, Rosh Hanikra on the Israel-Lebanese border. The sea carved caves into the mountain, something similar to the sea cave in Capri, Italy so I want you to enjoy them. From there we'll visit Batia's *Kibbutz*, Matzuba, a seven-mile drive from Rosh Hanikra. Batia and I were married there. We'll have a short visit with Batia's mom, Esther. We'll also visit Tsfat, the ancient city favored by the *kabbalists*. It is an interesting city, I guarantee."

"Sounds good to me," Glenn said while I showed him the places on the road map.

"After visiting Tsfat we'll descend to the Sea of Galilee and the city of Tiberias nestled on its shores. The Sea of Galilee is the lowest freshwater lake on earth, at 705 feet below sea level. The Jordan River connects it to the Dead Sea, which is the lowest point on earth, at 1380 feet below sea level. I believe you'll like my suggestions. Hopefully, it will whet your appetite for more visits in the future."

The next day, we hopped on the Egged Tours bus at the Dan Hotel for its daily guided tour to Jerusalem. The bus made a few more stops, picking up tourists from other hotels on Ha Yarkon Street. From there the bus ascended to Jerusalem, passing the remnants of the armored personnel vehicles destroyed during the Arabs' bloody siege on Jerusalem during Israel's 1948 War for Independence."

"Yes, I read all about it in *O Jerusalem*," Glenn whispered in my ear.

The tour guide took us to all the must-see attractions he felt the tourists in our group should see. We stopped at Mount Scopus for a panoramic postcard view of old Jerusalem and I pointed to where the first campus of the Hebrew University was established before Israel became a nation. I told him about my one-month military assignment at that campus when Mount Scopus and the campus was an Israeli enclave surrounded by Jordan. (See Chapter 6.)

We also walked the Via Dolorosa but Glenn wasn't moved because he was not of a practicing Christian. He was very moved, however, during our visit to the Holocaust museum at *Yad Vashem* and walked along the *Garden of the Righteous Among the Nations* where trees were planted to honor of gentiles who endangered their own lives

Figure 14.6 Glenn Rayburn wearing *tefillin*. I apologize for the blurry image. I took it in a hurry and without the elderly Jew's knowledge. Orthodox Jews are reluctant to have their picture taken.

and saved Jews during the Holocaust.

The most moving moment that would last for the rest of Glenn's life, was our visit to the Western Wall or by its other Hebrew name Ha'Kotel (Hebrew for the wall). When the Romans destroyed the last Jewish temple in Jerusalem, the Western Wall was the only remnant left. We walked toward the wall, touched its ancient lime stones, recited a silent pray and followed the tradition of inserting a small written note with a wish into a crevice between the huge stones. An elderly man stopped us and asked me in Hebrew if I would like to put on a *tefillin* (Jewish phylacteries). I agreed and whispered to Glenn in English, "I am sure that when I finish the ritual he will ask you to do the same. Just follow what I do and don't say anything. Let me handle it." I wrapped one *tefillin* around my arm and placed the other *tefillin* on my forehead. I recited the prayers associated with that *Mitzvah* (commandment).

Glenn watched what I did as attentively as a student. When I finished and returned the *tefillin* to the old man, he turned his attention to Glenn, as I predicted and asked him in Hebrew, "Did you put on your *tefillin* today?" so I jumped in and said, "Sir, my friend just arrived from America on his first visit to Israel. He does not speak Hebrew and you don't speak English, so I will translate. I am sure he did not put on *tefillin* today so let him do the *Mitzvah* here right now."

"But is he Jewish?" the old man asked

"Of course he is, I can tell you for sure that he got circumcised and had a very nice Bar Mitzvah," so he let Glenn put on the *tefillin* with a little bit of coaching from me.

I took pictures of Glenn wearing *tefillin*. (Figure 14.6) He was overwhelmed and speechless. We left the old man, after thanking him and putting a $20 bill in his hand. "Next year in Jerusalem," I told him, one of the customary blessings among the Jewish people.

"Amen," he replied while folding the $20 donation into his pocket.

Glenn sat quietly all through the ride to his hotel. I felt he was preoccupied with his own thoughts so I left him alone, pretending I was taking a short nap. Evidently, the *tefillin moment* at the Western Wall in Jerusalem, left an indelible impression on him. Several years later he confided to me that after his *tefillin moment* at the *Kotel* in Jerusalem he started feeling he was part of the Jewish people.

The next day I rented a car and we toured northern Israel. I dropped Glenn at the hotel and offered to come by the next morning and go with him to the souvenir shops along Ben Yehuda and Allenby streets, not too far from his hotel. I also invited him for a dinner at my home. I knew Ben Yehuda Street like the palm of my hand as it was my early childhood street." (See Chapter 1.)

Glenn was interested in buying *Judaica* souvenirs for himself and his family and he bought some nativity figurines carved of olive wood for his school secretary who was a devout Christian.

When he felt he'd bought enough souvenirs for everyone on his list, he said, "Sam, Israel and Antwerp are known as the world's diamond centers. The El Al brochure I read during my flight, claims that diamond and the diamond polishing business, are Israel's second largest industry and export. Do you know any reputable diamond stores that I can trust? I would like to surprise Margaret with a diamond ring from Israel. I am sure she would like it."

I assured Glenn that all jewelry stores selling diamonds in Israel were licensed and certified by the government so he should not worry about being taken advantage of. "Let me take you to a few stores and see if you find a ring you like. Then we'll negotiate a price you're comfortable with."

"Good idea," Glenn replied and we started our diamond expedition.

All the jewelry stores we visited had the government seal attesting to the store's certification. They all had an impressive inventory of diamond rings displayed inside their glass cabinets. Glenn finally found the ring he thought was the one Margaret would like. He had in his wallet one of Margaret's rings he managed to *steel* from her jewelry box so he showed it to the store owner, "Please make sure whatever ring I buy fits this size." Then he pointed to the ring he wanted to see.

"Sir, you can talk to me in English," the owner said which surprised Glenn. The owner double checked the size of Margaret's ring using his ring measuring gizmo, then pulled out the new ring Glenn chose.

"Here it is, sir," the owner said and jotted down the asking price on a small piece of paper. Glenn didn't negotiate very hard because when he converted the asking price listed in Israeli *shekel* to US dollars it sounded like a great deal. He pulled out his Visa card, paid for the ring, and started heading to the door. "Just a minute sir," the owner said. "What we sell here has pedigree. I would like to provide you with all the official certificates from the diamond polishing company that cut and polished the stones and the warranty of the craftsman who mounted the diamond into the ring. Our reputation is untarnished and we would like to keep it like that," he said and gave Glenn a folder with all the certifications papers inside.

Glenn was happy with the purchase. "I'll show it to Batia during dinner tonight and ask what she thinks."

I left Glenn at the hotel and rushed home, developed the film and prepared a presentation of the pictures I took during our guided tour to Jerusalem, which I planned to give him after dinner, especially the one with Glenn and his *tefillin moment*.

Glenn arrived and we had a lovely dinner after which he showed Batia the diamond ring he'd bought for Margaret. He had a wide smile when he heard Batia say, "Wow, that ring is gorgeous, where did you get it?"

"Oh, Sam took me to a jewelry store on Ben Yehuda street. You should go there with Sam one of these days," he told her and his twinkling eyes looked in my direction. I didn't want to ruin the moment by revealing that Batia preferred simpler things. *Simplicity is what I want in life*, was her motto.

Then, it was Glenn's turn to exclaim with a, "Wow," when I showed him the photographs of him wearing the *tefillin*. I took the liberty to brag that I used my own original chemical formulas to process the color negatives and prints.

"These are great and high-quality pictures," he said. "Just to remind you, I came here to discuss the idea of opening a 1-hour photofinishing lab. I visited the mall after you told me about the plan. As of now, there is no such store in the mall. I even talked to the mall manager about it and he showed a great interest of having one and said that no one else is planning to open one there. I am going to retire pretty soon, all the hard work in my cherry orchards is getting difficult for a person my age. I suggest that you return to Grandview, we form a partnership, and open that store at the Columbia Center Mall. I'll purchase the equipment and instruments needed, and you will do the processing and printing jobs using your processing chemicals. Just come back unless they offer you a permanent good paying position in Israel," he said to my very receptive ears as I was still recovering from the Richter Foundation fiasco.

"It makes sense to me," I replied. "Besides, we'll lose our green cards if we're not back in the USA by May 28."

Glenn browsed through his calendar and said, "Just let me know the minute you have the name of the airline, date and arrival time at Sea-Tac. I will be waiting to pick you up. You will stay with Margaret and me until you get settled in your own place. Wherever it might be. Staying in Grandview is beneficial because you and Batia already know the town. Raz can continue school at Harriet Thompson Elementary school where I'm still the Principal. I'll make sure he gets all the help he needs during the adjustment time."

Batia and I were overwhelmed by his foresight and willingness to help us during our *second coming* to Grandview so I accepted his offer and promised not to be a burden to them.

However thin you slice a good cake it does not last forever and so was Glenn's visit to our beloved Israel. He came to our apartment the evening before his departure. Raz and Shir gave him a big hug and promised to send him their drawings and he promised to display them on the walls at his school.

On the day of his departure, I accompanied him in the taxi from the Dan Hotel to the airport. He thanked me profusely for our hospitality and being his tour guide during his short visit.

"Your next visit to Israel will be even better and make sure to bring Margaret along," I replied. I promised to keep in touch and inform him of any development related to our plan. "I will start ordering the chemical ingredients I need for my formula and bring them with me until we establish our own supply sources in the USA."

"That's a smart idea," Glenn replied as we shook hands and he headed to the security area. I took the bus home to Tel Aviv. I had my work cut for me and began to prepare for our return to the USA.

Time was crucial as I had to order the most specific, hard-to-get chemical essentials, without which processing of photographic color materials could not be done. I call these ingredients, the *Exotic Chemicals* because they are crucial ingredients for the process despite their infinitesimal concentrations in the processing solution, on top of being hard to find. Luckily, I was able to order them is small containers that did not weigh much, nonetheless, I ended up shipping close to 500 kilos (½ a metric ton) of them to the USA in order to get me started. I used my Samuel Regev, Ph.D. title to impress the chemical supplier's sale representatives to sell them to me because they were not available to private citizens. I locked them in the small room I used as my dark room so Raz and Shir won't reach them accidentally.

Realizing that returning to the USA without a job offer, was risky, I decided to talk to my parents and get them involved. I laid out for them the pros and cons of returning to the USA and requested that they would not rent the apartment for six months which I thought would be enough time to determine what my next step should be. They agreed to do that despite the financial loss of having the apartment vacant. I promised to sell my household items before we left and store the essential items like the beds and mattresses in the apartment small room and lock it. I also offered to leave the washer and dryer and kitchen appliances. If we did not return, they could charge extra for the appliances. My parents agreed.

Breaking the news to Raz was the hardest thing to do and I felt guilty for a long time after that. We tried to break the news to him and Shir as close as possible to our departure day. Shir was too young to really care but Raz, sensed that something was going on just noticing all the commotion with people coming and leaving with items I sold.

Batia and I talked to Zehava, his first grade teacher, and explained our situation and that he won't finish the school year as we must leave by May 28. We requested that she do her best to maintain a *business-as-usual* attitude to reduce his apprehension and she promised to do so. "I will really miss him and so will the rest of the class, Raz has many friends." I felt guilty of all of a sudden realizing that I was the culprit that caused all of the heart break for everyone. I explained the circumstances leading to our decision to return to the USA. "I understand why you are doing it. They were not fair and honest with you," she said, and I felt somewhat vindicated.

It was time to purchase the airline tickets. As much as I preferred flying with El Al, I chose to fly with SAS, the Scandinavian airline as they offered us tickets from Israel to Copenhagen, an overnight stay, free of charge in their Copenhagen hotel, a free breakfast and then non-stop over Greenland to Seattle. Arrival time of that flight at the Sea-Tac airport, as listed on the itinerary was May 28 at 1:15 p.m.. I telegrammed the information to Glenn and he assured me he would be waiting for us at the airport. Three days before our departure day the Israeli contractor for the Bekins Transport, the mover that transported our belongings from Grandview to Israel, two years earlier came to pick up the load of ½ metric ton photographic chemicals along with other household items we wanted to take with us back to the USA. Next, I vacated the small room in the apartment and started cramming all of our belongings and personal items like books, LP records, clothing, into it. I left enough room to store our box springs and the mattresses on the morning of our departure.

I took a few hours to go to my office, clear my desk and take my personal belongings. I summoned all my strength to stay cool and went to have a final talk Professor Goren. I let him know I was returning to the USA in a few days. He looked or pretend to look surprise.

"I honestly believed that the faculty would keep its part of the deal with the government and grant me a permanent position after a year but instead, you expected me to accept a puny scholarship. I decline the offer and I'm going back to my former job at Washington State University. Here is my address in case Dr. Katz needs to contact me when he returns. I plan to publish the research work I did during my time here. Also, when Rami earns his Ph.D. diploma, I expect to get credit and acknowledgment for my professional help and guidance. Here are the keys to my office. Good luck to you," I waved goodbye and did not shake his hand.

✡

As I left Professor's Goren's office I felt a sudden need to visit the building where we first rented our apartment. I also wanted to visit, for the last time, the playground where Raz and Shir played. When I arrived, I noticed the lady that used to be Batia's companion while they watched the children play. One morning she had asked Batia where I worked. Batia had told her I worked at the Faculty of Agriculture and had a second job at the Kodak Photofinishing lab in Herzliya. "He also has his own original formula to process color photographic material," Batia had said to her. I greeted the lady and the man sitting by her side watching the children play. I told her we were leaving in a few days.

The man sitting by her sprung to life, extended his hand and said, "Hi, my name is Moshe Levine, Rivka's husband. She told me about your photographic formulas. What are you going to do with them?"

"I plan to sell them to the highest bidder in the USA," I replied.

"I am interested in these formulas and will talk to my friend about purchasing them from you and form our own company and produce them in Israel. Since you are leaving the country in a few days, I would like to come with my friend to Ramat Aviv this evening and present you with a written offer. If our offer is acceptable to you, we would all sign the contract before you leave."

I agreed to see their written offer at 7:00 p.m. at my apartment. Since understanding legal contracts was not my forte I asked my father to be present at the negotiation. A son of his childhood friend from Góra Kalwaria was a lawyer who consulted my father in the past and my father trusted him. I felt more comfortable if his lawyer would review the offer for my formulas before I signed a contract.

My father was at our apartment playing with Raz and Shir when Moshe Levine and his friend arrived. I introduced them to my father and apologized because the meeting would be short as I had other things to wrap up before leaving the country. "Leaving on Tuesday does not leave me enough time to review the contract you wrote so why don't you leave me a copy so my father can take it to his lawyer for a review or changes he deems necessary. I'm going to grant my father power of attorney to negotiate and sign on my behalf should our lawyer deem this contract acceptable. I'll leave all the formulas in my father's safe deposit box. They will be transferred to you when the contract is signed and executed. Just from my cursory browsing through the copy you just gave me, I don't see any discussion regarding royalties, should you use my formulas, or sell the kits. I would like our lawyer to put this stipulation into the contract, otherwise the deal is off.

It was obvious enough that Mr. Levine and his friend were not prepared for my observation but agreed to let our lawyer review the contract they drew. "Please leave us your phone number and address for our lawyer," I said when we all shook hands and they left.

"I'll call my lawyer first thing in the morning," my father promised, kissed Raz and Shir and took the bus home.

"The phone rang about noon. "Shmuel," said my father, "I just came from meeting with my lawyer and he told me these two crooks are trying to cheat you, big time. He advised against signing that contract and to sever any dealing with them, lest you find yourself in deep trouble later on." I could hear his blood boiling.

"Thank you *Aba* (Hebrew for father) for helping me and keeping me out of trouble. I will call Moshe Levine and tell him I'm not interested in doing any deal and that will be the end of it. We'll see you on Saturday for the last family dinner before we leave." I hung up and blessed God for giving me such loving and caring parents.

Friday May 26, 1978 was Raz's last day at Alonim Elementary School. For him it was the end of his school year but, the rest of the class had six weeks before starting the summer recess. His teacher Zehava and his classmates gave him a farewell party. Everyone was telling him how much they would miss him and hoped he would return from America to join them and start the second grade with them, after the summer recess or as it is known in Israel as *Ha chofesh Ha'gadol* (the large/long freedom). Zehava had asked each of his classmates to draw nice sketches with crayons and colored pencils, then she had tied it with a colorful ribbon to take with him to America. To this day I still keep it for him as a souvenir but it breaks my heart and riddles me with guilt feelings for taking him out of his class and the environment where he flourished.

Friday night was the last dinner we ate in our apartment. After washing the dishes, I emptied the cupboards and packed all our Corelle dishware. Batia loved the dishes and wanted to take them back with us. That of course, made the suitcase mighty heavy. We're still using them every day, forty-three years later.

On Saturday afternoon we went to my parents' house for the last family Sabbath dinner with my parents, my sister and her family. As always, Raz and Shir along with my sister's three children had their own table and were busy, not realizing it was their last time together as children. That last Sabbath dinner was the shortest one ever because we had to go home to continue packing and clean the apartment. I told my parents that the taxi would take us to the airport at 1:00 p.m. and the flight to Copenhagen departed at 5:00 p.m. My sister assured us that she and my parents would be there to bid us farewell.

I did not tell my parents I planned to paint the apartment's walls and leave it squeaky clean. I sent Raz and Shir to play with their friends in the backyard and I started painting while Batia was busy finishing packing. I was painting frantically trying to finish the job before the taxi driver came. And then, Rami and his wife dropped in to bid us farewell. I apologized for not being a good host but in less than three hours we were on our way to the airport. Rami thanked me for helping with the thesis and the research work and promised to keep me posted.

"As much as I hate losing you, you are doing the right thing. I will always be the eyewitness to the unfair way Dr. Katz and Professor Goren behaved toward you."

"Don't worry about me, Rami, I will be fine and once you get your Ph.D. diploma, I will do my best to arrange a Post Doctorate assignment for you at the WSU Research Center. You know me, I will move mountains to make that happen." (I fulfilled that promise two years later.) We all hugged each other and they left.

It was short of miracle, but the apartment was cleaned and painted. We cleaned ourselves and made sure to lock on the small room with our personal belongings were secure. We were ready when the taxi driver honked the horn at 1:00 p.m.

I let Batia and the children get into the car and stayed outside to make sure the driver loaded our four big suitcases. He managed to load the first three on the top of the car but could not lift the one with our Corelle dishware. It did not budge despite his huffing and puffing along with a few profanities. I don't know what happened at that moment but realizing we won't reach the airport in time if he got stuck with that suitcase, I just grabbed it from him and lifted it up to the top of the taxi. The driver looked at me as if I was *Popeye the Sailor* after munching on *spinach*. Batia was impressed as well.

My sister and my parents were waiting for us at the airport for a last farewell and long hugs. Although I was named after the biblical Hebrew prophet *Shmuel* (Samuel), I did not prophesize that this was our last farewell from my beloved father, a great husband, great father and a wonderful grandfather who always cared for his family. He passed away of a heart attack in 1981. He was seventy-four. I returned to Israel to bury him.

✡

We boarded the plane and buckled ourselves ready for the 4½ hour flight to Copenhagen. This one was easier than previous flights as Raz and Shir were older. We were all tired from our hectic last few days in Israel and hoped the overnight stay at the SAS hotel in Copenhagen would rejuvenate us for the long flight to Seattle. Flying at the cruising altitude was smooth and pleasant but the descent to the lower altitude approaching Copenhagen, was painful for Raz as he felt his ears were about to explode from the increased air pressure. He had the same problem a few years back when our friend Dr. Don Woods took us to Portland in his piper airplane. I gave Raz my soft drink and told him to sip the liquid through the straw to equalize the pressure in his ears. It alleviated the pain somewhat, but it continued to bother him until he went to sleep that evening.

We finally arrived at our hotel and enjoyed the hot showers and soft beds. We were dead tired and went to sleep after I asked the front desk to give us a wakeup call early enough the next morning to enjoy the complimentary breakfast.

Their shuttle bus took us to our flight. Flying over the vast, icy island of Greenland was interesting but I wondered who in his right mind would live in a place like that? Not me, a person spoiled by the sunny Mediterranean sea and its blue water.

We finally landed in Seattle and went through the immigration and border control station. It went smoothly. The White Booklet with the stamp of the American embassy in Athens, Greece, worked like magic and my green card was not taken away from me. We had plenty of time to contemplate our next move regarding our status with the Immigration and Naturalization office. We cleared customs and there was Glenn Rayburn waving to us, beaming with excitement to see us again. "Margaret can hardly wait to see you," he said as he drove Interstate 90 toward eastern Washington."

I whispered to Batia, "A new phase in our lives just started and I hope we made the right decision coming back. Only time will tell."

Chapter 15

Back in the USA and Moving to Tri-Cities, Washington

The ride from Sea-Tac airport to Glenn's house reintroduced us to the great scenery. There was a celebration when we entered his house and Margaret was waiting for us. She marveled at how much Raz and Shir had grown. Of course they remember her but coming back meant a language problem. They both spoke Hebrew. Raz knew English but seemed to have forgotten while living in Israel. "You can get situated and then we'll have a light dinner," Margaret said, showed us the room. "As you can see, our children flew out of the nest and Glenn and I are the only living souls in this house. You can stay with us until you find a place to rent."

"We really appreciate your generosity but I'm going to start looking for a place tomorrow morning and not be a burden," I assured them.

The next morning, I told Glenn during breakfast that living without a car for two years was hell. We wasted hours on the bus not to mention depending on the good will of friends and family to give us a ride. "I wish to buy my own car right now. Do you know of an honest used car agency where they won't sell me a lemon?"

"Yes, I know the perfect guy. I'll take you to Jim Regis Auto & Tractors. Jim will treat you like a king. He was my student at the Harriet Thompson Elementary School when I was the principal. He was born here and never left Grandview. I buy all my cars from him."

Glenn introduced me to Jim Regis. "Sam and his family lived in Grandview for four years and they just came back from his two-year sabbatical in Israel. They need a good dependable car," Glenn told him.

"So Sam, what kind of car do you have in mind?" Jim asked me.

He didn't have to ask because I spotted the car the minute I saw it. I always got a fuzzy feeling seeing the Ford Granada Eveline, the receptionist at the Irrigated Agriculture Research and Extension Center owned. The exact year, model and color was parked on Jim

Regis's lot beaming, *"Buy Me, Buy Me,"* and I sure did. It was in great shape and had law mileage. After squeezing into a VW with a noisy, air-cooled engine all my life, the Granada sounded and rode like a limousine. Jim was very generous and asked $1,900 for it and I paid him in cash. I made sure I had my Washington State driver's license and I drove the Granada to Glenn's house.

Glenn arrived before I did so everyone asked him where I was. "He bought a very nice car from Jim Regis and he's on his way here."

Batia's jaw dropped when she saw the Ford Granada, "Such a big car, do you even know how to drive it?" Evidently, I knew how to drive it as it served us for seventeen years until a young elementary school teacher failed to stop at a stop sign and totaled the car.

My children always poked fun at the big Granada and called it, *The Love Boat.* I didn't know where that nickname came from, but both Raz and Shir learned how to drive and passed the driving test in my beloved *Love Boat.*

Now that Raz and Shir were older and in school, Batia and I thought it would be better to live in the Tri-Cities where there was a thriving Jewish community. The synagogue had a Sunday School where Jewish kids learned Judaica as well as Hebrew and the community offered a better environment for Batia and I.

I told Glenn, "We're going to Richland to look for an apartment. If successful, I will leave the family at our new place and come back to pick up our luggage. "We need to find a place right away and register Raz in elementary school and Shir in kindergarten."

I was not familiar with the city of Richland except for the one visit to Dr. Milton Lewis's house a few years earlier. I remember that coming from Grandview I took a street named George Washington Way, so I decided to just meander along its path in search of an elementary school and apartment not too far from it. "You cannot go wrong with anything named after George Washington," I kept telling myself.

It was nice to have air-conditioning in our Ford Granada. All my previous cars did not have that luxury, but now, I felt on top of the world. "So far so good," I told myself and it got even better when we passed a building and a very large grassy play yard. A big sign screamed "Jefferson Elementary School." I guess it was my lucky day because not far from the school stood an apartment complex called The Manor House with a big banner NOW RENTING.

We parked the car and found the manager's office next to the swimming pool. When Raz and Shir saw children their age playing in the pool, they already liked the complex even before we checked out an apartment.

"Good morning, I'm Melinda, the manager, may I help you?"

"Yes, please. We just moved here from Israel. I saw your sign and wondered if you have a furnished apartment available on the third floor large enough to accommodate our family of four. We will take it provided your rental rates are reasonable."

"I'm sure our prices are reasonable but why do you prefer an apartment on the third floor when you have two children? All my tenants with small children take the ground floor, they feel it is safer for their children."

"Well, my wife is very sensitive to noise, and having tenants walking on the floor above us would drive her crazy, so we prefer the top floor if you have one available, otherwise we will continue to look someplace else."

"I have the exact apartment you're looking for and it is ready for renting. Would you like me to show you?"

"You bet," I said and she locked her office and took us to see the apartment.

We liked the nice clean furniture, and the laundry room on our floor, the apartment did not face the street so it was a quite location, and there was enough room for Raz and Shir to have their own rooms. "Unless the monthly rental is too high, we would like to rent it and move in right now."

"No problem, let's go back to my office and write the rental agreement," she said "I noticed your accent," she said while unlocking her office. "What nationality is that?"

"We are from Israel, and Hebrew is our language. The same language Jesus spoke and the same language used to write the Old Testament. We speak and read the original."

"WOW!" she exclaimed. "That is so wonderful."

"That calls for a good discount," I joked.

We signed the contract, and the manager gave us the keys. "Parking spots are not assigned specifically but we expect the tenants to park next to their own building. You also have a locked storage space for your belongings. The key to your apartment will unlock it. Let me show you where it is and if you have no further question I'll let you guys settled into your new home."

"Hey, I saw a McDonald's nearby, let's put our stuff in the apartment and go there to eat," I suggested to Raz and Shir. "After lunch you can stay in the apartment and I'll go back to Grandview, and bring our suitcases. Choose which room you'd like to have, but no fights, please."

After a short lunch we returned to the apartment. I started the air condition and left for Grandview. I told Glenn and Margaret that we found a very nice apartment, gave them our new address and promised to keep them posted. "Everything is in flux," I told them. "The most important issue is for me to find a job before our savings run out. We also need to register Raz in the elementary school. We worry about Raz because it looks like he's forgotten English."

"Don't worry about that, he'll start speaking English in no time. I know this school and if you want, I could talk to Betty Gold, the principal, I know her personally."

"I'll let you know if we need your intervention. My main concern is that the school might keep him in the first grade for another year until he catches up with the English." I thanked Glenn and Margaret for their help and hospitality and left.

We started unpacking the four huge suitcases that had traveled with us from Israel. We set up Raz and Shir's rooms and they were thrilled when we placed their favorite bedsheets with the pictures of their heroes from *Sesame Street*. We bought inexpensive pillows and very light summer blankets at the Pay N' Save and food items for supper and breakfast from the nearby 7-11.

I had written to Dr. Cone about my decision to return to Washington and promised to visit him as soon as I could to discuss writing up the scientific paper summarizing the research I completed just before leaving for Israel in July 1976.

The next morning, right after breakfast, I told Batia, "I'm going to drive to Prosser and try to see Wyatt. I'll stop at the manager's office and use their phone to call him and make sure he's there. While I'm gone you should spend some time at the pool so Raz and Shir can befriend some of the kids that live here."

Driving to meet Wyatt was somewhat of an emotional experience after not driving on that route for two years. I took the back roads to Prosser that stretched from Van Giessen Street through West Richland to Benton City. It brought sweet memories as I passed West Richland where the road to Benton City started. That spot was one of my family's favorites because its unique topography created wind streams that carried fine sand particles. There was plenty of this kind of sand for us to collect enough for Raz's sandbox when we lived in Grandview. That road took me through downtown Benton City where I entered the narrow two-lane Old Empire. I liked driving there except during harvest season when it was next to impossible to pass the farmers.

It felt like homecoming when I arrived at the research center, a place where I started my academic career. I couldn't resist playing a prank on Evelyn, the secretary and receptionist. The Ford Granada I bought was her car's identical twin, the same color and model. I bought a Ford Granada because I liked her car. I made sure to park next to her but I entered the building through the back door and not through the main lobby where she was sitting. I imagined her going home for lunch and trying to open my car door with her key.

Meeting with Wyatt was overwhelmingly emotional as this special guy had helped ensure my family's wellbeing. He was the one who offered me a post doctorate position and helped me get the coveted Green Card. I reciprocated by conducting the kind of research that put both of us on the map.

I told him just the highlights of what I did in Israel during the past two years and explained the reason for coming back. "It was more important for us to come back without having a job waiting for me than losing the Green Card. I have a plan to open a 1-hour photofinishing shop at the Columbia Center Mall in Kennewick, using my proprietary processing chemicals but I must wait for the ingredients I shipped from Israel to arrive. The most important issue for me, right now, is to write the scientific paper summarizing the research I did for you before I left. Is it possible for me to get a small desk and chair somewhere in the building where I can write?"

"You bet. I'll get you a desk and chair and a key to the building so you can come and go and work on the paper any time you want."

"Apropos to writing the scientific paper, let me show you something," Wyatt said and pulled a cardboard box from his cabinet and gave it to me. "These are the postcards requesting reprints of the research papers you wrote with my name as the co-writer. They kept coming after you left so I sent the reprints to the people who requested them and kept the cards for you as I remembered how you cherished them."

"Wow, what a pleasant surprise. It is rewarding to realize that people around the world showed interest in the research work that came out of your lab."

"OK Sam, we also need to discuss two important issues. The first one is to let you know that after you left for Israel, I hired a graduate student working on his master's degree so I support him a little bit with a token salary. He is not well versed in the type of research you did here. He evaluates different insecticides against mite infestations on Hops. Anyhow, I don't have funds to grant you another research position but I want to grant you some money while you write the paper. I know that right now you don't have a job so I want to help."

"Wyatt, it is very nice of you but you don't need to do that. If you remember, I was the one who told you that I will write a paper to document this research and I'm keeping my word. What I need from you is just the desk, the chair and the keys to enter the building."

"Leave it to me Sam, and remember, I am the guy who calls the shots here," Wyatt said to me, smiling from ear to ear.

"Now, a really pressing issue we need to discuss and get your reply before you leave my office today."

"What is it, Wyatt? Don't keep me in suspense."

"Well, a month ago I received a phone call from Dr. J.G. Rodriguez from the University of Kentucky, Department of Entomology, informing me that he was in charge of managing the Fifth International Congress of Acarology to be held August 6-12 at Michigan State University. He wanted you to be there and present the published research work you did while you were here. Your lecture should be written as a scientific paper to be included in the book titled *Recent Advances In Acarology Volume-1* with him as the editor and published by Academic Press. I told him that you left for a two-year research assignment in Israel and you might be back by the end of May. I promised to contact him as soon as I had more information. I hope you'll accept this invitation, since it is a vote of confidence in your work and a springboard opportunity for your academic career. You don't need to worry about the expenses. Dr. Rodriguez will provide you with the airline tickets and hotel stay. I would like to be there while you give the presentation. I will come to Richland and we'll fly to East Lansing from there. I need to call him as soon as possible. What do you say? Do you accept?"

"Yes but I can't stay through the entire week. Batia and I need to register Raz and Shir in the upcoming new school year, and we're worried that Raz has forgotten his English."

"I'll call Dr. Rodriguez and tell him you accept the invitation but won't mention that you will leave the day after your talk," Wyatt said and I agreed.

On my way out, I stopped by the counter to talk to Evelyn. "Hi Evelyn. It's nice to see you again. I missed you so much I came back. Not only that, I even bought a car like yours."

"Oh my gosh, I didn't even know you were here," she exclaimed. "Are you the owner of that Ford Granada parked next to mine?"

I answered in the affirmative.

"Welcome back Sam. Good to see you again."

"I need to write a scientific paper documenting the last research I did for Wyatt. I'll be here every once in a while, so we'll have the chance to talk. Right now, I'm leaving for Richland. We found an apartment there." I left her Ford Granada all by itself without its twin.

When I came home, Batia was busy preparing a light dinner as we still did not have all the utensils, pots and dishes other than what the apartment manager was able to provide. I could see that Raz and Shir had spent time in the swimming pool as both were burnt a bit from the sun. I told Batia about my meeting with Wyatt and my talk at the Fifth International Congress of Acarology. "

"How long will you be there?" she asked.

"It's a six-day conference. Wyatt and I will leave on August 1, but I'll give my talk and come home the next morning. My talk is scheduled for 10 a.m. August 2. I discussed this with Wyatt, but my participation won't be finalized until he talks to Dr. Rodriguez. Wyatt promised to call me as soon as he gets confirmation. The most important issue for us, though is to register Raz for the upcoming school year. We should all go to the Jefferson School first thing in the morning, introduce ourselves and talk to the principal about Raz not speaking English," I said.

The next morning, we walked to the school. Raz was not too happy going to the school instead of the swimming pool. "Don't you want to see your new school?" I asked.

"No! I want to go back to Alonim and Zehava."

"Sorry Raz, we have no choice, we live in Richland now. When we come back you and Shir can go swimming." We found the principal busy talking to a young teacher, who had came for her first orientation.

"Are you looking for me?" the principal asked us.

"Yes, we are new in town and would like to register our son for the upcoming school year but we also have a few issues we need to discuss with you," I said.

"Just give me ten more minutes to finish with our new teacher and then I am all yours," she said and sounded so friendly I felt we came to the right school for Raz.

When we came back the principal invited us in. "Hi, I am Patricia Mead, and you are........?"

"Sam and Batia Regev, and this is our son Raz and daughter Shir." We just moved into the Manor House Apartments across the street and would like to register Raz for the upcoming school year."

"Judging from your deep accent, your last name and your children's names it's apparent you are from a different country. What is your nationality, if I may ask?"

"Both Raz and Shir were born here in the USA but my wife and I are native Israelis. We just came back from Israel from my two-year research assignment. Raz attended first grade there. He missed one month of school because we had to come back to the USA before the school year ended. It is strange that we are facing the same problem."

"What problem you are talking about," Principal Mead asked.

"When time came to register him as a first grader in Israel, we realized he did not speak Hebrew. His teacher said not to worry about it and she was right. He started talking Hebrew the first day of school. Evidently, he picked it up at home. Now, school is about to start and he does not speak English. I worry that you will force him to repeat first grade until he speaks English," I confessed to Mrs. Mead.

"Mr. Regev, I am going to give you the same answer his Israeli teacher gave you, which is not to worry. He will start speaking in English very shortly after school starts."

We thanked Mrs. Mead for her time and encouraging words. She gave us printed instructions for parents enrolling their children for the first time. She also scheduled an appointment to see us a few days before school started to make sure everything was fine.

Afterward, I let the children spend some time at the pool as I had promised Raz earlier.

A few hours later, Dr. Cone called to let me know Dr. Rodriguez was thrilled that I agreed to be one of the speakers. "He requested the title of your presentation along with an abstract to add to the daily scheduled lectures. The sooner you come here the better."

I went to Prosser soon after his phone call. When I arrived at the research center Wyatt showed me my new spot, located in the room where I worked with the gas chromatograph.

"Please work on the title of your presentation and the abstract. I want to mail it to Dr. Rodriguez today and get him off our back," Wyatt pleaded. "I would also like to introduce you the graduate student, George Mathews, who is working on his master's degree."

It felt strange to see George in my former Office/Lab but George Mathews was a pleasant guy, a bit younger than me and still a bachelor. During our chat I happened to mention my plan to open my 1-hour photofinishing color lab at the Columbia Center Mall using the processing chemicals I formulated as my own propriety products. "I'm still waiting for most of the ingredients I need to arrive from Israel. I'll need to find a source for the exotic ingredients here in the USA, once my Israeli supplies are gone," I told George.

"At one time I was into color photography and purchased ingredients I needed from a Los Angeles company called Lauder. Call them and see if they carry what you need," he suggested. That was great advice as they became my sole supplier of two important hard-to find ingredients when I founded my own chemical company few months later.

It took me about an hour to select the title for my talk and to write a short abstract of my lecture. I asked Wyatt to browse through the color slides we produced out of my research and pick the best ones to use in the presentation. I set them aside and felt confident that all the logistics associated with my presentation were taken care of. I cleared my mind and started writing the scientific paper I promised.

On August fifth, I kissed Batia and the children good bye and drove to the tiny Richland airport to meet Wyatt and fly to East Lansing. Our new Ford Granada was too big and intimidating for Batia so I drove myself to the airport. I went inside but there was no waiting area or boarding counter and I didn't see an airplane that fit my expectation of a commercial airplane. I noticed a structure that could be defined as an air traffic control tower but that was all. I wondered if I was at the right airport.

When I saw Wyatt pull to the parking lot, I gave a sigh of relief. "I am so glad you came," I told him "I thought I was waiting for you at the wrong place."

"Why is that?"

"Because you told me to be at the Richland Airport but do you call this place an airport? I don't see any planes."

"This airline flies a small aircraft that carries six passengers. Do you see it over there?" he pointed to a small airplane about to taxi toward the airfield. "It will take us to Sea-Tac to catch the United flight to Chicago. From there we'll take a United flight to East Lansing. Here are your tickets. The boarding counter is over there."

Finally, our plane approached the building. The pilot greeted us, squeezed our small suitcases into the cargo compartment and we took off. All of a sudden, I re-lived the anxiety and discomfort I experienced when my Grandview friend, Dr. Donald Woods, took Batia, Raz and I to Portland in his Piper airplane. (See Chapter 11.)

In Seattle, we rushed to catch our United flight to Chicago. Wyatt enjoyed napping after they served us breakfast. I had no time for a nap. The next morning would be an important event in my academic life, i.e. presenting my research paper to an audience of international professionals. I spent the entire flight to East Lansing practicing my presentation.

Dr. Rodriguez greeted us at the hotel and showed us where the lecture hall was located. "Dr. Regev, please come for your presentation a bit early so the person in charge of operating the slide projector will have enough time to load your slides and get the projector ready for you."

"I'm impressed by how well organized you are, Dr. Rodriguez," I commended him.

In the lobby, I was surprised to see Dr. Katz, the person who hired me as a Research Team Leader at the Faculty of Agriculture in Israel. (See Chapter 13.) I introduced him to Dr. Cone and tried to be polite.

"I came from Fresno to attend the congress. I see that your lecture is tomorrow at 10 a.m. I'll be there. My presentation is scheduled for the next day, in case you're interested," he said.

"I would like to hear your presentation, but I'm leaving early tomorrow morning. I need to be back in Richland. We just came back from Israel, and have not settled yet. I'll read your presentation in Dr. Rodriguez's book. See you tomorrow morning," I told him and we left.

"Boy! You were cold," Wyatt said. "I expected kissing and hugging between two landsmen who have not seen each other for a long time."

I told him about Dr. Katz and Dr. Goren's dishonesty throughout of the entire scheme, "I was not in the mood to be nice to him."

"I see your point, Sam," he replied.

My presentation went well and generated interest as judged by the number of questions asked after I finished. Both Wyatt and I addressed the questions, and continued in the hallway as they readied the hall for the next speaker.

The organizer of the congress had a fancy outside barbecue dinner for all the participants providing me an opportunity to network with scientists in my field and inquire about open positions. Wyatt's fund was limited so I was bound to join the unemployed within a week or two when I finished writing the paper. After the barbecue dinner I retired to my room, packed my things and left the next morning while Wyatt stayed at the congress for another week.

When I arrived home, I slipped into my swimming suit, joined Raz and Shir in the pool, and listened to their report of what had happened during the time I was out of town.

Raz was apprehensive about attending Jefferson Elementary and wrote many letters to his former teacher, Zehava and his friends at Ramat Aviv School, telling the world how he missed Ramat Aviv, Israel and his classmates. We sent some of them to Zehava. His letters broke my heart and I realized writing was his way of coping with being homesick. To this day, I keep all his letters in a special binder.

Raz's first day at Jefferson Elementary was a pleasant surprise. Mrs. Mead had been right; Raz started speaking English without any Hebrew accent. It was a tremendous help that some of his swimming pool pals also attended Jefferson Elementary. They all walked to school and back together every day.

Shir attended a Montessori school Batia found for her not too far from where we lived, so for a few hours each morning I had the apartment to myself. I needed that time to write and send my resume to a myriad of ad's about job's available. I finished writing the paper, titled "The Monoterpene Citronellol, as a male sex attractant of the Two-Spotted Spider Mite, Tetranychus urticae (Acarina: Teranychidae)" and sent it for publication, adding Wyatt's name as the co-writer.

The paper was published in the February 1980 issue of *Environmental Entomology*. I found myself in the very awkward situation of being an unemployed scientist yet, the flood of postcards coming from around the world asking for reprints of my papers kept coming. Wyatt was kind enough to fill the requests and send the reprints but kept the cards for me, knowing how I treasured them.

Our savings account was dwindling fast. My salary in Israel was paid in Israeli currency but it was reduced considerably upon converting the Israeli Lira to US dollars. We had the Green Card so we could work but I could not find a job. Batia was luckier and started working for minimum wage at the laundry of a nursing home in Richland. At first I had to drive her to and from work but later on a co-worker gave her a ride.

Sunday mornings became busy and difficult days for me as Batia had to go to work and I had to take Raz and Shir to the Sunday school at the synagogue. It was important that Raz and Shir be with other Jewish kids their age. The entire Sunday school assembled at the sanctuary and had their morning service after which they dispersed to attend their own Hebrew and religious class. Just before the end of the general service at the sanctuary, the Sunday school principal gave the children a sermon on how important it is to help the Tri-Cities less fortunate people. At the end of the sermon and before dispersing to their own classed, the students placed cans of food and other non-perishable items into a special basket. I was not aware of the ritual the first time, so we came without anything to put in the basket, a rather embarrassing moment. From the next Sunday on, I made sure to bring a can or two.

I never took charity or welfare money in my life, but finding myself unemployed and our savings about to be depleted, I started thinking about requesting food stamps for Raz and Shir. One morning when the children were in school and Batia was at work, I drove to that office.

"May I help you sir" the person at the desk asked me.

"We are new to the Tri-Cities and I am unemployed and looking for a job. My seven-year old son and my five-year-old daughter were born in the USA, hence they are American citizens. I believe that based on our financial situation, they are qualified to receive food stamps every month until our financial situation changes for the better."

The guy at the desk heard my foreign accent and asked, "Where are you from?"

"We're from Israel sir, and I went to UC Davis for four years. I got my Ph.D. there but still could not get rid of my accent."

Most of the past similar encounters, the replies were friendly and warm when they heard I came from Israel, but this guy was cold, even colder than Antarctica at the peak of its winter. "I will have to ask you a few questions and you can take these forms home, fill them out, sign return to me. He then asked me few questions. "Sir what car do you drive?"

"We own a 1975 Ford Granada, sir."

To this day I am not sure if the guy lied to me, or simply did not like Israel and Israelis but his answer was, "Sir, owning and driving such a fancy car disqualifies you from getting food stamps."

I tried to protest his reasoning for denial, "I am not asking for food stamps for me. They are for my children who area American citizens," but the guy did not budge. I felt too proud to argue with the jerk and I left fuming at myself for even going to the welfare office.

I sent my resume to a not-for profit, Battelle Research Laboratory in Richland, Washington. They informed me that although my resume met their hiring standards, they could not offer me a position as I was not a USA citizen. "But I have a Green Card so I am allowed to work in the USA. What is your issue with my application?" I asked their Human Resources representative.

"Battelle is doing extensive nuclear research work for the Department of Defense, the candidates must be American Citizens with the highest security clearance. You are more than welcome to try again when you receive USA Citizenship."

One day I noticed an ad in the *Tri-City Herald,* advertising an open position at the Benton-Franklin Health District lab. "This job will be perfect for me," I surmised. A strong wave of optimism started going through my spine because Dr. Koren (not his real name) was the Head of Benton-Franklin Health District office and a member of our synagogue. Being naive coming from Israel with its life philosophy stating, *Your town's poor come first*, I thought that was the moto at our congregation and Dr. Koren would consider my qualifications and offer me the job or at least invite me for an interview. Everyone at Congregation Beth Shalom knew I was searching for a job. Then, an official letter came from Benton-Franklin Health District office, signed by Dr. Koren informing me that the position was filled and wishing me luck with my job search. I later on discovered that he hired someone who was way less qualified.

✡

A burning issue for a small Jewish community like ours was Jewish burial of deceased members of Congregation Beth Shalom. The congregation purchased a section of the existing commercial cemetery and made it the Jewish section. Burial plots within this section were sold to the families that needed to bury their loved ones. Since the cemetery was a Christian cemetery operated by Christians their funeral services were not considered a Jewish burial as far as the Jewish law was concerned. To resolve this issue, the congregation established its own burial services, comprised of men volunteers to bury the men and female volunteers to bury the women. This kind of Jewish burial group is known as *Chevra Kadisha* (or *Hevra Kadishah*) and I was, and I'm still one of the four to six men volunteers of Congregation Beth Shalom *Chevra Kadisha*.

✡

The *Chevra Kadisah* is an organization that makes sure that the bodies of the deceased Jews are prepared for burial according to the Halacha laws and the Jewish tradition. The bodies are protected from desecration until they are buried. Moreover, members of the *Chevra Kadisha* must show the proper and utmost respect for the corpse while cleansing and handling the deceased.

First we recited a special prayer asking the deceased for forgiveness, in advance, in case we inadvertently did something improper. Then we proceeded with the steps as stipulated in the instructions on how to prepare the body of the deceased for burial.

Most members of our synagogue were a bit squeamish and could not do it, so that is why it was carried out by volunteers like me. Yet, the task of *Chevra Kadisha* is considered a great laudable Jewish *mitzvah* (A good deed carried out from a religious duty). That is because tending to the dead is something the deceased cannot reciprocate. So, whatever I did through the years as a member of *Chevra Kadisha* was devoid of any ulterior motive. It was simply a *chesed shel emet* (Hebrew: a good deed of truth).

Then, thirty-six years later, on October 14, 2014 another member of our *Chevra Kadisha* volunteers called me. "Sam, I am sorry to bother you on a very short notice, but Dr. Koren just died. The hospital transferred his body to the Einan's Funeral home. Can you be at Einan's at 8 p.m. to prepare his body for burial? You are the first person I am calling. I'm not sure how many more will come but I will be there. I made the arrangements with the Einan's people, and they will stay in the building, open the preparation room for us and provide help if needed. Just come to the lobby and tell them that you are from Congregation Beth Shalom and they will take you downstairs to the room."

"Don't worry, I'll be there on time."

When I arrived, the director of the funeral home took me downstairs to the preparation room where Einan's people had placed Dr. Koren's on the washing table. It was covered with a white sheet ready for us to perform *Mitzva* for Dr. Koren.

Josh and David, the other members of our crew, were already there. The management of the funeral home had given us our own cabinets with all the items needed to perform the preparation for a Jewish burial, including the relevant prayers and instructions in laminated sheets, and *yarmulkes* (Jewish head covers). There was a simple pine wood coffin to place the body in after we finished.

I am not going to describe the process we went through to ensure Dr. Koren got his proper Jewish burial. But I would like to express the personal thoughts that ran through my head while the *Cevra Kadisha* volunteers performed the *Mitzva*, thirty-six years after Dr. Koren denied my application to work at Benton-Franklin Health District laboratory. There I was, 36 years later, washing and preparing a ninety-eight-year-old Jew who just passed away who did not give me a helping hand when I needed it the most. I never discussed this issue with him and moved on despite the deep scar it left in my heart. But now he was in front on me, a dead person, I was concentrating my efforts, giving my best, preparing him for his last voyage to meet his maker. While interacting with him, the resentment evaporated as I dressed him with the linen shroud and placed his *Teffilin* and the his prayer Shawl next to him inside the coffin.

I sprinkled Israel's soil on Dr. Koren's closed eyes. (We kept a bag of very reddish soil I brought from Israel during my last visit.)

"Sam, what are you doing?" the other volunteers asked.

"This is *hamra*, (Arabic for red) soil I collected in Israel. What you just saw me doing was a good will gesture to Dr. Koren, treating him like Joseph treated his father Jacob, who pleaded with him not to buried in Egypt. At the time of his death drew near, Jacob called for his son Joseph and said to him, 'Please do me this favor. Put your hand under my thigh and swear that you will treat me with unfailing love by honoring this last request: Do not bury me in Egypt.'" Genesis 47:29

Jacob wanted to be buried in Canaan (Israel) the country he came from and belonged to. I symbolically followed Joseph's act, to bury Dr. Koren in Israel instead of Richland.

"It is very interesting and nice of you," they said while we placed the coffin cover. There was one more act left for me to do before completing my *Chevra Kadisha Mitzva* and that was to affix a small Star of David made of pine wood at the center of the coffin.

We cleaned the place and let the funeral home director that the body was ready for the funeral the next day.

The burial service started at the sanctuary hall. Many people came to pay their last respect to Dr. Koren, a prominent physician in the Tri-Cities. Members of the Jewish community as well as non-Jews who knew him shared their memories of him. When this part of the funeral service ended we all marched to the freshly dug grave and waited for the coffin to arrive. It was lowered into the grave and members of Dr. Koren's family took a few shovel-fulls of dirt and emptied them onto the coffin.

It is customary for anyone who attends the funeral to show respect for the deceased. When the person ahead of me did his part and handed me the shovel, I emptied more shovel-fulls of dirt than other people as if I could not let him go. I found reciting inside me my own Jewish *Mourner Kadish*. I finally let go and whispered, "Rest in peace my friend," bringing the final closure to the hard feelings I felt toward him for thirty-six years and never shared with anyone other than my wife Batia.

✡

I found out by coincidence that the owner of our apartment complex also owned the condominium complex next to our building. It was known as Cherry Lane and with several two-story units with a nice grassy backyard and a community swimming pool. When I saw a U-hall parking near one of the units and the tenants loading their belongings, I told our manger that if there was a vacancy there, I'd like to move. She agreed but she was surprised that I was so eager to move. I said I would do so and not even wait for the management to paint the condominium before we moved in.

"When you first came to my office looking to rent an apartment, you insisted on having an apartment on the third floor. So why do you want to leave and go Cherry Lane?"

"Our apartment here is great but I believe we will have more privacy at Cherry Lane," I answered. I could not tell her that the cases of chemical ingredients I shipped from Israel were due to arrive any day. I needed a secluded place to start making them.

Moving to the Cherry Lane was a great move as it gave us more privacy and the other tenants were great. The McCool family had children the same age as Raz and Shir, and they were devout Christians who treated us royally for being members of The Chosen People, just like Judy and Wayne Gunther, our apartment managers and friends in Grandview.

The McCool's got very excited to have us living next to them. "We wish to know Hebrew," they kept telling us and still being unemployed I thought maybe I could earn a few dollars teaching Hebrew at my home. I posted a note (Figure 15.1) on the board at the entrance of the Osco-Buttery supermarket on George Washington. Both Mr. & Mrs. McCool registered for the class and brought their friend, a dentist. The note I posted at the Osco-Buttery supermarket brought me only one student, but it was a blessing in disguise as that sole student, Mr. Alan

Rither, became my close friend for life, and for many years he came to my house every Sunday night to chat and talk about Israel. Being a lawyer on the Battelle Research Laboratory legal team, he also became my legal advisor, keeping me out of trouble. I kept promising him that one day I would be his tour guide in Israel. I kept my word. In April 2019 we went to Israel and had a good time.

Back to the note I posted at the Osco-Buttery supermarket, I noticed that Alan took the liberty and without my knowledge added a few comments to my post and listed his phone number in case more people were interested and would call him for information.

Luckily, I had kept my class notes and information sheets I prepared for the Hebrew classes I taught at UC Davis foreign languages department. The notes saved preparation time and made teaching my Richland students easier. The class did not last long as my new students discovered that Hebrew was not an easy language to master and if these devout Christians students thought they would be able to read the Old Testament in Hebrew, they realized after a few classes that it was not going to happen. I terminated the class, but I gained my lifetime friend, Alan.

Figure 15.1 Notice offering Hebrew classes posted on the board at the entrance of the Osco-Buttery supermarket.

Needless to say, teaching Hebrew did not solve the unemployment problem. When the shipment with the photographic chemicals arrived, I called Glenn Rayburn and reminded him of our plan to open the 1-hour photofinishing store at the Columbia Center Mall in Kennewick.

"I am very excited to start. Just give me the list of the equipment we need and whom to contact and I'll set an appointment," he told me.

I prepared the list of the essential equipment we needed and the phone number of the Kodak office in Bellevue, near Seattle and Glenn scheduled an appointment with them. I drove to Glenn's house in Grandview and from there we headed to Bellevue in Glenn's car. The list I gave Glenn was very impressive. It was the first time he saw the instruments the Kodak representative showed us. Then we went to the office of the sales representative for the price quotations. As he punched the numbers into his adding machine, it made so much noise, I thought I could see smoke coming out of it. Glenn looked as if he was on the verge of having a heart attack. I realized that a 1-hour photo finishing lab at the Columbia Center Mall would happen right after the second coming of the messiah and not a minute before.

"Sir, we were very impressed with what we saw here so let us go back to the Tri-Cities, discuss the financial aspects, and check with the banks about securing a loan," I told the rep and we left.

Glenn seemed occupied with his thoughts as we drove back to Grandview. I surmised he felt bad for suggesting, while visiting us in Israel, that I should return, and we'd open the 1-hour photofinishing lab. Upon hearing the Kodak's sales representative price quotations, however, it was obvious he could not keep his promise. I broke the silence, "Glenn don't worry about it, we could establish a company that provides chemicals to printing shops, and newspapers."

"That's an idea, what name will you chose for that company?"

"Nothing cute or fancy. R&R Chemicals Corporation (Regev & Rayburn) would do."

"Let me see what I could do," he said and I felt a big boulder rolled off his chest.

Evidently, Glenn felt guilty for not being able to finance our 1-hour photofinishing store venture, so he channeled all his efforts to get R&R Chemicals Corporation started. A few days after our trip to Bellevue, he gave me a checkbook and said, "I just opened a joint bank account under the R&R Chemicals Corporation with our names as the officers authorized to sign the checks. Here is your checkbook. I also went to the Perfect Printing shop and here is our letterhead stationery. While there, I also talked to Eric Bernard, the owner and Rich Gay, the manager/editor of the *Prosser Record Bulletin* newspaper about our company and asked if they could use any of your chemicals in their business. Eric and Rich are members of the local Rotary Club. I am also a member and I know they will help us with the business if your chemicals work for them and are competitive. When they asked me about your credentials, I was not sure what to say. I told them you had a Ph.D. and worked as the manager of the Kodak Lab in Israel. Maybe I stretched the truth a bit but both of them, especially Eric Bernard the owner of Perfect Printing, want to talk to you as soon as possible."

I thanked Glenn for his efforts and promised to see Eric the next day. However, I had an issue with the checkbook he gave me. "Glenn, I thought about the finances and decided not to take any money from you. If I need some before I see any income, I would prefer considering it a loan. Money issues could ruin the best and deepest friendship in the world, and I don't want this to happen between us. I treasure our friendship and you being the proxy grandpa for Raz and Shir and I won't let this friendship get stained by money issues, so I am not going to use that checkbook. I am sure that sooner or later I will find a job so don't worry about us."

Glenn, took back the checkbook while protesting, "Remember, the account is at the bank for you to use in case you need some cash."

The next morning, I drove to Prosser to meet Erick Bernard at his Perfect Printing shop and found a very pleasant, soft-spoken person. Originally a Canadian, he had worked as a farm technician at the Irrigated Agriculture Research and Extension Center. He left them and opened a printing shop. He had no previous experience and was self-taught.

"Glenn Rayburn spoke very highly of you and then I heard you worked with Dr. Wyatt Cone at the research center, so the stars aligned for you. Let me show you what we're doing here and see how your processing chemicals can help us."

Eric took me to the back where he and his helper were working. "Here is our photo typesetting writer," Eric pointed to an instrument. A young lady was busy typing the text for a customer's order. However, unlike a regular typewriter where the text is printed on paper, this machine illuminated the text onto photographic paper strips that were processed using an *activator,* allowing for the text to show up, then fixed with a second solution called *stabilizer.* "Once the photographic typesetting is stabilized, we cut the strips onto a layout sheet and compose the material; then we photograph the layout sheet onto the kodalith film and image it onto the offset plate for our printer," Eric explained. "If you make activators and stabilizers that I can try, and I'm satisfied with their quality and price, I'll buy them from you."

He really caught me off guard since I had never heard about activators and stabilizers before as these chemicals were not chemicals any regular photographer or photo processing lab used. However, I could not afford to admit to him my total ignorance. I said, "Eric I would like to see the containers of these two chemicals so I know the size that fits your processing machine and the strength of the solutions you are using."

"Sure, here are the containers I haven't opened yet." He brought two containers called *cubitainers,* holding 2.5 gallon of each chemical. I pretended to inspect what they were, but I was fishing for the information about their chemical ingredients and commit them to memory." Let me go home and do my research of where I could get the empty containers and check with the shipment of chemicals I just received from Israel and see if I could be of service to you. Just give me a week if you don't mind."

"That would be fine," Eric assured me as I left. I had my work cut up for me.

When he showed me the containers, I noticed that the main ingredient of the activator was soda caustic so evidently a strong alkaline pH was needed so I chose sodium hydroxide crystals. I noticed that ammonium thiocyanate was listed on the stabilizer container so I used it in my version since I had this ingredient. I used that specific compound in the past on jobs requiring extremely short film fixing times. The next morning, I called Eric and asked if I could come right away with my samples.

"Of course," Eric said and added, "Boy, you were supper fast, I want to try your soups."

I showed up at Eric's Perfect Printing in less than an hour. "I am glad we are testing your samples; I was planning to replace the chemicals in the machine today. Let's dump the old chemical and put in one of your samples." Erick discarded the old solution and rinsed the activator tank. I brought two samples of my activator. The ingredients in sample #2 were twice the concentration in sample #1. The same was true with the two stabilizer samples I brought.

Eric poured sample #1 of activator and sample #1 of stabilizer into the processor and let it run for few minutes before processing a sample strip of the typesetting photographic paper. Next, he ran it through the processor loaded with my *soups* and inspected the result as the text strip came out of the machine, processed and dry. "Wow!! That is a great *soup* he exclaimed. I like the black fonts and the very white background. That's exactly what I need."

"I am very happy my chemicals work for you but there are two questions that we need to answer," I said. "The first one is the longevity of the solution. How long would it take before you need fresh solution? I would like to suggest don't dump sample #1 until it no longer processes your strips. Please track how many text strips you can process before the need to dump the solution. When that time comes, replace the solution with sample# 2 and see which one is better. The other test we need, and we can do right now, is to verify that the white background of the strip stays white and does not change to a brownish or off-white tint over time. Why don't we expose the strip you just processed to strong light and see if there is any change to the white background." It passed the test if the white background stayed unchanged.

Eric called me two weeks later to inform me that my sample #1 worked well and processed more typesetting strips than the commercial chemical he was using. He tried my sample#2, but did not notice a significant difference. "Besides, the less concentrated solution inside my equipment, the better," he said. "I already talked to Rich Gay, the manager of the *Prosser Record Bulletin* and told him that I'm satisfied with your products, and he wants you to stop and talk to Linda, his typesetter. They use a similar processor and would be interested in your activator and stabilizer."

"Thank you, Eric, for trying my chemicals and spreading the word to colleagues. I'm going to call Rich Gay right now and set an appointment to bring samples for Linda to try. Please let me know when you're ready to place an order if $XX/2.5 gallon of activator and $YY/2.5 gallon stabilizer is an attractive price for you."

"Well, when you have your meeting at the *Prosser Record Bulletin*, why don't you bring me one cubitainer each."

I landed my first customer.

My meeting at the *Prosser Record Bulletin* went very well. I asked Linda to use the sample of my activator and stabilizer and let me know her verdict. On the way back to the Tri-Cities I stopped at Eric's place and delivered the chemicals he ordered. I got my first check as a *Sam the Businessman* rather than *Sam the Scientist*. I also broke the news to Glenn and told him that I would continue the business on my own and suggested he close the R&R checking account. He sounded very happy to hear the news, but I also sensed he was relieved the business adventure he got himself into, ended on a positive note.

Linda from *Prosser Record Bulletin* called to let me know they were satisfied with the performance and price of my chemicals and placed an order. A few weeks later I received a phone call from the salesman who supplied these chemicals to *Prosser Record Bulletin* and *Perfect Printing,* after discovering that two of his clients switched to my processing chemicals. He introduced himself as salesman, Sam Hall, of *Printing Supplies, Inc.* based in Walla Walla, Washington and asked if he could stop by my house on his way back from Prosser to Walla Walla. "I want to explore with you the option of distributing your activator and stabilizer. I'm calling from *Prosser Record Bulletin*.

Linda and Eric just told me your chemicals perform very well."

I agreed and gave him directions to my Cherry Lane condominium.

When Mr. Sam Hall, a very pleasant grandpa-looking man in his sixties arrived I offered him coffee and cookies and we got down to business right away. "I cover the area between Walla Walla, the Tri-Cities and the lower Yakima Valley area up to Yakima. Most of my customers are small printing shops like Eric's so I don't need a huge volume but rather a secured supply of these chemicals. Based on what the major producers of these chemicals charge, I believe a $XX/2.5 gallon activator and $YY/2.5 gallon stabilizer should be competitive enough for my customers to switch to your products. My customers have been with me for many years and would be willing to take my suggestion to try yours. I would agree to distribute your products for a 35% mark-up he told me. Being unemployed and strapped for money, his offer sounded attractive. We started a business relationship that lasted for two years until he retired. It was a convenient deal for him as it was done on an as needed basis, but I requested a week notice for such orders. Since I wanted to do everything legally, I asked my friend and former Hebrew student Alan Rither, the attorney, to help me file my business as a corporation based in the State of Washington. I chose the name of the corporation to be *SBR Chemical Inc.* SBR stood for *Sam Batia Regev.*

I did not want to depend on making only two products. I explored the use of different version of the photographic developers on dental and medical X-Ray films. My first step in that direction was to visit Dr. Ronald Grow, DDS, from Grandview, who was our dentist during our four years of living there. Not only was he a great dentist but also a devout Christian who treated us royally just for being Jewish and natives of the holy land. He was a Grandview native and also a farmer during his off hours. As a farmer needing extension services, he knew all the scientists and the staff members that worked at The Irrigated Agriculture Research Center in Prosser. I made an appointment to see him feigning a tooth ache.

Arriving at Dr. Grow's office was a homecoming event. They treated me like a celebrity. I was pleased to find that the same staff members were still working for Dr. Grow. It felt like reuniting with family. "Where have you been for the last two years?" Dr. Grow asked me, pretending to be mad at me. "We kept sending you reminder cards, but the cards came back."

I told them about my two-year research assignment in Israel and our return to the Tri-Cities instead of Grandview. "It's not personal, we loved our time in Grandview but with Raz and Shir older now, Batia and I felt it would be better to be close to the Jewish synagogue.

"But please don't worry, Dr. Grow, you are still my favorite dentist and Linda is still my favorite dental assistant, so here I am. I believe that one tooth is acting up. I'm sure that you can fix it," I said. Dr. Grow checked and double checked and took two X-rays. "Sam, I don't see anything wrong with the tooth. Let's wait and see if it goes away or gets worse before doing anything." I couldn't tell him that the reason for my visit was really to seek his help with the photographic formula I concocted for processing dental and medical X-Ray films.

"So, what are you doing now?" Dr. Grow asked and I told him that my plan to open the 1-hour photofinishing shop at the Columbia Center Mall, did not work out. "However, I've started my own chemical corporation and make chemicals for phototypesetting. In fact, Perfect Printing and *The Prosser Record Bulletin* are my customers. I also have a small distributer from Walla Walla."

"What a coincidence, both Eric Bernard and Rich Gay are my patients. I'll talk to them about you next time they have their appointments."

Sensing his jovial mood, I brought up the topic of processing his dental X-ray films. "Dr. Grow, I wonder if you could help me with a new product I developed. I need an unbiased professional evaluation from a dentist."

"How can I help?"

"Well, next time you're ready to discard the old chemicals in your X-ray film processor, I'd like you to use my developer and fixer and see if the results satisfy your professional criteria and judgment. If the results are satisfactory just keep using that solution, if not, discard them and use the one from your supplier. I'm willing to make any adjustments to meet your standard if necessary. I would appreciate your help and input."

"I'd be more than happy to help you," Dr. Grow, replied, "but there would be a price to pay," he warned me.

"So what is your price?"

"I will be thrilled if you come to my church and talked to us about Israel. If you want to show slides, we have a great projector and a large screen."

I shook his hand and said, "That's a deal, just let me know when you're ready to try my chemicals."

A few days letter he called to let me know that he was ready. I brought three samples I formulated. We tried them all and the results were better than the commercial developer and fixer. I asked Dr. Grow, to shoot another batch of X-rays and evaluate again the results and he did. He was satisfied again with the definition and the sharp details shown on the film so I told him, "Let's make this sample as the one you are going to use because it cost me less to make it and I can give you a very competitive price. I prefer to sell it as a 4x1 gallon case comprised of 2x1 gallon Ready-to-Use Developer and 2x1 gallon Ready-to-use fixer."

Dr. Grow agreed and I was thrilled to add another customer to my list. "Have you thought about talking Dr. Bayam, our new chiropractor about using your X-ray processing chemicals? He's shooting lots of X-rays when patients complain about lower back pain."

"Thanks Doc," I said, "I'm on my way to talk to him."

"Well, you can't miss his office, it is just across from the city library."

Dr. Bayam was a very pleasant young man, eager to establish his clinic. I told him that I just came from Dr. Grow's office where he tried my X-ray film processing chemicals and Dr. Grow was satisfied with their performance. "So how about trying my chemicals on your X-ray films and save money?" He showed me how much he was paying for the Kodak chemicals and I assured him that I could beat their prices. "He agreed to buy five gallon cubitainers of X-ray film developer and fixer. I promised to refund his money if he was not happy with the product, but the chemical did a good job for him.

Word of mouth did it's wonders and pretty soon I had several loyal customers. It was time to advertise.

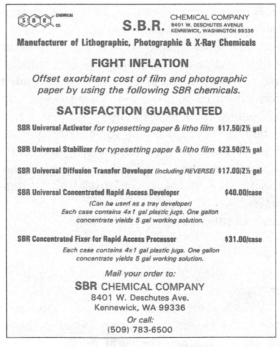

Figure 15.2 S.B.R. advertising

I placed ads in the professional magazines. (Figure 15.2) I also sent a personal first class mailing with my brochure and price list to potential customers I found listed in the yellow pages in cities in the State of Washington, Oregon, Idaho and Utah.

✡

One day, all of the tenants of the Cherry Lane condominium complex received a letter announcing the owner's decision to convert the rental units into private residences. We were to vacate a week after the school year ended. The owner was to compensate the tenants for the time still left on the annual contract and also to help the tenants find an apartment. Everyone was protesting but there was nothing we could do legally.

For me, the entire fiasco was a blessing in disguise because with all the orders that were coming in for my chemicals, I needed a larger space to produce them and my space at the Cherry Lane apartment had become too small. I found a house for rent on Davenport street that had all the features we needed. It had three bedrooms and a very large roofed working area attached to the kitchen at the back of the house. I could work there making my chemicals and also store the drums and 100 pound bags containing the ingredients. It had a separate basement apartment with its own entrance. We also had our own laundry room with brand new family size washer and dryer. Moreover, it was located not too far from the Lewis & Clark Elementary school

I grabbed it right away and we moved in. The owner provided the basic furniture and beds. The only piece of furniture I had to buy was a couch for the living room so I purchased a simple foamy couch that I could convert into a double bed in case I needed one.

The chemical business kept me busy but it was still not enough to live comfortably so I kept looking for a better paying regular job and keep making the chemicals. One day the phone rang and it was the Virologist at the Irrigated Agriculture Research and Extension Center in Prosser. "Hi Sam, this is Gaylord Mink calling. Do you still remember me?"

"Of course I remember you. How could I forget you after you poked fun at me and Dr. Cone during the first day I arrived from UC Davis."

"You're still holding that against me? When are you going to forgive me for that?"

"Never, unless you are making up to me" I answered.

"Well that is the reason I'm calling. Wyatt gave me your phone number and I know I reached the right person as you are the only person east of the Cascade Mountains with such a deep accent."

Before going any further, I would like to explain the *issue* I had with Dr. Gaylord Mink the morning Wyatt Cone introduced me during the coffee break. "So Sam, you're like Wyatt, using your thumb and index finger to pick mites off the Hop leaves and squash them with the sole of your shoes?" he said and imitated with his fingers and shoes what he described verbally. I was not sure at that moment if he was serious or just joking so I did not response. Later on, we became friends as I had to use his lab occasionally and discovered he was a smart and excellent scientist. I always gave Gaylord my manuscripts to review and make suggestion before I sent them for publication.

"Are you really calling me now to atone for embarrassing me when we first met?"

"Yes I am," he replied. "Do you have a few minutes to talk to me now or I should call you back at a more convenient time?"

"Now is a good time so what's on your mind, I am all yours."

"Well, I'm not sure if you're aware of the new problem our cherry growers are facing because of the Prunus Necrotic Ringspot Virus. The problem afflicts the cherry orchards but in California the almond growers are the ones impacted the most. Although we are talking about two different fruits, the problem is interrelated as it is the same virus that causes the problem and it is transmitted by the pollen grains gathered by honeybees. The connection between this problem in California and the problem we face here is very simple. Because California is south of us and closer to the equator, their growing season starts earlier than ours. They hire our bee keepers to secure pollination. Once the almond season is done, they move the beehives back here for cherry blossom season. Our enzyme-linked immunosorbent assay (ELISA) shows that the virus is present in the pollen grain these bees collected in California. The bees transmit the virus to our cherry orchards and fruit yields begin to deteriorate and the trees become useless as far as fruit production is concerned. My group at the Irrigated Agriculture Research Center is going to study ways to identify the presence of the virus using serological methods and establish a semi-commercial service where cherry growers send us random samples from the trees they suspect have the virus as judged by declining fruit production. At the lab, we'll analyze the samples for a nominal fee and advised them which trees in their orchard are infected."

I could not hold my curiosity any longer, "Gaylord, you know I am not a virologist by any stretch of imagination, so why you are calling me about the Prunus Necrotic Ringspot Virus, I don't know anything about it."

"To begin with, Wyatt told me that you are unemployed and looking for a job, aren't you?" Gaylord asked me, trying to impress upon me the notion that he was the "white Knight" going to save me so I told him I was busy selling my X-ray and lithographic chemicals, but he did not budge.

"I watched you using my lab equipment and analytical instruments so I am confident I could use your participation in this project. Time is of the essence for me, so just say *yes* to my job offer and it is all yours."

"Just a minute Gaylord," I exclaimed, "You gave me the big picture but failed to describe how I fit into it and what my responsibilities would be."

"Sam, the job will keep you extremely busy and your sole responsibility, with no technician's help. You will be the one to produce the anti-bodies (globulin) against the Prunus Necrotic Ringspot Virus and supply it to the commercial testing service lab we are establishing. It would be your job to propagate the virus on the greenhouse-grown Chenopodium quinoa seedlings my laborer George would grow for you. You would inoculate their leaves with the virus and harvest the leaves when they show the highest visible damage from the virus. After maceration of the leaves you would have to purify the extracts (*antigen*) and inject it into our rabbit for her to develop the anti-bodies in her serum. You let the rabbit rest for a week and then draw blood from her to eventually isolate the anti-bodies she developed against the virus. The end product should be the purified anti-bodies you prepared and we would use it for the ELISA tests the cherry growers order," Dr. Mink explained. "Are you up for the job?" he teased me.

"Well, being unemployed leaves me with no other options but to be the Phlebotomist or the Dracula to your poor rabbit," I told Gaylord and accepted his offer. "Just give me one day before reporting to work, so I can send the processing chemicals my customers ordered."

Once again I had to jump into a scientific field where I had no previous experience, yet Dr. Mink chose me, the *mite man* to carry out this significant part of his new project.

The day I came to work for Dr. Mink was a special day for me, not only because I was employed again but also it was sort of a homecoming. My first stop was to greet Wyatt Cone. He was glad to see me, "I'm happy Gaylord took my suggestion to hire you. Knowing you, I'm sure that one or two scientific papers for publication will come out of it. By the way, how are Batia, Raz and Shir doing?" I showed him a picture of Raz and Shir.

"Boy, they have grown so much since I last saw them. This is beautiful."

"What do you mean by beautiful? Did you mean to say the children are beautiful or the photograph I processed and printed using my photographic chemicals is beautiful?" I teased him.

"Both of them," he answered, like a skilled politician.

"See you later, Wyatt," I said and went downstairs to Dr. Mink's laboratory.

His lab had expanded since my post doctorate work, adding more instruments and equipment geared to research the Prunus Necrotic Ringspot Virus, especially the ultra-centrifuge I was about to use to produce the purified antibodies.

Gaylord introduced me to the people working with him. The only one I knew was his Research Technologist Bill Howell. Two of the new faces were of interest for me. The first one was Ahmed, a Jordanian Palestinian student finishing his master's degree in virology. Their association started during the sabbatical year Gaylord spent at the University of Jordan a few years earlier. I was not sure if Gaylord was joking or really meant it when he said while introducing us, "Ahmed, this is Sam Regev, an Israeli, and my request to both of you, please don't bring the Middle East fighting into my lab. I won't tolerate any political arguments." I felt his forewarning was not necessary and chose to ignore it.

Gaylord also introduced me to Henrik, a Polish researcher from the Polish Ministry of Agriculture, sent by his government to study the new advances in horticultural virology that Dr. Mink had developed. Since both of my parents were born in Poland, I spoke enough sentences in Polish, we became best friends from our first hand shake.

Poland was a communist country behind the Iron Curtain and was extremely watchful of its citizen so they couldn't defect to the west. In Henrik's case, they did not allow his wife to join him. When she visited him in Prosser, they forced her to leave their child with her parents.

Coming from a communist country where food was scarce or too expensive for most Polish citizens, made him addicted to meat, especially beef. Each barbecue event we had at the research center was like a national holiday for him.

Henrik's situation reminded me of a story my mother told me about her childhood friend from Golub-Dobrzyn. After the war, one member of her Betar Group became an official functionary in the government of communist Poland. The Polish government never let him travel with his wife to reunions in France, organized by another member, Daniel Piniek.

Daniel fled from Nazis-occupied Poland to France and joined the French partisans. He became a very successful surgeon but never forgot his Betar friends. He invited them to France at his expense for a reunion every few years. Only four of the eight people shown in Figure 3.7, page 99, survived the war, the rest perished in the Holocaust.

✡

The part of my job that complicated working for Gaylord was being *Dracula* to the rabbit that got injected with the saline solutions containing the virus and then *donated* its blood to our research group. I had to do that job and luckily, Batia did not see me make a living by drawing blood from that poor rabbit.

Dr. Mink showed me the *art* of drawing blood from a scared rabbit, "Pay attention because after today, you will do it."

He took me to the building where he kept the rabbit. "John, my technician takes care of her, as far as feeding her and cleaning her cage so you don't have to worry about that. As you can imagine, the rabbit does not like the procedure, so I built a special contraption to help us draw blood from her," Gaylord said and pulled a small wooden chamber with a sliding front wall. He pulled the rabbit out of her cage and placed her inside the blood drawing contraption and slide the u-shaped front wall over the rabbit's neck. Needless to say, she was protesting by tapping her legs inside the box, but her head was accessible for drawing the blood. "Next you use a new razor blade to nick one of the veins in the rabbit's earlobe and collect the dripping blood into this test tube."

The test tube looked very large so I asked, "Are you sure this is the one to use for a rabbit and not an elephant?"

"Trust me, it is not a big deal and if the test tube is still not full, God created the rabbit with two ears, so you can use the other ear to fill the tube," Gaylord assured me while finishing drawing the blood and returning the rabbit to her cage. "Store the test tube full of blood in the refrigerator until the serum separates from the blood cells. Discard the blood cell layer and bring the serum to our lab. I'll show you the rest of the steps to isolate the antibodies."

The next blood draw was my job from start to finish. I was not apprehensive but felt bad for the rabbit so I said out loud, "Hey girl! Count your blessing that it's me drawing a sample of your blood and not a technician doing a lab tests for a gynecologist. Have you heard the saying, *the rabbit died* associated with pregnancy tests? Well, no one will say, "the rabbit died" after I'm done with you today."

It usually took me two to three days to isolate and purify the antibodies (or more scientifically precise anti-Necrotic Ringspot Virus globulin). Description of the methodology is somewhat complicated and beyond the scope of this book so I won't delve into it. Nonetheless, it produced a scientific paper that was published in 1982 in *Phytopathology* Vol 72, No. 12: 1542-1545.

Meanwhile, the commercial services for the cherry growers was about to start operating on a daily basis. I was not sure it was my *cup of tea* so to speak. I didn't see the opportunity for me to carry out scientific research that produced papers in the peer-reviewed scientific journals. The daily round trip commute between Richland and Prosser was getting to me especially during the winter with its snowstorms and icy roads. I preferred to find a decent paying job in the Tri-Cities and kept looking and letting people know I was available.

✡

One of the impacts the 1973-1974 Arab oil embargo imposed on the USA by the Arab members of OPEC (Organization of Petroleum Exporting Countries) for supporting Israel in the 1973 Yom Kippur War was a shortage of fuel in the USA along with increased prices. The USA government started a concerted effort to wean itself from depending on the Middle East for its energy supply. Domestic oil explorations and production zoomed as a result. Building commercial nuclear reactors was accelerated as well. In the State of Washington, the construction of five nuclear energy reactors started in earnest, three plants (WNP-1, WNP-2 WNP-3) north of Richland, close to the Hanford Reservation and two generating plants (WNP-4 and WNP-5) at Satsop located in Grays Harbor county on the west side of the Cascade mountains. A semi-public company by the name Washington Public Power Supply System (WPPSS), was established to build these nuclear generating plants, each one with the capacity of 1,240 MW. The company funded its operation and construction by selling bonds in the open market. It was a booming time at the Tri-Cities as so many workers, engineers and scientist were flocking to the Tri-Cities so I hoped to find a job there eventually.

Among the many engineers that came to the Tri-Cities to work on the construction was David Shooha, who came from Chicago but was born in Khartoum, the capital of Sudan. I guess his family immigrated to the USA when he and his brother were young and they attended schools here as I could not trace any foreign accent when he talked. Also he was fluent in Arabic. He became an engineer and his brother became a prominent heart surgeon in Chicago. David was a bachelor, at least during the time he lived in Richland.

Luckily for me he came to our synagogue. We both found common ground; both being somewhat different from the other members because we came from a different country.

David Shooha had family members who lived in Israel so it was natural for him to associate with me and Batia. One day I told him about my wish to leave academia and find a job at WPPSS. "Please keep your eyes open and let me know if you come across any open position for me." I gave him my resume.

"I'll see what I can do."

One weekend David Shooha stopped by my house carrying a cardboard box filled with rather thick textbooks. *"Ma Hadha?"* (Arabic: *what is that*) I asked him.

"These are books I took from the WPPSS library, and I suggest you browse through them and absorb as many buzz words as you can. You don't have much time as I need to return them within three days. Bob Wright is a supervisor at the WPPSS Health Physics/Radiation Protection Department, and also my tennis partner at the Tri-Cities Health Club in Kennewick. I gave him your resume and he suggested that you browse through these books and promised to look into the possibility to plug you into their organization. I know Bob as a person who stands behind his word so I strongly recommend you heed his advice and browse through these books. Try to understand the key concepts listed here."

I followed David Shooha's advice, perused the books and waited patiently to hear from Bob Wright. When David Shooha came to take back the books, he told me to expect a phone call from Bob Wright shortly. "I'm almost sure he and Dan Harrison, his manager, are going to offer you a spot in their organization but don't jump for joy until it happens."

"Please ask him to call me at home in the evening. I don't like to discuss potential job offerings while I'm at Dr. Mink's lab."

He called the next evening. "Hi, this is Bob Wright calling. David Shooha gave me your resume and said that you were looking for a job with us at WPPSS. Although your resume indicates you have no experience in Health Physics and Radiation Protection, we believe that with your education and research experience you could be trained on the job. I would like to schedule an interview with you this coming Friday. Our department is located on George Washington Way. Would 9:00 a.m. be OK for you?"

I told him I would be there.

"See you then and enjoy the rest of the evening."

I called David Shooha right away. "I played tennis with him last night and he told me he was going to call you. I wanted to keep him happy so I let him beat me in the tennis game. Congratulations and good luck with the interview on Friday. And take it from me, they will offer you a job," he said.

It was music to my ears.

Chapter 16

Washington Public Power Supply Systems (WPPSS)

"**M**ake sure to come to your interview with Bob Wright dressed *properly* Davis Shooha called me to wish me luck the day before my interview.

"What do you mean by 'dressed properly?'" I asked.

"Well, WPPSS is a semi-public company and their dress code requires employees like you to wear a suit and tie. I always see Bob Wright dressed like that at work. I wear a suit and tie, so better get used to it, my friend," he explained. It forced me to look frantically for the black fancy suit I wore for my sister's wedding sixteen years earlier. It was sort of ironic because, I didn't wear a suite for my own wedding in 1967 but was going to wear one for the interview with Bob Wright.

I met Bob Wright at the WPPSS headquarters. "Nice to meet you. Our department is located in the building across the street from here so let's go there. My boss, Dan Harrison, will join us," Bob said while shaking my hand. Dan was the manager of the Health Physics/ Radiation Protection Department. He closed the door to his office so we wouldn't be interrupted.

Bob Wright introduced me to Dan, who shook my hand and said, "Sam, it is nice meeting you. I know plenty about you already, believe it or not."

I was a bit surprised and asked, jokingly "How come? Did you check with the FBI?"

"No, I did not need the FBI to know about you. I live in Prosser and read the articles the Grandview and Prosser papers published about you and your family during the time you worked at the research center. I have many friends working there so I asked them about you. I like what I heard. Bob Wright is our supervisor and the subject matter expert so I'll let him describe what the job would entail," Dan stopped and let Bob continue with the interview.

"There are three generating nuclear reactors under construction here at the Hanford. They are designated as, WNP-1, WNP-2 and WNP-4. The WNP-2, is a BWR (Boiling Water Reactor) designed and built by General Electric, WNP-1 and WNP-4 are PWR (Pressurized Water Rector) and have different designs. We will send you to a week-long course to study the basics about the WNP-2 BWR reactor because this plant is getting closer to finishing construction, and become operational and licensed by the Nuclear Regulatory Commission (NRC). WPPSS must demonstrate that the radioactivity from it, once routinely operational, won't be harmful to the population within a 50-mile radius. The NRC developed a computer program called LADTAP II to estimate radiation doses to individuals, population groups and the biota from the isotopes WNP-2 expected to be released to the environment via its liquid effluents. The NRC also developed the GASPAR II computer program to estimate the radiation doses to individuals and population groups from the airborne isotopes released into the environment via the plant's gaseous effluents. Your job would be to run these two computer programs to show that the dose from these isotopes released to the population and the environment are within the NRC limits. Once WNP-2 reactor is licensed and operational, you will run LADTAP II and GASPAR II once a month using the actual concentrations inside the reactor vessel. These monthly reports will be filed with the NRC. That, in a nutshell, is the essence of the job," Bob Wright explained.

The job appeared more intricate to me than it sounded from Bob's description. Granted, there were the LADTAP II and the GASPAR II computer programs. I asked Bob to elaborate more on the definition and what constitutes *individuals* used by these programs.

"As far as the US government believes and implements through the NRC regulations, there are two kinds of *individuals* they are concerned with, the *average individual* and the *maximum individual.* The NRC defines them as living in the 50 miles radius around our nuclear generation plant. You will formulate, calculate and document the many parameters to input into the LADTAP II and GADSPAR II. Your data must be real, substantiated and documented as to how it was obtained. The NRC needs to have the ability to verify your data at any time if they so choose. Dan Harrison feels that the numerous scientific papers you have published in the peer-review journals, including documenting observation, data, methodology, etc. is equivalent to NRC requirements. It should keep us out of trouble in case the NRC arrives unannounced. As far as we're concerned, your past research and publishing experience makes you the perfect candidate, even though you are coming from a different professional sphere."

I was ready to tell him right then, that I would accept their job offer but I wanted more information on what kind of data they expected me to collect and document so I asked Bob to elaborate.

"Basically speaking, the NRC is concerned with the radiological effects on the population and the environment within the 50-mile radius from the reactor," Bob started his mini lecture. "They *invented* the so-called *average individual*. That person ingests radioactive particulates such as cobalt, cesium, chromium and manganese from the reactor's gaseous effluents that drop on the leafy vegetables grown inside the 50-mile zone. Additionally, the *average individual* gets more of these isotopes into his body from drinking milk from the local cows grazing in that area and feeding on forage grown inside the zone. The Iodine-131 isotope the cows ingest through grazing ends up in their milk. The radioactive iodine accumulates in the individuals thyroid gland which incorporates it into the very important thyroxine hormone in the human body. Then, there is the special case of an *average individual* who prefers goat's milk over cow's milk and drinks it on a regular basis. The NRC wants you to address that special person separately," Bob added.

"Why is that?" I asked. "Milk is milk, isn't it?"

"Not really," Bob replied. "The individual who drinks the goat milk gets higher radioactivity into his thyroid gland because iodine-131 gets incorporated into goat's milk more efficiently compared to cow's milk resulting in higher exposure to his thyroid.

"Our poor individual is also getting *zapped*"with X-Ray (gamma) radiation emanating from the Nobel gases krypton and xenon also released in the plant's gaseous effluent. The impacted organ in this exposure is the person's skin. The hydrogen isotope tritium is also problematic. It is released into the environment through the gaseous effluent and reacts with oxygen to form water which the *average individual* drinks. These are the main issues associated with the gaseous effluents the WNP-2 reactor releases to the environment.

The GASPAR II computer program will generate all the information you need in the report for the NRC. Your job would be to determine the quantity of leafy and other kinds of vegetables harvested within the 50-mile radius. You will determine how much milk is produced, also locate where the nearest goat milk farm is and how much goat milk is produced there. This information will be input into GASPAR II. And please remember, you would be required to document that information and where you obtained it," Bob Wright said.

When we came back from a short break, Bob continued with the job description. "Thus far we talked about the reactor's gaseous effluents and GASPAR II computer program associated with it, but WNP-2 liquid effluents are as challenging as its gaseous ones. The reactor's liquid effluents affect the *average individual* by delivering a dose to his/her body from the isotopes in liquid effluents released into the nearby Columbia River. Yes, you heard it right. We are going to release radioactive stream into a river, which is widely accessible to the public, hence exposing the public to radioactive isotopes. However, as the saying goes, *dilution is the solution*. We know the average annual flow rate of the Columbia River so we can determine the release flow rate of WNP-2 liquid effluent to guarantee a 2000 river dilution factor at the slough where the effluents are discharged. Further away from the plant the river dilution factor should be at least 20,000 fold which is a very large dilution ratio, thus bringing the potential dose from the liquid effluents it to a minuscule level.

Other exposure routes to our *average individual* from WNP-2 liquid effluents are through drinking water, consuming fish caught in the river, as well as recreational boating and swimming. This is where you need to run the LADTAP II computer program to estimate the dose to the *average individual* from the reactor's liquid effluents. The results should show compliance with the NRC's limiting dose levels," Bob Wright showed me a printout from the LADTAP II they ran the previous month. "This is what the printed data looks like."

Despite Bob's excellent presentation, I still had questions about the differences between the *average individual* and the *maximum individual*, so I asked for clarification.

"These are consumption rates the scientists commissioned by NRC consider to be realistic for the *average individuals*. There are also individuals within the 50-mile radius who consume more of these food items, drink more milk and water than the *average individual* and spend more time on recreational activities on the Columbia River. These are defined by the NRC as the *maximum individual*. *Maximum individuals* take their boat to the WNP-2 slough area where the reactor discharges its liquid effluents into the river. In that particular spot, the river dilution factor is only 2,000 instead of 20,000 we factor for the *average individual*. These fishermen believe they will catch more fish because they think the warm effluents attract the fish. We have no legal way to prevent them from being there because the Columbia River is open to the public. The NRC's experts estimated the annual fish consumption rates of these people and incorporated these factors into the GASPAR II and LADTAP II computer programs." Bob paused for a minute, looked at me and said, "Looks overwhelming, doesn't it Sam?"

"Yes it does, but I find it very interesting and challenging at the same time."

"You will need the cooperation of two other people in order to run the GASPAR II and LADTAP II analyses. One is Mr. Henry King, our meteorologist. The second is Mr. Albert Percy, from the WNP-2 Health Physics group. Albert will provide you with the data known as the *source terms* which is the current list of the radioactive isotopes identified in both the gaseous and liquid effluents and their activity measured in curies. You need to input that data into the two computer programs. Mr. Henry King, the meteorologist will provide you with atmospheric dispersion (X/Q) and deposition factors (D/Q) of the isotopes in the gaseous effluent at each location within the 50-mile zone. You need this data for your GASPAR II run."

Dan Harrison interjected, "Sam, in a nutshell this is what the job entails. We are offering you a $27,000 annually, with full medical and dental insurance coverage. We are also providing you enrollment in the company pension plan. Are you interested and willing to accept our offer?"

Not having a permanent and steady job, the $27,000 salary looked like a huge upgrade from my earnings at the research center in Prosser. I took their offer without thinking twice.

"Just give me two weeks to wrap up the work I'm doing for Dr. Mink and let him know about your offer. I would like to know when to report to work."

"Monday two weeks from today will be just fine," Dan Harrison said. "My gut feeling told me you would accept our offer, so I asked the secretary to prepare the application papers for you. Please take them home, fill in the information and bring them back with you upon reporting for work and don't forget, the dress code here is a suit and tie," Dan said and gave me a manila envelope. I thanked him and Bob Wright for their job offer, shook their hands and rushed home.

"God shined on us today," I told Batia and showed her the manila envelope with the job offer.

Dr. Mink was not surprised at all when I told him about my job offer from WPPSS. "That is a neck-breaking switch from being a plant virologist to a professional working in a nuclear reactor generating electricity. I hope you won't start glowing in the dark from the radiation you will be exposed to," he joked and asked what my salary there would be. I gave him the figure and the information spread like a wildfire. Several scientists working at the research center came to me with a copy of their resume and asked me to find them a job with WPPSS. "I'll do my best but an annual salary of $27,000 would be attractive enough for you?" I asked Dr. Kevin Boyd, the plant pathologist working on his post doctorate assignment.

"I would take it in a heartbeat," he replied.

My last working day at the research center finally came. It was time to say farewell again to the place and people. I spent close to six years of my life as a member of the academic world and would soon divorce myself from the world driven by the *Publish or Perish* mantra and delve into the nuclear energy health physics/radiation protection arena. Saying farewell to Henrik, my Polish friend was especially difficult because I knew what kind of life was awaiting him upon returning to communist Poland. I wished him well and thanked him for our friendship. I lost tract of him after he returned to Poland, never to hear from him again.

It took me a few days of considerable effort standing in front of the mirror, practicing the art of putting a tie around my neck as I had not done so for many years. As much as I hated it, I had to go along. My new employer required me to come to work with a leash around my neck.

On my first day at WPPSS, I looked like a groom walking down the aisle. I gave the secretary the completed paperwork. Bob Wright introduced me to my new co-workers, all of them dressed in suits and ties. The place looked more like a board meeting of a big corporation than a group of health physicists working for a nuclear generating plant. Next, he took me to a cubicle and said, "Sam, here is your desk and all the items you need to perform your job." Then he dropped a thick folder on my desk. "I give you three days to familiarize yourself with this material. It will become the bread and butter of your job."

The folder contained the NRC user's guides for the LADTAP II and GASPAR II. I almost fainted when I saw all the extremely long mathematical equations; I felt I needed an 18-wheeler truck just to hall them. "Bob, are you serious? Do you expect me to use all of these scary mathematical equations?"

"What's wrong with that?" he asked smiling from ear to ear.

"Not only are you forcing me to show up for work wearing a suit and tie, but also barefoot so I can use my toes and fingers to do these calculations," I explained. Maybe I was exaggerating a little bit, but these equations looked formidable to me.

Bob was not too moved by my protest and added more fuel to the fire by saying, "The NRC provided you with the GASPAR II and LADTAP II programs to estimate the dose to the public but it also requires us, meaning YOU, to write an elaborate manual for us to calculate dose estimates manually in case the GASPAR II and LADTAP II programs don't work or are not available. Dan Harrison and I delegated this task to you. You will have to write it along with the associated procedures. It is called Offsite Dose Calculation Manual or ODCM, but don't worry, I'll help you."

I felt I made the wrong decision accepting the job and told Batia that night that I was not sure I would last another day.

For the next two weeks, I got myself busy working on the input parameters for the GASPAR II and LADTAP II programs, such as production of leafy vegetables, milk production, etc. I documented their values and referenced the sources they came from. Evidently, both Dan Harrison, my manager, and Bob Wright, my supervisor were pleased with the job I was doing and called me to Dan's office.

"What did I do wrong this time?" I asked, jokingly.

"You have done nothing wrong but Bob and I did," Dan said. "The corporate Human Resources Department called us and stated that WPPSS is a semi-public corporation and as such, must comply with all Equal Opportunity (EO) regulations, both, Federal and the State of Washington. They want us to justify hiring you, a person with a Ph.D. degree and yet, paying you only $27,000 per year which is way below the salary range WPPSS pays its employees with a Ph.D. and similar credentials. I informed the Human Resources people that we would look into it and correct our mistake, if necessary. I talked to Bob and we decided to raise your initial annual salary to $45,000/year even though you are not well versed yet in Health Physics and Energy generating nuclear reactors.

"To justify the raise, you will attend the company's week-long BWR course. The course should get you up to speed on our WNP-2 Boiling Water Reactor. At the end of this class, you must pass a test with a grade of 80% or higher. It starts on Monday next week at the WNP-2 administration building training room. As for getting familiar with the health physics and radiation protection aspects of your job, we are going to enroll you in Harvard's Environmental and Occupational Radiation Protection four-day course, taught by the Department of Environmental Health Sciences of the Harvard School of Public Health. Please mark it on your calendar, you are going to be there from August 24 through August 28. These two assignments should keep you busy for the next few weeks."

It dawned on me that my professional life had changed course again. I already wore the hats of a Biologist, Acarologist, Physiologist, Plant Virologist and my new hat would be the one of Health Physicist. I felt sorry for whoever read my resume and tried to follow my professional path.

I attended the WNP-2 Boiling Water Reactor class and scored 95% on the test. Dan and Bob did not have to worry about that part of justifying the salary raise they gave me. The next hurdle, i.e. attending the four-day course at Harvard (Figure 16.1 a) was great as well, and gave me the opportunity to explore the city of Boston. In May 1987 they sent me to Harvard again for an additional training class (Figure 16.1 b.) when I took charge of the WPPSS whole counting task.

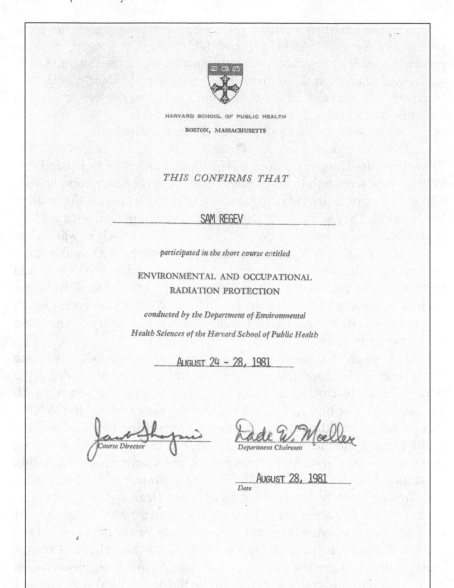

Figure 16.1 a August 24-28 1981, Certificate from Harvard's Environmental and Occupational Radiation Protection four-day course, taught by the Department of Environmental Health Sciences of the Harvard School of Public Health.

HARVARD SCHOOL OF PUBLIC HEALTH

BOSTON, MASSACHUSETTS

THIS CONFIRMS THAT

SAMUEL REGEV

participated in the short course entitled

CONTROL OF OCCUPATIONAL EXPOSURES
IN NUCLEAR POWER PLANTS

conducted by
the Department of Environmental Science and Physiology
and the Office of Continuing Education

May 11, 1987   *to*   May 15, 1987

Course Co-Leader

Course Co-Leader and
Associate Dean for
Continuing Education

Figure 16.1 b May 11-15, 1987, Certificate from Harvard's
Environmental and Occupational Radiation Protection four-day
course, taught by the Department of Environmental Health Sciences
of the Harvard School of Public Health.

✡

As the time flew by, I felt more confident with my job and made peace with the impressively long and intimidating mathematical equations beaming at me from the NRC GASPAR II and LADTAP II manuals. The Friday following my return from Harvard, Bob Wright stopped at my cubicle to chat.

"*Shabbat Shalom*," he said to me before leaving. That threw me off.

"Why are you greeting me in Hebrew and without a trace of American accent?" I asked.

"It is Friday today, so I want to greet you with a *Shabbat Shalom* like any good Jew should do," he said to me. It was a clever way to let me know he was Jewish too.

It took me by surprise, so I asked why we don't see him at the synagogue. "I was born to a very liberal and progressive Jewish family. My father is a family doctor, and my mother is a successful lawyer. I married a devout Catholic lady who does not skip even one Sunday going to church. She is raising our children as Catholics. I am a complete atheist so that is why you don't see me at the synagogue." His personal life did not place any barrier between us as our families became friends through the years that followed. His son and my daughter Shir attended the same high school.

Then, there was our colorful meteorologist Mr. Henry King, an extremely smart guy. When he saw something that looked stupid to him, he would let you know what he thought in his unique in-your-face manner. Henry and I collaborated because, as the company's meteorologist, he ran the NRC XOQDOQ computer program to generate the X/Q and D/Q values I needed as input for the GASPAR II program I oversaw. He had served as a meteorologist in the US Air Force until he retired. His Air Force duties took him all over the world, so it was not too strange for him to associate with a foreigner like me who spoke English with a deep accent. We became friends.

✡

One Monday morning after our weekly staff meeting, Henry King barged into my cubicle all excited and exclaimed, "Wow! My Southern Company stock went up this morning and I'm also getting 5% discount on dividend reinvested in my DRIP account."

"Henry, I don't know what you're talking about, please explain if you don't mind."

"I bought the stock of Southern Company, a gas and electric utility company, headquartered in Atlanta Georgia. It serves the southern United State. I joined its DRIP plan and get a 5% discount on any stock I purchase with the quarterly dividend. The stock jumped up a few dollars per share today and made me a nice profit. I feel rich."

"Wait a minute Henry, you lost me. I don't know anything about this staff. I am familiar with *drip irrigation* but I never heard about the Southern Company or its DRIP plan."

"DRIP stands for Dividend Reinvestment Plan. After you buy stock from a company that pays dividends, its DRIP plan gives you the option to buy additional stock with that dividend. Southern Company sells me these shares at a 5% discount. It is a great deal because unlike the brokerage companies, they don't charge commission on the transactions. "Boy, you are a Ph.D. and know squat about the stock market. What's wrong with you Sam? You better catch up fast or you'll end up poor when you retire."

I took Henry's advice and started studying what stocks represented, where and how to buy them. I started reading about DRIP programs, brokerage agents, commission fees, etc. I also learned about investing in the stock market through buying mutual funds vs. buying individual stocks in the stock market. The level of my complete ignorance regarding investment and the stock market was overwhelming and I felt insecure and dumb all of a sudden. I made a decision right there to close this gap as soon as possible. It was easier said than done because I was too busy catching up with my new job.

✡

With a nice paying job, I felt it was time to purchase our own home. A young couple we knew from the synagogue had just moved to a new neighborhood called Kennewick Park close to the Columbia Center Mall. There were several brand-new empty houses on their street.

Batia and I drove there the next day and found a 3-bedroom rambler we liked. The real estate agent had it nicely staged. Coming from the old house we were renting in Richland, this one looked very fancy and beautiful. The asking price was very reasonable but the going interest rate at that time was 12%. I was a novice at buying homes and paying mortgages. I did not catch the trick the real estate agency did to us, namely, charging us less than the actual monthly mortgage payment. After five years they zapped us with a balloon payment, forcing me to refinance.

Being a homeowner for the first time in my life helped me with my SBR Chemical business as I did not have to worry about a landlord objecting. I was very discreet and kept the area squeaky clean. The garage had a water faucet and a laundry sink, so I was able to produce my chemicals without bothering the neighbors. I leased a water softener unit thus eliminating the potential of sludge that normally formed in high alkaline photographic solutions.

I received a phone call from George Clement, the local service man of a Spokane-based company that provided weekly maintenance services to three Tri-Cities hospitals and medical clinics in eastern Washington, as well as Hermiston, Umatilla area in Oregon. "I would like to try your chemicals for our client's 90-second X-Ray film machines. If they meet our standards, we'll order from you on a weekly basis. I'd like to get a sample this weekend and try them." He came the next day to pick up the samples.

Around noon on Monday, George called to let me know my chemicals performed to his QA standards. "Are you capable of supplying me with 400 gallons of x-ray developer and 400 gallons of x-ray fixer every Monday morning?" he asked and I replied with a definite yes, not realizing that I was committing myself to a life sentence with hard labor. Every Friday, upon coming home from my job at WPPSS, 5-gallon cubical containers stood like soldiers in front of the garage.

My association with George Clement gave me the opportunity to work on improving my X-Ray film developer. X-ray films were processed at high temperatures in order to shorten the processing time. One of the problems was the swelling of the photographic emulsion of the x-ray film. The rollers of the processing machine pinched the soft gelatin making the processed x-ray film useless, as it obscured the fine details the radiologist needed. George took me with him on one of his weekly service calls at the local hospital.

He filled the tanks with my chemicals which included my *magic potion* that hardened the emulsion as it entered the processor. It worked and the processed film came out without any roller marks. I remember that experiment very well as we did it at 2:00 o'clock in the morning. I needed less than one fluid ounce in my formula but the ingredient was extremely expensive to buy from one of my photographic suppliers so I ended up buying a 50-gallon barrel from the manufacture because it was much cheaper. I still have plenty left as I write this chapter.

The mushrooming chemical manufacturing in my garage convinced me that I should obtain a business license from the City of Kennewick. I called their office and was advised that because my business activities were performed in a residential zone, I needed the consent of my neighbors before the city would issue me the license. My neighbors did not object and signed the consent forms. I submitted the consent forms and received my business license. I had to renew it annually.

✡

Two significant events occurred during that time. On June 2, 1982 Batia and I became naturalized American citizens. It was nice to receive a letter from Slade Gorton, the US Senator for the state of Washington, acknowledging that milestone and congratulating and welcoming us as US citizens.

Then, on January 1983, Batia, the mother of two young children, was diagnosed with cancer. She chose to make peace with the cancer and *offered* the cancer a *deal* by which she promised not to bother the cancer and in return the cancer not to bother her. As of this writing, it seems the *deal* is still on . . . .

✡

Our residential neighborhood had been growing fast and a new school, named Sunset Elementary, was built. The Kennewick School Board gave an aptitude test to elementary school age children in Kennewick and established a special program called KOG (Kennewick Opportunity for the Gifted). The students who passed the aptitude test were bussed to Lincoln Elementary. The KOG program had specially trained teachers and a special curriculum tailored for gifted students. Shir passed the test and attended the KOG program until she finished elementary school and moved on to Middle School.

✡

I was a Senior Health Physicist at WPPSS during the day and a manufacturer of radiographic, lithographic and photographic processing chemicals during my off hours. There were times when the two hats I wore merged and I was both at the same time.

Such was the case when an Israeli family arrived from Santa Barbara, California where the husband, Nathan, had finished a professional photography school and was hired by WPPSS to be their official professional photographer. Batia and I helped Nathan and his family settle and found them a brand new house in our neighborhood which they bought. Nathan became a very popular photographer at work but also earned a nice living taking professional photographs for manufacture's catalogs and user manuals. I took advantage of that and asked him to test samples of my photographic chemicals at the WPPSS lab. I asked Nathan not to reveal where these samples came from because I worked for the same company. As it turned out, the lab and its manager liked my products better than the Kodak products they were using, especially the high-definition developer I formulated for my Ph.D. thesis. They used this particular formula to process the aerial photos taken by a U-2 reconnaissance plane. They also used my processing chemical in their printing the company's brochures.

The way I supplied them my chemicals was sort of funny because, although the lab manager knew where these products came from, he placed the orders through the company's procurement department. The procurement department had no clue that the chemicals were produced by me. The routine was simple: When the WPPSS procurement guy called my home to place an order, Batia told him that I was out of the office but would call them shortly to verify what they needed. Then she called me right away. Next, I called them back and took their order and promised the chemicals would be delivered, free of charge, to their shipping/receiving deck the next day at noon. I took the cubitainers with me to work the next day and delivered them during lunch time. Everyone was happy.

✡

The activities at my Health Physics/Radiation protection department got hectic as we got closer to WNP-2 startup date. One of the bitter lessons learned from the Three Mile Island nuclear reactor accident was the need to have an independent off-site facility to evaluate and control the reactor should a similar accident occur. Hence, WPPSS built its off-site facility 1.5 miles from WNP-2. The off-site facility had its own radiation shielding walls along with internal closed filtered airflow system to protect the staff from the radiation and contamination outside air caused by a potential nuclear accident at WNP-2. Our Health Physics/Radiation Protection Department moved from Richland to the off-site facility upon its completion. Each one of us got his own office, a nice upgrade from the tiny cubicle we had in Richland. (Figure 16.2)

As our workload got heavier and the job responsibility mounted, Mitch, in charge of the whole-body counter and the back-up

Figure 16.2 Here I am in the radiochemistry lab.

radiochemistry lab quit his job without advance notice. He simply did not show up for work let alone, train someone to replace him. Dan and Bob came to my office and said, "Sam, as much as we hate putting you on the spot, we have no one else. Your new job assignment is to take Mitch's place in addition to the GASPAR II and LADTAP II. Granted, your workload will increase but your paycheck will increase as well."

The computers that operated the whole-body counting chairs and the one operating the radiochemistry lab computer were produced by Nuclear Data Inc. Bob Wright browsed through a folder he had with him and found a business card. "Here is the name and phone number of their local representative. His name is Ben Morton. He lives in Richland. Give him a call and see if he will give you a hand with their computers. We have an annual service contract with them. Besides, Ben is a great guy."

✡

Whole-body Counter. Our department built three whole-body counting chairs by using car seats and placed two shielded detectors next to them. One detector is to detect x-ray emitted from the person's thyroid gland. The other one is placed by the person's torso to detect the x-ray emitted from the rest of the person's body. The source of the radiation emitted, is the X-Ray (gamma) emitting isotopes that entered into the person's body either as a result of a contamination accident at work or through the routine working activities at the WNP-2 reactor. Each worker at a nuclear reactor has a quarterly annual and lifetime exposure allowance as

Figure 16.3 Whole-body Counter.

> stipulated by the NRC regulations. These exposures are monitored by personal dosimeter the worker wears at work in addition to his/her data obtained from whole-body counting. Each worker has a "bank" of how much he/she has been exposed to and takes this bank to wherever they work.

✡

Occasionally, contamination accidents did occur at WNP-2 and the contaminated person was sent to our facility for a whole-body count. First we made him/her take a decontamination shower. The water that washed their body drained into a special tank to avoid release into the environment. The decontamination shower cleaned radioactive contaminants off the person's skin so that ascertaining the isotopes detected by the whole-body counting chair came from what the person inhaled or ingested into their body. Sometimes several decontamination showers, each one followed by a whole-body counting were needed until I was sure the person's skin was clean.

Some contamination accidents required several follow-up whole-body counts for a few days until the results showed radiation within acceptable levels. The reduction was the result of physical decay and biological decay eliminating the radioactive particles through excretion. In addition to using the whole-body counter to evaluate each contamination incident, I also analyzed the clothes they wore during the accident as well as the towels they used at the decontamination showers. For this I used a special detector and a dedicated computer and program in the radiochemistry lab.

Ben Morton, the Nuclear Data representative was a huge help during the first few weeks following the abrupt departure of my predecessor. The friendship between our families strengthened through the years and it is still going strong to this day. Ben suggested to my boss that they should send me to the Nuclear Data's three-day training class at their Atlanta Georgia headquarters.

Dan Harrison concurred. Putting me in charge of the whole-body counting and running the radiochemistry lab added more feathers to my hat, but also complicated my life at work as I had to write procedures on how to perform various daily routines.

For example, a written procedure for performing a daily QA/QC check, for routine whole-body counting as well as for those following contamination accidents. I had to write similar procedures for operating the computers at the radiochemistry lab.

Although the whole-body counting and the radiochemistry lab were my responsibilities, the actual work performing the operations belonged to the Health Physics/Rad Chem Technicians of our department. They were union members and got paid on an hourly basis whereas I was on an exempt annual salary. I also had the privilege of working on a flexed time schedule. However, being an exempt employee also meant getting in deep trouble had I carried out any routine considered a *union job*.

For example, being on a flex work schedule, I showed up to work at 6:00 a.m. instead of 8:00 a.m. It enabled me to perform QA/QC checks on my counting systems and make adjustments if needed. I also needed to perform the same running routines as per the procedures I wrote for the technicians to make sure the system was operational at the start of the day. However, I was not allowed to use my runs of these procedures as the official QA/QC daily checks, lest the union file a grievances complaint against me for doing a *union job*, I had to wait for the Health Physics/Rad Chem Technician to show up at 8:00 a.m. and re-do the daily QA/QC routine, sign the print-out and give it to me for a review and my signature.

Yet, one day, I performed that *union job* myself and logged the report in to the official logbook to indicate the three whole-body counting chairs passed the QA/QC test and declared the chairs operational. It was not my intention to antagonize the Union members by doing job assigned to that particular technician. On the contrary, I was simply trying to spare him from disciplinary action filed against him by the corporation. To be specific, three NRC auditors from Washington DC scheduled a week-long audit of WNP-2 and needed to have their entry *whole-body counting* before entering the plant. I came to work at 6:00 a.m. to verify that all three counting chairs were performing well and passed the QA/QC check. I obtained the printouts and put them in my drawer. The clock was ticking and I got very concerned when it was 7:45 and yet, the technician assigned to count the NRC auditors was not there. There was still no sign of him at 8:00 a.m., the official start time.

The three NRC auditors started looking nervously at their watches wondering what was going on as he was still not there. I went to the Health Physics/Rad Chem Technician room and could not find him or any technician to take his place. I was afraid that the irate auditors would penalize our department with a nasty audit report along with a compliant letter about our services, so I seated them in the whole-body counting chairs and did the counting routine myself. I sent them to the plant with my report signed by me so that they would be allowed into WNP-2 and start their audit.

The technician showed up after 9:00 a.m. and admitted that he overslept. I told him I covered him and saved him from trouble because his clients were three NRC auditors from the Washington DC. "What happened should stay between you, me and the walls, so no one knows about it and you aren't disciplined. Here are the printouts from the daily QA/QC, for you to sign."

"Unfortunately, I had to give them the whole-body counting report signed by me so that they could enter the plant," I told him.

He thanked me profusely for saving his butt, and signed the daily QA/QC, report.

I have no idea how the senior Health Physics/Rad Chem Technician found out but he was furious and started the grievance complaint motion against me because I did not wait for the technician assigned for that job. He finally withdrew it after my technician begged him not to file against me because I did it to protect his job.

✡

Grandview, a small town populated mostly by farmers and devout Christians who loved and supported Israel, was a kind and warm place for us to live. The Tri-Cities on the other hand, had its own share, albeit tiny, of anti-Semites/Israel haters who kept sending venomous letters to the editor of the *Tri-Cities Herald* newspaper. These hate letters did not show any sophistication or intelligence on the part of the people who penned them, yet they forced me to write rebuttals. It took a lot of effort and time to answer them. It became a never-ending task because they kept sending more letters in response to mine. After a while I stopped that cycle realizing that by responding to their letters, I was providing the anti-Semites a podium to air their venom.

Then on Sunday, January 17, 1991 I left the house on my daily jog. That was the date the United State and its allies started the Golf War against Iraq's Saddam Hussein who invaded Kuwait and took its oil fields. When I came back from jogging Batia was about to drive to the synagogue and take Shir with her to the Sunday school where they both taught Hebrew. "Did you see this," Batia asked me and pointed to front right window by the passenger seat of our Ford Granada. I got closer and discovered to my dismay, that someone carved with his/her fingernail, "I am going to kill you," in the frost that covered window. "You were out jogging and I did not know what to do so I asked Jim (our neighbor) to come and see it. Jim called the Kennewick police department. They sent an officer who asked a few questions and said he would write a report for the police records and left," Batia told me.

To this day we don't know who the culprit was, but I suspected he was the anti-Semite who kept me engaged in the "Letters to the Editor" game. It was easy for him to find my address because of the newspaper's policy requiring letters to the editor be signed with the writer's full name and phone number. Whoever carved this message on my car window, got my phone number and called me few days later at 3:00 in the morning to repeat his, "I am going to kill you," threat and hung up. I did not call the Kennewick police to report it as I was not impressed with their reaction handling the case when Batia reported it a few days earlier. I did not own a gun and never intended to own one. However, I had the huge scary machete, my friend Rami brought me from the Dominican Republic when he was there. I kept that machete next to me for a few days until the crises subsided and no more phone calls were received. The culprit's letters to the editor stopped as well.

✡

Batia and I were invited to a New Year's Eve party. A few guests were in a heated debate over what would be the best stocks to buy in the coming year. Again I felt stupid for not having even the basic knowledge required to invest in the stock market, so I avoided these guests. When we came home, I discussed with Batia that shortcoming of mine and vowed to jump into the stormy waters of trading stocks. I gave her my word that I won't let our family go broke because of my getting into the stock market.

I decided to play it safe and invested a small amount of money in two mutual funds managed by the now defunct Twentieth Century Mutual Funds Company from Kansas, Missouri. I chose that investment company based of their investment return compared to that of their peers listed in Fortune magazine. I was very pleased with the returns of my initial investment, albeit *on paper* as I did not sell anything and kept investing more money with these two funds until the company elected to become a private investment company and stopped serving small private investors like me. With the nice returns of my investment it was my turn to brag to Henry about my prowess as an investor.

I felt confident and decided to dive into the stock market. It required opening an account with a stockbroker, but I did not know who to choose out of the many brokerage firms on the market. Each one claimed to be the best and promised me the moon and the constellations included. Talking to some of these brokers required taking tranquilizers after they told you how much their commission fee was. Although it was my policy not to do business with personal friends or family members, I opened a brokerage account with the Israeli Bank Leumi in New York city where my brother-in-law was a stockbroker. Without any stock trading experience, I felt I should start learning under his umbrella.

The first step was to research a stock to start with, buy ten shares and join their dividend reinvestment plan (DRIP). I rationalized that people will always need electricity, hence buying a stock of an electric utility that pays quarterly dividends, higher than a commercial bank CD paid, would be a safe choice. I bought ten shares of Philadelphia Electric company. It changed its name to Excelon a few years later.

I also felt that people would always need medications so a stock of a pharmaceutical company that payed a dividend would serve me well. I purchased ten shares of Abbott Laboratory, the minimum required to join its DRIP. Abbott Laboratory, looked attractive because aside from its prescription drugs business they also manufactured the Similac baby formula and Ensure liquid food for adults. Another division made the counting instruments for blood tests and the comprehensive metabolic analyses for commercial laboratories serving doctors and hospitals.

I felt I could not go wrong with these two stocks. Their DRIP plans also allowed me to purchase additional stock with a minimum of $50 per purchase so I purchase more whenever I had some extra cash to invest. Both my brokerage account and the DRIP accounts were set as joint accounts with me and Batia as equal owners so both signatures were required for important activities associated with these accounts.

One of my WPPSS co-workers, Tom Chase, who came from Omaha, Nebraska, subscribed to the daily newspaper to keep abreast of what was going on in his home town. He still owned a farm and properties and planned on retiring there eventually. One day, I noticed an ad on the paper's front page from the Perelman-Carley Brokerage, Inc. "Tom, are you familiar with these people?" I asked him and pointed to the ad.

"Not at all but why do you ask?"

"Well, the name Perelman is usually a Jewish last name so I bet you a million dollars this Perelman guy is a member of my tribe," I explained.

Tom took scissors out of his drawer, cut the ad from the newspaper, gave it to me and said, "Sam, it is all yours. There is a toll-free phone number, call them and find out."

At lunch time, I dialed the toll-free phone number listed in the ad. Bob Perelman answered my call. I introduced myself as an investor, a novice to the stock market and with very little trading experience, looking for information about opening an account with them. "We are a low-cost brokerage firm and charge only $25 per trade, for buy or sell orders and as such we don't do any stock research or trade recommendations to our clients. You will have to do these tasks yourself. If this is OK with you and you still want to open an account with us, I'll send you the application form or you can download it from the Internet."

I was still eager to find out whether or not Mr. Perelman was Jewish so I said, "Mr. Perelman, you probably noticed my accented English. I am originally from Israel, and I wish I had $1 for every

Perelman listed in the Tel Aviv phone directory. I would be a rich man. Are you by any chance Jewish?"

"Yes. I am and my wife Betty is Jewish too. She has family in Seattle and will be thrilled when I tell her about you. She also works here as a broker, so in the future, if you need to trade or have any problem with the account, she can help you."

I was still curious and asked, "Your firm is called Perelman-Carley & Associates so is Mr. Carley also a Jew?".

"No, we both worked at Merrill Lynch and retired. Bob Carley wanted to open his own brokerage firm and said he would do so only if I'd join him. Bob Carley is not Jewish but he says he likes *Gefilte Fish* (stuffed carp)," Bob Perelman said with a laugh.

A few days later he called to let me know my new account was approved and ready for trades. Opening an account with Perelman-Carley started many years of friendship that lasted until the company was purchased by StockCross, a California investment firm. Through the years I brought Perelman-Carley twenty-five clients, all friends of mine who were new to the stock market. I became my friends' free-of-charge advisor. Both Bob Perelman and Bob Carley retired a few years later.

I considered myself a value-oriented investor who never paid attention to what so many charlatans posted on their Internet websites. All that I needed was the daily price quotation for the stocks I owned or wished to acquire. I decided to subscribe to the *Wall Street Journal* and was pleasantly surprised that it was, in my opinion, the best newspaper in the USA. It had so many reports about what was going on in the world in addition to the investment data. Moreover, I found it to be very pro-Israel at that time.

I liked to read its daily account of what happened on Wall Street the day before and discovered that the newspaper treated the individual stocks as they were human beings and not just pieces of paper denoting partial ownership in the corporation. So I learned that stock ABC *soared* because the company received a big order for its product. Poor stock XYZ on the other hand *went south* because of its poor just-released quarterly earnings.

One more fact I learned from that column on the *Wall Street Journal* was how influential and omnipotent we, the Jewish people were. For example, one of the columns describing what happened the day before stated that, "The stock market fell yesterday due to a very light trading volume because it was Yom Kippur and the Jewish investors attended their synagogues." Was this line an admission of how significant members of my tribe were to the stock market? Or God forbid, an overt anti-Semitic remark blaming the Jewish people for the low price of stocks traded that day?

With all its greatness, the *Wall Street Journal* had one shortcoming; stocks prices listed were the closing prices of the previous trading day. I had to call Perelman-Carley for an up-to-the-minute quotation. Next, via the telephone line and a special modem, I subscribed to the now defunct Prodigy service that offered access to a broad range of network services, including stocks, travel, and a variety of other features.

I also took it upon myself to introduce American investors to Israeli stocks traded in the USA. It was a great opportunity for a positive PR for Israel. Moreover, the Israeli stocks were great companies with popular products and services sold in the USA. The American public was not even aware that they were Israeli products. In fact, the third largest country with stocks traded in the USA was and still is Israel. I wrote about these stocks and their products and received many responses and questions from individual investors. It kept me busy and my phone line busy as well.

My writings on the Israeli stocks was purely informational besides being my patriotic drive to let more people appreciate Israel. I did not intend to make one cent out of these writings. But there were many charlatans who manipulated their innocent followers by posting glowing reports on many worthless penny stocks. They hyped these worthless stocks telling the unsuspecting followers stock XYZ was *the next Microsoft* or stock ABC was *the next Apple.* The scheme pushed the price of these junk stocks higher so the charlatans made money by dumping the stock on the innocent followers of their website. The innocent followers ended up losing their money because these worthless stocks went nowhere but down and no one in his/her right mind would buy them back. The cycle repeated itself as the charlatans found a new worthless stock to hype and made more money, leaving the innocent followers holding the bag.

Although watching these kind of postings by the charlatans was kind of entertaining, I realized that there were many innocent and naïve people who got stung by that trap and I began feeling sorry for the victims. I felt I should do something about it. I noticed that one lady in particular, kept following the *buy* advice of one nasty charlatan and I knew for sure that she would lose money on each purchase she made following his advice. And sure enough she did, yet she thanked the charlatan by writing on the Internet page how great his free advice was.

This scheme continued for quite some time. I could no longer be a bystander and let it continue because the last name of that particular lady, Vicki (first name) from St. Louis, sounded Jewish to me. I decided it was time for me to be my *brother/sister's keeper*. I wrote her a long email, introduced myself and expressed my humble opinion that she was a victim of a charlatan's scheme who hyped worthless penny stocks by writing a fake glorified news releases. "His promises of these stocks going up and making you rich won't, in my opinion, materialized," I wrote her and explained why I was convinced. I let her know she could write to me if she wanted more information. I could not resist the temptation of checking whether or not she was Jewish so I ended my email by saying *"Your last name sounds Jewish to me. Are you by any chance Jewish?"* and pressed the ENTER key. It started a close and interesting relationship between our families.

Vicki replied swiftly, "Yes, you guessed right, my husband and I are Jewish but we hardly visit any synagogue. We don't deal or read much about Israel and have never been there. I have no investment experience and buy what that guy on the Internet recommends. It would be interesting to hear what you recommend I should do," she wrote.

My reply was swift and somewhat blunt as I felt she was in a dire situation. "It is none of my business, but if you don't mind I wish to know how much money you have lost thus far from following that guy's BUY recommendations?"

"More than $12,000 so far," she replied.

I was mad but not surprised. "I am sorry to hear that you lost so much money following the advice of that charlatan. However, if you agree to follow my investment advice, I would do my best to help you recuperate that loss. I cannot guarantee that, but you stand a better chance following my advice. People helped me and my family when I was in a bad situation so I would like to do the same for you. I am from Israel and that is the way most Israelis behave," I wrote and hit the ENTER key.

"Wow! What a kind gesture from you," Vicki wrote. "I will take your offer to help me but how are we going to expedite that?" she asked.

"There are two conditions that you must accept in order to get my help. The first one is to open a brokerage account with Perelman-Carley and Associates. The second condition is to follow my instructions and investment plan to the letter and not to second-guess me. If you don't feel comfortable with that, then my offer is off and there would be no hard feelings on my part. I would like to suggest that when you call Perelman-Carley and Associates, ask to talk to Betty Perelman, Bob Perelman's wife and mention my name. Ask her to be your personal broker who takes your trade orders." I was not a bit surprised that the chemistry between these two ladies was perfect and Betty Perelman treated Vicki like a queen.

Our email communication became a daily routine where we discussed the health and wealth of her stock portfolio built through buying and holding the stocks I recommended and purchased through Perelman-Carley. I walked like a super-proud peacock the day her

$12,000 investment loss was erased by the performance of the portfolio I built for her. It took almost a year for that to happen. She shared my investment advice with her friends and they shared with their friends so I became, unintentionally popular figure in St. Louis of all places.

I did not mind giving my advice for free as long as the investors followed the plan I drew and agreed it was for the long term and not for the frantic frequent daily trades which I abhorred. I was not shy about expressing my displeasure when people agreed to take my investment advice but then became day traders the minute the portfolio I built for them started making nice returns. A few of them started playing the stock market as if they were sitting in front of the Las Vegas slot machines. I made sure to admonish them and explained why I stopped advising them. Some of them saw my reasoning and returned back to be serious, long-term investors. The following letter received from Vicki's friend, also my "client," demonstrates that point:

Shalom Sam,

I know you will be sitting down when you get this letter so that you won't pass out from hitting your head because you fainted from getting two emails from me so close together. I hope that I have been able to express my thanks for everything you have done for my family financially in the past but, if I have or not done an adequate job it bears repeating. I know that you cannot be aware of the influence that you have had on so many lives in St. Louis. You are a legend here. You will be greeted warmly by many people when you visit St. Louis (and you will) because there are so many people that feel as if they know you personally. I know that neither Rick and I, nor my children could ever hope to repay you for the financial education you have given us. Both from your letters directly to me and thru your letter to Vicki that she was generous enough to share with me. I bought my first stock, Abbott Labs, in 1993 on your recommendation. I have added to my position since I am reaping great rewards. The other stocks I bought that year, Texaco and Exxon again on your recommendation have rewarded me greatly also. I now have 22 stocks in my portfolio and am very proud of every one of them and do not intend to sell any of them until retirement when we will need the extra cash. I still own mutual funds because of my lack of confidence in my ability to pick good stock but any new money is now going only into my stocks thru the DRIPS. I don't blame you for being frustrated with all of us. Investing is a scary business and we needed you to hold our hands and you did for a long time. You showed soooo much more patience than I ever could. I think you should let your investing children try their wings and concentrate on yourself and your family. You have done more than enough for us. Again it is the financial education that is the important thing that I will have forever. That and just creating an interest in the market in general. The stock market is about life and the day to day things that happen to all of us. So many people think it is about greed. I disagree. My way of repaying you and Vicki is to try to educate as many people as I can, especially kids. Also Rick does dentistry free for Vicki, Jack, and Vicki's mom. There really aren't words to express my deep thanks but I hope you are getting my message. Sorry to hear about your grapes. Keep babysitting them so you can squeeze out at least one bottle of wine for the fall. My flowers are looking exceptionally good this year as are my tomato plants. I am hoping for a good harvest. I have substituted swimming for racquetball for the time being but swimming is so boring and I like competition.

Hi to Batia.
Shalom, Dot

✡

Vicki and her husband, Jack, started showing great interest in Israel and rekindled their affinity to Judaism. I suggested that they should join a local synagogue as I was not a qualified rabbi to answer the avalanche of questions they asked me about Judaism.

They joined the St. Louis chapter of *Aish HaTorah*, a Jewish orthodox organization founded in Jerusalem in 1974 and branched out world-wide later on. It was formed to provide Jewish education to non-observant Jews like Vicki and Jack to get them back to Judaism. Jack, who was still working full time as a mail carrier for the St. Louis postal services, was trained by *Aish HaTorah* to become a kosher inspector and worked part time as such.

With her investment portfolio doing so well, Vicki and Jack felt comfortable to plan a visit to Israel for the first time in their lives. I planned and arranged a two-week visit recommending where to go and where to stay on the Sabbath as they became observant Jews and refused to travel on the Sabbath. I asked Vicki to contact my sister

Chaya who owned a travel agency at that time, and my sister finalized the details of their Israel visit. Vicki also consulted me on a few medical issues she or her mother were facing or needed my input or explanation associated with the medical reports or test results.

More than a year of intensive daily emailing exchanges between Vicki and I had passed. Actually, I didn't even know what she or her husband Jack looked like. She never attached any photographs. I did not send pictures of me, Batia or my children. In fact, Batia was not aware of these email exchanges or me helping others with investment advice. Then one day an email from Vicki arrived saying, "Jack and I have friends in Seattle. We have never visited Seattle or the Pacific Northwest so we would like to come and visit you in the Tri-Cities for a weekend. Our Seattle friends will come to Kennewick to pick us up and take us to Seattle after our visit with you. Is this OK with you and your wife? And if it is OK, what would be the best weekend for our visit?" she asked. That was a complete surprised as I had to break the news to Batia, let alone tell her about my year-long correspondence with Vicki.

I told Batia the story about Vicki's investment fiasco and how I got involved extricating her out of the financial nightmare she got herself into. Batia took it in stride. We selected a date for Vicki and Jack's visit. Batia and I were the only ones residing at our house at that time since Raz was living in Seattle and Shir was in Namibia, Africa serving in the Peace Corps. I wrote to Vicki that we would love to host them and picked a date convenient for them and their Seattle friend.

"We never saw you or your picture before so how we are going to recognize you at the airport when we land?" she wrote.

"Not a problem" I wrote back. "First, make sure you buy the airline tickets to Pasco, Washington, the airport that serves Richland, Kennewick and Pasco, otherwise known as the Tri-Cities. This is a very small airport so you won't get lost. You should not have any problem recognizing me. Just look for a fat, short, bald, middle-aged man. There is no way in the world for you to miss me. Besides, I will hold a copy of the Jerusalem Post newspaper in my hand to ensure you recognize me," I assured Vicki. To this day I don't know what possessed me to concoct a prank like that. It did not fit my look during that era of my life.

Finally their flight landed in Pasco. After the last passengers claimed their suitcases, I was still sitting on the bench at the waiting area and feeling bad watching a couple walking nervously looking for me in all directions. Finally, my guilt-ridden feelings took over so I got up from the bench and walked behind them and said, "Excuse me, are you by any chance looking for a short, fat, bald, middle-aged man?"

"Yes!" Vicki replied, "He was supposed to meet us here more than fifteen minutes ago but we are the only ones here except for you."

"Well, you must be the famous Vicki and Jack Leschen from St. Louis, Missouri. I'm Sam Regev from Kennewick, Washington. I am very pleased to meet you, finally."

Vicki protested vehemently the minute I finished my sentence. "But you are not a short, fat, bald, middle-aged man," she said to me. "And you aren't holding a copy of the *Jerusalem Post*. That is why we didn't recognize you."

We all hugged each other and I said, "Let's go home, Batia is waiting for us. Your visit is the first time she learned about our Internet correspondence, just to let you know."

It took us ten minutes to drive from the airport to my house, and Vicki did not stop saying, "I like the mountains here. We don't have these high mountains in St. Louis." It was funny she called the hills in our area mountains so I told her, "When your Seattle friends come to pick you up on Sunday, they will drive through Snoqualmie Pass in the Cascades and there you will see real mountains."

It was a warm reception when we entered my house. Vicki hugged Batia and started talking to her as if these two ladies were close childhood friends. I showed them my large backyard with all the apple trees, plums and my Thompson seedless grapevines, something they were not accustomed to seeing in their neighborhood in St. Louis. I found both of them to be attractive, pleasant and warm people. "Why don't you rest a little bit, and after Sabbath dinner we will drive around the Tri-Cities and stroll along the bank of the Columbia River. Jack decided he needed a short nap and headed to our guest room. Vicki stayed in the kitchen and talked with Batia who was putting the final touches on Sabbath dinner.

The Sabbath dinner was a great experience for our guests. We lit the Sabbath candles and made a *Kiddush* over the wine. We also had a fresh *challah* from the local supermarket. Everyone enjoyed the get-together as if we had known each other for decades. After the Sabbath dinner we drove to Amon Park in Richland and walked along the bank of the Columbia River enjoying the clean fresh air and the tranquility. "You have a very tranquil life here, it is so quiet and beautiful," Vicki commented as a slim lady jogger passed us.

"Yes, I agree, and that is why we don't live in a big city," I replied. "The state of Washington is not very populated to begin with, so as you can see, we have a vast land here, with only six million of us populating it," I said. "Tomorrow we will drive to the synagogue for the Sabbath morning service and after a quick lunch at home I'll take you to the nuclear reactor where I work. You will see what I do for a living."

Batia and I rarely attended the Sabbath services, but Vicki and Jack wanted to see how a Sabbath service is performed by laymen and not by an ordained rabbi. "We are a small community comprised of different Jewish backgrounds, so we are not affiliated with any branch of Judaism. We are not Orthodox, Conservatives or Reforms so we run our services our way," I explained. After the service we rushed back home for a quick lunch.

I wanted to take them to the WNP-2 off-site facility and show them and Batia what I do at work. We had a tasty lunch and enjoyed my must-have strong espresso and headed to my workplace, twelve miles north. On the way there I made a short stop at one of the hills, or mountains as Vicki defined them, to give Vicki and Jack a view of the Tri-Cities area. It was very scenic and I am sure Vicki told her friends upon returning back to St. Louis that she climbed one of the mountains in the State of Washington.

Very few people where in the building when we arrived as it was the weekend. I showed them my three whole-body counting chairs and the computer that controlled them. I seated Vicki, Jack and Batia in the counting chairs and performed our ten-minute routine whole-body count. They were alarmed to see a few radioactive isotopes listed on their report. "Don't worry, the activity is low and coming from the ambient background." I let them look at the printout and then shredded it. I also showed them the radiochemistry lab and its instruments and explained why we needed it as a back-up lab to that at the plant itself. Vicki was impressed with what I was doing besides emailing my daily investment advice to her.

We returned back to my house and waited for the Leschen's friends from Seattle to arrive and we all went to one of the local diners for dinner. The friends from Seattle commented, "The Tri-Cities is unbelievably clean."

"What do you mean?"

"So far we have not seen a single graffiti carved or drawn on the walls here. People are very polite while driving," the husband explained so I told him he was more than welcome to move to the Tri-Cities. "We still have a three-hour drive back to Seattle so we better leave soon," the friend said so we went back to my house for Vicki and Jack to pick up their suitcases.

Vicki was very emotional when we walked with them to the friend's car. "We will never forget both of you," she said. "Sam, you don't know that you changed our lives. Please let's stay close and keep writing to me." Then she hugged Batia and said, "This is a personal present from me," and handed Batia a gold necklace. At first, I thought Vicki's words about me changing their lives was said at a height of an emotional storm soon to dissipate, but when she sent me a copy of an article from the January 9, 1994 issue of the *St. Louis Dispatch*. (Figure 16.4) I realized she really meant it.

r young son to Paul McCartney tickets on the "net."

ɔnnections on the
ɘr superhighway

aby.   understand.   community of the electronic highway   Vicki E.B. Leschen said her com-
Coun-   But to someone like Steven K. Rob-   "isn't a substitute for having friends   puter has opened up a "whole new
ional   erts, who lives a kind of nomadic exis- whose faces you know."   world" for her. A man from the state
ork)   tence on a strange-looking half-bicy-   Wendy Miller, 17, a Jefferson   of Washington whom she met via her
y free   cle, half-spaceship contraption with a County high school student, said she computer now helps her manage her
sers to   fully equipped computer, it is as com- has been communicating through   stock portfolio. He has inspired her to
d tele-   fortable as an overstuffed easy chair. computers for a year and a half. Her   turn back to Judaism, has given her
er the   "My home is the Net," Roberts   interest in sports, particularly hockey, up-to-date information on medications
           said in an article in the January edition led her to computer friendships with for her and her family and has even
d baby   of Internet World, a magazine that   high school students in Wisconsin, Ar- introduced her to a travel consultant
on-   deals with the developing Internet   izona, California, New Jersey, Vir-   who is helping her and her husband
seek   communications system.   ginia and Alabama. She said she has   plan an Israeli vacation.
other   "When I meet someone new in   since met some of these people, but   She has shopped for clothing, cho-
           physical space and I realize that we others she knows only through the   sen and mailed holiday cards and
d her   should remain in touch, I quickly warn computer. Still, she said, in some   found lost family members — all via
ig for   them that I cannot maintain an effec- ways she feels closer to them than   computer.
me up   tive relationship with anyone who is some of the friends she sees every day   "Why leave the house?" she said.
ping   not online — the meager bandwidth in school. Since she has been commu-   Joe C. Angert, owner of Apex soft-
row   of occasional paper mail and the an- nicating with them, she said, two have ware and a junior college instructor
con-   noyance of telephone tag are just too lost parents. Miller herself lost a   who writes a monthly column for a St.
           inhibiting."   friend in a car accident.   Louis County-based newspaper, the
t in-   Rheingold, author of the just-pub-   "I could come home, sit down at my   Personal Computer Journal, said that
the   lished book "The Virtual Communi-   computer and talk to them about it,"   while he is excited about the future of
           ty," said in a telephone interview that she said.   the new communications network, he
mem-   everyday people in everyday commu- Terry DeSmet, a computer pro-   is also worried.
an   nities are finding roofing contractors, grammer from West County, said she He said he is concerned at what the
and   automobile mechanics and schools for first began communicating via com- system may be doing to interpersonal
uthor   their children — all through their puter from her home in 1989, but it   relationships.
tual   computers.   wasn't until her husband was diag-   "We shouldn't be inside our homes
ople,   But possibly most importantly, he   nosed with cancer in 1992 that it   on a Sunday evening, chatting on bul-
reci-   said, they are finding community.   became a crucial link to the outside   letin boards," Angert said. "We
           "We have a hunger for communi-   world. Initially, she communicated   should be out on our front porches
now   ty," Rheingold said. "We've lost the with people on a cancer support line; talking to our neighbors."
l.   old town square, the corner grocery after her husband died in October, she Angert said the amount of informa-
r way   store. Our cities have become danger- began "talking" on a grief support   tion available on local bulletin boards,
puter   ous. There are people who want to   line.   through pay online services like
world   meet other people, connect with other "You realize there are other people CompuServe, Prodigy and America on
gy too   people and they're tired of going to who have gone through the same loss   Line, and through the Internet system
           bars."   that you have," she said. "You realize See COMPUTERS, Page 10
           Still, Rheingold said, the virtual you're not losing your mind."

> "Vicki E. B. Lechen said her computer has opened up a "whole new world" for her. A man from the state of Washington who she met via her computer now helps her manage her stock portfolio. He has inspired her to turn back to Judaism, has given her up-to-date information on medications for her and her family and has even introduced her to a travel consultant who is helping her and her husband plan an Israeli vacation."

Figure 16.4 Excerpt from January 9, 1994 issue of the
St. Louis Dispatch

We continued our daily email communication through the Prodigy Internet service and Vicki's investment portfolio kept growing. She and Jack became more involved with the *Aish HaTorah* activities and started practicing Orthodox Judaism. Next, they joined the *Aish HaTorah* tour to Israel. It made such a huge impact on them and they entertained the idea of moving to Israel upon Jack's retirement.

Unfortunately, only Jack fulfilled this dream, as Vicki died of cancer in 1998 at the age of 61. Jack, a widower, met a widow from *Aish HaTorah*, got married and they still live in Jerusalem. I write to him occasionally, and he already admitted that he has a better life living in Israel compared to the quality of life in St. Louis.

✡

Dark clouds started to hover over our head as early as January 1982 when the WPPSS board of directors stopped all construction activities on WNP-4 and WNP-5 at Satsop, Washington, located on the west side of the Cascade mountains. The board's decision was driven by the fact that the total cost for all WPPSS five generating plants was projected to exceed $24 billion.

These plants were not generating revenues forcing WPPSS to default on its $2.25 billion in municipal bonds. It was the largest bond default in American history. Only WNP-2 became operational, but the company started to tighten its belt.

Then on January 1, 1994 the North American Free Trade Agreement (NAFTA) was signed by Canada, Mexico and the USA, creating a trilateral trade block in North America. It pressured WPPSS to cut costs. Because of NAFTA, the constant threat to cut cost by layoff was real because the electricity generated by our WNP-2 nuclear reactor was not competitive and cost more per kilowatt to produce compared to generating turbines that ran on Canadian natural gas. Rumors about a massive pending layoff started flying around and turned out to be true when management informed us that they would evaluate manpower and decide who would be laid off. The ones selected to be laid off would find a letter to that effect on their desk on Monday morning. The company also scheduled an orientation processing meeting at the company headquarters to set the mechanism for the laid off employees to receive their unemployment benefit checks for the next thirty weeks. The company also offered a class on how to write resumes.

Batia and I had a large barbecue party in our backyard and invited many friends just to ease a bit the anxiety of the possibility of losing my job the next day. Then, upon showing up at my office my fears came true when I opened the envelope I found on my desk telling me that my job with the Washington Public Power Supply System was terminated. I was instructed to attend the company's termination and orientation processing meeting. No sooner than I finished reading my termination letter, my friend and colleague, Henry King, the company's meteorologist entered my office fuming like hell and showed me a similar letter he found on his desk. Our supervisor was not spared either, and got his letter as well. Overall, more than 300 exempt employees were laid off on that day. The only ones spared where technicians and members of other unions. All of a sudden the notion of being a union member became a very attractive advantage for me to consider while looking for a new job.

Seeing so many laid off people in one room commiserating together, was not a very pleasant setting. A few were close to retiring so did not agonize over it too much. A few others like my friend Henry King, were not too worried about it either as they were already getting their monthly pension checks after serving twenty years in the armed forces. But for most of us the layoff put a monkey wrench in our wheels.

There were some who could not resist the temptation to buy expensive toys like a new pick-up truck or entertainment center in their home, by liquidating their pension money and 401K plans. Not only did they lose their jobs but they had to pay the IRS 20% penalty for cashing their tax-deferred 401-K funds before the age of 59½ as stipulated by law. Henry King and I, avoided that temptation and rolled over our 401-K funds to a new self-directed IRA account that we opened at Perelman-Carley and Associates.

An unemployed placement center was established in Kennewick to help the newly laid off people locate a new job. The placement center had several advisers on its staff to help us tailor our resume. They also posted a list of open positions available nation-wide. The center also provided us with the use of computers, laser printers and a fax machine. I also used that office to satisfy the requirement stipulated in the regulations pertaining to my unemployment benefit check. The regulations required me to prove that I was actively looking each week for a job. Applying for the weekly unemployment check of $340/week, if I remember correctly, was a weekly ritual of going on the phone, each Sunday evening, answering the prompts and attesting to the fact that I was actively looking for a job. Visiting the unemployment placement center served this purpose.

Receiving the unemployment check was not an open-ended benefit; it terminated after thirty payments. However, I became aware of the fact that the NAFTA agreement stipulates that anyone who lost his/her job as a result of the agreement, was entitled to be trained in a different industry and search for a job in his/her new vocation. In that case, the government would pay for the tuition and the cost associated with it, such as textbooks and supplies and would continue sending the weekly unemployment checks until graduation.

I took that route and enrolled in the Columbia Basin Community College (CBC) and received an AA degree in Environmental Restoration Management Technology after finishing its two-year program. I suggested to my WPPSS supervisor who was also laid off, to take that plan and join me at CBC but he was reluctant, saying chemistry was not his forte. Nonetheless, he joined me after I promised to help him.

Batia and I tried to maintain normalcy during the time I was unemployed and a CBC student. I also continued making and selling my photographic and lithographic chemicals, but the volume started dwindling down as everyone was switching to digital photography and digital radiographic. This trend pushed the old fashion chemical processing industry to the brink of extension. We tried to keep ourselves busy as before. Batia volunteered for few organizations. Through one of them, Volunteer Chore Service, she volunteered, on some weekends, to clean houses/apartments for people who "were too rich to qualify to receive this needed help from the State or the Government, yet could not afford to hire someone to clean their house/apartment.

Chapter 17

Working for the US Department of Energy (DOE) at Hanford

B eing unemployed was a situation I knew too well. No one can prepare you, because each unemployment situation is different and occurs at different stages in your life. When you're laid off at an older age, you're not very attractive to potential employers.

I didn't have too much time to commiserate with my friends who were also laid off. I had three days before the start of my two-year program toward the AA degree in Applied Science, Environmental Hazardous Material Management at Columbia Basin College (CBC). I used those three days to reinvent my resume and tailor it to fit each open position I found.

I was forced to write many different versions of my resume after receiving a wide spectrum of replies that indicated, between the lines, that I was too old, overqualified or had a last name that they could not pronounce. With so many versions of my resume I had to introduce myself to myself, to make sure I knew who I was.

I don't know what kind of experience, mentally or emotionally, other people who got laid off undergo, but for me, it was a sobering, cruel reality. People and co-workers whom I considered to be my best friends seemed to disappear when I needed their support. At first, I was excited when one of my friends called. I hoped they had good news that they found me a job or a lead for me to contact. As the conversation progressed it became clear however, that they called seeking my advice on how to manage their investment portfolio. Others called to get advice on a new stock.

✡

I found going back to school interesting and I took it seriously. It was UC Davis all over again. I spent hours studying hard and shooting for the highest grades.

I was not the only one in the classroom who spoke English with a deep foreign accent. Dr. Jin, our Chemistry instructor, was a Korean native, who also spoke English with a heavy accent. Four of us did well in Dr. Jin's chemistry course, the rest of the students struggled and failed the tests, not because he was a bad teacher but simply because they did not take the time to prepare for the tests. They never blamed themselves for flunking the tests, they claimed they didn't understand his lectures because of his English. They were very vocal about it, and I was afraid they would complain about him to the dean of the science. To prevent this situation, I offered to tutor the vocal complainers before each test and the final exam to make sure they would pass. It worked.

One day when Dr. Jin dismissed us, he asked me to stay and talk to him. "I have a hunch you have a college degree, am I right?"

I confessed to having a Ph.D. degree, like him, and the reason I ended up studying for the AA degree. I requested that he keep the information confidential and not share it with my classmates. "Since you are a faculty member at CBC, please watch and let me know if there is an open position available," I asked him.

"I promise to do that. If you can provide me with a resume tailored for an instructor/lecturer position, I'll deliver it to Debbie, the Dean of the Science Department." I followed his advice and met Debbie at her office.

"Dr. Jin told me all about you and gave me a copy of your resume. It is very impressive," she said. "Unfortunately, we don't have an open position to offer you at the moment, but I am going to keep your resume on top of the file," she said, and I went back to the classroom.

My *pilgrimage* to the WPPSS placement center turned out to be a boring and discouraging routine. It never generated even the tiniest glimpse of hope that I would find a job through their services. Every time, I saw the same co-workers, desperate like me to find a job. Then I remembered that during my many visits to the UPS depot to ship my chemicals, I noticed that there was a food bank and employment placement services office across the street. It was operated by the Mormon Church.

"Good morning, sir," the man at the Mormon employment placement office greeted me. "My name is George Damian. This is a one-man-show, I volunteer my time and help members of our church find jobs. We also let them visit our food bank to pick items they need for their family until their situation improves. Our service is free but we expect the recipients to help during the harvest season. What brought you here today?"

I introduced myself and gave him a short summary of my situation as a newly unemployed person laid off from WPPSS. I mentioned my unsuccessful attempts to find a job through the employment placement center WPPSS established for us. "I am not a Mormon so I guess I'm not eligible to get help from your office."

"Sam, we help anyone who needs help and not just members of our church. By the way, you look familiar to me. I believe I see you jogging in the neighborhood where I live. What is your nationality?"

"I am from Israel." I noticed a gleam in his eyes.

"What a pleasant coincidence," George Damian said. "The Mormon Church just opened a new educational campus on Mount Scopus overlooking Jerusalem. In fact, the late Mr. Teddy Kollek, the Mayor of Jerusalem, was a great friend of the Mormon Church, and helped our church build the educational center, but that is beside the point. I have spent many years in the corporate world and gained plenty of experience with the job market. I would like to help you find a job. Why don't you come here tomorrow morning and bring a copy of your best resume."

The next morning, I brought a new version of my resume to George's office. "I omitted my Ph.D. title, should I put it back?"

"Yes, you should. I am going to enter your data and personal profile into our data base so that all the employers can access to your information. I need every small detail to be included." After entering the data, George glossed over my resume and made some suggestions for revising it, which I did the minute I got home. "I'll send an alert to the data base users that it was just updated and indicate that you are available. I'll keep you posted if a job opening comes up."

I visited his office frequently but unfortunately, he did not find a suitable a job for me. Nonetheless, it did not diminish my respect and appreciation for him as he was the only one who tried hard to help a total stranger and not even a member of his church.

I continued to visit the company's employment placement center to use their fax machine and laser printers, and I was still a full-time student at CBC.

✡

A year passed and no job offer came my way. I began doubting my self-worth. "See Sam, you're not that great after all," I kept telling myself. "No one shows interested in hiring you, no matter what version of your resume you send them." Then, on Friday, September 27, 1996, my phone rang around 6 p.m.

"Hi Sam, this is Debbie, the Dean of the Science Department, do you have a minute to talk to me?"

"It's Friday evening, I'm surprised you're still working. What is this all about?" I asked Debbie.

"Do you remember asking me to let you know when we had a teaching job for you? Well today is your lucky day as I have a job that matches your qualifications perfectly. I hope you will agree to accept it," she said and sounded a bit apprehensive.

"What is your offer?"

"I would like you to be our Biology 221.1 instructor teaching Human Anatomy and Physiology. Your students will be different from our regular students. This particular group is comprised of Tri-Cities first responders wanting to be certified as EMTs and paramedics. This class also includes the nursing school students as it is a requirement towards their certification. It is a two hour class twice weekly, followed by a two-hour lab twice weekly. I'm aware that you are a student halfway done with your AA degree, however, I trust that you can manage being a CBC student and CBC Instructor at the same time."

I felt good about her offer because I was asked to teach topics which I knew well. It also had the potential of becoming a permanent job at the Columbia Basin College (CBC). I told Debbie I would be honored to accept the offer.

"Great. I must tell you how this offer came about and why I'm calling you this late on Friday. Mrs. Francis, who taught the course for the last five years, called to say she left for California and is not coming back to Washington. I tried all afternoon to find a replacement. Then I remembered your inquiry about a teaching job. I am relieved that you are willing to take the job on such short notice. Thirty students are registered and waiting to take the course. Unfortunately, you don't have much time to prepare because the course starts in four days, on Tuesday October 1, at 4:00 p.m."

I was concerned by the lack of time to prepare the lectures, and anything else associated with the course. I asked Debbie, "I'm a full time CBC student myself. How am I going to find the time for all of this?"

"Here is my suggestion. Please don't attend your AA degree class on Monday morning. Just come to my office as I need to give you the textbook. I will also give you a copy of the syllabus Mrs. Francis handed to her students. I'm going to talk to your instructors and let them know I instructed you to skip their classes on Monday and the reason why. On Monday morning I'll show you the classroom and give you the key to the microscope cabinet. "So Sam, are you still willing to take the offer after all I've told you about the job? Please don't say no!"

I took the offer and discovered that it was more work than I bargained for.

Monday morning was hectic even though I skipped my classes as per Debbie's instructions. Textbooks and a tray of color slides were on her table for me to pick up. "These are all yours to use and here is the course syllabus Mrs. Francis used. You'll need to write your own and bring it to me tomorrow morning so we can make enough copies to hand out to your students.

"Here is the list of your students. Please verify they are present at each class. Since these classes are a prerequisite for the student's certification as EMTs, paramedics or nurses, skipping class is not allowed without my prior approval," Debbie warned me. "The first class and the lab are taught on Tuesday and Thursday each week, starting on October 1 and ending on December 10. Please make sure the dates listed in your syllabus are correct. If you feel you need some extra time to prepare, let me know and I'll tell your instructors that I suggested that you skip their class. I'm fully aware of the awkward situation you are in and appreciate that you accepted this assignment. I promise to return the favor in the feature. In the meantime, unless you have questions for me, I suggest you go home and start preparing the lecture notes for the first class and lab session tomorrow. I believe your first class and lab deals with cell structure and functions. A box with tissue slides for watching under the microscope will be ready for you on the podium. Good luck."

At home, I reviewed the chapter dealing with the cell structure and cell physiology and wrote my lecture notes, soon to become an attraction to my students as my notes were peppered with my comments in Hebrew.

Most of my students invested lots of time and effort to succeed in the course. They were working full time, some as fire fighters or members of the Hanford security forces, besides having their own families. One or two were not serious students and dropped after the first or second class. I wanted all of my students to successfully finish the course.

The formalin-preserved cats the students used to study the different parts of the body made teaching the two-hour lab session an olfactory challenge. My students chose their lab partners and each pair received one cat to use until the course ended. They had to wrap their cats at the end of the lab session and store them safely for the next session in a special storage room. The smell of formaldehyde (formalin) stuck to our hair and clothing and lingered for a long time.

As mentioned earlier, because of the very short notice by which I got that teaching job, I hardly had time to write my lecture notes for the one I was about to teach. Finishing writing the lecture was almost always completed half an hour before my class started. This half an hour included the driving time from my home to the classroom at CBC. It was extremely difficult not to speed a little bit.

There was nothing more rewarding than the final exam I gave them on December 10, 1996. The last student finished the final test around 6 p.m. I rushed home to correct the tests, and recorded the final grades. The next morning I went to Debbie's office to give her the form and the corrected tests for the students to pick up if they desired to do so. No one flunked the test; the average final score of that particular group of students was around 90%.

Debbie was very pleased with the job I did and the high grades my student received. "Now you can go back to being a full time student at CBC. I promise you'll hear from me again in the near future." I put the class and lab textbooks on her desk, ready to leave her office. "No Sam, these books are yours now as a token of appreciation for a job well done. Please take them with you. I'm sure you will use them again in the future."

I thanked her for the teaching job, "Have a Merry Christmas and Happy New Year."

Back at home I put all my lecture notes and syllabus in a large folder. "Who knows, maybe I'll need them again."

I finished my own studies at CBC and received the Associate Degree in Applied Science, Environmental Hazardous Material Management in August 1997. (Figure 17.1) I had to reinvent myself, write a new version of my resume and search for a job in the Environmental Hazardous Material Management field. Once again, no one contacted me with a job offer.

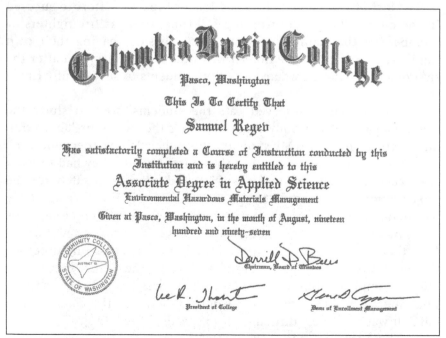

Figure 17.1 Associate Degree in Applied Science, Environmental Hazardous Material Management

✡

One of the problems I still faced was lack of medical insurance. I had to buy insurance for me and Batia. I reached a point where I no longer cared what kind of job I found as long as it provided medical/dental insurance. Desperation set in and before I knew it, I found myself affixing stamps to envelopes containing my application for janitorial jobs, night shifts included. Even that route proved to be completely barren. I received not even a single reply. I was even willing to go into exile and work on cleaning up the nasty hazardous chemicals left at Johnston Atoll, a 3200-acre island in the North Pacific Ocean. I applied for the open position they advertised but never heard from them.

The long period of being unemployed gnawed at my confidence. Thoughts of *What is wrong with me?* reverberated in my head and I started looking into other fields that might have something to offer. One day, while sitting in the doctor's waiting room, I noticed a patient talking to an interpreter and later discovered the interpreter was paid by the state to help the Spanish-speaking patients communicate in English. It made sense to become a Hebrew/English medical interpreter. I called the Washington Department of Social and Health Services (DSHS) for information and received a large package with the material I needed to study in order to pass their written and oral exams. The exams were designed to check understanding and familiarity with medical terms as well as translating correctly diagnostic report into plain English so the patients could understand. It also evaluated my ability to translate the patient's complaints. The patient described his/her symptoms, using a layman's language and terms, often peppered with slang words. My job was to convert what was said, into a medical version with the proper diagnostic terms the physician used. I passed both tests and got certified. (Figure 17.2) I wondered where the state found a medical doctor fluent in Hebrew to evaluate the quality of my interpretation.

I got my first medical interpreter job at a Portland, Oregon hospital's pediatric department. The pediatrician was scheduled to examine a toddler whose Israeli mother did not speak English. The doctor felt he needed an interpreter.

On the scheduled date, the pediatrician was on the phone introducing himself and asked me to talk to the young mother. I relayed back to him what she told me and used the correct medical terms applicable to her story and the symptoms she noticed. He asked questions, clarifying what she said, so I had to translate that into Hebrew and relay it to the young mother. We went back and forth until the pediatrician was satisfied and thanked me for my service. "Now I know who to call next time," he said.

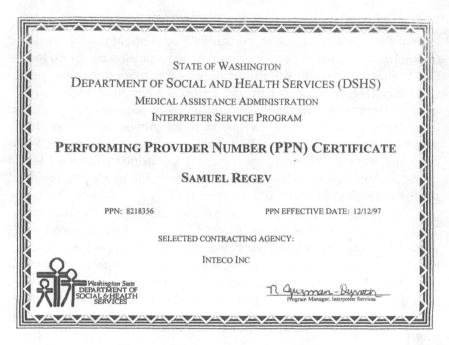

Figure 17.2 Interpreter certificate

"I will be more than happy to be of service to you." I continued to receive more orders for my services but most of the requests were for English translation of Israeli official documents such as marriage certificates, birth certificates, etc. Although these jobs were not exactly medically related, the state of Washington referred these cases to me as I was the only certified Hebrew/English translator at that time.

I was still looking for a job, a boring routine, to say the least, when my phone rang and Jane Wright, the wife of Bob Wright, who hired me at WPPSS was on the phone. Jane was a veteran registered nurse who joined the administration department at Kadlec Hospital in Richland. "Hi Sam, do you have a minute to talk?"

"Of course I have. You can call me anytime. What's up?"

"Well, I know that you're looking for a job. I believe I have something here at Kadlec that you should consider taking until something better comes your way. This job will provide you and Batia with medical coverage. Are you interested?" she asked, sort of rhetorically as she perfectly well knew I would accept it.

"Since you whet my appetite, what kind of job are you offering?"

"Our Medical Records Department needs someone to take charge of handling reports the physicians dictate for the transcribers.

You'll need to make sure they are transcribed and distributed to the applicable wards at the hospitals. These transcribed dictations are also needed by the Kadlec medical coders who read the medical procedure the doctor performed on the patient and the physicians' current procedural terminology (CPT) code. These CPT codes are needed for billing statements but for other purposes as well. Each procedure has its own unique code." Jane paused for a brief moment and asked, "Do you have any questions thus far or would you like me to stop right here because you are not interested."

"Just the contrary. I love talking to doctors about medical issues, and I'm sure I would like the job. Besides, any source of income will help. Is it a full-time job?"

"The job is Monday through Friday from 7:00 a.m. to noon. You will get medical coverage for you and Batia but no pension plan. Unfortunately, it is less than a forty-hour work week. Are you still interested?"

"Yes! Of course I'll take it," I exclaimed.

"Great. Please meet me tomorrow morning at my office. Bring your resume with you."

On Monday morning, Jane introduced me to Nancy, the Medical Records supervisor. Nancy glanced at my resume and said, "I know almost everything about you. Jane told me that you worked with her husband for fifteen years. Let me show you what kind of work we're doing here. I'll be thrilled if you accept. Hopefully, you won't turn it down after seeing all the commotion that is a daily occurrence in this department."

"Please don't worry about me. It will be great to interact with the doctors and from what Jane Wright described, I would like to accept your job offer."

"Wonderful! Let me introduce you to Mary, the lady you are replacing. Today is her last day, so unfortunately, there is not much time left to train you. Nonetheless, I am sure you will survive."

I filled out and signed all the paperwork associated with my new job. The Human Resources people took my picture and made my badge. "Using this badge at the cafeteria will give you a big discount on lunch or anything else they serve at the hospital," Nancy said. "I need to show you your daily route around the hospital. One of your tasks is to deliver the documents the nurses and the physicians need. The hospital has four floors served by four elevators."

"I would probably use the stairs and skip the elevators to stay in shape" I replied. "Anyhow, just for my curiosity, I would like to know why the morning shift starts at 8 a.m. whereas I must report to work at 7 a.m.?"

"Kadlec runs a same-day-surgery ward where minor surgeries and procedures such as colonoscopies, are performed as they do not require hospitalization afterwards. They start at 7 a.m. The physician performing a specific procedure comes to the Medical Records office first and dictates the H&P Report (History and Physical) describing the medical history and medical conditions of the patient. The dictation is then transcribed by our transcribing services into a hard copy. You should find these reports on your desk when you come to work at 7 a.m. You'll need to take them right away to the same-day–surgery staff. The doctor won't be allowed to start the procedure without that H&P Report," Nancy explained and looked at her watch. "It is getting late. Let's return to our office. I want you to meet Mary before she leaves. This is her last day with us so ask her as many questions about the job you can think of."

Mary was still sitting at the desk, soon to be mine, enjoying the chocolate cake her co-workers brought for the farewell party. "Hey Sam, hurry up and grab a piece of cake before it's all gone, then I'll show you how to run this kingdom," she suggested. The cake was indeed tempting so I nabbed a small piece and returned to my mentor. Mary looked in all directions to ensure no one was listening and whispered, "Sam, I don't like to rain on your parade, but this job has the potential to drive you crazy. Especially when most of the hospital beds are occupied, mostly towards the end of the calendar year."

"Why is that?"

"Towards the end of the year, people have satisfied their annual deductible. The end result is that everyone tries to squeeze as many procedures or treatments as possible before the current year ends," she explained and it made sense to me.

"Then, you have to deal with this damn phone ringing and 99.9% of time a receptionist from a doctor's office complaining that they have not received a copy of the doctor's dictation. Your *escape route* is to promise that you will personally see to it that they receive a copy today. I cannot overemphasize the need for you to use the word *personally* as it has some magical power to mitigate the crisis. A second later you'll receive a similar call from a different office but the complaint is the same. You will also find that some doctors are not easy to deal with. But let me stop at that because I don't want to depress you on your first day at work. Try to stay calm and take each crisis in stride. Good luck." She collected her personal belongings and left. I realized that my new job would not be easy but I consoled myself knowing that I had medical insurance for Batia and me.

✡

Watching the doctors' body language while they dictated their reports told me something about their personality as well as their professionalism. For example, the doctors who always came on time to dictate their reports, gave the transcribing service ample time to produce the written report.

Compare that to other doctors who were consistently late, forcing Nancy, our Medical Records manager to go after them. She was not shy to admonish them for delaying a procedure, especially the ones at the Same-Day-Surgery center.

I suspected that the "on time" doctors were more professional and better doctors. Another yardstick I used to judge the doctors was their behavior upon entering our office. I was willing to bet that those who always stopped to chat and thank us for our services before entering the dictation room, also had great bed-side manners and genuinely cared for their patients. A few of them behaved more like peacocks than physicians. One more specific group of doctors I liked were the ones from my synagogue. There were quite a few and they made sure to stop at my desk to chat before entering the dictation room.

The part of my job which I considered most rewarding was the access I had to the reports the physicians dictated detailing the medical procedures. With some patients, the primary doctor also sought the opinion of another specialist, so a Consultation Report accompanied their report. I felt that my past research work in academia provided me with an unbiased ability to judge the quality of the physician's reports. Using the quality of their dictated report to gauge the quality of their service was substantiated later on by talking to some of my personal friends who were Tri-Cities physicians. They knew personally, most of the doctors in the Tri-Cities and verified my theory.

There was one physician, Dr. Harry Towers, whom I liked the most. He was in a different league, way above of his peers. In my opinion he was a *mensch*. A *mensch* is a Yiddish term for someone of high integrity and honor, to be admired and emulated. Dr. Towers was relatively young, and listened to his patience concerns without lecturing. Professionally speaking, he had the reputation of being an excellent general surgeon who always called his patients at home to check how they were doing or allay their concerns.

Barbara Towers was a registered nurse by training and met Dr. Towers when they both worked at the same hospital somewhere on the east coast. They got married and moved to the Tri-Cities. He opened his own clinic and she became the manager of his clinic. She spent most of her time on billing. She needed to have copies of Dr. Tower's transcribed dictations as soon as possible so she could bill the patients or the insurance company. She was not a bit shy about raising hell if she did not receive the documents on time. In most cases it was the fault of staff members at the front section of our office. They were either too busy or overwhelmed with work. They just didn't get the chance to pick up the transcribed copies and distribute them to the doctors.

No one warned me about Barbara's wrath if she did not get the copies she needed. One morning I answered the phone, "Kadlec Medical Records office, Sam speaking, may I help you?"

"Who the heck is Sam?" Barbara Towers asked me. "I need to talk to Mary, please find her for me."

"Ma'am, from the sound of your voice I sense that you are mad at something but I am new here and took Mary's job when she quit. Please introduce yourself and tell me what the problem is. I would be more than happy to help you," I assured her.

"I am Barbara Towers, Dr. Towers wife and the manager his clinic. The Medical Records Department is constantly late delivering copies of Dr. Towers transcribed dictations. I need to have them on my desk every day. Mary promised to do so many times but it is still an on-going problem. It shouldn't be this way."

"Mrs. Towers, I will look into a way to resolve this problem but please give me a week to work on it since I just started working here."

"Well, I wish you luck. I hope that you are better than your predecessors," she replied and hung up.

The onus was on me to live up to the promise I made to her, so I developed a routine to assure Mrs. Towers received her husband's transcribed reports on time.

Seeing him in the dictation room prompted me to search the next morning for his transcribed report the minute I came to work. I pulled out all of Dr. Towers transcribed reports and put them in a special folder. If I had seen Dr. Towers dictating a report and the transcribed copy was not ready the next morning, I called the transcribing services to get an explanation as to why it was not ready yet. The system seemed to work well. Every day, I stopped at her office on my way home and gave her the folder with the documents she needed. Under my watch, all of her reports were delivered on time.

A week after I started personally delivering Dr. Towers reports, she thanked me for resolving her problem, "It's obvious from your last name and accent that you are a foreign national, so what is your nationality?"

You're right, I'm a native of Israel, and Hebrew is my language. I speak and read the Old Testament in its original," I replied almost like a tape recorder as I had been asked that question so many times before.

"Wow! How about that!!" she exclaimed. "Both Harry and I are devout Christians and would like to hear more about Israel and the Holy Land. I'll ask him to stop by your desk and introduce himself if you don't mind." She planted the seed for the warm relationship that followed. This warm relationship was augmented further because Dr. Towers was a good friend Dr. Robert Green. MD, my friend from the synagogue.

✡

Two weeks into my new job at Kadlec, I got a phone call, "Hi Sam, this is Debbie from the Science Department at CBC. Do you remember me?"

"Of course, I remember you. How are you, and what is this call all about?"

"Did you find a new job after you graduated from CBC?"

I told her about my job at Kadlec but I would quit in favor of a higher paying job at the first opportunity.

"There is a great shortage of nurses and paramedics in the Tri-Cities right now and CBC was asked to add an extra Biology 221.1, Human Anatomy and Physiology course that you taught during fall quarter 1996 and winter quarter 1997. All my biology instructors are teaching other classes. I called you to see if you are willing to bail me out one more time."

"I don't see any compelling reason to turn your offer down so when do you need me to start?"

"We need you to teach our 1998 spring and summer quarters. Are you available?"

I accepted her offer.

"Great!! The first class and its associated lab work assignment starts on April 1. Please come to my office ASAP to get the textbook for the class and the lab manual. You will need to write a new syllabus and change your lecture notes, because, unfortunately we changed the textbook for the lecture part of the course. When you come to my office you'll need to sign all the paperwork like we did last time except this time around you're getting a 10% increase in your salary."

"I always like getting a raise," I assured her. "I'm working at Kadlec until 12:30 p.m. every day so any time after 1:30 p.m. is convenient."

"So how about 2:00 p.m. at my office?"

I started teaching the Human Anatomy and Physiology course and the two-hour lab associated with it on April 1, 1998. Once again I had to squeeze myself between two daily activities, working at Kadlec and teaching at CBC.

I rewrote my lecture notes and incorporated the information I gained from reading the Kadlec doctors' transcribed reports into my lectures. It made the lecture more interesting and useful when I described to my students the medical problems unique to each organ, how they are treated, and the medical procedure(s) involved. On some occasions I was able to bring the MDs to talk to my students and answer their questions.

✡

Getting access to many transcribed copies of doctors' dictations through my job at the Kadlec's Medical Records department was a bonus for me. I learned valuable and practical medical information which I used later on, as a certified Medical Interpreter for the State of Washington Department of Social and Health Services (DSHS). I already had many medical textbooks at home, gifted to me by my MD friends when they replaced their old editions with up-to-date versions.

Still, the transcribed copies of the doctor's dictations were much better. Whenever I had questions about some medical issue or procedure discussed in a report, especially the ones dictated by Dr. Towers, I felt comfortable asking him for an explanation and he never turned me down. I reciprocated by answering all the questions he and his wife Barbara had regarding the Holy Land, modern Israel, and Judaism. Being very devout Christians it meant a lot to them.

✡

I didn't consider my job at Kadlec to be a long-term occupation as it did not pay enough to cover our expenses. Occasionally, I needed to borrow more money against my investment margin account. I kept sending out my resume but no employer replied.

Then, I got a phone call. "May I speak to Sam Regev."

"This is Sam, who is calling, please?"

"I am Jim Presley from Fluor Hanford Corporation here at the Hanford Reservation. I'm looking at your resume and I would like to talk to you about a potential job offer with us if you are interested."

"Wait a minute, Mr. Presley," I replied almost cutting him short, "I have so many versions of my resume, I no longer recognize who I am, would you please be kind enough to read a few lines from the resume so I recognize what Sam Regev you are interested in hiring?"

"The Sam Regev I am looking at is the one with fifteen years' experience at the WPPSS WNP-2 Nuclear plant. Are you still available or did you find a job?" Mr. Presley asked.

"I'm currently have a part time job at Kadlec hospital but I am available for a better paying job."

Jim Presley went on to explain a new project at Hanford called the Hanford Spent Nuclear Fuel Project (SNF) to be carried out at the Hanford K-Basins.

"The K-Basins are the DOE's largest collection of spent nuclear fuel, wastes, debris, sludge, and ion-exchange resins, etc., results of the defense-related nuclear activities associated mainly with the production of weapon plutonium. They have been stored for many years in metallic canisters, under water in a concrete–walled pool, very much like a swimming pool. The urgent issue right now is that these K-basins were built a few yards away from the Columbia River. The concrete walls started leaking. The contaminated radioactive water is migrating towards the Columbia River and the water table underneath the basins. We are heading toward a real environmental disaster. The Department of Energy (DOE) initiated this Spent Nuclear Fuel (SNF) project to remove the fuels, sludge and everything associated with it out of the pool. It will be followed by solidifying the liquid inside the pools and eventually demolishing the K-basin.

"Fluor Hanford was commissioned to do the project. We badly need health physicists and other people with radiation protection experience to work on the project. Fluor Hanford is willing to train candidates we deem qualified. The training involves six-months of classes, five days a week, eight hours a day with full salary and benefits, after which the candidates that pass both the academic and practical tests will be hired as full-time Fluor Hanford employees. Time is of the essence. Looking at your resume I'm sure you are a perfect candidate for us. Are you interested?"

When Jim concluded his rather lengthy explanation, I felt like a drowning person given a life jacket. I didn't think twice, "Yes sir. Please, count me in."

The wheels started moving fast after I accepted Jim Presley's offer. "Sam, as far as I'm concerned, you got the job so I am adding your name to the course roster. Unlike the candidates we already hired, you come with a different work background in line with the US Nuclear Regulatory Commission (NRC) requirements and not what the Department of Energy (DOE) requires. Hence we need to place some conditions to make sure we are offering the job to the right person. Here is the deal for you to consider: The job offer and participation in our six-month training course is contingent upon satisfying these conditions:

1. I am sending you the training book that deals with the academic aspects of the course i.e. calculus, chemistry, math, etc. You have one week to study the material on your own. You will be tested at our training center by one of the instructors assigned to teach this course. It is a two-hour test and you will get a phone call from them to schedule the date. The test starts at 10:00 a.m. You must pass with a 80% grade. There won't be a second chance to take the test. I gambled

on you passing it and scheduled a medical appointment for you at Kadlec hospital.

2. The appointment at Kadlec hospital is for a psychological evaluation to verify that you are mentally fit to work at the Hanford site. They will also draw blood samples to verify you are not using recreational drugs. As you can see, you must be *squeaky clean* to work for us.

3. Later on, after you pass the training and get your badge, a DOE inspector/detective will check your past and current work history. I trust that you don't have a checkered past that could disqualify you from getting Hanford security clearance.

"That's the gist of the requirements. Are you still interested?"

I reaffirmed my interest in getting the job.

"Great! I'll call you after you pass these three requirements."

The thick book dealing with the academic aspects of the six-month course, was delivered to my house the next day. I started studying right away as I was to be tested a week later. The book came with an official letter informing me of the date for the test, where to go and whom to contact. I was advised that although the test was a multiple-choice format, a great portion of it included problem solving questions that required calculations. The test was scheduled on the upcoming Monday 10:00 a.m. I took the morning off from my Kadlec job.

During the test itself, I took my time making sure not to make stupid mistakes and ruin my chances. When I finished, I handed the test to the trainer who proctored me. "It is almost lunch time so why don't you have lunch while I grade your test. Please be here at 1:00 p.m."

I came back at 1:00 and found the trainer smiling at me. "You did a great job, Sam, scoring 92%. The first hurdle is behind you, here are the documents you need to take to Kadlec for your drug test and the psychological evaluation. I'm sure you will pass them as well, so I expect to see you here when the course starts two weeks from today."

"Here is your book," I said. "I kept it clean and didn't mark on it so it is in its pristine shape."

"No, it is yours now and better keep it because it's the one we will use in the course."

I passed the drug test and the psychological evaluation. Two days later I received an official letter from Jim Presley informing me that I was admitted to the Fluor Hanford six-month course and would get my badge on the first day of class. The timing was perfect as it provided me with the two-week advance notice to let the Kadlec Medical Records department know that I was quitting my job.

Starting the six-month Fluor Hanford Health Physic/Radiation

Protection course presented me with an opportunity to learn a new vocation but most importantly it paid well and provided medical insurance. My classmates had already been working as Radiation Control Technicians (RCT) at different DOE sites across the country or served as RCT's on the US Navy nuclear submarines. Still, Fluor Hanford needed more RCT's keeping Jim Presley busy looking through the pile of resumes on his desk. Almost every day a new student joined our group. The trainers did not mind that the newcomers missed the earlier classes because all of them were already working as RCT's someplace else.

We became a close-knit group and worked together at the K-West Basin upon graduating from the course. Graduation required passing two major exams, each lasted about 1½ hours and required quite a bit of calculus. The first test was centered on the academic portion of the course, similar to the test I took after studying the textbook for one week. It was given in the morning. The second two-hour test was given in the afternoon and centered on the instruments required on the job, how to use them, and how to perform the daily QA tests before using them. It also dealt with the site-specific characteristics of the K-Basins. Here too, the passing grade was set at 80% or higher. We all became Fluor Hanford employees on a ninety-day probation, after which we became full-fledged K-West Basin workers. The K-Basins were the farthest site at Hanford, almost an hour drive in each direction so we formed carpools.

We were issued our Hanford badges that we had to show the security guards. A Department of Energy security clearance was required to work at most of the sites inside the reservation, the K-Basins included. My classmates received their clearance the day their badge was issued as they worked at different DOE nuclear sites prior to joining Fluor Hanford.

My situation was more complicated. The first inkling I got indicated that I was treated differently than my co-workers. They were sent inside the K-West basin to work while I was left in the office area, taking care of our instruments and monitors.

Then one day someone knocked on my door at home, showed me his FBI badge with his picture and said he came to interview me as part of the security requisites associated with hiring me. He took a seat on the sofa and started to ask me questions. He had a copy of my resume, provided by Jim Presley. Every once in a while he consulted my resume. "Just to let you know, I already talked to all of your neighbors, even the ones you hardly know. I also talked to people down the street a few blocks, like the houses next to Sunset View Elementary school. I have plenty of information about you already. Do you want to change any input you gave me today or should I write my report to the DOE's Hanford Security Department."

"No changes to what you heard from me today," I replied. "But what should I expect next?"

"You will probably get a phone call from the DOE's security people at the federal building in Richland to let you know about their decision regarding your L-Security Clearance."

A few days later I received a confidential letter from the DOE Hanford Security Department informing me that their background check did not reveal any troubling information to prevent them from granting me the L-Security Clearance. Nonetheless they were temporarily withholding their final approval in order to look further into my case because I was a *binational* holding citizenship of both the USA and Israel. The letter instructed me to call for more details. Once again I found myself at the brink of losing my job.

I called the number listed in the letter, talked to a nice lady and requested an explanation as to what their problem was and what I needed to do to resolve it. "I don't understand why having dual citizenship is troublesome for you. You already investigated me inside and out along with taking my finger prints. The FBI agent checked me out, talked to my entire neighborhood and could not find any incriminating evidence against me, so what's the hold up?"

"The problem is that you need the L-Security clearance so you can work at the Hanford site, unescorted. Don't forget, the Hanford site is the place where the plutonium was produced for the atomic bombs," she explained. "We are not going to instruct Fluor Hanford to terminate your employment. You could still do your job as long as you are escorted by someone with the L-Security clearance. However, since you are on a ninety-day probation period, I am afraid Fluor Hanford might deem you a liability and terminate your job at the end of the probation period." She spelled the cruel reality about to haunt me.

"So do you have any suggestion for me in order to allay your concern and grant me the clearance."

"The best solution is for you to renounce your Israeli citizenship. We would need an official document from Israel that you did so before granting you the L-security clearance".

Her instructions hit me like a brick, I was speechless and there was a long silence on my side of the phone line.

"Are you still there, sir?" she asked, bringing me back to the real world.

"Yes, I'm still here but I don't know how to do what you are asking me to do. Please give me some time to find out from the Israeli government how to renounce my Israeli citizenship. I will call you back with the update the minute I have the information."

There I was, a person born to parents who believed in the Zionist idea of immigrating to then Eretz Israel/Palestine. They endured the dangerous ordeal sailing on board of the dilapidated ship Parita. (See Chapter 3.) They escaped the horrors of the Holocaust while their families were murdered by the Nazis. Then Israel was founded, survived its Arab enemies and became a safe haven for the Jewish people. I did not see my father for more than a year when he was fighting during that war. I fought as a paratrooper for Israel survival in the 1967 Six-Day War. Now the DOE security people wanted me to renounce my Israeli citizenship. It was an overpowering dilemma.

I had only two choices, either refuse to renounce my Israeli citizenship or renounce my citizenship in the country I loved so much. And I had to face the harsh reality that I was not the only player in that drama. I had a family to support as well as providing my children with college education and a chance for a better future. Moreover, I was getting older so it behooved me to keep the job I just got, stay with it until retirement and earn the fixed income from the company pension. My new job sounded very attractive because it was a union job and I still remembered that 300 exempt employees like me who were laid off but not the union members at WPPSS.

The moment of truth finally came when I told Batia about my painful decision to go along with the DOE security department requirement. I would renounce my Israeli citizenship and get the L-Security Clearance I needed for my job. I called their office to let them know I was willing to comply. "I need to contact the Israeli consulate in San Francisco and get their instructions on how to do it."

"You better do it fast because we are not sure how long Fluor Hanford will be willing to employ you without the L-Security Clearance."

I called the Israeli consulate in San Francisco to explain my situation. I don't know what possessed me to turn on the answering machine and record the conversation while we talked. When the guy from the consulate asked the reason for calling, I felt like a traitor, but I managed to explain my dilemma. "I was just hired at the US Department of Energy at the Hanford reservation, after five years of unemployment. That site is associated with plutonium nuclear weapons. My employer told me to renounce my Israeli citizenship, or I would be laid off. Please give me the instructions on how to do that. I have no other choice but to go along with their demand." I explained, almost apologizing to the guy who answered my phone call.

"Mr. Regev, please tell your employer that Israel does not take renunciation of its citizenship lightly," he told me in a very authoritative voice. "First of all, we don't do it via the phone or the mail. You need to appear in person here in San Francisco, or at any other Israeli consulate in the USA. You can also travel to Washington DC and do it at the Israeli embassy there. This is a very long interview that must be done in person. Then it takes six months or even longer for the Israeli interior ministry office to review your case and make a decision. I cannot give any precise timeline. You should relay this information to your employer."

Next, I called the DOE Security department informing them about my attempt to renounce my Israeli citizenship. "I am aware that you want this to be done as soon as possible but I just got off the phone with the Israeli consulate in San Francisco and found out the process is complex and time consuming. First, I must be there in person for a lengthy face-to-face interview after which, they will send the recoded interview and the documents to the Israeli Ministry of the Interior to approve or disapprove my request. It would take at least six months or longer. I have my conversation with the consulate in San Francisco recorded on a tape to back me up. I am still willing to go along with your directive and renounce my Israeli citizenship. However, it requires a 1,474 mile round trip on my part as they want me to appear in person. The trip would require at least one night at a motel plus meals. Are you going to reimburse these expenses?" I said to my contact at the DOE Security office.

"Well, let me pass this information to the manager of our department, and we'll contact you soon. In the meantime, continue to doing your job at the K-basin."

"Just to let you know, I will be in training in Richland for the next three days so please ask the secretary there to page me if you need to contact me."

During my second day at the company's training center, the receptionist came into the room and gave the instructor a small note. "Sam Regev, you are needed at the office," he said and waited for me to leave the classroom.

All eyes followed me as if I was a convict on his way to the gallows. When I entered the office, the same FBI agent that did the background inspection was waiting for me.

"Good morning Mr. Regev" he said while shaking my hand. "I need to wrap up my report. Let's go to the conference room so we can talk." He led me to conference room he'd prearranged with the secretary. "Just to let you know, in addition to talking to residents in your neighborhood, I also talked to your instructors, classmates, supervisors and co-workers. So far there is nothing negative or alarming about you to prevent hiring you. Besides, you already spent fifteen years at the WNP-2 nuclear generating plant. Your managers there spoke highly of you, and the

Nuclear Regulatory Commission gave you clearance to work there and get access inside the reactor itself. I feel that I have all the information I need to write my report and submit it to the DOE Security Department. You should hear from them soon. Thanks for your corporation and patience. Sorry to take you out in the middle of your class. Good luck with your job."

I was puzzled; he didn't mention anything about renunciation of my Israeli citizenship and I didn't raise the issue either.

A few days later a confidential letter came from the DOE's Hanford Security Department instructing me to go to the Hanford Badging building with my current Hanford ID badge. "A new Hanford ID badge marked with L-Security Clearance has been granted," the letter said. From that moment on I was allowed to do all my tasks, unescorted.

This coveted badge adorned my chest for the twelve years that followed until I retired from Hanford in 2012. No one ever mentioned my dual citizenship. The only time my Israeli citizenship came up was when I planned to visit Israel. I was required to meet with the DOE security officer. I had to meet with them again upon returning from the visits. This requirement applied to anyone visiting a country that was on the DOE list of *sensitive countries*. These were pleasant chats, as most of my interviewers had been to Israel while serving in the US military.

I loved my Hanford job very much. When I worked as a Senior Health Physicist at WPPSS WNP-2, I complained about wearing a suit and tie. My job at the Hanford site required me to wear all kinds of strange outfits. (Figure 17.4)

I gained many friends while working there, some of them became friends for life. I had the pleasure of helping my co-worker with investment advice and building their 401-K portfolios or their brokerage accounts. They are still seeking my advice.

My daughter, Shir, who also works there as RCT (Radiation Control Technician) keeps relaying their regards to me. It is heartwarming when she says, "I took the xyz course today and John Murphy took the class too. He asked me how you were doing and sent his regards." She gave us her tickets to the company's annual Christmas party. It gave me the opportunity to meet my friends who were still working there and reminisce about the old days when we all worked together.

The most important impact of my twelve-year tenure at Hanford were the overtime hours I worked there, close to 1300 hrs/year. As mentioned earlier, being without a job for five years forced me to borrow money against my margin account. It was a substantial amount and the many hours of overtime at Hanford bailed me out of that debt and provided me with a smooth financial sailing into my "Golden Years."

Figure 17.4 A few examples of the strange outfits
Hanford required me to wear

Chapter 18

The Moldy Bread

Another Monday and the beginning of a new work week. It was my turn to drive the van pool the eighty-mile round trip from home to our trailer MO-438 at the Hanford reservation. We usually arrived early each day leaving enough time for those who were too lazy to get up early enough to cook breakfast before leaving for work. When we arrived, Cindy Linn, the *Mother Superior* of our trailer was determined that our two refrigerators were in dire need of cleaning which meant getting rid of the *old stuff*. The refrigerator doors were wide opened while she checked the expiration dates and shot the expired items into the garbage bin. I inspected what she threw out and retrieved the items I felt would be a crime to waste.

My aversion toward throwing food in the garbage has been part of my personal life experience. For example, my practice of never paying attention to expiration dates, goes back to my time as a penniless foreign student at the University of California at Davis when I browsed the contents of garbage cans in the neighborhood fishing for food. (See Chapter 8.)

✡

During my childhood, following the War for Independence, there was a severe food shortage. Existing farms had been ravaged by the war or the farmers fought instead of running their farms. The period of food shortages has become to be known as *T'kufat Hatzena,* the austerity period.

Food shortages forced the new government to ration basic and staple food by using coupon books. The coupons represented your allotment for the specific food for that time period and were clipped by the owner of the grocery store where the food was purchased. Meat was purchased at the butcher shop using a different coupon book. The meat ration, for the general public was very small but a bit larger for those whom the government deemed as hard laborers, construction workers for example. The distribution of the ration coupon books was controlled against fraud. Verification of distribution was done by stamping your ID Card with a special stamp.

In spite of the difficult food shortage and the fair distribution of whatever food was available, the government did its best to maintain our nutrition. It provided us with vitamins and fish oil to be taken daily. I still have the funny after taste of the *Bevitex* chewable vitamins lingering in my mouth.

Sugar was very scarce forcing the government to supply us with cans of molasses instead. When the molasses also became scare, we had to use saccharine. Just to think about it's bitter after taste still makes me shiver. Forget eggs and milk; we saw them in pictures in magazines and books but never on our table. We had to settle for milk powder and powdered eggs supplied through the ration coupon books. I still vividly remember my attempts to make an omelet causing the oil in the frying pan to spatter all over the kitchen because I added too much water to the powdered eggs, teaching me my first lesson in chemistry, namely that water and oil don't mix. The powdered eggs never tasted good.

And there was the help from the American people who were and still are most generous people on earth, willing to help other people in need across the globe. Thanks to their generosity, we munched on cheddar cheese and enjoyed butter. The cheese was distributed to the store in large round cardboard containers very much like you see nowadays in the bulk food section of large supermarket in the USA. These cardboard containers had the US Foreign Aid logo of *shaking hands* printed on them so we knew who to thank. The butter was distributed as ½ pound bricks. It was salty as my poor mother found out the hard way trying to bake a cake for the Sabbath using the American butter.

Oftentimes, American taxpayers complain about *wasting* tax dollars on foreign aid but from my personal experience and the Israelis who lived through the food scarcity following the War for Independence, the generosity of the American people has not been forgotten.

As mentioned before, meat was very scarce, so the government made herring available as a relatively inexpensive source of protein. It came from Norway in oak barrels similar to the ones used by wineries. The fish inside those barrels where *swimming* in muddy brine. The herring purchased at the grocery store was so salty, it had to be soaked in water to leach out the salt. Paper products were in short supply during the austerity era and many years after, so it was customary for the owner of the grocery store to wrap the salty herring in old newspaper. No matter how careful I tried to be, it always dripped on my clothes all the way home. I smelled like an owner of the largest fish stand at the Seattle famous Pike Place market. Wrapping the smelly herring in newspaper was not only a way to save on an item of short supply but it found its way into the folklore of the new nation and a way to critique journalists and their articles. So if you did not like an article you just read or wanted to take issue with the journalist who penned it, you would say that the article and the paper it was printed on was good only for wrapping herring.

To sweeten our life with deserts, the government rationed cans of various fruits packed in heavy syrup. The most popular fruits were peaches, pears and my favorite, figs. The canned figs were imported from South Africa. I was addicted to these fruity deserts.

✡

I have described the food shortages I experienced just to shed some light on the reason for being a scavenger of the garbage can at Trailer MO-438 when Cindy did her refrigerator cleaning ritual. She was happy when the refrigerators were glowingly clean and I was happy salvaging whatever I dimmed valuable. One day however, the refrigerator cleaning ritual was a bit different as she tossed a loaf of French bread into the garbage. I fished it out. "Why are you doing that?" she exclaimed. "Don't you see how old and moldy it is?" Cindy lambasted at me in disbelief.

I told her that I can't see people tossing bread into the garbage as it makes me emotional. I was not capable of elaborating but promised to explain in the future.

I am doing so now.

As far back as I can remember, bread was a special item in our house, almost a sacred, treated with the utmost respect. My parents conversed mostly in Yiddish or Polish. Polish was the preferred language when my aunt and uncle were visiting so I picked up a few words of these two languages. They either used the Yiddish word *Broit (Broyt)* or the Polish word *Chl'eb* (bread).

My father's childhood close friend from the Polish town of Góra Kalwaria, Yehezkel Goldberg was, by vocation an accomplished artisan baker who immigrated to Israel a few years before my father. Yehezkel Goldberg became a member of the *Achdut* cooperative which was the largest bakery cooperative in Tel Aviv. He was a short man with a big heart and a true friend of my father's, always making sure that fresh hot bread was delivered to us either by a friend or his son Dovik. Fridays were special treats as he baked Challah for our Sabbath.

At times he got creative and made a round loaf with big pieces of onions embedded in the soft crust. My father had a ritual whenever he sliced a loaf of fresh bread. He made a tiny cut on one edge of the bread before slicing pieces. To this day I don't know where this ritual originated or what it meant yet it has been ingrained in my mind ever since. Perhaps it was a symbolic act of sharing bread with your hungry and less fortunate fellowman.

My mother had a worship-like attitude toward bread. To her, throwing bread into the garbage was a crime against humanity. Any leftover beard that became rock hard was grated into crumbs and sprinkled onto whatever was sizzling in the frying pan. The moldy pieces were fed to the birds. She had vivid childhood memories of winters in Poland where the ground froze and vegetation was covered with heavy snow making it hard for the birds to survive. She fed the tiny creatures during the harsh winter and drilled this practice into my tiny head while I was growing up.

✡

Allow me to digress a bit and tell you another story related to the moldy bread issue. It is about Yula, a Holocaust survivor whom I knew very well while growing up. She arrived in Israel with her son and daughter right after the War for Independence. She lost her husband and all of her relatives during the Holocaust. The only familiar face she found in Israel was my father as they came from the same little Polish town of Góra Kalwaria. My parents tried to help her adopt to her new homeland.

I still remember my first encounter with Yula, a small-stature lady with blond hair who spoke *Yiddish* with a noticeable lisp. She had a great affection for my father.

As a child I noticed that other survivors from Góra Kalwaria showed a measure of coldness toward Yula. There was an implicit accusation in the air blaming her for the death of her husband.

Yula, her husband Yanek, and their two small children, Yoseph and Chana, were hiding in the attic of a ghetto building. They were starving while the situation deteriorated by the minute. Chana, the youngest child was crying, non-stop, pushing Yula to the brink of losing her mind.

Then, one morning as she peeked through the window, she noticed a moldy loaf of bread on the garbage heap in the alley. No one in their right mind would even contemplate consuming this moldy bread. But at that moment the moldy bread was her *mana* sent from heaven. She asked her husband to go outside and snatch it from the garbage heap.

He declined at first, knowing with 100% certainty that he would be shot but the crying kept on and so did Yula's determination to have that loaf of bread. Yula begged him until he finally submitted.

It was getting dark and he prayed that no one was watching. He finally reached the garbage pile, grabbed the bread and hid it under his heavy coat. He was heading back towards their hiding place when a single gunshot pierced the eerie silence and echoed through the buildings. He fell to the ground. A streak of blood gushing from his head painted the white snow red.

Poor Yula was watching and realized that her life had changed forever. She was left alone with hungry children. She did not believe she would survive this horrible war.

I don't know how Yula's children managed to survived but Yula was caught and sent to Auschwitz. Eventually they were brought to Israel.

Starting a new life as a widow with two small children in Israel was difficult for Yula who did not speak or read Hebrew. She could communicate in Yiddish or Polish but not with the young *natives*, born in Israel who spoke Hebrew.

Everyone who just immigrated to Israel was called either as *ole hadash* (Hebrew for new immigrant) or by the nickname *yarok* (Hebrew for green).

It is noteworthy that with so many immigrants from all over the world, Hebrew was spoken with at least seventy different accents. Numerous daily newspapers published in these languages kept the new immigrants informed.

Yula's broken Hebrew made it difficult for her to perform daily errands such as going to the grocery store or the *souk*, (Hebrew for open market) to buy food. Most difficult of all was going to the government office in charge of allocating and distributing the monthly ration coupons so she always came to my parents for help. My parents were busy at their own jobs so they delegated the task to me. I accompanied her during shopping trips and helped her get her monthly ration coupons.

Children can be cruel at times and mock their cohorts for activities not considered *cool*. My friends never missed an opportunity to ridicule me for accompanying what they called "that Yiddishe (slang for Jewish) lady" instead of playing with them. So one day I confronted my parents protesting the roll of being Yula's *babysitter*. "She is a grownup lady. Not a baby," I protested.

In doing so I put my parents through a difficult dilemma forcing them to share with me another painful fact about Yula's complex personality. The trauma of seeing her husband killed by the German soldier triggered a lifelong paranoia. She believed she was being followed by the Nazis who won't stop until they killed her. She was living in Israel by then, free and far away from the Germans, yet in her mind, the Holocaust continued and Germany was still undefeated. My parents told me that I was Yula's *bodyguard*, protecting her from the Nazis. This was a huge burden and difficult for me, an elementary school student, to comprehend.

Accompanying Yula to the office distributing the ration coupon books was the most difficult for me. She was a nervous wreck before we even boarded the public bus heading downtown were the office was located. Once on board the bus she would gaze in all directions looking for the Nazis she believed were there to kill her.

This sad ritual repeated itself at every bus stop along the way as passengers got off and on. She inspected each one from head to toe. For the brief moments when she wasn't watching for Nazis, she looked frantically at the very large wrist watch she wore on her thin arm. It had been retrieved from her husband's body by a friend who was a member of the Jewish crew tasked with removing the bodies of Jews who died of starvation, diseases or execution. When he too was brought to Israel after the war, he gave her Yanek's wrist watch.

She feared we would be late, the office would be closed and then what?

At first I didn't pay too much attention to Yula's gazing at her watch but after several visits to the ration coupon distribution office, I noticed that the watch always showed the same time. Finally, it occurred to me she had never rewound it. Perhaps it was her way of expressing the sad reality that their normal lives ended at the moment he was murdered.

Yula had her own unique way of gazing at her watch every time we were entering the distribution office. She would roll up her sleeve just enough to expose the watch. Still, it was wide enough for me to notice that her skin was as white as a fresh snow indicating to me that she avoided exposing her skin to the sun. Then, on a hot, muggy summer day while we were on our routine visit to the coupons distribution office, she was sweating profusely. I asked, "Yula, why don't you take off this long sleeve sweater or at least roll up the sleeves. There is no need to torture yourself."

"Oh, no, no, no! *Shmulikoole* (nickname she invented just for me). You don't understand that, but it is hard for me to do what you suggest I do." And then she rolled up her left sleeve exposing enough of her arm to show me the rather long number tattooed into her skin. She was no longer a human being but German property with a SERIAL NUMBER very much like a serial number engraved on products in a production line. "I am ashamed of this number," she told me, "It brings too much bad memories and agony so that is why I don't roll up my sleeves and exposed it, *Shmulikoole*."

She always called me *Shmulikoole* instead of my Hebrew name *Shmuel*, after the biblical prophet Shmuel (Samuel). One of the most common derivatives of the name Shmuel is *Shmulik*. But for Yula, addressing me as *Shmulik* was not sufficient to express her deep appreciation. It was a token of, "Thank you" for my willingness to be her *bodyguard*. I guess that in her mind, I must have done a great job as nothing bad happened under my watch.

My *Shmulikoole* heydays are gone now and Yula is gone too but every once in a while *Shmulikoole* still reverberates in my ears. My wife Batia calls me *Mulik* which is her way of expressing affection but I have to work hard and be supper nice to earn her *Mulik*.

✡

The years flew by, and Israel's financial and economic situation improved dramatically. Agriculture developed making rationing a thing of the past. Israel became Europe's main supplier of fruits and vegetables, sent daily via air cargo.

During my stint in a *kibbutz* (agricultural farming community) we grew bananas and shipped them to Europe from the city port of Haifa at least three times a week. To my knowledge, this export is still going on today. Israel's big advantage is that the Jordan Valley and Arava regions have near-tropical weather while Europe has its cold snowy winter.

With the end of food rationing and Yula's learning Hebrew, I was no longer needed as Yula's bodyguard.

However, Yula didn't notice the tremendous improvement in the quality of life in Israel, its social life, or the abundance of food. Her paranoia worsen bringing her to the brink of mental break down. Not only did it destroy her mentality but also financially as she would sell an apartment she had just bought and buy another one in a different location. This selling and buying cycle repeated itself losing money in each real-estate transaction. A big chunk of the reparation money she received from the German government for her Holocaust ordeal was almost gone because of it. Eventually she convinced herself that there was no place in Israel safe enough for her to hide from the Nazis so she sold her last apartment, packed some of her belongings and left for the United States. Hanna, her daughter did not join her as she was already married with her own family in Israel.

Yula's son Yoseph, could not come with her as he was still doing his mandatory service in the Israeli Army as a heavy truck driver. He used to spend nights with us whenever his job assignment brought him to Tel Aviv. Upon his discharge, he joined Yula in Chicago. He attended college and upon earning a law degree, he moved to California and became a lawyer. My wife Batia and I met him in 1969 in Chicago. He was still a bachelor. We did not maintain contact with him and lost his whereabouts.

Yula's immigration to the USA did not provide her a sense of security. She still believed that the Germans were after her and won't stop until they killed her.

Her paranoia got even worse. She sold her new house and bought another one in a different state, still losing money in the process.

My wife and I witnessed for ourselves one of her real estate transactions. We were on our way from New York to Davis California and stopped at her new house in Chicago. Tired from the long bus ride, we decided to take a short afternoon nap. We were asleep when the door opened abruptly and Yula entered with potential buyers inspecting the room and us as well. We hopped on the next Greyhound bus available and headed for California.

My memories of Yula were triggered by various scenes, like a homeless person sleeping on a bench. There were several homeless people at the park but this particular homeless man had adopted one bench and made it his home. He usually slept there and I saw his toes sticking out through the holes in his sucks. That bench became his specific spot under the sun. More fortunate members of society have homes and usually driveways to park cars but the homeless man claimed ownership of that spot by parking the shopping cart he *borrowed* from the supper market. His cart was filled with the items he salvaged from the garbage cans he encountered along his daily route— his work day. On rainy days he took cover under the cardboard box he snatched from the back of a furniture store. I had empathy for him and often wondered what brought him to homelessness.

I was silently furious, when I saw him browsing through a garbage can where he found half a loaf of bread, then threw it back in utter contempt because it was moldy.

"Wait a minute," I muttered to myself, "I knew a woman who didn't have the luxury of wasting a moldy loaf of bread. Her husband lost his life while trying to recover it to feed his hungry children. Please treat this moldy bread with the utmost respect."

In my favorite park along the river next to my hometown, Kennewick, Washington, I watched flocks of gulls or geese fighting for every crumb of bread, moldy or not. What a gorgeous day and a lively show of Mother Nature. On moments like that I am sure that my late mother, God bless her soul, is watching me from her heavenly kingdom above where all its residents are hovering around above the clouds flipping their white wings, making sure that I follow to the letter the *commandment* she ingrained in me, *never* throw bread, fresh, moldy or in between, in the garbage.

It is ironic that bread almost killed my mother. In her early sixties she started losing weight at an alarming pace. She looked like a survivor of the Holocaust concentration camps. Mostly skin and bone. At first the doctors could not pinpoint the diagnosis. Then one doctor with the gift of attention to detail suspected that she had developed a malabsorption syndrome where her digestive system had become allergic to gluten, the main protein in flour made from wheat, barley and the like. This autoimmune reaction kept killing the cells in her digestive system responsible for absorbing the nutrients her body needed. No wonder she was suffering weight and muscle loss during those years of missed diagnosed, *celiac disease.*

Her doctor ordered her to stop eating any kind of bread or flour products containing gluten. I am sure that it was torture for her, but she started gaining weight and came back to being herself.

It was so difficult for her, especially when the yeasty smell of freshly baked bread wafted through the streets of Tel Aviv. She cheated occasionally like the poor kid caught with his hand in the cookie jar.

✡

Well, every story must end, including my "Moldy Bread Story" augmented by my personal accounts of food scarcity during various periods of my life. This story was began when I witnessed moldy bread being tossed into the garbage by a dear friend while she cleaned our refrigerator at work. Telling the story has rekindled different moments in my life that were ingrained in my mind. As I grow older I often wonder who I am, who I was or how I would like to be remembered. I am getting confused.

For my parents I was *Moo-Li-Le.*

For my friends and the public in general I was *Shmuel, Samuel or Shmulik.*

For my dear wife I was *Mulik* and for my dear children Raz and Shir I was simply *Aba.*

And there was Yula, who called me *Shmulikoole* as I protected her from the Nazis she believed were trying to kill her.

As for how I define myself—I am simply a salty teardrop in the Ocean of Humanity.

Chapter 19

A Vineyard Story

My maternal great grandfather, Rabbi Fiebush Lipka was an ordained Orthodox rabbi, the religious leader of the Jewish community in Golub-Dobrzyń, Poland. Historically, Dobrzyń, was a part of Poland. The Golub section, however, was a Polish territory until it was conquered and annexed by Prussia. Later on, it was retaken by Poland. The Jews of Golub-Dobrzyń, were engaged in the lumber, wheat and grains commodity trade and the fur business.

My great grandfather was also a successful businessman, well versed in mechanical engineering and excelled in business administration and management. His business knowhow was the equivalent of our modern day MBA. His first business project was to purchase timber forests, build a lumber mill, and cut his trees into lumber. He built and owned grain silos and flour mills that served the city and its nearby communities. My great grandfather also built, owned, and operated the city and surrounding areas' only electric power plant. As he grew older, he delegated the responsibilities of running the family business empire to his two sons—my grandfather and my mother's uncle. But he remained the community's sole Rabbi.

My great grandfather was a practicing Zionist, who firmly believed that the Jews living in the diaspora, and Poland in particular, should return to their ancestral homeland in what was then known as Palestine. Once settled there, they should reclaim and cultivate the land, and rebuild a new Jewish State. The new state would be the safe haven and refuge for Jewish people escaping anti-Semitism and persecution. He attended the first Zionist Congress in Basel, Switzerland, where Theodor Herzel, the founder of the Zionist movement, presented a fiery manifesto describing his vision of what the reborn Jewish state would look like. My great grandfather was so moved by Herzel's speech and enthusiasm that he immediately traveled to Palestine, toured the land, searching for a place where the entire Lipka clan could move and start a new life. He planned to buy land and plant a large vineyard where the Lipka family would fulfill the prophesies of the great Biblical

Jewish prophets like Micah, promising that at the end of time, the Jewish people would return to their homeland and each one will live under his own vine and fig tree. (Micah 4:4) True to his conviction, he purchased enough acreage to accommodate a large vineyard and the Lipka's family dwelling. Oddly enough, the land he purchased was at the fertile valley of Megiddo, otherwise known as Armageddon, the battle ground of the Gog and Magog War.

The transaction was done when Palestine was still part of the Ottoman (the Turkish Empire). After visiting Palestine and purchasing the land, my great grandfather returned to Poland. The family business was thriving and expanding, especially after his oldest daughter (my mother's sister) married Zigi Hirsch from a well-to-do Jewish family living in the Golub section of town. Zigi's brother was a prominent family doctor. The Hirsh family was the sole importer of agricultural equipment such as tractors, ploughs, fertilizers and cement machines. They also sold ammunition and dynamite to mining and excavating companies.

The Lipka family was doing very well financially under the guidance of my great grandfather. As years went by, his regular visits to the famous mineral spas in Switzerland grew more frequent as his health deteriorated. He died in 1921 at the age of seventy-nine. After his death, the family's business kept flourishing. In the meantime, World War I erupted. The Ottoman Empire and its German ally lost the war and Palestine came under the British mandate assigned to it by the International League of Nations. The economic and financial situation in Germany worsened after World War I, ushering the rise of Nazism and Hitler. One of the Zionist leaders, Ze'Ev Jabotinsky predicted the looming disaster to the Polish Jewry and urged them to leave while it was still possible to do so. My mother who belonged to the youth movement Betar founded by Jabotinsky, heeded his advice, left home and sneaked into Palestine illegally. (See Chapter 3.)

The German army invaded Poland at the outbreak of World War II. They took over Golub-Dobrzyń, claiming that it was a German/Prussian territory to begin with. After overrunning the city, they confiscated the Lipka's power plant claiming that it was a travesty for the Germans to purchase electricity from a Jewish-owned business. Later on, they confiscated the rest of the family assets. The Nazis massacre of the Jewish community started as well.

The Lipka's realized it was time to escape or they would be killed. My mother's brother, Heniek, was married to an elementary schoolteacher from Lamasha, (a small Russian town on the Polish-Russian border). The family fled to Mir, another small town on the Polish-Russian border. The Lipka clan's sole source of income was her salary as a teacher and Dr. Hirsch's house calls treating patients. My grandfather, Mordecai Lipka acted as Dr. Hirsh's chauffeur, taking him from patient to patient using horse and a buggy.

As the Germans invaded Russia and advanced closer to where the Lipkas lived, the family sent urgent postcards to my mother in Palestine, requesting that she go to the British authorities to ensure that the documents associated with the land purchased were in effect. I found four postcards while cleaning my mother's apartment after her death in 2011. (Figure 19.1a, 1b)

The story had its bitter and cruel end as eventually the Germans stormed the home where my family had taken refuge. They rounded them up, took them to a nearby ditch and murdered them one by one, including my uncle's small baby, Yeshik. My great grandfather's dream for his beloved family to dwell under the grapevines and fig tree, was shattered, execution style. There was no longer a family vineyard in that utopic dream but a cruel reality of a burial ditch with the dead bodies of an entire family riddled with bullets just because they were Jews.

I learned about that story for the first time when I was in my late fifties. It was during my mother's last visit to my home in Kennewick, WA. I needed information about the people shown in the family photo album she gave me. It did not go too well. She refused to provide more details, so the facts described here are the extent of the story I heard from her. The emotional burden was too much for her to bear so I dropped the inquiry and never asked her again. She is dead now but the story of the way my family perished still echoes in my head. The beautiful vineyard in that story became engraved in my memory.

When the British left Palestine in 1948, seven Arab armies invaded Israel. This was Israel's War for Independence. We won and, after the war was over, the acres purchased by my great grandfather were incorporated into the rural town of Afula, Israel. The municipality divided the land into five parcels, designated as industrial land. In the following years, the city started sending my parents, who lived more than 150 miles away, huge property tax bills. Then came the flood of cleaning charges for removing the garbage and debris dumped by the public on the empty lots. My parents struggled, financially, just to make ends meet, and did not have money to pay these hefty tax bills. This situation created a never-ending argument between my parents. My father wanted to sell the lots, claiming that they would ruin us. My mother, on the other hand, was adamantly against doing so. Her emotional attachment to the land overrode any realistic thinking about the financial impact on our family.

Figure 19.1a, Front of one of the post cards I found in my
mother's apartment in 2011

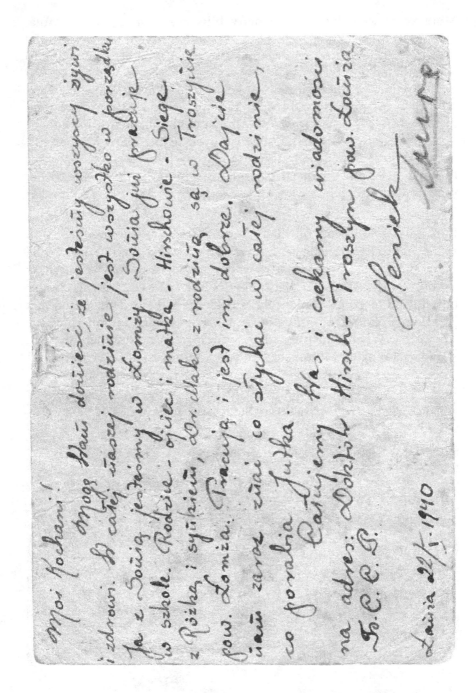

Figure 19.1b Back of one of the post cards I found in my
mother's apartment in 2011

✡

More years went by and the hefty bills kept coming from Afula, bringing us closer to poverty. Still, my mother would not yield to the pressure to sell exerted by my father. It was her tangible connection to her murdered family.

Eventually, the financial burden reached its peak. It forced my mother to compromise and sell all but one lot that she would keep no matter what. (My sister owns it now and does not intend to sell it either.)

Still more years passed and I moved to the USA. My parents' financial situation turned around and they lived comfortably after the many years of financial struggle. My mother still watched that remaining lot like a hawk.

✡

But the story was not finished. Our American-born daughter, Shir, spent time in Italy during her military service with the US Navy. While there, she granted us power of attorney and requested that we purchase a house with acreage in Washington. Her idea was to raise water buffalo and make mozzarella cheese like the Italians. I suggested that planting a vineyard would be a more practical option and she concurred. When I mentioned the vineyard to my mother, she was elated, claiming that it was the fate of her family to have a vineyard.

Figure 19.2 Badger Canyon Vineyard

In 2005 I leased two acres from Shir and planted a vineyard. (Figure 19.2.) I did it all by myself with my own bare hands and no equipment or tools to speak of. I trained and pruned original varieties I ordered from an Italian nursery and from UC Davis. It took me almost ten years. We harvested

Figure 19.3 Batia helped with the harvest

the grapes, and finally, I made more than fifteen different varietal wines and sold them at local supermarkets and the farmer's market under Badger Canyon Vineyard brand. (Figure 19.4.) Batia thought that a bottle of wine with a meaningful and beautiful quotation would be a great combination so she designed small tags, each one with a different quotation from her collection and affixed it to each bottle with a colorful ribbon. (Figure 19.5.)

Many friends thought I was crazy, yet I felt at peace, knowing that this living, growing vineyard was a great legacy to the family I never knew. It was my legacy as well.

Financially speaking, it was our family vineyard but emotionally, it was a monument more powerful than the Nazis' bullets. The vineyard was a life commitment on my part, an *in-your-face* to the Germans who killed my mother's family in Poland just for being Jews. The Nazis failed to destroy my great grandfather's dream of a family vineyard.

Figure 19.4 Batia sand I selling wine at farmer's market

In 2016 my daughter sold the property and moved to Richland. I hoped that the new owner would keep the vineyard since he agreed to pay the asking price, which included the cost of the vineyard. Two days after the title changed hands, a friend in the neighborhood told me the new owner had hired a contractor to uproot the entire vineyard, destroying all the vines and trellises, and ripping out the underground irrigation system. It took the new owner less than three days to kill a dream.

Even worse, the property went back on the market within a month.

Had the Nazis won after all?

But then, every time I enjoy a bottle of the wine made from the grapes I grew in my vineyard, I taste my great-grandfather's dream come true.

Figure 19.5 Four of my wines and the quotes on their tags.

Barbara: "To the world you may be one person but to one person you may be the world." ~ Rural Pearls

Amarone: We have come into being to praise, to labor, and to love." ~ The Jewish Sidur

Aglianico: "You can't control the wind but you can adjust your sails." ~ Yiddish proverb

Primitivo: "In WATER one sees one's face. But in WINE one beholds the heart of another." ~ French proverb

Epilogue

Every beginning has an end and what started as an attempt on my part to document the milestones in my life as well as paying tribute to my family members who were executed by the Nazis during the Holocaust, has mushroomed into a rather lengthy book. I hope readers will enjoy reading it and find it informative as well.

I feel fortunate to be born in a time and place unique and significant in world history and Israeli history in particular. I was exposed to wars, and Holocaust survivors and their sad stories, yet, all of this did not mar my happy childhood and adolescence. Writing this book presented me with the opportunity to tell these stories for the first time as they had been bottled inside me for many years.

As stated in the Preface, fairly early in my adult life I made the decision to come to the USA in pursuit of a higher education. It was not a capricious decision. I carefully drafted a simple PLAN: "Go to the USA, get the Ph.D. degree and returned to my beloved Israel the minute I earn my diploma." However, I discovered, to my dismay, John Lennon's phrase "Life is what happens to us while we are making other plans" definitely applies to my life. The simple plan I made 53 years ago, never materialized for various reasons, most of them compelling and justifiable, and the others fit what I call the "That's Life" category.

Taking inventory of what I have done throughout my life and squeezing most of the events into a book, left me with the inescapable question, "Was it worth it?"

Granted, I fulfilled my dream but maybe there was a measure of unfairness to my own family. Take for example my wife, Batia, then my girlfriend with whom I was upfront from the very beginning, telling her about my decision to study for a Ph.D. degree in the USA. She elected to join me and adopt MY PLAN as OUR MUTUAL PLAN after we were married.

I look in the mirror and ask myself whether or not fulfilling my dream was fair. Was it fair to take Batia away from *Kibbutz* Matzuba where she was born and raised, leaving her widowed mother, Esther, all by herself. I know for sure that it was extremely difficult for both of them. Batia took solace by telling me time and time again that the moment I got my Ph.D. diploma, "We are going back to Matzuba."

We never did.

As the years passed, living in the USA, she adopted the country. The USA became her home and integral part of her. Nowadays, it pains her deeply that the USA we knew for many years, is changing in an alarming pace and in the wrong direction and further away from the America we loved.

Was I fair to my son Raz and my daughter Shir? Both of them were born in the USA but we took them to Israel just because I had ANOTHER PLAN. They flourished in Israel during the two years we lived there, but then I brought them back to the USA. They are grownup now and very happy to be Americans, Nonetheless, I often wondered whether or not staying in Israel would have been better for them. I will let them be the judge of that.

Was I fair to my own parents who worked so hard and lived an austere life to make ends meet so they could raise me and my sister and provide us with the ability and discipline to survive the challenges we would face? Then MY PLAN took me across the ocean never to come back so they could enjoy their grandchildren. Numerous times I apologized to my mother, but she kept reassuring me that "a mother is always happy and proud when her son or daughter succeeds in life." My parents always bragged about "our son with the Ph.D." and their daughter who turned out to be an entrepreneur and business woman, but it never mitigated the guilt feelings that haunt me to this day.

And finally, how about me? Was I fair to myself? Granted, I executed MY PLAN and earned the Ph.D. but was it worth leaving the country I was born in, loved and fought for in the Six-Day War? I left it and adopted the USA as the new country that I also love. I am still trying to find the answer to that question. "Was it worth it?"

In conclusion, this book is about one man's life story. You are probably familiar with the saying *everyone has a story*. What's yours?

Wishing you a life filled with meaning, health and love.

In Memory Of

Mordehai Mendel Lipka: age 61
Grandfather

Bluma Lipka nee Cohen: age 58
Grandmother

Heniek Lipka: age 28
Uncle

Rozka Hirsch nee Lipka: age 27
Aunt

Jerzyk Yehuda Hirsch: age 4
Cousin

YAD VASHEM
The Holocaust Martyrs' and Heroes Remembrance Authority

יד ושם
רשות הזיכרון לשואה ולגבורה
היכל השמות · ת.ד. 3477, ירושלים 91034

Page of Testimony — דף עד

Victim's family name: **LIPKA**

First name (also nickname): **MORDEHAI**

Approx. age at death: **61** | Date of birth: **1878** | Gender: **M** | Title: **M**

Nationality: **POLAND** | Country: **POLSKA** | Region: **POMORZE** | Place of birth: **DOBRZYN - GOLUB**

Victim's father — Family name: **LIPKA** | First name: **FAIVIS**

Victim's mother — Maiden name | First name: **RIZEL**

Victim's wife / husband: No. of children **4** | Maiden name: **COHEN** | First name: **BLIME**

Address: **RYNEK 5** | Country: **POLSKA** | Region: **POMORZE** | Permanent residence: **DOBRZYN - GOLUB**

Place of work: **Golub, DOBRYN str. RYNEK 5**

Address: **RYNEK 5** | Country: **POLSKA** | Region: **POMORZE** | Residence before deportation: **DOBRZYN - GOLUB**

Date of death: **9. XI. 1941** | Country: **U.S.S.R.** | Place of death: **MIR**

I, the undersigned, hereby declare that this testimony is correct to the best of my knowledge.

Previous/maiden name: **Jutka LIPKA** | First name:

State/zip code: **64284** | Phone no.: **26**

Tel.: **03 - 5281854** | Country: **ISRAEL**

Date: **22. 6. 1999** | Place:

"And I shall give them in My house and within My walls a memorial and a name...that shall not be cut off"

Example of the original Testimonial Forms my mother (Jutka Lipka Polonecki) filed at the *Vad va Shem* Memorial Museum in Jerusalem.

MORDEHAI NENDEL LIPKA
Mordehai Nendel Lipka was born in Golub-Dobrzyń, Poland in
1878 to Faivis and Rizel. He was the owner of a grain mill, a lumber
mill, and an electric power plant. Prior to WWII he lived in Golub-
Dobrzyń, Poland. During the war he was in Golub-Dobrzyń, Poland.
Mordehai Nendel Lipka was murdered in the Shoah
(Hebrew term for The Holocaust).
He was my grandfather.

BLUMA LIPKA

Bluma Lipka nee Cohen was born in Ripin, Poland in 1883 to Leib and Dwora. She was a housewife and married to Mordehai. Prior to WWII she lived in Golub-Dobrzyń, Poland. During the war she was in Golub-Dobrzyń, Poland. Bluma was murdered in the Shoah (Hebrew term for The Holocaust).

She was my grandmother.

HENIEK LIPKA

Heniek Lipka was born in Golub-Dobrzyń, Poland, in 1913 to Mordehai and Blima. He was a bookkeeper and married to Sonia nee Oldak. Prior to WWII he lived in Golub-Dobrzyń, Poland. During the war he was in Golub-Dobrzyń, Poland. Heneik was murdered in the Shoah (Hebrew term for The Holocaust).

He was my uncle.

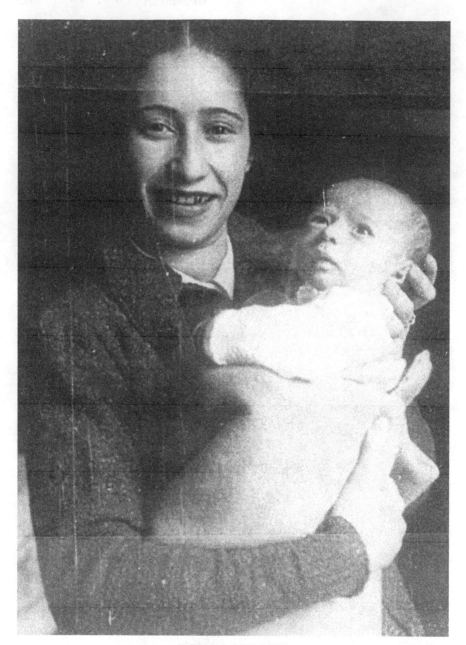

ROZKA HIRSCH
Rozka Hirsch nee Lipka was born in Golub-Dobrzyń, Poland, in 1914
to Mordehai and Bluma. She was a trade house owner, and married
to Zigi Hirsch. Prior to WWII she lived in Dobrzyn Golub, Poland.
During the war she was in Dobrzyn Golub, Poland.
Rozka was murdered in the Shoah (Hebrew term for The Holocaust).
She was my aunt.

JERZYK YEHUDA HIRSCH
Jerzyk Yehuda Hirsch was born in Golub-Dobrzyń, Poland in 1937
to Zigi and Rozka. He was a child. Prior to WWII he lived in Golub-
Dobrzyń, Poland. During the war he was in Golub-Dobrzyń, Poland.
Jerzyk was murdered in the Shoah (Hebrew term for The Holocaust).
He was my cousin.

CPSIA information can be obtained
at www.ICGtesting.com
Printed in the USA
LVHW081135190422
716614LV00008B/305

9 781944 887674